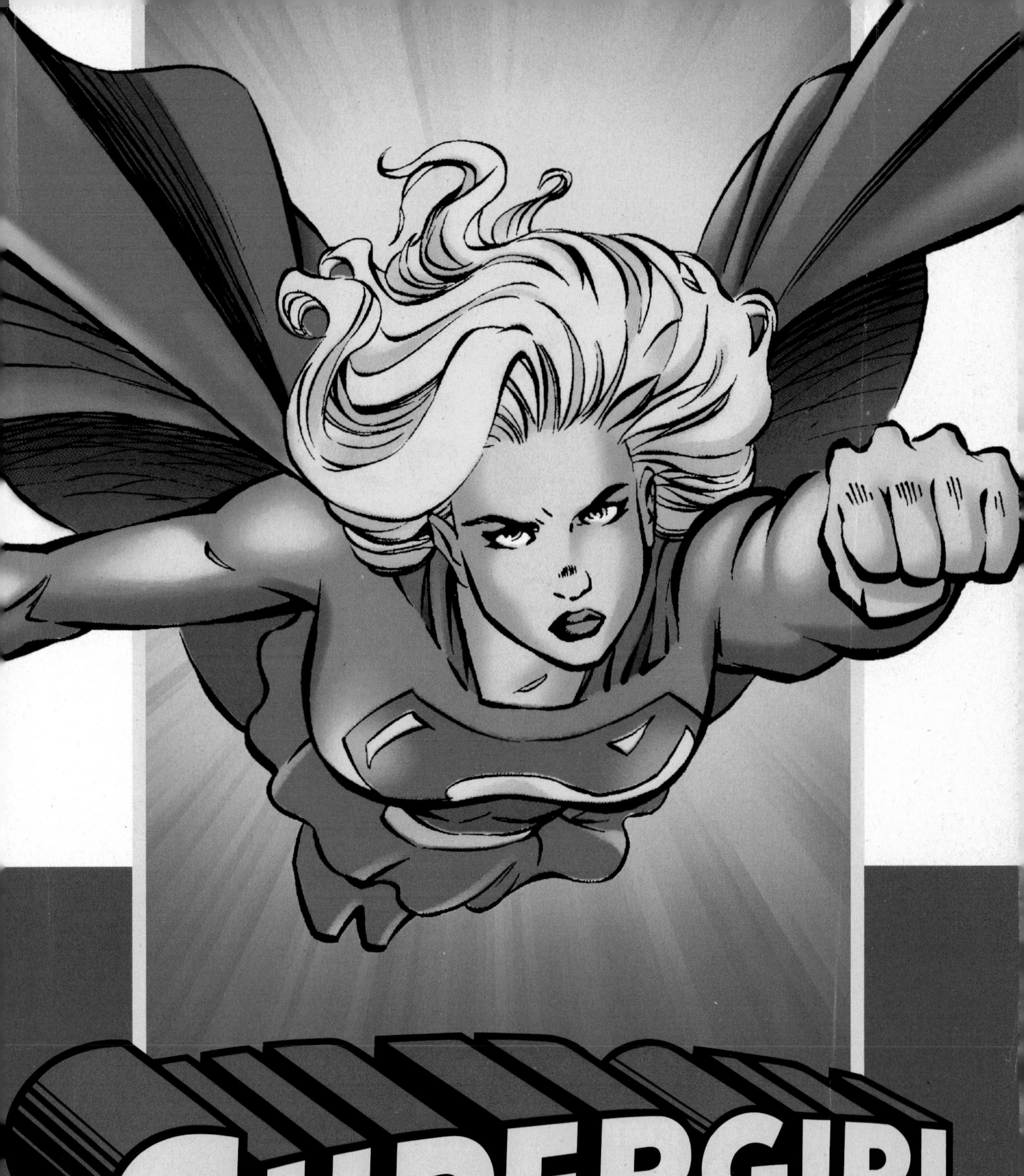

SUPERGIRL

BOOK TWO

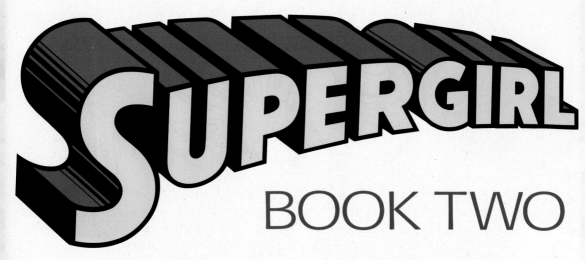

SUPERGIRL
BOOK TWO

PETER DAVID
DARREN VINCENZO
TOM PEYER
CHUCK DIXON
writers

LEONARD KIRK
GREG LAND
ANTHONY CASTRILLO
pencillers

CAM SMITH
PRENTIS ROLLINS
CHUCK DROST
DOUG HAZLEWOOD
JORDI ENSIGN
inkers

GENE D'ANGELO
TOM ZIUKO
colorists

PAT PRENTICE
BOB LAPPAN
ALBERT DEGUZMAN
letterers

DIGITAL CHAMELEON
separations

GARY FRANK
CAM SMITH
PATRICK MARTIN
collection cover artists

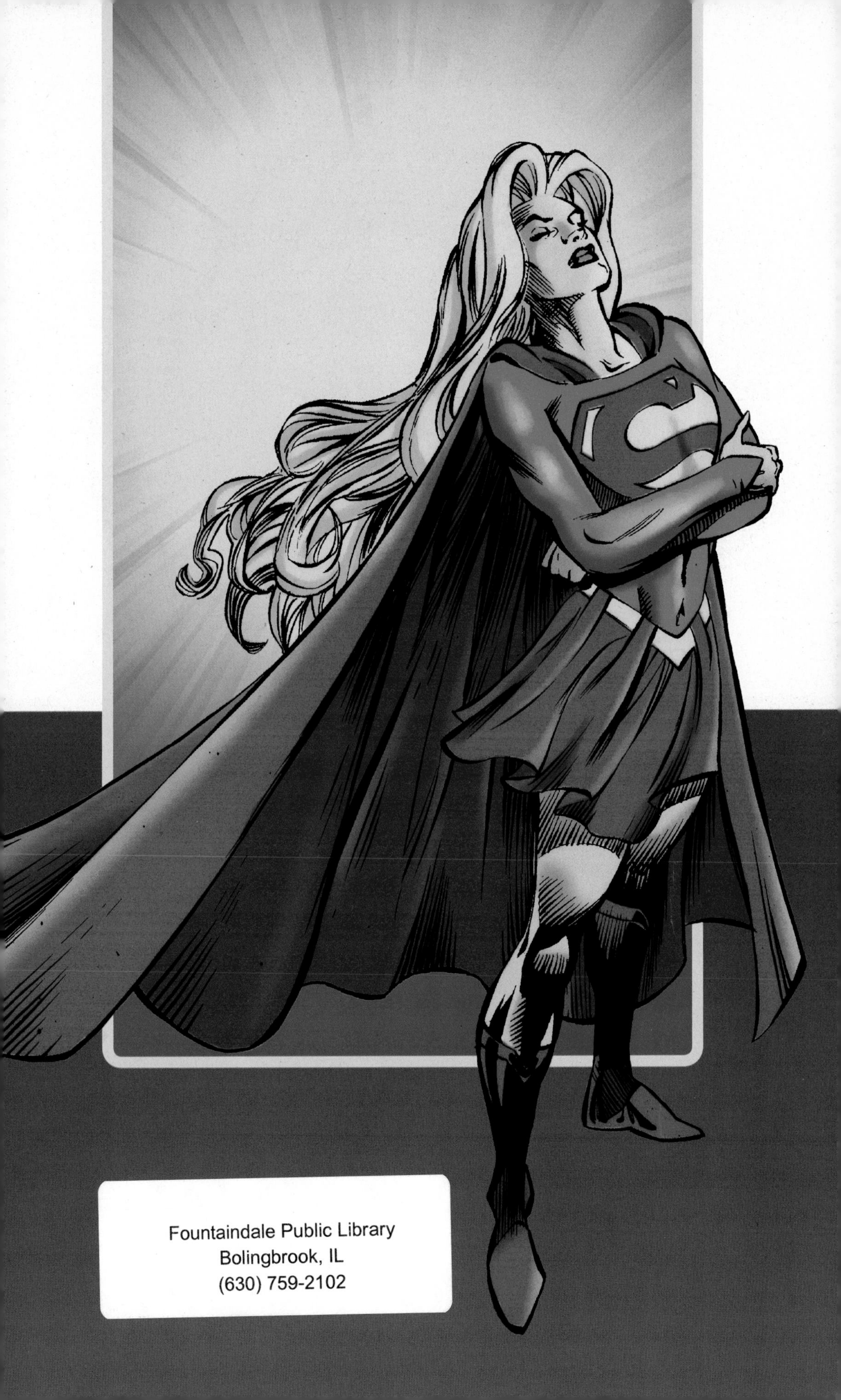

FRANK PITTARESE CHRIS DUFFY
MIKE McAVENNIE
Editors – Original Series
MAUREEN McTIGUE EDDIE BERGANZA
ROBERT GREENBERGER
Assistant Editors – Original Series
JEB WOODARD
Group Editor – Collected Editions
ERIKA ROTHBERG
Editor – Collected Edition
STEVE COOK
Design Director – Books
CURTIS KING JR.
Publication Design
BOB HARRAS
Senior VP – Editor-in-Chief, DC Comics
DIANE NELSON
President
DAN DIDIO and JIM LEE
Co-Publishers
GEOFF JOHNS
President & Chief Creative Officer
AMIT DESAI
Executive VP –Business & Marketing Strategy, Direct to
Consumer & Global Franchise Management
SAM ADES
Senior VP – Direct to Consumer
BOBBIE CHASE
VP – Talent Development
MARK CHIARELLO
Senior VP – Art, Design & Collected Editions

JOHN CUNNINGHAM
Senior VP – Sales & Trade Marketing
ANNE DePIES
Senior VP – Business Strategy, Finance &
Administration
DON FALLETTI
VP – Manufacturing Operations
LAWRENCE GANEM
VP – Editorial Administration & Talent Relations
ALISON GILL
Senior VP – Manufacturing & Operations
HANK KANALZ
Senior VP – Editorial Strategy & Administration
JAY KOGAN
VP – Legal Affairs
THOMAS LOFTUS
VP – Business Affairs
JACK MAHAN
VP – Business Affairs
NICK J. NAPOLITANO
VP – Manufacturing Administration
EDDIE SCANNELL
VP – Consumer Marketing
COURTNEY SIMMONS
Senior VP – Publicity & Communications
JIM (SKI) SOKOLOWSKI
VP – Comic Book Specialty Sales & Trade Marketing
NANCY SPEARS
VP – Mass, Book, Digital Sales & Trade Marketing

SUPERGIRL BOOK TWO

Published by DC Comics. Compilation and all new material Copyright © 2017 DC Comics. All
Rights Reserved. Originally published in single magazine form in SUPERGIRL 10-20, SUPERGIRL
ANNUAL 2. Copyright © 1997, 1998 DC Comics. All Rights Reserved. All characters, their
distinctive likenesses and related elements featured in this publication are trademarks of DC
Comics. The stories, characters and incidents featured in this publication are entirely fictional. DC
Comics does not read or accept unsolicited submissions of ideas, stories or artwork.

DC Comics, 2900 West Alameda Ave., Burbank, CA 91505
Printed by Solisco Printers, Scott, QC, Canada. 2/24/17. First Printing.
ISBN: 978-1-4012-6553-3

Library of Congress Cataloging-in-Publication Data is available.

SUPERGIRL #10 cover by Phil Jimenez and Patrick Martin

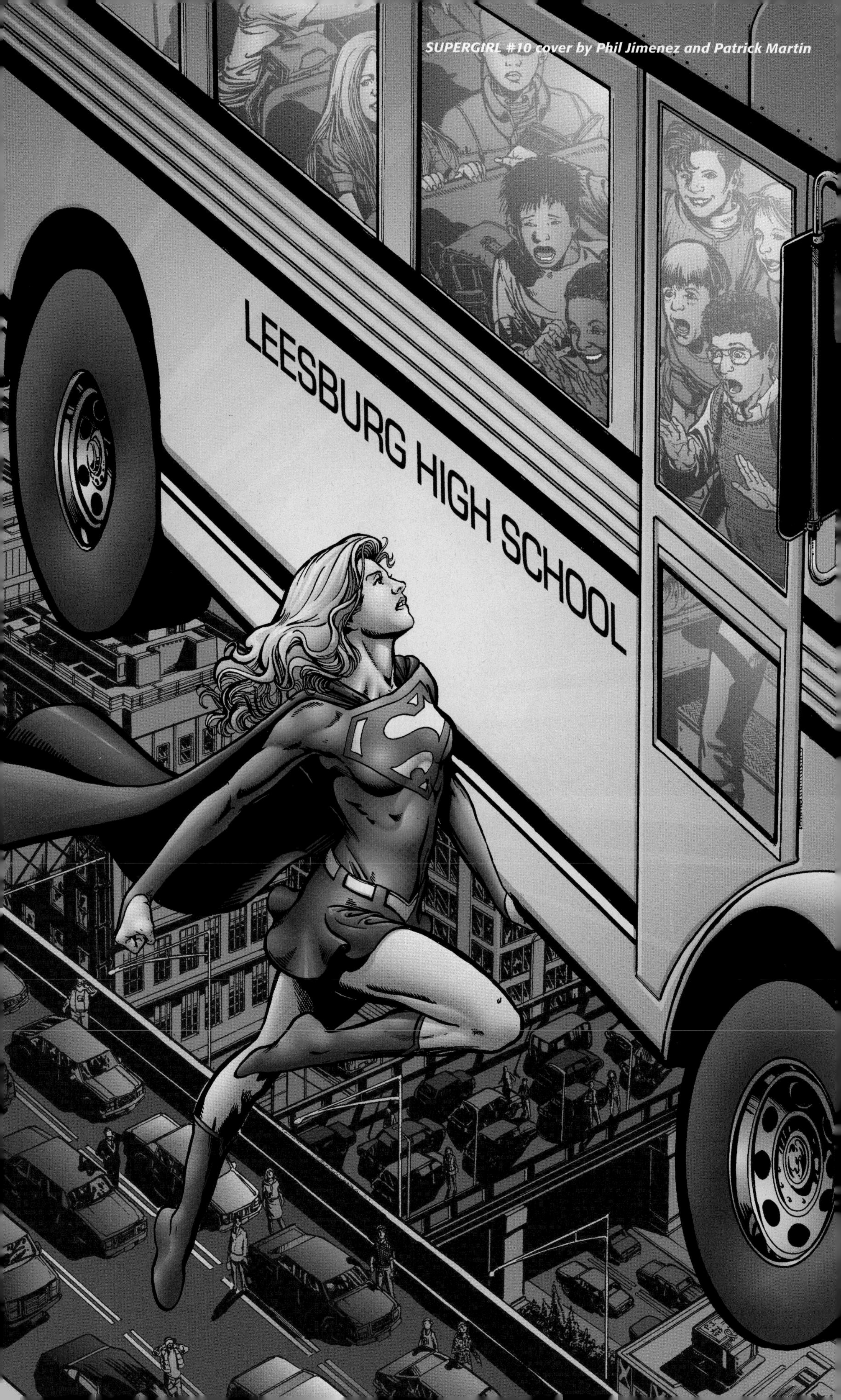
LEESBURG HIGH SCHOOL

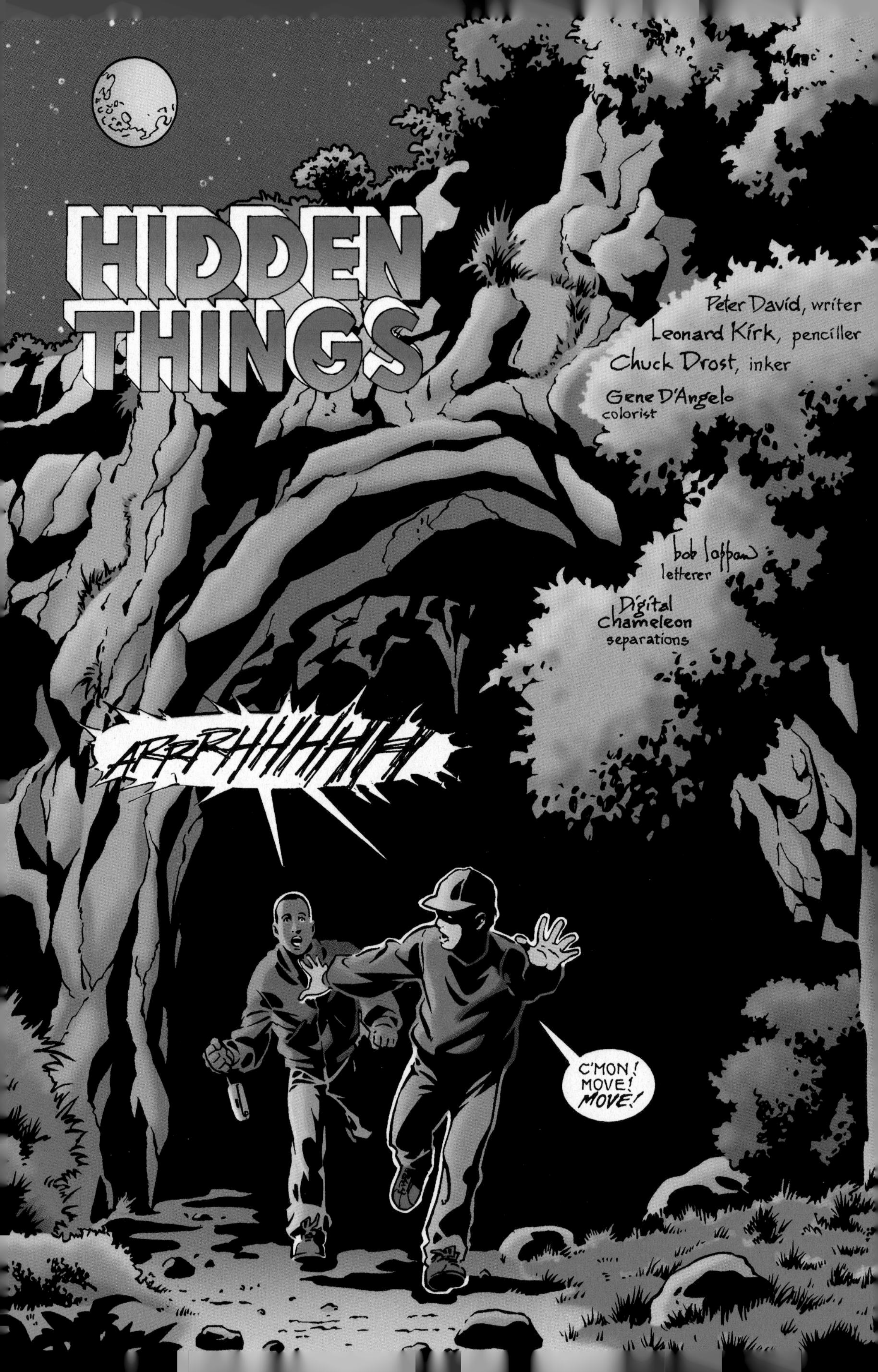
HIDDEN THINGS
Peter David, writer
Leonard Kirk, penciller
Chuck Drost, inker
Gene D'Angelo colorist
bob lappan letterer
Digital Chameleon separations
ARRRHHHHHH
C'MON! MOVE! MOVE!

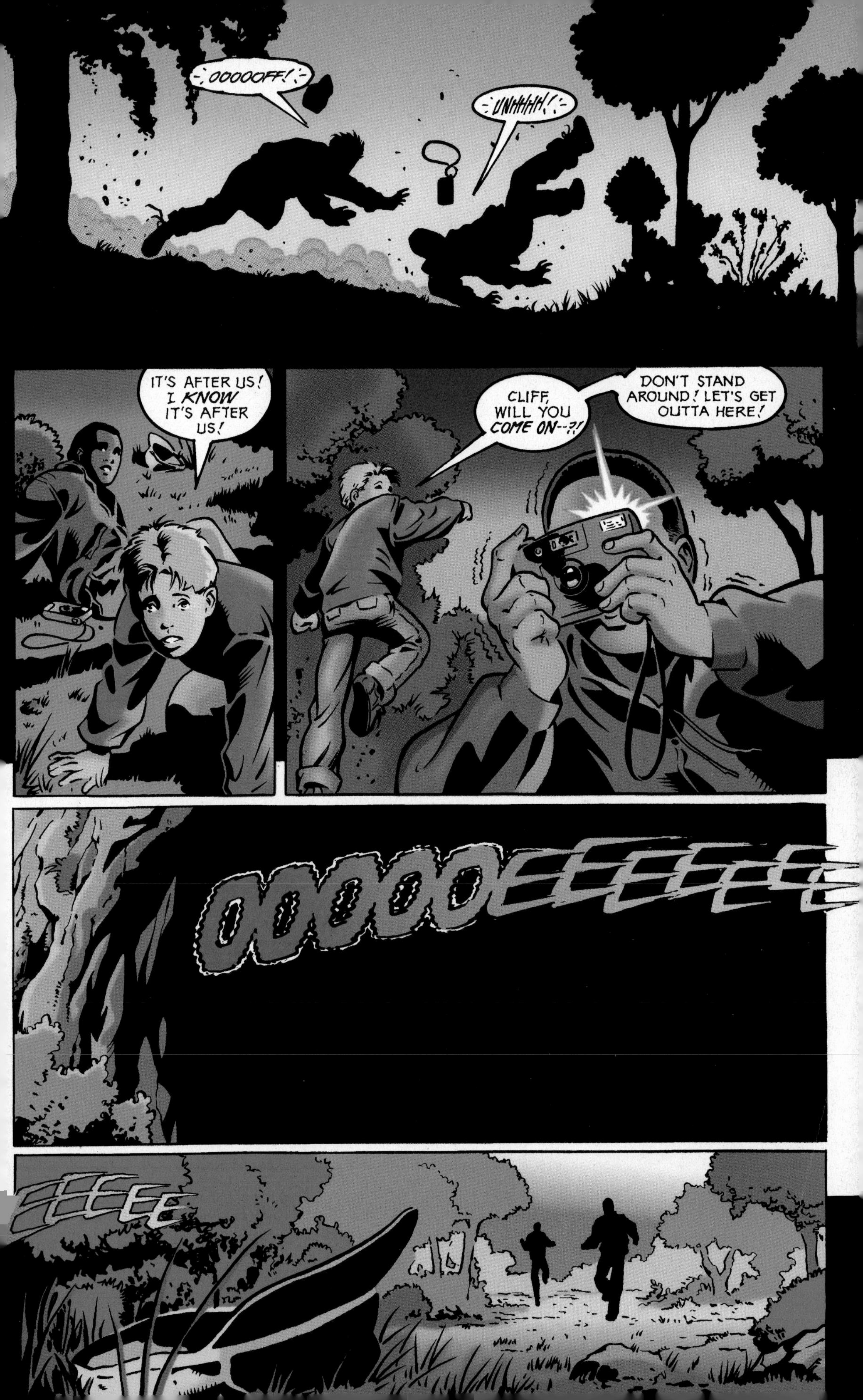
OOOOOFF!
UNHHHH!
IT'S AFTER US! I KNOW IT'S AFTER US!
CLIFF, WILL YOU COME ON--?!
DON'T STAND AROUND! LET'S GET OUTTA HERE!
OOOOOEEEEEEEE
EEEEE

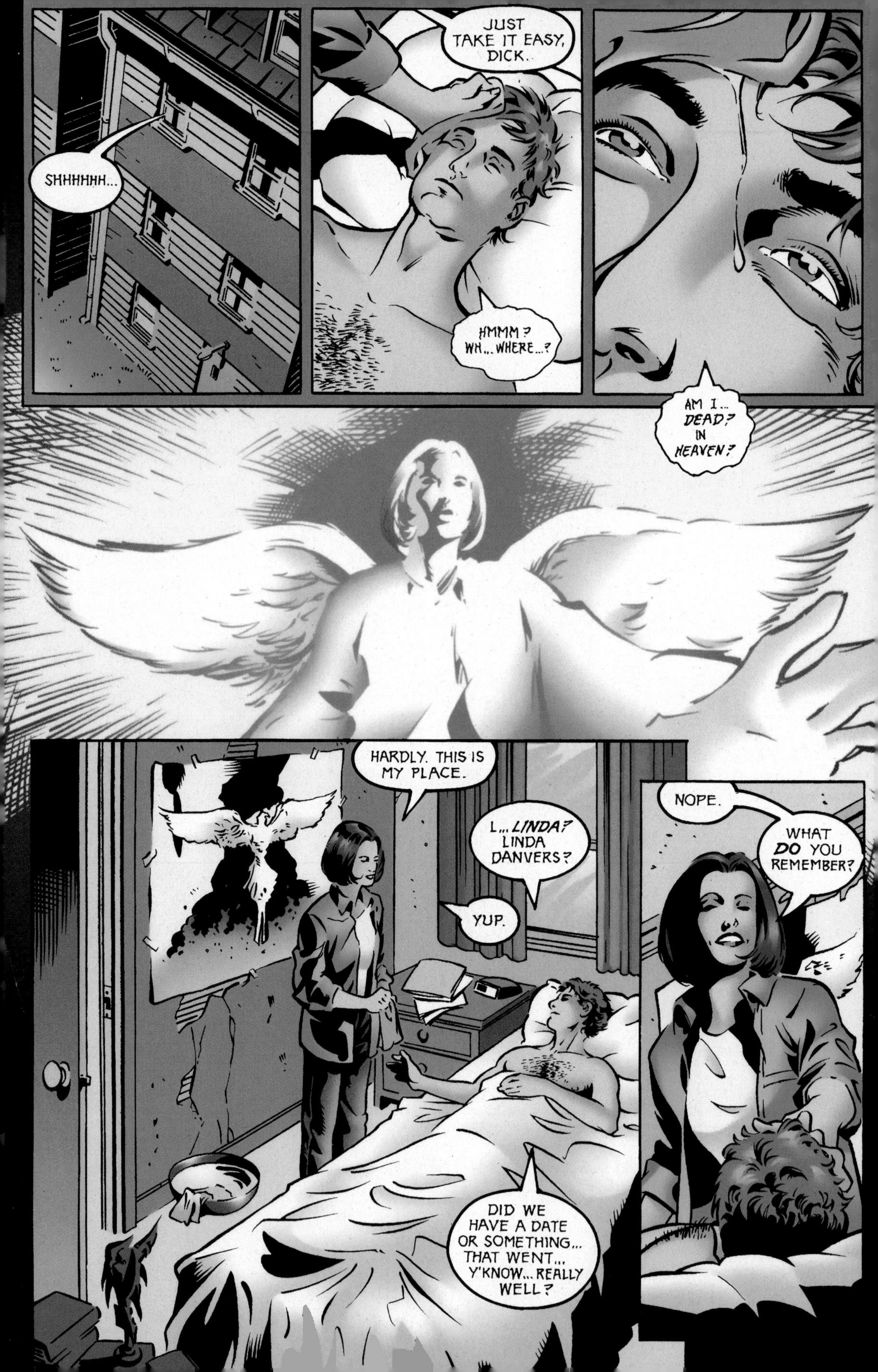
SHHHHHH...
JUST TAKE IT EASY, DICK.
HMMM? WH... WHERE...?
AM I... DEAD? IN HEAVEN?
HARDLY. THIS IS MY PLACE.
L... LINDA? LINDA DANVERS?
YUP.
DID WE HAVE A DATE OR SOMETHING... THAT WENT... Y'KNOW... REALLY WELL?
NOPE.
WHAT DO YOU REMEMBER?

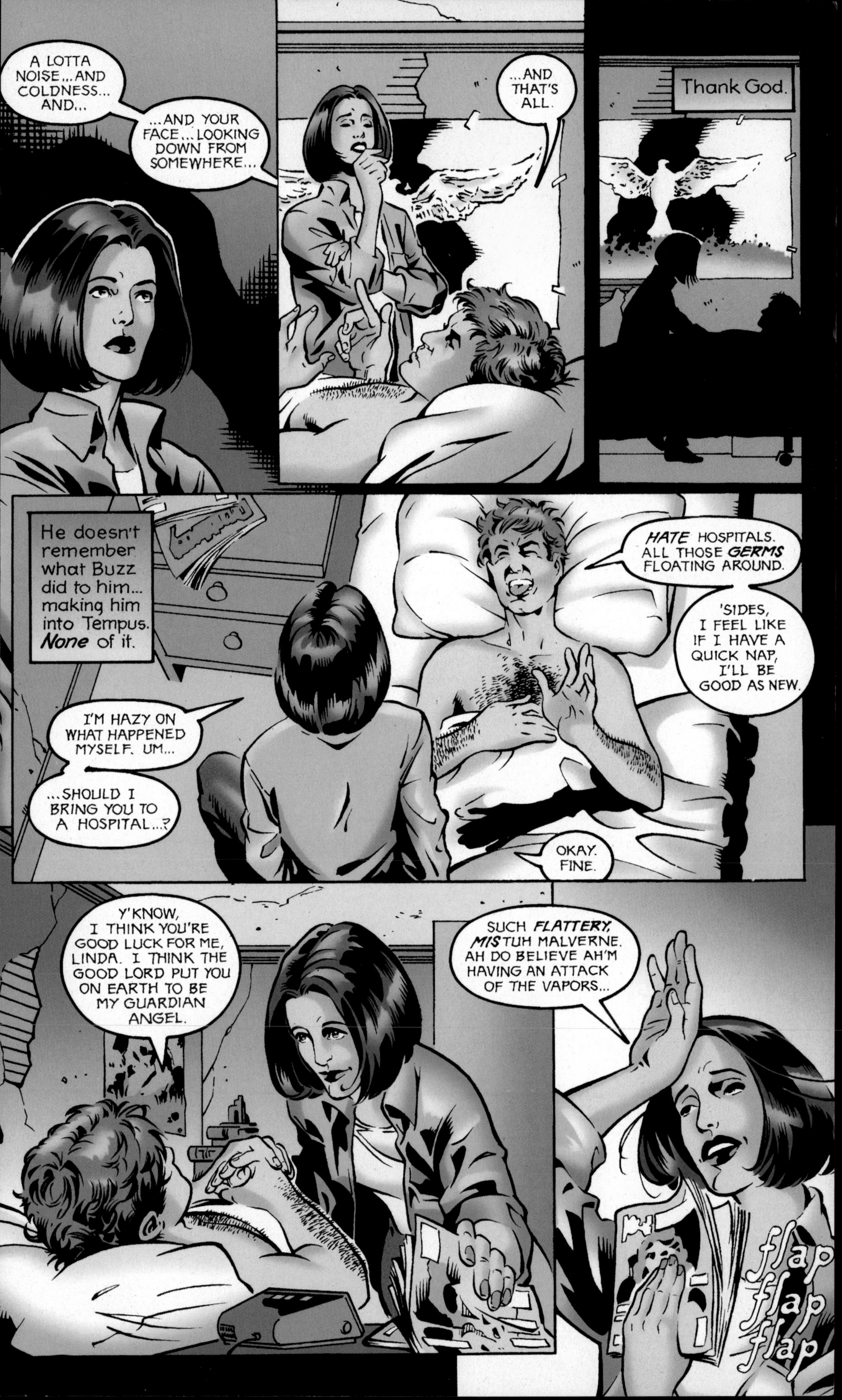
A LOTTA NOISE... AND COLDNESS... AND...
...AND YOUR FACE... LOOKING DOWN FROM SOMEWHERE...
...AND THAT'S ALL.
Thank God.
He doesn't remember what Buzz did to him... making him into Tempus. None of it.
HATE HOSPITALS. ALL THOSE GERMS FLOATING AROUND.
'SIDES, I FEEL LIKE IF I HAVE A QUICK NAP, I'LL BE GOOD AS NEW.
I'M HAZY ON WHAT HAPPENED MYSELF. UM...
...SHOULD I BRING YOU TO A HOSPITAL...?
OKAY. FINE.
Y'KNOW, I THINK YOU'RE GOOD LUCK FOR ME, LINDA. I THINK THE GOOD LORD PUT YOU ON EARTH TO BE MY GUARDIAN ANGEL.
SUCH FLATTERY, MISTUH MALVERNE. AH DO BELIEVE AH'M HAVING AN ATTACK OF THE VAPORS...
flap flap flap

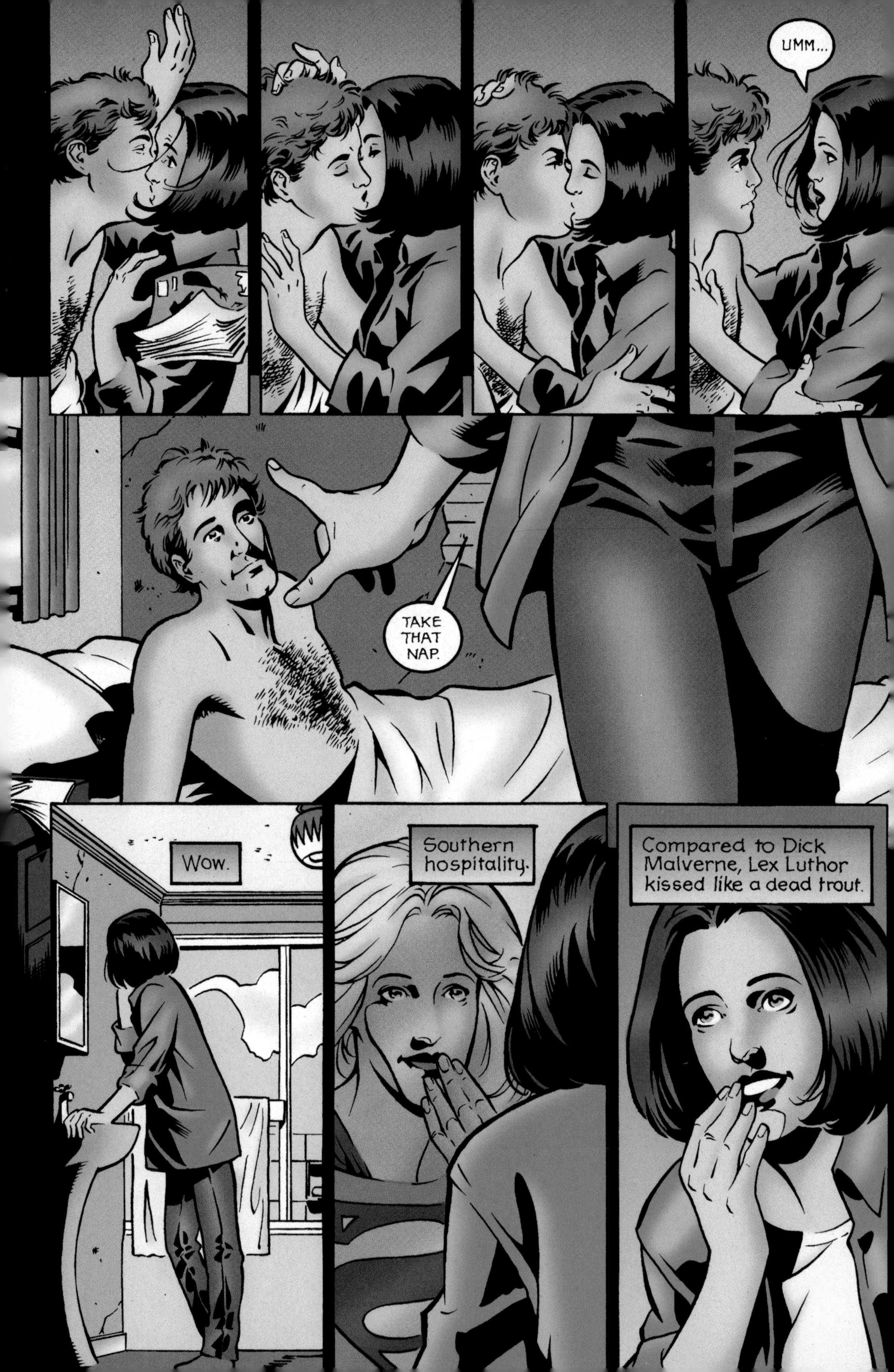
UMM...
TAKE THAT NAP.
Wow.
Southern hospitality.
Compared to Dick Malverne, Lex Luthor kissed like a dead trout.

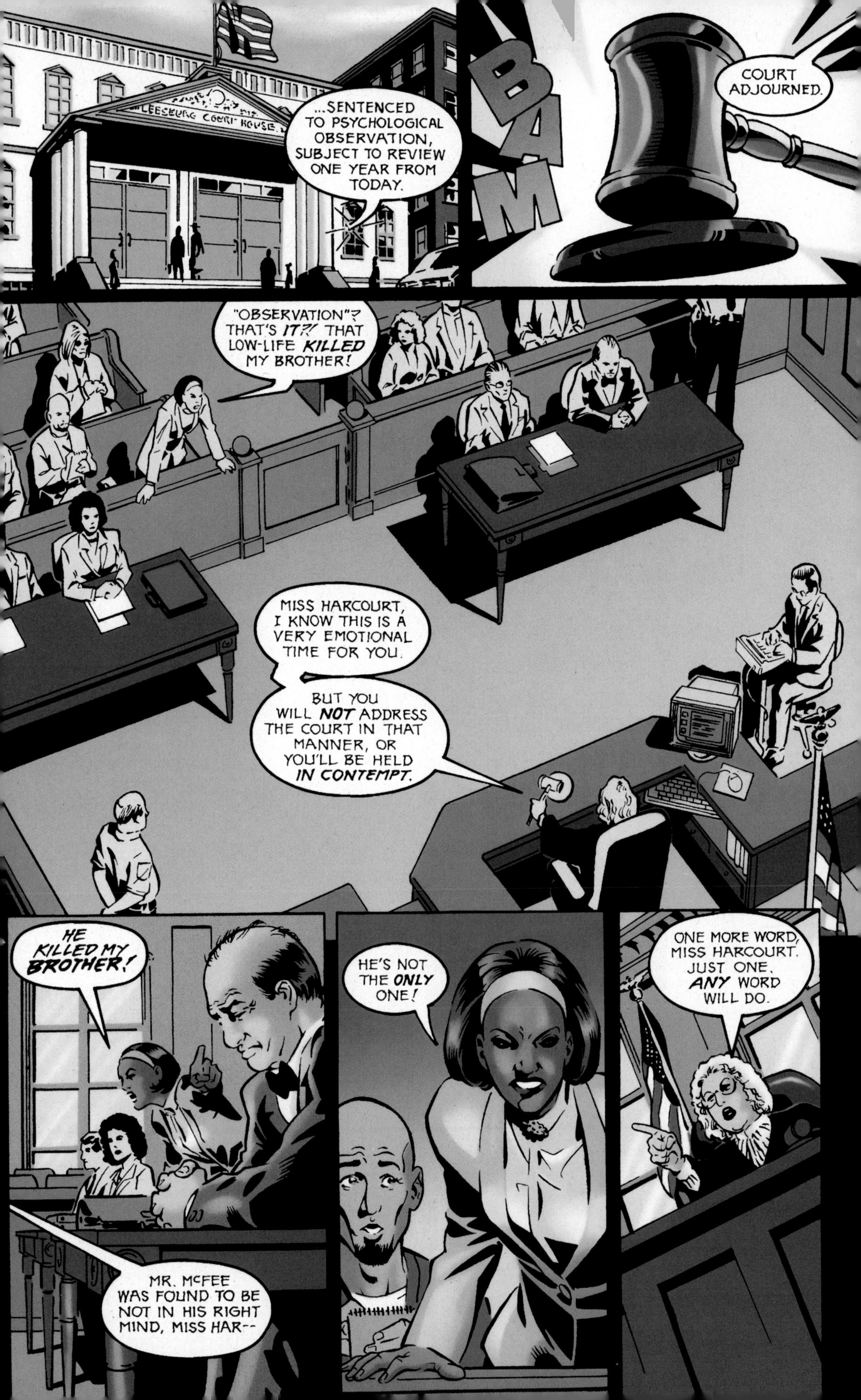
LEESBURG COURT HOUSE
...SENTENCED TO PSYCHOLOGICAL OBSERVATION, SUBJECT TO REVIEW ONE YEAR FROM TODAY.
BAM
COURT ADJOURNED.
"OBSERVATION"? THAT'S IT?! THAT LOW-LIFE KILLED MY BROTHER!
MISS HARCOURT, I KNOW THIS IS A VERY EMOTIONAL TIME FOR YOU.
BUT YOU WILL NOT ADDRESS THE COURT IN THAT MANNER, OR YOU'LL BE HELD IN CONTEMPT.
HE KILLED MY BROTHER!
MR. McFEE WAS FOUND TO BE NOT IN HIS RIGHT MIND, MISS HAR--
HE'S NOT THE ONLY ONE!
ONE MORE WORD, MISS HARCOURT. JUST ONE. ANY WORD WILL DO.

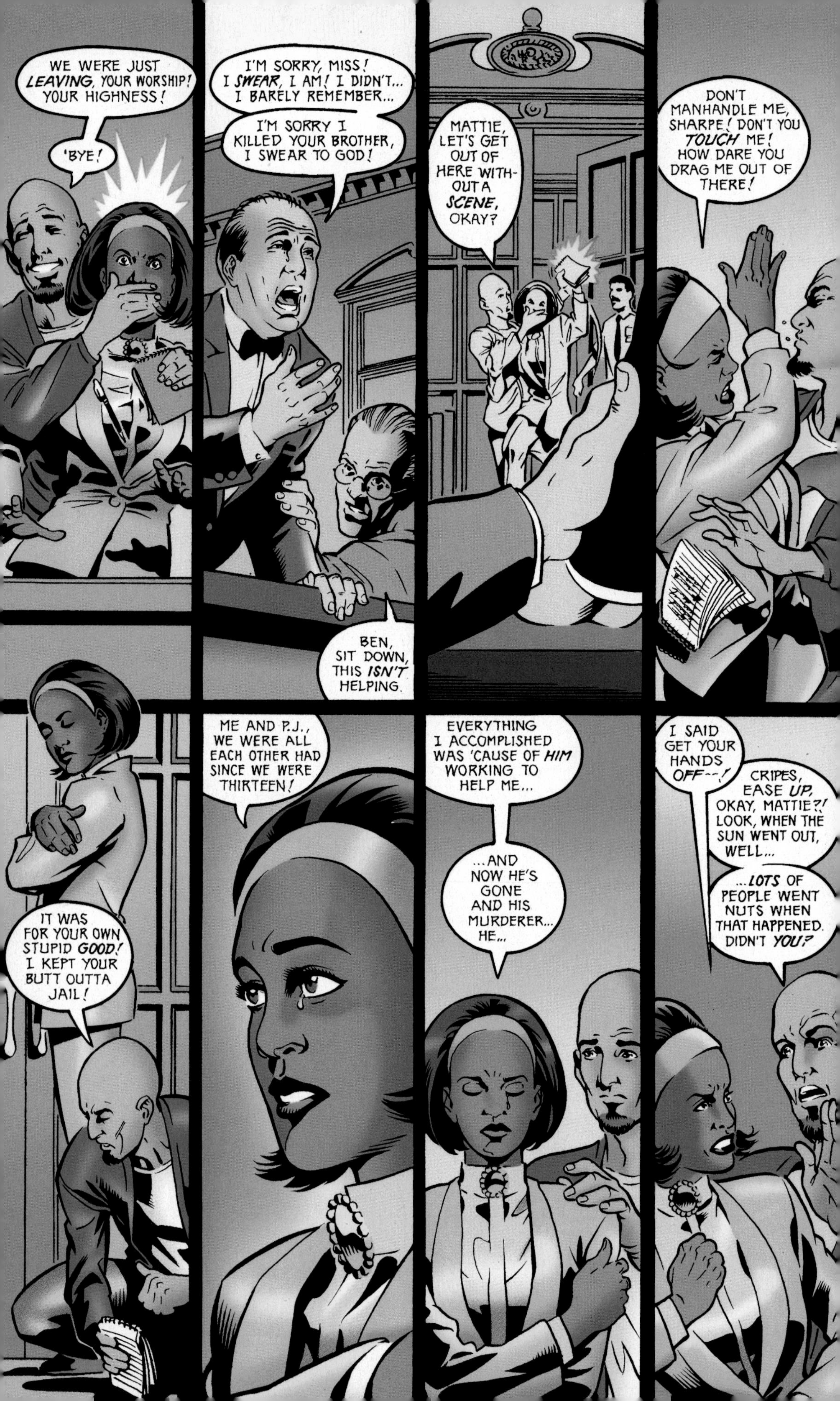
WE WERE JUST LEAVING, YOUR WORSHIP! YOUR HIGHNESS!
'BYE!
I'M SORRY, MISS! I SWEAR, I AM! I DIDN'T... I BARELY REMEMBER...
I'M SORRY I KILLED YOUR BROTHER, I SWEAR TO GOD!
BEN, SIT DOWN, THIS ISN'T HELPING.
MATTIE, LET'S GET OUT OF HERE WITH-OUT A SCENE, OKAY?
DON'T MANHANDLE ME, SHARPE! DON'T YOU TOUCH ME! HOW DARE YOU DRAG ME OUT OF THERE!
IT WAS FOR YOUR OWN STUPID GOOD! I KEPT YOUR BUTT OUTTA JAIL!
ME AND P.J., WE WERE ALL EACH OTHER HAD SINCE WE WERE THIRTEEN!
EVERYTHING I ACCOMPLISHED WAS 'CAUSE OF HIM WORKING TO HELP ME...
...AND NOW HE'S GONE AND HIS MURDERER... HE...
I SAID GET YOUR HANDS OFF--!
CRIPES, EASE UP, OKAY, MATTIE?! LOOK, WHEN THE SUN WENT OUT, WELL...
...LOTS OF PEOPLE WENT NUTS WHEN THAT HAPPENED. DIDN'T YOU?

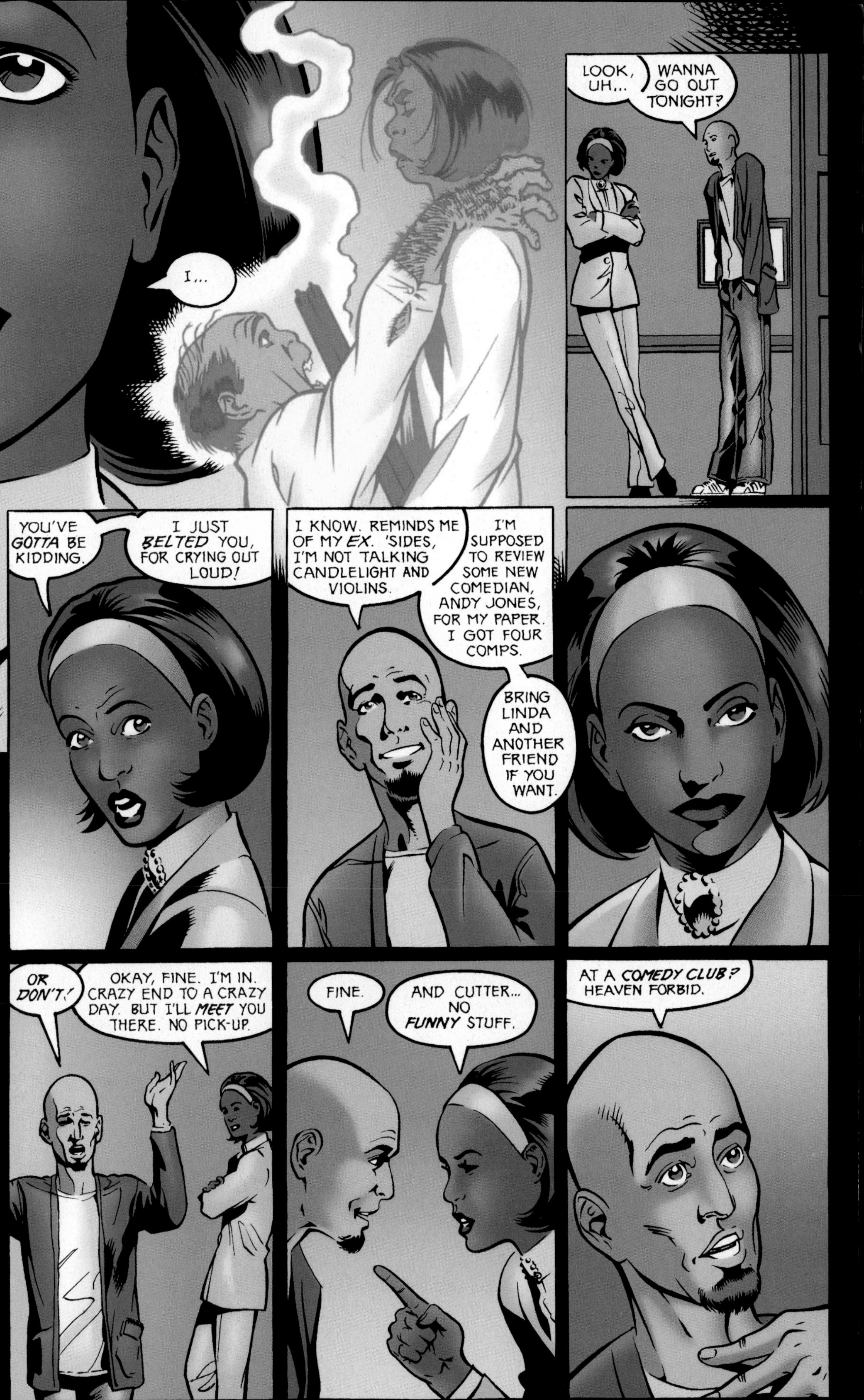
I...
LOOK, UH...
WANNA GO OUT TONIGHT?
YOU'VE GOTTA BE KIDDING.
I JUST BELTED YOU, FOR CRYING OUT LOUD!
I KNOW. REMINDS ME OF MY EX. 'SIDES, I'M NOT TALKING CANDLELIGHT AND VIOLINS.
I'M SUPPOSED TO REVIEW SOME NEW COMEDIAN, ANDY JONES, FOR MY PAPER. I GOT FOUR COMPS.
BRING LINDA AND ANOTHER FRIEND IF YOU WANT.
OR DON'T!
OKAY, FINE. I'M IN. CRAZY END TO A CRAZY DAY. BUT I'LL MEET YOU THERE. NO PICK-UP.
FINE.
AND CUTTER... NO FUNNY STUFF.
AT A COMEDY CLUB? HEAVEN FORBID.

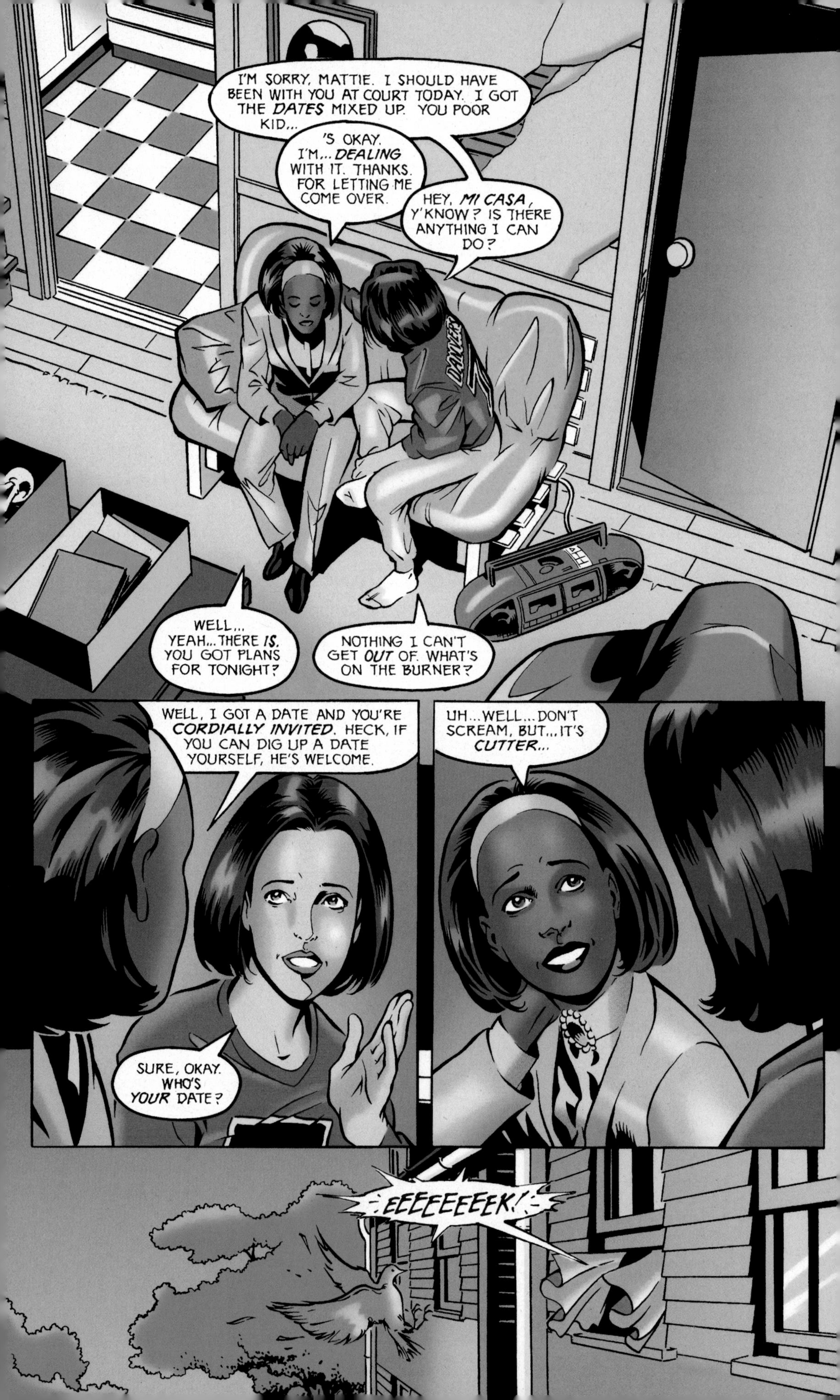
I'M SORRY, MATTIE. I SHOULD HAVE BEEN WITH YOU AT COURT TODAY. I GOT THE DATES MIXED UP. YOU POOR KID...
'S OKAY. I'M... DEALING WITH IT. THANKS. FOR LETTING ME COME OVER.
HEY, MI CASA, Y'KNOW? IS THERE ANYTHING I CAN DO?
WELL... YEAH... THERE IS. YOU GOT PLANS FOR TONIGHT?
NOTHING I CAN'T GET OUT OF. WHAT'S ON THE BURNER?
WELL, I GOT A DATE AND YOU'RE CORDIALLY INVITED. HECK, IF YOU CAN DIG UP A DATE YOURSELF, HE'S WELCOME.
SURE, OKAY. WHO'S YOUR DATE?
UH... WELL... DON'T SCREAM, BUT... IT'S CUTTER...
EEEEEEEEEK!

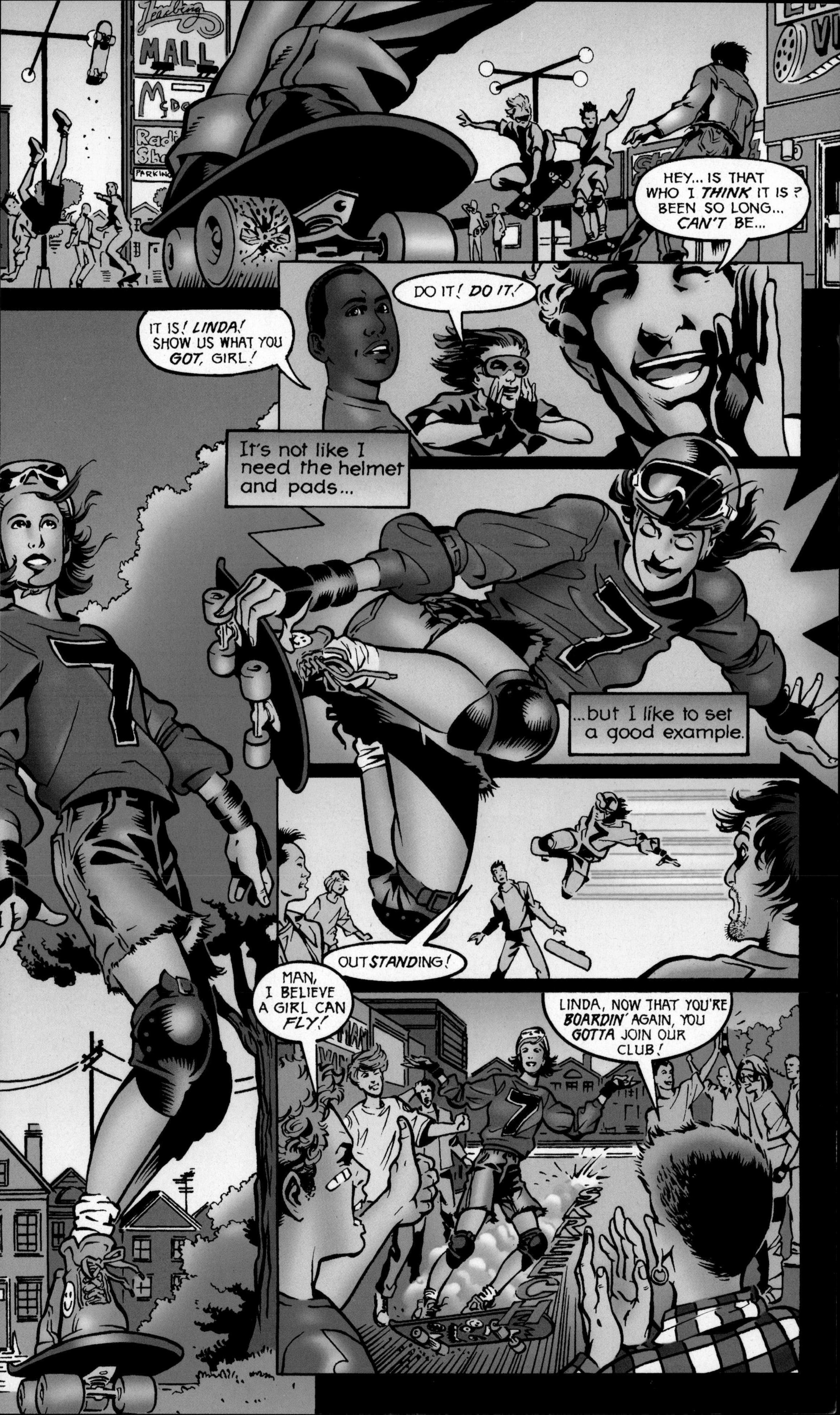

HEY... IS THAT WHO I THINK IT IS? BEEN SO LONG... CAN'T BE...
DO IT! DO IT!
IT IS! LINDA! SHOW US WHAT YOU GOT, GIRL!
It's not like I need the helmet and pads...
...but I like to set a good example.
OUTSTANDING!
MAN, I BELIEVE A GIRL CAN FLY!
LINDA, NOW THAT YOU'RE BOARDIN' AGAIN, YOU GOTTA JOIN OUR CLUB!

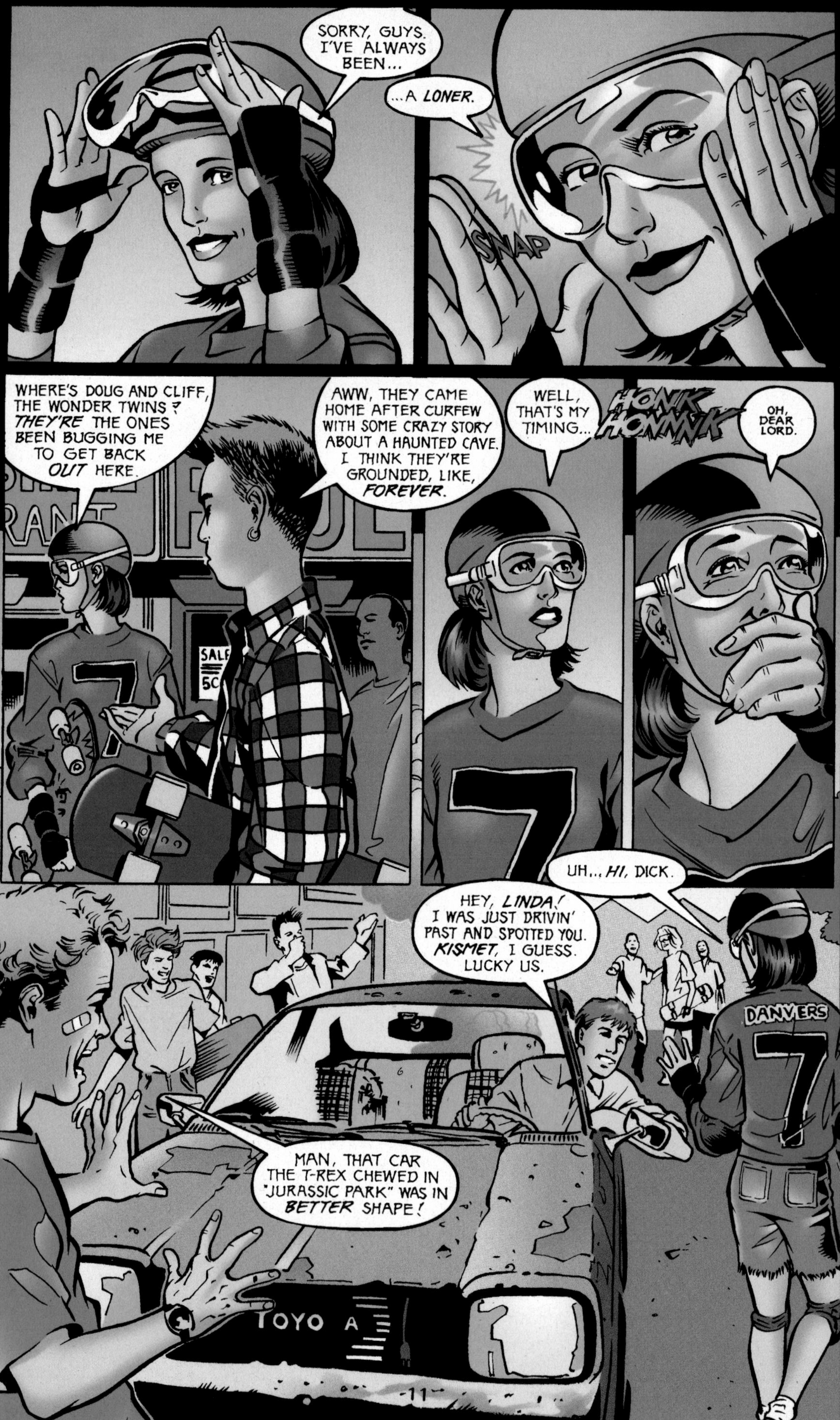
SORRY, GUYS. I'VE ALWAYS BEEN...
...A LONER.
SNAP
WHERE'S DOUG AND CLIFF, THE WONDER TWINS? THEY'RE THE ONES BEEN BUGGING ME TO GET BACK OUT HERE.
AWW, THEY CAME HOME AFTER CURFEW WITH SOME CRAZY STORY ABOUT A HAUNTED CAVE. I THINK THEY'RE GROUNDED, LIKE, FOREVER.
SALE
WELL, THAT'S MY TIMING...
HONK HONNNK
OH, DEAR LORD.
UH... HI, DICK.
HEY, LINDA! I WAS JUST DRIVIN' PAST AND SPOTTED YOU. KISMET, I GUESS. LUCKY US.
DANVERS
MAN, THAT CAR THE T-REX CHEWED IN "JURASSIC PARK" WAS IN BETTER SHAPE!
TOYO A

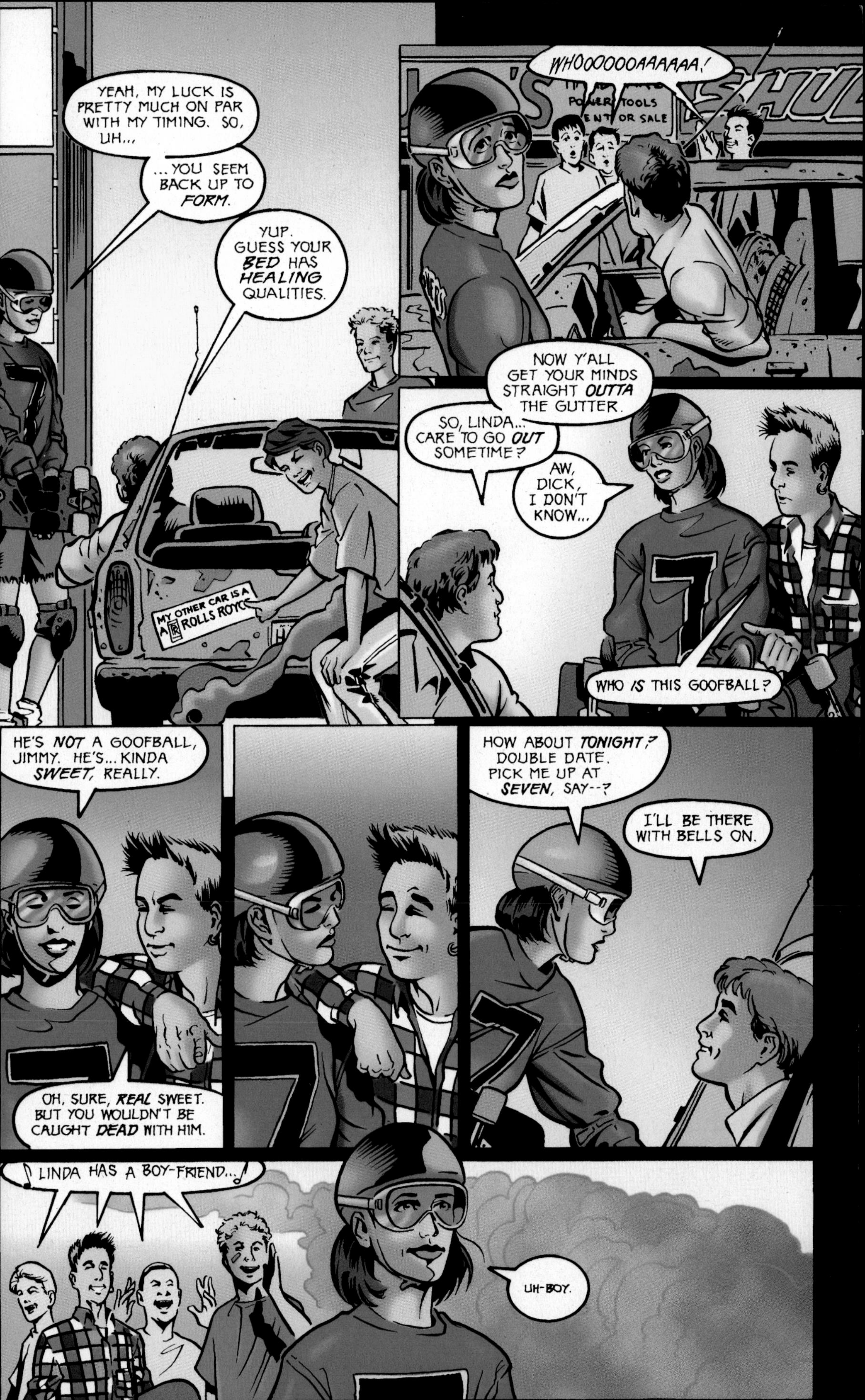
YEAH, MY LUCK IS PRETTY MUCH ON PAR WITH MY TIMING. SO, UH...
...YOU SEEM BACK UP TO FORM.
YUP. GUESS YOUR BED HAS HEALING QUALITIES.
MY OTHER CAR IS A ROLLS ROYC
WHOOOOOOAAAAAA!
POWER TOOLS
ENT OR SALE
NOW Y'ALL GET YOUR MINDS STRAIGHT OUTTA THE GUTTER.
SO, LINDA... CARE TO GO OUT SOMETIME?
AW, DICK, I DON'T KNOW...
WHO IS THIS GOOFBALL?
HE'S NOT A GOOFBALL, JIMMY. HE'S... KINDA SWEET, REALLY.
OH, SURE, REAL SWEET. BUT YOU WOULDN'T BE CAUGHT DEAD WITH HIM.
HOW ABOUT TONIGHT? DOUBLE DATE. PICK ME UP AT SEVEN, SAY--?
I'LL BE THERE WITH BELLS ON.
LINDA HAS A BOY-FRIEND...
UH-BOY.

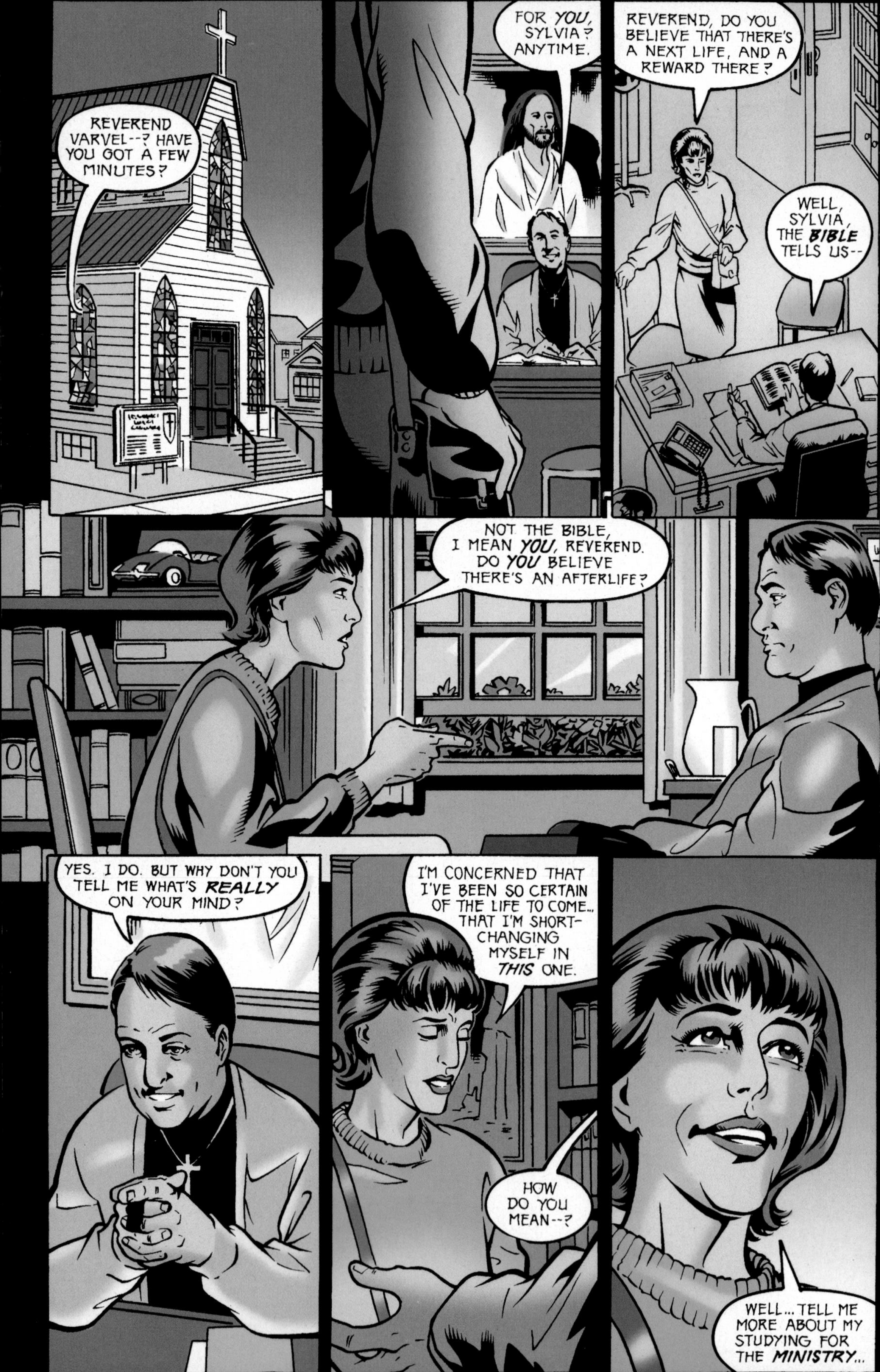
REVEREND VARVEL--? HAVE YOU GOT A FEW MINUTES?
FOR *YOU*, SYLVIA? ANYTIME.
REVEREND, DO YOU BELIEVE THAT THERE'S A NEXT LIFE, AND A REWARD THERE?
WELL, SYLVIA, THE ***BIBLE*** TELLS US--
NOT THE BIBLE, I MEAN *YOU*, REVEREND. DO *YOU* BELIEVE THERE'S AN AFTERLIFE?
YES. I DO. BUT WHY DON'T YOU TELL ME WHAT'S ***REALLY*** ON YOUR MIND?
I'M CONCERNED THAT I'VE BEEN SO CERTAIN OF THE LIFE TO COME.. THAT I'M SHORT-CHANGING MYSELF IN *THIS* ONE.
HOW DO YOU MEAN--?
WELL... TELL ME MORE ABOUT MY STUDYING FOR THE ***MINISTRY***...

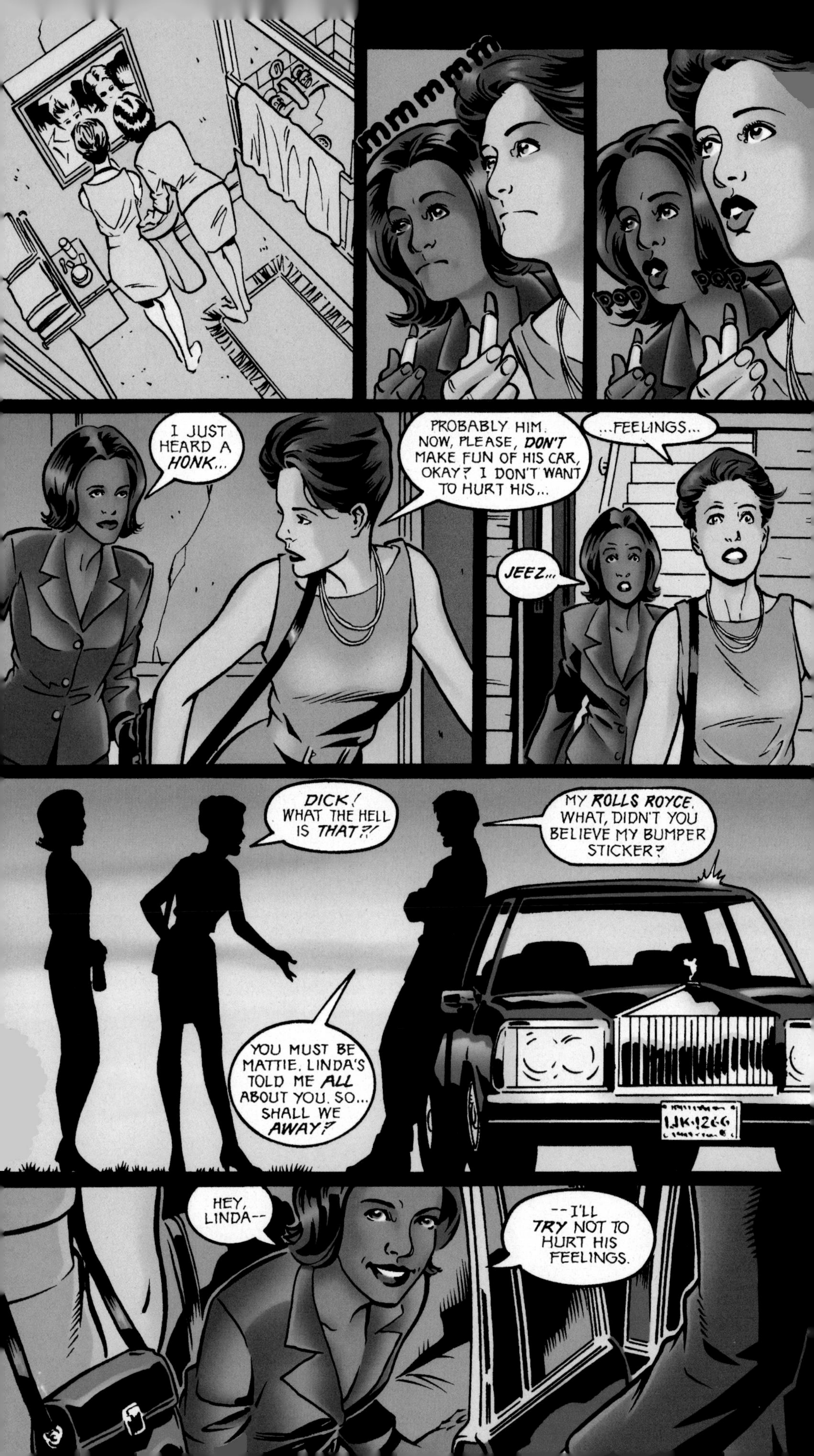
MMMMM
POP
POP
I JUST HEARD A HONK...
PROBABLY HIM. NOW, PLEASE, DON'T MAKE FUN OF HIS CAR, OKAY? I DON'T WANT TO HURT HIS...
...FEELINGS...
JEEZ...
DICK! WHAT THE HELL IS THAT?!
MY ROLLS ROYCE. WHAT, DIDN'T YOU BELIEVE MY BUMPER STICKER?
YOU MUST BE MATTIE. LINDA'S TOLD ME ALL ABOUT YOU. SO... SHALL WE AWAY?
1JK-1266
HEY, LINDA--
--I'LL TRY NOT TO HURT HIS FEELINGS.

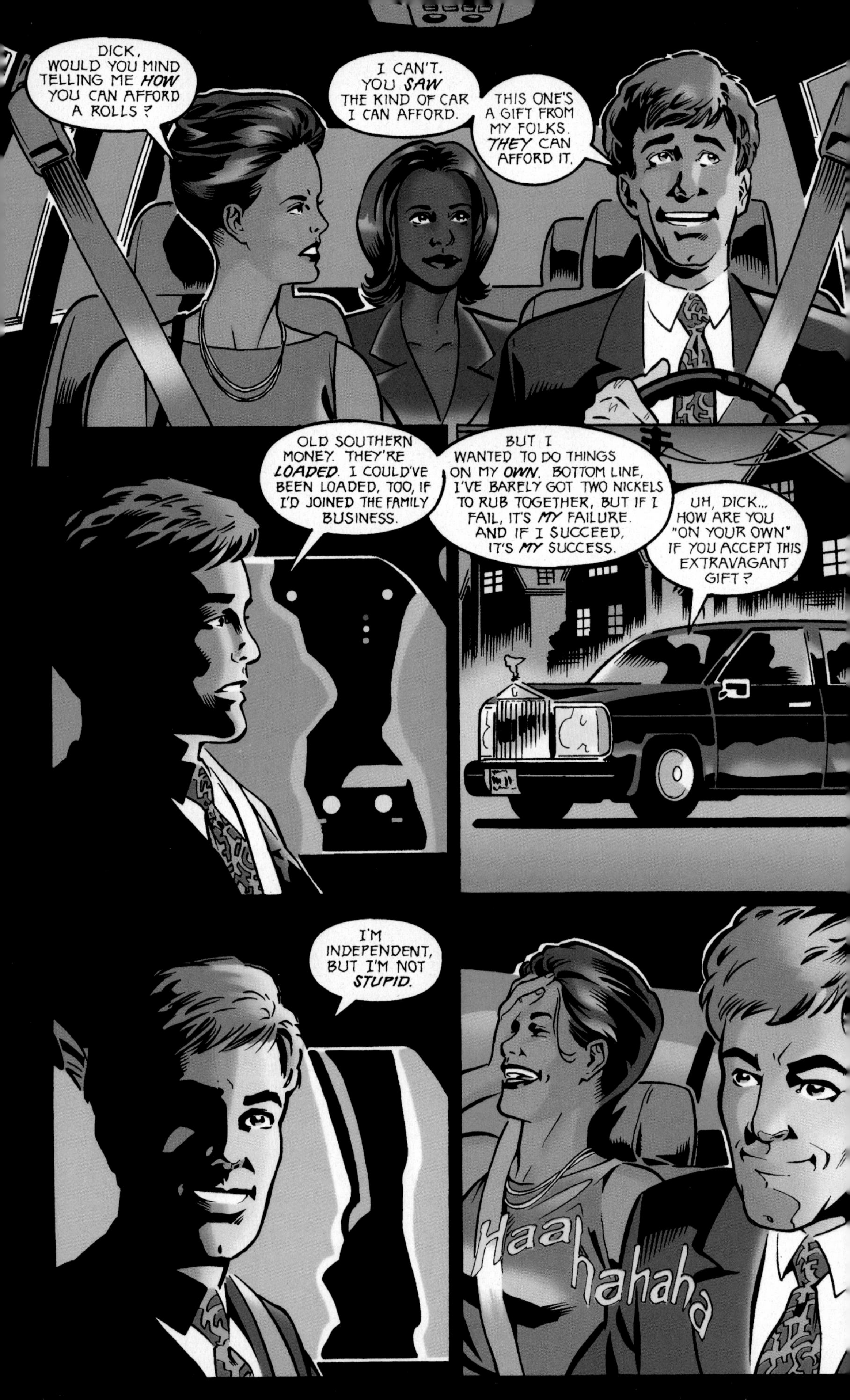
DICK, WOULD YOU MIND TELLING ME HOW YOU CAN AFFORD A ROLLS?
I CAN'T. YOU SAW THE KIND OF CAR I CAN AFFORD.
THIS ONE'S A GIFT FROM MY FOLKS. THEY CAN AFFORD IT.
OLD SOUTHERN MONEY. THEY'RE LOADED. I COULD'VE BEEN LOADED, TOO, IF I'D JOINED THE FAMILY BUSINESS.
BUT I WANTED TO DO THINGS ON MY OWN. BOTTOM LINE, I'VE BARELY GOT TWO NICKELS TO RUB TOGETHER, BUT IF I FAIL, IT'S MY FAILURE. AND IF I SUCCEED, IT'S MY SUCCESS.
UH, DICK... HOW ARE YOU "ON YOUR OWN" IF YOU ACCEPT THIS EXTRAVAGANT GIFT?
I'M INDEPENDENT, BUT I'M NOT STUPID.
Haa hahaha

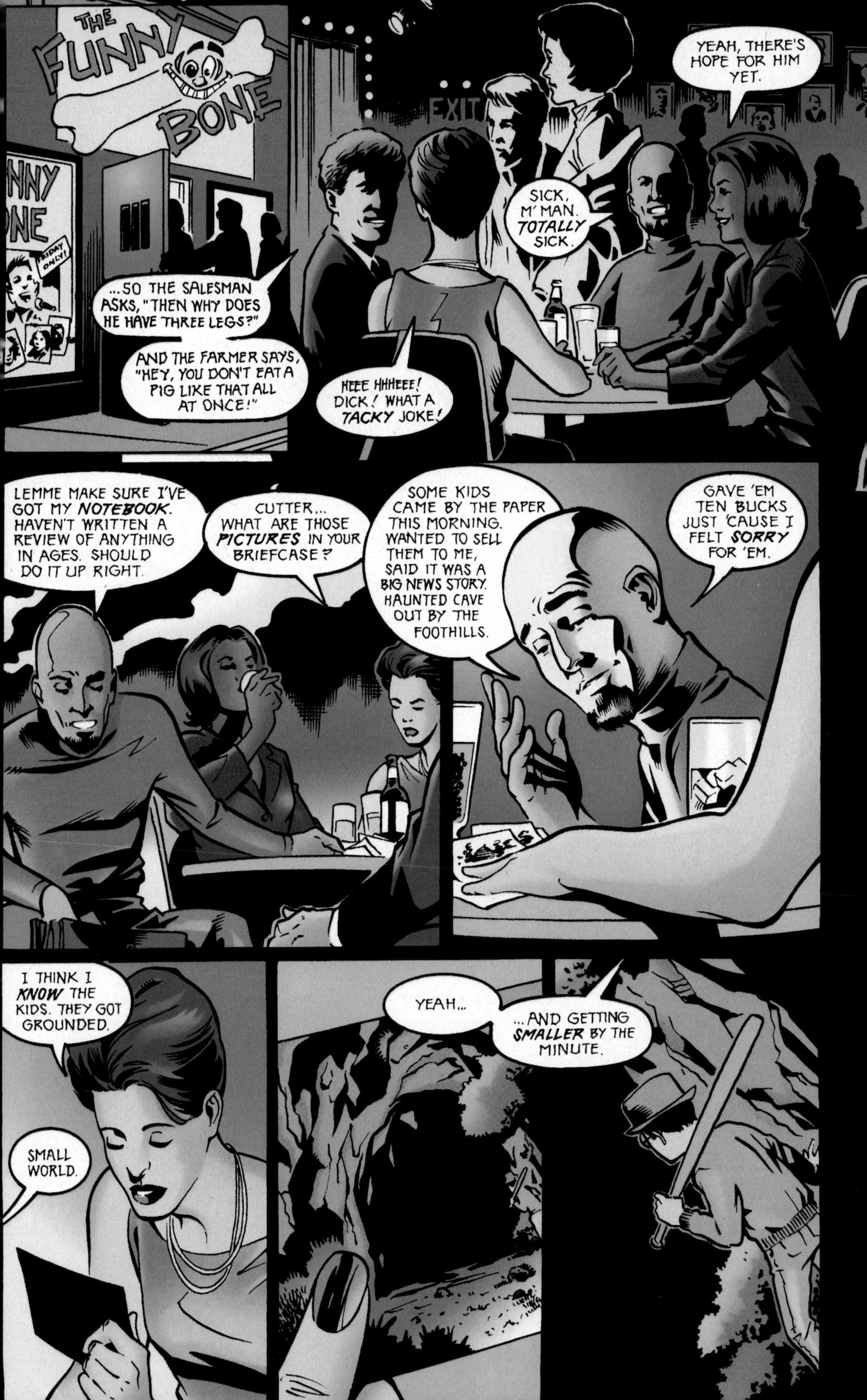
THE FUNNY BONE
NNY ONE
FRIDAY ONLY!
EXIT
YEAH, THERE'S HOPE FOR HIM YET.
SICK, M' MAN. TOTALLY SICK.
...SO THE SALESMAN ASKS, "THEN WHY DOES HE HAVE THREE LEGS?"
AND THE FARMER SAYS, "HEY, YOU DON'T EAT A PIG LIKE THAT ALL AT ONCE!"
HEEE HHHEEE! DICK! WHAT A TACKY JOKE!
LEMME MAKE SURE I'VE GOT MY NOTEBOOK. HAVEN'T WRITTEN A REVIEW OF ANYTHING IN AGES. SHOULD DO IT UP RIGHT.
CUTTER... WHAT ARE THOSE PICTURES IN YOUR BRIEFCASE?
SOME KIDS CAME BY THE PAPER THIS MORNING. WANTED TO SELL THEM TO ME, SAID IT WAS A BIG NEWS STORY. HAUNTED CAVE OUT BY THE FOOTHILLS.
GAVE 'EM TEN BUCKS JUST 'CAUSE I FELT SORRY FOR 'EM.
I THINK I KNOW THE KIDS. THEY GOT GROUNDED.
SMALL WORLD.
YEAH...
...AND GETTING SMALLER BY THE MINUTE.

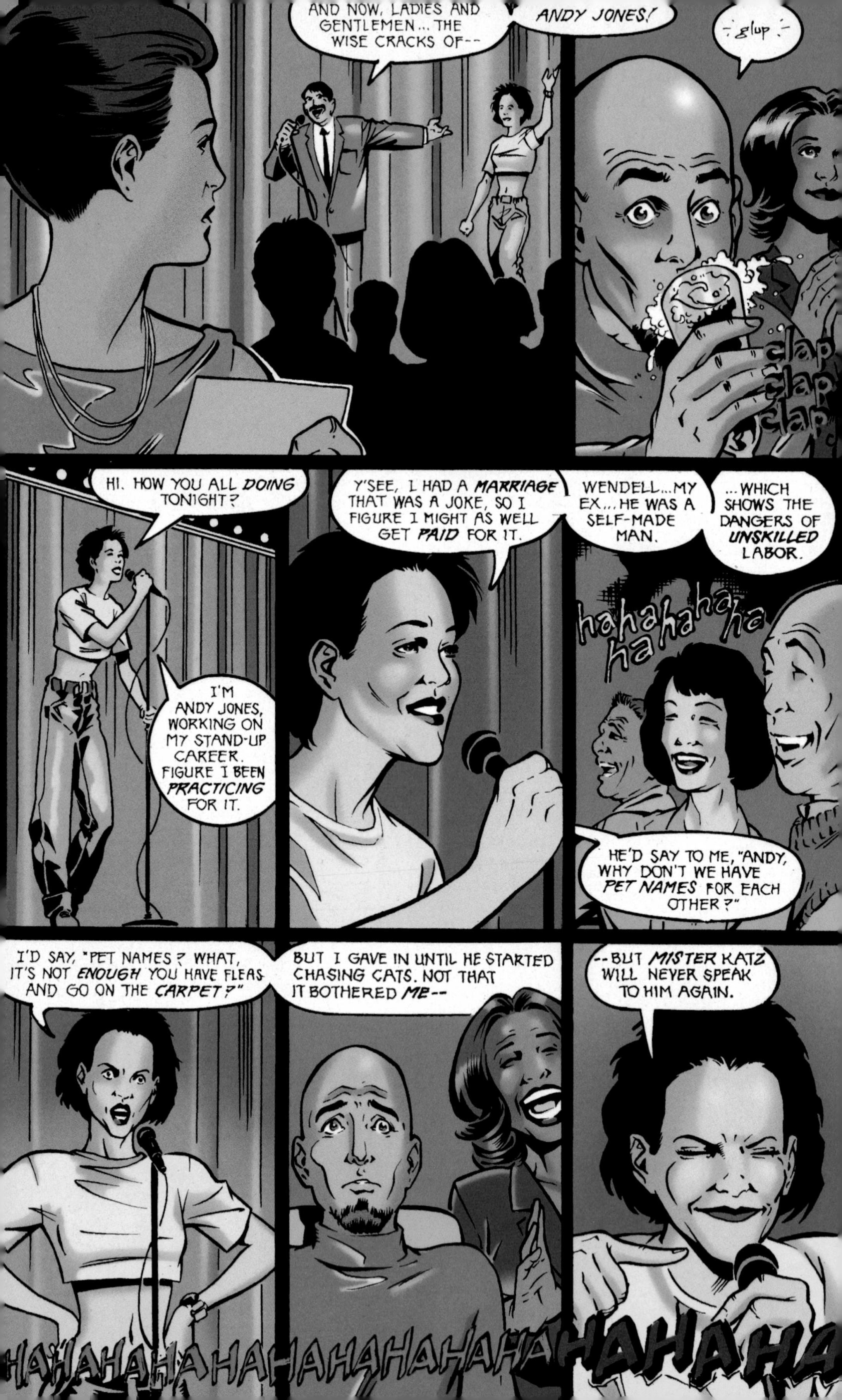

AND NOW, LADIES AND GENTLEMEN... THE WISE CRACKS OF--
ANDY JONES!
glup
clap clap clap
HI. HOW YOU ALL DOING TONIGHT?
I'M ANDY JONES, WORKING ON MY STAND-UP CAREER. FIGURE I BEEN PRACTICING FOR IT.
Y'SEE, I HAD A MARRIAGE THAT WAS A JOKE, SO I FIGURE I MIGHT AS WELL GET PAID FOR IT.
WENDELL...MY EX... HE WAS A SELF-MADE MAN.
...WHICH SHOWS THE DANGERS OF UNSKILLED LABOR.
hahahahaha ha
HE'D SAY TO ME, "ANDY, WHY DON'T WE HAVE PET NAMES FOR EACH OTHER?"
I'D SAY, "PET NAMES? WHAT, IT'S NOT ENOUGH YOU HAVE FLEAS AND GO ON THE CARPET?"
BUT I GAVE IN UNTIL HE STARTED CHASING CATS. NOT THAT IT BOTHERED ME--
--BUT MISTER KATZ WILL NEVER SPEAK TO HIM AGAIN.
HAHAHAHAHAHAHAHAHAHAHAHAHAHAHA

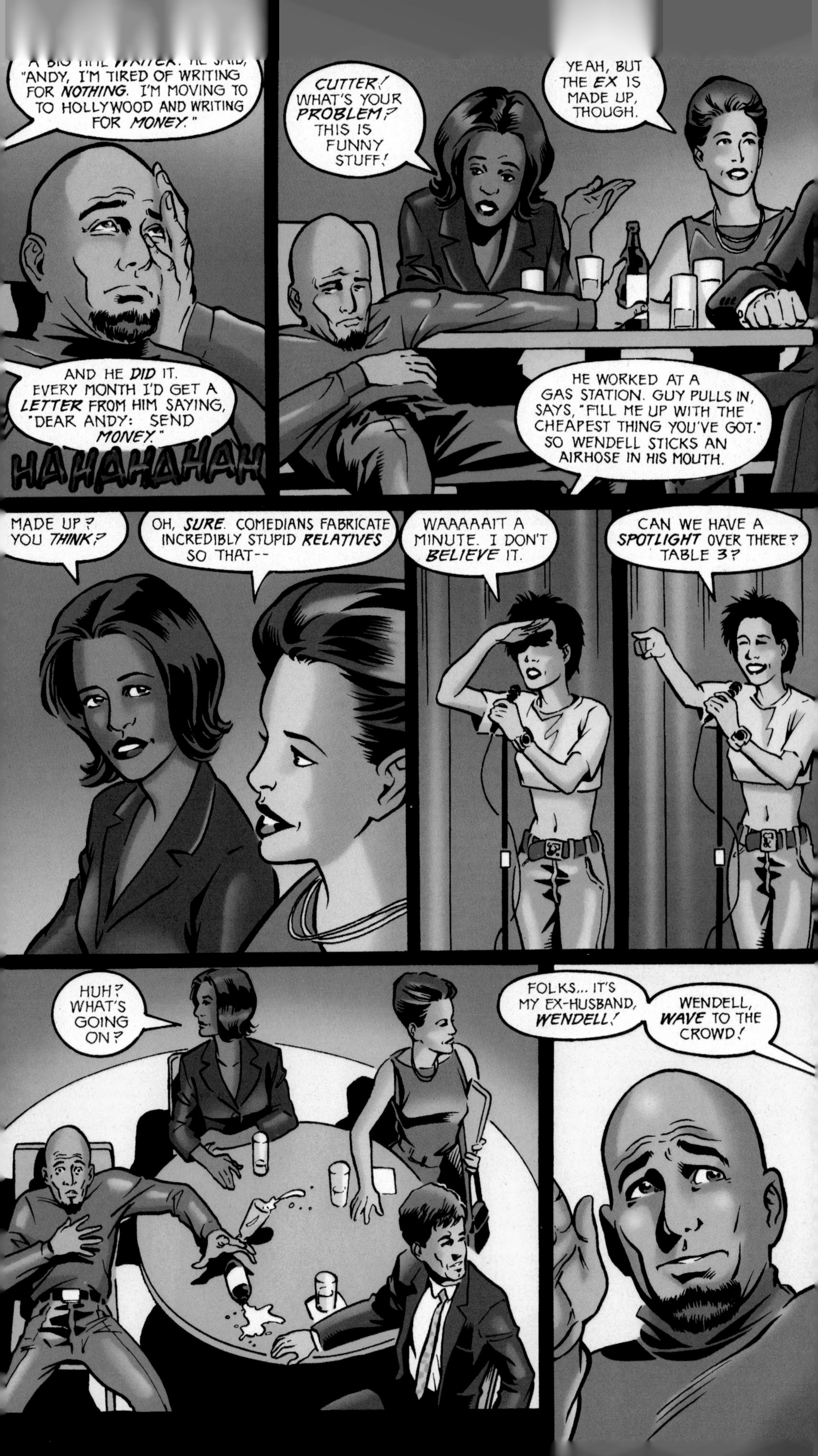

"ANDY, I'M TIRED OF WRITING FOR NOTHING. I'M MOVING TO TO HOLLYWOOD AND WRITING FOR MONEY."
AND HE DID IT. EVERY MONTH I'D GET A LETTER FROM HIM SAYING, "DEAR ANDY: SEND MONEY."
HAHAHAHAH
CUTTER! WHAT'S YOUR PROBLEM? THIS IS FUNNY STUFF!
YEAH, BUT THE EX IS MADE UP, THOUGH.
HE WORKED AT A GAS STATION. GUY PULLS IN, SAYS, "FILL ME UP WITH THE CHEAPEST THING YOU'VE GOT." SO WENDELL STICKS AN AIRHOSE IN HIS MOUTH.
MADE UP? YOU THINK?
OH, SURE. COMEDIANS FABRICATE INCREDIBLY STUPID RELATIVES SO THAT--
WAAAAAIT A MINUTE. I DON'T BELIEVE IT.
CAN WE HAVE A SPOTLIGHT OVER THERE? TABLE 3?
HUH? WHAT'S GOING ON?
FOLKS... IT'S MY EX-HUSBAND, WENDELL!
WENDELL, WAVE TO THE CROWD!

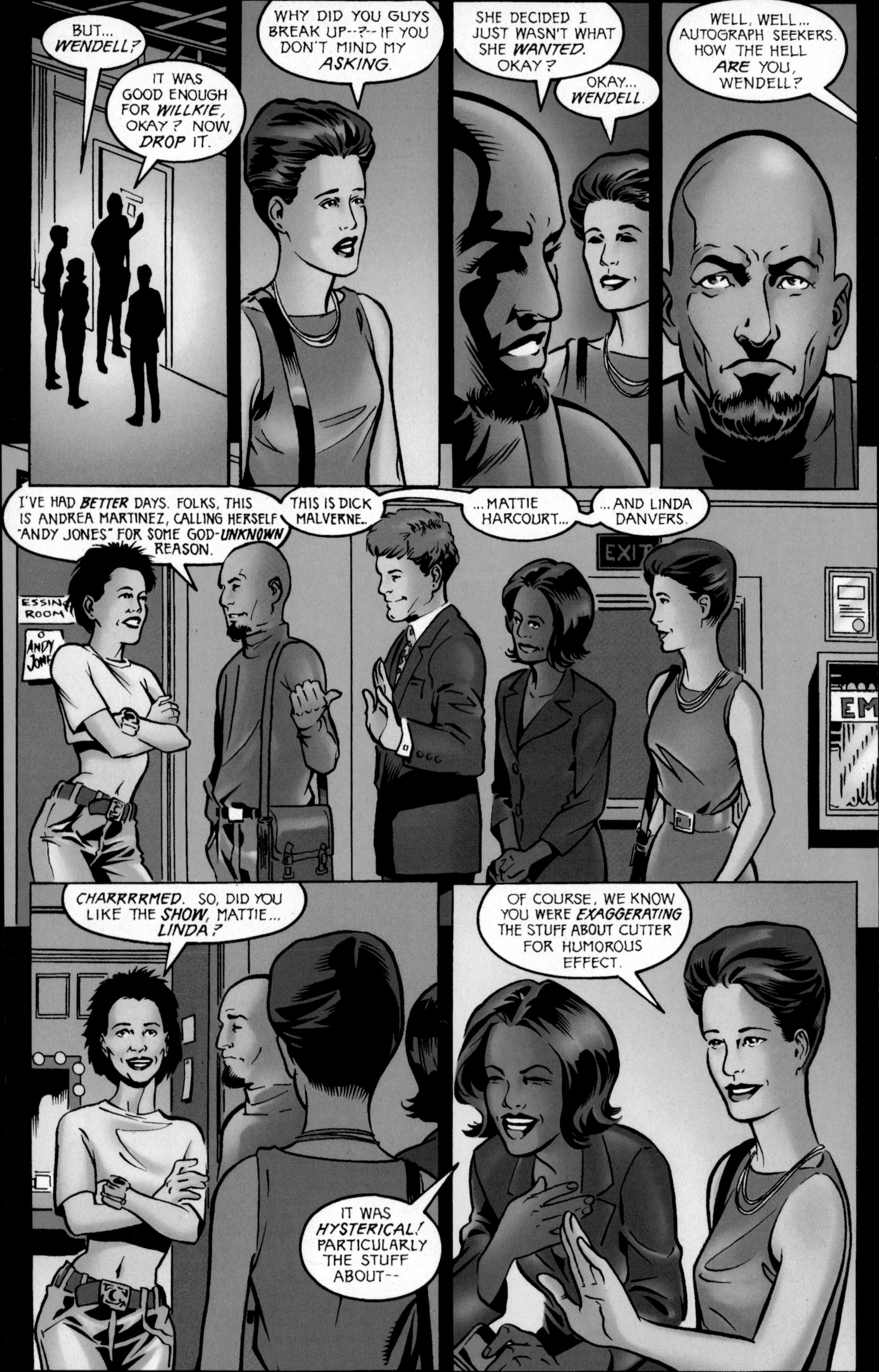
BUT... WENDELL?
IT WAS GOOD ENOUGH FOR WILLKIE, OKAY? NOW, DROP IT.
WHY DID YOU GUYS BREAK UP--?--IF YOU DON'T MIND MY ASKING.
SHE DECIDED I JUST WASN'T WHAT SHE WANTED. OKAY?
OKAY... WENDELL.
WELL, WELL... AUTOGRAPH SEEKERS. HOW THE HELL ARE YOU, WENDELL?
I'VE HAD BETTER DAYS. FOLKS, THIS IS ANDREA MARTINEZ, CALLING HERSELF "ANDY JONES" FOR SOME GOD-UNKNOWN REASON.
THIS IS DICK MALVERNE...
...MATTIE HARCOURT...
...AND LINDA DANVERS.
EXIT
ESSING ROOM
ANDY JONES
CHARRRRMED. SO, DID YOU LIKE THE SHOW, MATTIE... LINDA?
IT WAS HYSTERICAL! PARTICULARLY THE STUFF ABOUT--
OF COURSE, WE KNOW YOU WERE EXAGGERATING THE STUFF ABOUT CUTTER FOR HUMOROUS EFFECT.

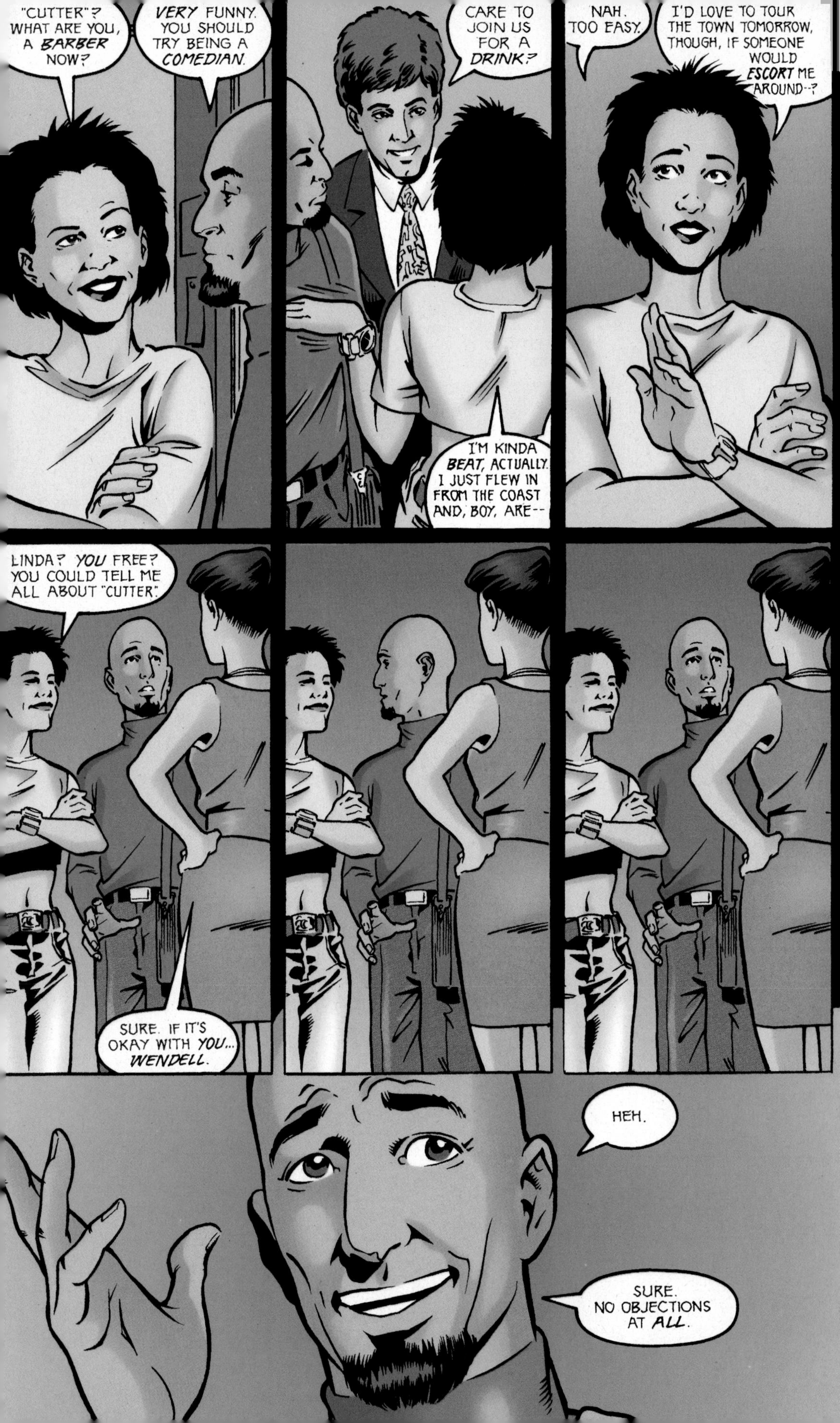
"CUTTER"? WHAT ARE YOU, A BARBER NOW?
VERY FUNNY. YOU SHOULD TRY BEING A COMEDIAN.
CARE TO JOIN US FOR A DRINK?
I'M KINDA BEAT, ACTUALLY. I JUST FLEW IN FROM THE COAST AND, BOY, ARE--
NAH. TOO EASY.
I'D LOVE TO TOUR THE TOWN TOMORROW, THOUGH, IF SOMEONE WOULD ESCORT ME AROUND--?
LINDA? YOU FREE? YOU COULD TELL ME ALL ABOUT "CUTTER".
SURE. IF IT'S OKAY WITH YOU... WENDELL.
HEH.
SURE. NO OBJECTIONS AT ALL.

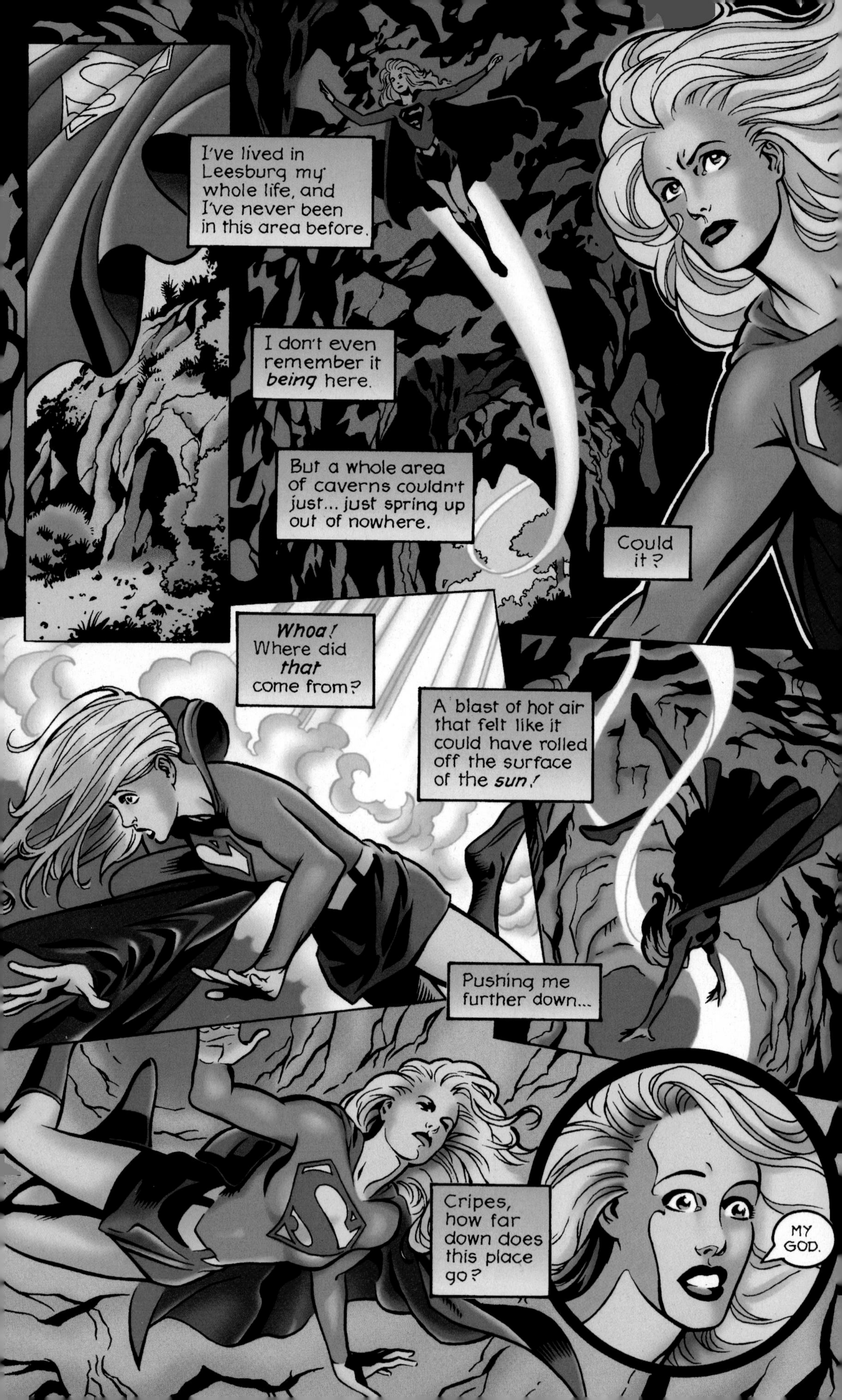

I've lived in Leesburg my whole life, and I've never been in this area before.
I don't even remember it *being* here.
But a whole area of caverns couldn't just... just spring up out of nowhere.
Could it?
Whoa! Where did *that* come from?
A blast of hot air that felt like it could have rolled off the surface of the *sun!*
Pushing me further down...
Cripes, how far down does this place go?
MY GOD.

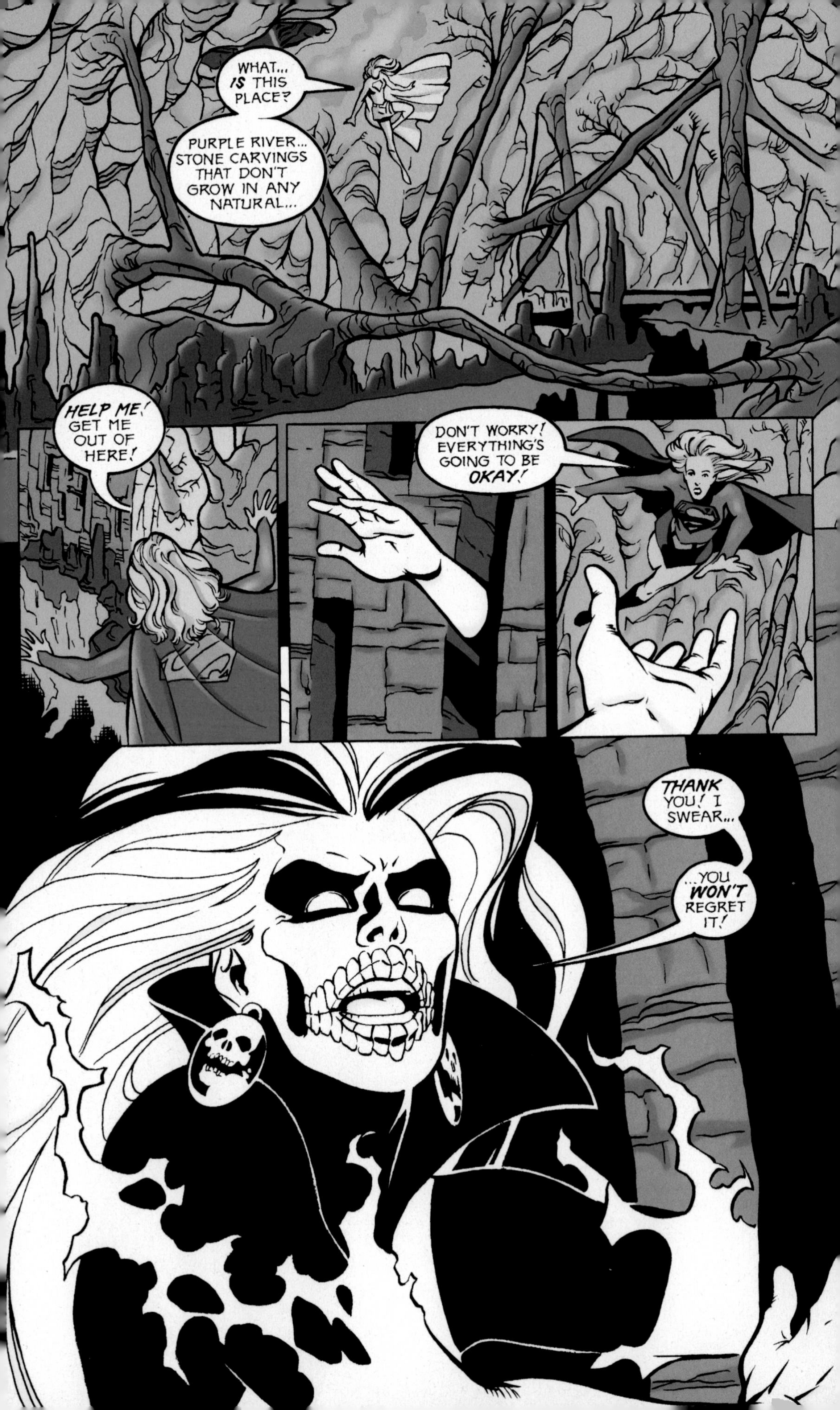
WHAT... IS THIS PLACE?
PURPLE RIVER... STONE CARVINGS THAT DON'T GROW IN ANY NATURAL...
HELP ME! GET ME OUT OF HERE!
DON'T WORRY! EVERYTHING'S GOING TO BE OKAY!
THANK YOU! I SWEAR...
...YOU WON'T REGRET IT!

***SUPERGIRL* #11 cover by Gary Frank, Cam Smith and Patrick Martin**

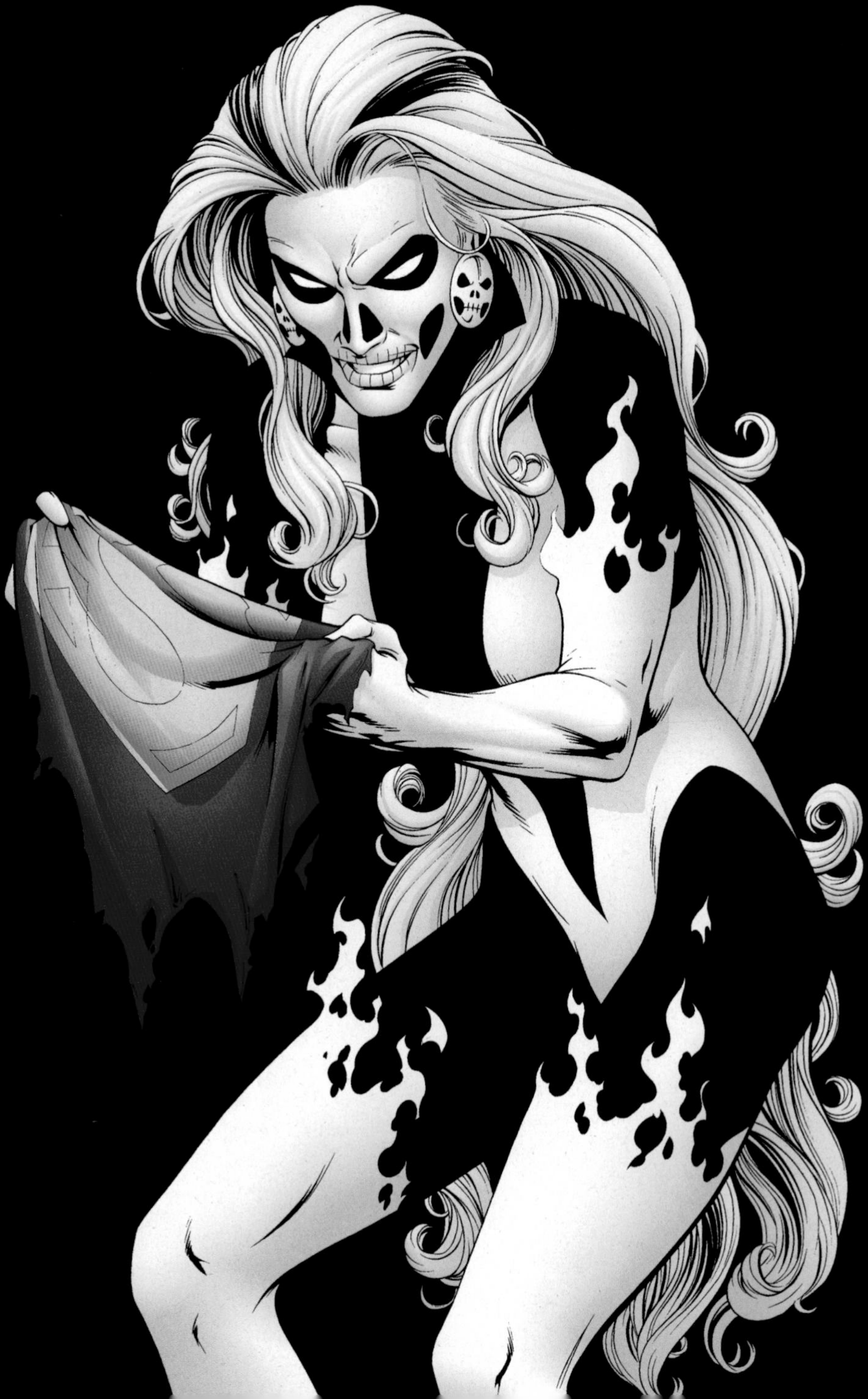

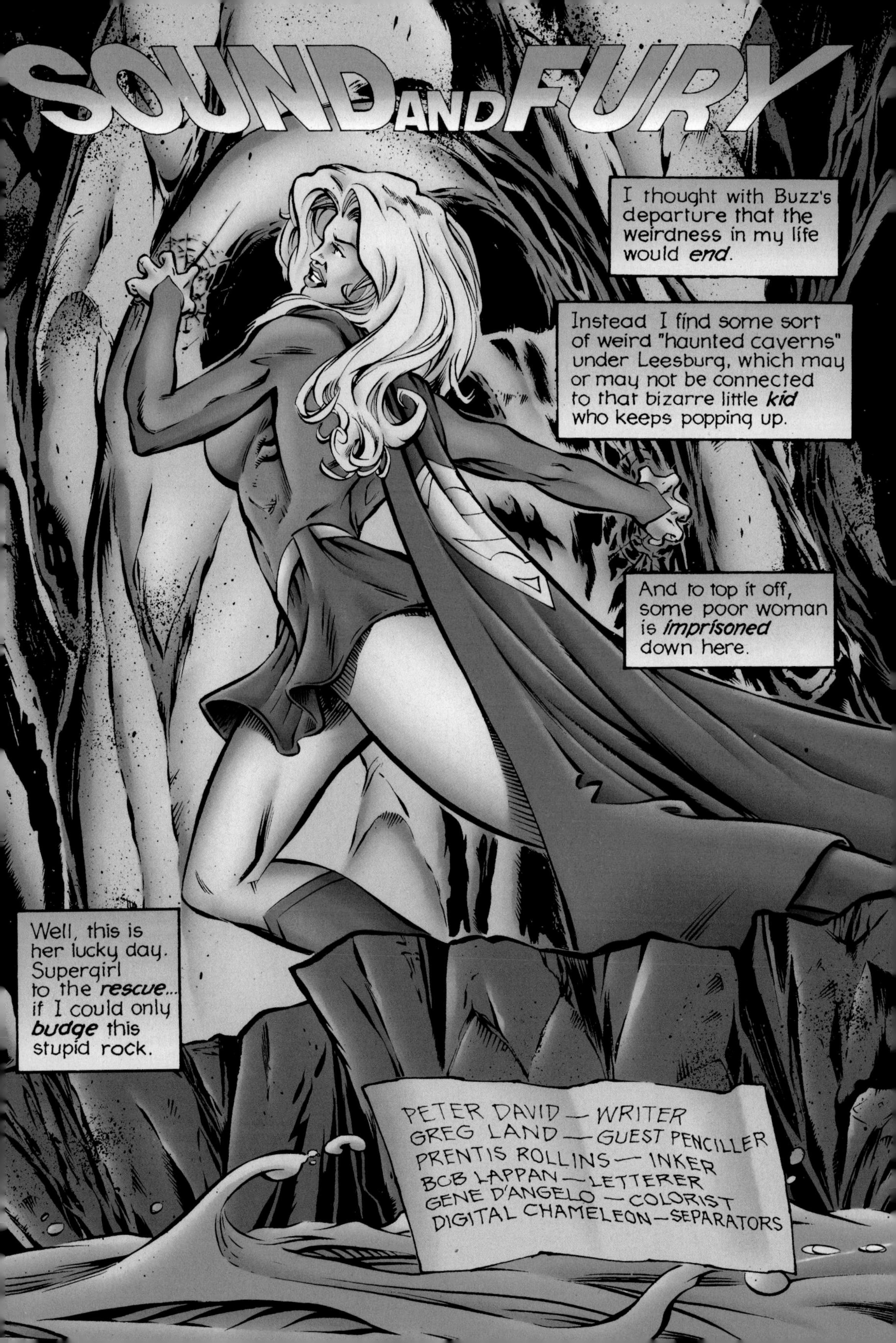
SOUND AND FURY
I thought with Buzz's departure that the weirdness in my life would *end*.
Instead I find some sort of weird "haunted caverns" under Leesburg, which may or may not be connected to that bizarre little *kid* who keeps popping up.
And to top it off, some poor woman is *imprisoned* down here.
Well, this is her lucky day. Supergirl to the *rescue*... if I could only *budge* this stupid rock.
PETER DAVID — WRITER
GREG LAND — GUEST PENCILLER
PRENTIS ROLLINS — INKER
BOB LAPPAN — LETTERER
GENE D'ANGELO — COLORIST
DIGITAL CHAMELEON — SEPARATORS

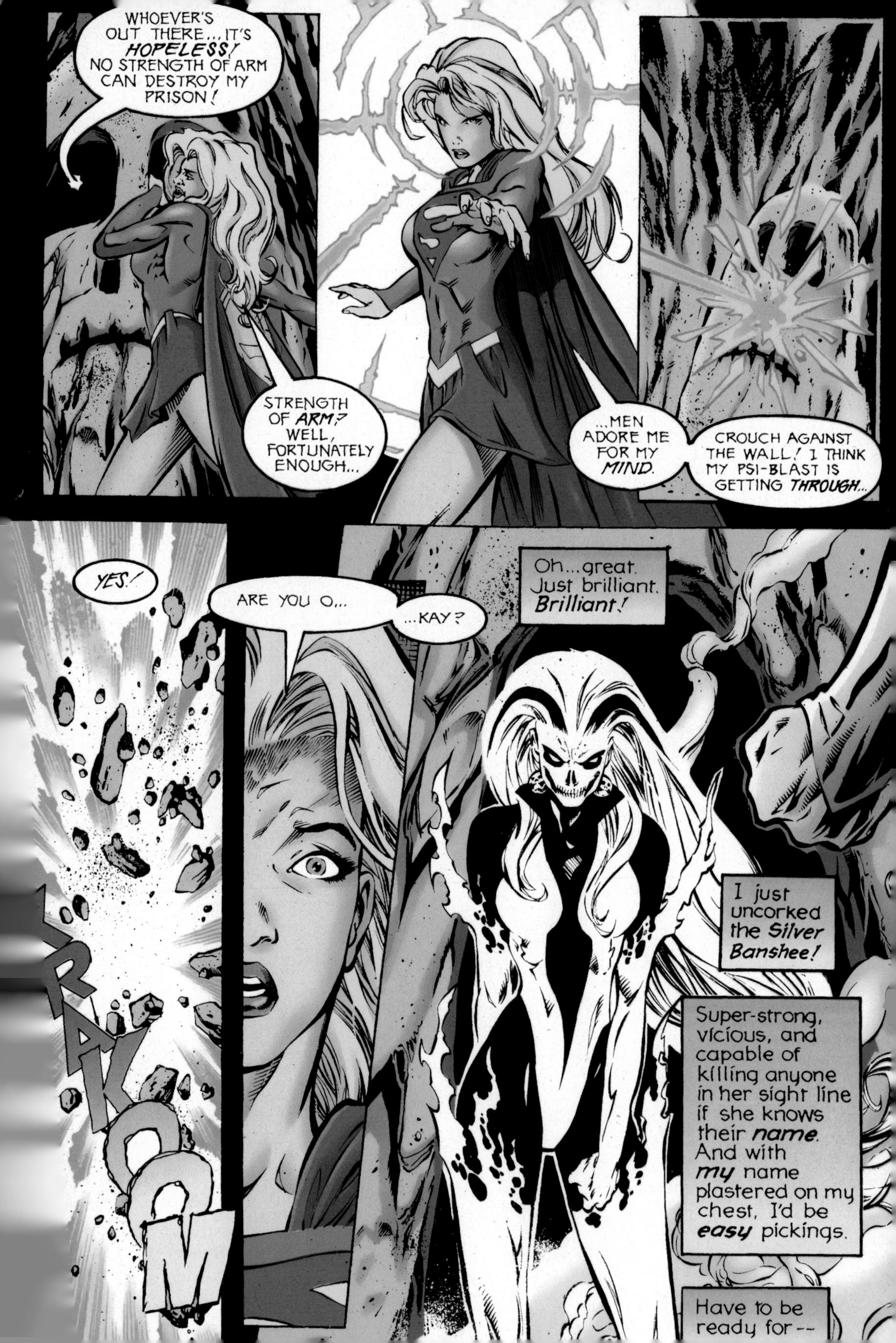
WHOEVER'S OUT THERE... IT'S HOPELESS! NO STRENGTH OF ARM CAN DESTROY MY PRISON!
STRENGTH OF ARM? WELL, FORTUNATELY ENOUGH...
...MEN ADORE ME FOR MY MIND.
CROUCH AGAINST THE WALL! I THINK MY PSI-BLAST IS GETTING THROUGH...
YES!
KRAKOOM
ARE YOU O...
...KAY?
Oh...great. Just brilliant. Brilliant!
I just uncorked the Silver Banshee!
Super-strong, vicious, and capable of killing anyone in her sight line if she knows their name. And with my name plastered on my chest, I'd be easy pickings.
Have to be ready for--

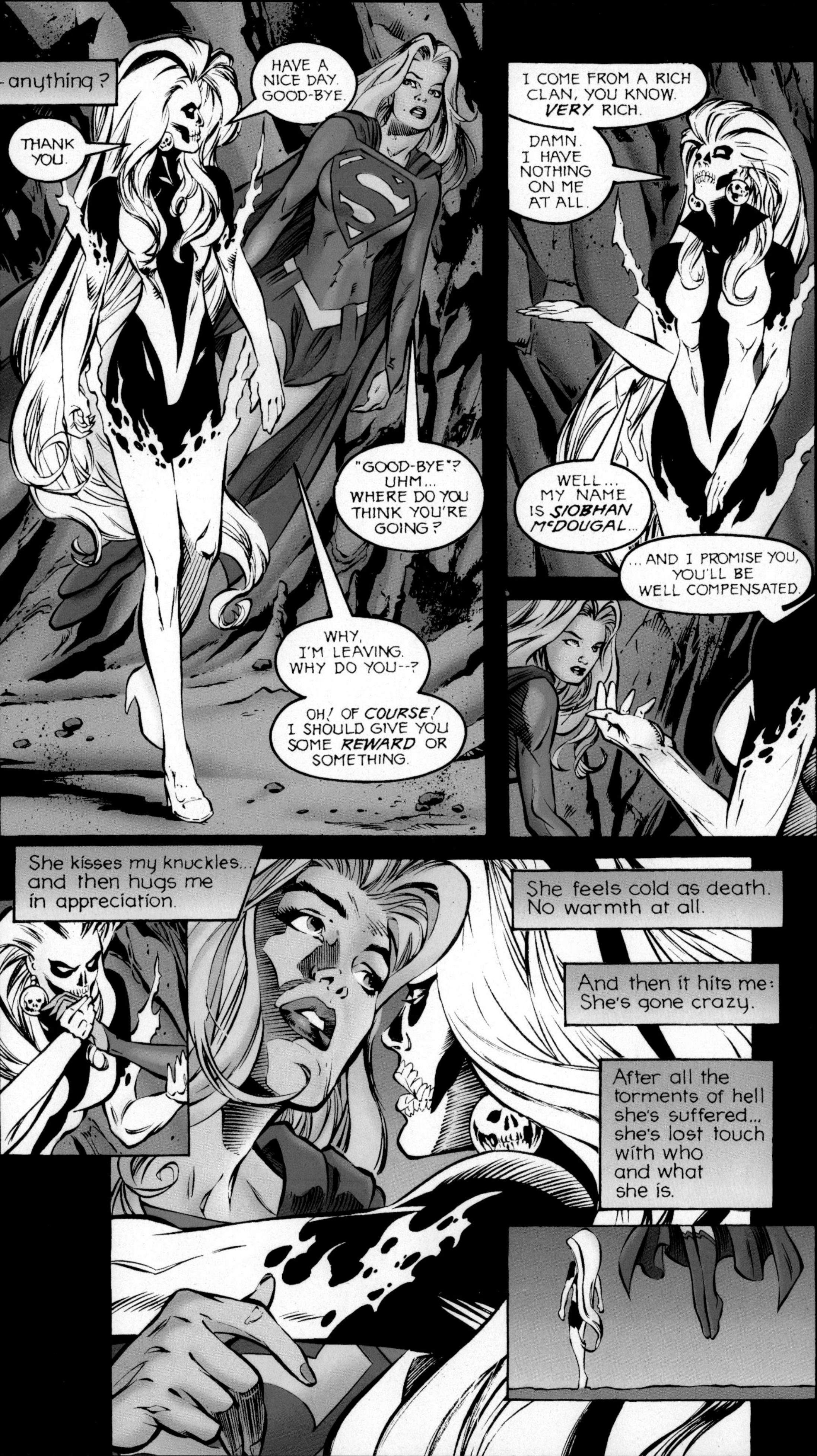
-anything?
THANK YOU.
HAVE A NICE DAY. GOOD-BYE.
"GOOD-BYE"? UHM... WHERE DO YOU THINK YOU'RE GOING?
WHY, I'M LEAVING. WHY DO YOU--?
OH! OF COURSE! I SHOULD GIVE YOU SOME REWARD OR SOMETHING.
I COME FROM A RICH CLAN, YOU KNOW. VERY RICH.
DAMN. I HAVE NOTHING ON ME AT ALL.
WELL... MY NAME IS SIOBHAN McDOUGAL...
...AND I PROMISE YOU, YOU'LL BE WELL COMPENSATED.
She kisses my knuckles... and then hugs me in appreciation.
She feels cold as death. No warmth at all.
And then it hits me: She's gone crazy.
After all the torments of hell she's suffered... she's lost touch with who and what she is.

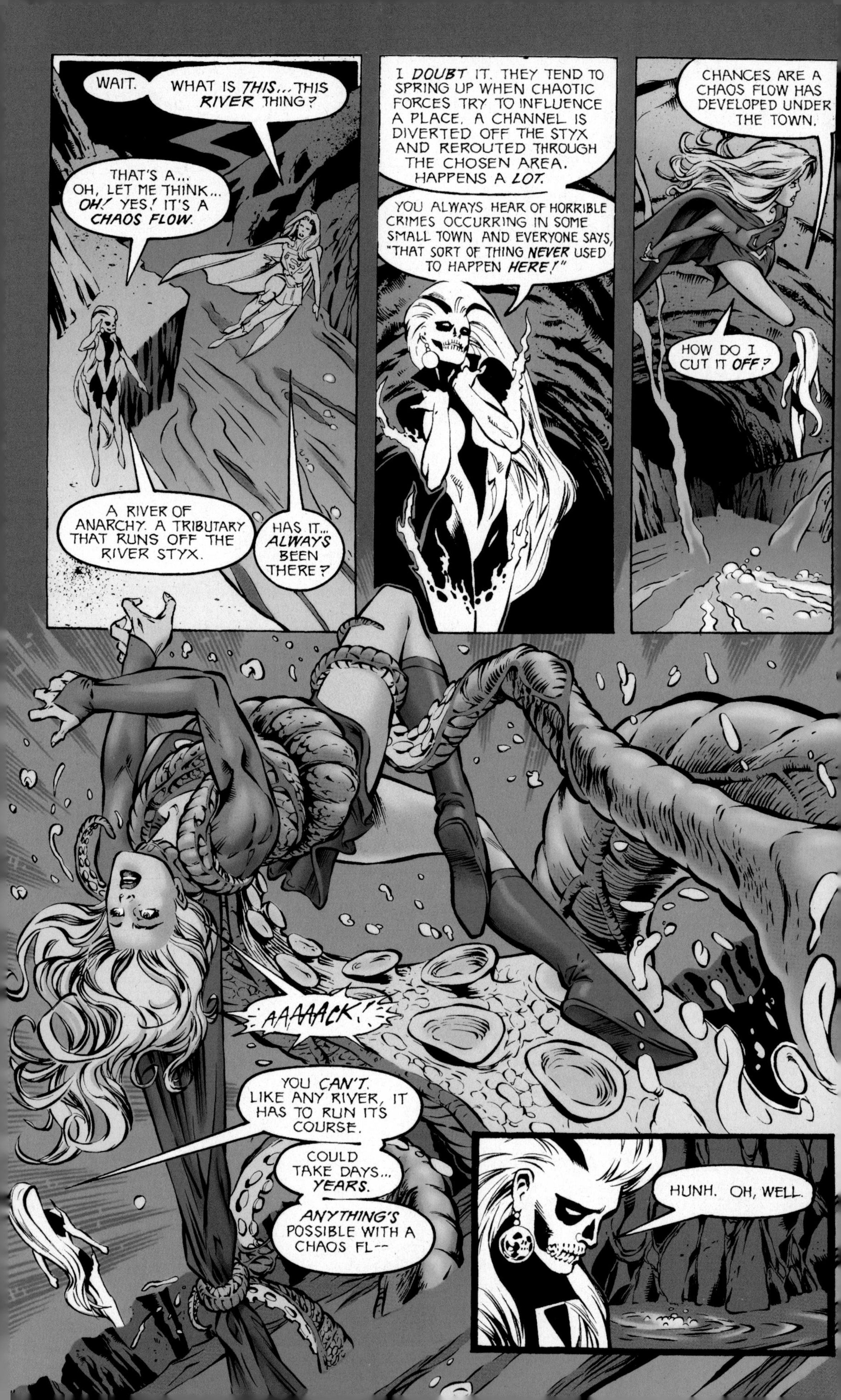
WAIT.
WHAT IS THIS... THIS RIVER THING?
THAT'S A... OH, LET ME THINK... OH! YES! IT'S A CHAOS FLOW.
A RIVER OF ANARCHY. A TRIBUTARY THAT RUNS OFF THE RIVER STYX.
HAS IT... ALWAYS BEEN THERE?
I DOUBT IT. THEY TEND TO SPRING UP WHEN CHAOTIC FORCES TRY TO INFLUENCE A PLACE. A CHANNEL IS DIVERTED OFF THE STYX AND REROUTED THROUGH THE CHOSEN AREA. HAPPENS A LOT.
YOU ALWAYS HEAR OF HORRIBLE CRIMES OCCURRING IN SOME SMALL TOWN AND EVERYONE SAYS, "THAT SORT OF THING NEVER USED TO HAPPEN HERE!"
CHANCES ARE A CHAOS FLOW HAS DEVELOPED UNDER THE TOWN.
HOW DO I CUT IT OFF?
AAAAACK!
YOU CAN'T. LIKE ANY RIVER, IT HAS TO RUN ITS COURSE.
COULD TAKE DAYS... YEARS.
ANYTHING'S POSSIBLE WITH A CHAOS FL--
HUNH. OH, WELL.

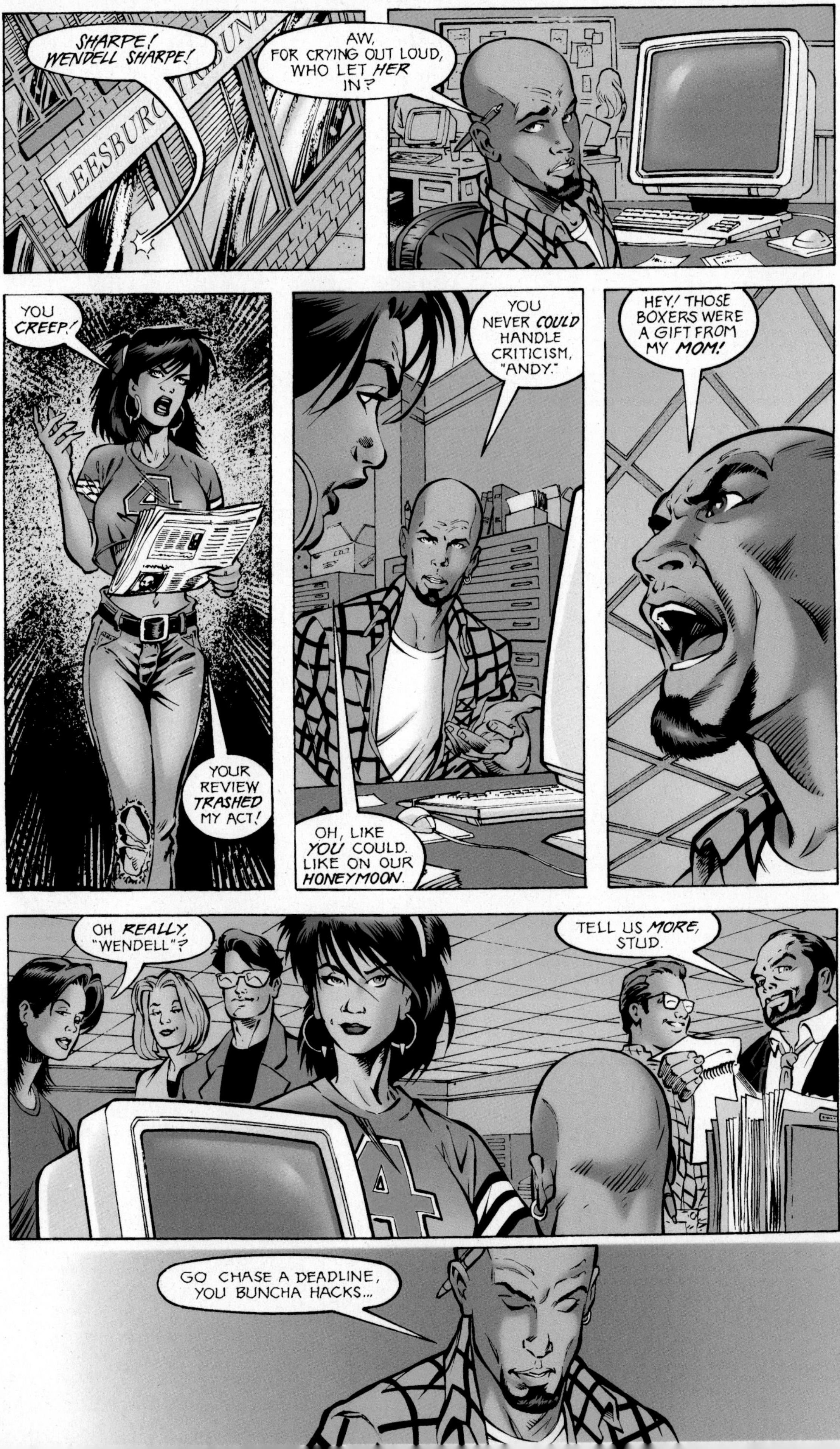
SHARPE! WENDELL SHARPE!
LEESBURG TRIBUNE
AW, FOR CRYING OUT LOUD, WHO LET HER IN?
YOU CREEP!
YOUR REVIEW TRASHED MY ACT!
YOU NEVER COULD HANDLE CRITICISM, "ANDY."
OH, LIKE YOU COULD. LIKE ON OUR HONEYMOON.
HEY! THOSE BOXERS WERE A GIFT FROM MY MOM!
OH REALLY, "WENDELL"?
TELL US MORE, STUD.
GO CHASE A DEADLINE, YOU BUNCHA HACKS...

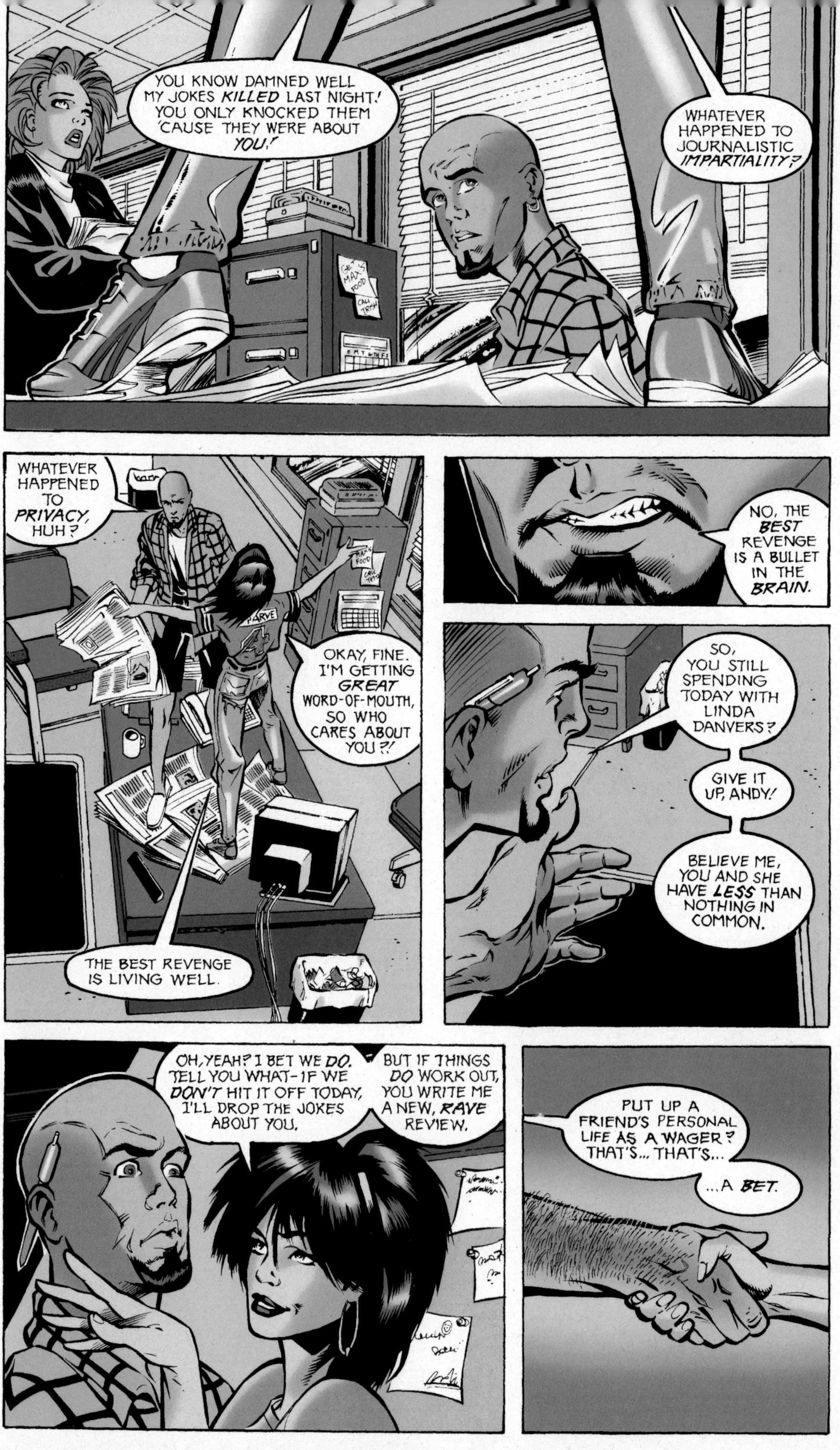

YOU KNOW DAMNED WELL MY JOKES KILLED LAST NIGHT! YOU ONLY KNOCKED THEM 'CAUSE THEY WERE ABOUT YOU!
WHATEVER HAPPENED TO JOURNALISTIC IMPARTIALITY?
GET MAX'S FOOD
CALL TRISH
WHATEVER HAPPENED TO PRIVACY, HUH?
OKAY, FINE. I'M GETTING GREAT WORD-OF-MOUTH, SO WHO CARES ABOUT YOU?!
THE BEST REVENGE IS LIVING WELL.
NO, THE BEST REVENGE IS A BULLET IN THE BRAIN.
SO, YOU STILL SPENDING TODAY WITH LINDA DANVERS?
GIVE IT UP, ANDY!
BELIEVE ME, YOU AND SHE HAVE LESS THAN NOTHING IN COMMON.
OH, YEAH? I BET WE DO. TELL YOU WHAT-IF WE DON'T HIT IT OFF TODAY, I'LL DROP THE JOKES ABOUT YOU.
BUT IF THINGS DO WORK OUT, YOU WRITE ME A NEW, RAVE REVIEW.
PUT UP A FRIEND'S PERSONAL LIFE AS A WAGER? THAT'S... THAT'S...
...A BET.

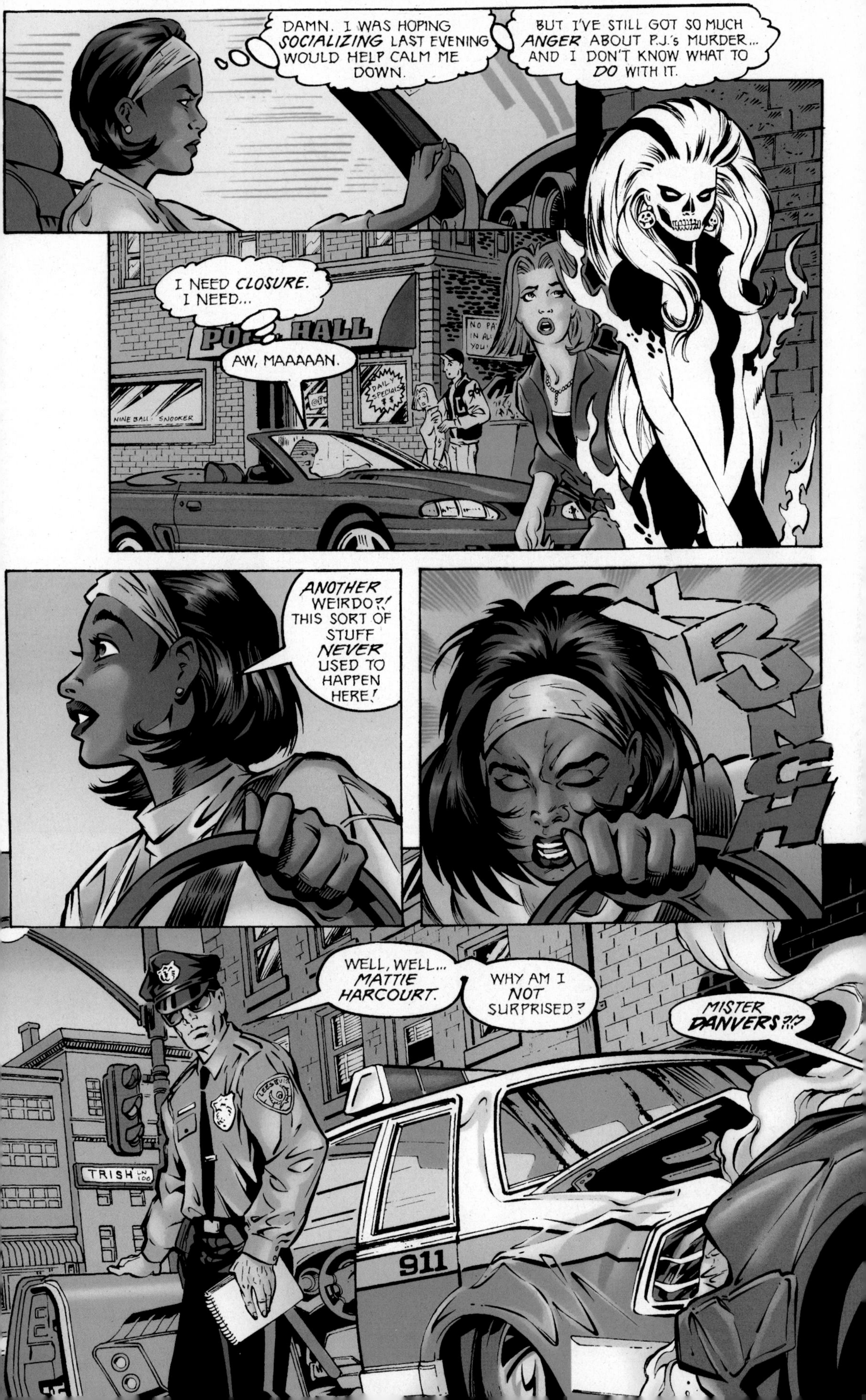
DAMN. I WAS HOPING SOCIALIZING LAST EVENING WOULD HELP CALM ME DOWN.
BUT I'VE STILL GOT SO MUCH ANGER ABOUT P.J.'s MURDER... AND I DON'T KNOW WHAT TO DO WITH IT.
I NEED CLOSURE. I NEED...
AW, MAAAAAN.
POOL HALL
NINE BALL · SNOOKER
DAILY SPECIALS
ANOTHER WEIRDO?! THIS SORT OF STUFF NEVER USED TO HAPPEN HERE!
KRUNCH
WELL, WELL... MATTIE HARCOURT.
WHY AM I NOT SURPRISED?
MISTER DANVERS?!?
TRISH LN 100
911

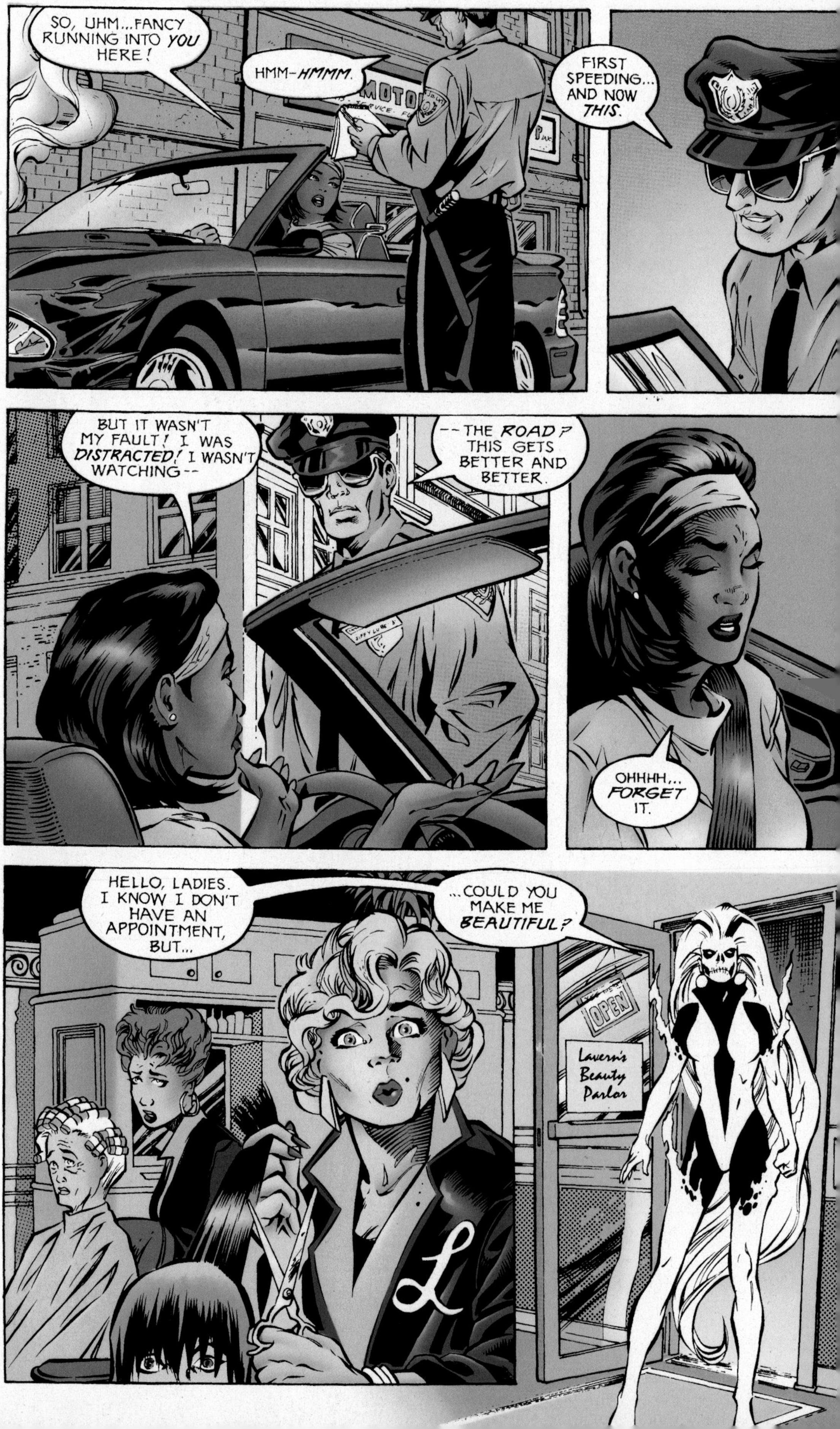

SO, UHM...FANCY RUNNING INTO YOU HERE!
HMM-HMMM.
MOTO
FIRST SPEEDING... AND NOW THIS.
BUT IT WASN'T MY FAULT! I WAS DISTRACTED! I WASN'T WATCHING--
--THE ROAD? THIS GETS BETTER AND BETTER.
OHHHH,.. FORGET IT.
HELLO, LADIES. I KNOW I DON'T HAVE AN APPOINTMENT, BUT...
...COULD YOU MAKE ME BEAUTIFUL?
OPEN
Lavern's Beauty Parlor

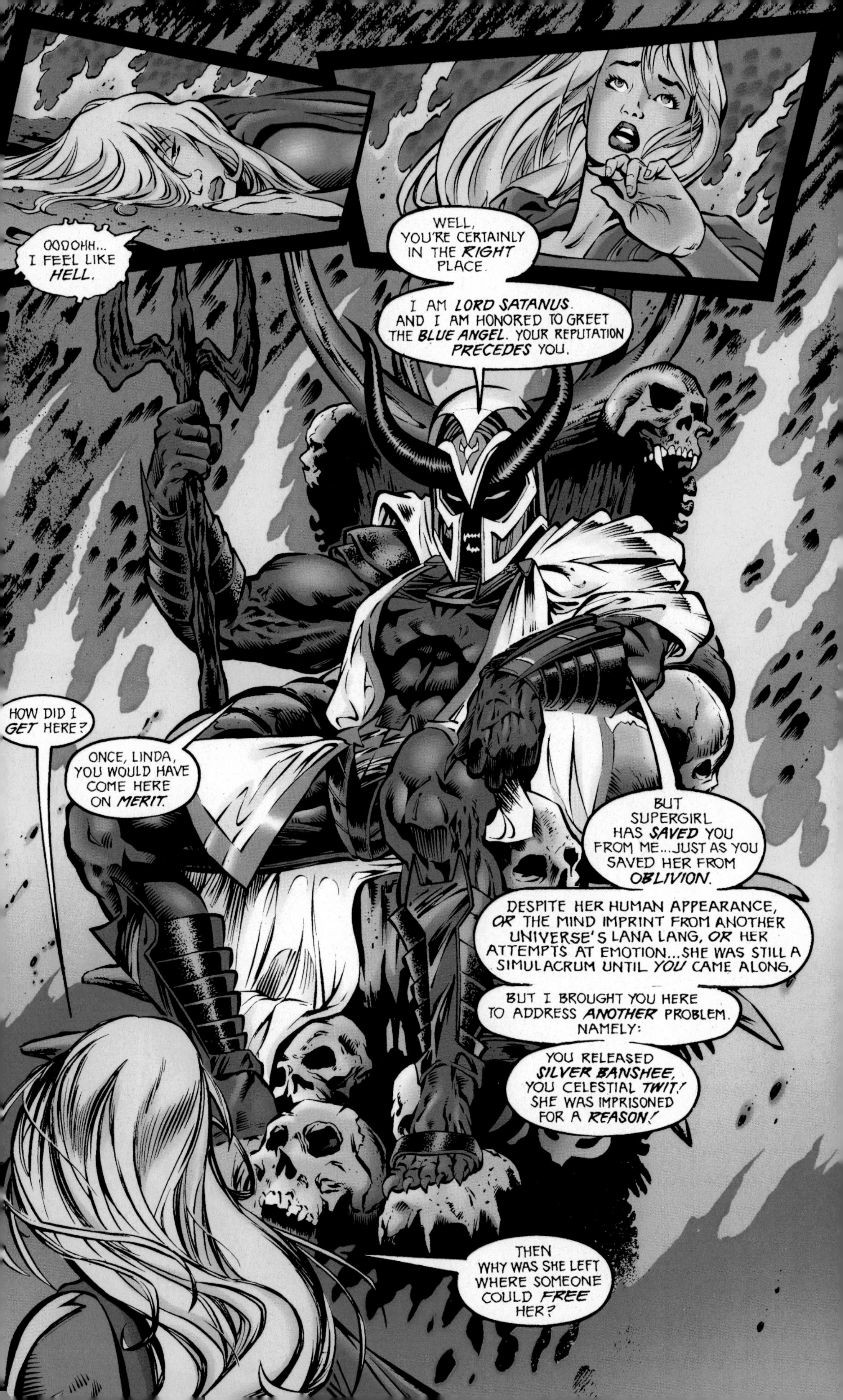

OOOOHH... I FEEL LIKE HELL.
WELL, YOU'RE CERTAINLY IN THE RIGHT PLACE.
I AM LORD SATANUS. AND I AM HONORED TO GREET THE BLUE ANGEL. YOUR REPUTATION PRECEDES YOU.
HOW DID I GET HERE?
ONCE, LINDA, YOU WOULD HAVE COME HERE ON MERIT.
BUT SUPERGIRL HAS SAVED YOU FROM ME...JUST AS YOU SAVED HER FROM OBLIVION.
DESPITE HER HUMAN APPEARANCE, OR THE MIND IMPRINT FROM ANOTHER UNIVERSE'S LANA LANG, OR HER ATTEMPTS AT EMOTION...SHE WAS STILL A SIMULACRUM UNTIL YOU CAME ALONG.
BUT I BROUGHT YOU HERE TO ADDRESS ANOTHER PROBLEM. NAMELY:
YOU RELEASED SILVER BANSHEE, YOU CELESTIAL TWIT! SHE WAS IMPRISONED FOR A REASON!
THEN WHY WAS SHE LEFT WHERE SOMEONE COULD FREE HER?

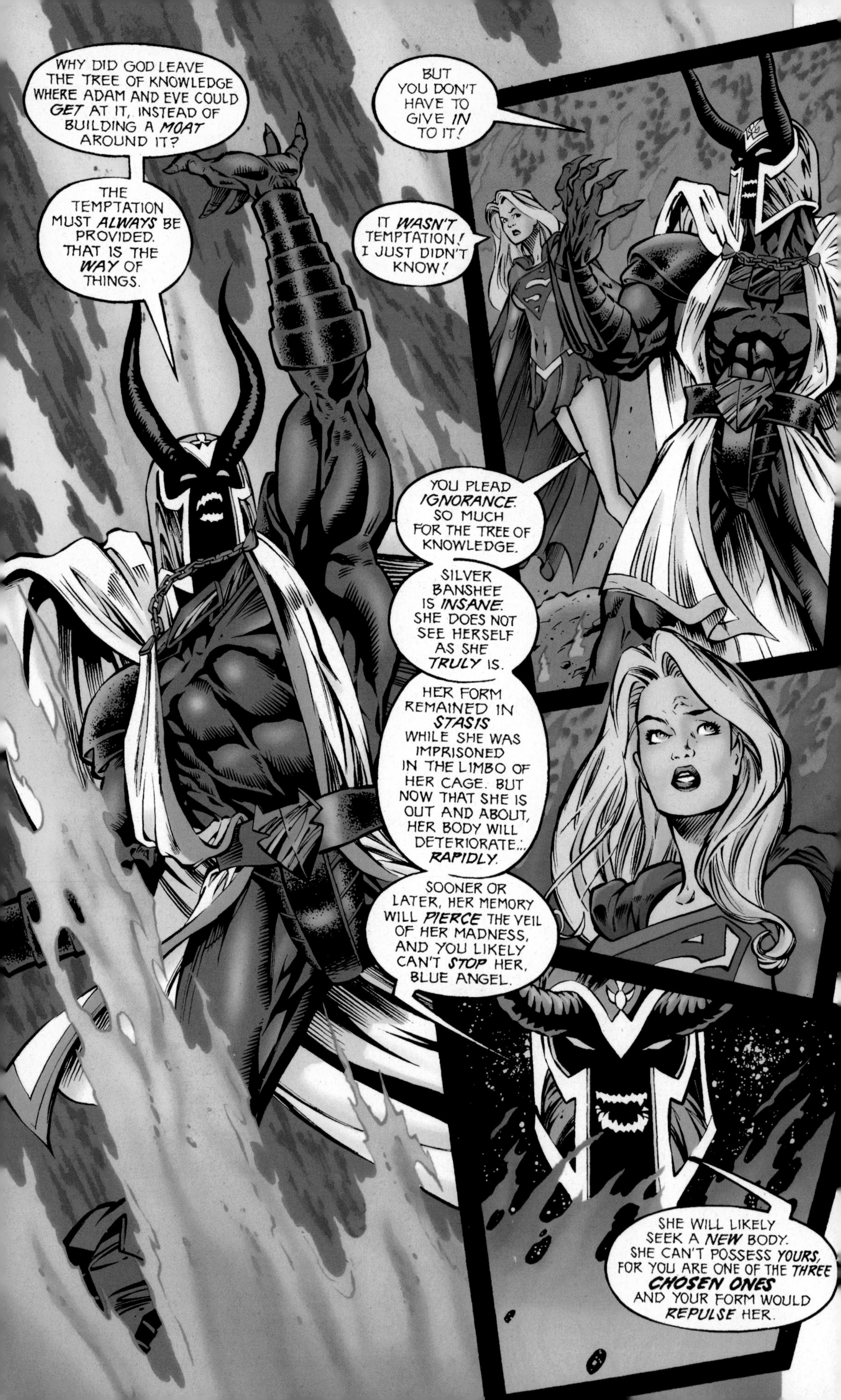

WHY DID GOD LEAVE THE TREE OF KNOWLEDGE WHERE ADAM AND EVE COULD GET AT IT, INSTEAD OF BUILDING A MOAT AROUND IT?
THE TEMPTATION MUST ALWAYS BE PROVIDED. THAT IS THE WAY OF THINGS.
BUT YOU DON'T HAVE TO GIVE IN TO IT!
IT WASN'T TEMPTATION! I JUST DIDN'T KNOW!
YOU PLEAD IGNORANCE. SO MUCH FOR THE TREE OF KNOWLEDGE.
SILVER BANSHEE IS INSANE. SHE DOES NOT SEE HERSELF AS SHE TRULY IS.
HER FORM REMAINED IN STASIS WHILE SHE WAS IMPRISONED IN THE LIMBO OF HER CAGE. BUT NOW THAT SHE IS OUT AND ABOUT, HER BODY WILL DETERIORATE... RAPIDLY.
SOONER OR LATER, HER MEMORY WILL PIERCE THE VEIL OF HER MADNESS, AND YOU LIKELY CAN'T STOP HER, BLUE ANGEL.
SHE WILL LIKELY SEEK A NEW BODY. SHE CAN'T POSSESS YOURS, FOR YOU ARE ONE OF THE THREE CHOSEN ONES AND YOUR FORM WOULD REPULSE HER.

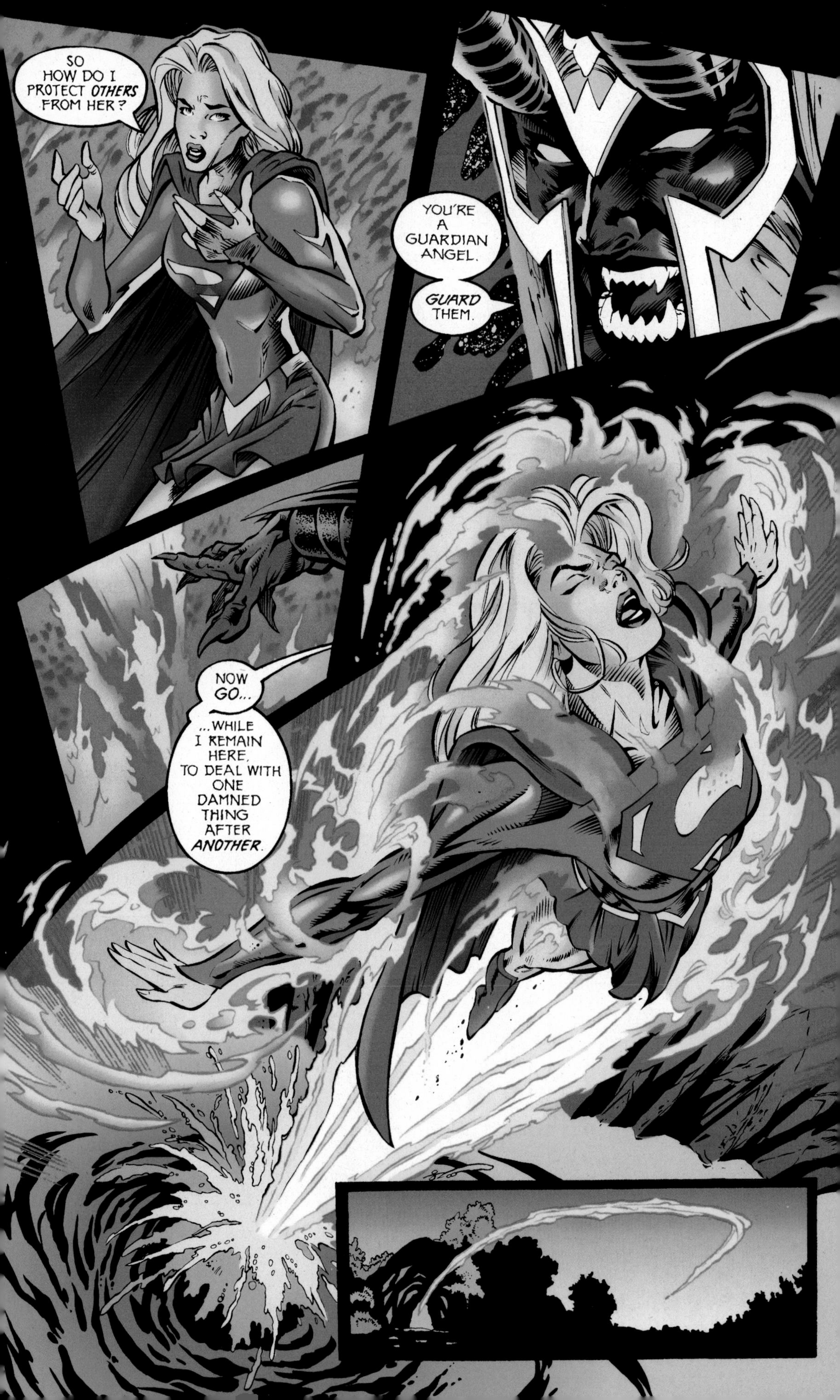
SO HOW DO I PROTECT OTHERS FROM HER?
YOU'RE A GUARDIAN ANGEL.
GUARD THEM.
NOW GO...
...WHILE I REMAIN HERE, TO DEAL WITH ONE DAMNED THING AFTER ANOTHER.

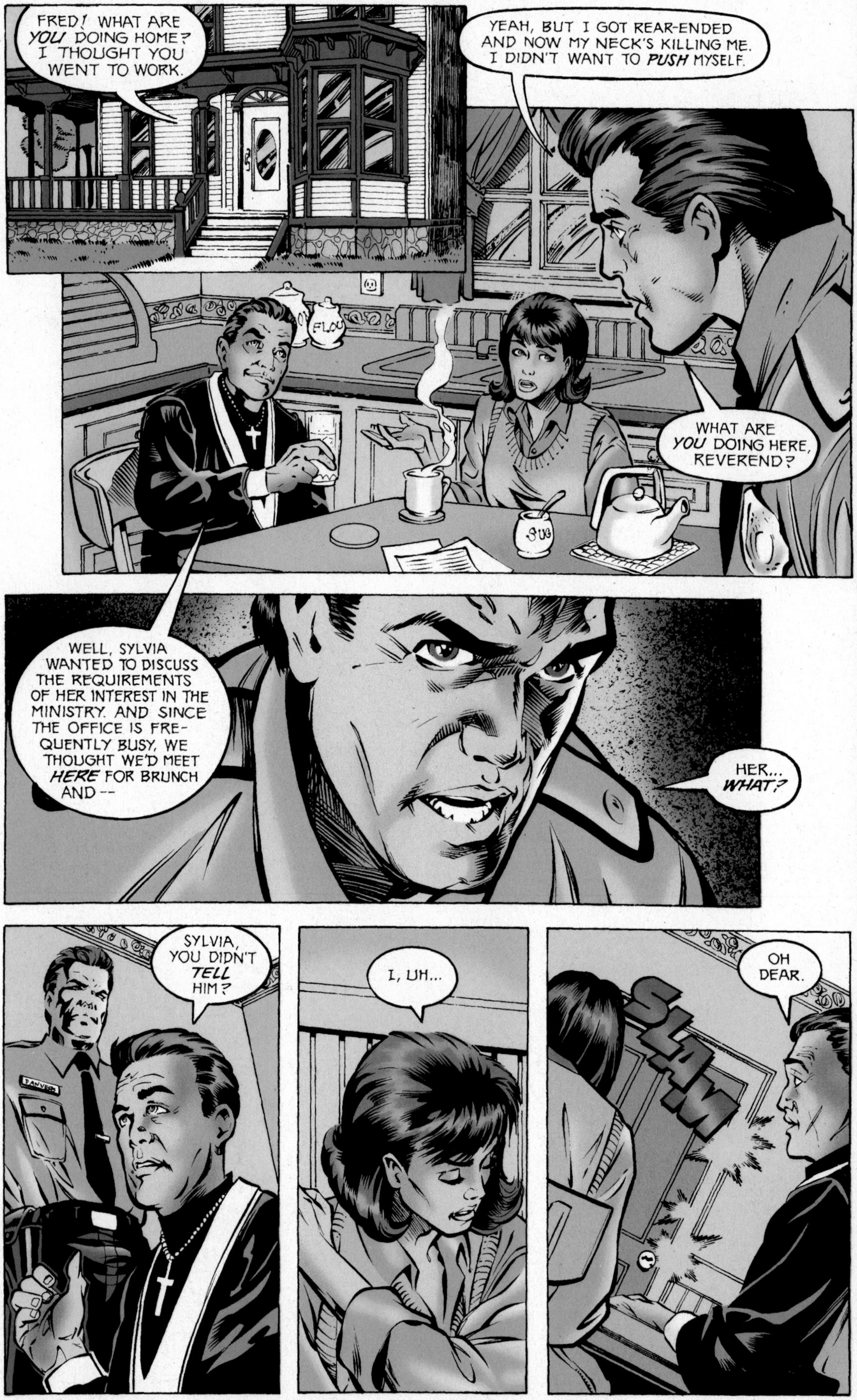
FRED! WHAT ARE YOU DOING HOME? I THOUGHT YOU WENT TO WORK.
YEAH, BUT I GOT REAR-ENDED AND NOW MY NECK'S KILLING ME. I DIDN'T WANT TO PUSH MYSELF.
WHAT ARE YOU DOING HERE, REVEREND?
WELL, SYLVIA WANTED TO DISCUSS THE REQUIREMENTS OF HER INTEREST IN THE MINISTRY. AND SINCE THE OFFICE IS FRE-QUENTLY BUSY, WE THOUGHT WE'D MEET HERE FOR BRUNCH AND --
HER... WHAT?
SYLVIA, YOU DIDN'T TELL HIM?
I, UH...
SLAM
OH DEAR.

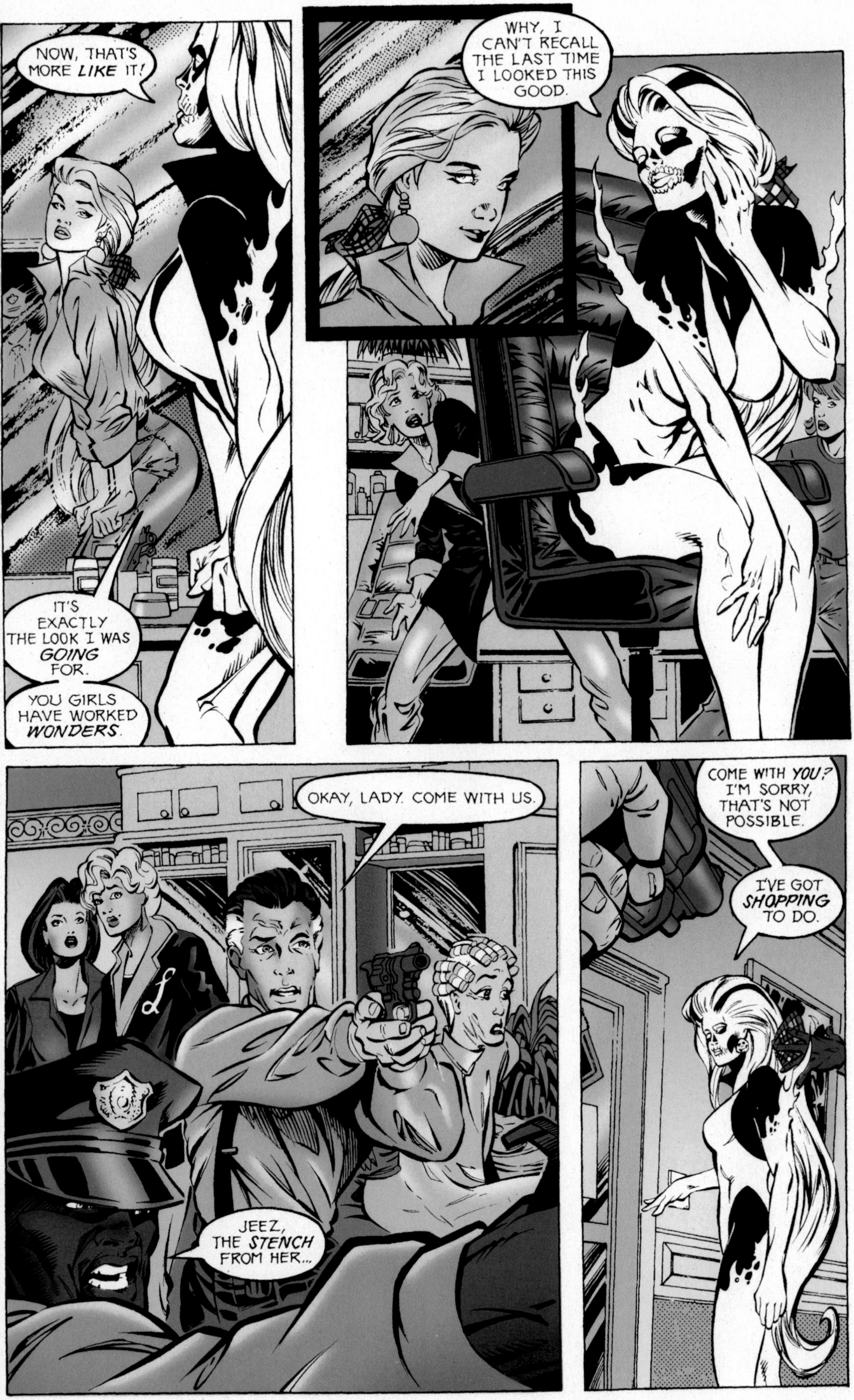
NOW, THAT'S MORE *LIKE* IT!
IT'S EXACTLY THE LOOK I WAS *GOING* FOR.
YOU GIRLS HAVE WORKED *WONDERS*.
WHY, I CAN'T RECALL THE LAST TIME I LOOKED THIS GOOD.
OKAY, LADY. COME WITH US.
JEEZ, THE *STENCH* FROM HER...
COME WITH *YOU?* I'M SORRY, THAT'S NOT POSSIBLE.
I'VE GOT *SHOPPING* TO DO.

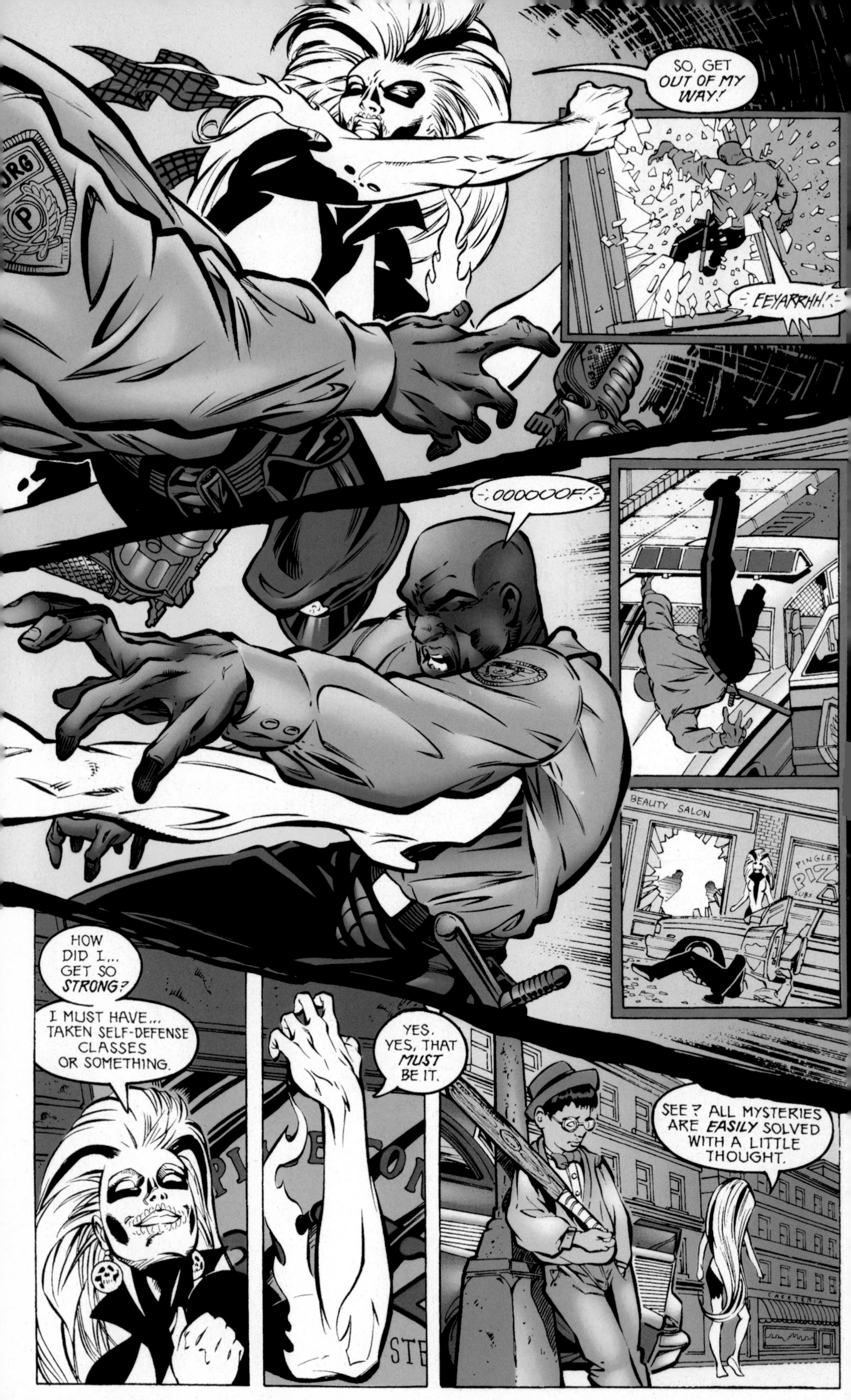
SO, GET OUT OF MY WAY!
EEYARRHH!
OOOOOOF!
BEAUTY SALON
HOW DID I... GET SO STRONG?
I MUST HAVE... TAKEN SELF-DEFENSE CLASSES OR SOMETHING.
YES. YES, THAT MUST BE IT.
SEE? ALL MYSTERIES ARE EASILY SOLVED WITH A LITTLE THOUGHT.

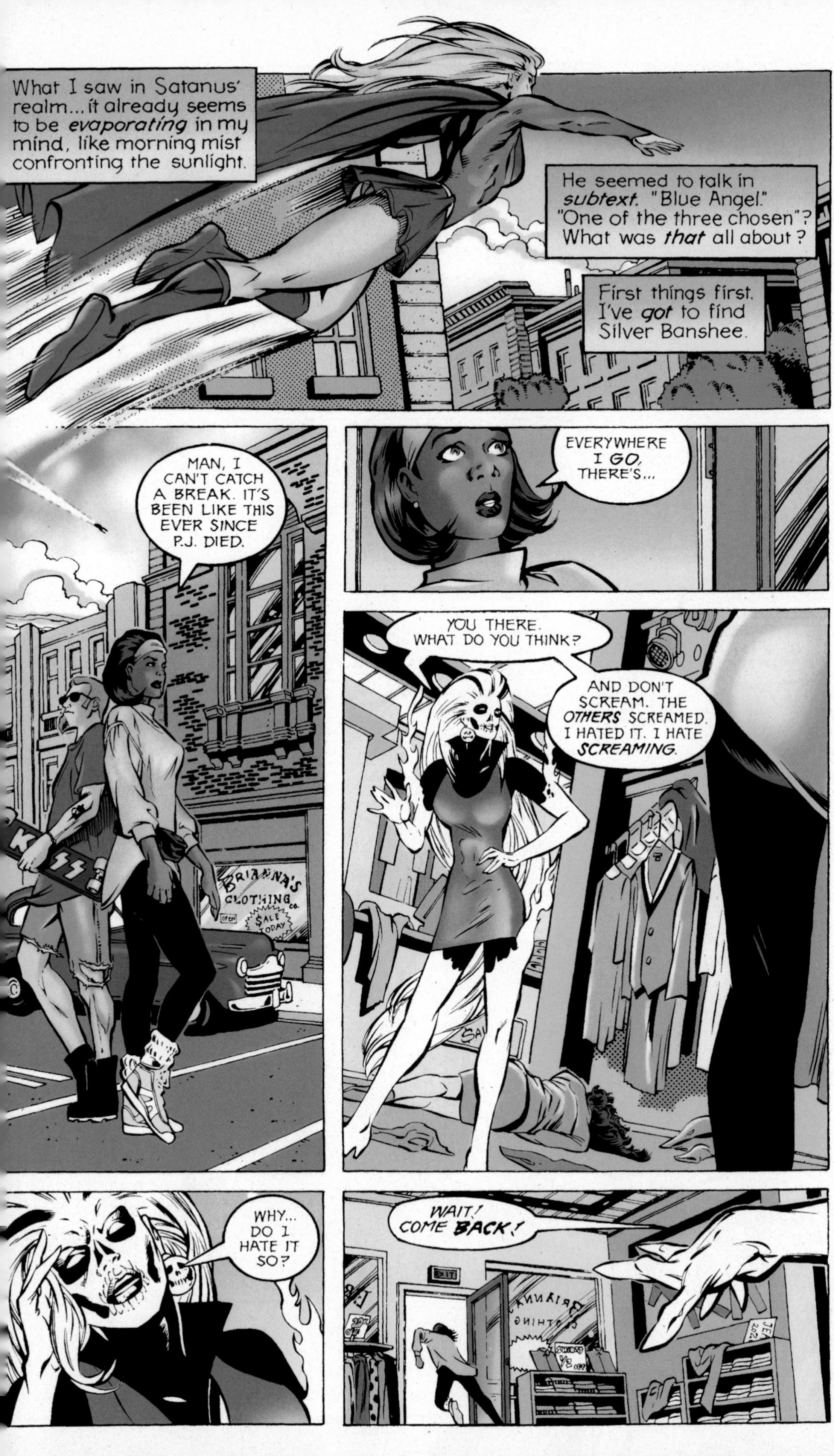
What I saw in Satanus' realm... it already seems to be *evaporating* in my mind, like morning mist confronting the sunlight.
He seemed to talk in *subtext*. "Blue Angel." "One of the three chosen"? What was *that* all about?
First things first. I've *got* to find Silver Banshee.
MAN, I CAN'T CATCH A BREAK. IT'S BEEN LIKE THIS EVER SINCE P.J. DIED.
BRIANNA'S CLOTHING CO.
OPEN
SALE TODAY
EVERYWHERE I *GO*, THERE'S...
YOU THERE. WHAT DO YOU THINK?
AND DON'T SCREAM. THE *OTHERS* SCREAMED. I HATED IT. I HATE *SCREAMING*.
WHY... DO I HATE IT SO?
WAIT! COME *BACK*!
EXIT

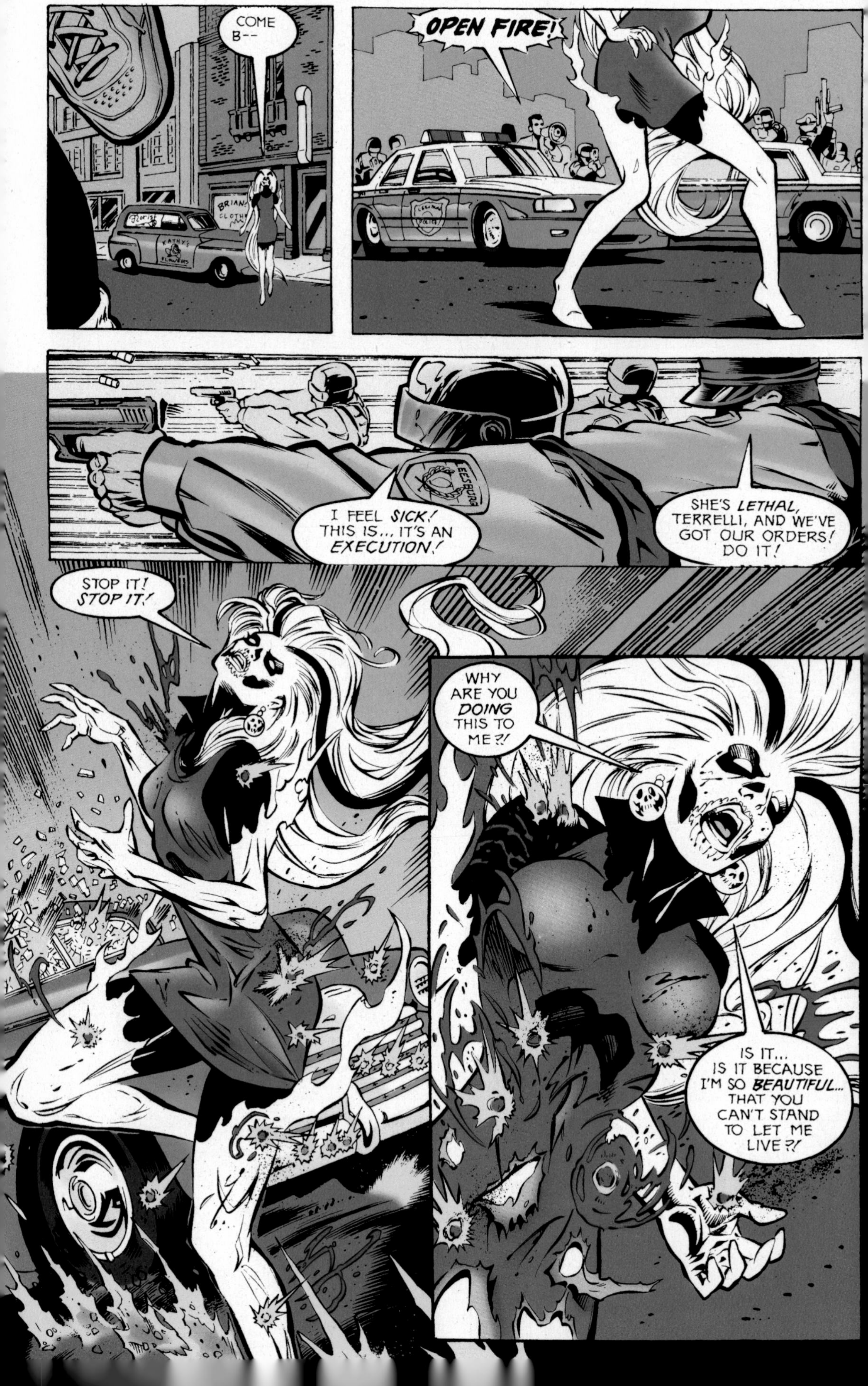
COME B--
OPEN FIRE!
I FEEL SICK! THIS IS... IT'S AN EXECUTION!
SHE'S LETHAL, TERRELLI, AND WE'VE GOT OUR ORDERS! DO IT!
STOP IT! STOP IT!
WHY ARE YOU DOING THIS TO ME?!
IS IT... IS IT BECAUSE I'M SO BEAUTIFUL... THAT YOU CAN'T STAND TO LET ME LIVE?!

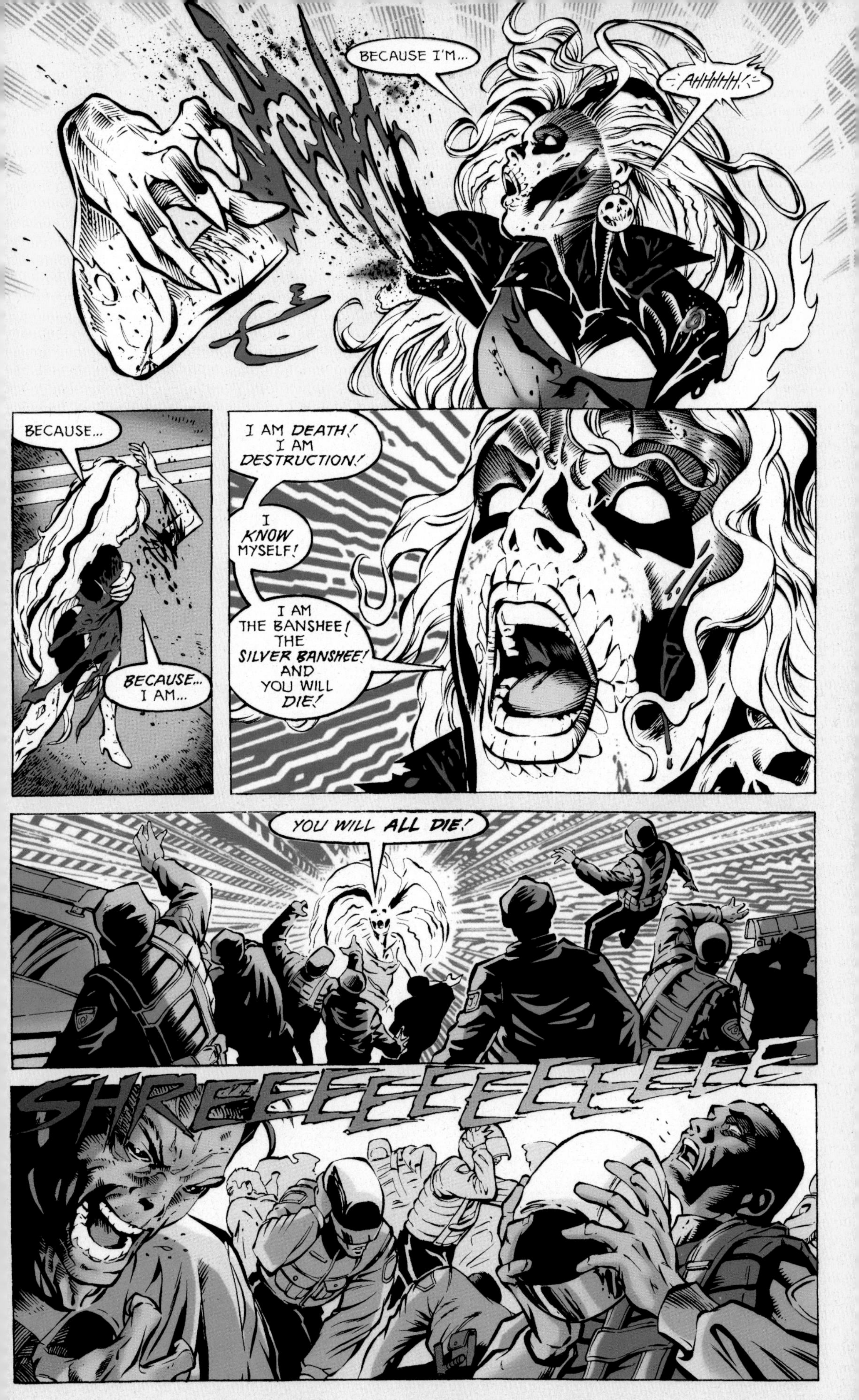
BECAUSE I'M...
AHHHHH!
BECAUSE...
BECAUSE... I AM...
I AM DEATH! I AM DESTRUCTION!
I KNOW MYSELF!
I AM THE BANSHEE! THE SILVER BANSHEE! AND YOU WILL DIE!
YOU WILL ALL DIE!
SHREEEEEEEEEEEEE

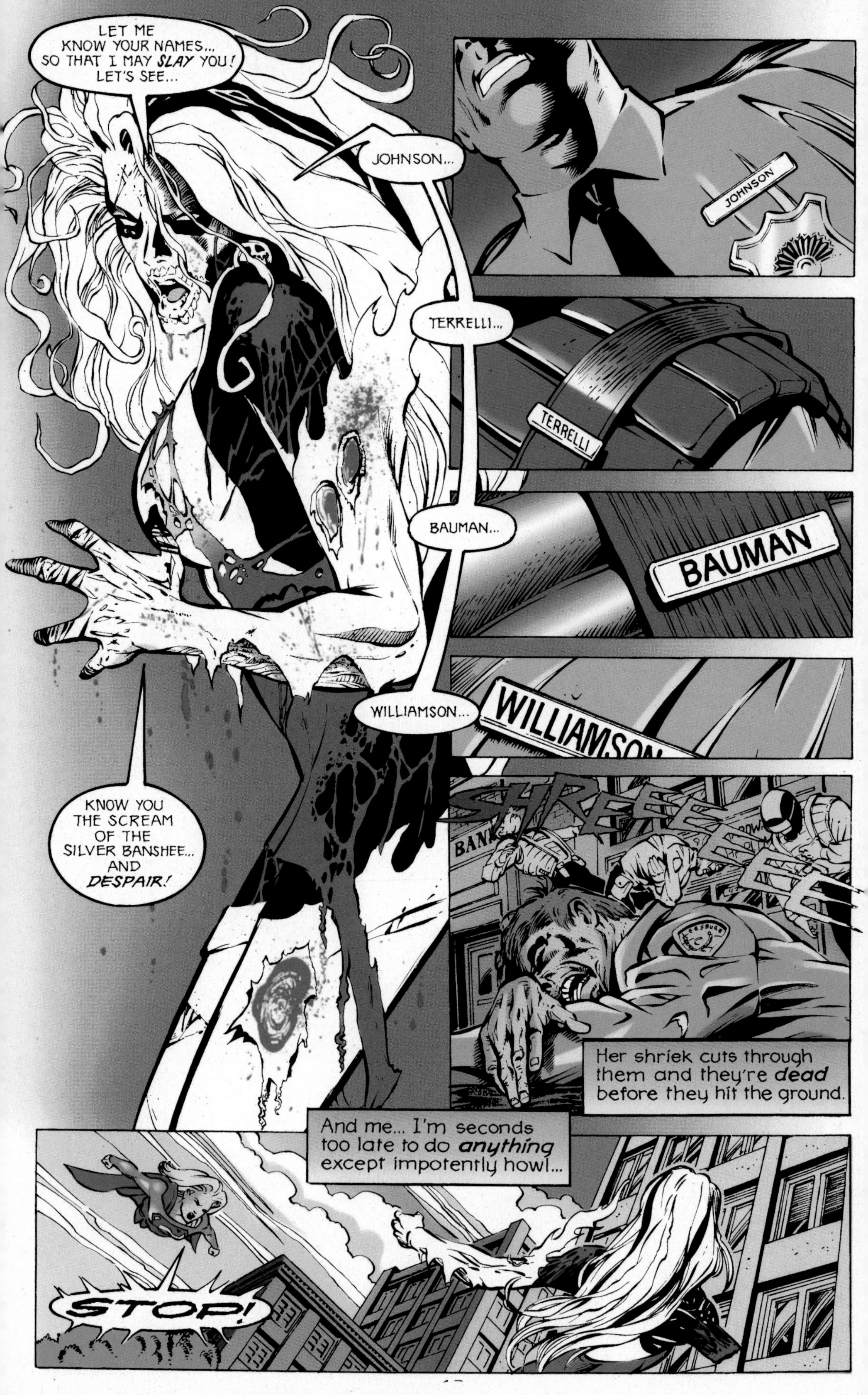
LET ME KNOW YOUR NAMES... SO THAT I MAY *SLAY* YOU! LET'S SEE...
JOHNSON...
JOHNSON
TERRELLI...
TERRELLI
BAUMAN...
BAUMAN
WILLIAMSON...
WILLIAMSON
KNOW YOU THE SCREAM OF THE SILVER BANSHEE... AND *DESPAIR!*
SHREEEEEE
Her shriek cuts through them and they're *dead* before they hit the ground.
And me... I'm seconds too late to do *anything* except impotently howl...
STOP!

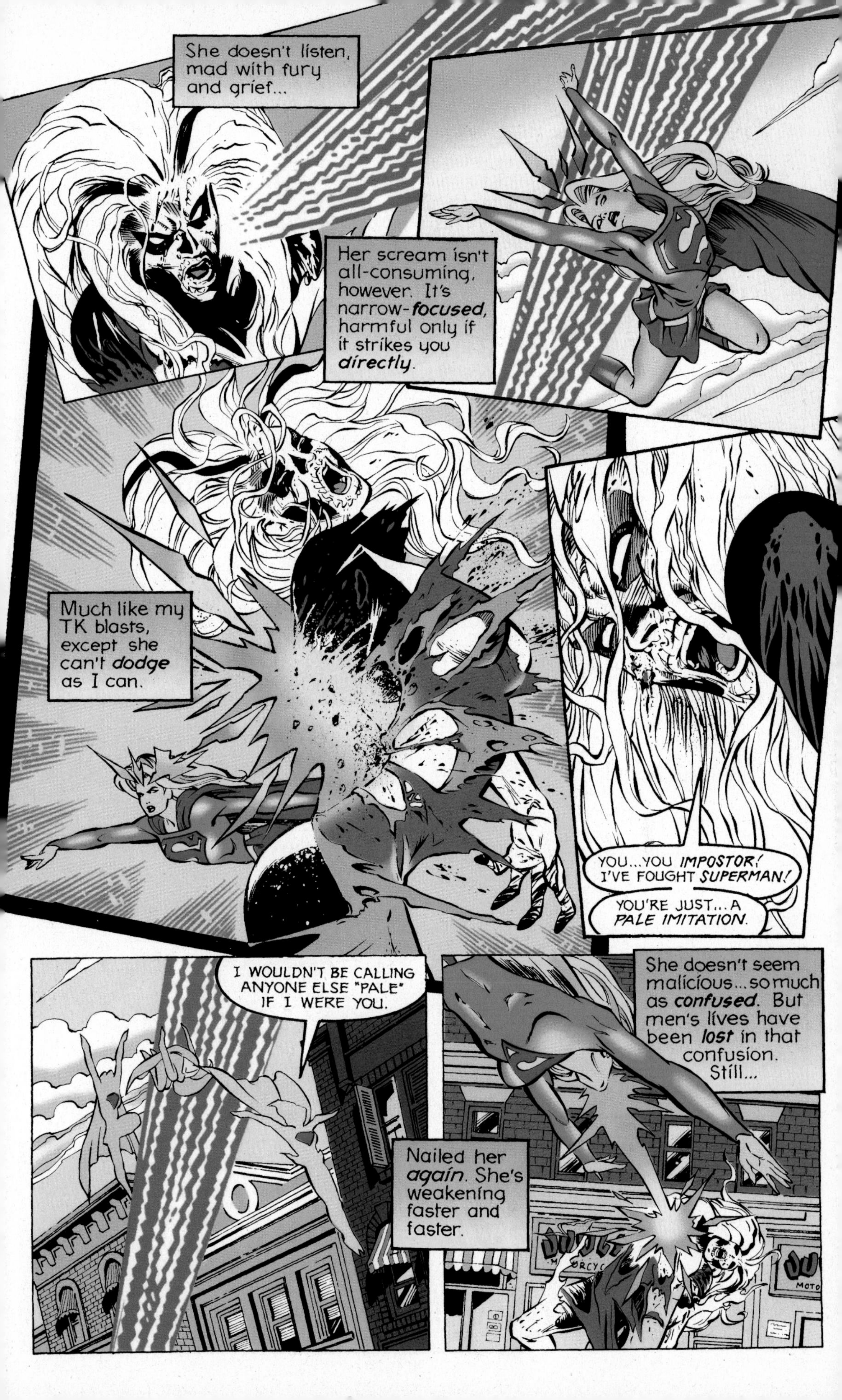
She doesn't listen, mad with fury and grief...
Her scream isn't all-consuming, however. It's narrow-*focused*, harmful only if it strikes you *directly*.
Much like my TK blasts, except she can't *dodge* as I can.
YOU...YOU *IMPOSTOR!* I'VE FOUGHT *SUPERMAN!*
YOU'RE JUST... A *PALE IMITATION*.
I WOULDN'T BE CALLING ANYONE ELSE "PALE" IF I WERE YOU.
Nailed her *again*. She's weakening faster and faster.
She doesn't seem malicious...so much as *confused*. But men's lives have been *lost* in that confusion. Still...

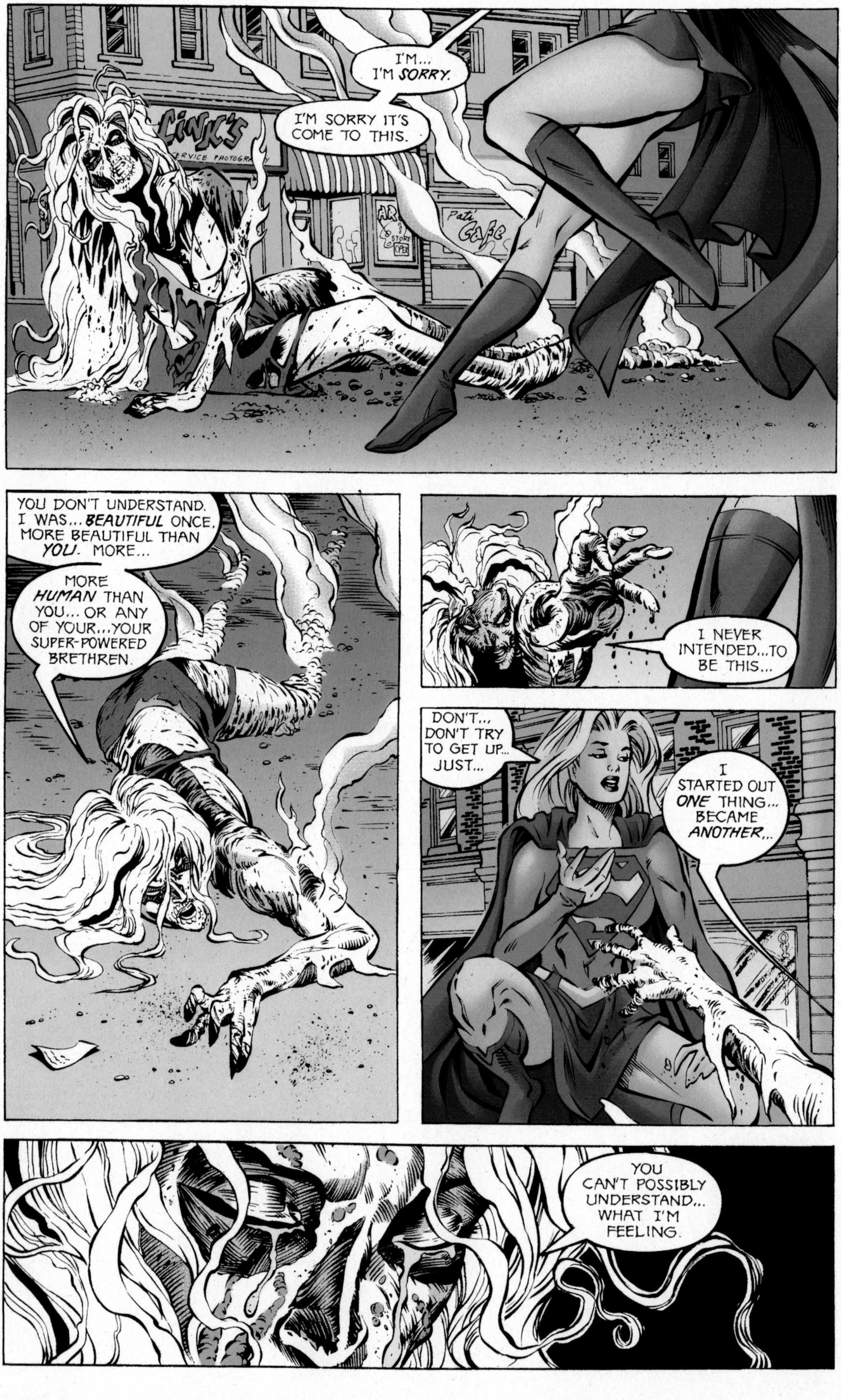
I'M... I'M SORRY.
I'M SORRY IT'S COME TO THIS.
YOU DON'T UNDERSTAND. I WAS... BEAUTIFUL ONCE. MORE BEAUTIFUL THAN YOU. MORE...
MORE HUMAN THAN YOU... OR ANY OF YOUR... YOUR SUPER-POWERED BRETHREN.
I NEVER INTENDED... TO BE THIS...
DON'T... DON'T TRY TO GET UP... JUST...
I STARTED OUT ONE THING... BECAME ANOTHER...
YOU CAN'T POSSIBLY UNDERSTAND... WHAT I'M FEELING.

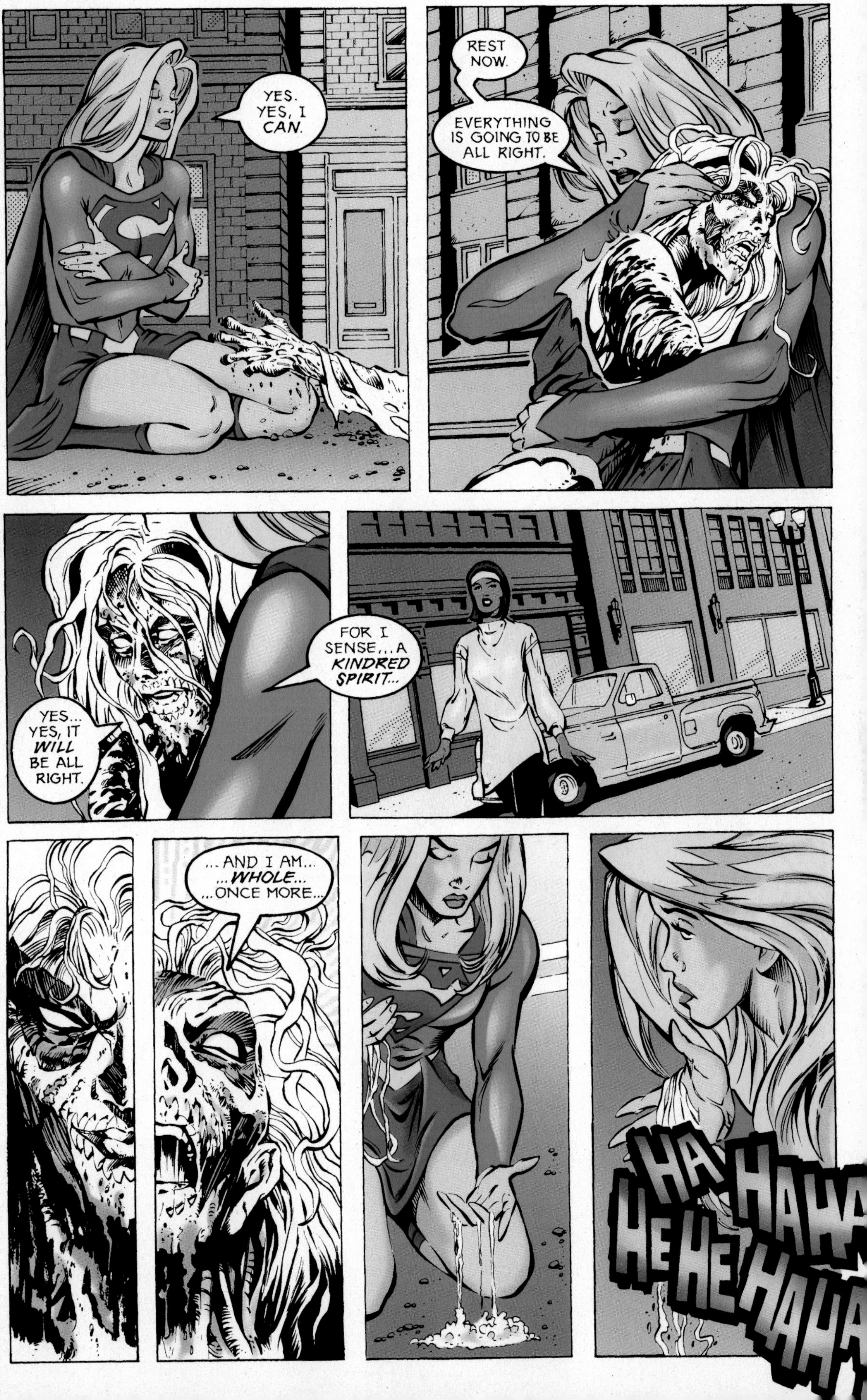
YES.
YES, I
CAN.
REST
NOW.
EVERYTHING
IS GOING TO BE
ALL RIGHT.
YES...
YES, IT
WILL
BE ALL
RIGHT.
FOR I
SENSE... A
KINDRED
SPIRIT...
...AND I AM...
...WHOLE...
...ONCE MORE...
HA
HAHA
HE HE HAHA

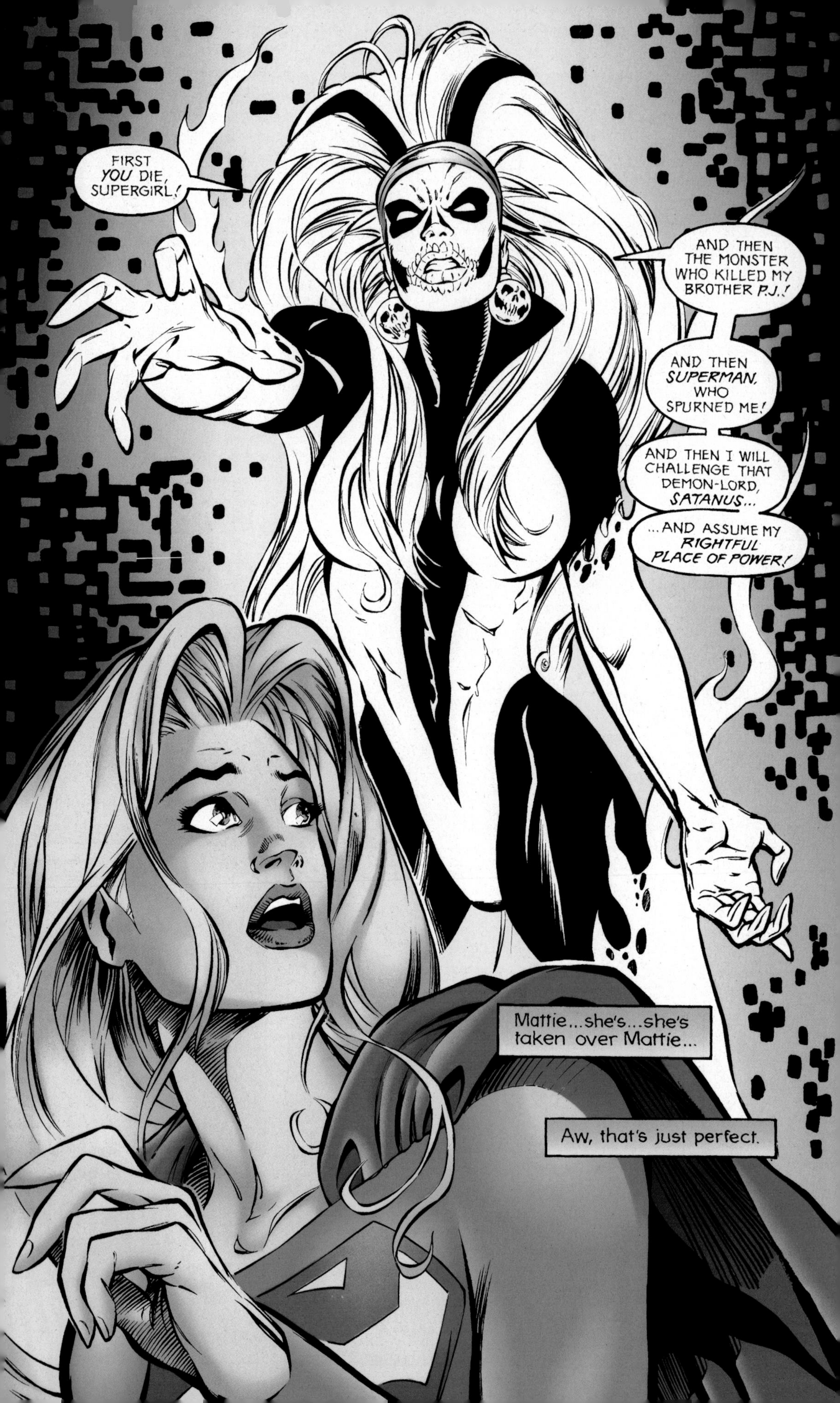
FIRST YOU DIE, SUPERGIRL!
AND THEN THE MONSTER WHO KILLED MY BROTHER P.J.!
AND THEN SUPERMAN, WHO SPURNED ME!
AND THEN I WILL CHALLENGE THAT DEMON-LORD, SATANUS...
...AND ASSUME MY RIGHTFUL PLACE OF POWER!
Mattie...she's...she's taken over Mattie...
Aw, that's just perfect.

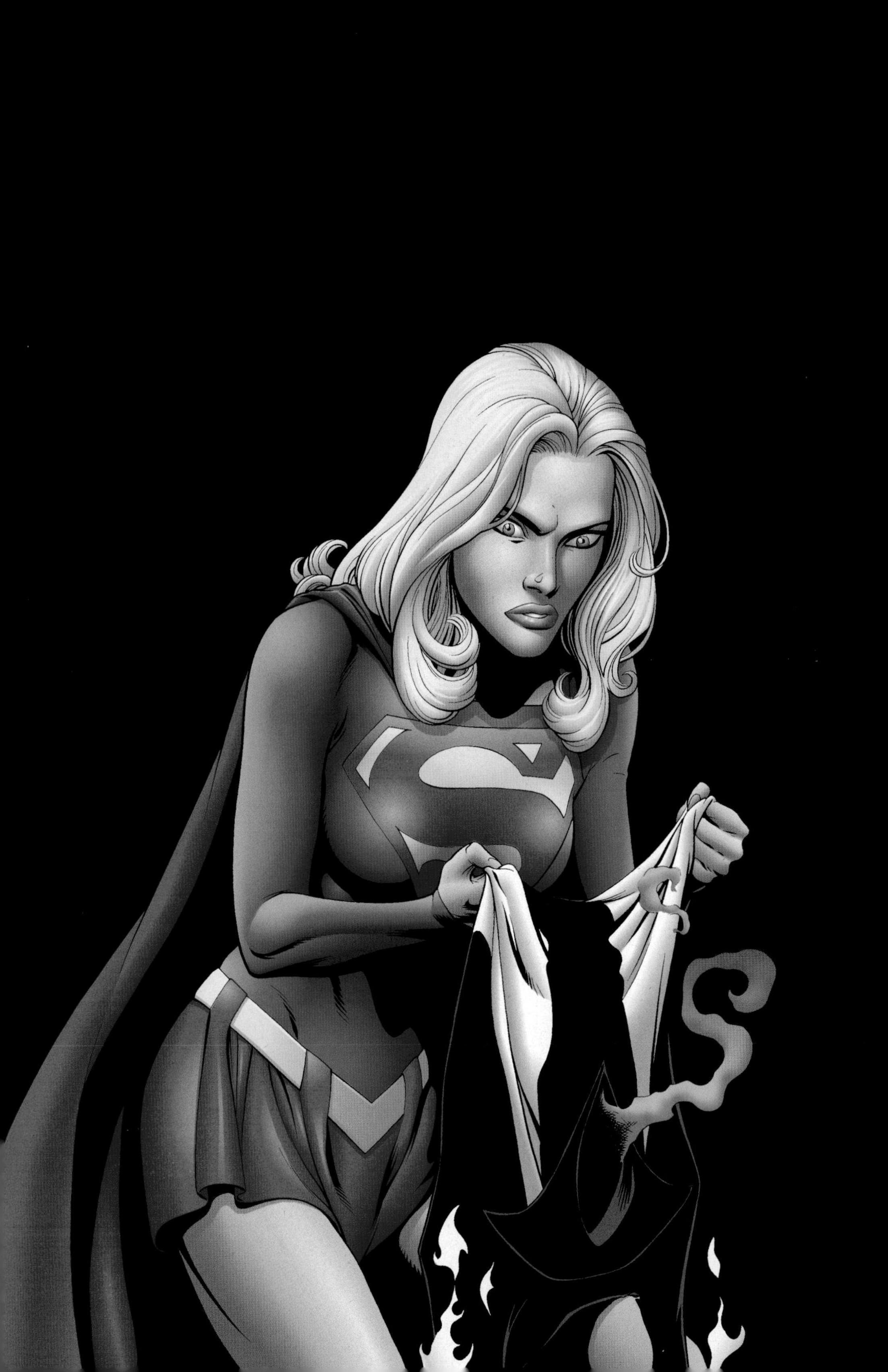

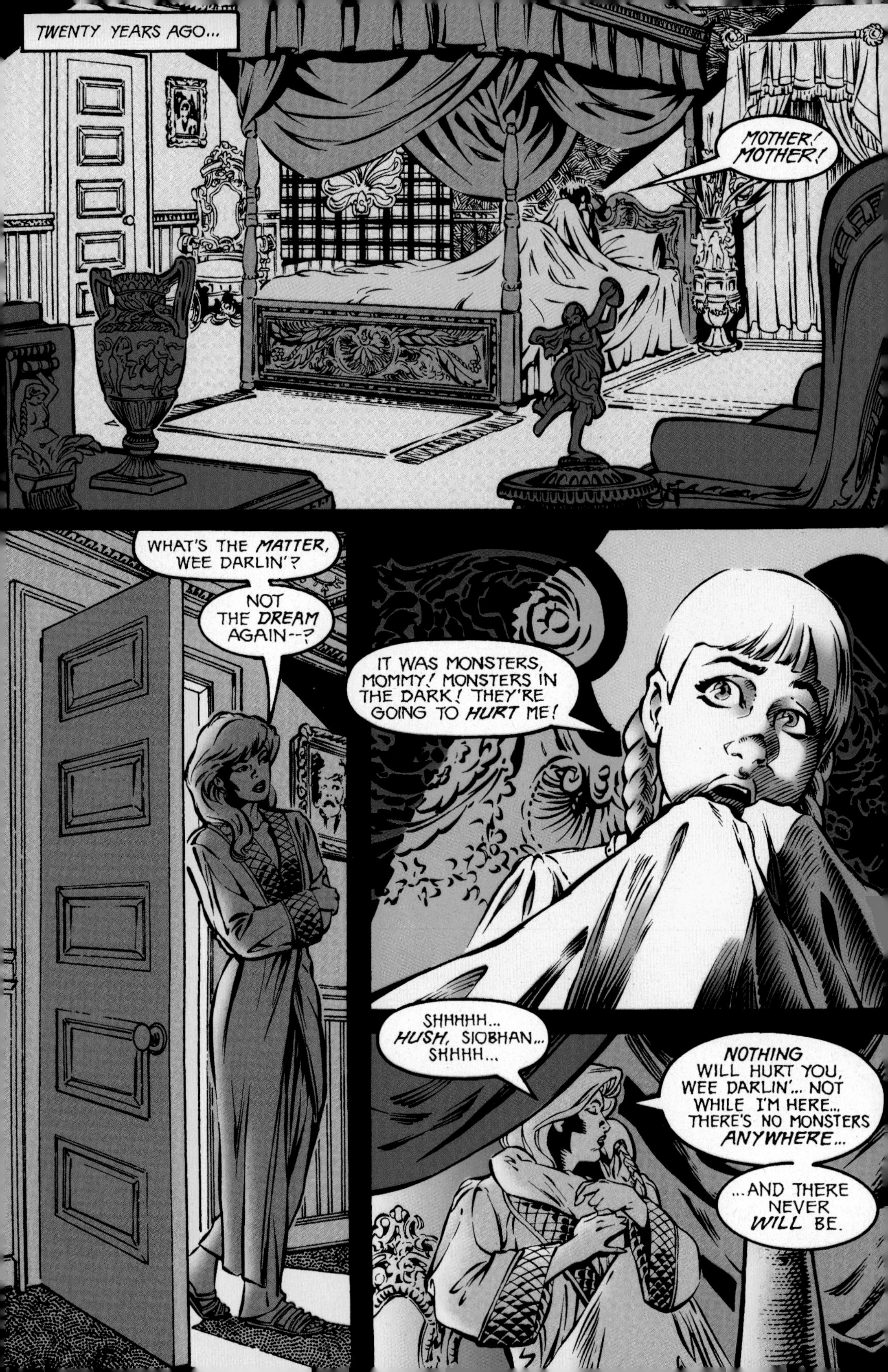

TWENTY YEARS AGO...
MOTHER! MOTHER!
WHAT'S THE MATTER, WEE DARLIN'?
NOT THE DREAM AGAIN--?
IT WAS MONSTERS, MOMMY! MONSTERS IN THE DARK! THEY'RE GOING TO HURT ME!
SHHHHH... HUSH, SIOBHAN... SHHHH...
NOTHING WILL HURT YOU, WEE DARLIN'... NOT WHILE I'M HERE... THERE'S NO MONSTERS ANYWHERE...
...AND THERE NEVER WILL BE.

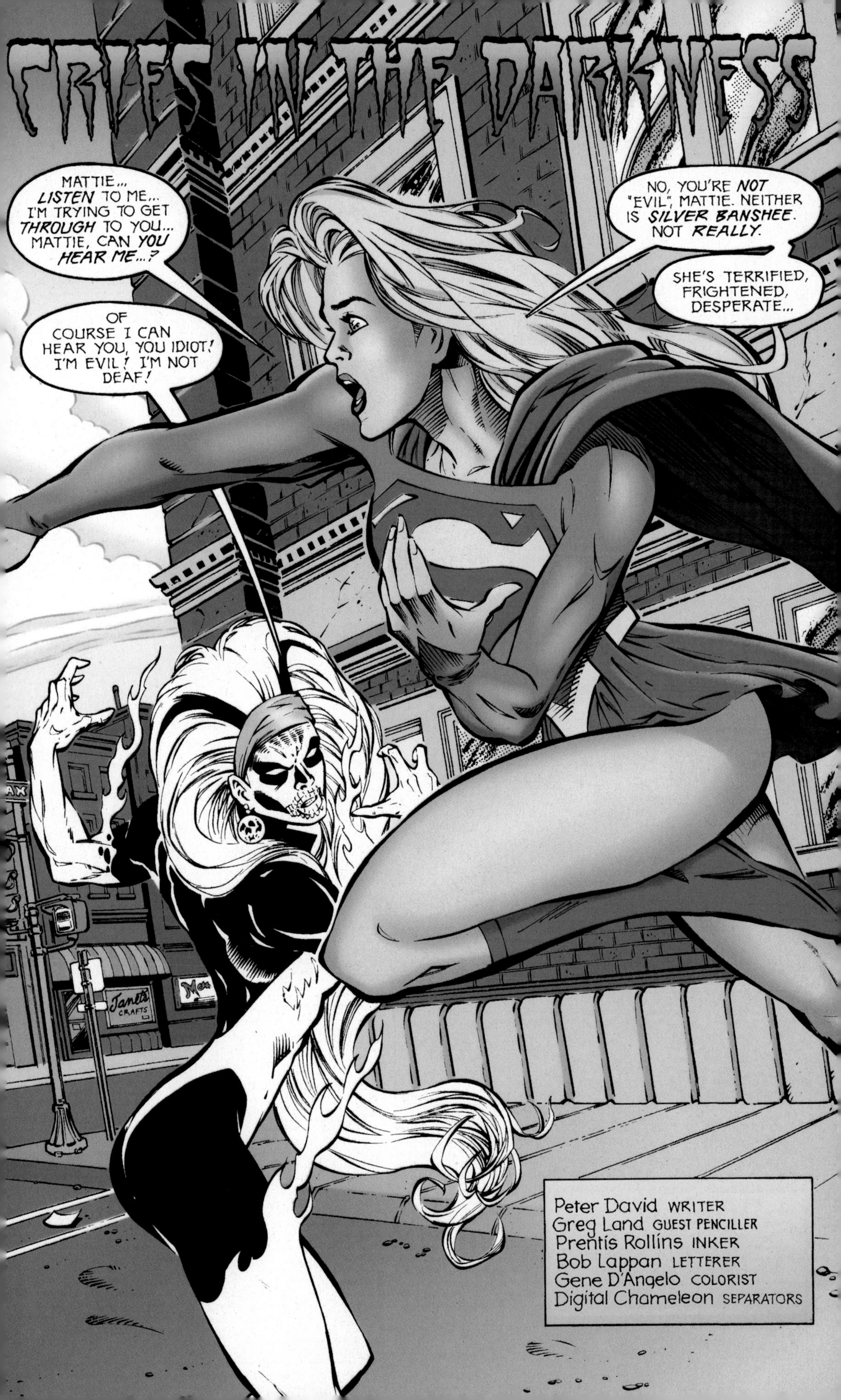

CRIES IN THE DARKNESS
MATTIE... LISTEN TO ME... I'M TRYING TO GET THROUGH TO YOU... MATTIE, CAN YOU HEAR ME...?
OF COURSE I CAN HEAR YOU, YOU IDIOT! I'M EVIL! I'M NOT DEAF!
NO, YOU'RE NOT "EVIL", MATTIE. NEITHER IS SILVER BANSHEE. NOT REALLY.
SHE'S TERRIFIED, FRIGHTENED, DESPERATE...
Janet's CRAFTS
Peter David WRITER
Greg Land GUEST PENCILLER
Prentis Rollins INKER
Bob Lappan LETTERER
Gene D'Angelo COLORIST
Digital Chameleon SEPARATORS

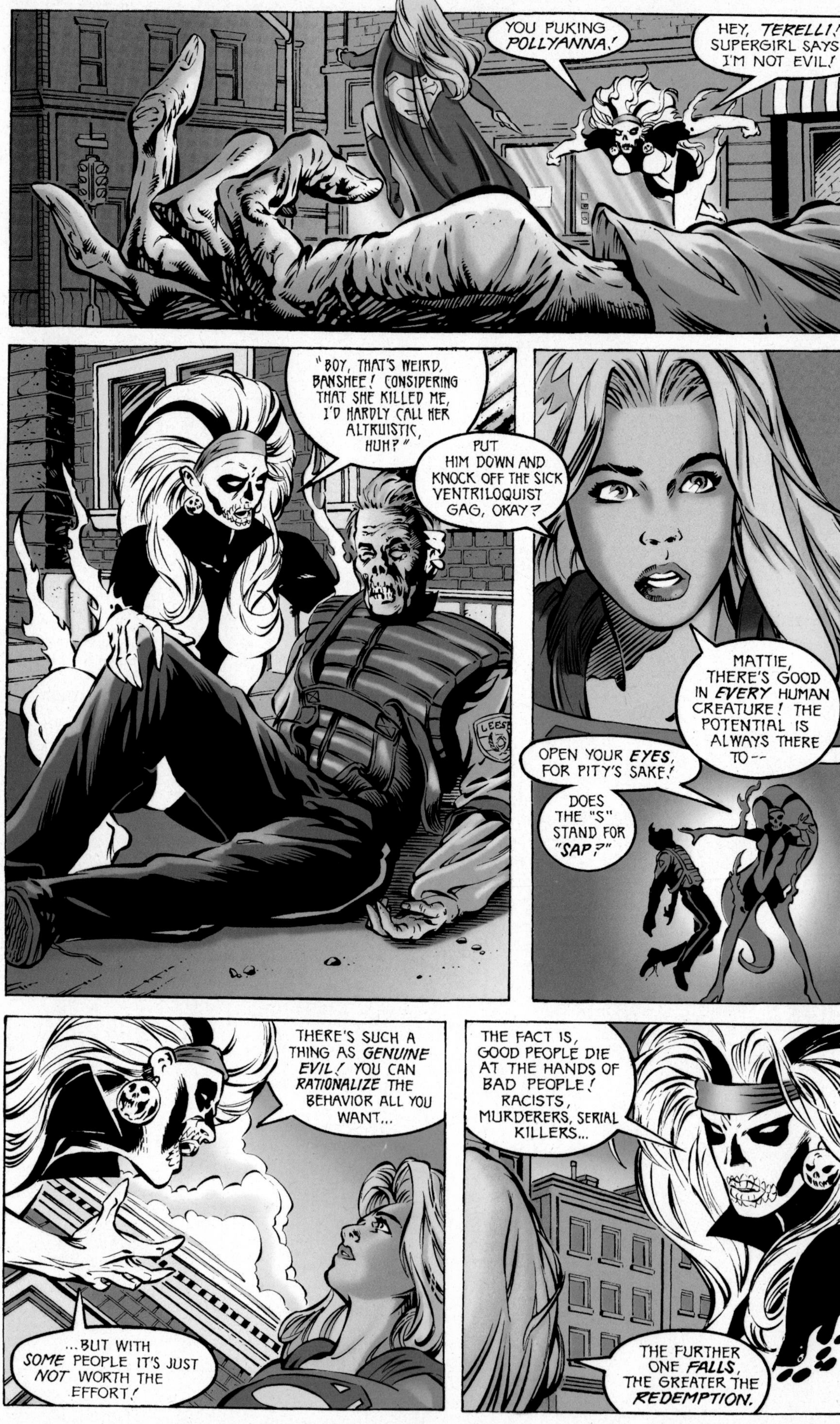
YOU PUKING POLLYANNA!
HEY, TERELLI! SUPERGIRL SAYS I'M NOT EVIL!
"BOY, THAT'S WEIRD, BANSHEE! CONSIDERING THAT SHE KILLED ME, I'D HARDLY CALL HER ALTRUISTIC, HUH?"
PUT HIM DOWN AND KNOCK OFF THE SICK VENTRILOQUIST GAG, OKAY?
MATTIE, THERE'S GOOD IN EVERY HUMAN CREATURE! THE POTENTIAL IS ALWAYS THERE TO--
OPEN YOUR EYES, FOR PITY'S SAKE!
DOES THE "S" STAND FOR "SAP?"
THERE'S SUCH A THING AS GENUINE EVIL! YOU CAN RATIONALIZE THE BEHAVIOR ALL YOU WANT...
...BUT WITH SOME PEOPLE IT'S JUST NOT WORTH THE EFFORT!
THE FACT IS, GOOD PEOPLE DIE AT THE HANDS OF BAD PEOPLE! RACISTS, MURDERERS, SERIAL KILLERS...
THE FURTHER ONE FALLS, THE GREATER THE REDEMPTION.

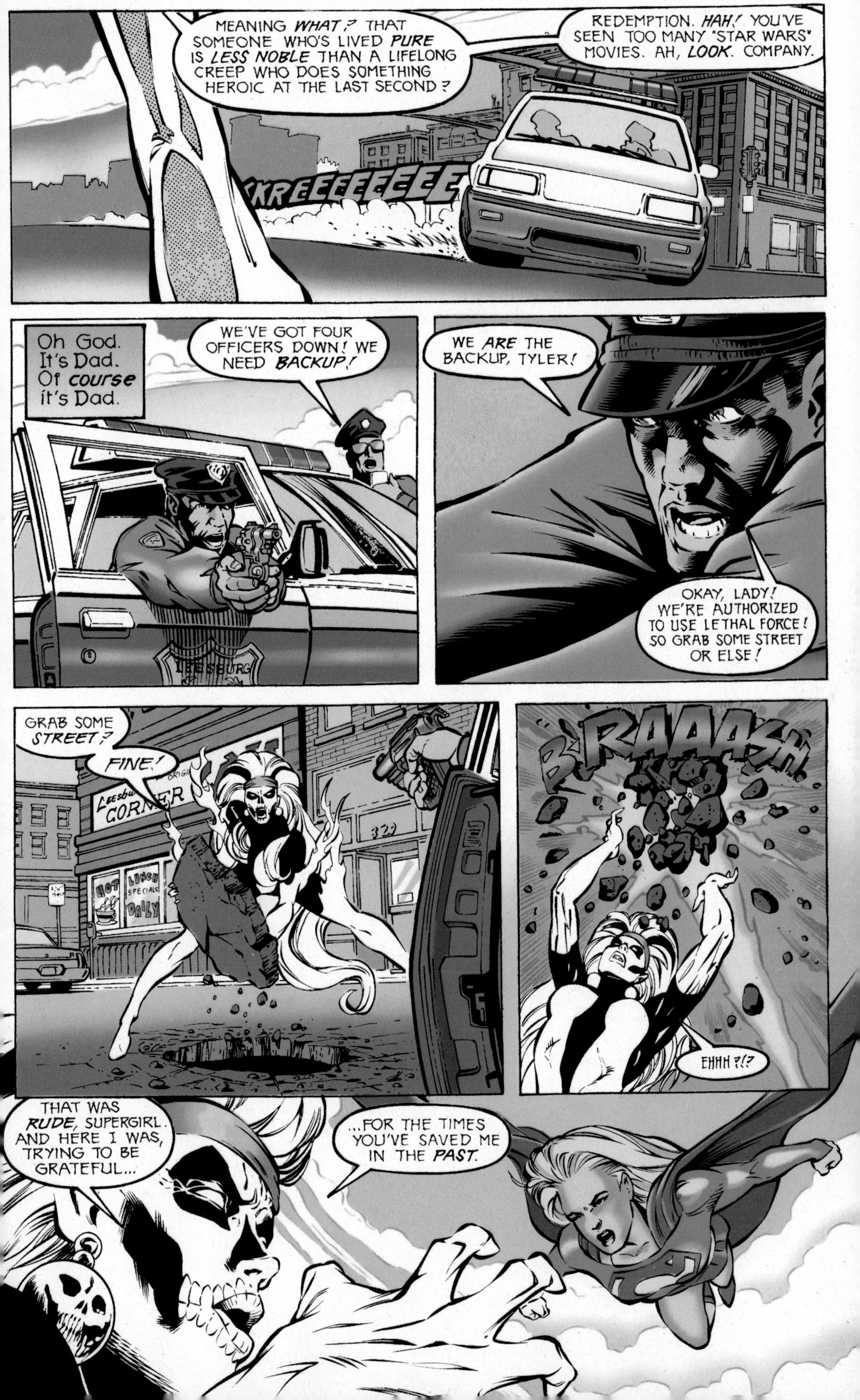

MEANING WHAT?! THAT SOMEONE WHO'S LIVED PURE IS LESS NOBLE THAN A LIFELONG CREEP WHO DOES SOMETHING HEROIC AT THE LAST SECOND?
REDEMPTION. HAH! YOU'VE SEEN TOO MANY "STAR WARS" MOVIES. AH, LOOK. COMPANY.
KREEEEEEEEE
Oh God. It's Dad. Of course it's Dad.
WE'VE GOT FOUR OFFICERS DOWN! WE NEED BACKUP!
LEESBURG
WE ARE THE BACKUP, TYLER!
OKAY, LADY! WE'RE AUTHORIZED TO USE LETHAL FORCE! SO GRAB SOME STREET OR ELSE!
GRAB SOME STREET?!
FINE!
CORNER
HOT LUNCH SPECIALS DAILY
BRAAASH
EHHH?!?
THAT WAS RUDE, SUPERGIRL. AND HERE I WAS, TRYING TO BE GRATEFUL...
...FOR THE TIMES YOU'VE SAVED ME IN THE PAST.

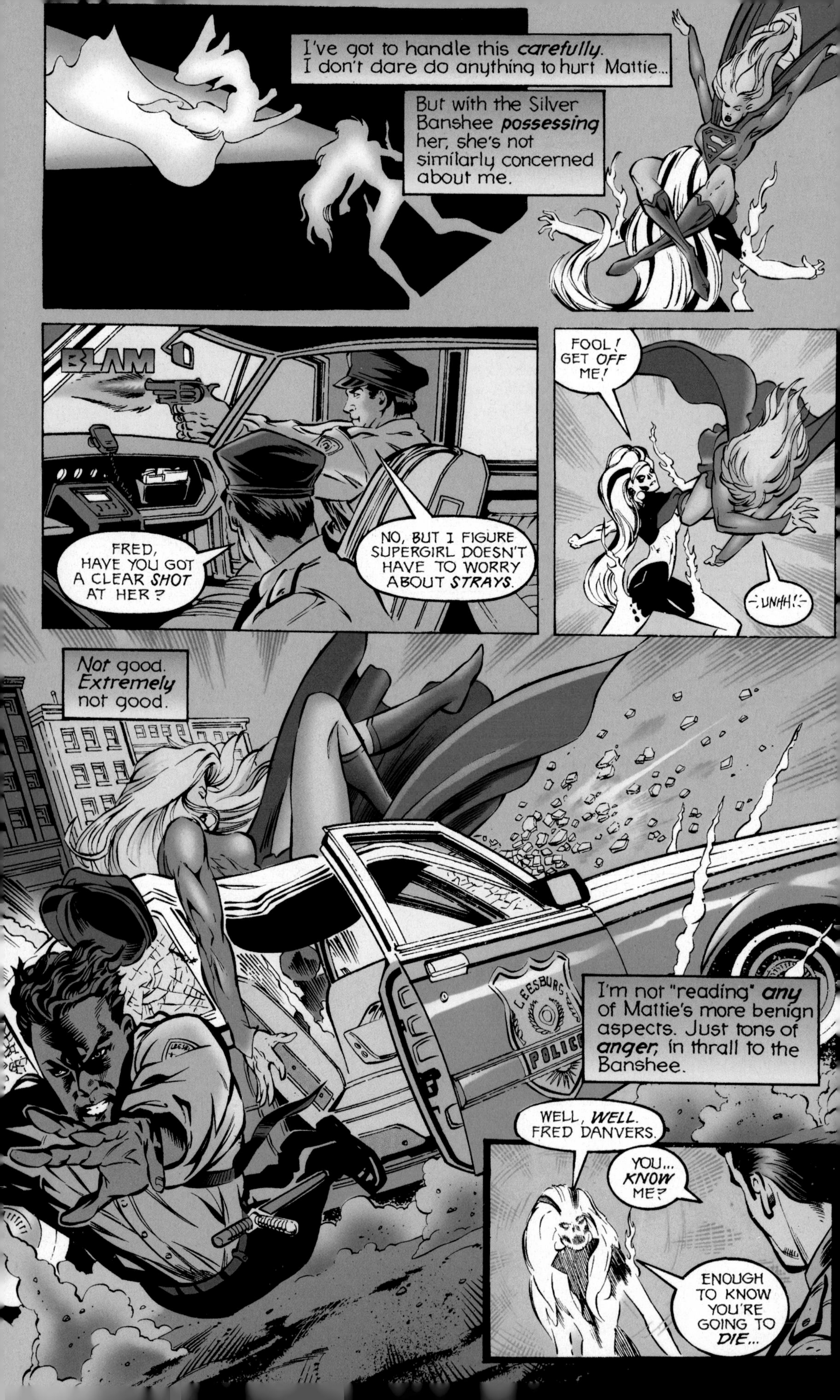

I've got to handle this *carefully*. I don't dare do anything to hurt Mattie...
But with the Silver Banshee *possessing* her, she's not similarly concerned about me.
BLAM
FRED, HAVE YOU GOT A CLEAR *SHOT* AT HER?
NO, BUT I FIGURE SUPERGIRL DOESN'T HAVE TO WORRY ABOUT *STRAYS*.
FOOL! GET *OFF* ME!
-UNHH!-
Not good. *Extremely* not good.
LEESBURG POLICE
I'm not "reading" *any* of Mattie's more benign aspects. Just tons of *anger*, in thrall to the Banshee.
WELL, *WELL*. FRED DANVERS.
YOU... *KNOW* ME?
ENOUGH TO KNOW YOU'RE GOING TO *DIE*...

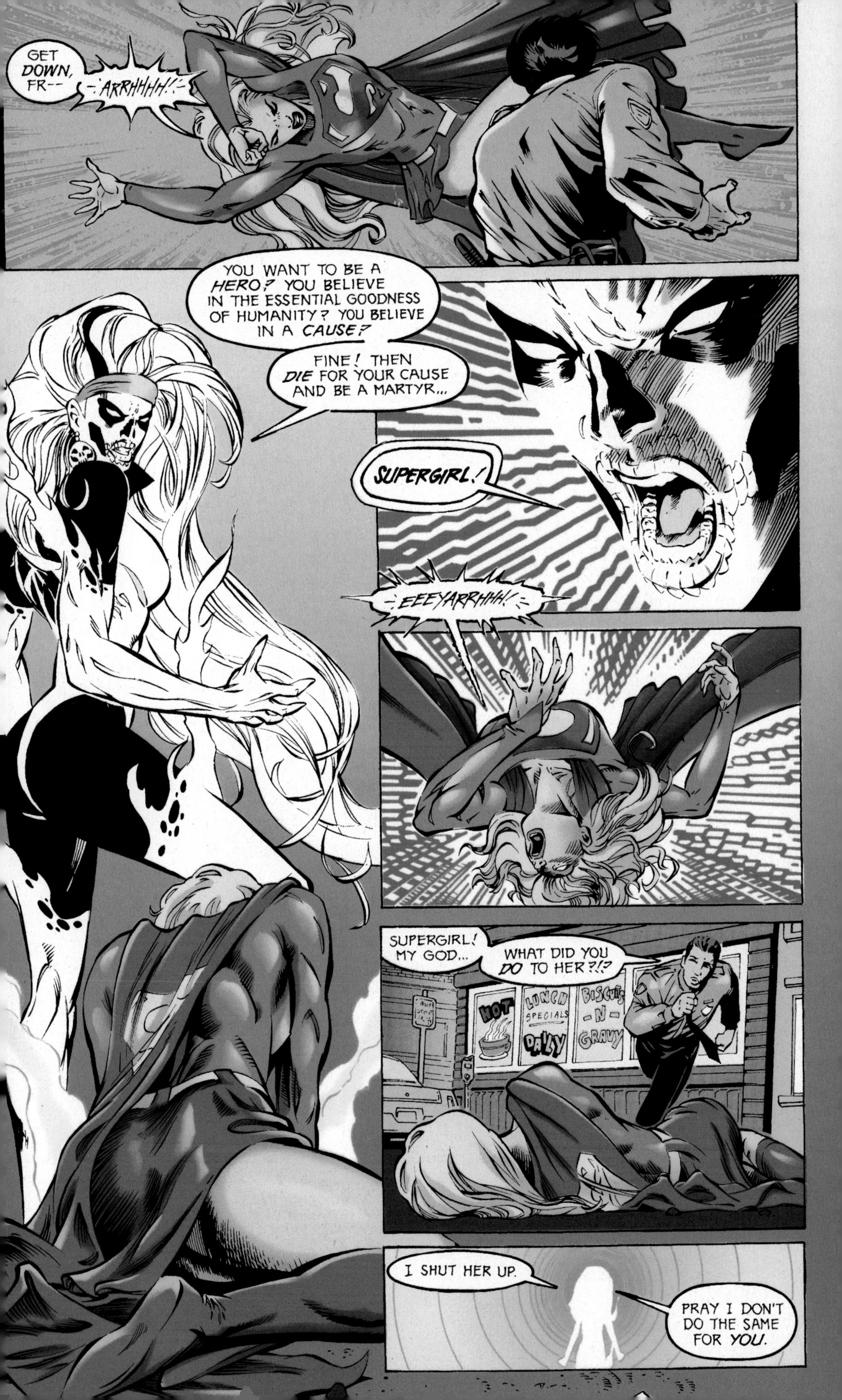
GET DOWN, FR--
-ARRHHHH!-
YOU WANT TO BE A HERO? YOU BELIEVE IN THE ESSENTIAL GOODNESS OF HUMANITY? YOU BELIEVE IN A CAUSE?
FINE! THEN DIE FOR YOUR CAUSE AND BE A MARTYR...
SUPERGIRL!
-EEEYARRHHH!-
SUPERGIRL! MY GOD...
WHAT DID YOU DO TO HER?!?
HOT
LUNCH SPECIALS DAILY
BISCUITS -N- GRAVY
I SHUT HER UP.
PRAY I DON'T DO THE SAME FOR YOU.

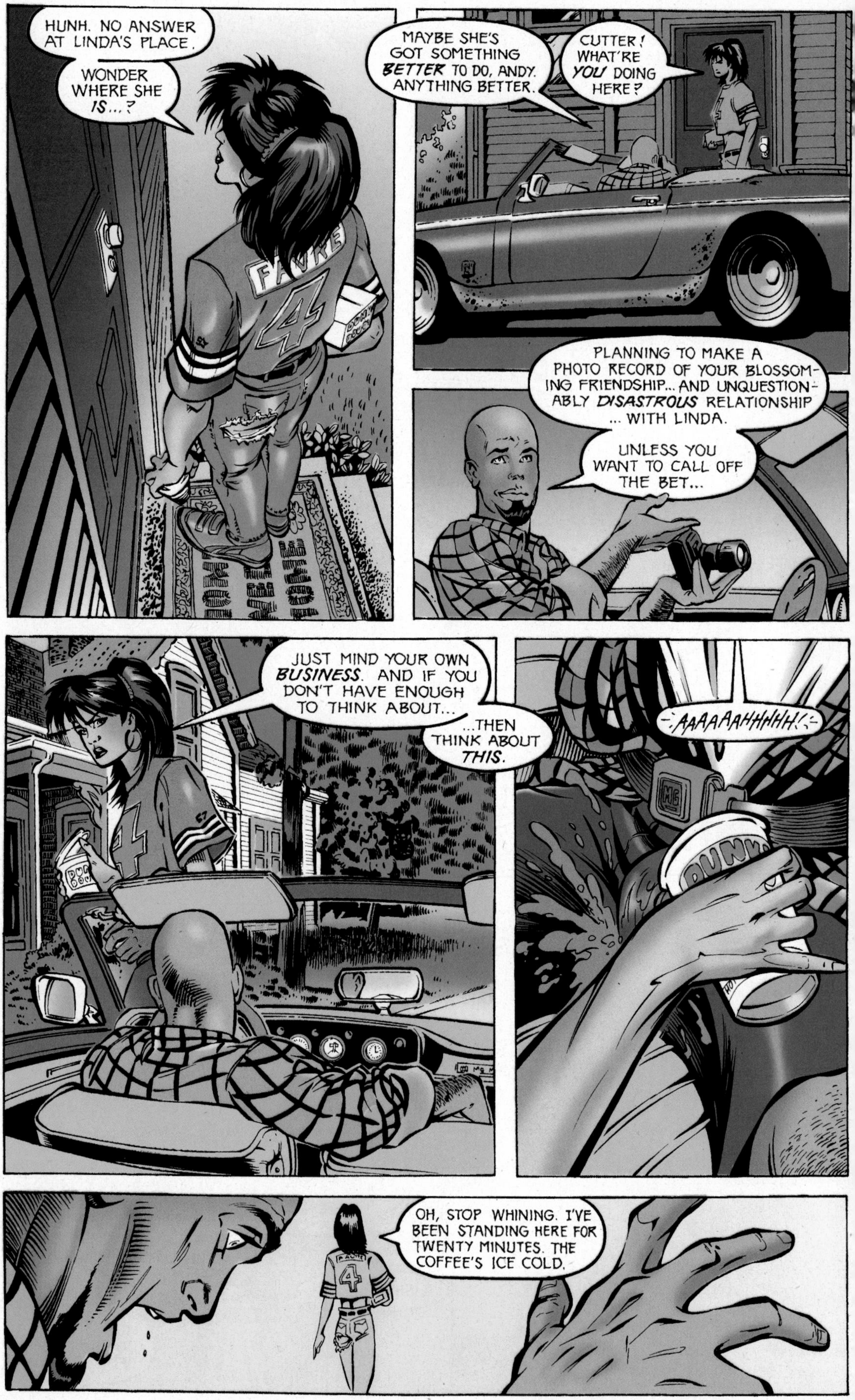
HUNH. NO ANSWER AT LINDA'S PLACE.
WONDER WHERE SHE *IS*...?
MAYBE SHE'S GOT SOMETHING *BETTER* TO DO, ANDY. ANYTHING BETTER.
CUTTER! WHAT'RE *YOU* DOING HERE?
PLANNING TO MAKE A PHOTO RECORD OF YOUR BLOSSOMING FRIENDSHIP... AND UNQUESTIONABLY *DISASTROUS* RELATIONSHIP ... WITH LINDA.
UNLESS YOU WANT TO CALL OFF THE BET...
JUST MIND YOUR OWN *BUSINESS*. AND IF YOU DON'T HAVE ENOUGH TO THINK ABOUT...
...THEN THINK ABOUT *THIS*.
AAAAAAHHHHH!
OH, STOP WHINING. I'VE BEEN STANDING HERE FOR TWENTY MINUTES. THE COFFEE'S ICE COLD.

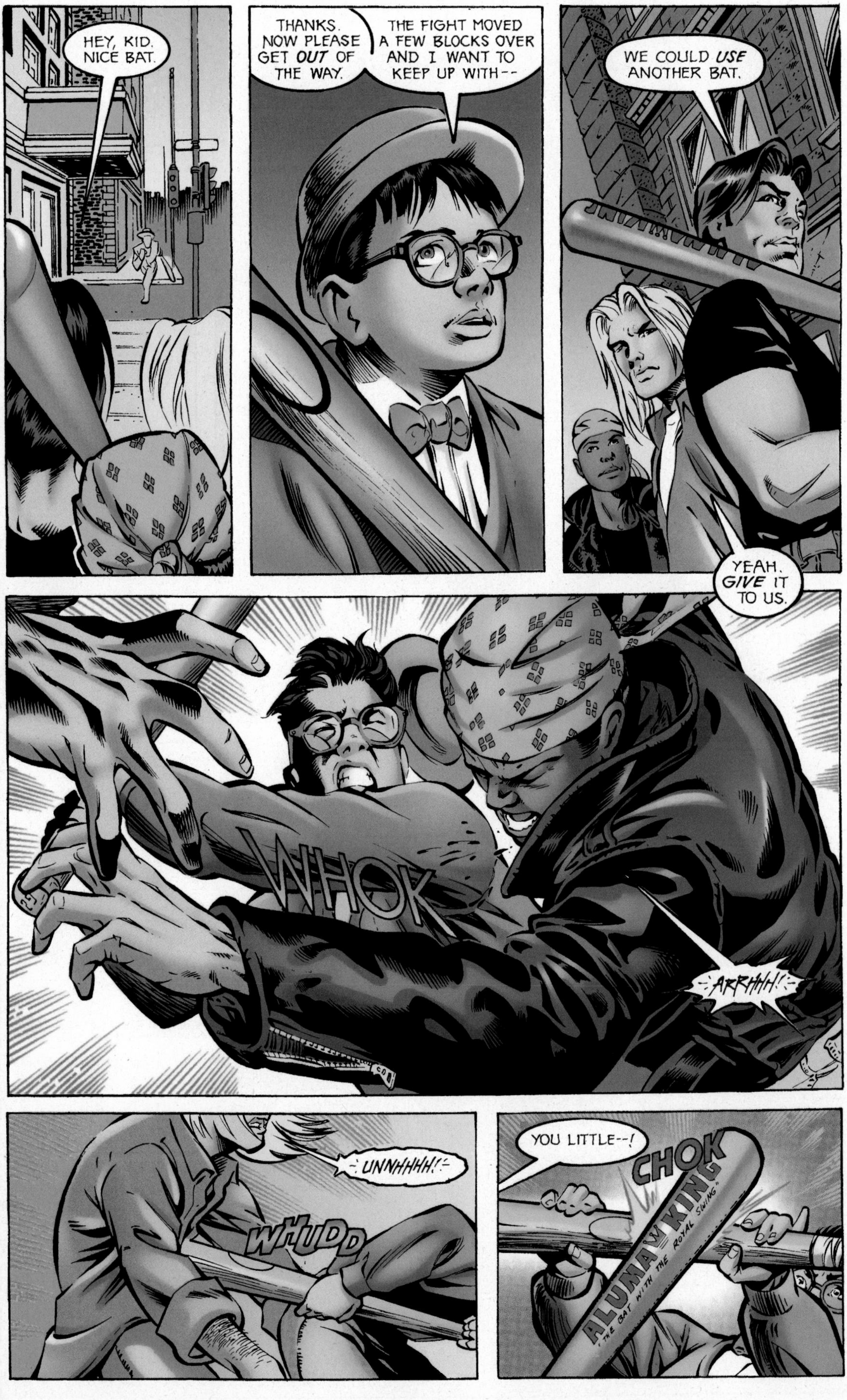
HEY, KID. NICE BAT.
THANKS. NOW PLEASE GET OUT OF THE WAY.
THE FIGHT MOVED A FEW BLOCKS OVER AND I WANT TO KEEP UP WITH--
WE COULD USE ANOTHER BAT.
YEAH. GIVE IT TO US.
WHOK
ARHHH!
UNNHHHH!
WHUDD
YOU LITTLE--!
CHOK
ALUMA KING
"THE BAT WITH THE ROYAL SWING"

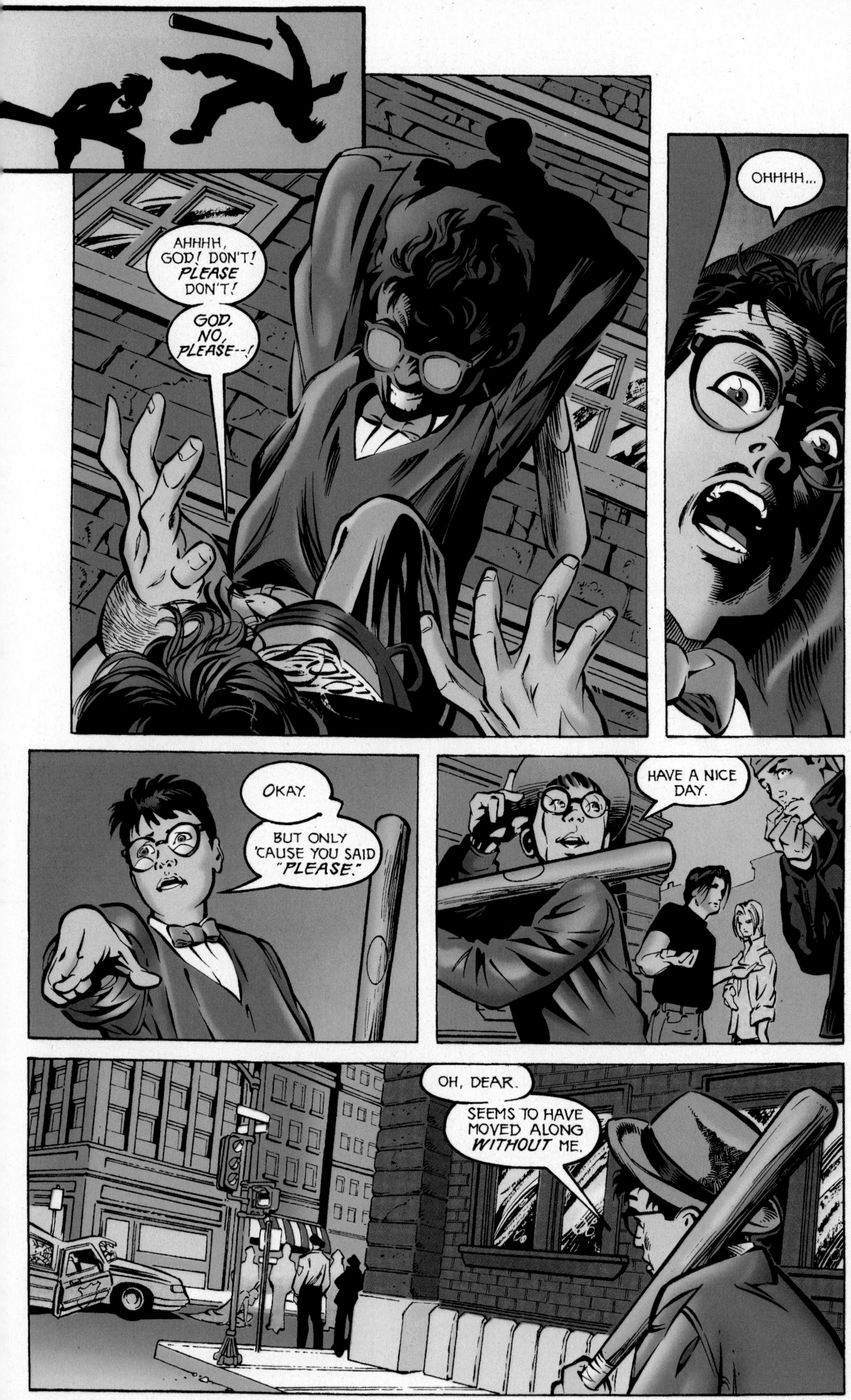
AHHHH, GOD! DON'T! PLEASE DON'T!
GOD, NO, PLEASE--!
OHHHH...
OKAY.
BUT ONLY 'CAUSE YOU SAID "PLEASE."
HAVE A NICE DAY.
OH, DEAR.
SEEMS TO HAVE MOVED ALONG WITHOUT ME.

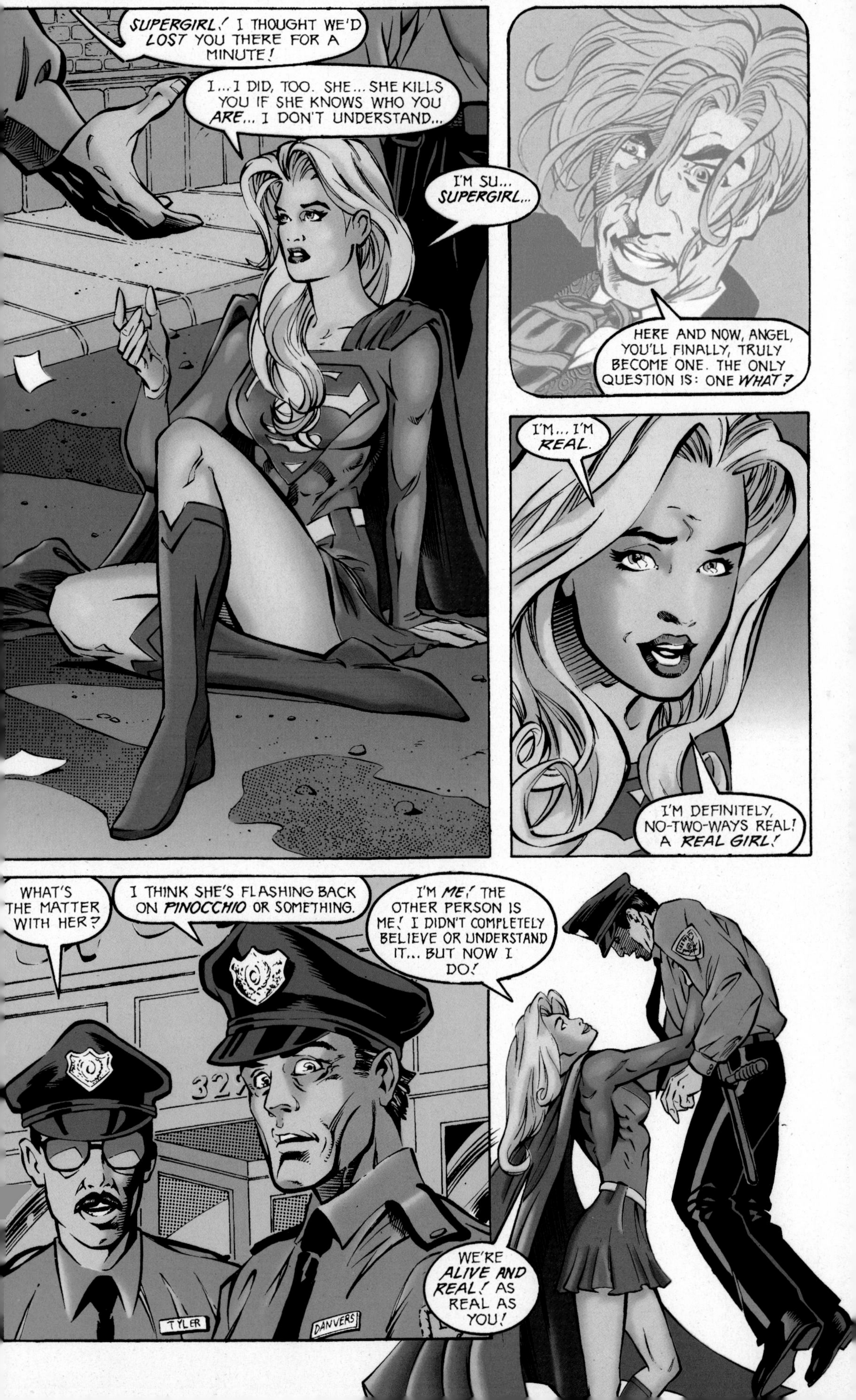
SUPERGIRL! I THOUGHT WE'D LOST YOU THERE FOR A MINUTE!
I... I DID, TOO. SHE... SHE KILLS YOU IF SHE KNOWS WHO YOU ARE... I DON'T UNDERSTAND...
I'M SU... SUPERGIRL...
HERE AND NOW, ANGEL, YOU'LL FINALLY, TRULY BECOME ONE. THE ONLY QUESTION IS: ONE WHAT?
I'M... I'M REAL.
I'M DEFINITELY, NO-TWO-WAYS REAL! A REAL GIRL!
WHAT'S THE MATTER WITH HER?
I THINK SHE'S FLASHING BACK ON PINOCCHIO OR SOMETHING.
I'M ME! THE OTHER PERSON IS ME! I DIDN'T COMPLETELY BELIEVE OR UNDERSTAND IT... BUT NOW I DO!
WE'RE ALIVE AND REAL! AS REAL AS YOU!
TYLER
DANVERS

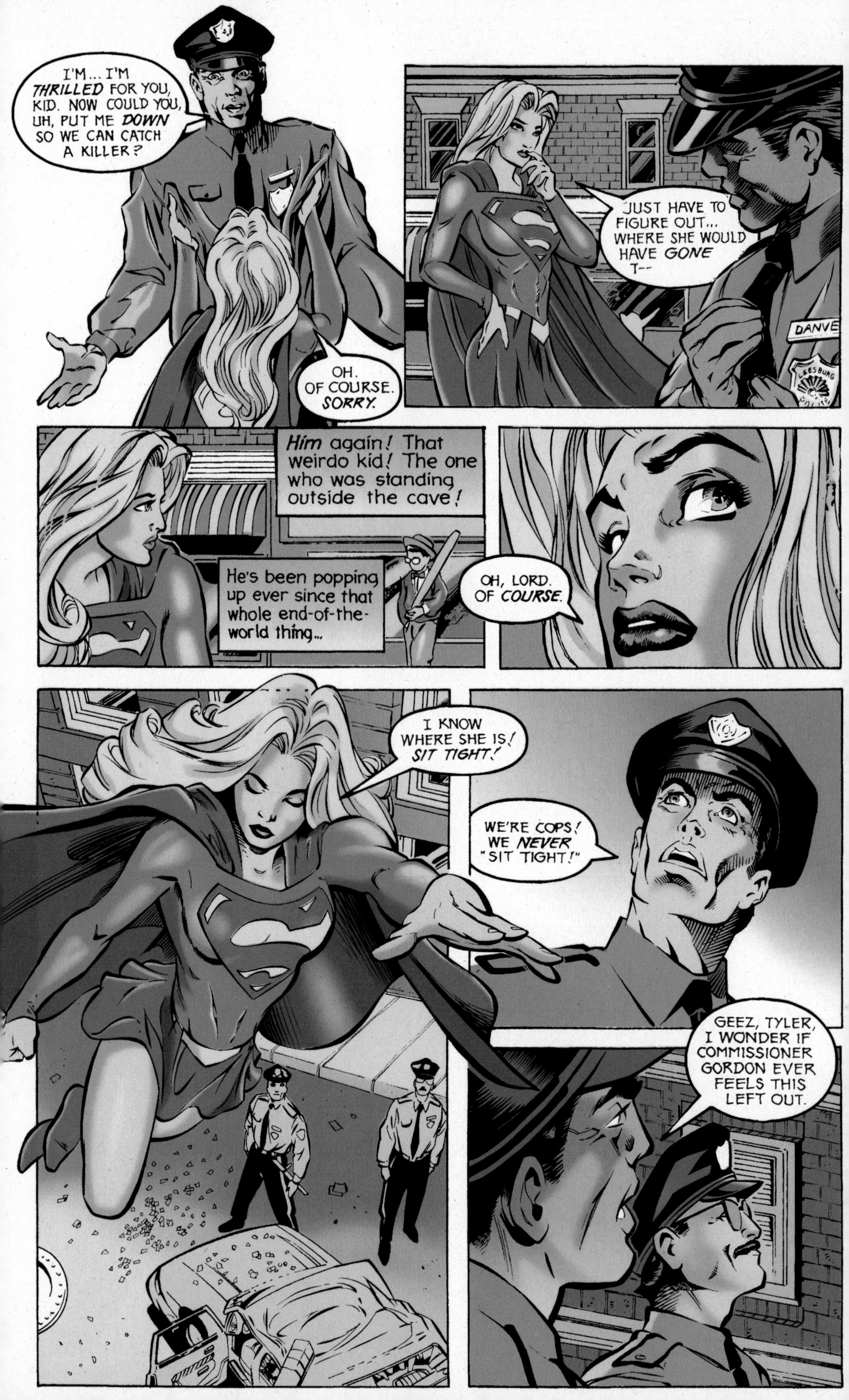

I'M... I'M THRILLED FOR YOU, KID. NOW COULD YOU, UH, PUT ME DOWN SO WE CAN CATCH A KILLER?
OH. OF COURSE. SORRY.
JUST HAVE TO FIGURE OUT... WHERE SHE WOULD HAVE GONE T--
DANVE
LEESBURG POLICE
Him again! That weirdo kid! The one who was standing outside the cave!
He's been popping up ever since that whole end-of-the-world thing...
OH, LORD. OF COURSE.
I KNOW WHERE SHE IS! SIT TIGHT!
WE'RE COPS! WE NEVER "SIT TIGHT!"
GEEZ, TYLER, I WONDER IF COMMISSIONER GORDON EVER FEELS THIS LEFT OUT.

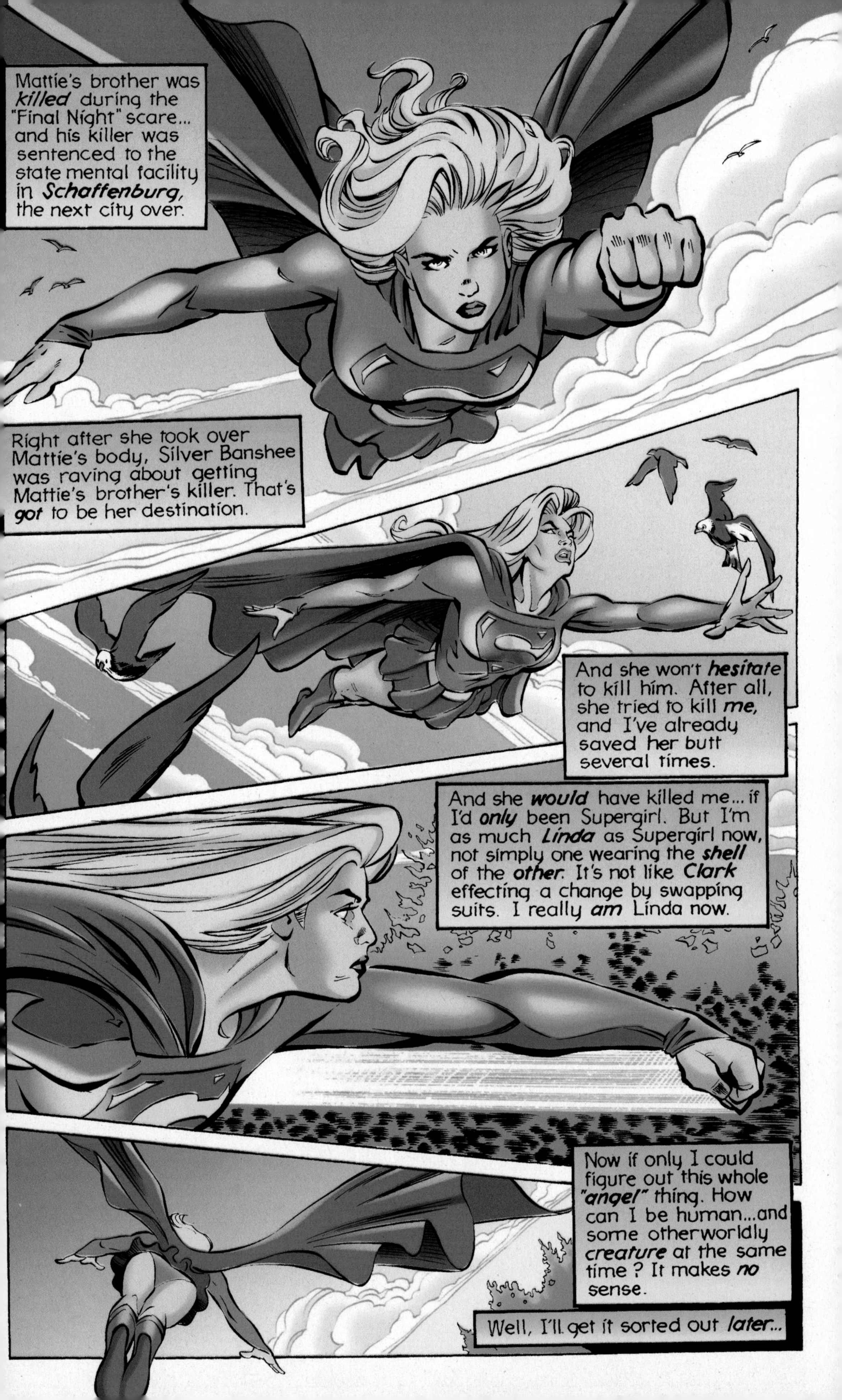
Mattie's brother was killed during the "Final Night" scare... and his killer was sentenced to the state mental facility in Schaffenburg, the next city over.
Right after she took over Mattie's body, Silver Banshee was raving about getting Mattie's brother's killer. That's got to be her destination.
And she won't hesitate to kill him. After all, she tried to kill me, and I've already saved her butt several times.
And she would have killed me... if I'd only been Supergirl. But I'm as much Linda as Supergirl now, not simply one wearing the shell of the other. It's not like Clark effecting a change by swapping suits. I really am Linda now.
Now if only I could figure out this whole "angel" thing. How can I be human...and some otherworldly creature at the same time? It makes no sense.
Well, I'll get it sorted out later...

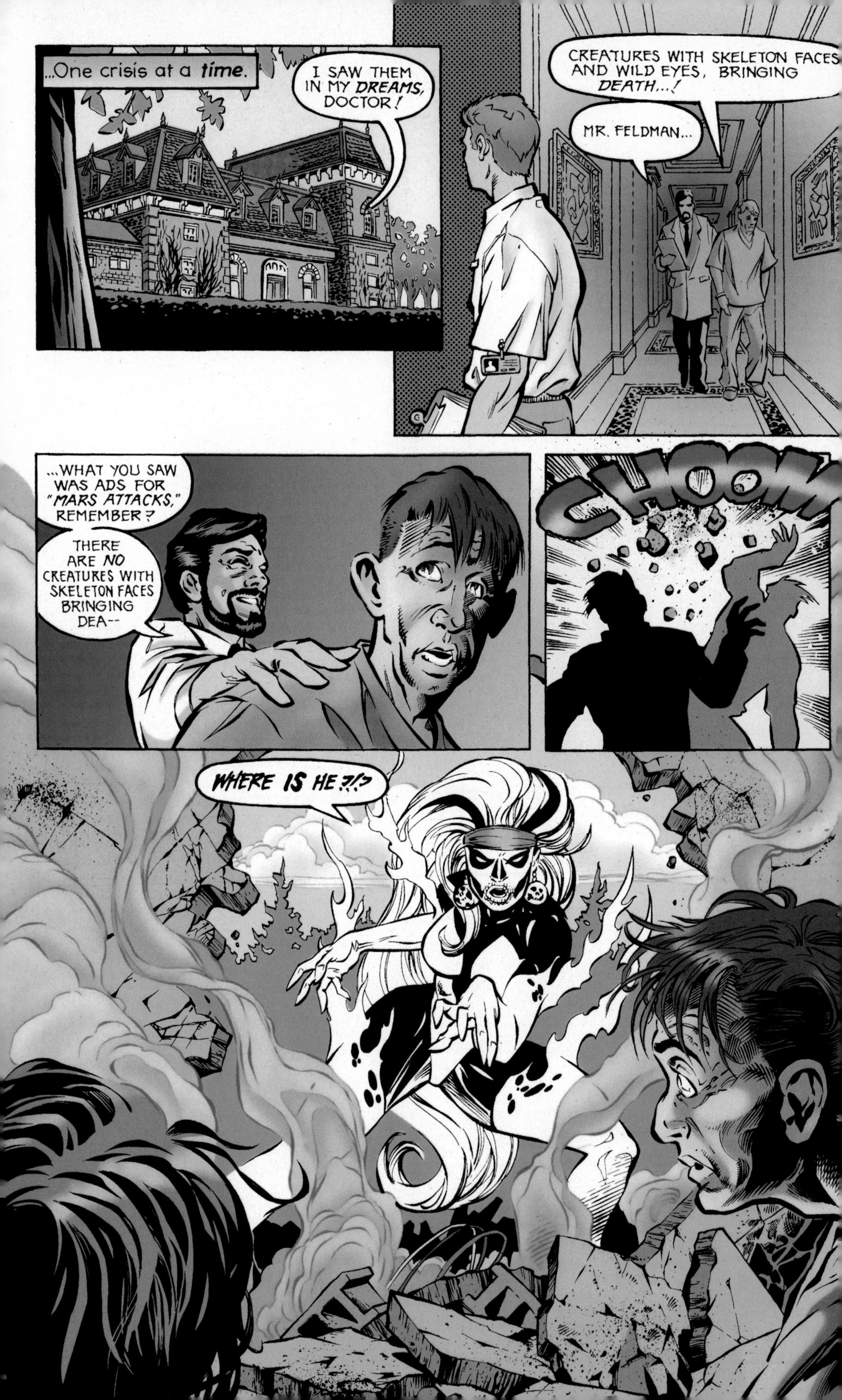
...One crisis at a *time*.
I SAW THEM IN MY *DREAMS*, DOCTOR!
CREATURES WITH SKELETON FACES AND WILD EYES, BRINGING *DEATH*...!
MR. FELDMAN...
...WHAT YOU SAW WAS ADS FOR *"MARS ATTACKS,"* REMEMBER?
THERE ARE *NO* CREATURES WITH SKELETON FACES BRINGING DEA--
CHOOM
WHERE IS HE?!?

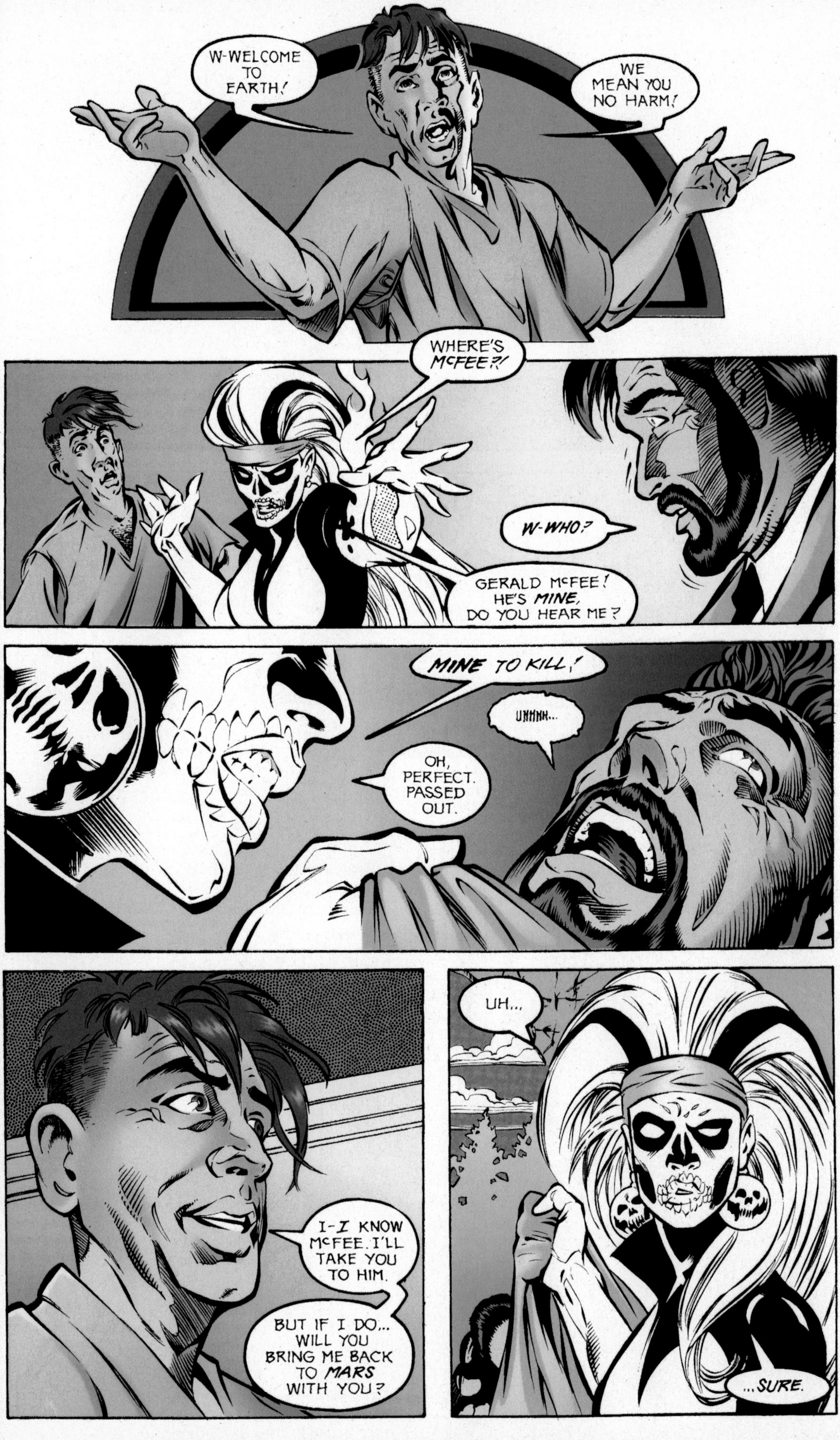

W-WELCOME TO EARTH!
WE MEAN YOU NO HARM!
WHERE'S McFEE?!
W-WHO?
GERALD McFEE! HE'S MINE, DO YOU HEAR ME?
MINE TO KILL!
UNNNH...
OH, PERFECT. PASSED OUT.
I-I KNOW McFEE. I'LL TAKE YOU TO HIM.
BUT IF I DO... WILL YOU BRING ME BACK TO MARS WITH YOU?
UH...
...SURE.

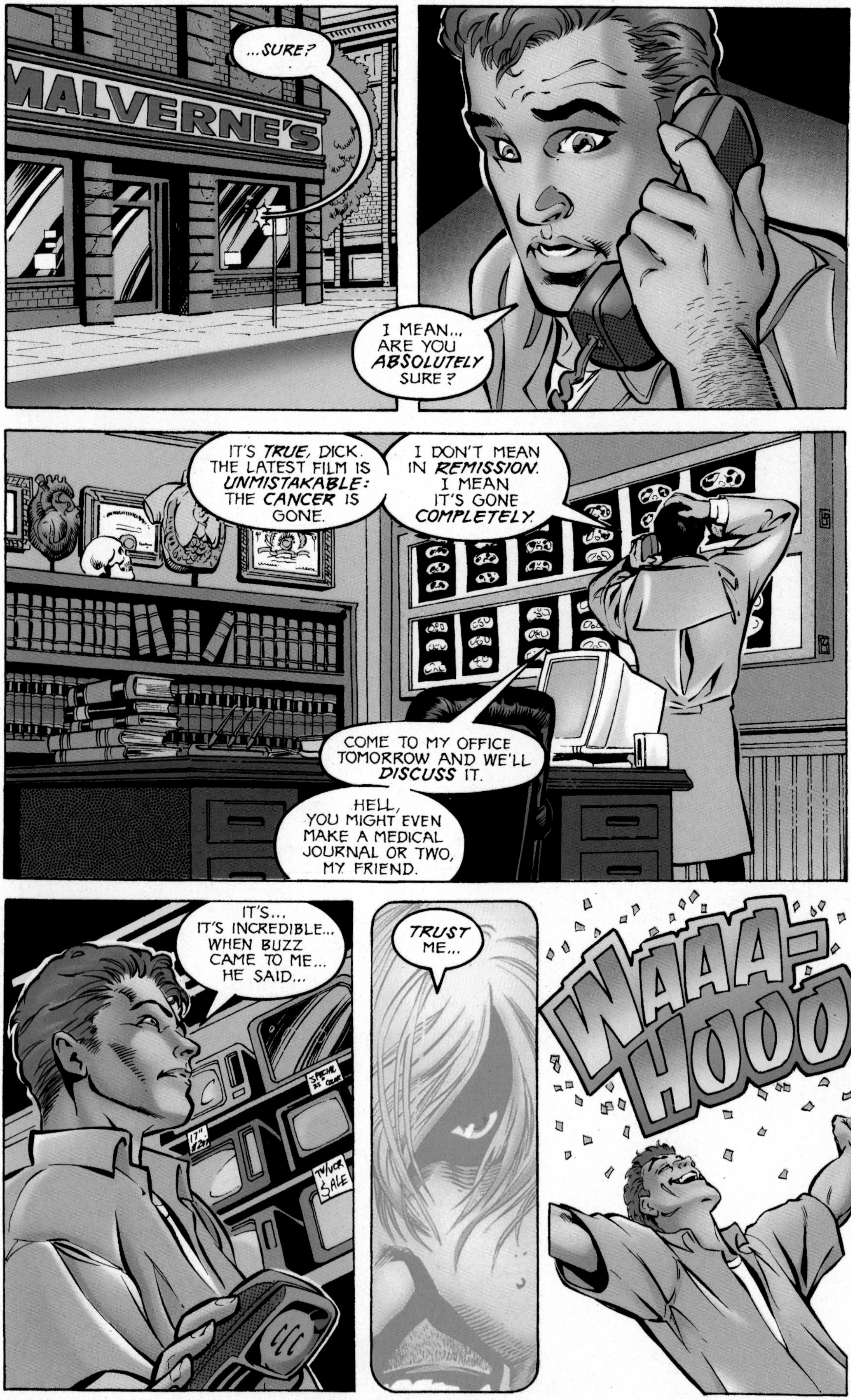
MALVERNE'S
...SURE?
I MEAN... ARE YOU ABSOLUTELY SURE?
IT'S TRUE, DICK. THE LATEST FILM IS UNMISTAKABLE: THE CANCER IS GONE.
I DON'T MEAN IN REMISSION. I MEAN IT'S GONE COMPLETELY.
COME TO MY OFFICE TOMORROW AND WE'LL DISCUSS IT.
HELL, YOU MIGHT EVEN MAKE A MEDICAL JOURNAL OR TWO, MY FRIEND.
IT'S... IT'S INCREDIBLE... WHEN BUZZ CAME TO ME... HE SAID...
TV/VCR SALE
TRUST ME...
WAAA-HOOO

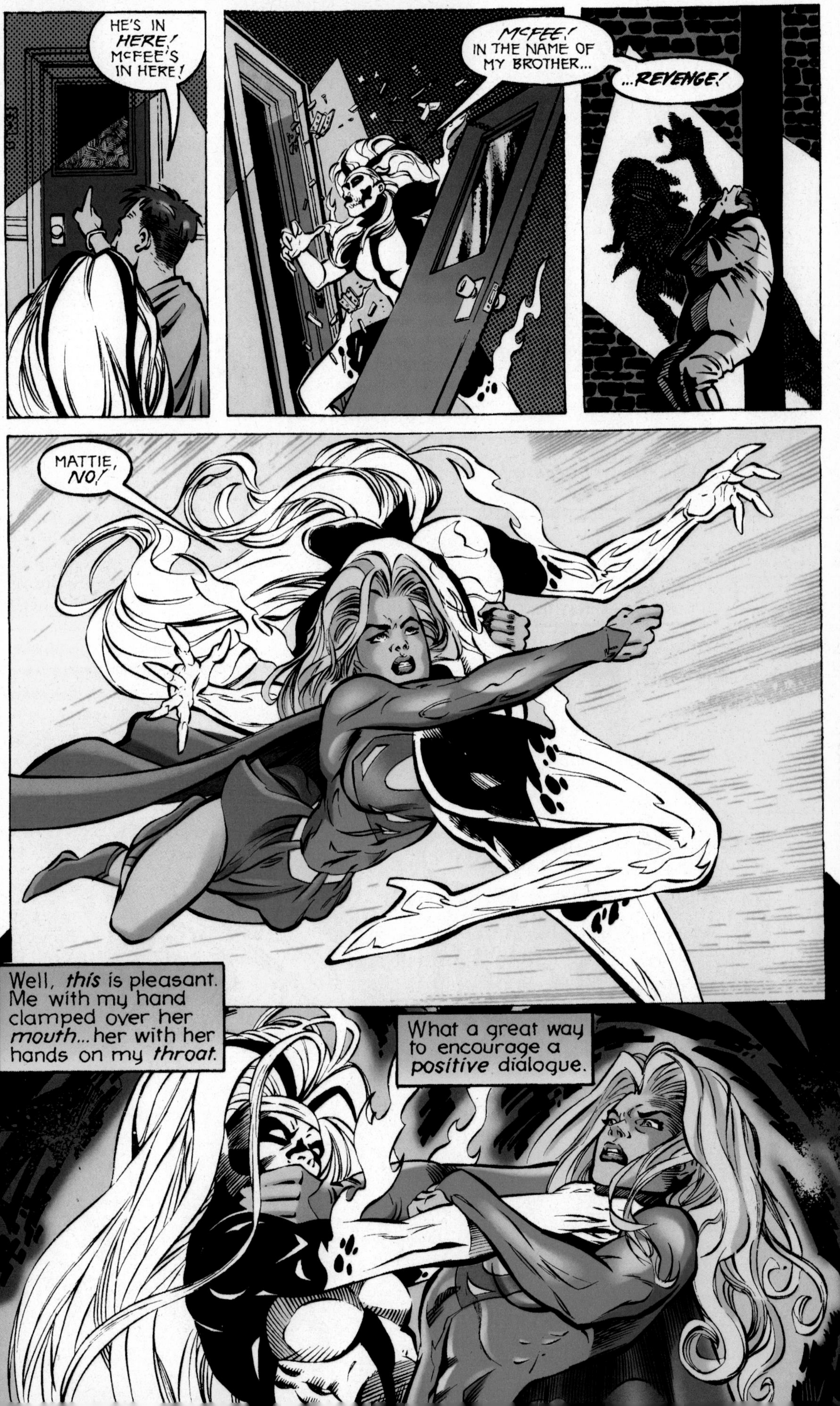

HE'S IN
HERE!
McFEE'S
IN HERE!
McFEE!
IN THE NAME OF
MY BROTHER...
...REVENGE!
MATTIE,
NO!
Well, this is pleasant. Me with my hand clamped over her mouth... her with her hands on my throat.
What a great way to encourage a positive dialogue.

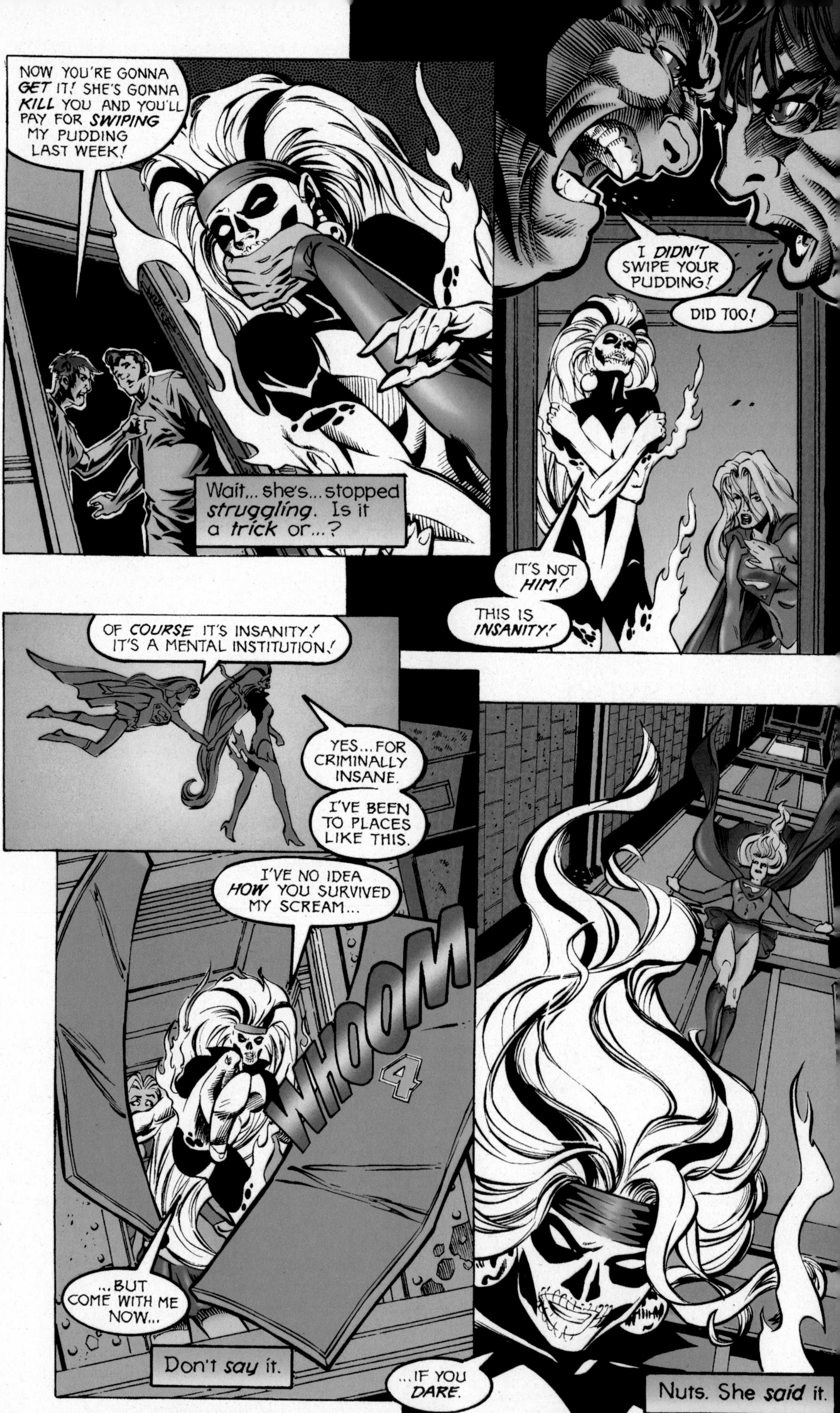

NOW YOU'RE GONNA GET IT! SHE'S GONNA KILL YOU AND YOU'LL PAY FOR SWIPING MY PUDDING LAST WEEK!
Wait... she's... stopped struggling. Is it a trick or...?
I DIDN'T SWIPE YOUR PUDDING!
DID TOO!
IT'S NOT HIM!
THIS IS INSANITY!
OF COURSE IT'S INSANITY! IT'S A MENTAL INSTITUTION!
YES... FOR CRIMINALLY INSANE.
I'VE BEEN TO PLACES LIKE THIS.
I'VE NO IDEA HOW YOU SURVIVED MY SCREAM...
WHOOM
...BUT COME WITH ME NOW...
Don't say it.
...IF YOU DARE.
Nuts. She said it.

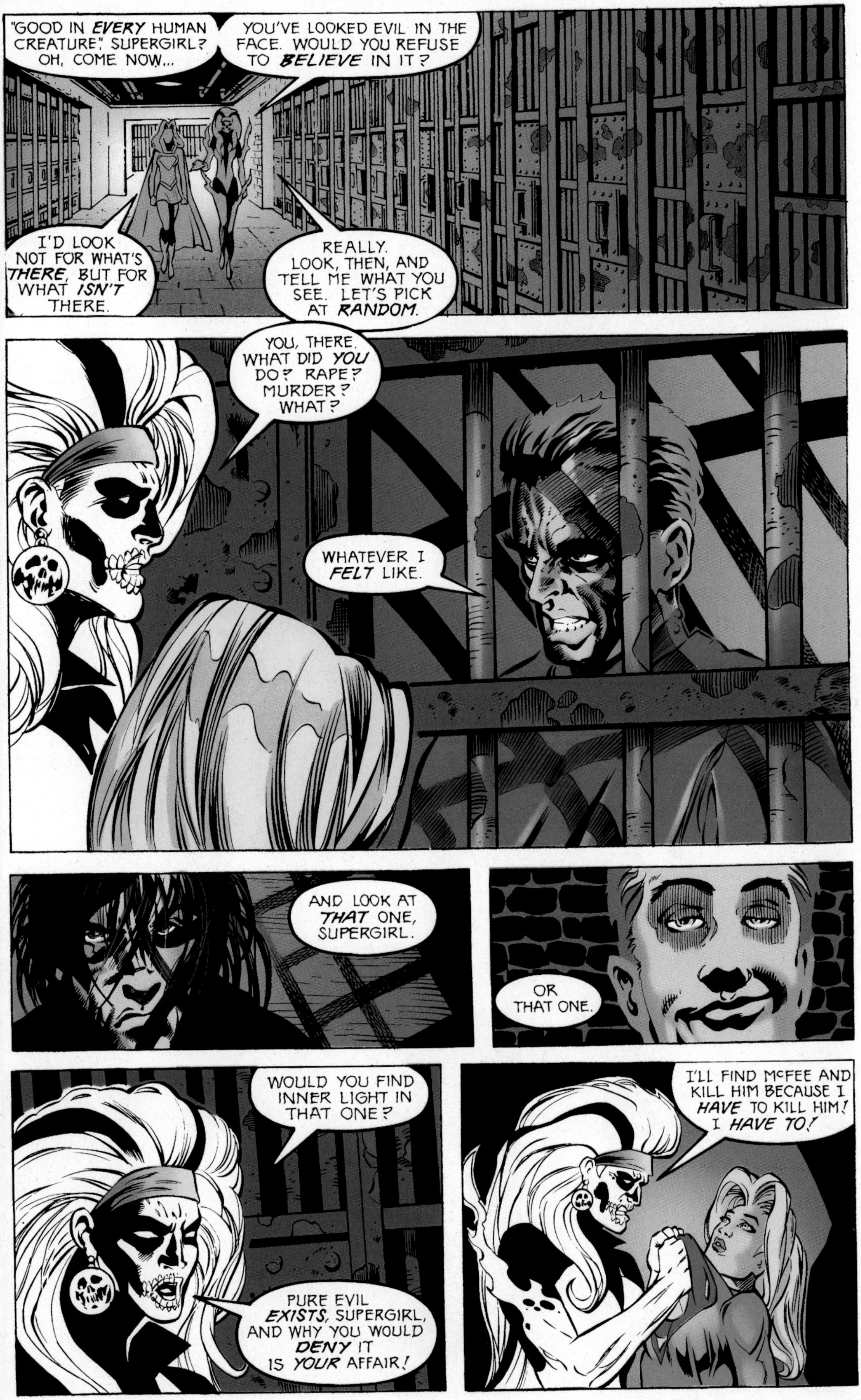
"GOOD IN EVERY HUMAN CREATURE," SUPERGIRL? OH, COME NOW...
YOU'VE LOOKED EVIL IN THE FACE. WOULD YOU REFUSE TO BELIEVE IN IT?
I'D LOOK NOT FOR WHAT'S THERE, BUT FOR WHAT ISN'T THERE.
REALLY. LOOK, THEN, AND TELL ME WHAT YOU SEE. LET'S PICK AT RANDOM.
YOU, THERE. WHAT DID YOU DO? RAPE? MURDER? WHAT?
WHATEVER I FELT LIKE.
AND LOOK AT THAT ONE, SUPERGIRL.
OR THAT ONE.
WOULD YOU FIND INNER LIGHT IN THAT ONE?
PURE EVIL EXISTS, SUPERGIRL, AND WHY YOU WOULD DENY IT IS YOUR AFFAIR!
I'LL FIND McFEE AND KILL HIM BECAUSE I HAVE TO KILL HIM! I HAVE TO!

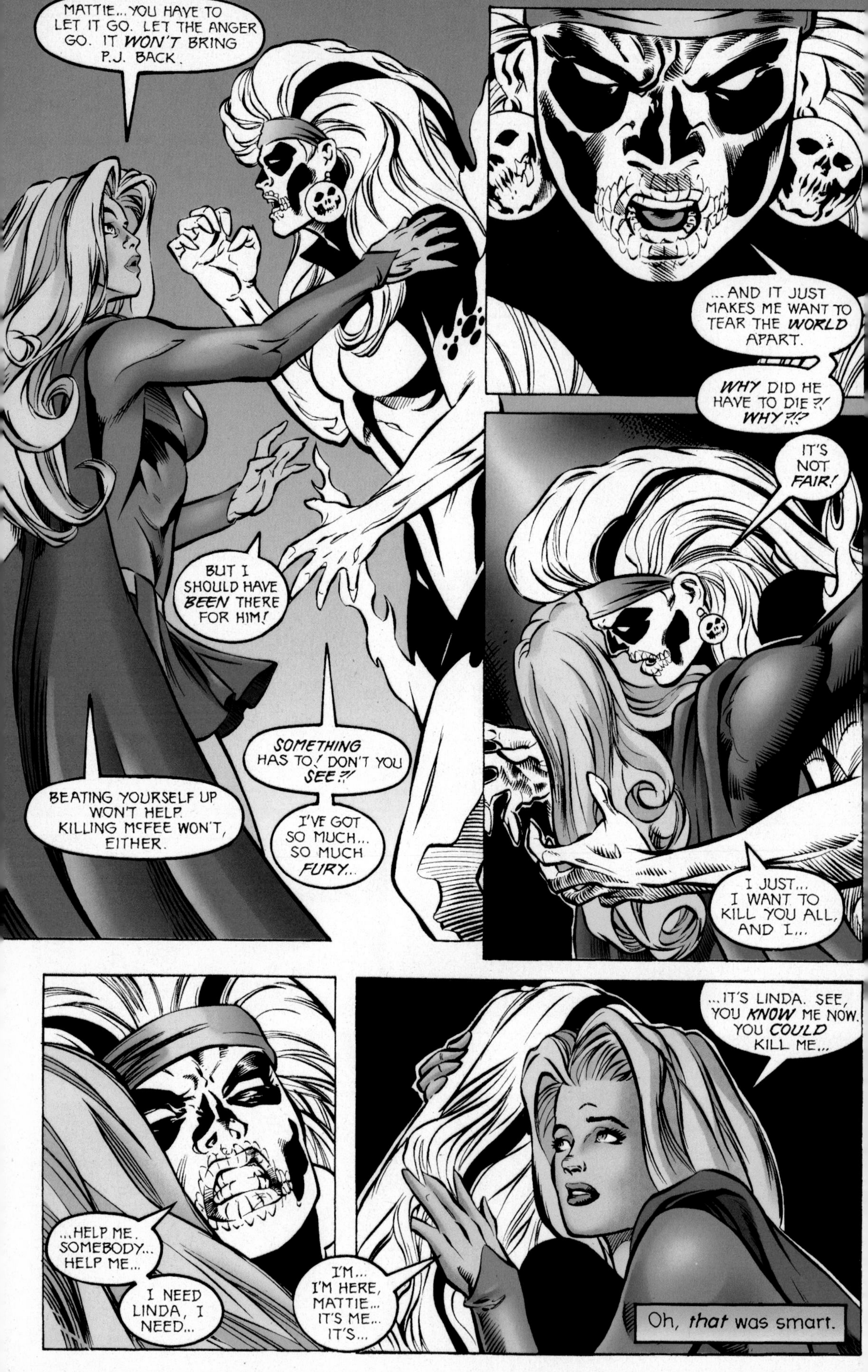
MATTIE... YOU HAVE TO LET IT GO. LET THE ANGER GO. IT WON'T BRING P.J. BACK.
BUT I SHOULD HAVE BEEN THERE FOR HIM!
BEATING YOURSELF UP WON'T HELP. KILLING MCFEE WON'T, EITHER.
SOMETHING HAS TO! DON'T YOU SEE?!
I'VE GOT SO MUCH... SO MUCH FURY...
...AND IT JUST MAKES ME WANT TO TEAR THE WORLD APART.
WHY DID HE HAVE TO DIE?! WHY?!?
IT'S NOT FAIR!
I JUST... I WANT TO KILL YOU ALL, AND I...
...HELP ME. SOMEBODY... HELP ME...
I NEED LINDA, I NEED...
I'M... I'M HERE, MATTIE... IT'S ME... IT'S...
...IT'S LINDA. SEE, YOU KNOW ME NOW. YOU COULD KILL ME...
Oh, that was smart.

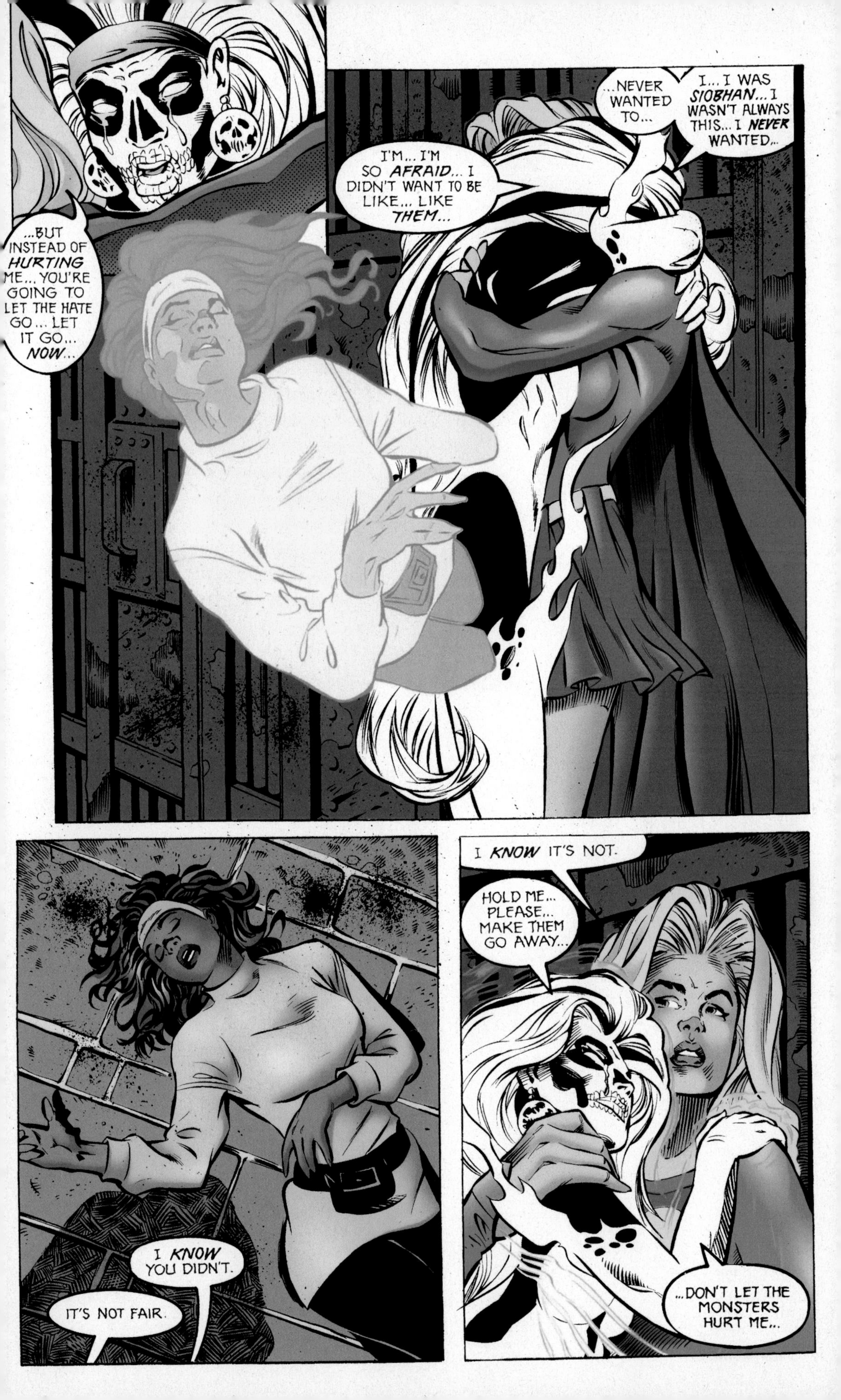
...BUT INSTEAD OF HURTING ME... YOU'RE GOING TO LET THE HATE GO... LET IT GO... NOW...
I'M... I'M SO AFRAID... I DIDN'T WANT TO BE LIKE... LIKE THEM...
...NEVER WANTED TO...
I... I WAS SIOBHAN... I WASN'T ALWAYS THIS... I NEVER WANTED...
I KNOW YOU DIDN'T.
IT'S NOT FAIR.
I KNOW IT'S NOT.
HOLD ME... PLEASE... MAKE THEM GO AWAY...
...DON'T LET THE MONSTERS HURT ME...

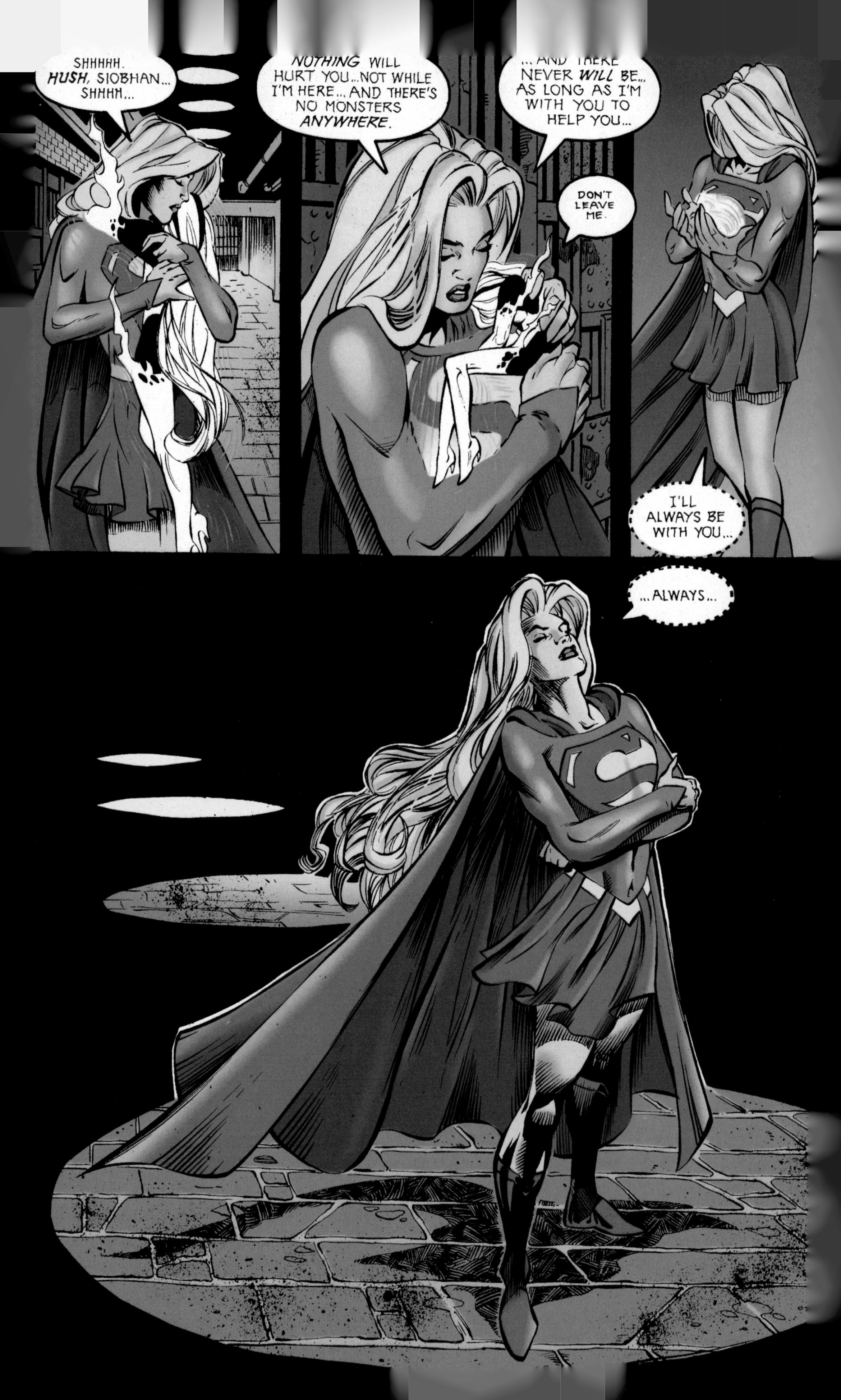
SHHHHH. HUSH, SIOBHAN... SHHHH...
NOTHING WILL HURT YOU...NOT WHILE I'M HERE... AND THERE'S NO MONSTERS ANYWHERE.
...AND THERE NEVER WILL BE... AS LONG AS I'M WITH YOU TO HELP YOU...
DON'T LEAVE ME.
I'LL ALWAYS BE WITH YOU...
...ALWAYS...

***SUPERGIRL* #13 cover by Gary Frank, Cam Smith and Patrick Martin**

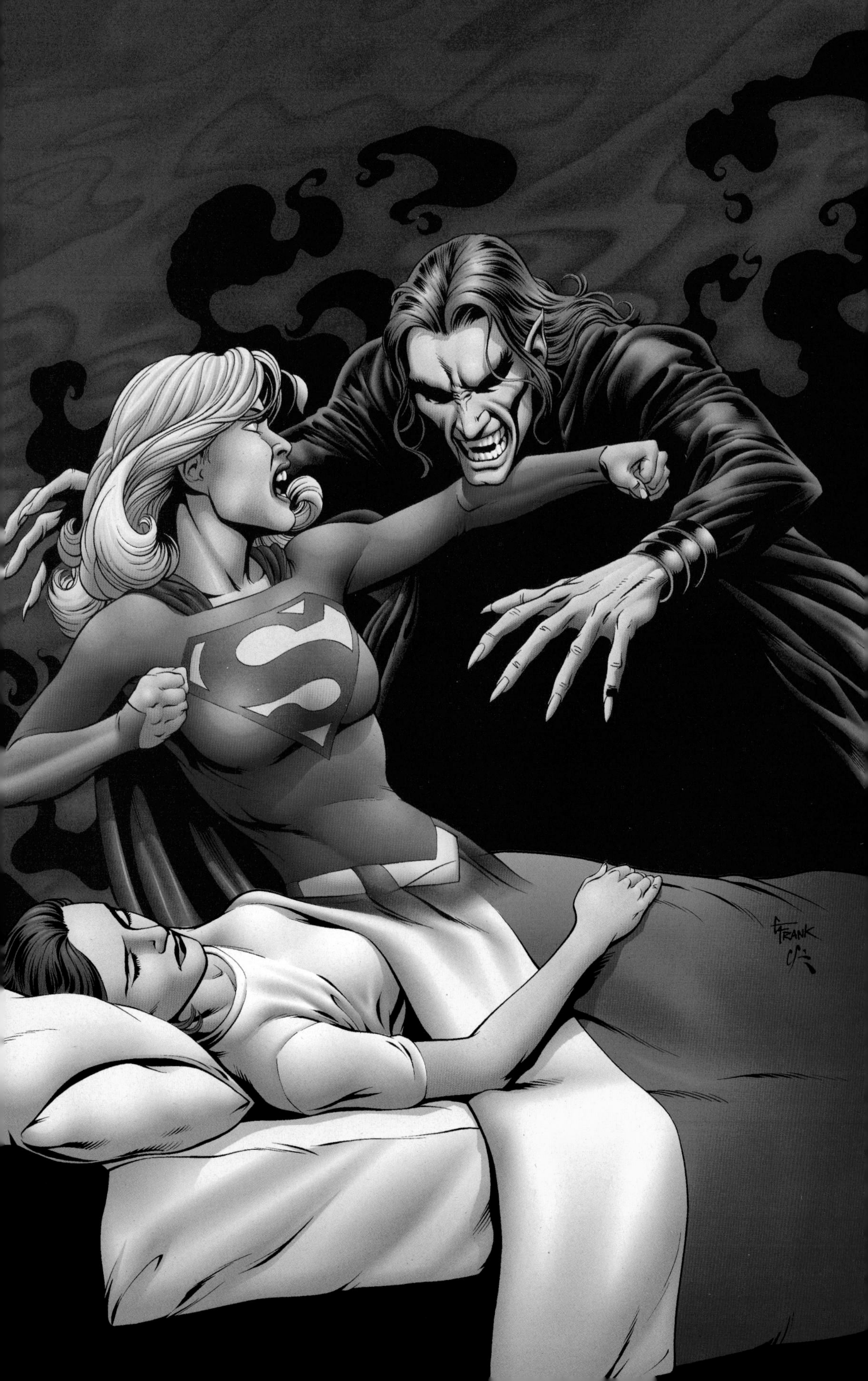

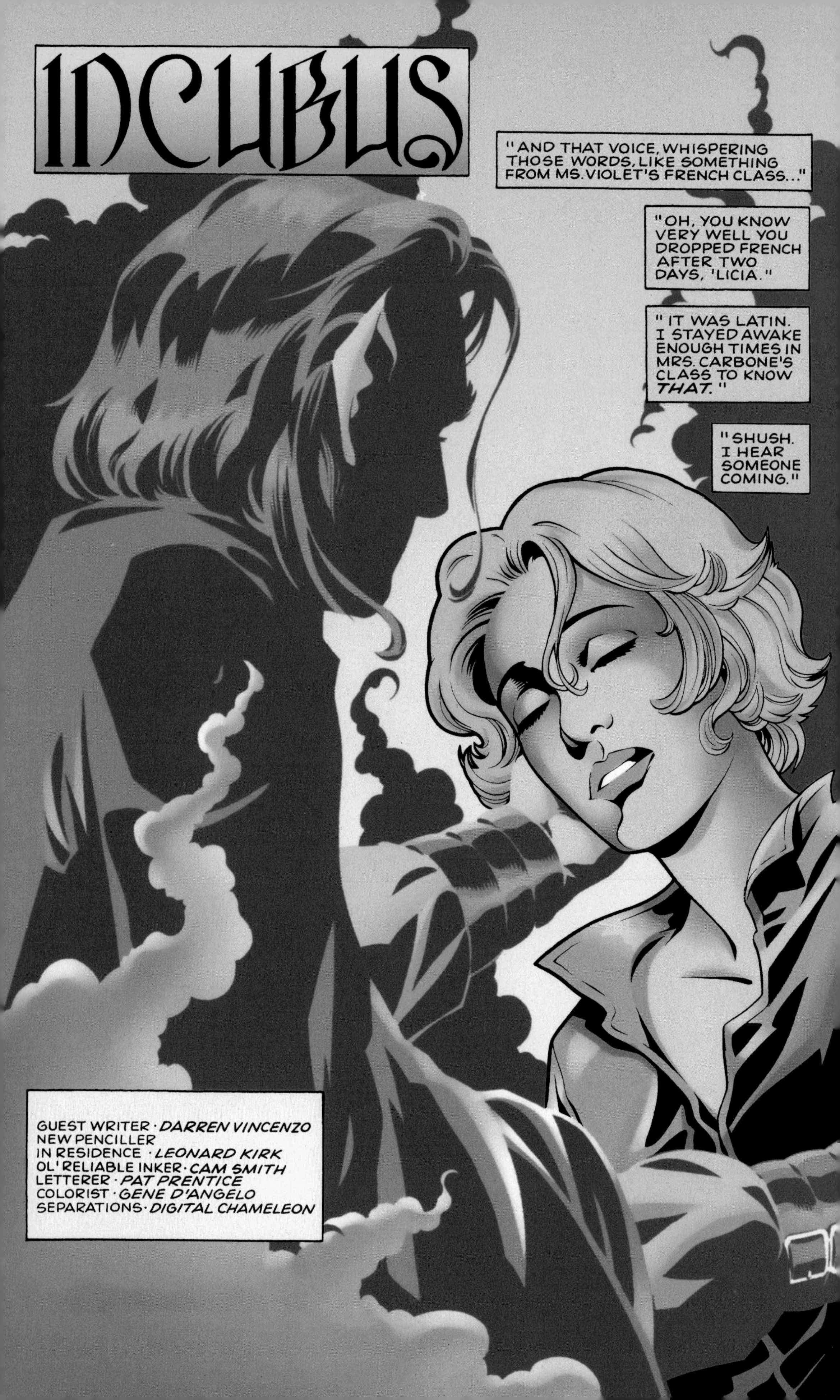
INCUBUS
"AND THAT VOICE, WHISPERING THOSE WORDS, LIKE SOMETHING FROM MS. VIOLET'S FRENCH CLASS..."
"OH, YOU KNOW VERY WELL YOU DROPPED FRENCH AFTER TWO DAYS, 'LICIA."
"IT WAS LATIN. I STAYED AWAKE ENOUGH TIMES IN MRS. CARBONE'S CLASS TO KNOW THAT."
"SHUSH. I HEAR SOMEONE COMING."
GUEST WRITER · DARREN VINCENZO
NEW PENCILLER IN RESIDENCE · LEONARD KIRK
OL' RELIABLE INKER · CAM SMITH
LETTERER · PAT PRENTICE
COLORIST · GENE D'ANGELO
SEPARATIONS · DIGITAL CHAMELEON

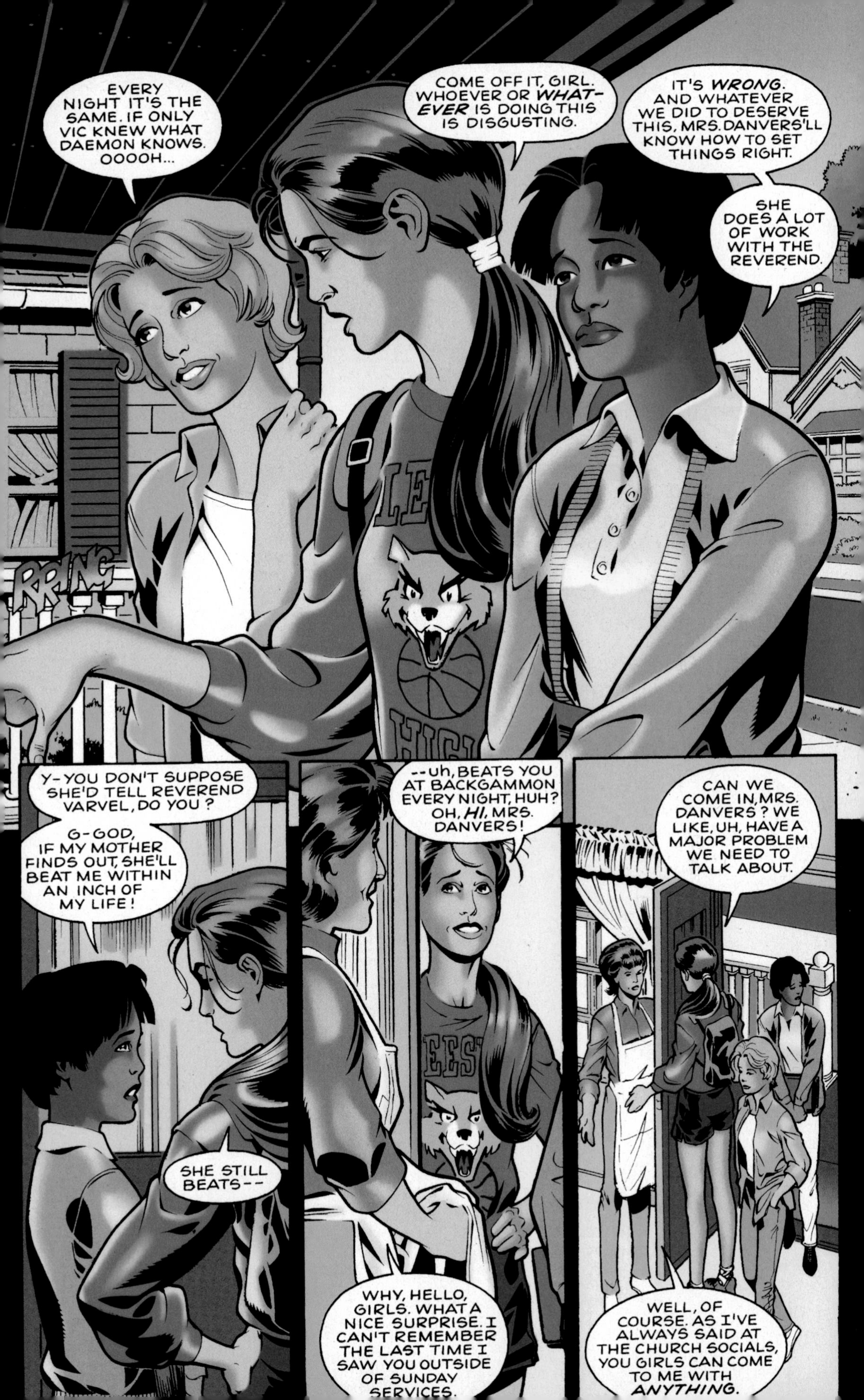
EVERY NIGHT IT'S THE SAME. IF ONLY VIC KNEW WHAT DAEMON KNOWS. OOOOH...
COME OFF IT, GIRL. WHOEVER OR *WHAT-EVER* IS DOING THIS IS DISGUSTING.
IT'S *WRONG*. AND WHATEVER WE DID TO DESERVE THIS, MRS. DANVERS'LL KNOW HOW TO SET THINGS RIGHT.
SHE DOES A LOT OF WORK WITH THE REVEREND.
RRING
Y-YOU DON'T SUPPOSE SHE'D TELL REVEREND VARVEL, DO YOU?
G-GOD, IF MY MOTHER FINDS OUT, SHE'LL BEAT ME WITHIN AN INCH OF MY LIFE!
SHE STILL BEATS--
--uh, BEATS YOU AT BACKGAMMON EVERY NIGHT, HUH? OH, *HI*, MRS. DANVERS!
WHY, HELLO, GIRLS. WHAT A NICE SURPRISE. I CAN'T REMEMBER THE LAST TIME I SAW YOU OUTSIDE OF SUNDAY SERVICES.
CAN WE COME IN, MRS. DANVERS? WE LIKE, UH, HAVE A MAJOR PROBLEM WE NEED TO TALK ABOUT.
WELL, OF COURSE. AS I'VE ALWAYS SAID AT THE CHURCH SOCIALS, YOU GIRLS CAN COME TO ME WITH *ANYTHING*.

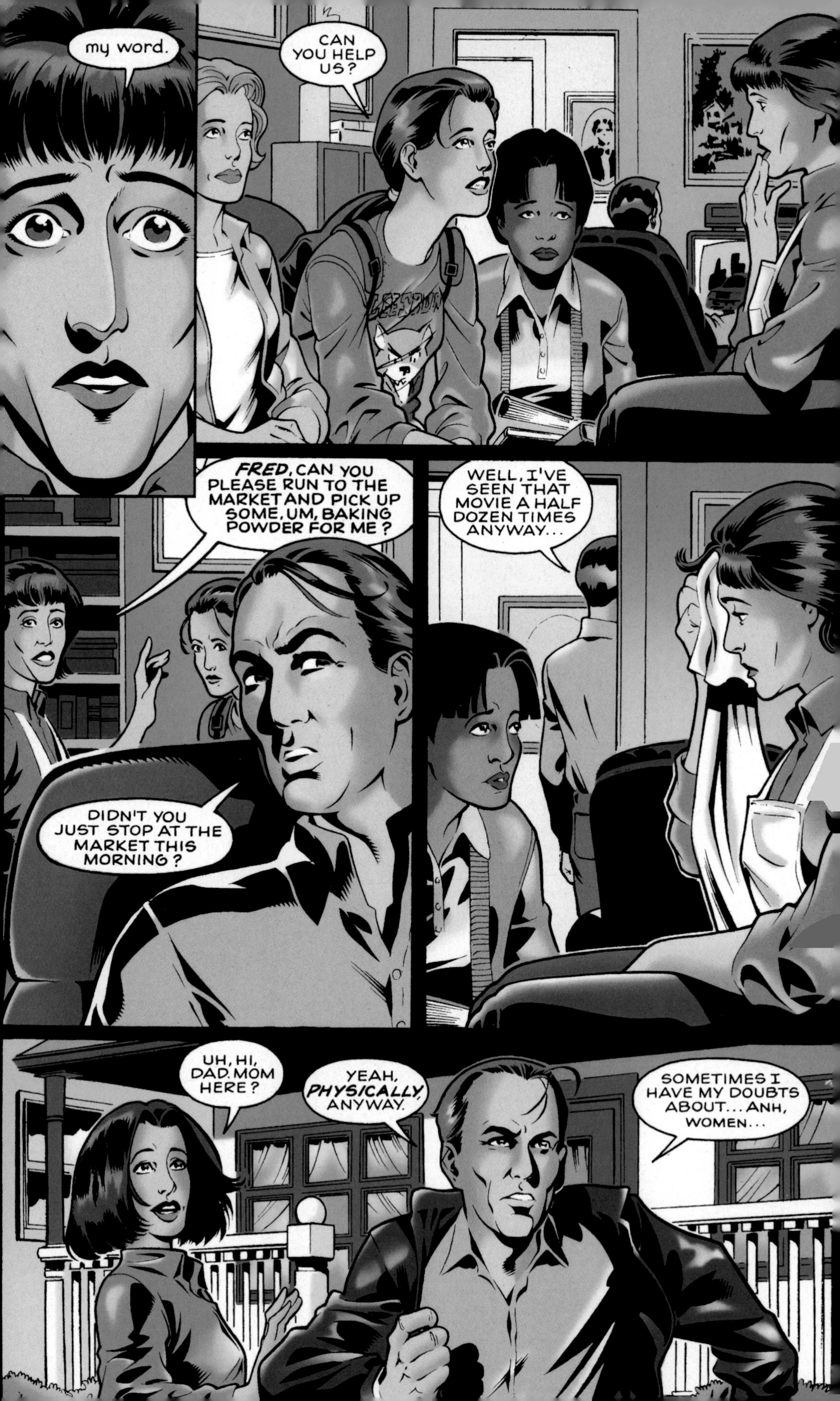
my word.
CAN YOU HELP US?
FRED, CAN YOU PLEASE RUN TO THE MARKET AND PICK UP SOME, UM, BAKING POWDER FOR ME?
DIDN'T YOU JUST STOP AT THE MARKET THIS MORNING?
WELL, I'VE SEEN THAT MOVIE A HALF DOZEN TIMES ANYWAY...
UH, HI, DAD. MOM HERE?
YEAH, PHYSICALLY, ANYWAY.
SOMETIMES I HAVE MY DOUBTS ABOUT... ANH, WOMEN...

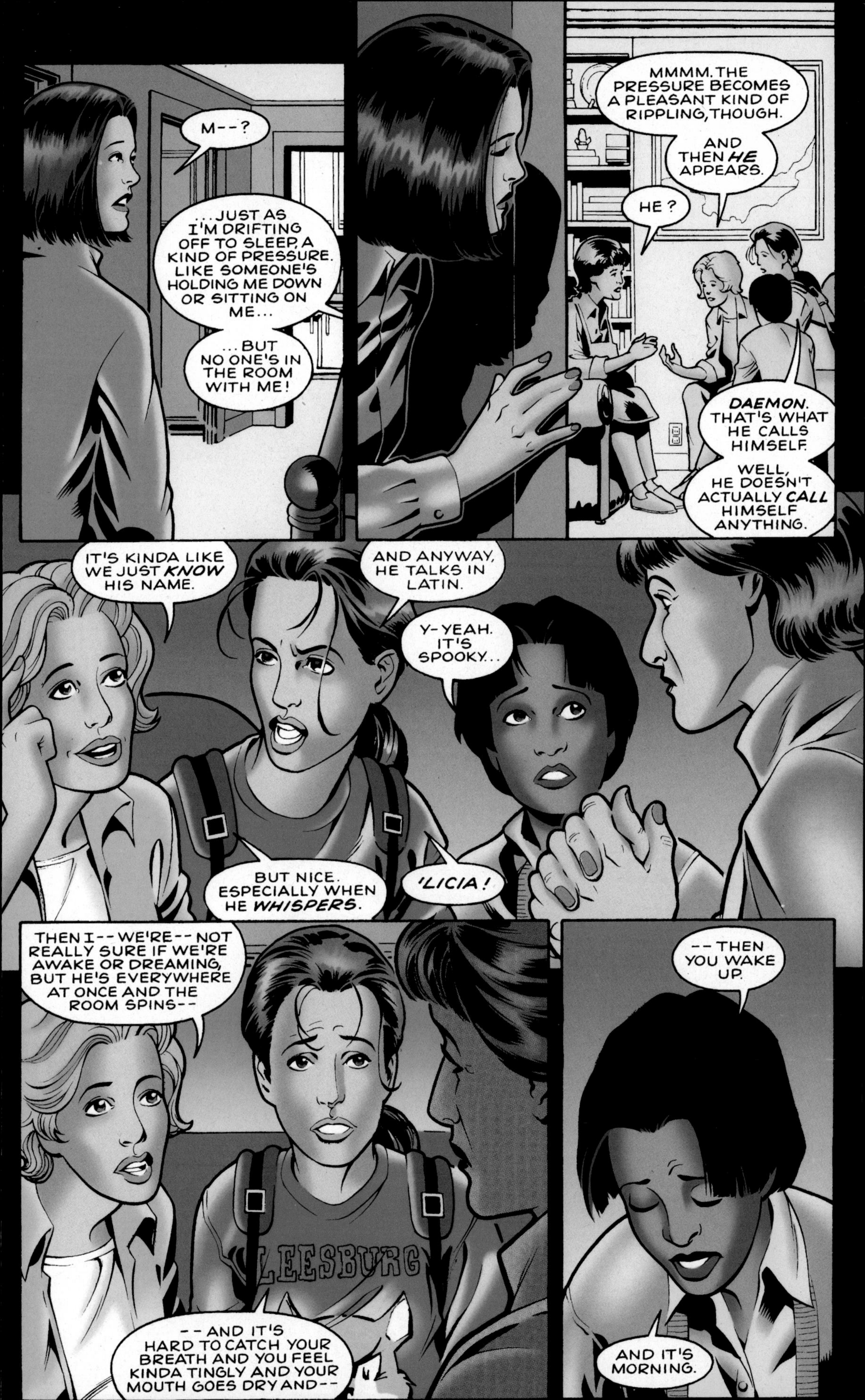
M--?
...JUST AS I'M DRIFTING OFF TO SLEEP, A KIND OF PRESSURE. LIKE SOMEONE'S HOLDING ME DOWN OR SITTING ON ME...
...BUT NO ONE'S IN THE ROOM WITH ME!
MMMM. THE PRESSURE BECOMES A PLEASANT KIND OF RIPPLING, THOUGH.
AND THEN *HE* APPEARS.
HE?
DAEMON. THAT'S WHAT HE CALLS HIMSELF.
WELL, HE DOESN'T ACTUALLY *CALL* HIMSELF ANYTHING.
IT'S KINDA LIKE WE JUST *KNOW* HIS NAME.
AND ANYWAY, HE TALKS IN LATIN.
Y-YEAH. IT'S SPOOKY...
BUT NICE. ESPECIALLY WHEN HE *WHISPERS*.
'LICIA!
THEN I--WE'RE--NOT REALLY SURE IF WE'RE AWAKE OR DREAMING, BUT HE'S EVERYWHERE AT ONCE AND THE ROOM SPINS--
--AND IT'S HARD TO CATCH YOUR BREATH AND YOU FEEL KINDA TINGLY AND YOUR MOUTH GOES DRY AND--
--THEN YOU WAKE UP.
AND IT'S MORNING.
LEESBURG

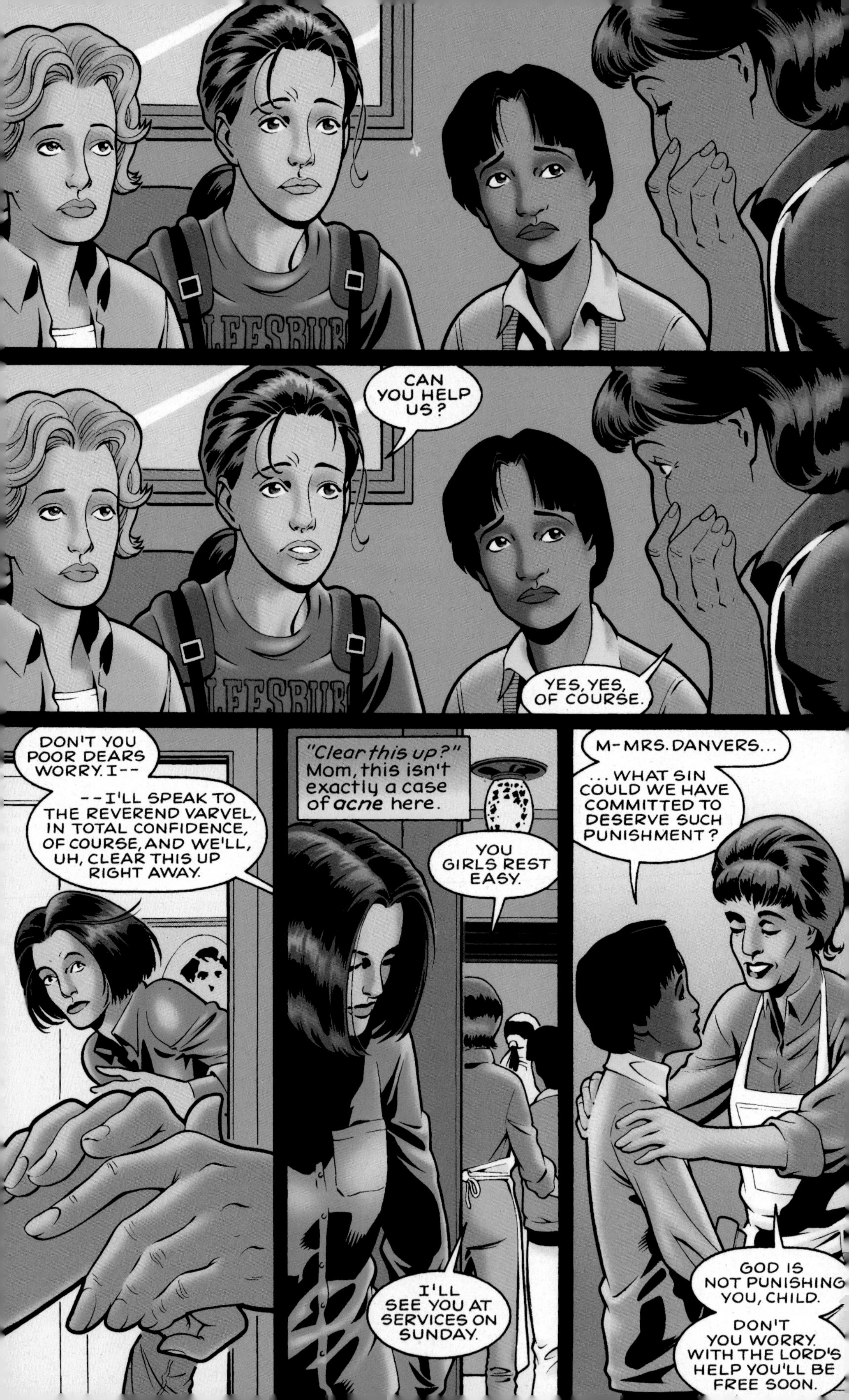
CAN YOU HELP US?
YES, YES, OF COURSE.
DON'T YOU POOR DEARS WORRY. I--
--I'LL SPEAK TO THE REVEREND VARVEL, IN TOTAL CONFIDENCE, OF COURSE, AND WE'LL, UH, CLEAR THIS UP RIGHT AWAY.
"Clear this up?" Mom, this isn't exactly a case of acne here.
YOU GIRLS REST EASY.
I'LL SEE YOU AT SERVICES ON SUNDAY.
M-MRS. DANVERS...
...WHAT SIN COULD WE HAVE COMMITTED TO DESERVE SUCH PUNISHMENT?
GOD IS NOT PUNISHING YOU, CHILD.
DON'T YOU WORRY. WITH THE LORD'S HELP YOU'LL BE FREE SOON.

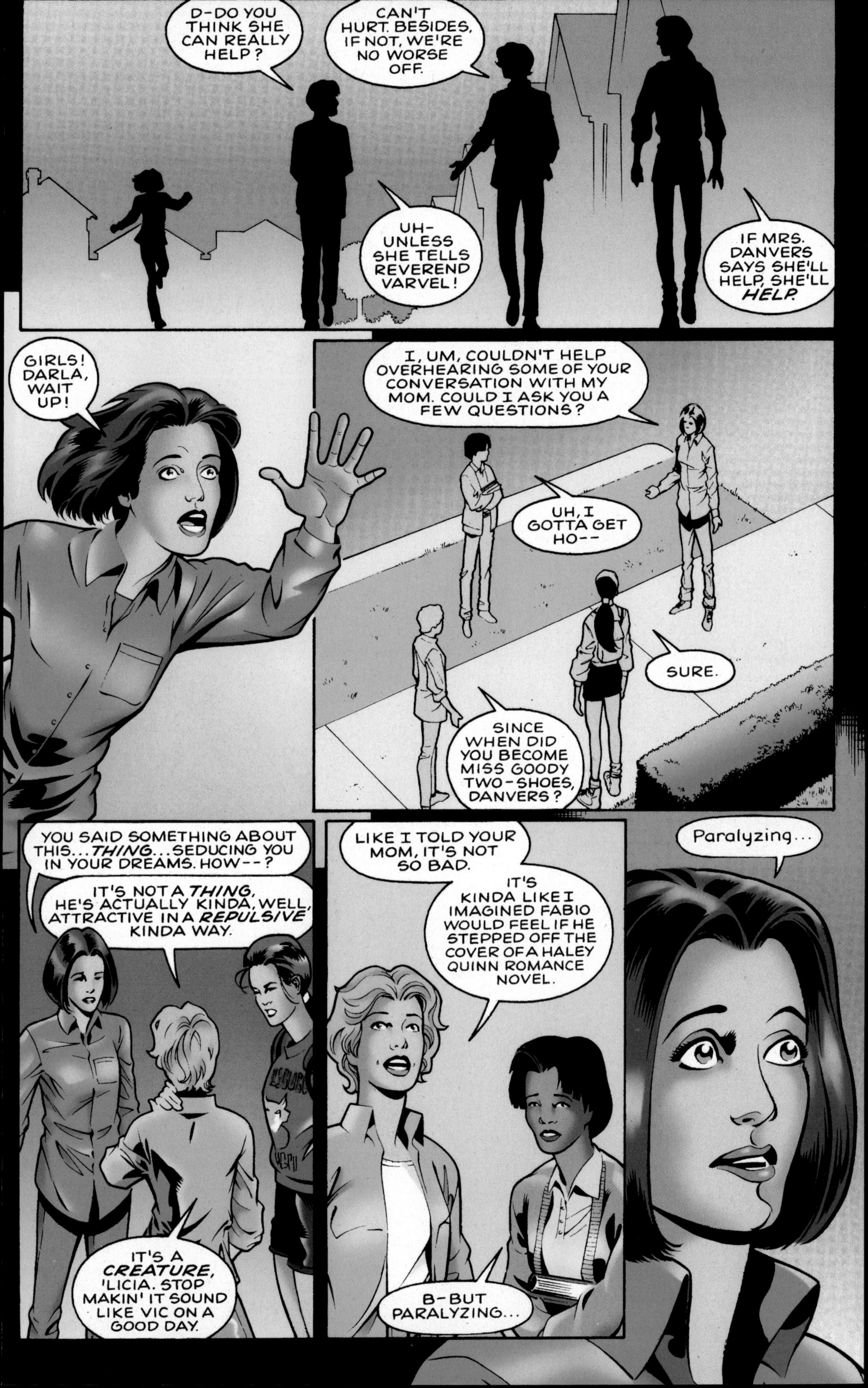
D-DO YOU THINK SHE CAN REALLY HELP?
CAN'T HURT. BESIDES, IF NOT, WE'RE NO WORSE OFF.
UH-UNLESS SHE TELLS REVEREND VARVEL!
IF MRS. DANVERS SAYS SHE'LL HELP, SHE'LL HELP.
GIRLS! DARLA, WAIT UP!
I, UM, COULDN'T HELP OVERHEARING SOME OF YOUR CONVERSATION WITH MY MOM. COULD I ASK YOU A FEW QUESTIONS?
UH, I GOTTA GET HO--
SURE.
SINCE WHEN DID YOU BECOME MISS GOODY TWO-SHOES, DANVERS?
YOU SAID SOMETHING ABOUT THIS...THING...SEDUCING YOU IN YOUR DREAMS. HOW--?
IT'S NOT A THING. HE'S ACTUALLY KINDA, WELL, ATTRACTIVE IN A REPULSIVE KINDA WAY.
IT'S A CREATURE, 'LICIA. STOP MAKIN' IT SOUND LIKE VIC ON A GOOD DAY.
LIKE I TOLD YOUR MOM, IT'S NOT SO BAD.
IT'S KINDA LIKE I IMAGINED FABIO WOULD FEEL IF HE STEPPED OFF THE COVER OF A HALEY QUINN ROMANCE NOVEL.
B-BUT PARALYZING...
Paralyzing...

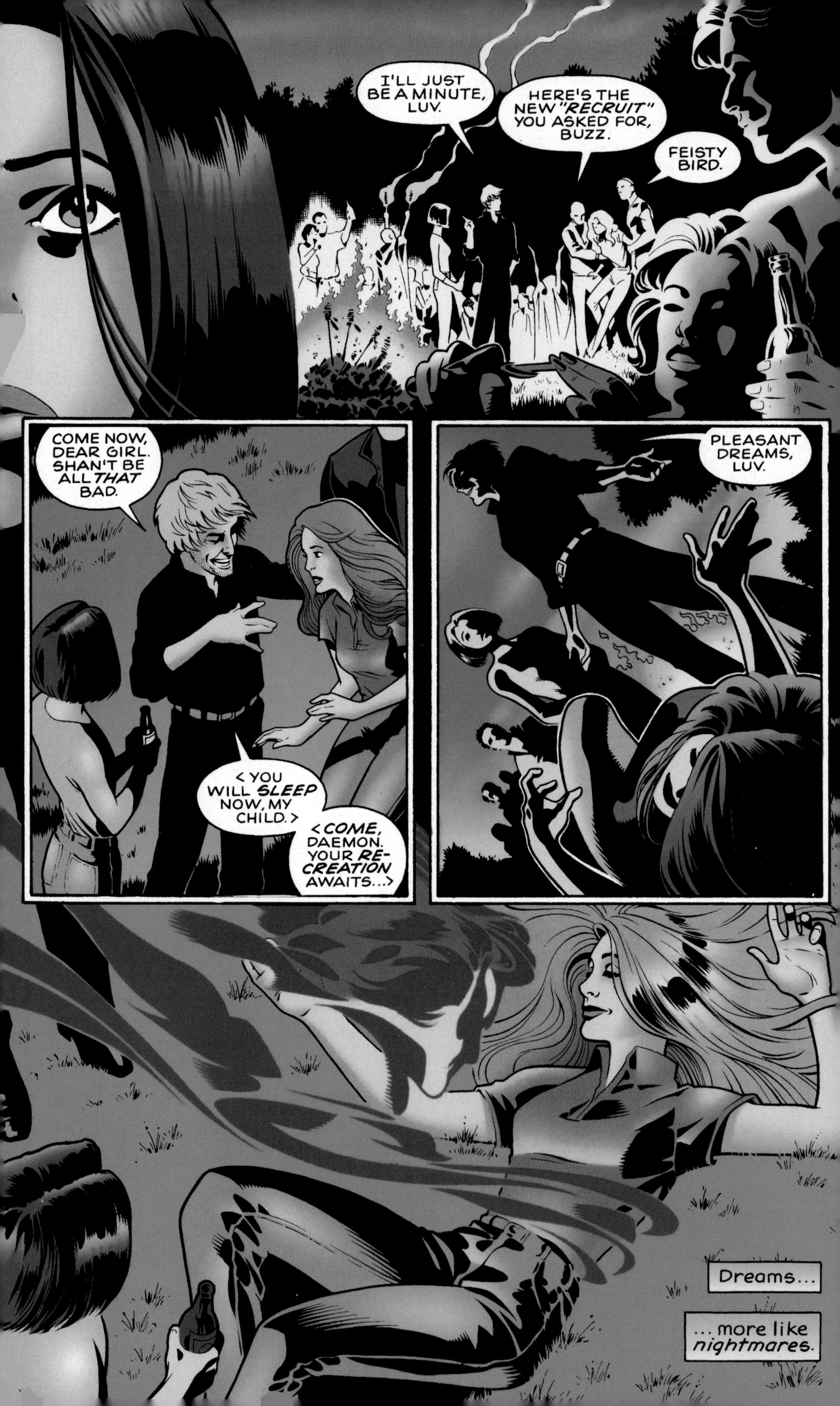
I'LL JUST BE A MINUTE, LUV.
HERE'S THE NEW "RECRUIT" YOU ASKED FOR, BUZZ.
FEISTY BIRD.
COME NOW, DEAR GIRL. SHAN'T BE ALL THAT BAD.
<YOU WILL SLEEP NOW, MY CHILD.>
<COME, DAEMON. YOUR RE-CREATION AWAITS...>
PLEASANT DREAMS, LUV.
Dreams...
...more like nightmares.

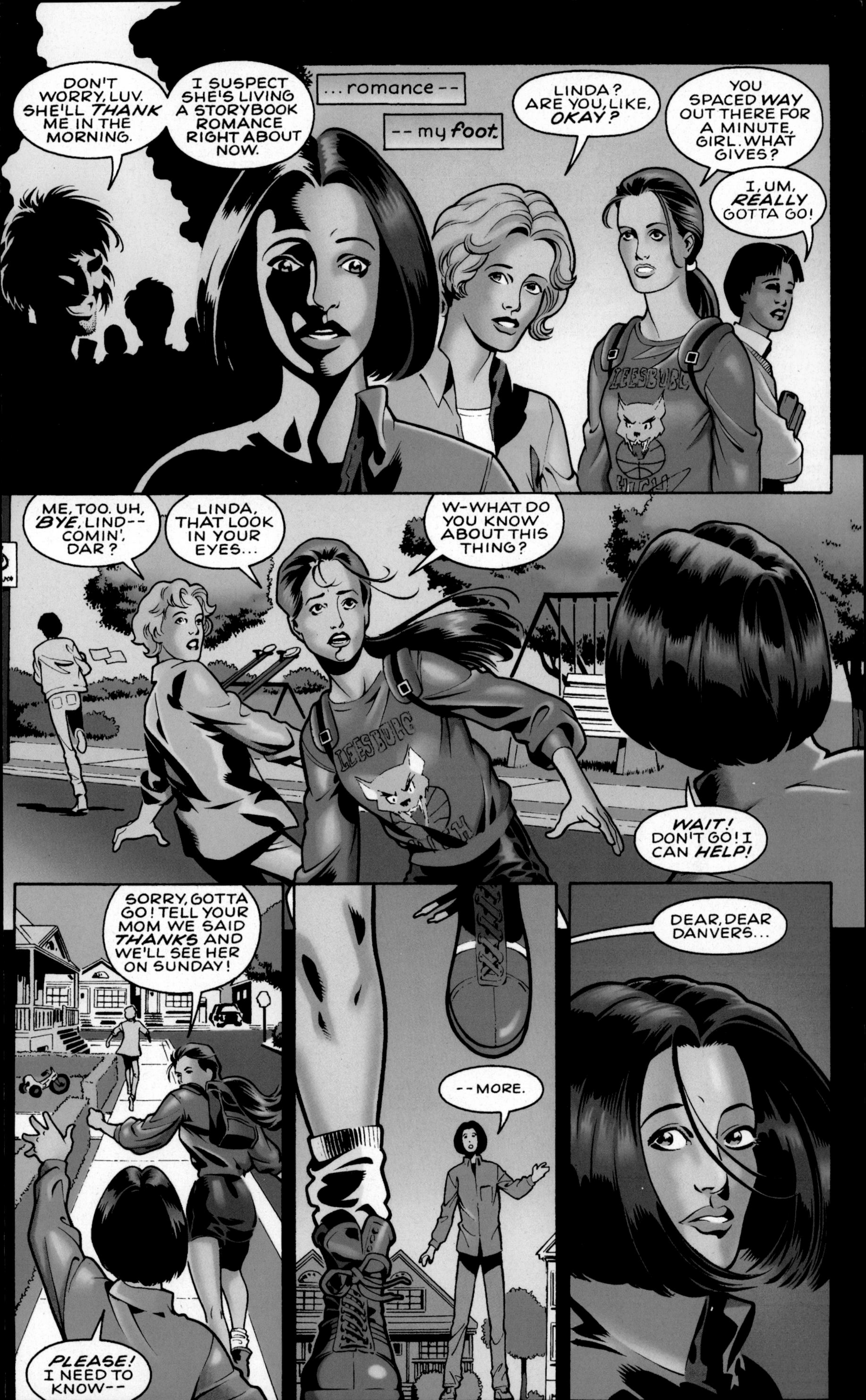
DON'T WORRY, LUV. SHE'LL THANK ME IN THE MORNING.
I SUSPECT SHE'S LIVING A STORYBOOK ROMANCE RIGHT ABOUT NOW.
...romance--
--my foot.
LINDA? ARE YOU, LIKE, OKAY?
YOU SPACED WAY OUT THERE FOR A MINUTE, GIRL. WHAT GIVES?
I, UM, REALLY GOTTA GO!
ME, TOO. UH, 'BYE, LIND-- COMIN', DAR?
LINDA, THAT LOOK IN YOUR EYES...
W-WHAT DO YOU KNOW ABOUT THIS THING?
WAIT! DON'T GO! I CAN HELP!
SORRY, GOTTA GO! TELL YOUR MOM WE SAID THANKS AND WE'LL SEE HER ON SUNDAY!
PLEASE! I NEED TO KNOW--
--MORE.
DEAR, DEAR DANVERS...

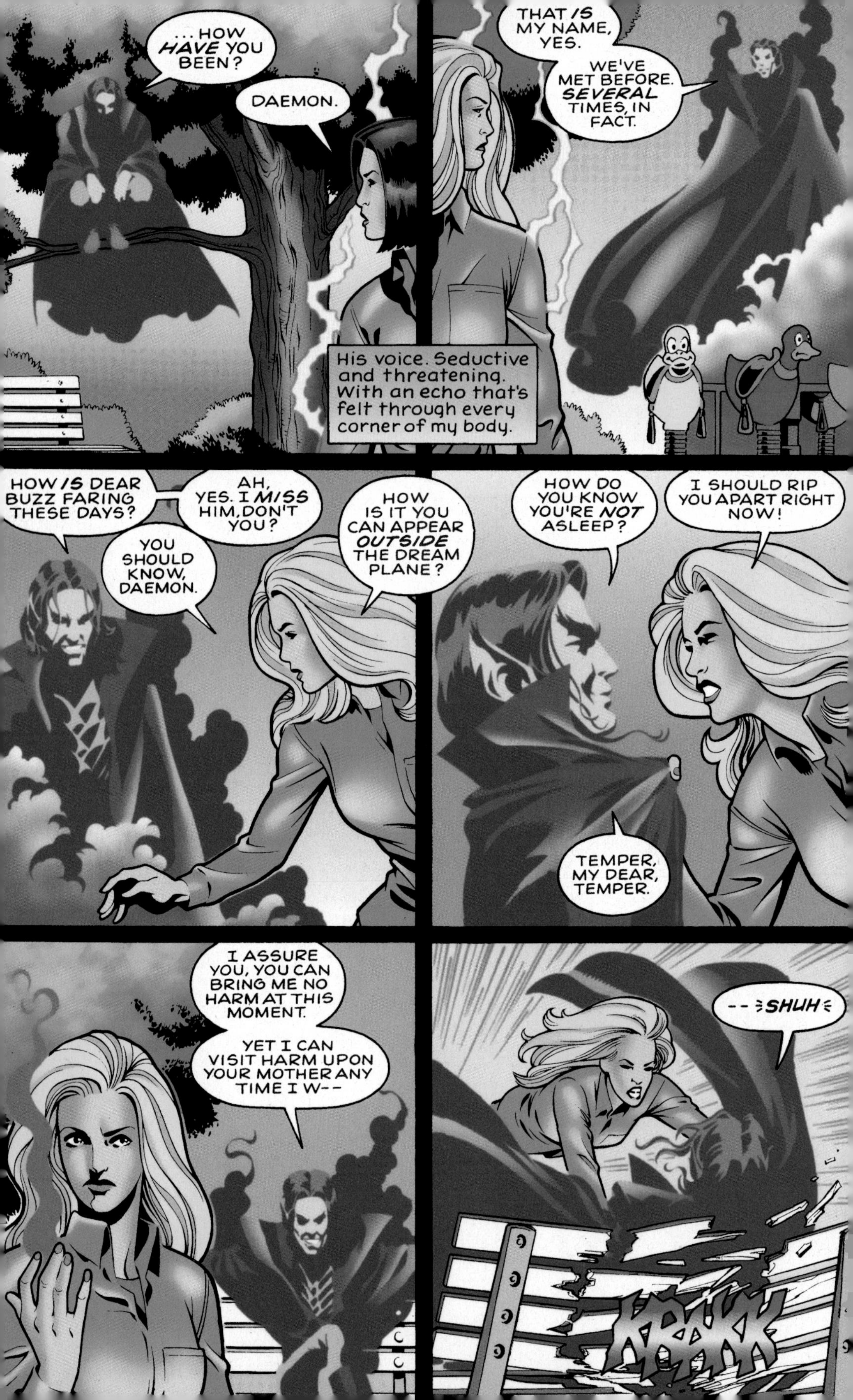
...HOW HAVE YOU BEEN?
DAEMON.
THAT IS MY NAME, YES.
WE'VE MET BEFORE. SEVERAL TIMES, IN FACT.
His voice. Seductive and threatening. With an echo that's felt through every corner of my body.
HOW IS DEAR BUZZ FARING THESE DAYS?
YOU SHOULD KNOW, DAEMON.
AH, YES. I MISS HIM, DON'T YOU?
HOW IS IT YOU CAN APPEAR OUTSIDE THE DREAM PLANE?
HOW DO YOU KNOW YOU'RE NOT ASLEEP?
I SHOULD RIP YOU APART RIGHT NOW!
TEMPER, MY DEAR, TEMPER.
I ASSURE YOU, YOU CAN BRING ME NO HARM AT THIS MOMENT.
YET I CAN VISIT HARM UPON YOUR MOTHER ANY TIME I W--
--SHUH
KRAKK

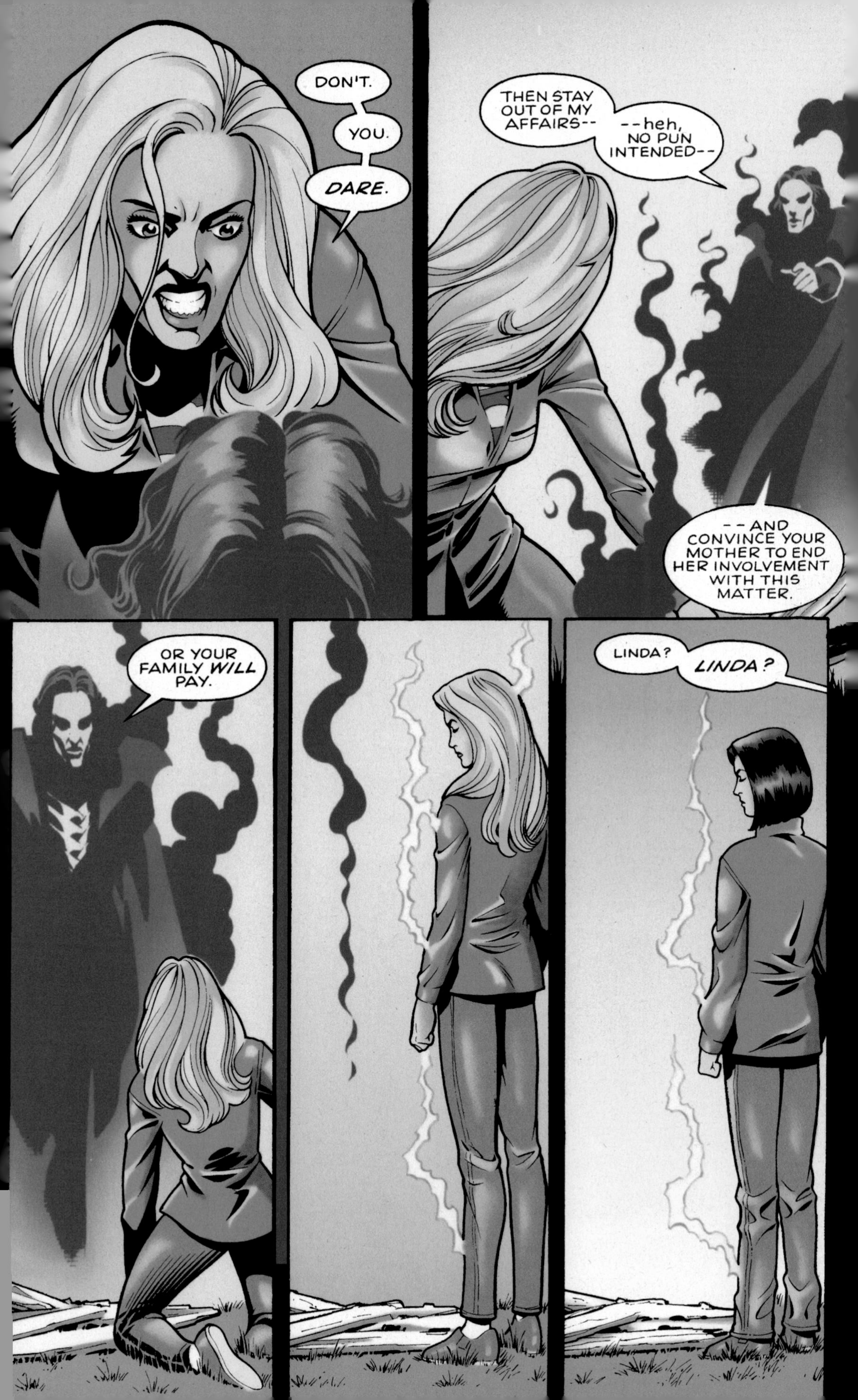
DON'T.
YOU.
DARE.
THEN STAY OUT OF MY AFFAIRS--
--heh, NO PUN INTENDED--
--AND CONVINCE YOUR MOTHER TO END HER INVOLVEMENT WITH THIS MATTER.
OR YOUR FAMILY WILL PAY.
LINDA?
LINDA?

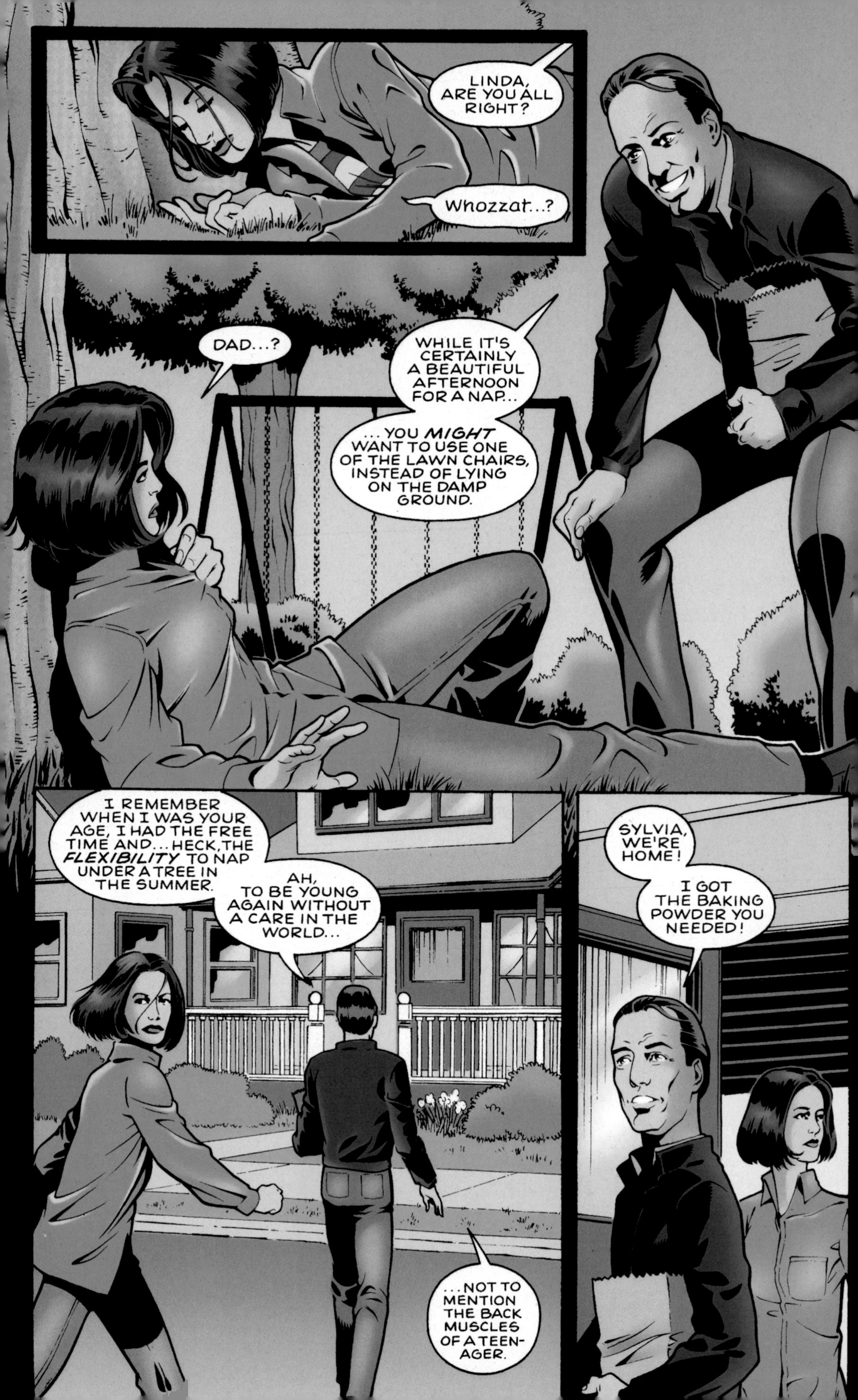
LINDA, ARE YOU ALL RIGHT?
Whozzat...?
DAD...?
WHILE IT'S CERTAINLY A BEAUTIFUL AFTERNOON FOR A NAP...
...YOU *MIGHT* WANT TO USE ONE OF THE LAWN CHAIRS, INSTEAD OF LYING ON THE DAMP GROUND.
I REMEMBER WHEN I WAS YOUR AGE, I HAD THE FREE TIME AND... HECK, THE *FLEXIBILITY* TO NAP UNDER A TREE IN THE SUMMER.
AH, TO BE YOUNG AGAIN WITHOUT A CARE IN THE WORLD...
...NOT TO MENTION THE BACK MUSCLES OF A TEEN-AGER.
SYLVIA, WE'RE HOME!
I GOT THE BAKING POWDER YOU NEEDED!

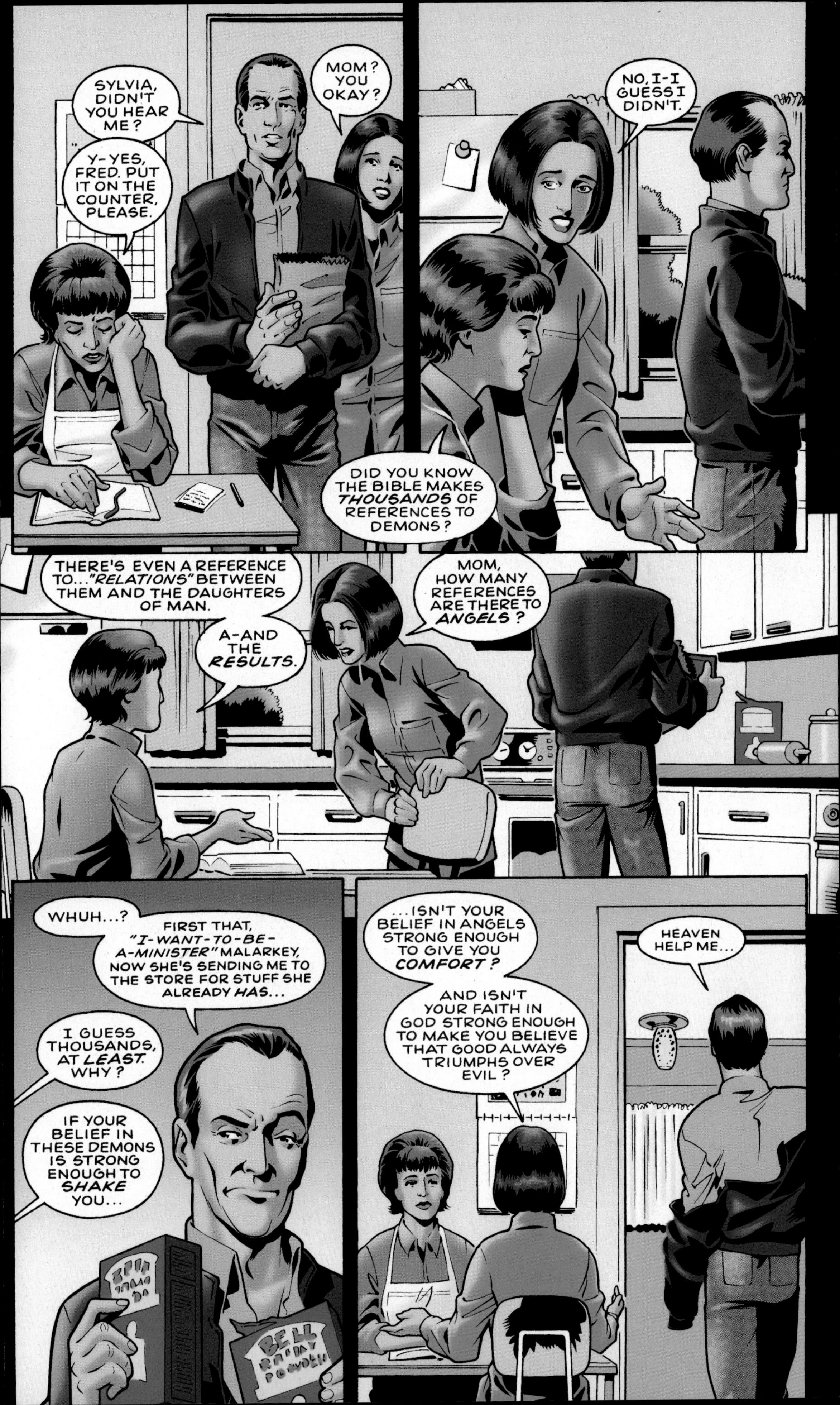

SYLVIA, DIDN'T YOU HEAR ME?
Y-YES, FRED. PUT IT ON THE COUNTER, PLEASE.
MOM? YOU OKAY?
NO, I-I GUESS I DIDN'T.
DID YOU KNOW THE BIBLE MAKES THOUSANDS OF REFERENCES TO DEMONS?
THERE'S EVEN A REFERENCE TO..."RELATIONS" BETWEEN THEM AND THE DAUGHTERS OF MAN.
A-AND THE RESULTS.
MOM, HOW MANY REFERENCES ARE THERE TO ANGELS?
WHUH...?
FIRST THAT, "I-WANT-TO-BE-A-MINISTER" MALARKEY, NOW SHE'S SENDING ME TO THE STORE FOR STUFF SHE ALREADY HAS...
I GUESS THOUSANDS, AT LEAST. WHY?
IF YOUR BELIEF IN THESE DEMONS IS STRONG ENOUGH TO SHAKE YOU...
...ISN'T YOUR BELIEF IN ANGELS STRONG ENOUGH TO GIVE YOU COMFORT?
AND ISN'T YOUR FAITH IN GOD STRONG ENOUGH TO MAKE YOU BELIEVE THAT GOOD ALWAYS TRIUMPHS OVER EVIL?
HEAVEN HELP ME...

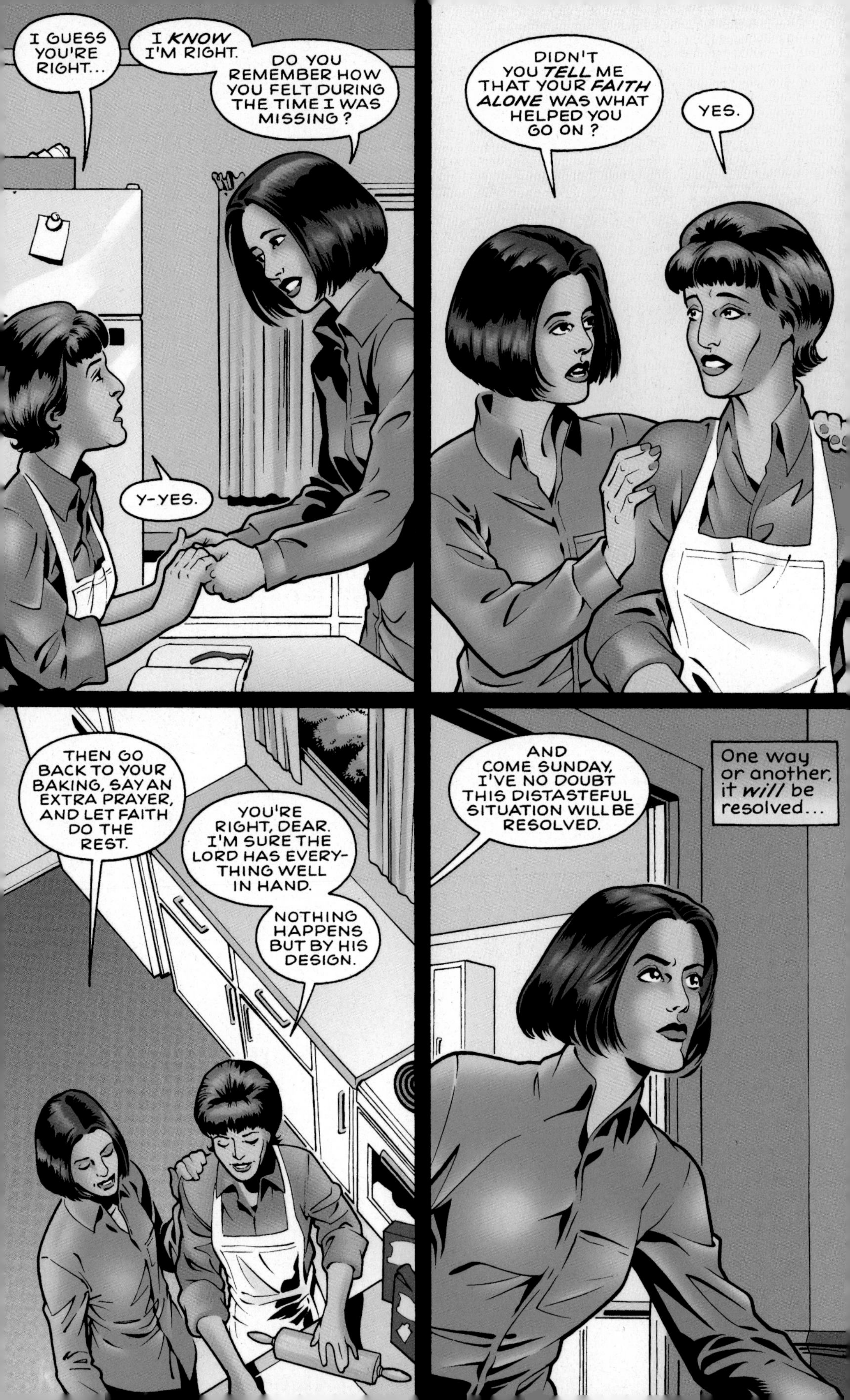

I GUESS YOU'RE RIGHT...
I KNOW I'M RIGHT.
DO YOU REMEMBER HOW YOU FELT DURING THE TIME I WAS MISSING?
Y-YES.
DIDN'T YOU TELL ME THAT YOUR FAITH ALONE WAS WHAT HELPED YOU GO ON?
YES.
THEN GO BACK TO YOUR BAKING, SAY AN EXTRA PRAYER, AND LET FAITH DO THE REST.
YOU'RE RIGHT, DEAR. I'M SURE THE LORD HAS EVERY-THING WELL IN HAND.
NOTHING HAPPENS BUT BY HIS DESIGN.
AND COME SUNDAY, I'VE NO DOUBT THIS DISTASTEFUL SITUATION WILL BE RESOLVED.
One way or another, it will be resolved...

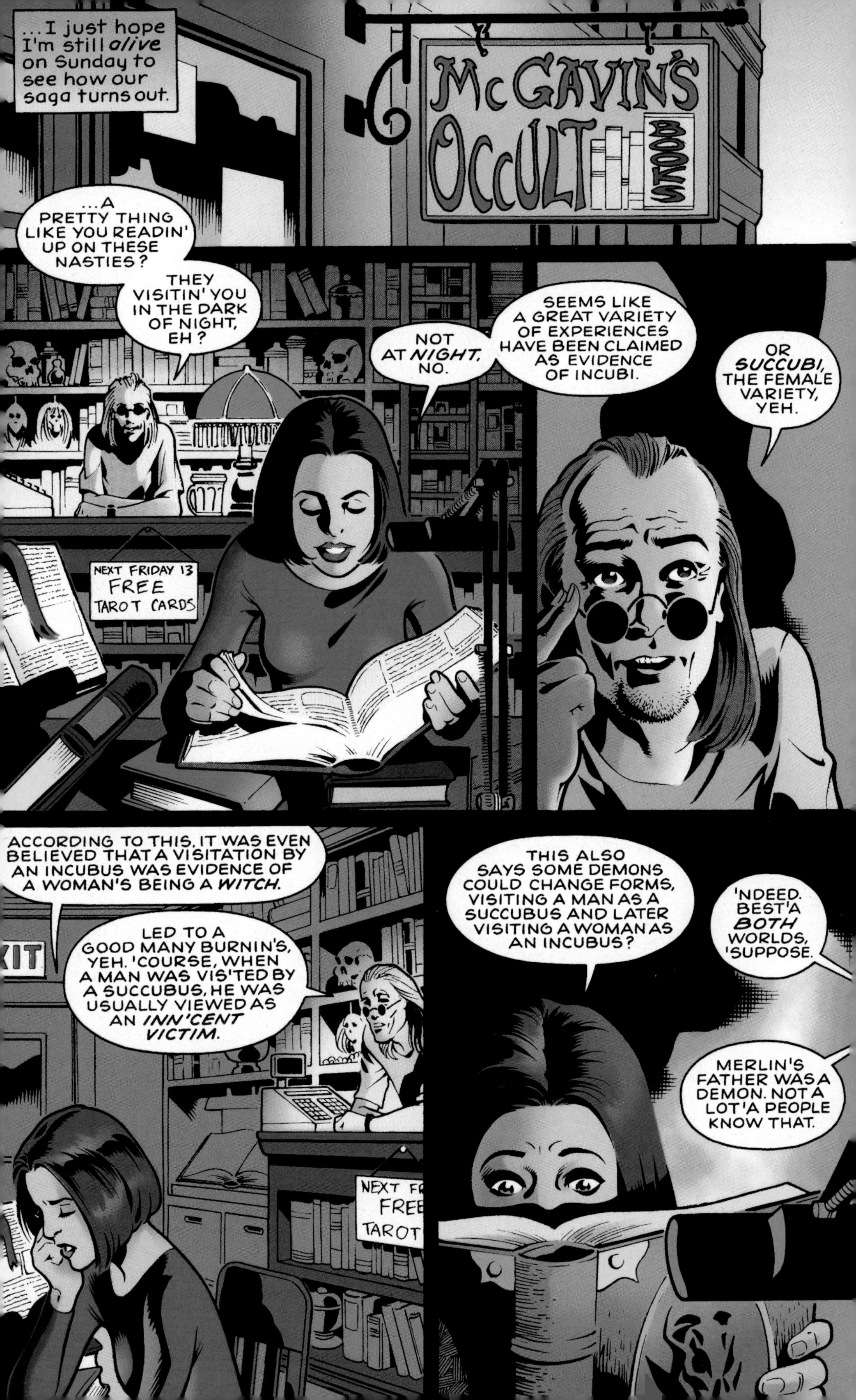
...I just hope I'm still *alive* on Sunday to see how our saga turns out.
McGAVIN'S OCCULT BOOKS
...A PRETTY THING LIKE YOU READIN' UP ON THESE NASTIES?
THEY VISITIN' YOU IN THE DARK OF NIGHT, EH?
NOT AT *NIGHT*, NO.
SEEMS LIKE A GREAT VARIETY OF EXPERIENCES HAVE BEEN CLAIMED AS EVIDENCE OF INCUBI.
NEXT FRIDAY 13 FREE TAROT CARDS
OR *SUCCUBI*, THE FEMALE VARIETY, YEH.
ACCORDING TO THIS, IT WAS EVEN BELIEVED THAT A VISITATION BY AN INCUBUS WAS EVIDENCE OF A WOMAN'S BEING A *WITCH*.
LED TO A GOOD MANY BURNIN'S, YEH. 'COURSE, WHEN A MAN WAS VIS'TED BY A SUCCUBUS, HE WAS USUALLY VIEWED AS AN *INN'CENT VICTIM*.
THIS ALSO SAYS SOME DEMONS COULD CHANGE FORMS, VISITING A MAN AS A SUCCUBUS AND LATER VISITING A WOMAN AS AN INCUBUS?
'NDEED. BEST'A *BOTH* WORLDS, 'SUPPOSE.
MERLIN'S FATHER WAS A DEMON. NOT A LOT'A PEOPLE KNOW THAT.

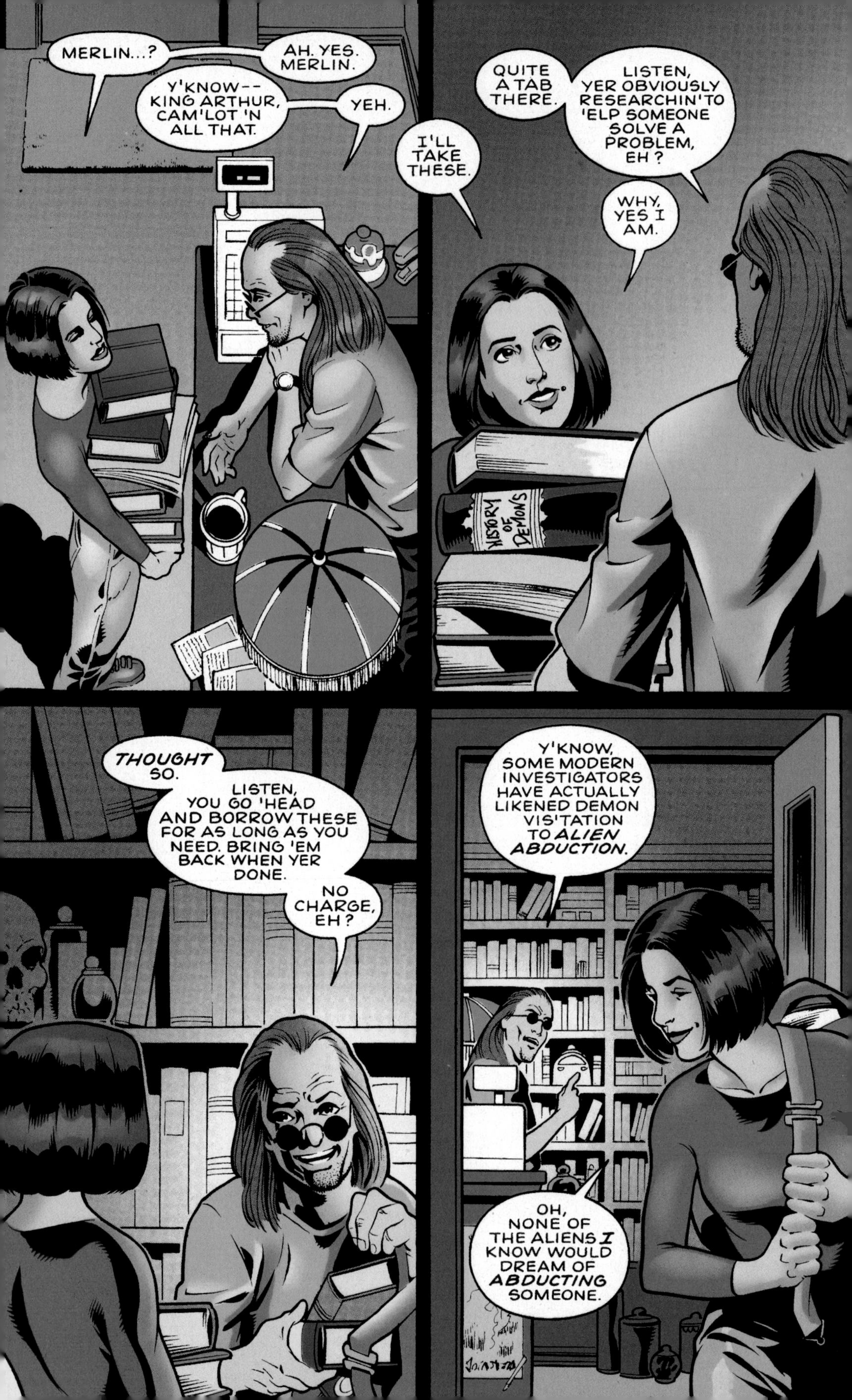
MERLIN...?
AH. YES. MERLIN.
Y'KNOW-- KING ARTHUR, CAM'LOT 'N ALL THAT.
YEH.
I'LL TAKE THESE.
QUITE A TAB THERE.
LISTEN, YER OBVIOUSLY RESEARCHIN' TO 'ELP SOMEONE SOLVE A PROBLEM, EH ?
WHY, YES I AM.
HISTORY OF DEMONS
THOUGHT SO.
LISTEN, YOU GO 'HEAD AND BORROW THESE FOR AS LONG AS YOU NEED. BRING 'EM BACK WHEN YER DONE.
NO CHARGE, EH ?
Y'KNOW, SOME MODERN INVESTIGATORS HAVE ACTUALLY LIKENED DEMON VIS'TATION TO *ALIEN ABDUCTION*.
OH, NONE OF THE ALIENS *I* KNOW WOULD DREAM OF *ABDUCTING* SOMEONE.

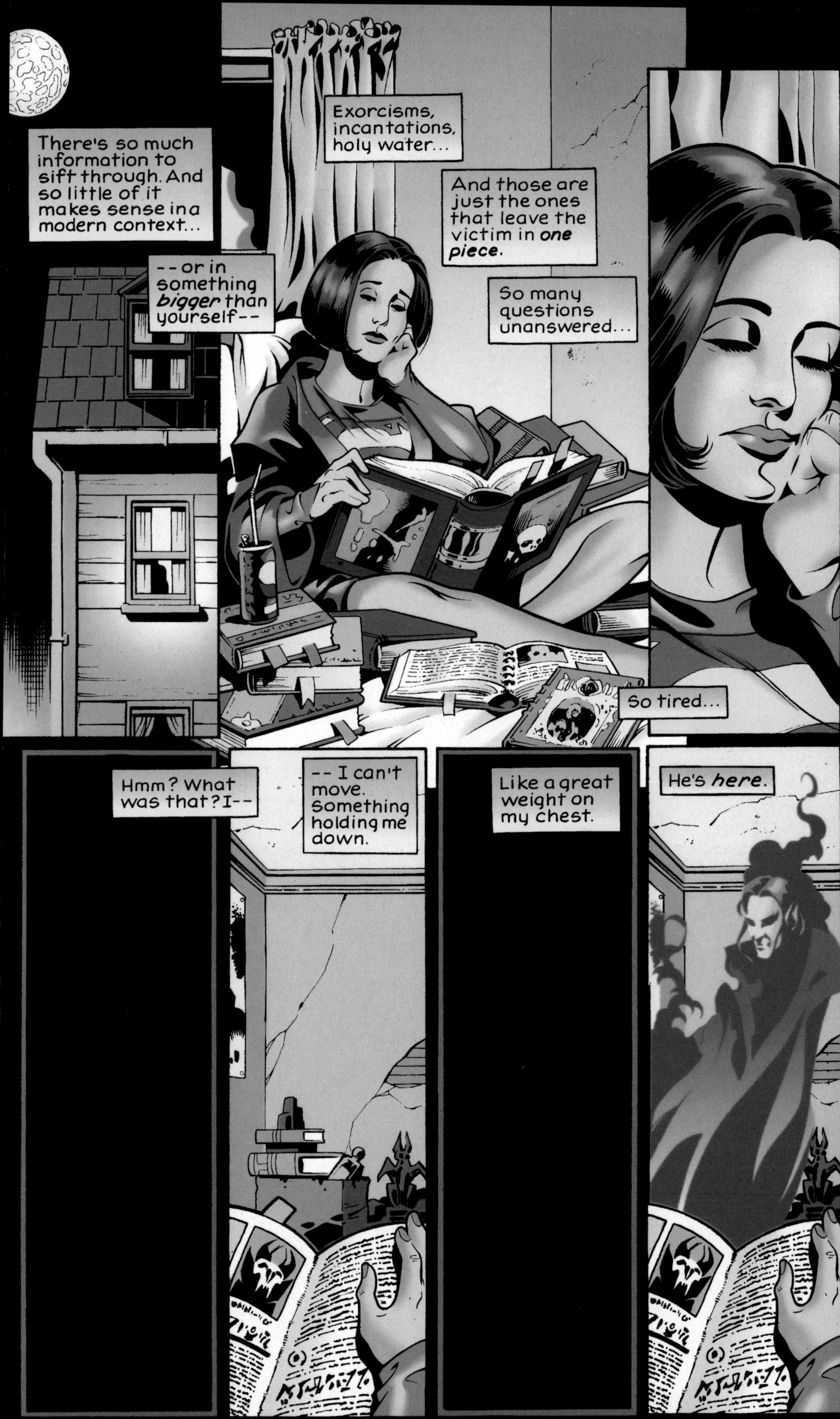

There's so much information to sift through. And so little of it makes sense in a modern context...
--or in something *bigger* than yourself--
Exorcisms, incantations, holy water...
And those are just the ones that leave the victim in *one piece.*
So many questions unanswered...
So tired...
Hmm? What was that? I--
-- I can't move. Something holding me down.
Like a great weight on my chest.
He's *here*.

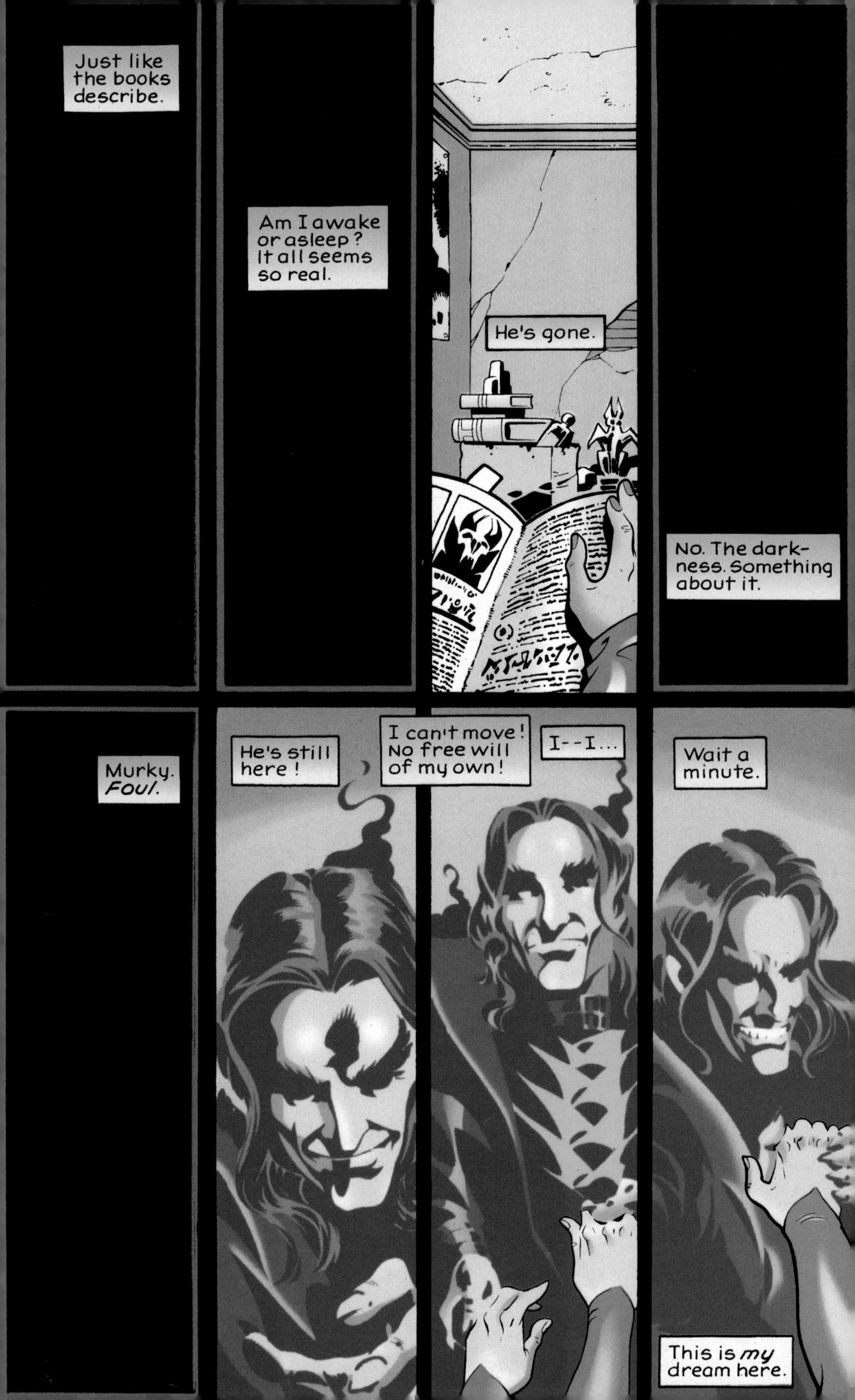
Just like the books describe.
Am I awake or asleep? It all seems so real.
He's gone.
No. The dark-ness. Something about it.
Murky. *Foul.*
He's still here!
I can't move! No free will of my own!
I--I...
Wait a minute.
This is *my* dream here.

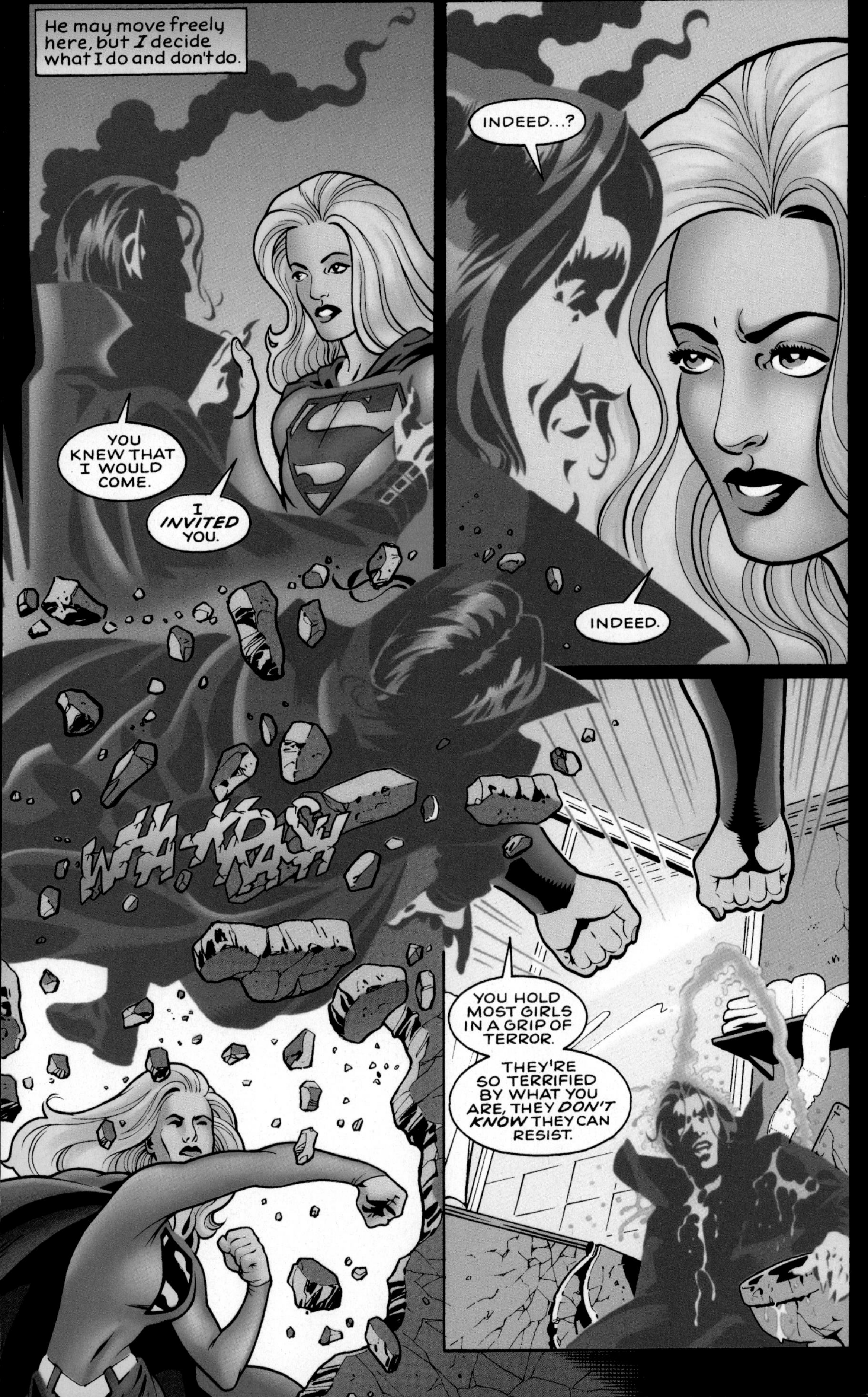
He may move freely here, but *I* decide what I do and don't do.
YOU KNEW THAT I WOULD COME.
I *INVITED* YOU.
INDEED...?
INDEED.
WHA-KRASH
YOU HOLD MOST GIRLS IN A GRIP OF TERROR.
THEY'RE SO TERRIFIED BY WHAT YOU ARE, THEY *DON'T KNOW* THEY CAN RESIST.

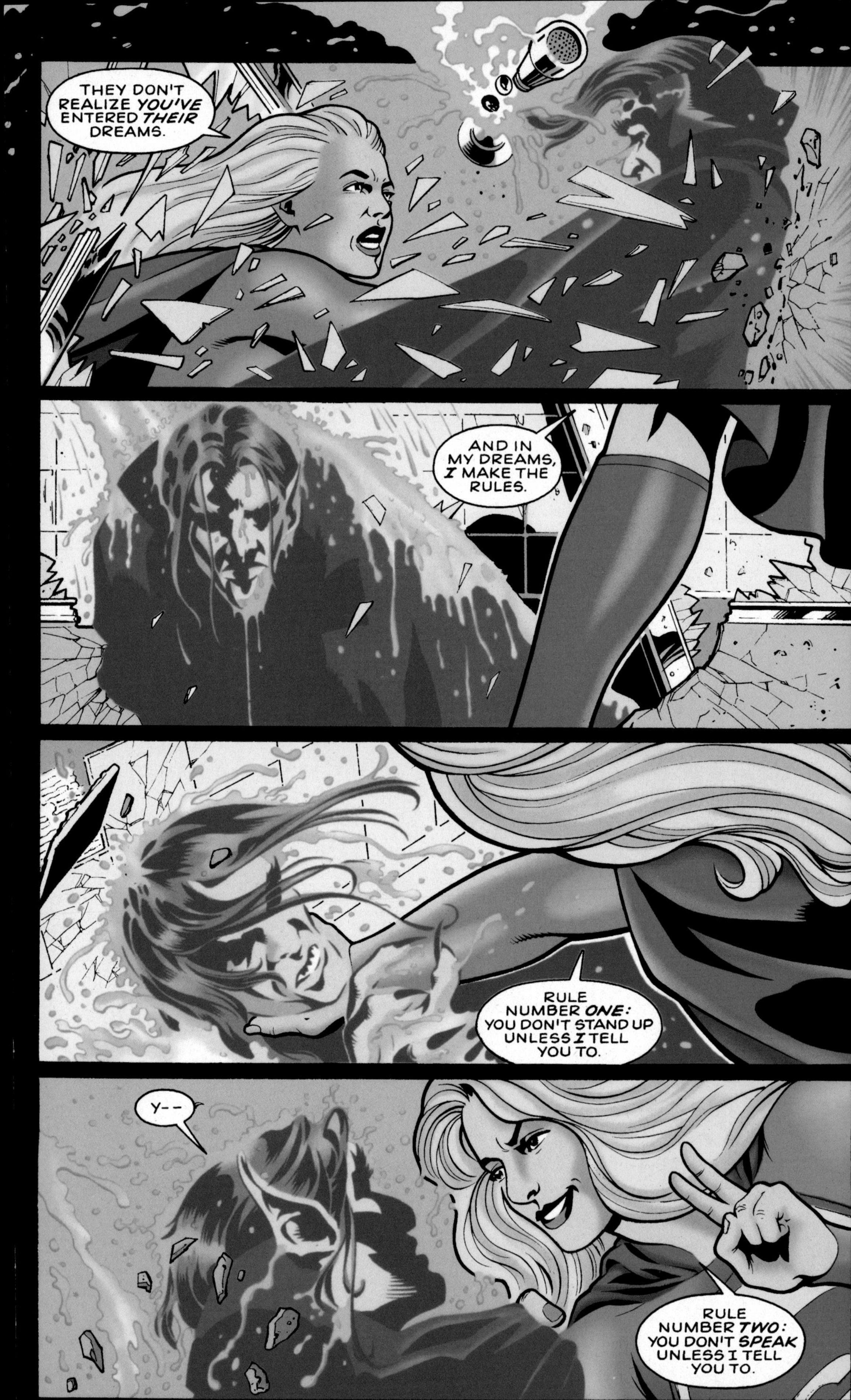
THEY DON'T REALIZE YOU'VE ENTERED THEIR DREAMS.
AND IN MY DREAMS, I MAKE THE RULES.
RULE NUMBER ONE: YOU DON'T STAND UP UNLESS I TELL YOU TO.
Y--
RULE NUMBER TWO: YOU DON'T SPEAK UNLESS I TELL YOU TO.

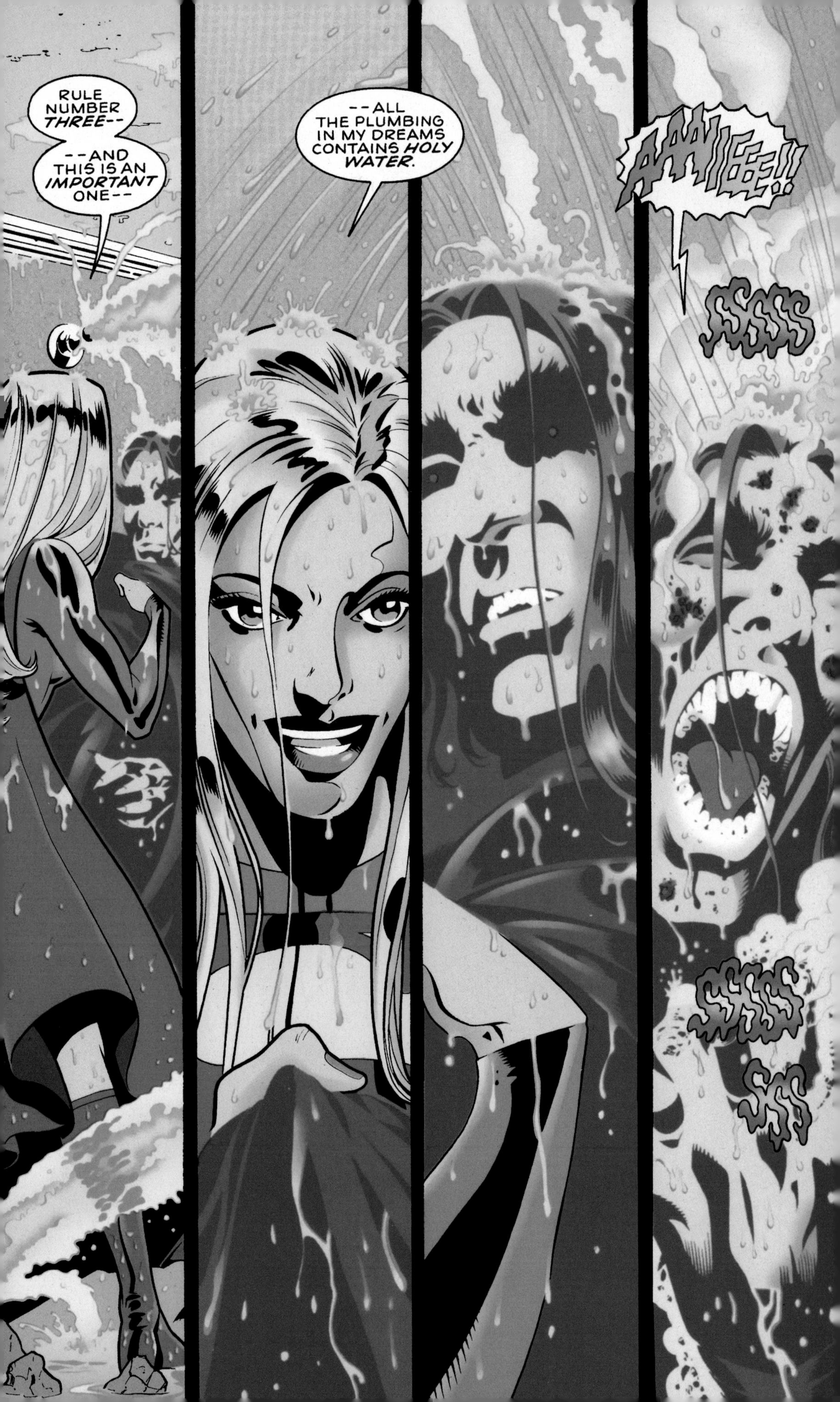
RULE NUMBER *THREE*--
--AND THIS IS AN *IMPORTANT* ONE--
--ALL THE PLUMBING IN MY DREAMS CONTAINS *HOLY WATER*.
AAAIEEE!!
SSSSS
SSSS
SSS

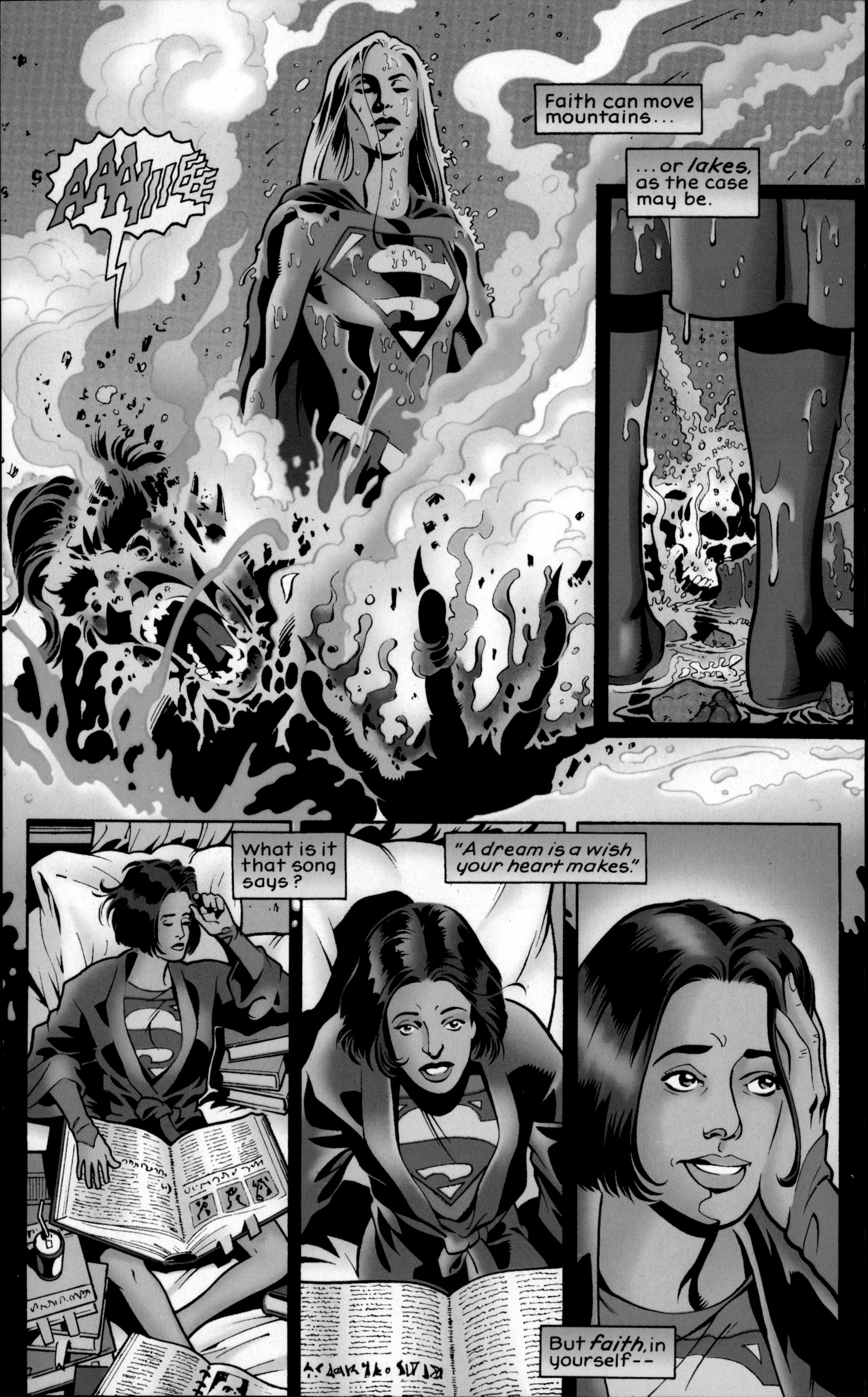
AAAIIEEE
Faith can move mountains...
...or *lakes*, as the case may be.
What is it that song says?
"A dream is a wish your heart makes."
But *faith*, in yourself--

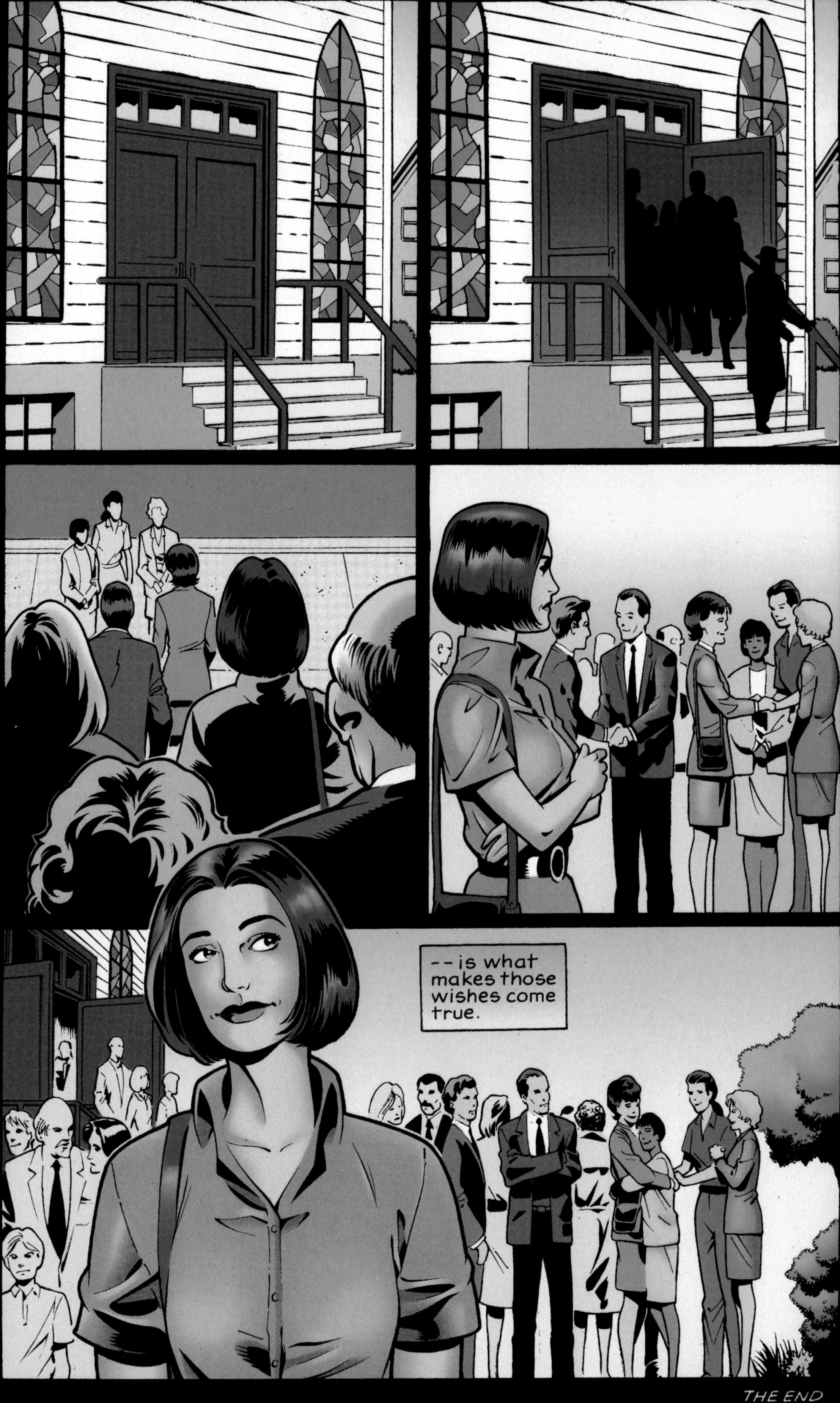
--is what makes those wishes come true.
THE END

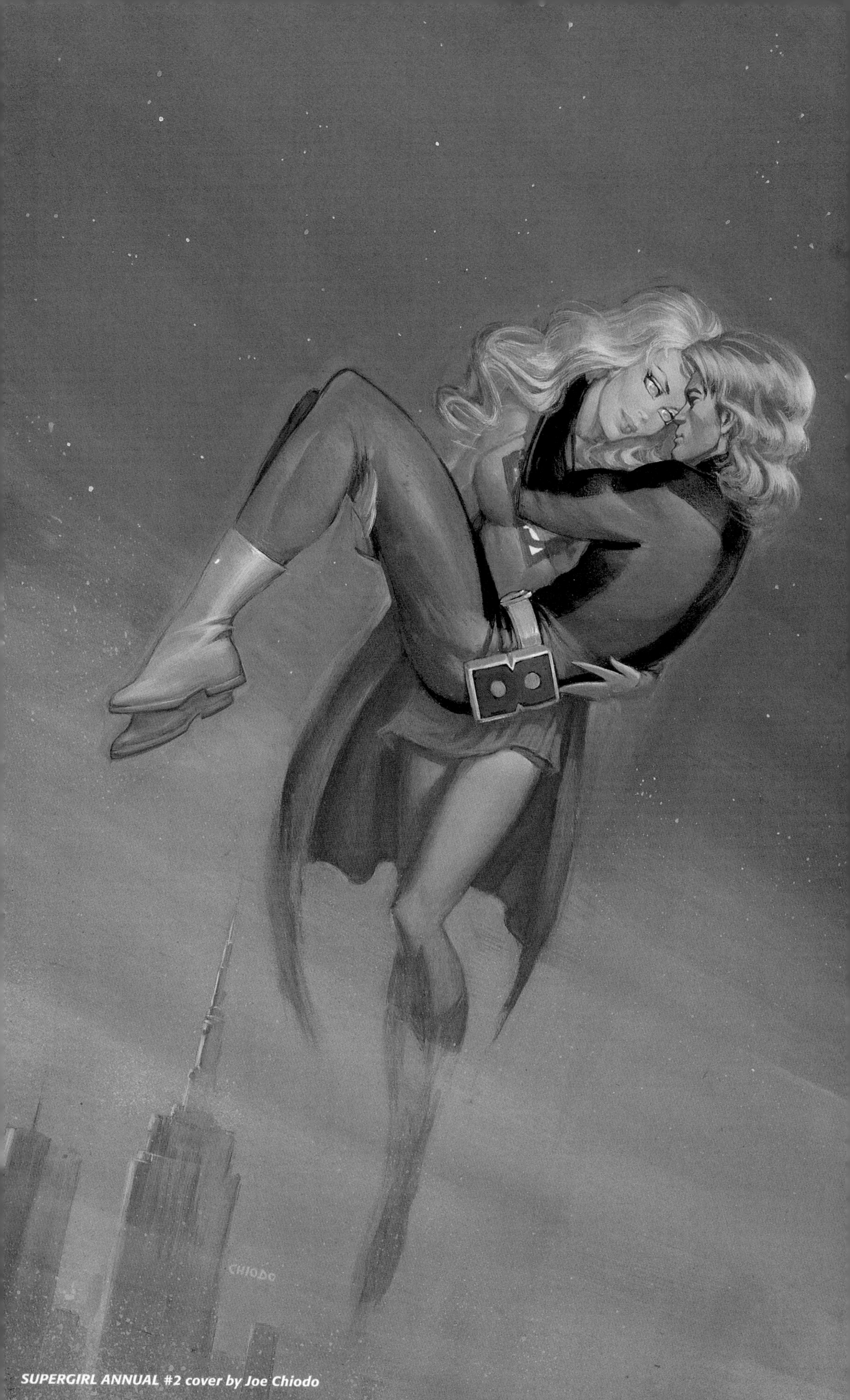
CHIODO

SUPERGIRL ANNUAL #2 cover by Joe Chiodo

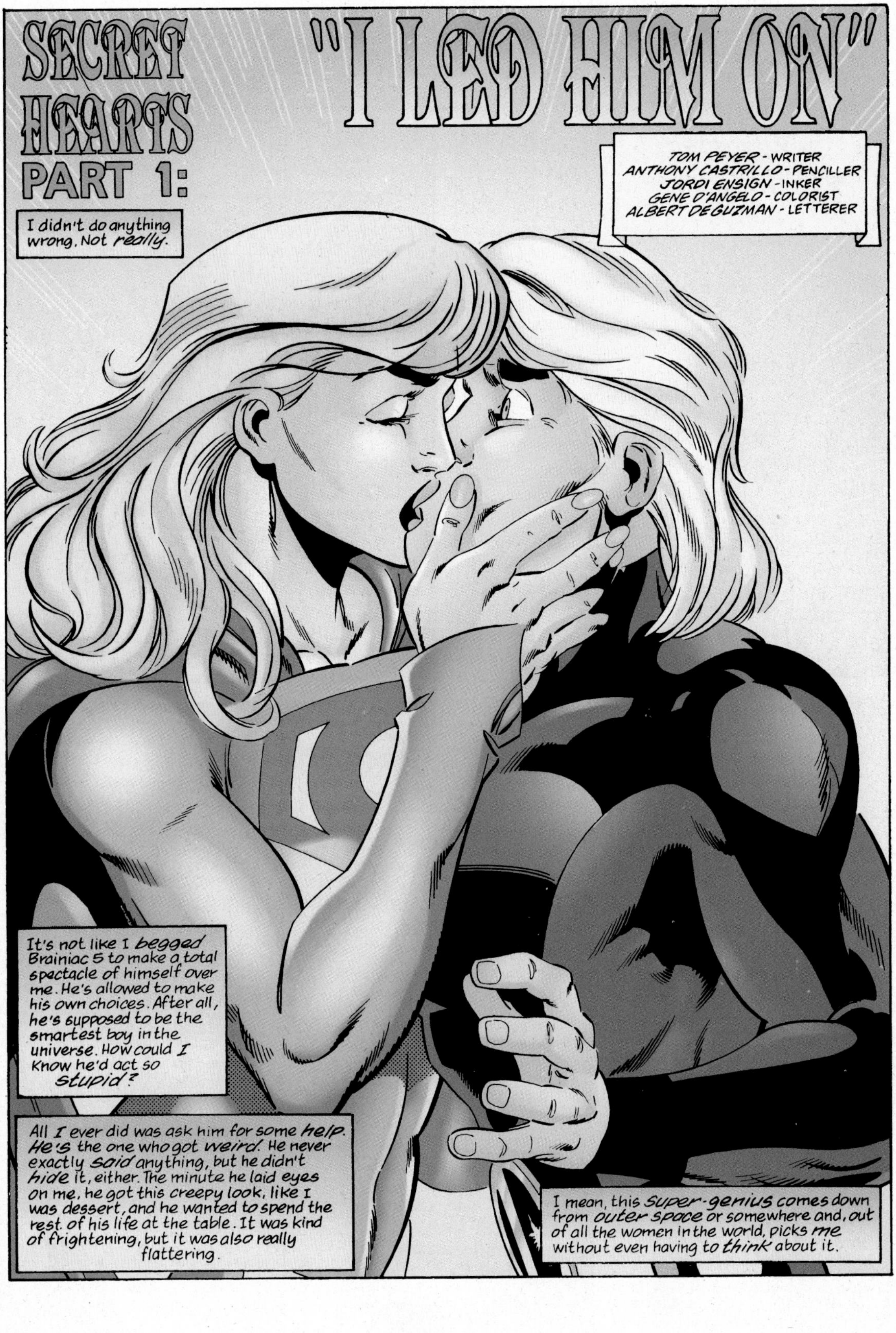
SECRET HEARTS PART 1:
"I LED HIM ON"
TOM PEYER - WRITER
ANTHONY CASTRILLO - PENCILLER
JORDI ENSIGN - INKER
GENE D'ANGELO - COLORIST
ALBERT DE GUZMAN - LETTERER
I didn't do anything wrong. Not really.
It's not like I begged Brainiac 5 to make a total spectacle of himself over me. He's allowed to make his own choices. After all, he's supposed to be the smartest boy in the universe. How could I know he'd act so stupid?
All I ever did was ask him for some help. He's the one who got weird. He never exactly said anything, but he didn't hide it, either. The minute he laid eyes on me, he got this creepy look, like I was dessert, and he wanted to spend the rest of his life at the table. It was kind of frightening, but it was also really flattering.
I mean, this super-genius comes down from outer space or somewhere and, out of all the women in the world, picks me without even having to think about it.

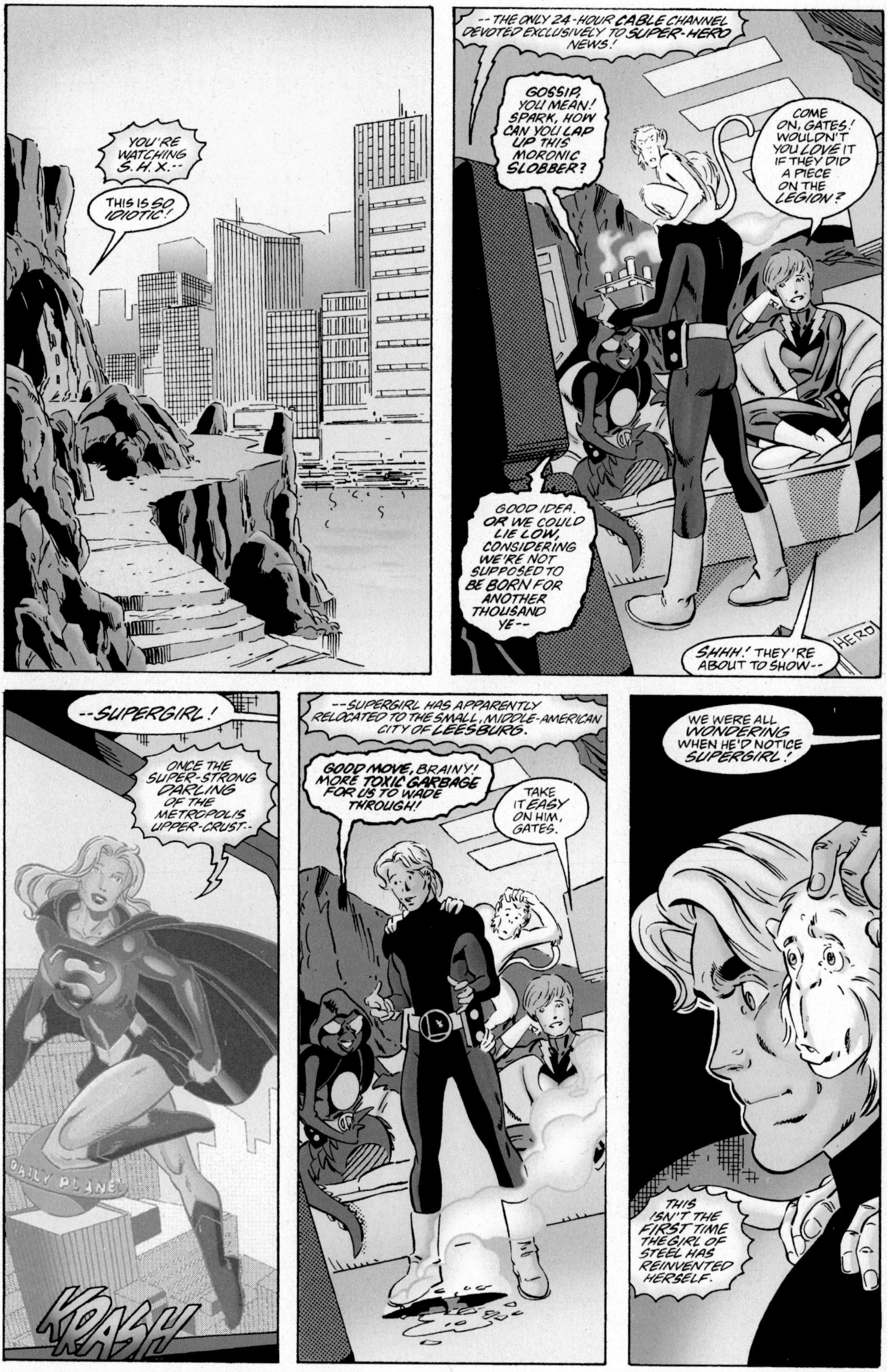
YOU'RE WATCHING S.H.X.--
THIS IS SO IDIOTIC!
--THE ONLY 24-HOUR CABLE CHANNEL DEVOTED EXCLUSIVELY TO SUPER-HERO NEWS!
GOSSIP, YOU MEAN! SPARK, HOW CAN YOU LAP UP THIS MORONIC SLOBBER?
COME ON, GATES! WOULDN'T YOU LOVE IT IF THEY DID A PIECE ON THE LEGION?
GOOD IDEA. OR WE COULD LIE LOW, CONSIDERING WE'RE NOT SUPPOSED TO BE BORN FOR ANOTHER THOUSAND YE--
SHHH! THEY'RE ABOUT TO SHOW--
HERO
--SUPERGIRL!
ONCE THE SUPER-STRONG DARLING OF THE METROPOLIS UPPER-CRUST--
DAILY PLANET
KRASH
--SUPERGIRL HAS APPARENTLY RELOCATED TO THE SMALL, MIDDLE-AMERICAN CITY OF LEESBURG.
GOOD MOVE, BRAINY! MORE TOXIC GARBAGE FOR US TO WADE THROUGH!
TAKE IT EASY ON HIM, GATES.
WE WERE ALL WONDERING WHEN HE'D NOTICE SUPERGIRL!
THIS ISN'T THE FIRST TIME THE GIRL OF STEEL HAS REINVENTED HERSELF.

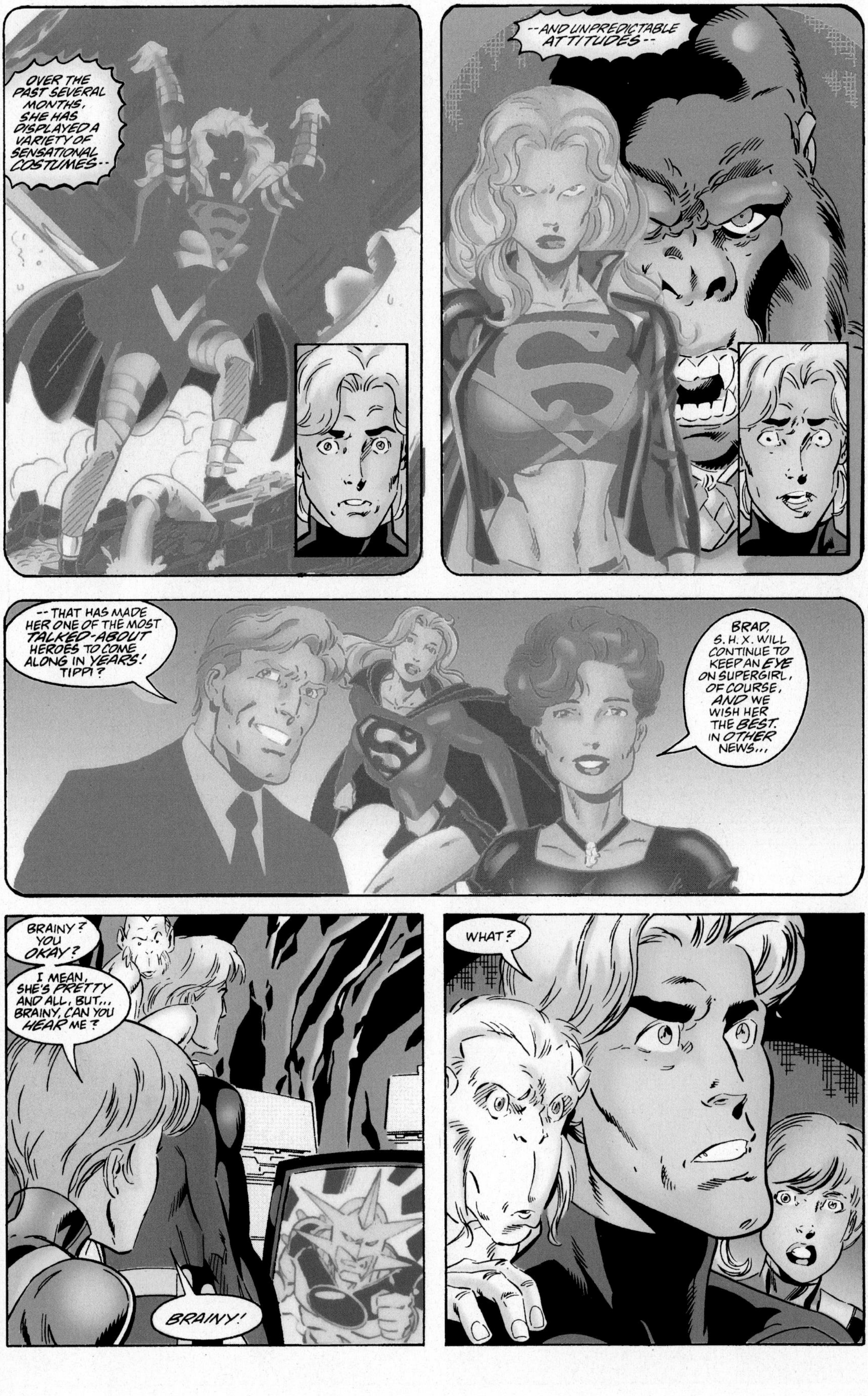
OVER THE PAST SEVERAL MONTHS, SHE HAS DISPLAYED A VARIETY OF SENSATIONAL COSTUMES--
--AND UNPREDICTABLE ATTITUDES--
--THAT HAS MADE HER ONE OF THE MOST TALKED-ABOUT HEROES TO COME ALONG IN YEARS! TIPPI?
BRAD, S.H.X. WILL CONTINUE TO KEEP AN EYE ON SUPERGIRL, OF COURSE, AND WE WISH HER THE BEST. IN OTHER NEWS...
BRAINY? YOU OKAY?
I MEAN, SHE'S PRETTY AND ALL, BUT... BRAINY, CAN YOU HEAR ME?
BRAINY!
WHAT?

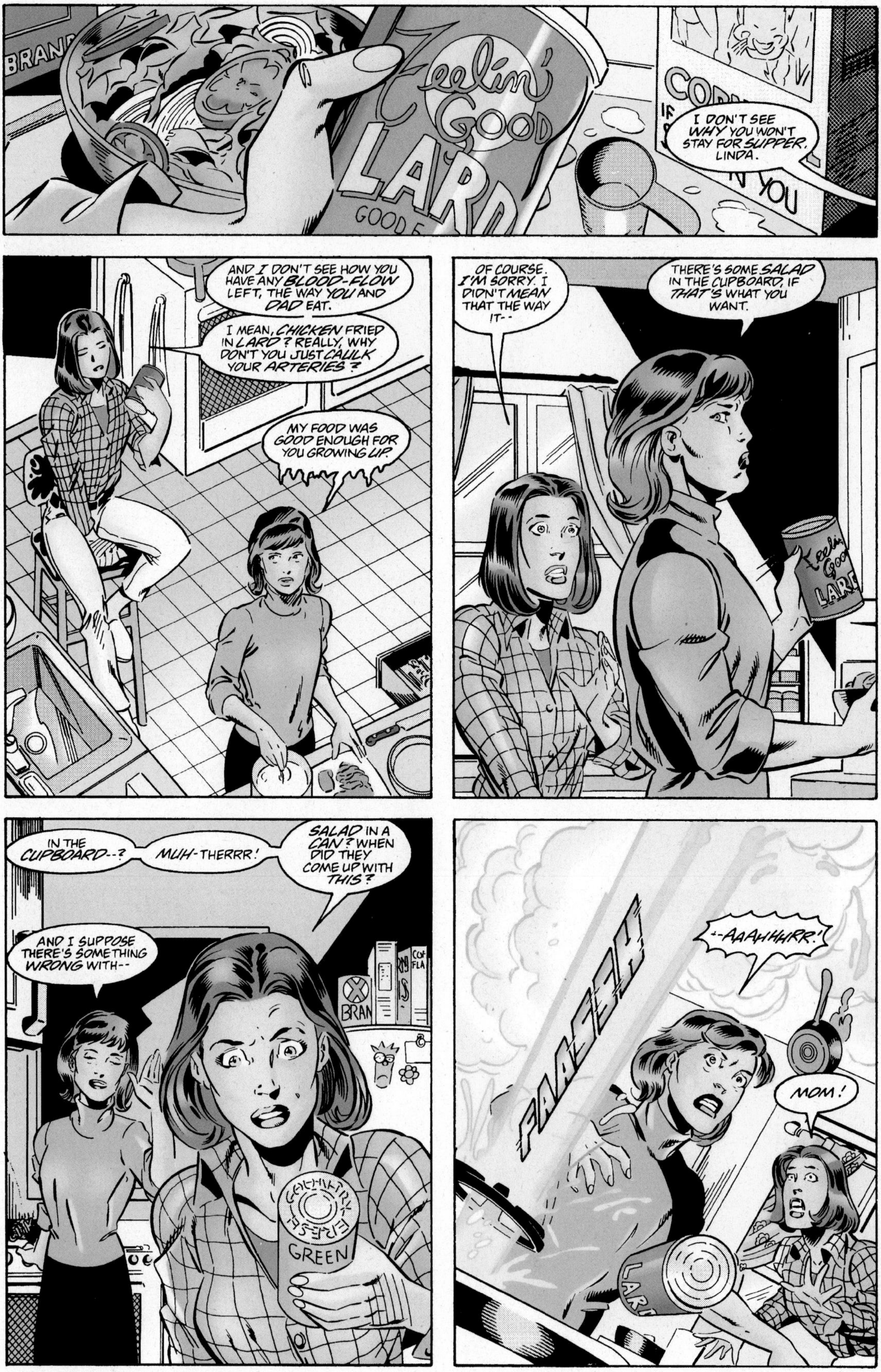
Feelin' GOOD LARD
GOOD F
BRAND
CORN
IF
N YOU
I DON'T SEE WHY YOU WON'T STAY FOR SUPPER, LINDA.
AND I DON'T SEE HOW YOU HAVE ANY BLOOD-FLOW LEFT, THE WAY YOU AND DAD EAT.
I MEAN, CHICKEN FRIED IN LARD? REALLY, WHY DON'T YOU JUST CAULK YOUR ARTERIES?
MY FOOD WAS GOOD ENOUGH FOR YOU GROWING UP.
OF COURSE. I'M SORRY. I DIDN'T MEAN THAT THE WAY IT--
THERE'S SOME SALAD IN THE CUPBOARD, IF THAT'S WHAT YOU WANT.
IN THE CUPBOARD--?
MUH-THERRR!
SALAD IN A CAN? WHEN DID THEY COME UP WITH THIS?
AND I SUPPOSE THERE'S SOMETHING WRONG WITH--
GREEN
FAASSSH
--AAAHHHRR!
MOM!

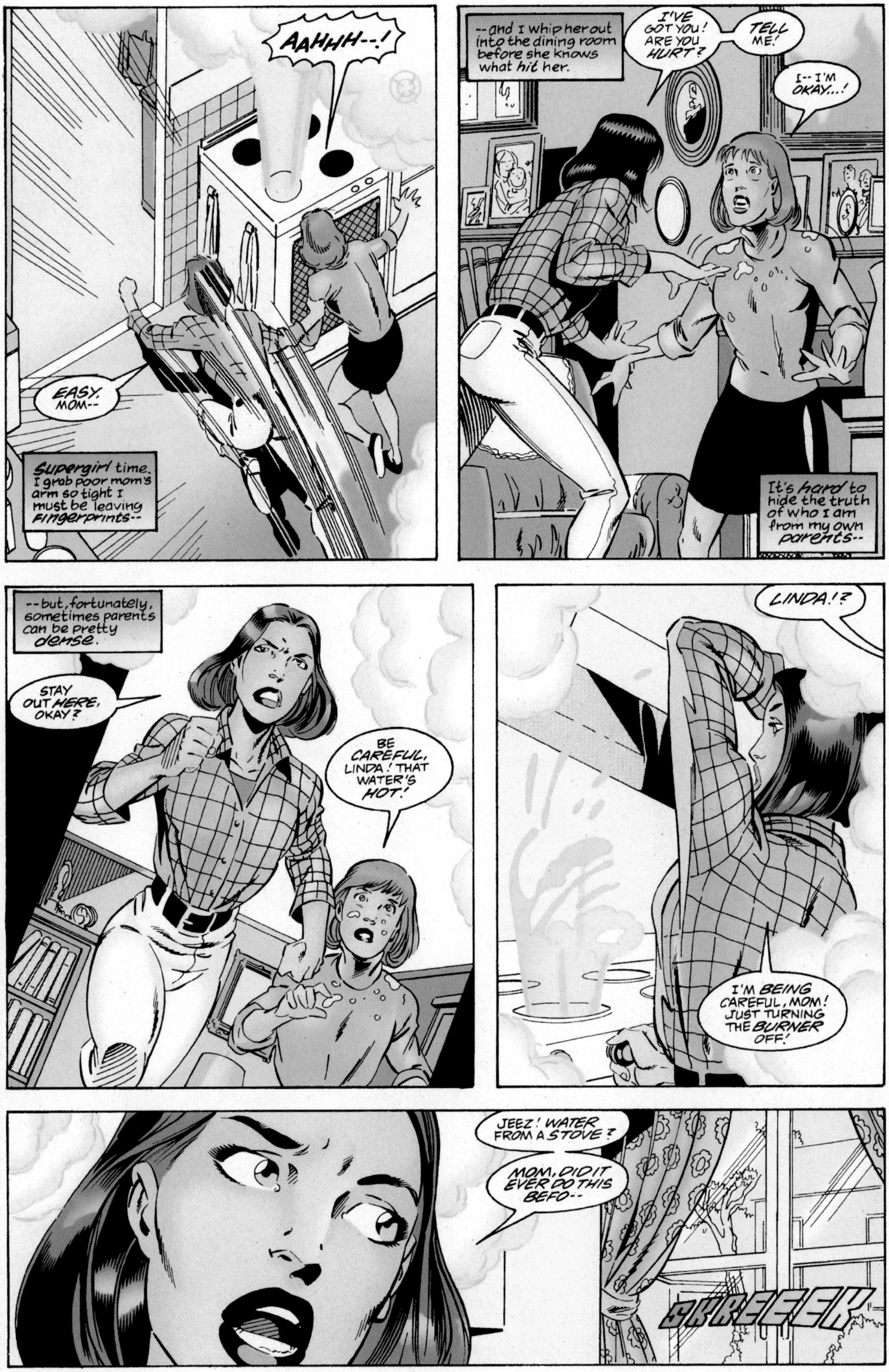
AAHHH--!
EASY. MOM--
Supergirl time. I grab poor mom's arm so tight I must be leaving fingerprints--
--and I whip her out into the dining room before she knows what hit her.
I'VE GOT YOU! ARE YOU HURT?
TELL ME!
I-- I'M OKAY...!
It's hard to hide the truth of who I am from my own parents--
--but, fortunately, sometimes parents can be pretty dense.
STAY OUT HERE, OKAY?
BE CAREFUL, LINDA! THAT WATER'S HOT!
LINDA!?
I'M BEING CAREFUL, MOM! JUST TURNING THE BURNER OFF!
JEEZ! WATER FROM A STOVE?
MOM, DID IT EVER DO THIS BEFO--
SKREEEK

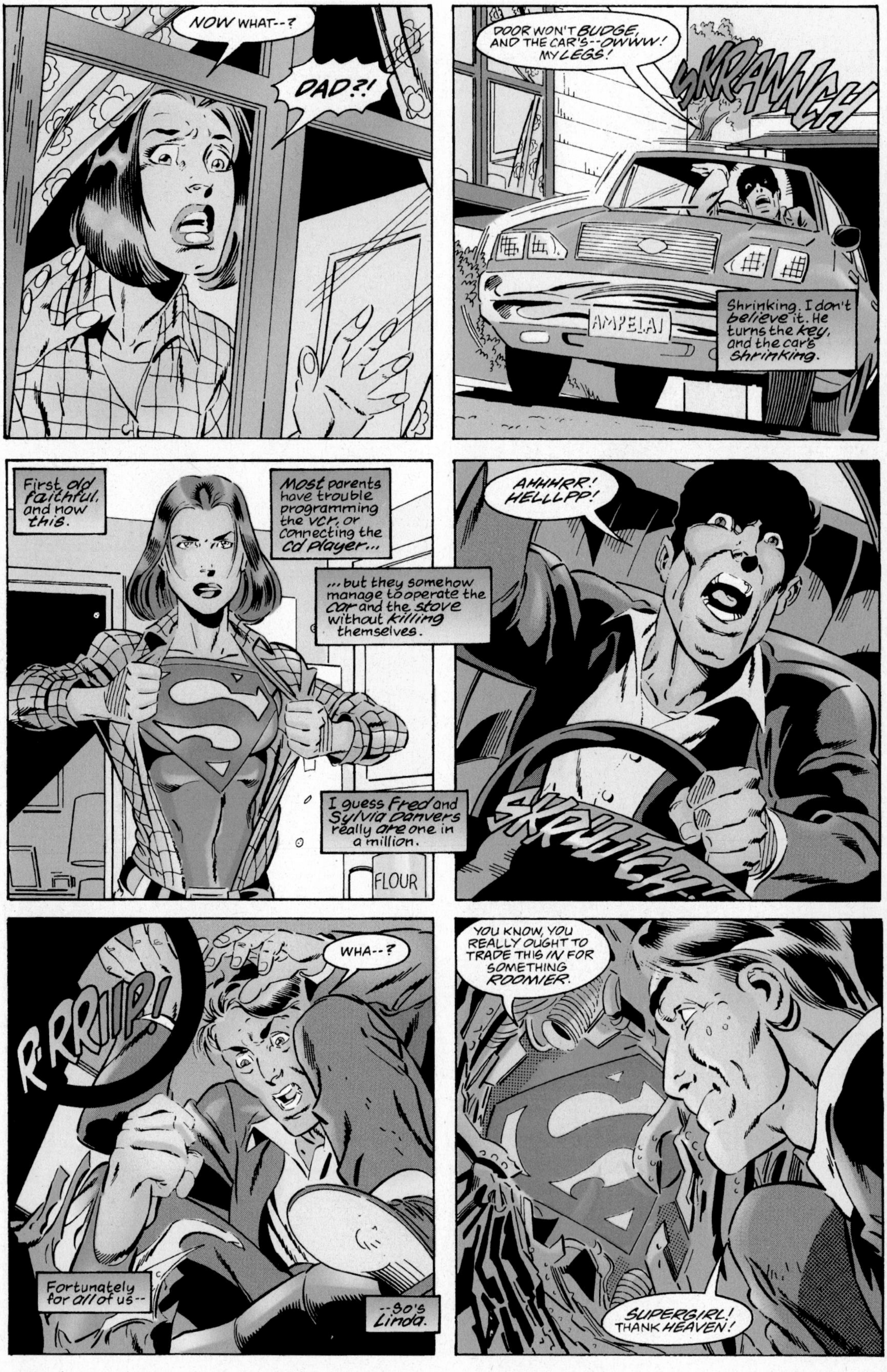
NOW WHAT--?
DAD?!
DOOR WON'T BUDGE, AND THE CAR'S--OWWW! MY LEGS!
SKRANNCH
AMPELAI
Shrinking. I don't believe it. He turns the key, and the car's shrinking.
First old faithful, and now this.
Most parents have trouble programming the vcr, or connecting the cd player...
...but they somehow manage to operate the car and the stove without killing themselves.
I guess Fred and Sylvia Danvers really are one in a million.
FLOUR
AHHHRR! HELLLPP!
SKRUTCH!
WHA--?
R-RRIIP!
Fortunately for all of us--
--so's Linda.
YOU KNOW, YOU REALLY OUGHT TO TRADE THIS IN FOR SOMETHING ROOMIER.
SUPERGIRL! THANK HEAVEN!

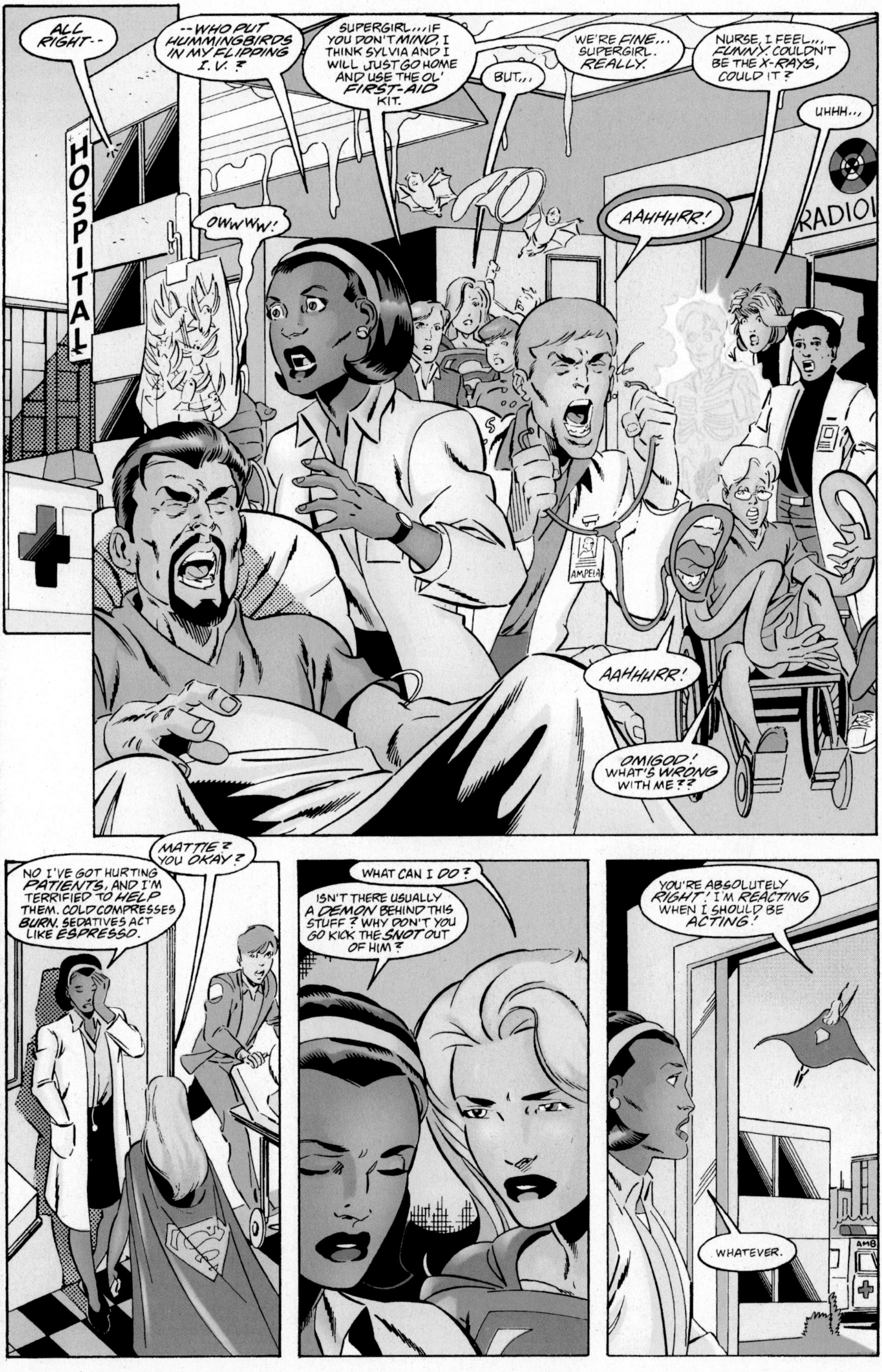
ALL RIGHT--
--WHO PUT HUMMINGBIRDS IN MY FLIPPING I.V.?
SUPERGIRL... IF YOU DON'T MIND, I THINK SYLVIA AND I WILL JUST GO HOME AND USE THE OL' FIRST-AID KIT.
BUT...
WE'RE FINE... SUPERGIRL. REALLY.
NURSE, I FEEL... FUNNY. COULDN'T BE THE X-RAYS, COULD IT?
UHHH...
HOSPITAL
OWWWW!
AAHHHRR!
RADIOL
AAHHURR!
OMIGOD! WHAT'S WRONG WITH ME??
NO I'VE GOT HURTING PATIENTS, AND I'M TERRIFIED TO HELP THEM. COLD COMPRESSES BURN. SEDATIVES ACT LIKE ESPRESSO.
MATTIE? YOU OKAY?
WHAT CAN I DO?
ISN'T THERE USUALLY A DEMON BEHIND THIS STUFF? WHY DON'T YOU GO KICK THE SNOT OUT OF HIM?
YOU'RE ABSOLUTELY RIGHT! I'M REACTING WHEN I SHOULD BE ACTING!
WHATEVER.

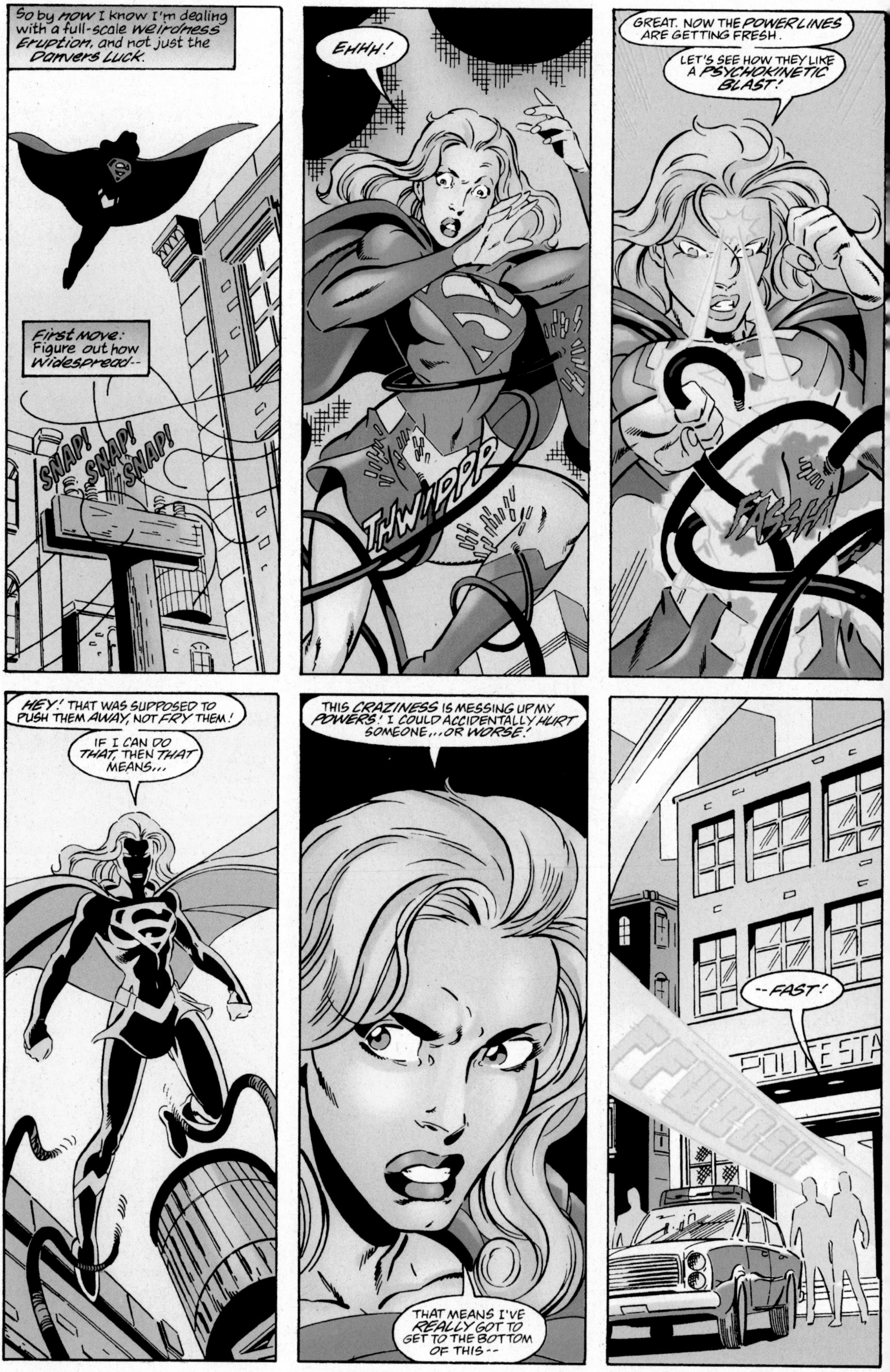

So by now I know I'm dealing with a full-scale Weirdness Eruption, and not just the Danvers Luck.
First move: Figure out how widespread--
SNAP! SNAP! SNAP!
EHHH!
THWIPPP
GREAT. NOW THE POWERLINES ARE GETTING FRESH.
LET'S SEE HOW THEY LIKE A PSYCHOKINETIC BLAST!
FASSHH
HEY! THAT WAS SUPPOSED TO PUSH THEM AWAY, NOT FRY THEM!
IF I CAN DO THAT, THEN THAT MEANS...
THIS CRAZINESS IS MESSING UP MY POWERS! I COULD ACCIDENTALLY HURT SOMEONE... OR WORSE!
THAT MEANS I'VE REALLY GOT TO GET TO THE BOTTOM OF THIS--
--FAST!
FFWOOSH
POLICE STA

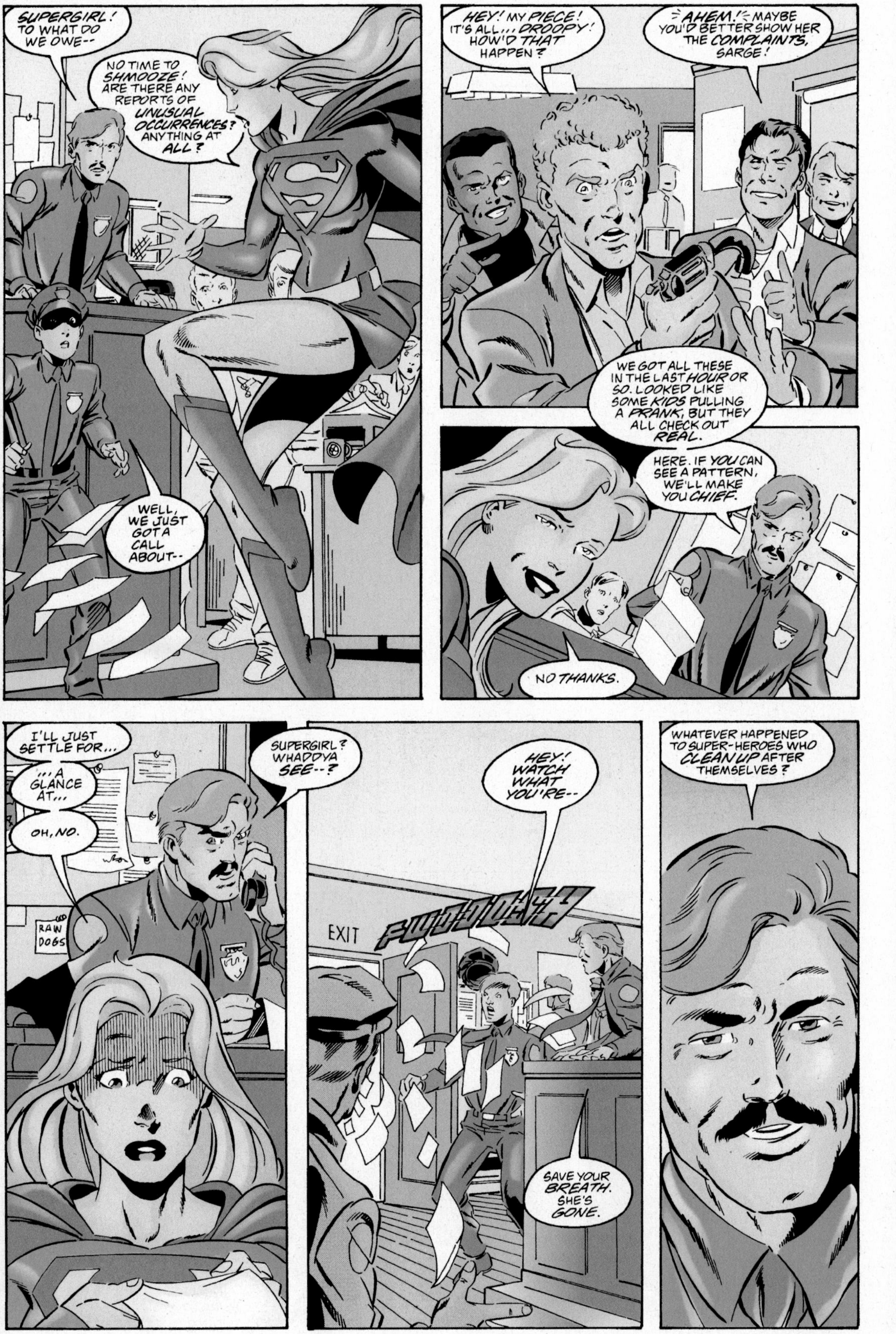
SUPERGIRL! TO WHAT DO WE OWE--
NO TIME TO SHMOOZE! ARE THERE ANY REPORTS OF UNUSUAL OCCURRENCES? ANYTHING AT ALL?
WELL, WE JUST GOT A CALL ABOUT--
HEY! MY PIECE! IT'S ALL... DROOPY! HOW'D THAT HAPPEN?
AHEM! MAYBE YOU'D BETTER SHOW HER THE COMPLAINTS, SARGE!
WE GOT ALL THESE IN THE LAST HOUR OR SO. LOOKED LIKE SOME KIDS PULLING A PRANK, BUT THEY ALL CHECK OUT REAL.
HERE. IF YOU CAN SEE A PATTERN, WE'LL MAKE YOU CHIEF.
NO THANKS.
I'LL JUST SETTLE FOR...
...A GLANCE AT...
OH, NO.
RAW DOGS
SUPERGIRL? WHADDYA SEE--?
HEY! WATCH WHAT YOU'RE--
EXIT
FWOOOOSH
SAVE YOUR BREATH. SHE'S GONE.
WHATEVER HAPPENED TO SUPER-HEROES WHO CLEAN UP AFTER THEMSELVES?

I *heard* that.

If that cop only knew about the *real* mess... and how desperately I *want* to clean it up.

I just wish I knew *how.*

The reports showed *a pattern* to the disturbances, all right. They all happened near *me.* What if they're all *my fault?*

I don't know where to *begin* sorting this out, and until I *do,* I'm scared to lift a *finger.*

Scared to pick up the *phone* and ask for *help.*

GREAT.

ALL RIGHT... IF THE PHONE'S A *BLOWTORCH,* THEN MAYBE SOMETHING *ELSE* IS THE *PHONE.*

MY GOD, THE LAMP'S *RINGING.*

COME *ON,* PICK *UP...*

CLARK? MAE.

SORRY. I MEAN TO CALL MORE OFTEN... LISTEN, WHO'S THE *SMARTEST* PERSON YOU KNOW?

LET'S SEE... MOST OF THE *GENIUSES* I'VE MET ARE PRETTY *NASTY CHARACTERS...*

OH, *WAIT.* I'M FORGETTING THE *SMARTEST* PERSON ON *EARTH.*

LITTLE V UNIVERS

CLARK

WHKR

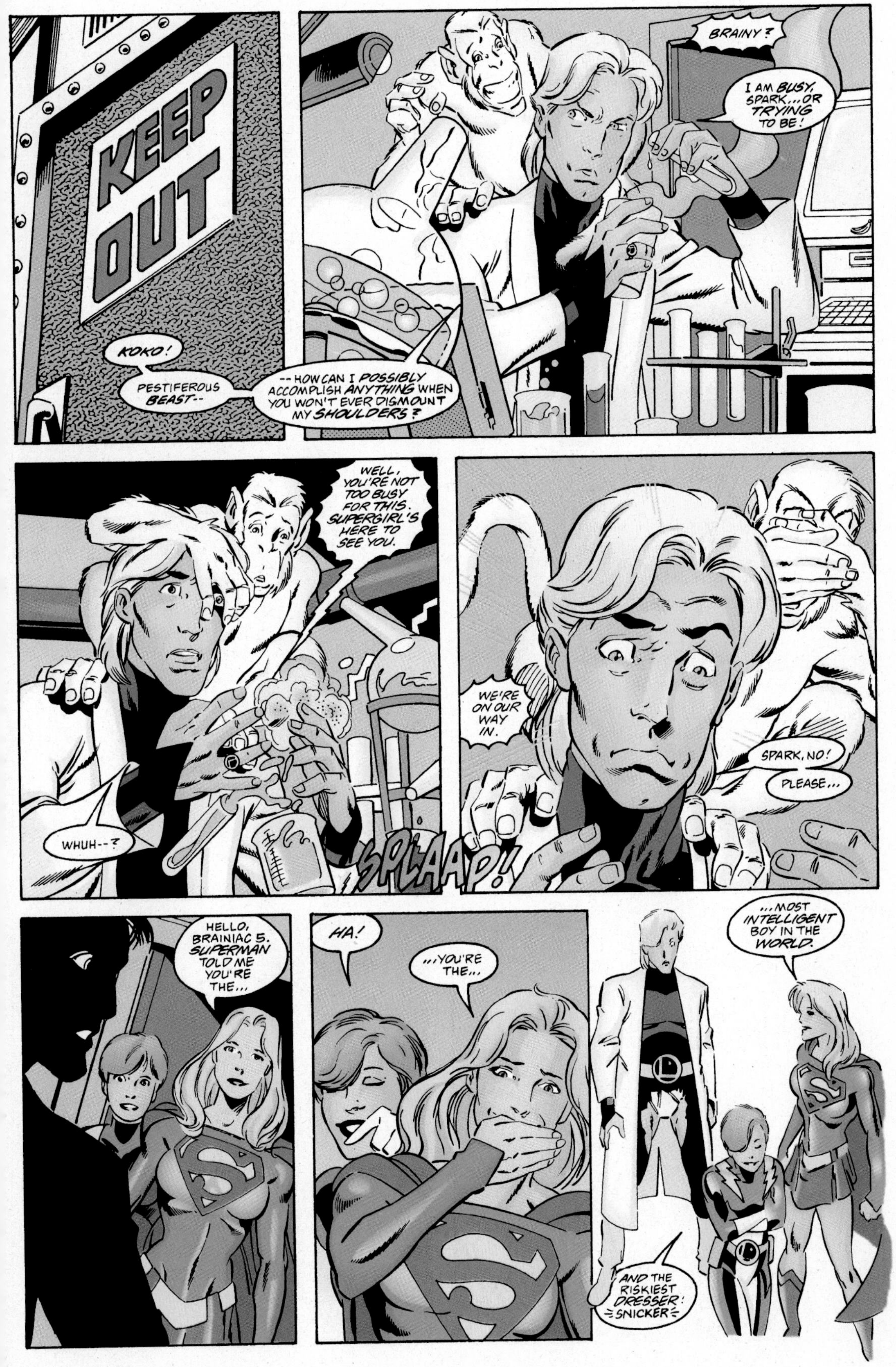
KEEP OUT
BRAINY?
I AM BUSY, SPARK... OR TRYING TO BE!
KOKO!
PESTIFEROUS BEAST--
--HOW CAN I POSSIBLY ACCOMPLISH ANYTHING WHEN YOU WON'T EVER DISMOUNT MY SHOULDERS?
WELL, YOU'RE NOT TOO BUSY FOR THIS. SUPERGIRL'S HERE TO SEE YOU.
WHUH--?
SPLAAP!
WE'RE ON OUR WAY IN.
SPARK, NO!
PLEASE...
HELLO, BRAINIAC 5. SUPERMAN TOLD ME YOU'RE THE...
HA!
...YOU'RE THE...
...MOST INTELLIGENT BOY IN THE WORLD.
AND THE RISKIEST DRESSER!
SNICKER

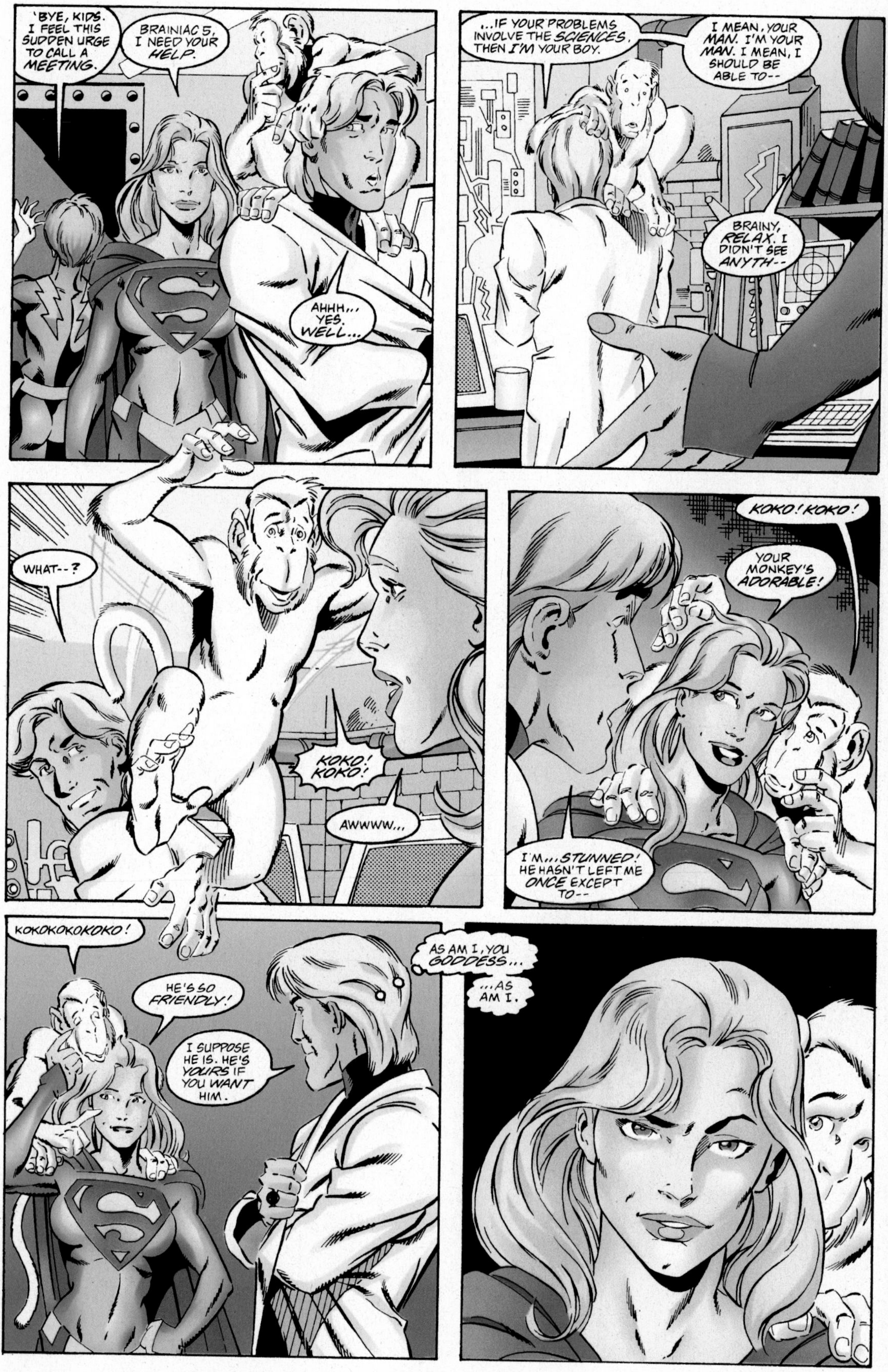

'BYE, KIDS. I FEEL THIS SUDDEN URGE TO CALL A MEETING.
BRAINIAC 5, I NEED YOUR HELP.
AHHH... YES. WELL...
...IF YOUR PROBLEMS INVOLVE THE SCIENCES, THEN I'M YOUR BOY.
I MEAN, YOUR MAN. I'M YOUR MAN. I MEAN, I SHOULD BE ABLE TO--
BRAINY, RELAX. I DIDN'T SEE ANYTH--
WHAT--?
KOKO! KOKO!
AWWWW...
KOKO! KOKO!
YOUR MONKEY'S ADORABLE!
I'M... STUNNED! HE HASN'T LEFT ME ONCE EXCEPT TO--
KOKOKOKOKOKO!
HE'S SO FRIENDLY!
I SUPPOSE HE IS. HE'S YOURS IF YOU WANT HIM.
AS AM I, YOU GODDESS...
...AS AM I.

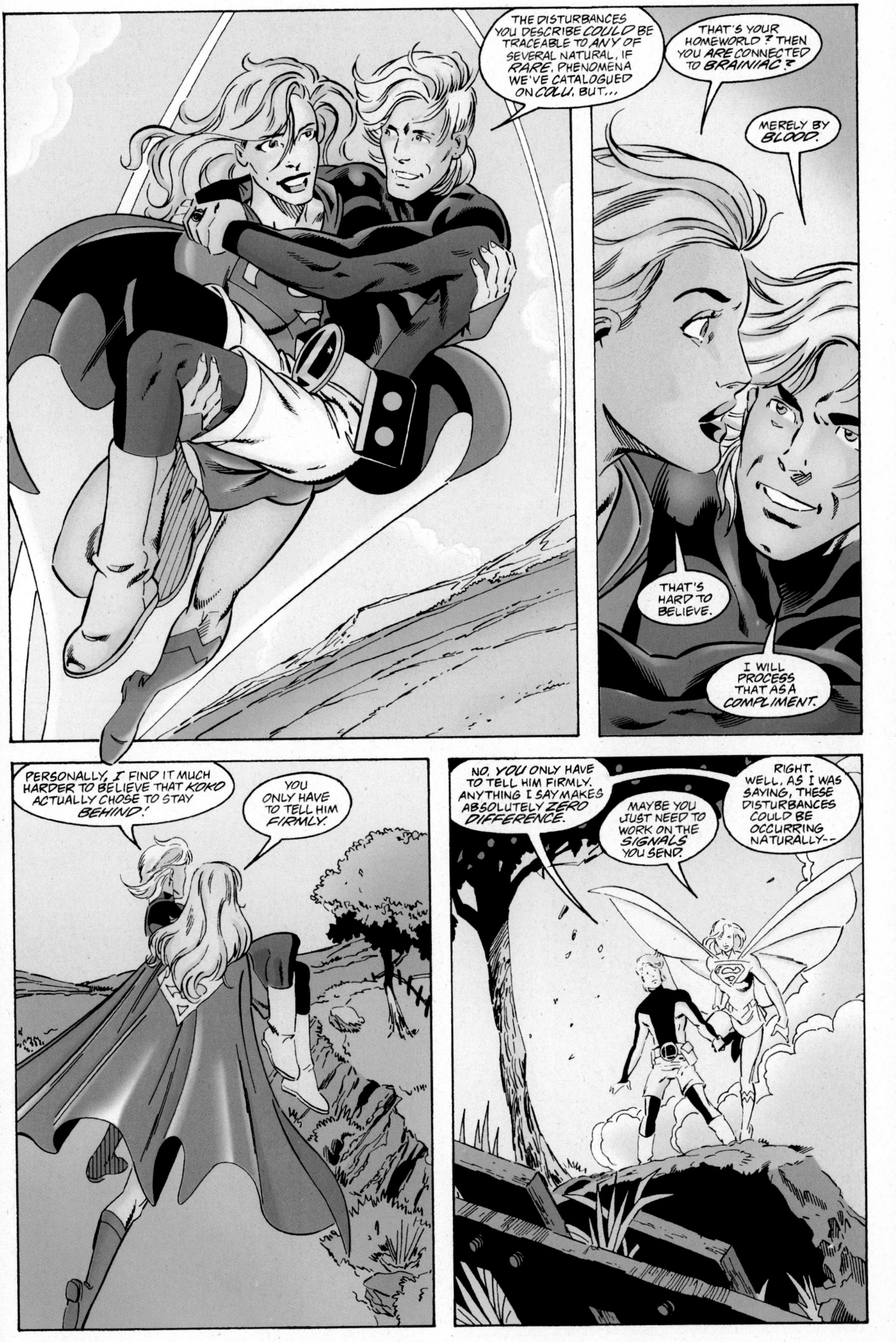
THE DISTURBANCES YOU DESCRIBE COULD BE TRACEABLE TO ANY OF SEVERAL NATURAL, IF RARE, PHENOMENA WE'VE CATALOGUED ON COLU. BUT...
THAT'S YOUR HOMEWORLD? THEN YOU ARE CONNECTED TO BRAINIAC?
MERELY BY BLOOD.
THAT'S HARD TO BELIEVE.
I WILL PROCESS THAT AS A COMPLIMENT.
PERSONALLY, I FIND IT MUCH HARDER TO BELIEVE THAT KOKO ACTUALLY CHOSE TO STAY BEHIND!
YOU ONLY HAVE TO TELL HIM FIRMLY.
NO, YOU ONLY HAVE TO TELL HIM FIRMLY. ANYTHING I SAY MAKES ABSOLUTELY ZERO DIFFERENCE.
MAYBE YOU JUST NEED TO WORK ON THE SIGNALS YOU SEND.
RIGHT. WELL, AS I WAS SAYING, THESE DISTURBANCES COULD BE OCCURRING NATURALLY--

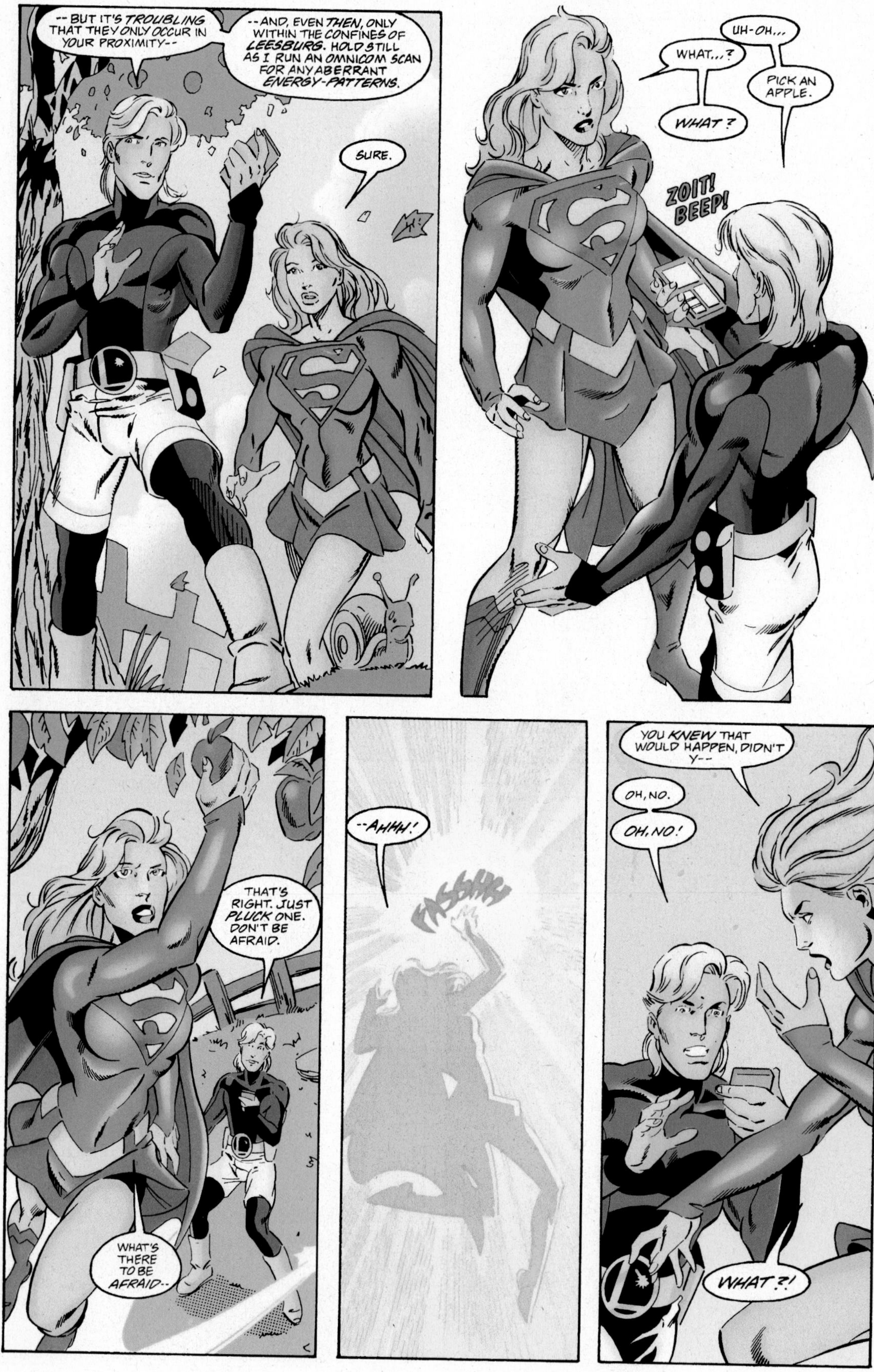

-- BUT IT'S TROUBLING THAT THEY ONLY OCCUR IN YOUR PROXIMITY--
--AND, EVEN THEN, ONLY WITHIN THE CONFINES OF LEESBURG. HOLD STILL AS I RUN AN OMNICOM SCAN FOR ANY ABERRANT ENERGY-PATTERNS.
SURE.
WHAT...?
WHAT?
UH-OH...
PICK AN APPLE.
ZOIT! BEEP!
THAT'S RIGHT. JUST PLUCK ONE. DON'T BE AFRAID.
WHAT'S THERE TO BE AFRAID--
--AHHH!
FASSHH
YOU KNEW THAT WOULD HAPPEN, DIDN'T Y--
OH, NO.
OH, NO!
WHAT?!

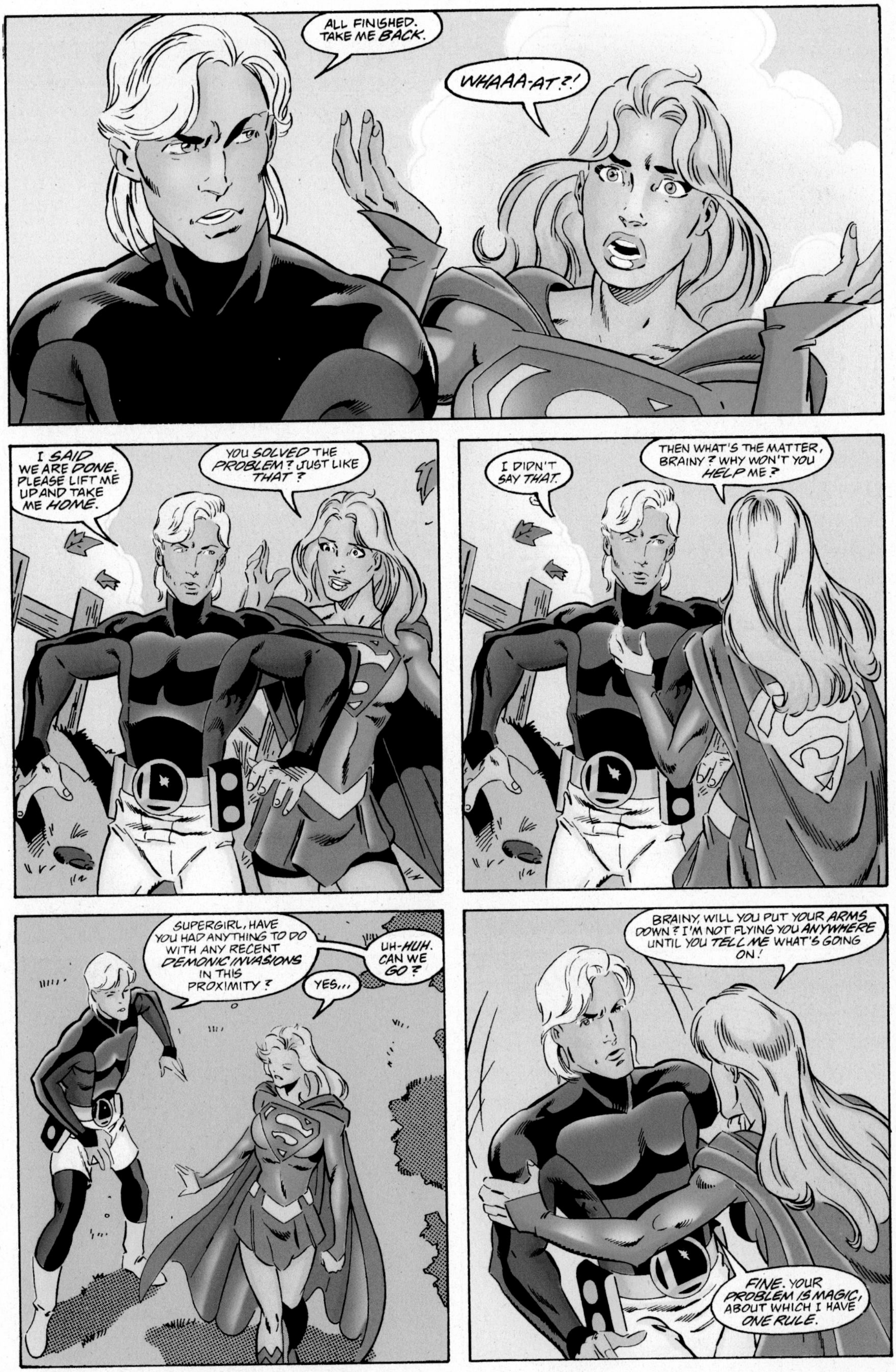
ALL FINISHED. TAKE ME BACK.
WHAAA-AT?!
I SAID WE ARE DONE. PLEASE LIFT ME UP AND TAKE ME HOME.
YOU SOLVED THE PROBLEM? JUST LIKE THAT?
I DIDN'T SAY THAT.
THEN WHAT'S THE MATTER, BRAINY? WHY WON'T YOU HELP ME?
SUPERGIRL, HAVE YOU HAD ANYTHING TO DO WITH ANY RECENT DEMONIC INVASIONS IN THIS PROXIMITY?
YES...
UH-HUH. CAN WE GO?
BRAINY, WILL YOU PUT YOUR ARMS DOWN? I'M NOT FLYING YOU ANYWHERE UNTIL YOU TELL ME WHAT'S GOING ON!
FINE. YOUR PROBLEM IS MAGIC, ABOUT WHICH I HAVE ONE RULE.

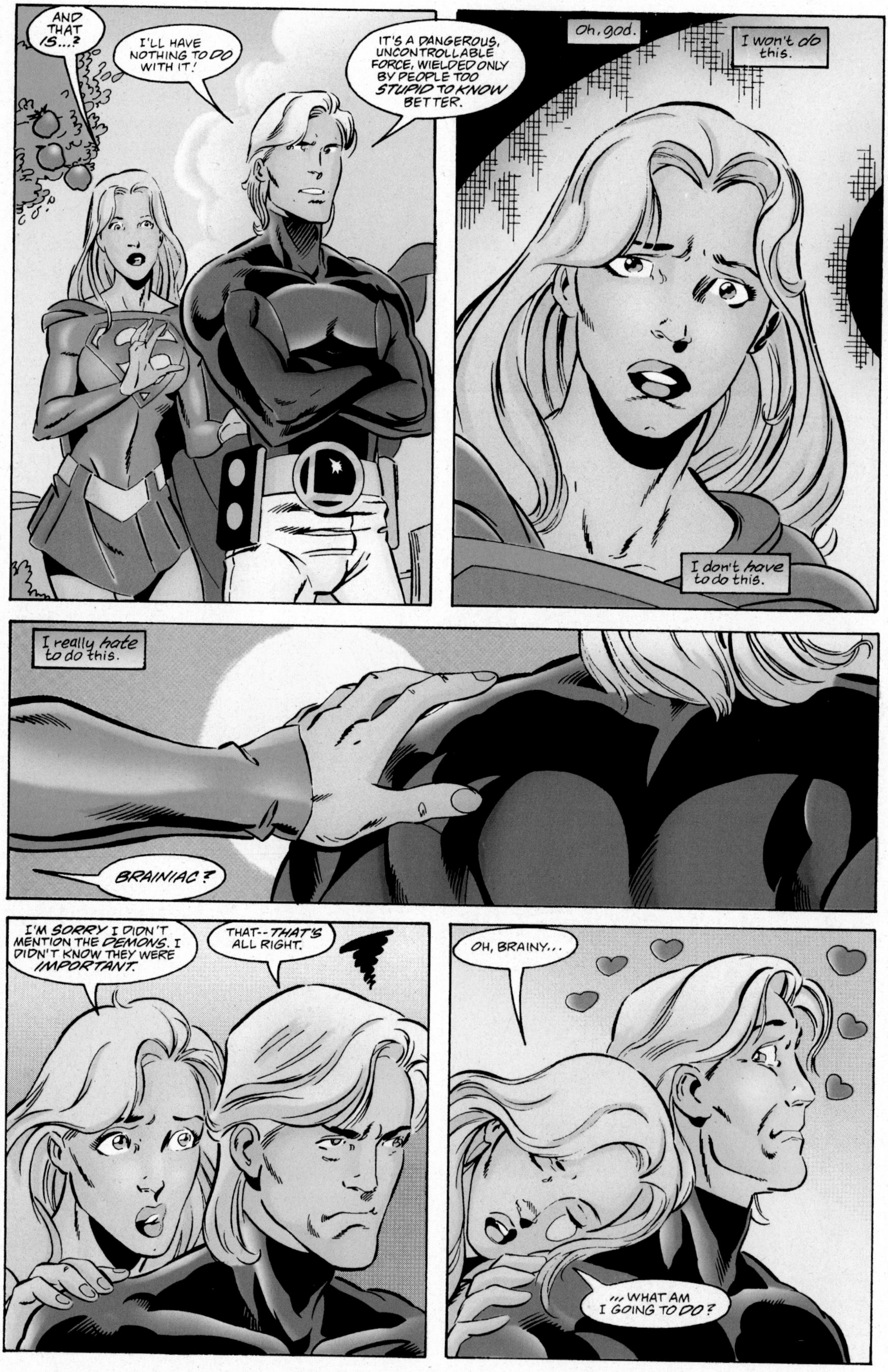
AND THAT IS...?
I'LL HAVE NOTHING TO DO WITH IT!
IT'S A DANGEROUS, UNCONTROLLABLE FORCE, WIELDED ONLY BY PEOPLE TOO STUPID TO KNOW BETTER.
Oh, god.
I won't do this.
I don't have to do this.
I really hate to do this.
BRAINIAC?
I'M SORRY I DIDN'T MENTION THE DEMONS. I DIDN'T KNOW THEY WERE IMPORTANT.
THAT--THAT'S ALL RIGHT.
OH, BRAINY...
...WHAT AM I GOING TO DO?

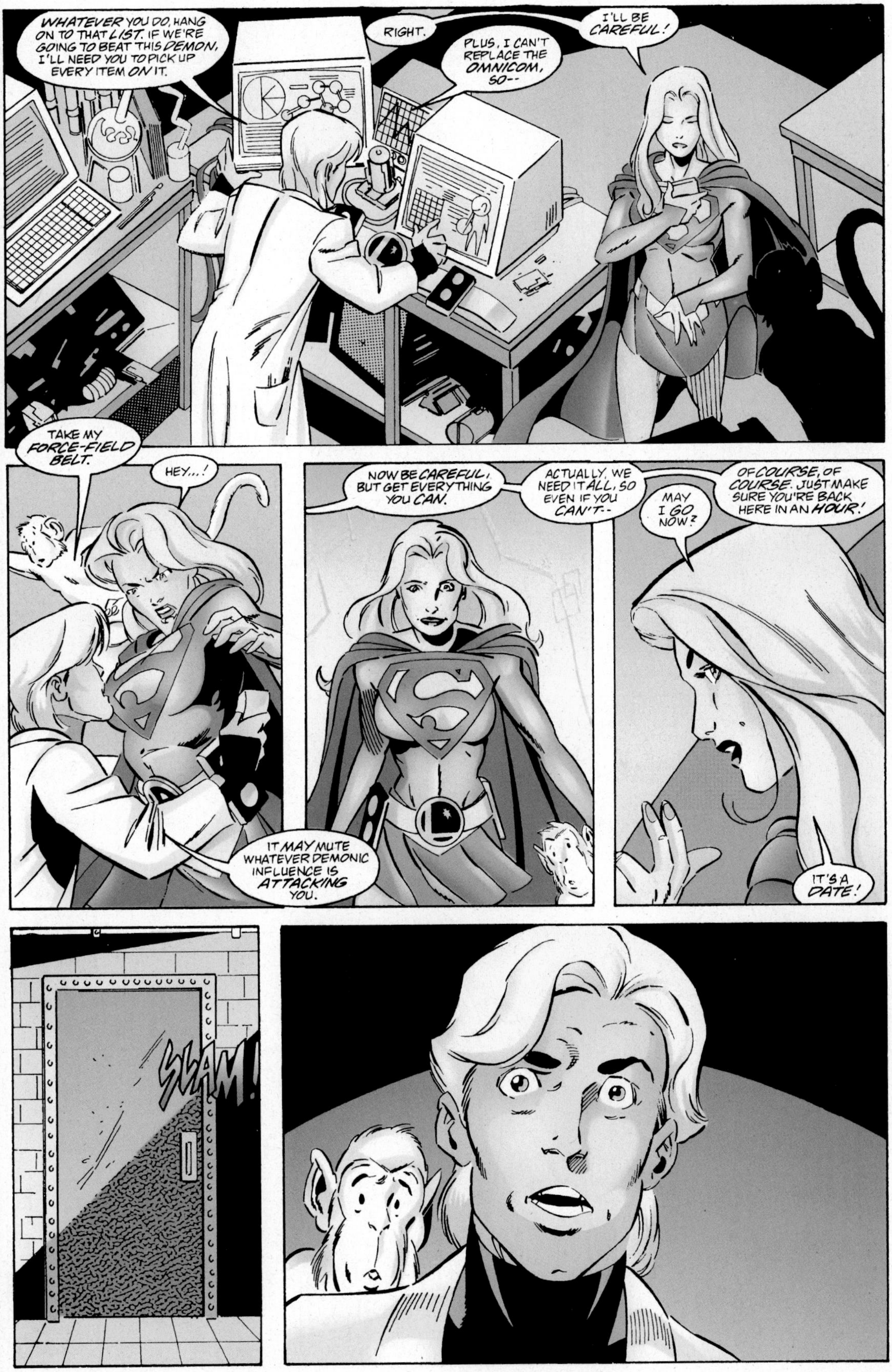
WHATEVER YOU DO, HANG ON TO THAT LIST. IF WE'RE GOING TO BEAT THIS DEMON, I'LL NEED YOU TO PICK UP EVERY ITEM ON IT.
RIGHT.
PLUS, I CAN'T REPLACE THE OMNICOM, SO--
I'LL BE CAREFUL!
TAKE MY FORCE-FIELD BELT.
HEY...!
IT MAY MUTE WHATEVER DEMONIC INFLUENCE IS ATTACKING YOU.
NOW BE CAREFUL, BUT GET EVERYTHING YOU CAN.
ACTUALLY, WE NEED IT ALL, SO EVEN IF YOU CAN'T--
MAY I GO NOW?
OF COURSE, OF COURSE. JUST MAKE SURE YOU'RE BACK HERE IN AN HOUR!
IT'S A DATE!
SLAM!

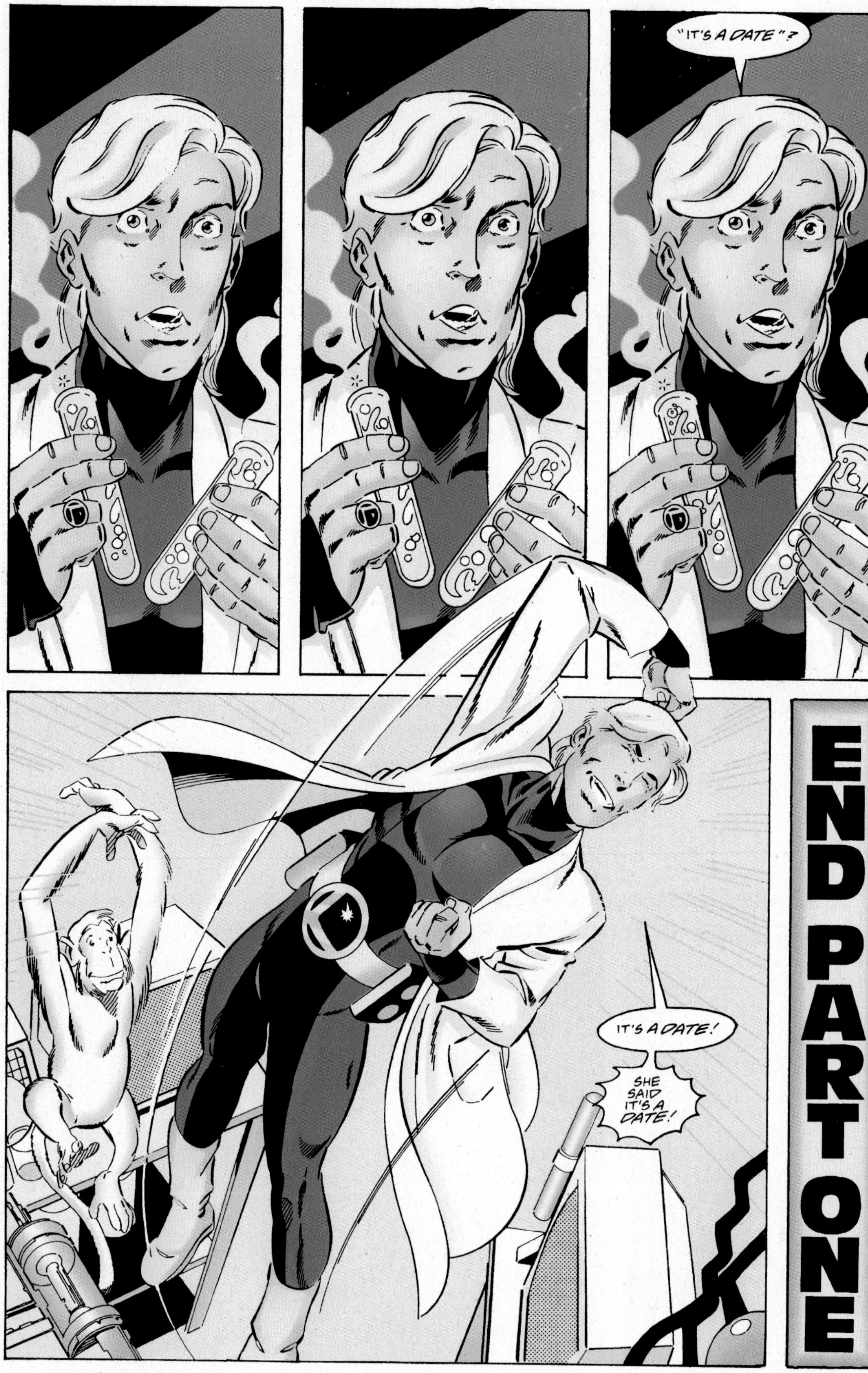
"IT'S A DATE"?
IT'S A DATE!
SHE SAID IT'S A DATE!
END PART ONE

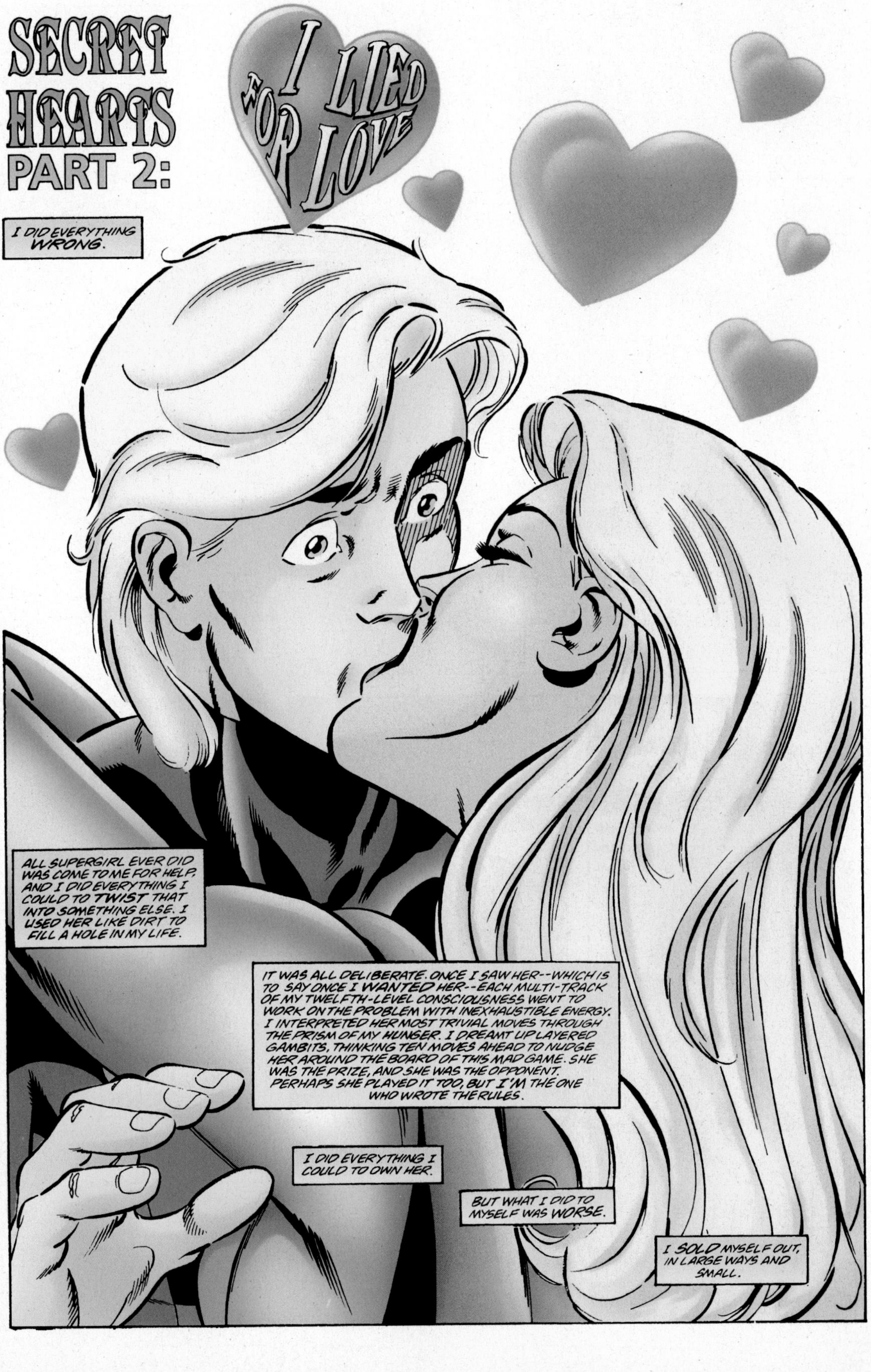
SECRET HEARTS
PART 2:
I LIED FOR LOVE
I DID EVERYTHING WRONG.
ALL SUPERGIRL EVER DID WAS COME TO ME FOR HELP, AND I DID EVERYTHING I COULD TO TWIST THAT INTO SOMETHING ELSE. I USED HER LIKE DIRT TO FILL A HOLE IN MY LIFE.
IT WAS ALL DELIBERATE. ONCE I SAW HER--WHICH IS TO SAY ONCE I WANTED HER--EACH MULTI-TRACK OF MY TWELFTH-LEVEL CONSCIOUSNESS WENT TO WORK ON THE PROBLEM WITH INEXHAUSTIBLE ENERGY. I INTERPRETED HER MOST TRIVIAL MOVES THROUGH THE PRISM OF MY HUNGER. I DREAMT UP LAYERED GAMBITS, THINKING TEN MOVES AHEAD TO NUDGE HER AROUND THE BOARD OF THIS MAD GAME. SHE WAS THE PRIZE, AND SHE WAS THE OPPONENT. PERHAPS SHE PLAYED IT TOO, BUT I'M THE ONE WHO WROTE THE RULES.
I DID EVERYTHING I COULD TO OWN HER.
BUT WHAT I DID TO MYSELF WAS WORSE.
I SOLD MYSELF OUT, IN LARGE WAYS AND SMALL.

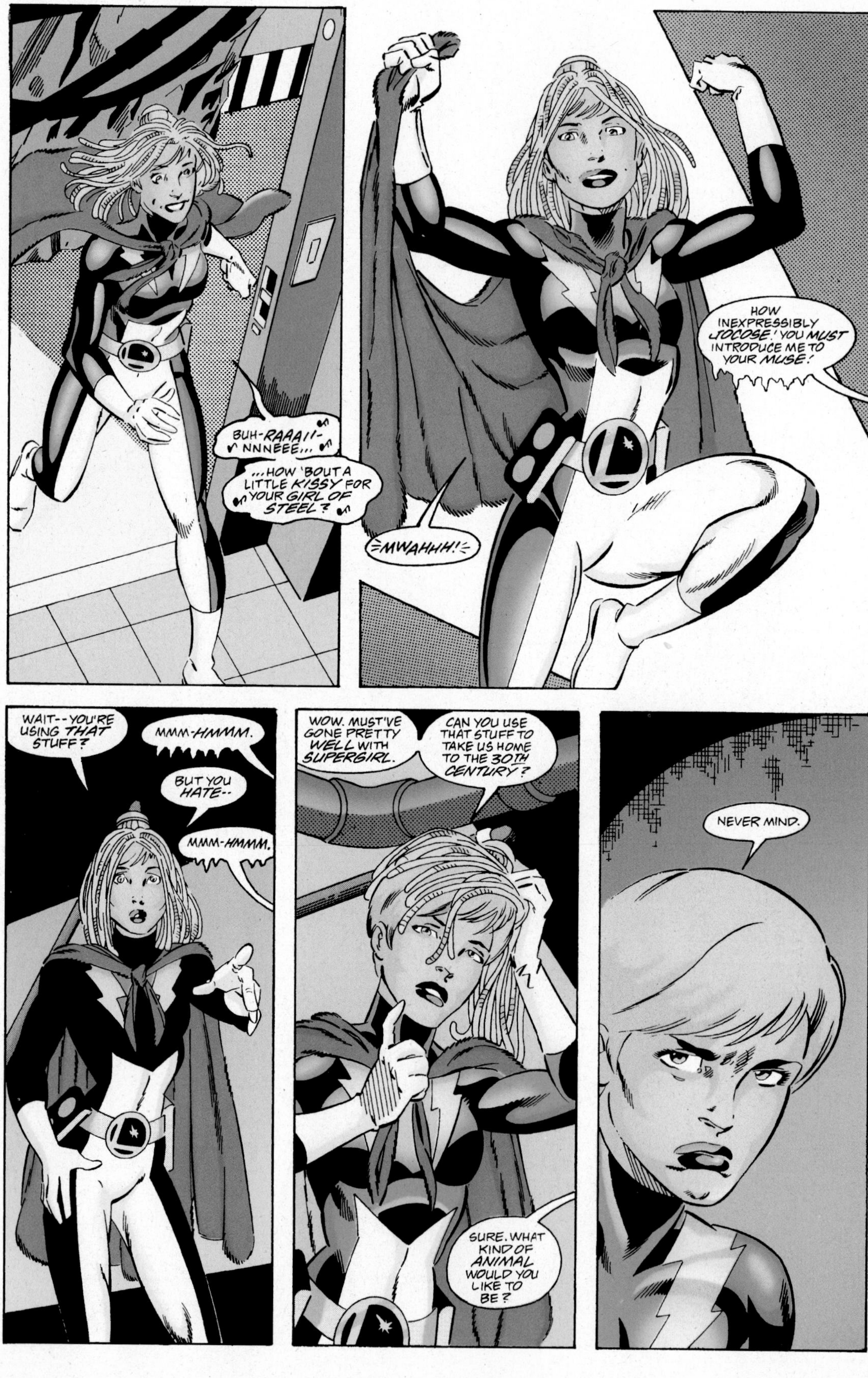

BUH-RAAAII-NNNEEE...
...HOW 'BOUT A LITTLE KISSY FOR YOUR GIRL OF STEEL?
MWAHHH!
HOW INEXPRESSIBLY JOCOSE! YOU MUST INTRODUCE ME TO YOUR MUSE!
WAIT--YOU'RE USING THAT STUFF?
MMM-HMMM.
BUT YOU HATE--
MMM-HMMM.
WOW. MUST'VE GONE PRETTY WELL WITH SUPERGIRL.
CAN YOU USE THAT STUFF TO TAKE US HOME TO THE 30TH CENTURY?
SURE. WHAT KIND OF ANIMAL WOULD YOU LIKE TO BE?
NEVER MIND.

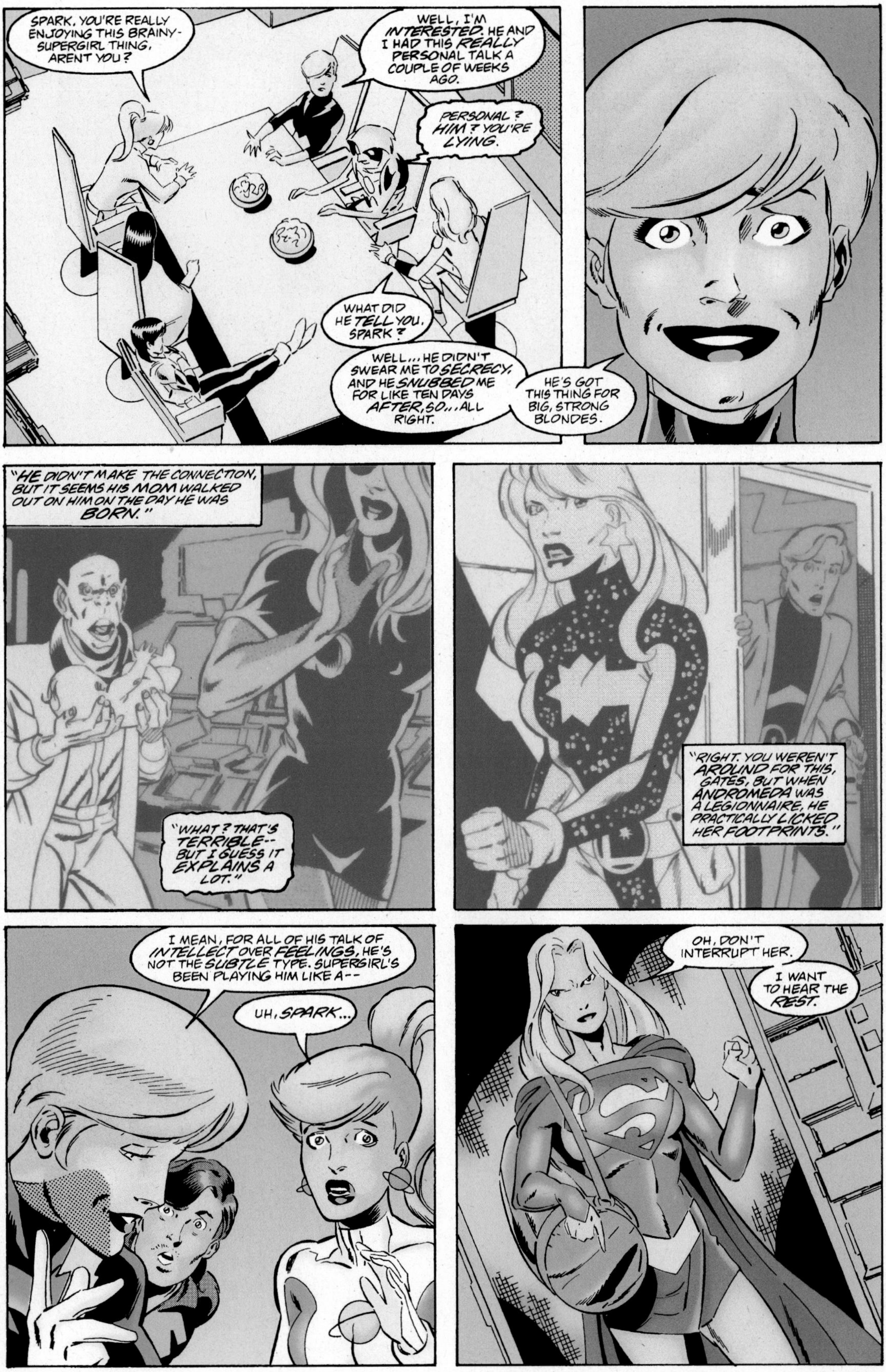
SPARK, YOU'RE REALLY ENJOYING THIS BRAINY-SUPERGIRL THING, ARENT YOU?
WELL, I'M INTERESTED. HE AND I HAD THIS REALLY PERSONAL TALK A COUPLE OF WEEKS AGO.
PERSONAL? HIM? YOU'RE LYING.
WHAT DID HE TELL YOU, SPARK?
WELL... HE DIDN'T SWEAR ME TO SECRECY. AND HE SNUBBED ME FOR LIKE TEN DAYS AFTER, SO... ALL RIGHT.
HE'S GOT THIS THING FOR BIG, STRONG BLONDES.
"HE DIDN'T MAKE THE CONNECTION, BUT IT SEEMS HIS MOM WALKED OUT ON HIM ON THE DAY HE WAS BORN."
"WHAT? THAT'S TERRIBLE-- BUT I GUESS IT EXPLAINS A LOT."
"RIGHT. YOU WEREN'T AROUND FOR THIS, GATES, BUT WHEN ANDROMEDA WAS A LEGIONNAIRE, HE PRACTICALLY LICKED HER FOOTPRINTS."
I MEAN, FOR ALL OF HIS TALK OF INTELLECT OVER FEELINGS, HE'S NOT THE SUBTLE TYPE. SUPERGIRL'S BEEN PLAYING HIM LIKE A--
UH, SPARK...
OH, DON'T INTERRUPT HER.
I WANT TO HEAR THE REST.

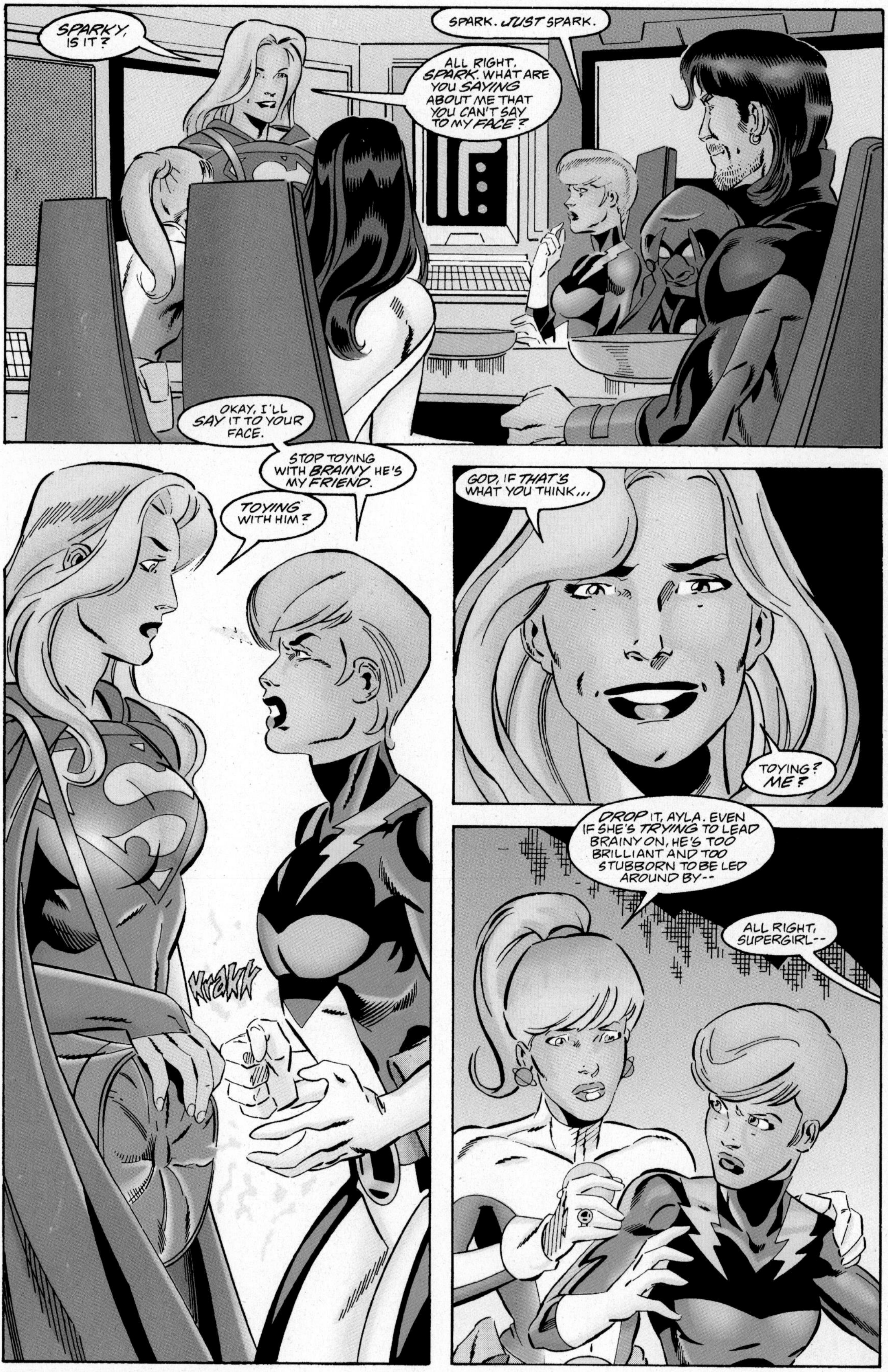
SPARKY, IS IT?
SPARK. JUST SPARK.
ALL RIGHT. SPARK. WHAT ARE YOU SAYING ABOUT ME THAT YOU CAN'T SAY TO MY FACE?
OKAY, I'LL SAY IT TO YOUR FACE.
STOP TOYING WITH BRAINY. HE'S MY FRIEND.
TOYING WITH HIM?
KRAKK
GOD, IF THAT'S WHAT YOU THINK...
TOYING? ME?
DROP IT, AYLA. EVEN IF SHE'S TRYING TO LEAD BRAINY ON, HE'S TOO BRILLIANT AND TOO STUBBORN TO BE LED AROUND BY--
ALL RIGHT, SUPERGIRL--

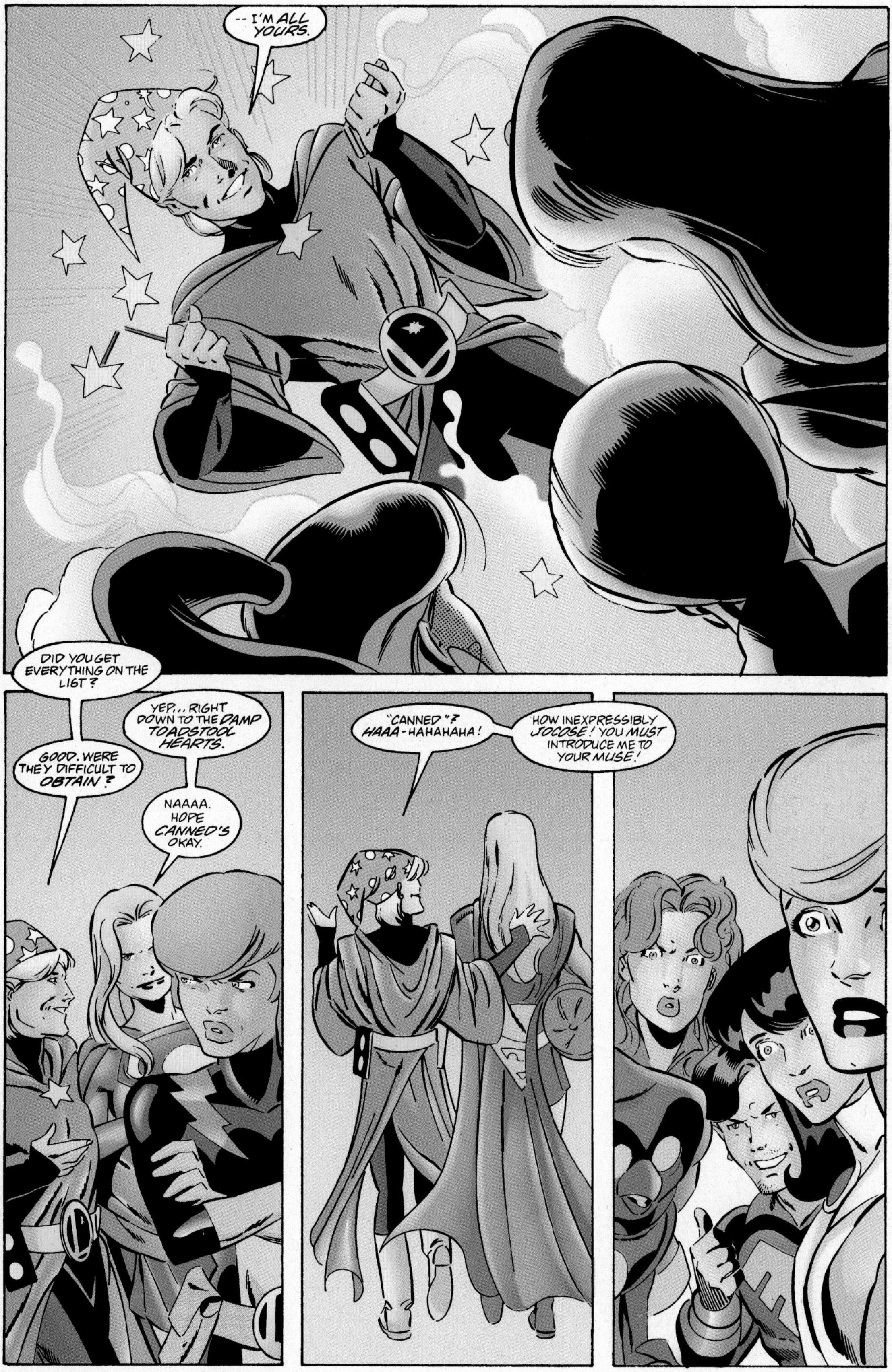
-- I'M ALL YOURS.
DID YOU GET EVERYTHING ON THE LIST?
YEP... RIGHT DOWN TO THE DAMP TOADSTOOL HEARTS.
GOOD. WERE THEY DIFFICULT TO OBTAIN?
NAAAA. HOPE CANNED'S OKAY.
"CANNED"? HAAA-HAHAHAHA!
HOW INEXPRESSIBLY JOCOSE! YOU MUST INTRODUCE ME TO YOUR MUSE!

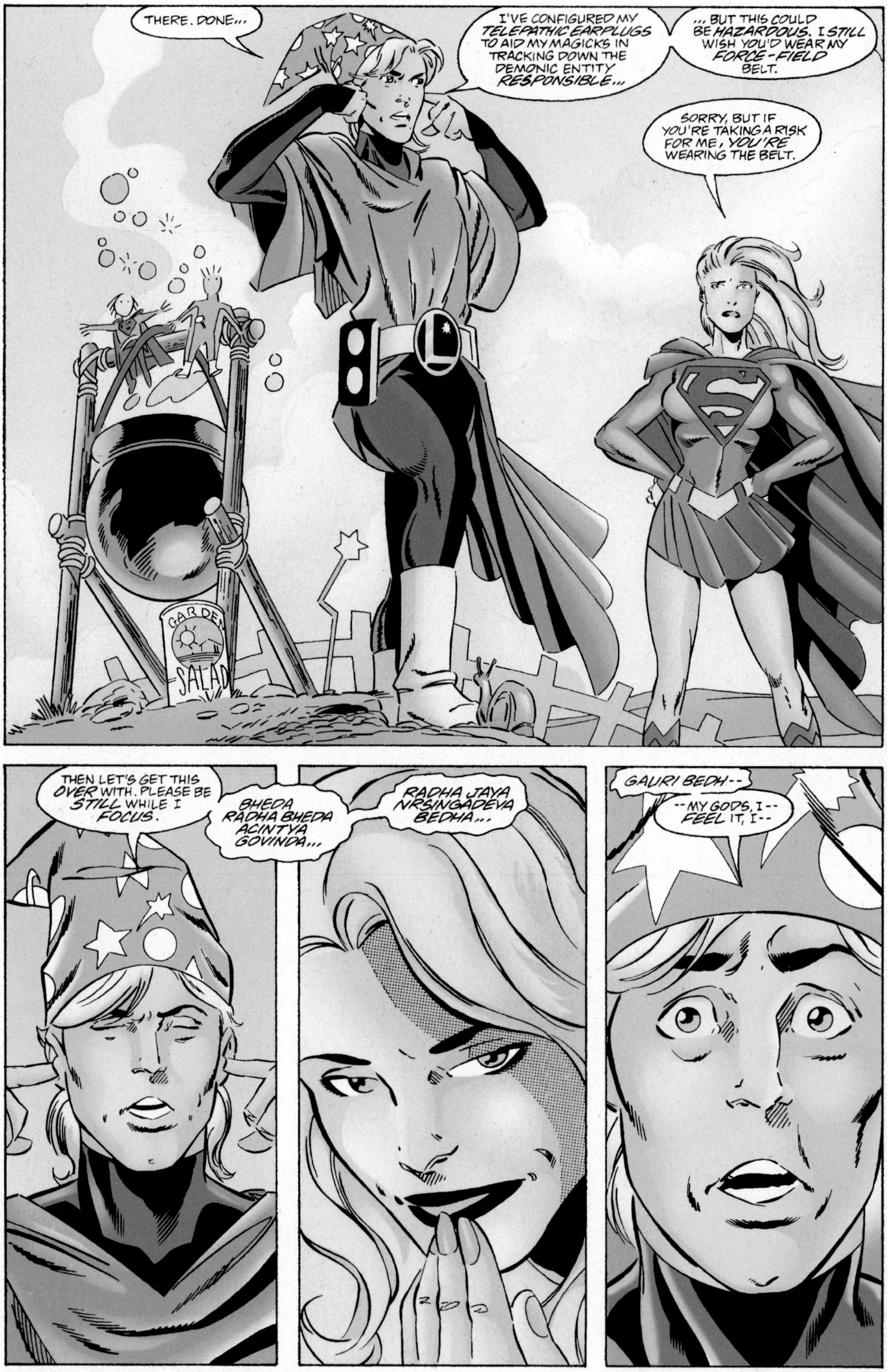
THERE. DONE...
I'VE CONFIGURED MY TELEPATHIC EARPLUGS TO AID MY MAGICKS IN TRACKING DOWN THE DEMONIC ENTITY RESPONSIBLE...
...BUT THIS COULD BE HAZARDOUS. I STILL WISH YOU'D WEAR MY FORCE-FIELD BELT.
SORRY, BUT IF YOU'RE TAKING A RISK FOR ME, YOU'RE WEARING THE BELT.
GARDEN SALAD
THEN LET'S GET THIS OVER WITH. PLEASE BE STILL WHILE I FOCUS.
BHEDA RADHA BHEDA ACINTYA GOVINDA...
RADHA JAYA NRSINGADEVA BEDHA...
GAURI BEDH--
--MY GODS, I--FEEL IT, I--

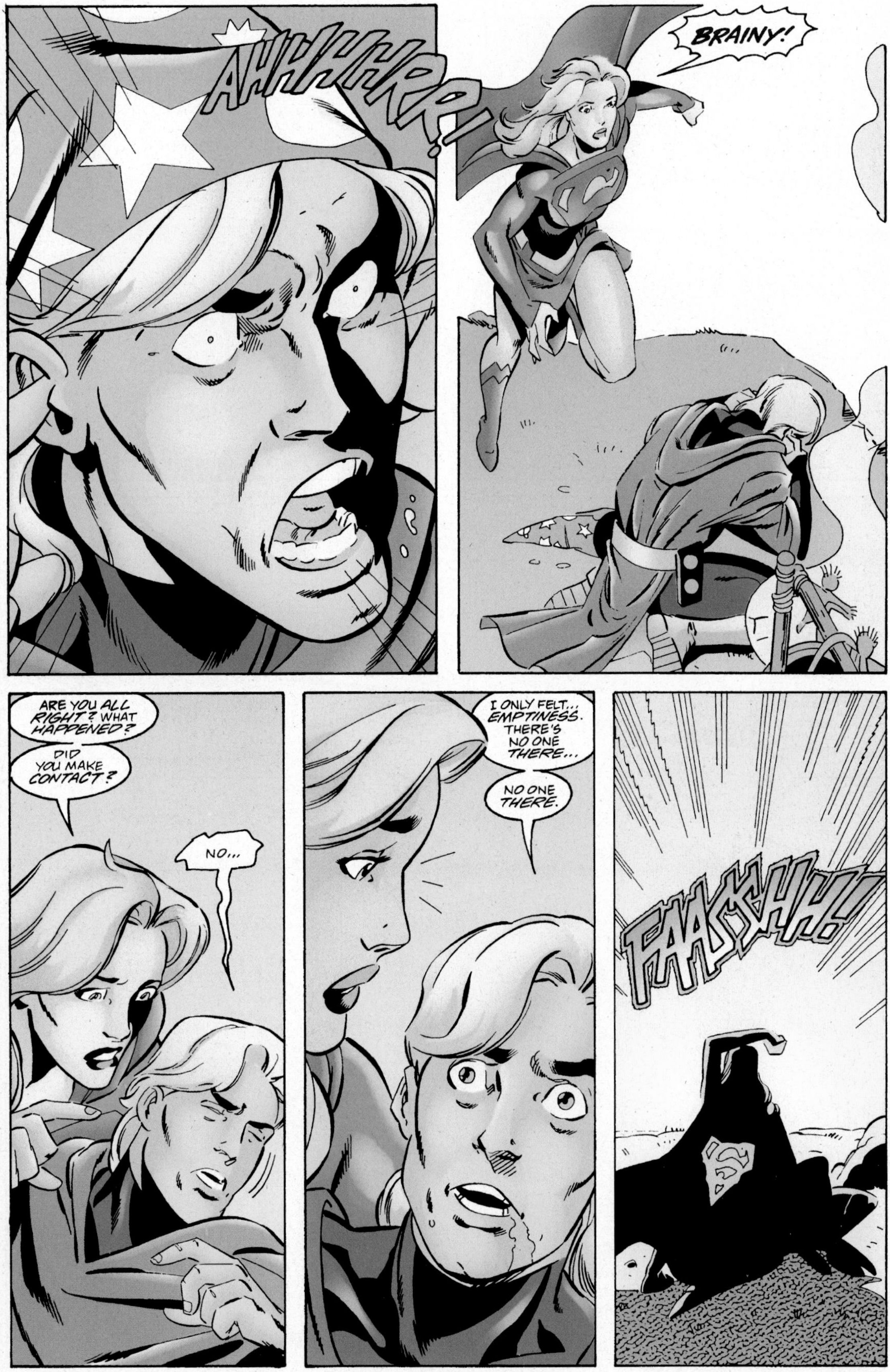
AHHHHRR!
BRAINY!
ARE YOU ALL RIGHT? WHAT HAPPENED?
DID YOU MAKE CONTACT?
NO...
I ONLY FELT... EMPTINESS. THERE'S NO ONE THERE...
NO ONE THERE.
FAASHH!

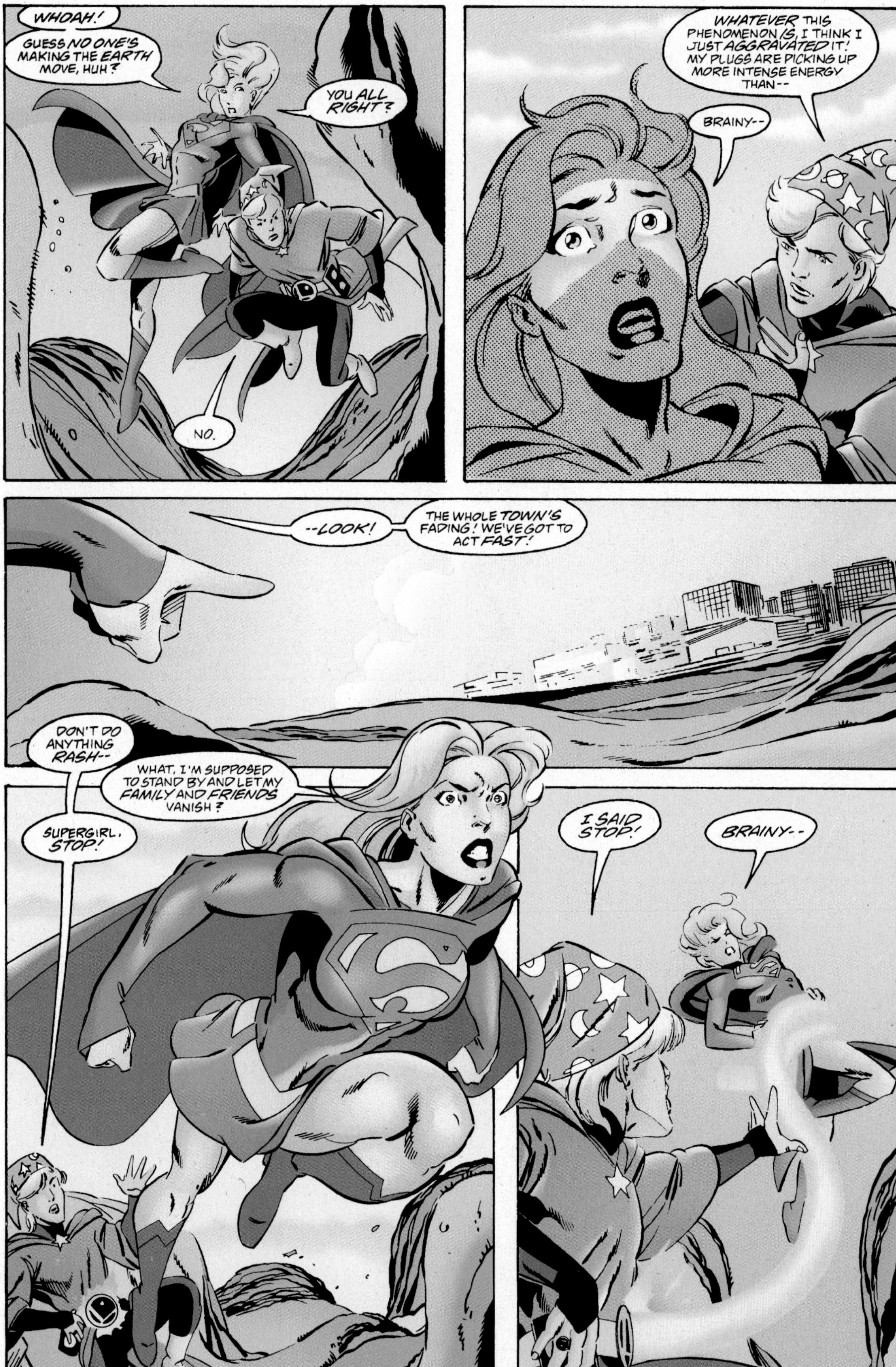
WHOAH!
GUESS NO ONE'S MAKING THE EARTH MOVE, HUH?
YOU ALL RIGHT?
NO.
WHATEVER THIS PHENOMENON IS, I THINK I JUST AGGRAVATED IT! MY PLUGS ARE PICKING UP MORE INTENSE ENERGY THAN--
BRAINY--
--LOOK!
THE WHOLE TOWN'S FADING! WE'VE GOT TO ACT FAST!
DON'T DO ANYTHING RASH--
WHAT, I'M SUPPOSED TO STAND BY AND LET MY FAMILY AND FRIENDS VANISH?
SUPERGIRL, STOP!
I SAID STOP!
BRAINY--

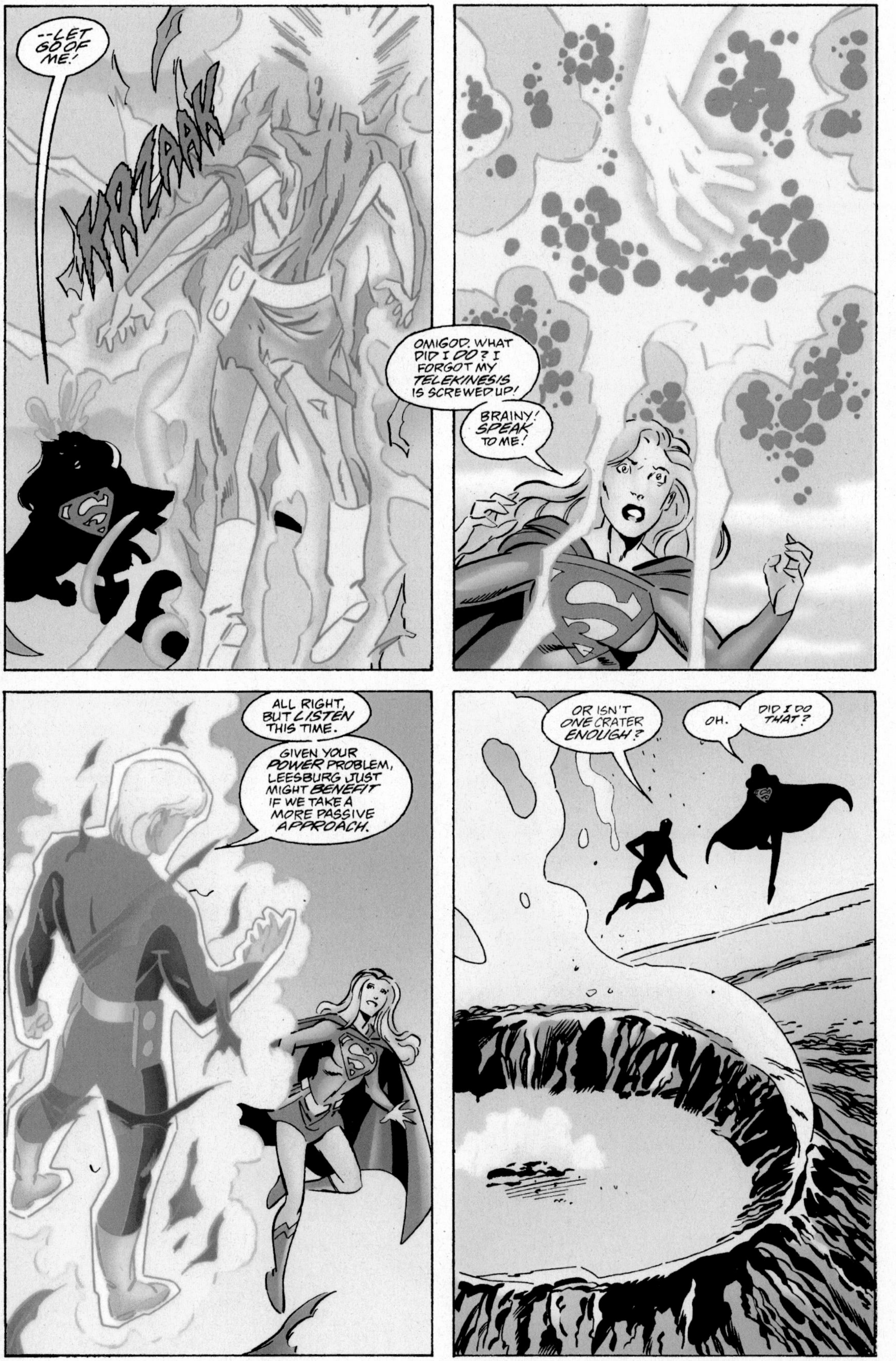
--LET GO OF ME!
KRZAAK
OMIGOD. WHAT DID I DO? I FORGOT MY TELEKINESIS IS SCREWED UP!
BRAINY! SPEAK TO ME!
ALL RIGHT, BUT LISTEN THIS TIME.
GIVEN YOUR POWER PROBLEM, LEESBURG JUST MIGHT BENEFIT IF WE TAKE A MORE PASSIVE APPROACH.
OR ISN'T ONE CRATER ENOUGH?
OH.
DID I DO THAT?

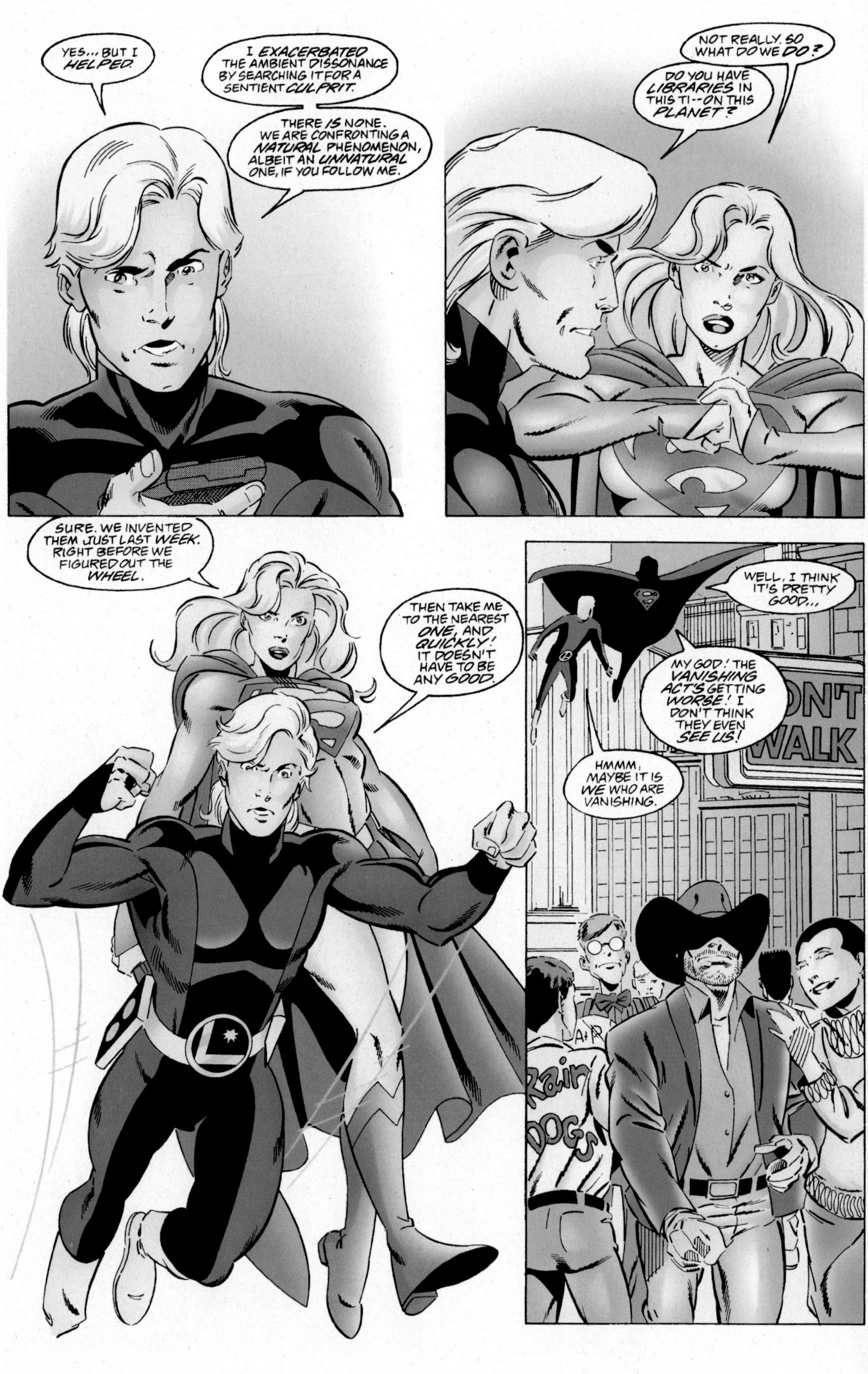
YES... BUT I HELPED.
I EXACERBATED THE AMBIENT DISSONANCE BY SEARCHING IT FOR A SENTIENT CULPRIT.
THERE IS NONE. WE ARE CONFRONTING A NATURAL PHENOMENON, ALBEIT AN UNNATURAL ONE, IF YOU FOLLOW ME.
NOT REALLY. SO WHAT DO WE DO?
DO YOU HAVE LIBRARIES IN THIS TI--ON THIS PLANET?
SURE. WE INVENTED THEM JUST LAST WEEK. RIGHT BEFORE WE FIGURED OUT THE WHEEL.
THEN TAKE ME TO THE NEAREST ONE, AND QUICKLY! IT DOESN'T HAVE TO BE ANY GOOD.
WELL, I THINK IT'S PRETTY GOOD...
MY GOD! THE VANISHING ACT'S GETTING WORSE! I DON'T THINK THEY EVEN SEE US!
HMMM, MAYBE IT IS WE WHO ARE VANISHING.
DON'T WALK

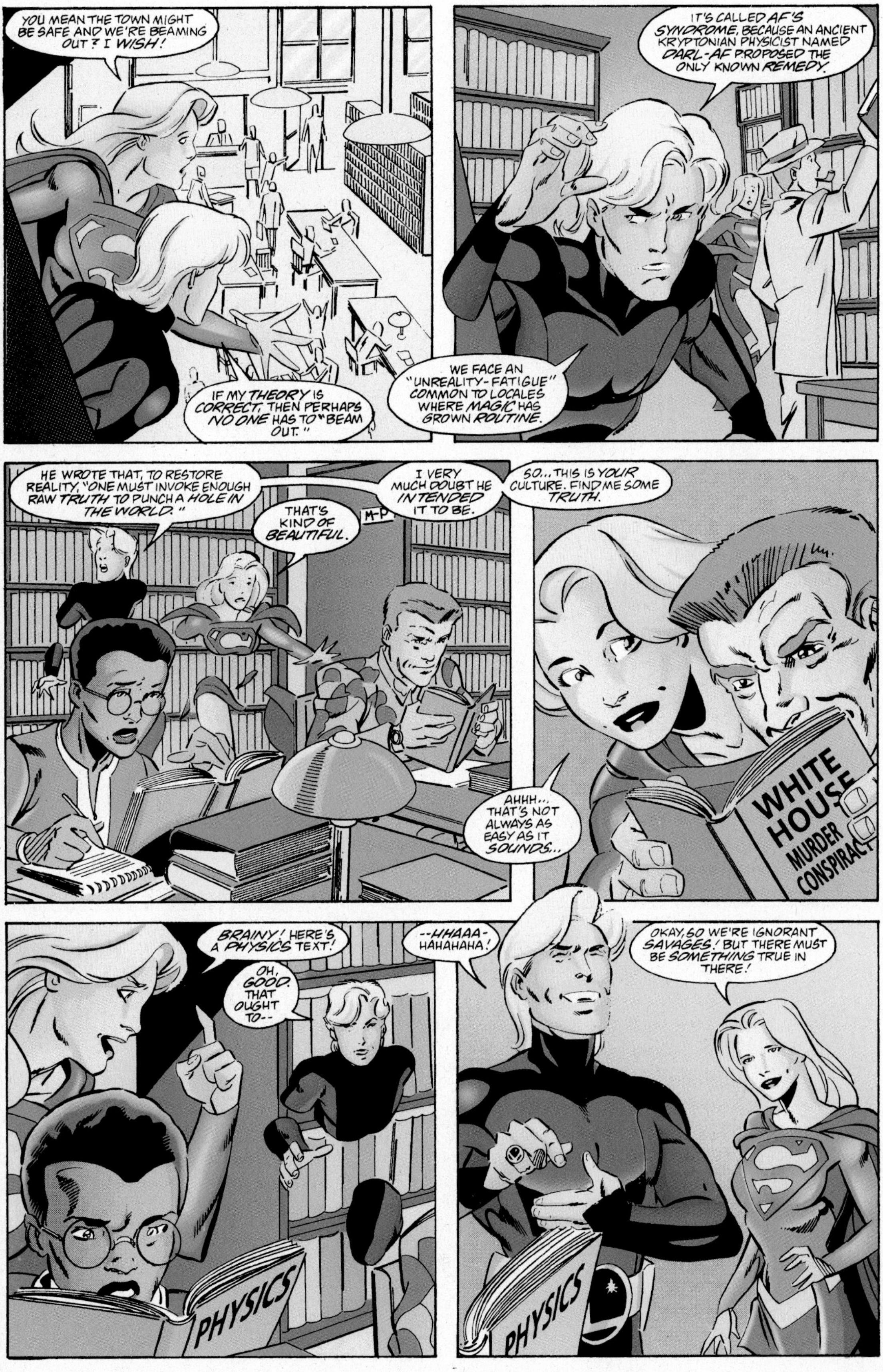
YOU MEAN THE TOWN MIGHT BE SAFE AND WE'RE BEAMING OUT? I WISH!
IT'S CALLED AF'S SYNDROME, BECAUSE AN ANCIENT KRYPTONIAN PHYSICIST NAMED DARL-AF PROPOSED THE ONLY KNOWN REMEDY.
IF MY THEORY IS CORRECT, THEN PERHAPS NO ONE HAS TO "BEAM OUT."
WE FACE AN "UNREALITY-FATIGUE" COMMON TO LOCALES WHERE MAGIC HAS GROWN ROUTINE.
HE WROTE THAT, TO RESTORE REALITY, "ONE MUST INVOKE ENOUGH RAW TRUTH TO PUNCH A HOLE IN THE WORLD."
THAT'S KIND OF BEAUTIFUL.
I VERY MUCH DOUBT HE INTENDED IT TO BE.
M-P
SO... THIS IS YOUR CULTURE. FIND ME SOME TRUTH.
AHHH... THAT'S NOT ALWAYS AS EASY AS IT SOUNDS...
WHITE HOUSE MURDER CONSPIRACY
BRAINY! HERE'S A PHYSICS TEXT!
OH, GOOD. THAT OUGHT TO--
--HHAAA-HAHAHAHA!
OKAY, SO WE'RE IGNORANT SAVAGES! BUT THERE MUST BE SOMETHING TRUE IN THERE!
PHYSICS
PHYSICS

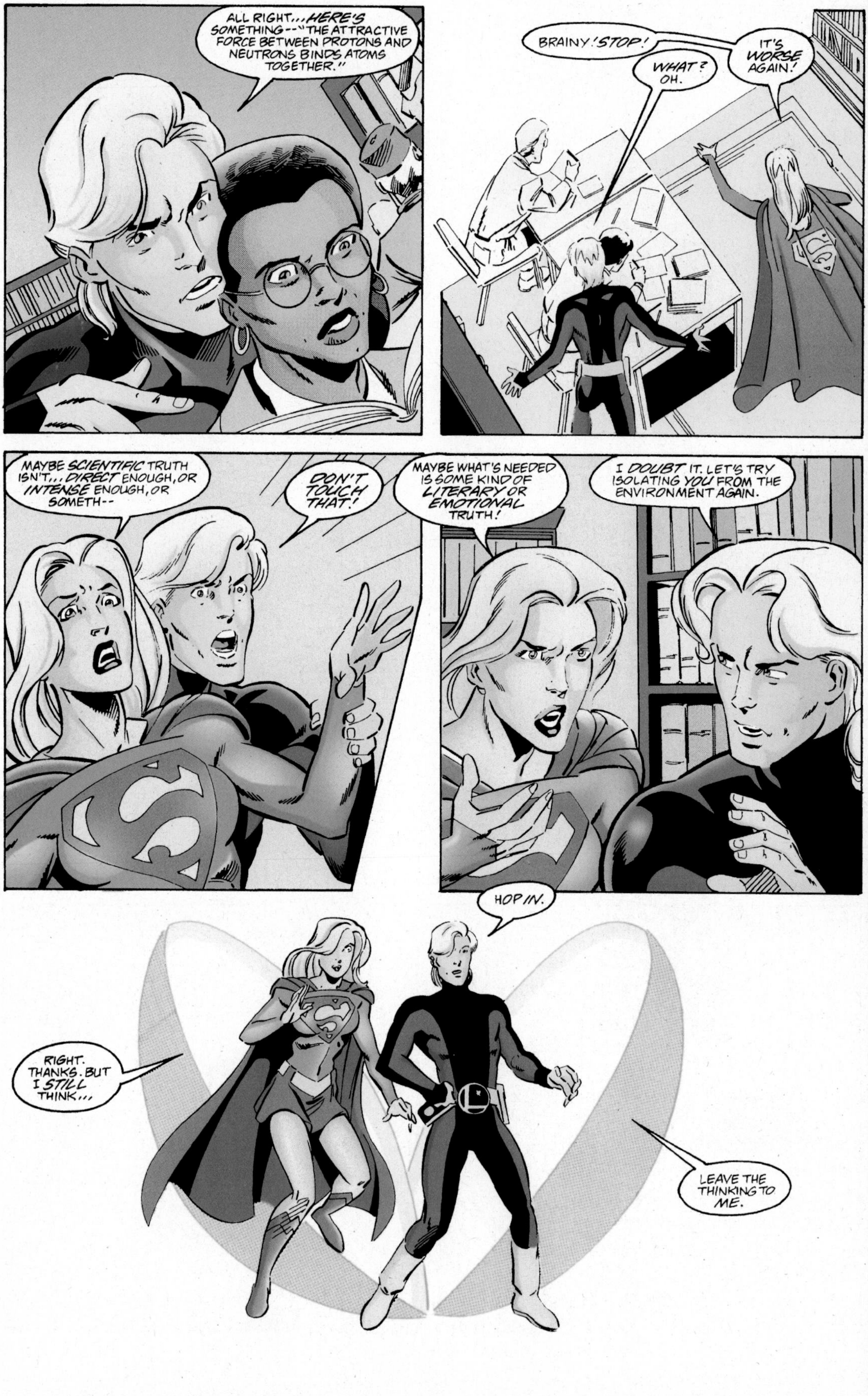
ALL RIGHT... HERE'S SOMETHING--"THE ATTRACTIVE FORCE BETWEEN PROTONS AND NEUTRONS BINDS ATOMS TOGETHER."
BRAINY! STOP!
IT'S WORSE AGAIN!
WHAT? OH.
MAYBE SCIENTIFIC TRUTH ISN'T... DIRECT ENOUGH, OR INTENSE ENOUGH, OR SOMETH--
DON'T TOUCH THAT!
MAYBE WHAT'S NEEDED IS SOME KIND OF LITERARY OR EMOTIONAL TRUTH!
I DOUBT IT. LET'S TRY ISOLATING YOU FROM THE ENVIRONMENT AGAIN.
HOP IN.
RIGHT. THANKS. BUT I STILL THINK...
LEAVE THE THINKING TO ME.

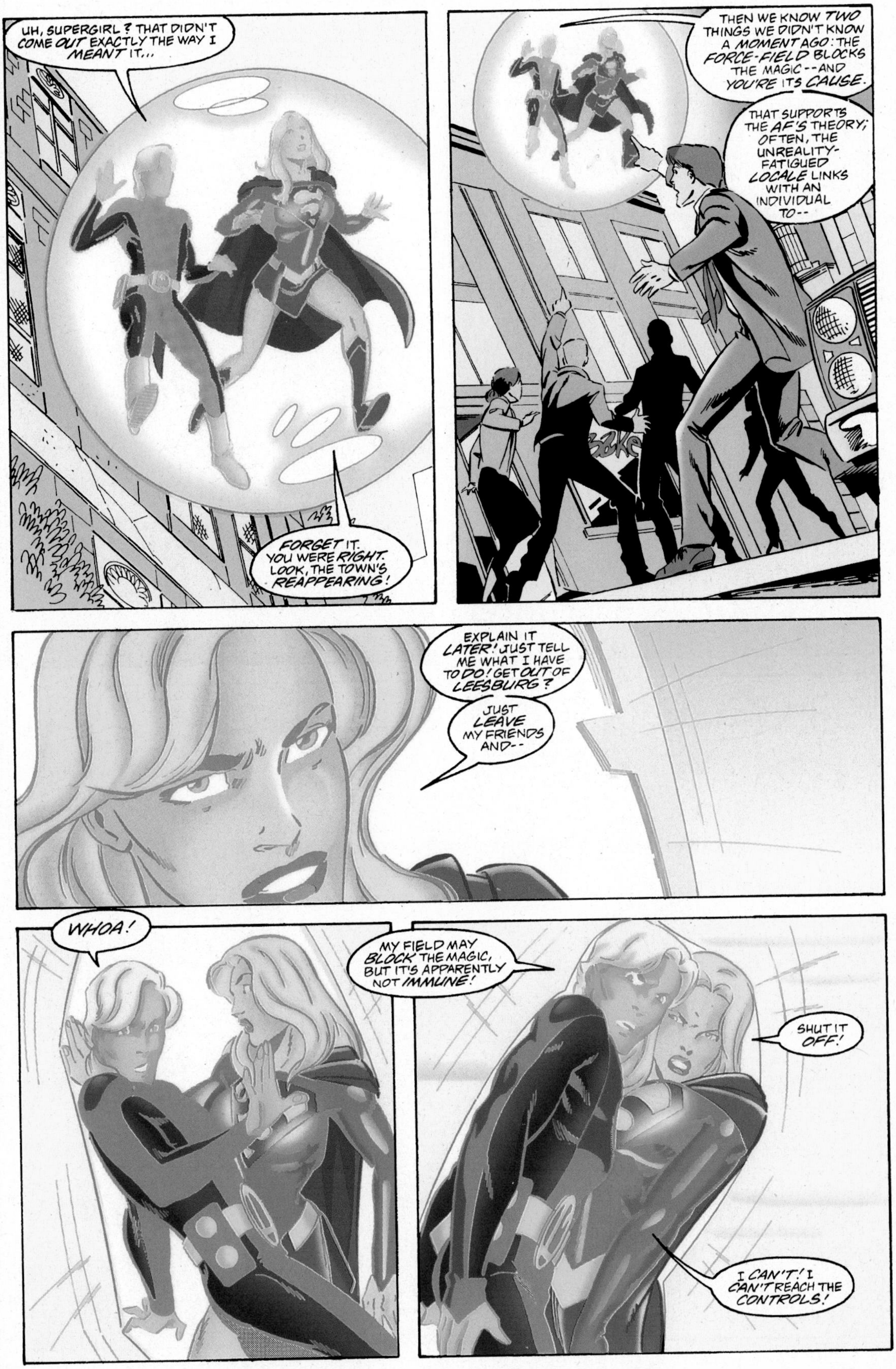

UH, SUPERGIRL? THAT DIDN'T COME OUT EXACTLY THE WAY I MEANT IT...
FORGET IT. YOU WERE RIGHT. LOOK, THE TOWN'S REAPPEARING!
THEN WE KNOW TWO THINGS WE DIDN'T KNOW A MOMENT AGO: THE FORCE-FIELD BLOCKS THE MAGIC--AND YOU'RE ITS CAUSE.
THAT SUPPORTS THE AF'S THEORY; OFTEN, THE UNREALITY-FATIGUED LOCALE LINKS WITH AN INDIVIDUAL TO--
EXPLAIN IT LATER! JUST TELL ME WHAT I HAVE TO DO! GET OUT OF LEESBURG?
JUST LEAVE MY FRIENDS AND--
WHOA!
MY FIELD MAY BLOCK THE MAGIC, BUT IT'S APPARENTLY NOT IMMUNE!
SHUT IT OFF!
I CAN'T! I CAN'T REACH THE CONTROLS!

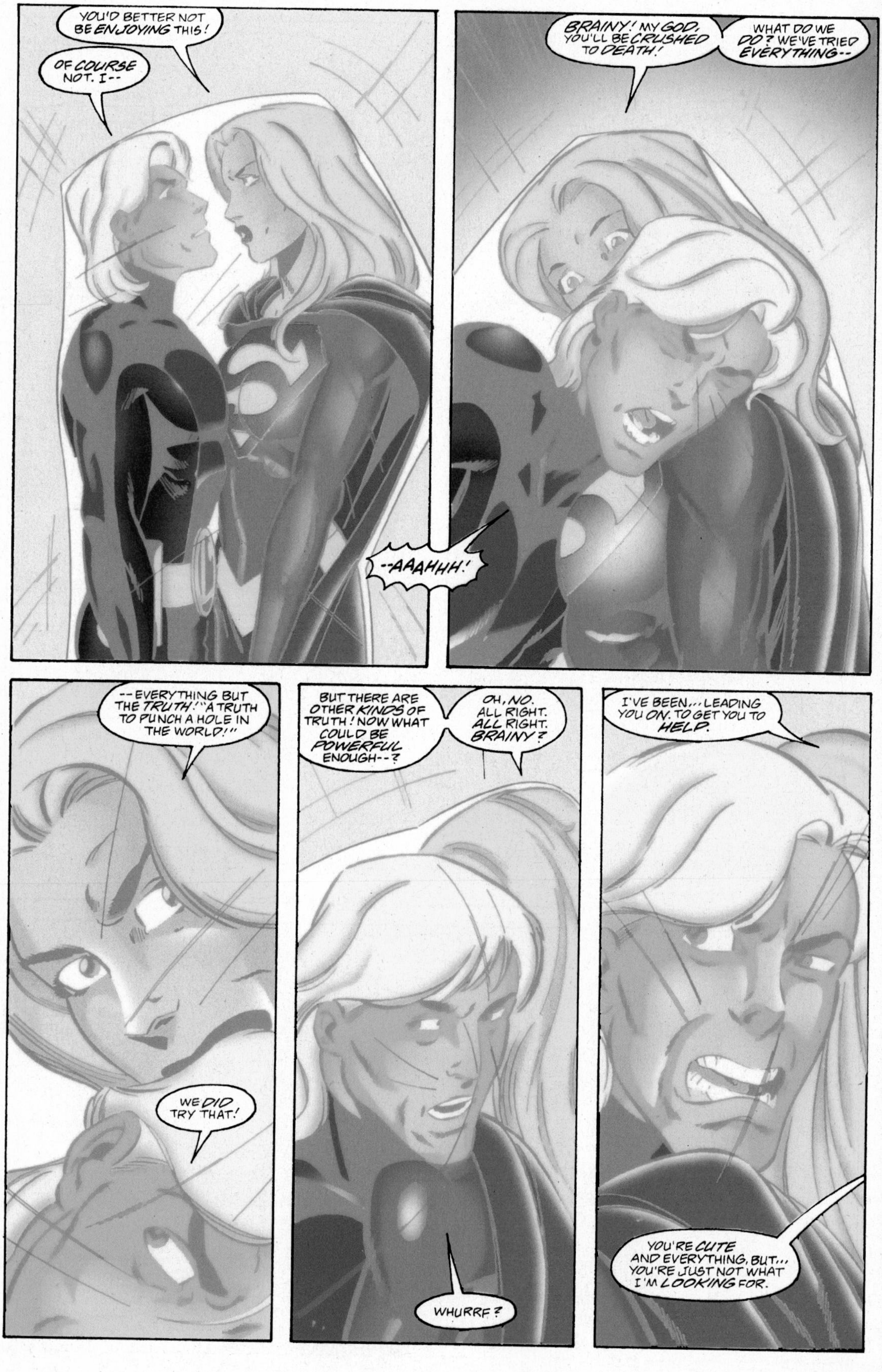

YOU'D BETTER NOT BE ENJOYING THIS!
OF COURSE NOT. I--
BRAINY! MY GOD, YOU'LL BE CRUSHED TO DEATH!
WHAT DO WE DO? WE'VE TRIED EVERYTHING--
--AAAHHH!
--EVERYTHING BUT THE TRUTH!' "A TRUTH TO PUNCH A HOLE IN THE WORLD!"
WE DID TRY THAT!
BUT THERE ARE OTHER KINDS OF TRUTH! NOW WHAT COULD BE POWERFUL ENOUGH--?
OH, NO. ALL RIGHT. ALL RIGHT. BRAINY?
WHURRF?
I'VE BEEN... LEADING YOU ON. TO GET YOU TO HELP.
YOU'RE CUTE AND EVERYTHING, BUT... YOU'RE JUST NOT WHAT I'M LOOKING FOR.

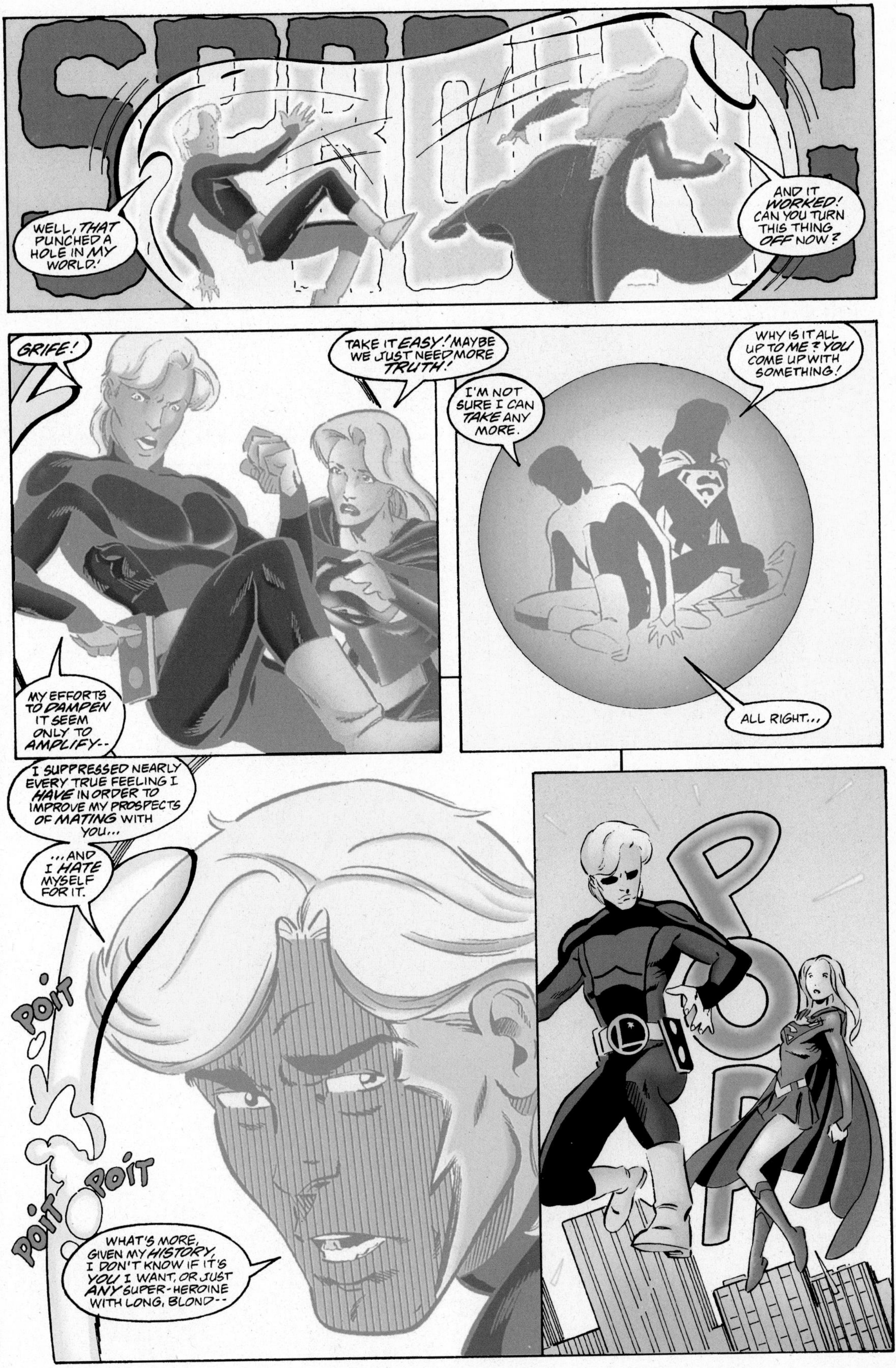

WELL, THAT PUNCHED A HOLE IN MY WORLD!
AND IT WORKED! CAN YOU TURN THIS THING OFF NOW?
GRIFE!
TAKE IT EASY! MAYBE WE JUST NEED MORE TRUTH!
MY EFFORTS TO DAMPEN IT SEEM ONLY TO AMPLIFY--
WHY IS IT ALL UP TO ME? YOU COME UP WITH SOMETHING!
I'M NOT SURE I CAN TAKE ANY MORE.
ALL RIGHT...
I SUPPRESSED NEARLY EVERY TRUE FEELING I HAVE IN ORDER TO IMPROVE MY PROSPECTS OF MATING WITH YOU...
...AND I HATE MYSELF FOR IT.
POIT
POIT
POIT
WHAT'S MORE, GIVEN MY HISTORY, I DON'T KNOW IF IT'S YOU I WANT, OR JUST ANY SUPER-HEROINE WITH LONG, BLOND--

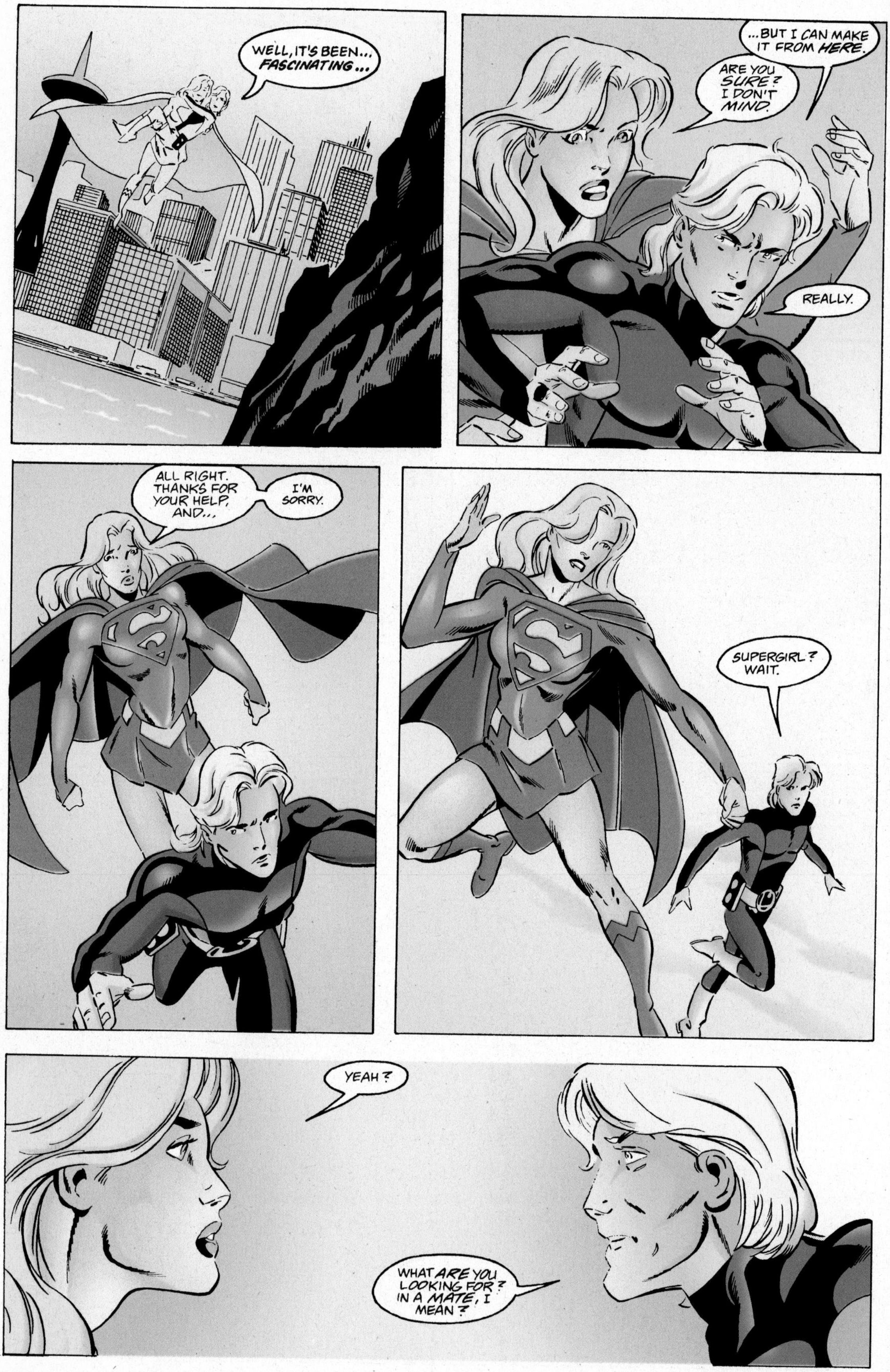
WELL, IT'S BEEN... FASCINATING...
...BUT I CAN MAKE IT FROM HERE.
ARE YOU SURE? I DON'T MIND.
REALLY.
ALL RIGHT. THANKS FOR YOUR HELP, AND...
I'M SORRY.
SUPERGIRL? WAIT.
YEAH?
WHAT ARE YOU LOOKING FOR? IN A MATE, I MEAN?

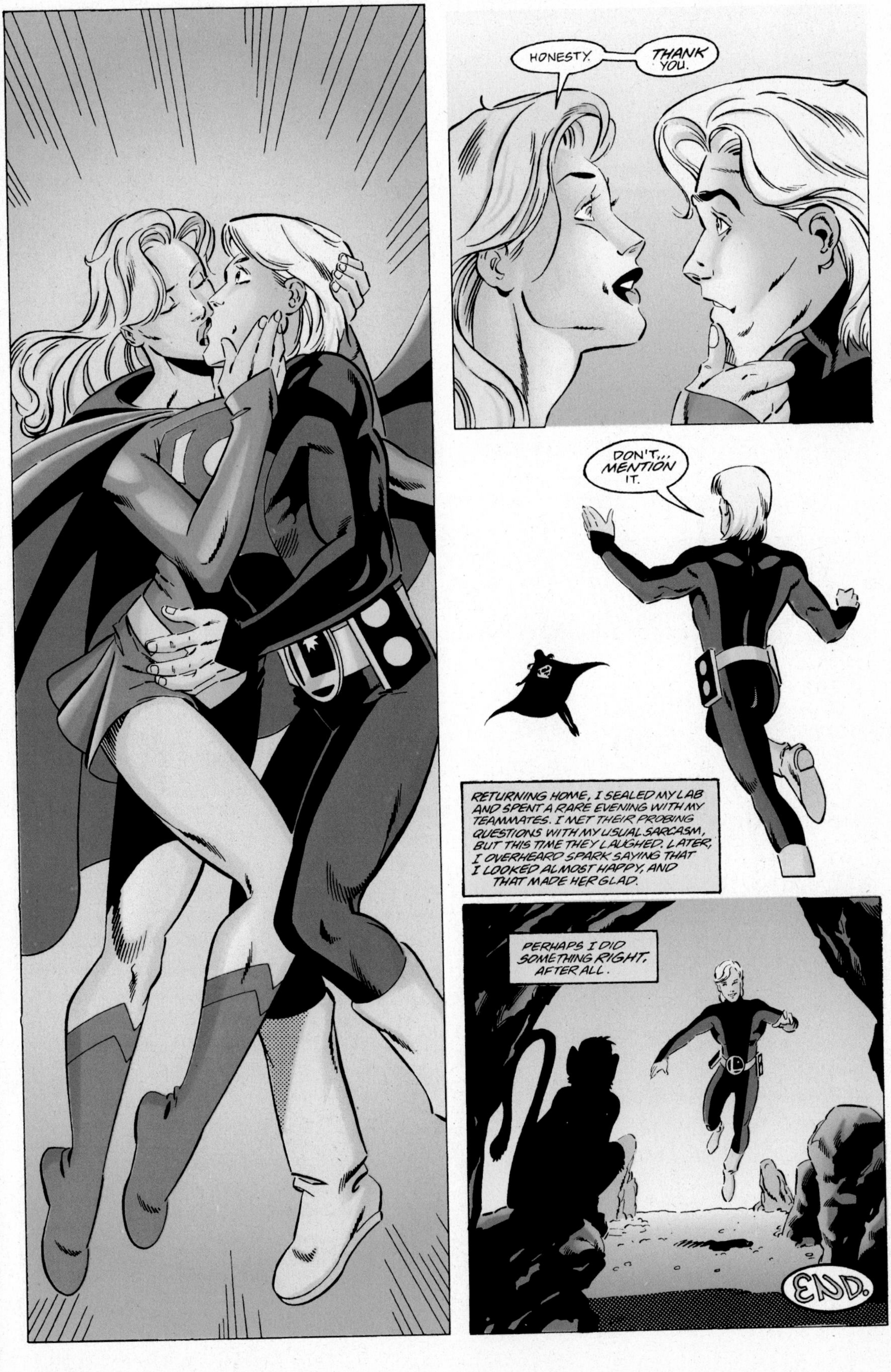
HONESTY.
THANK YOU.
DON'T... MENTION IT.
RETURNING HOME, I SEALED MY LAB AND SPENT A RARE EVENING WITH MY TEAMMATES. I MET THEIR PROBING QUESTIONS WITH MY USUAL SARCASM, BUT THIS TIME THEY LAUGHED. LATER, I OVERHEARD SPARK SAYING THAT I LOOKED ALMOST HAPPY, AND THAT MADE HER GLAD.
PERHAPS I DID SOMETHING RIGHT, AFTER ALL.
END.

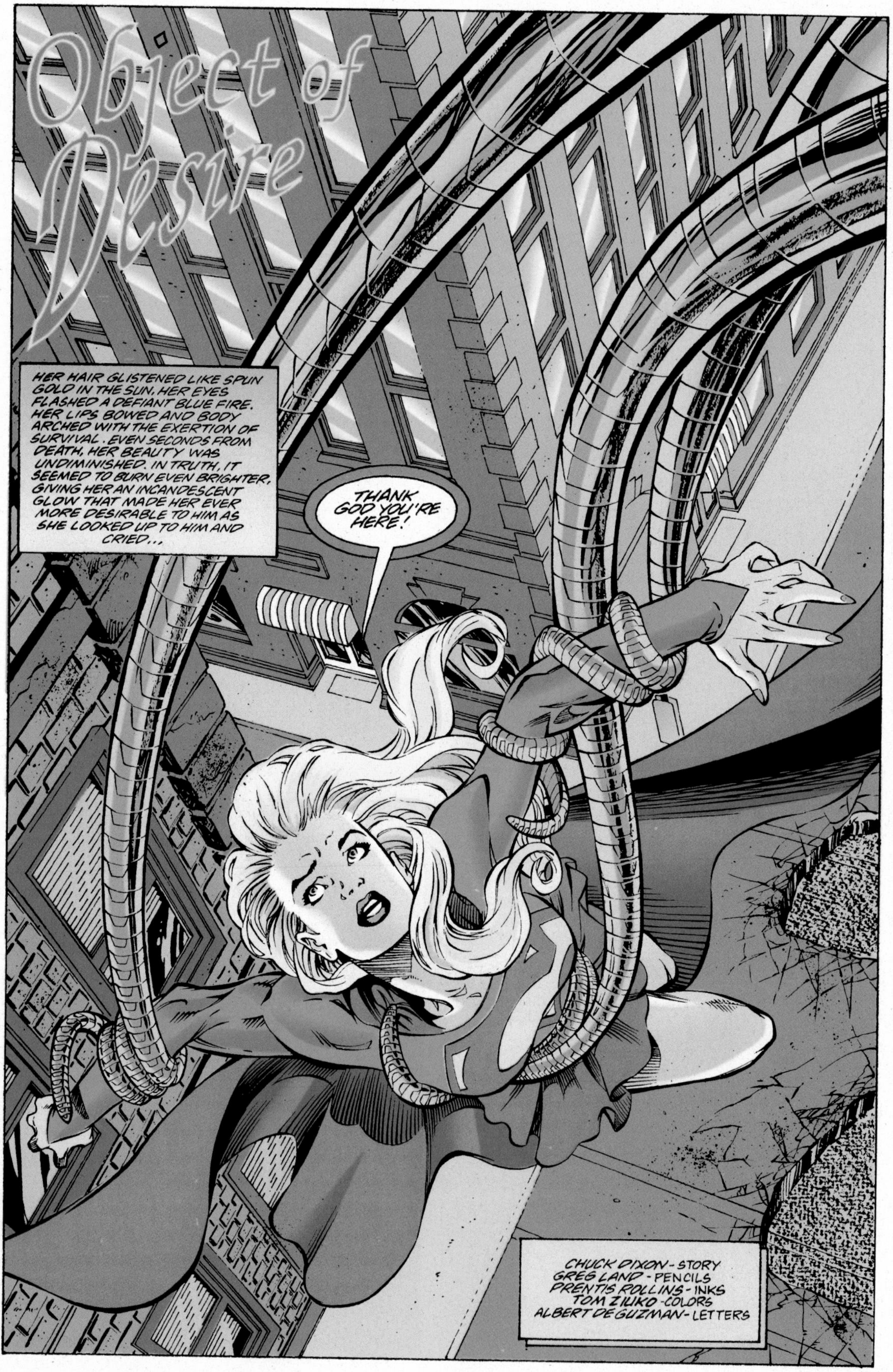
Object of Desire
HER HAIR GLISTENED LIKE SPUN GOLD IN THE SUN. HER EYES FLASHED A DEFIANT BLUE FIRE. HER LIPS BOWED AND BODY ARCHED WITH THE EXERTION OF SURVIVAL. EVEN SECONDS FROM DEATH, HER BEAUTY WAS UNDIMINISHED. IN TRUTH, IT SEEMED TO BURN EVEN BRIGHTER, GIVING HER AN INCANDESCENT GLOW THAT MADE HER EVER MORE DESIRABLE TO HIM AS SHE LOOKED UP TO HIM AND CRIED...
THANK GOD YOU'RE HERE!
CHUCK DIXON - STORY
GREG LAND - PENCILS
PRENTIS ROLLINS - INKS
TOM ZIUKO - COLORS
ALBERT DE GUZMAN - LETTERS

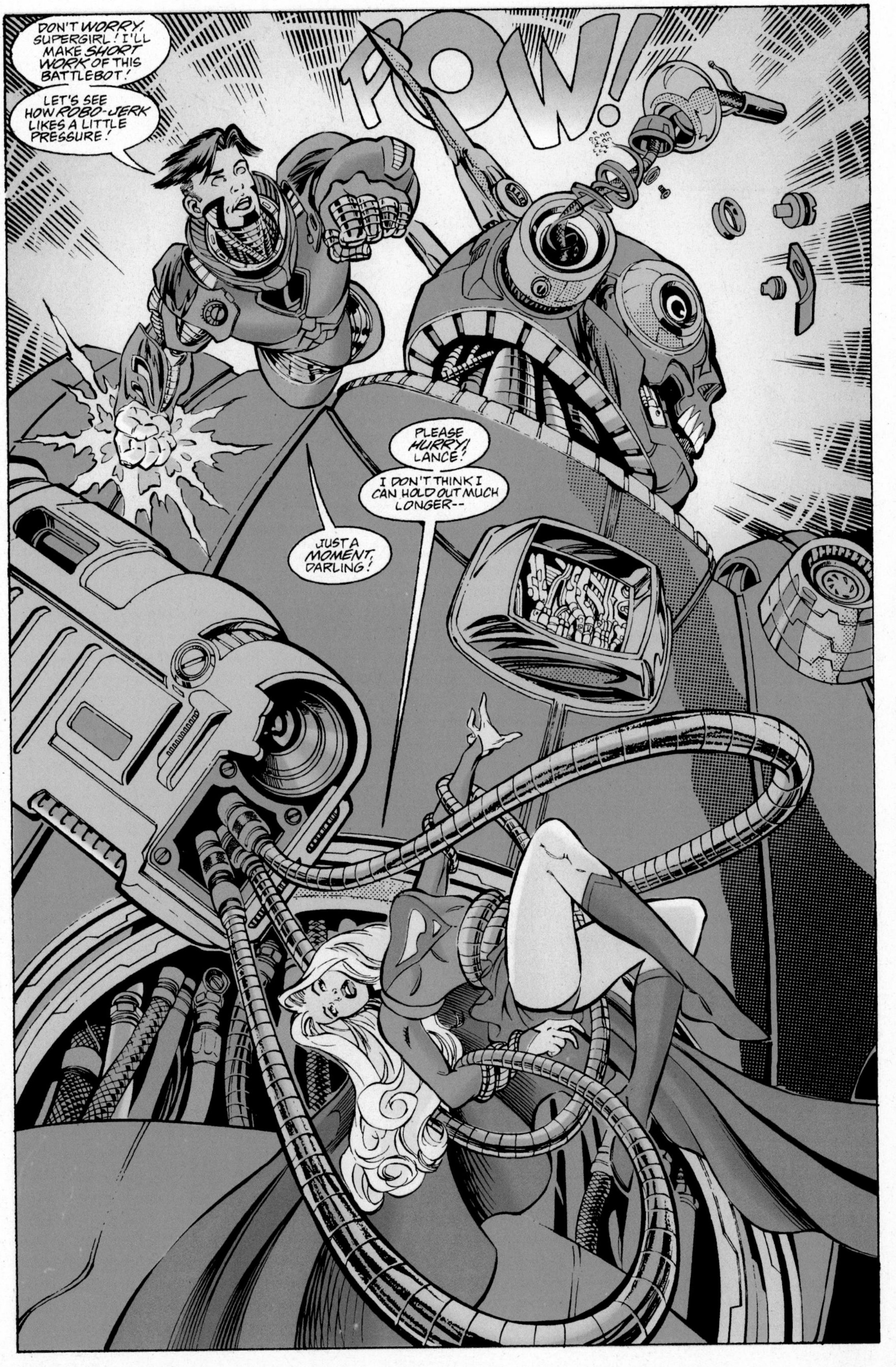

DON'T WORRY, SUPERGIRL! I'LL MAKE SHORT WORK OF THIS BATTLEBOT!
LET'S SEE HOW ROBO-JERK LIKES A LITTLE PRESSURE!
POW!
PLEASE HURRY, LANCE!
I DON'T THINK I CAN HOLD OUT MUCH LONGER--
JUST A MOMENT, DARLING!

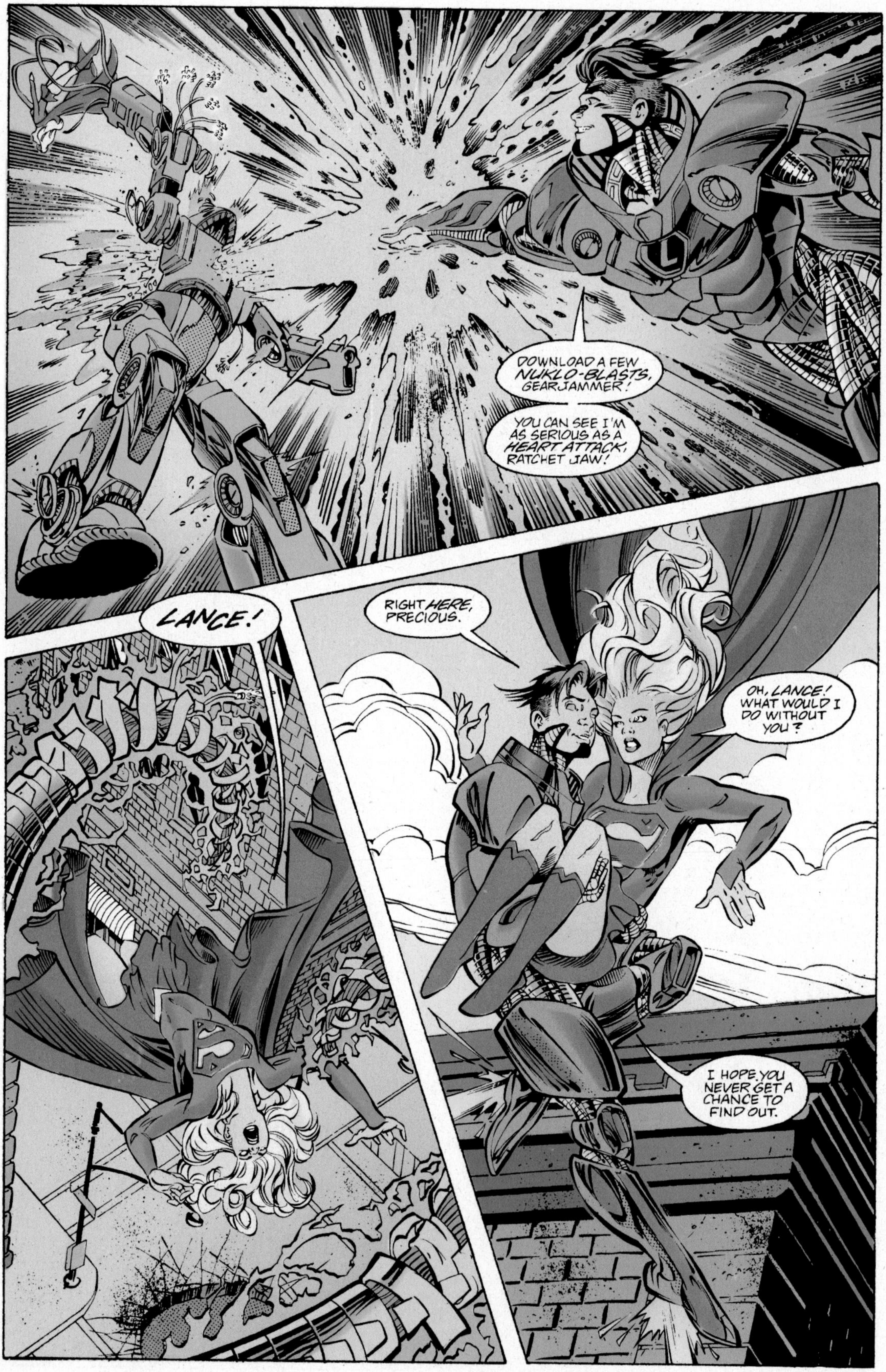
DOWNLOAD A FEW NUKLO-BLASTS, GEARJAMMER!
YOU CAN SEE I'M AS SERIOUS AS A HEART ATTACK, RATCHET JAW!
LANCE!
RIGHT HERE, PRECIOUS.
OH, LANCE! WHAT WOULD I DO WITHOUT YOU?
I HOPE YOU NEVER GET A CHANCE TO FIND OUT.

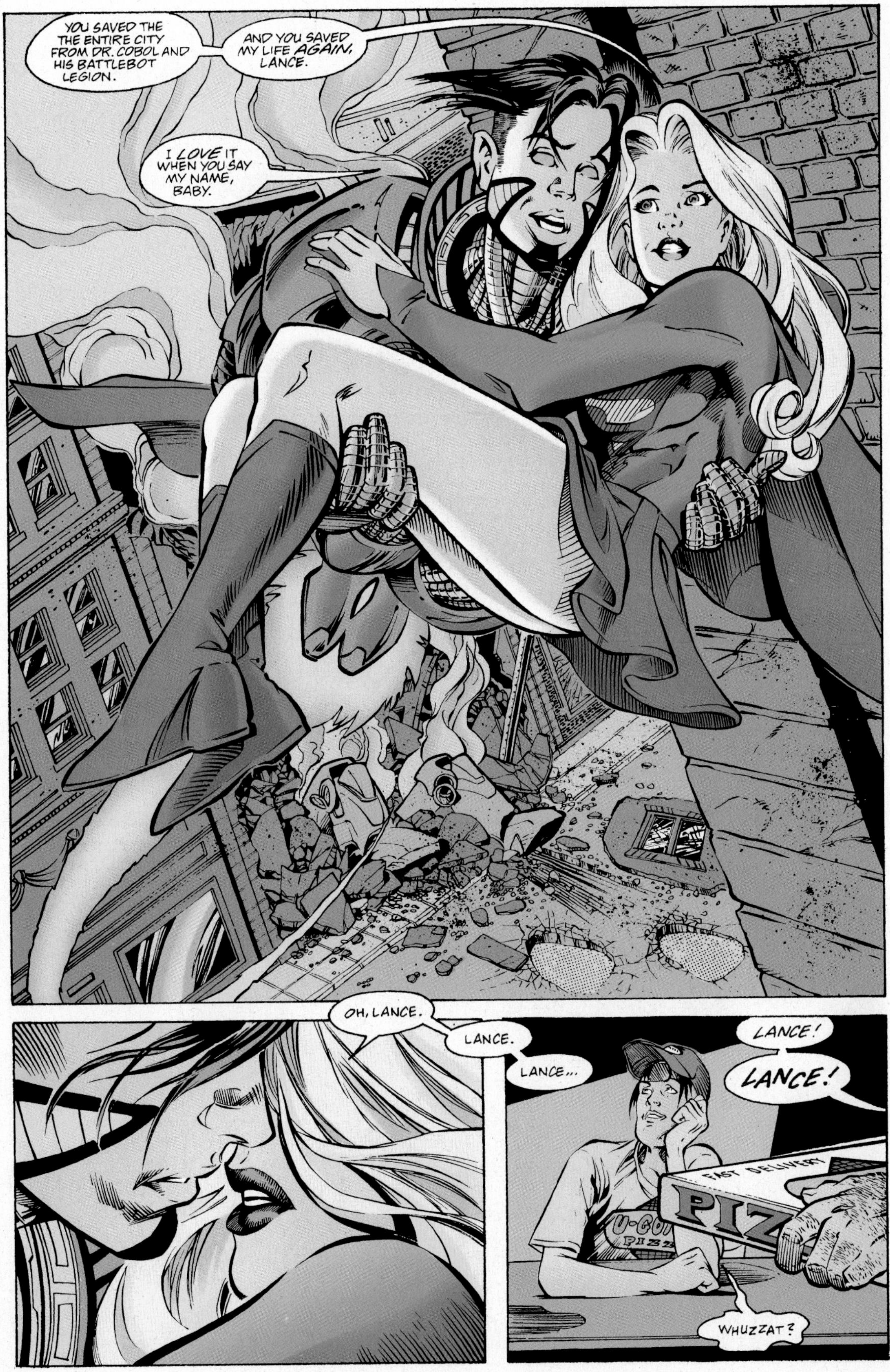

YOU SAVED THE THE ENTIRE CITY FROM DR. COBOL AND HIS BATTLEBOT LEGION.
AND YOU SAVED MY LIFE AGAIN, LANCE.
I LOVE IT WHEN YOU SAY MY NAME, BABY.
OH, LANCE.
LANCE.
LANCE...
LANCE!
LANCE!
FAST DELIVERY
PIZ
WHUZZAT?

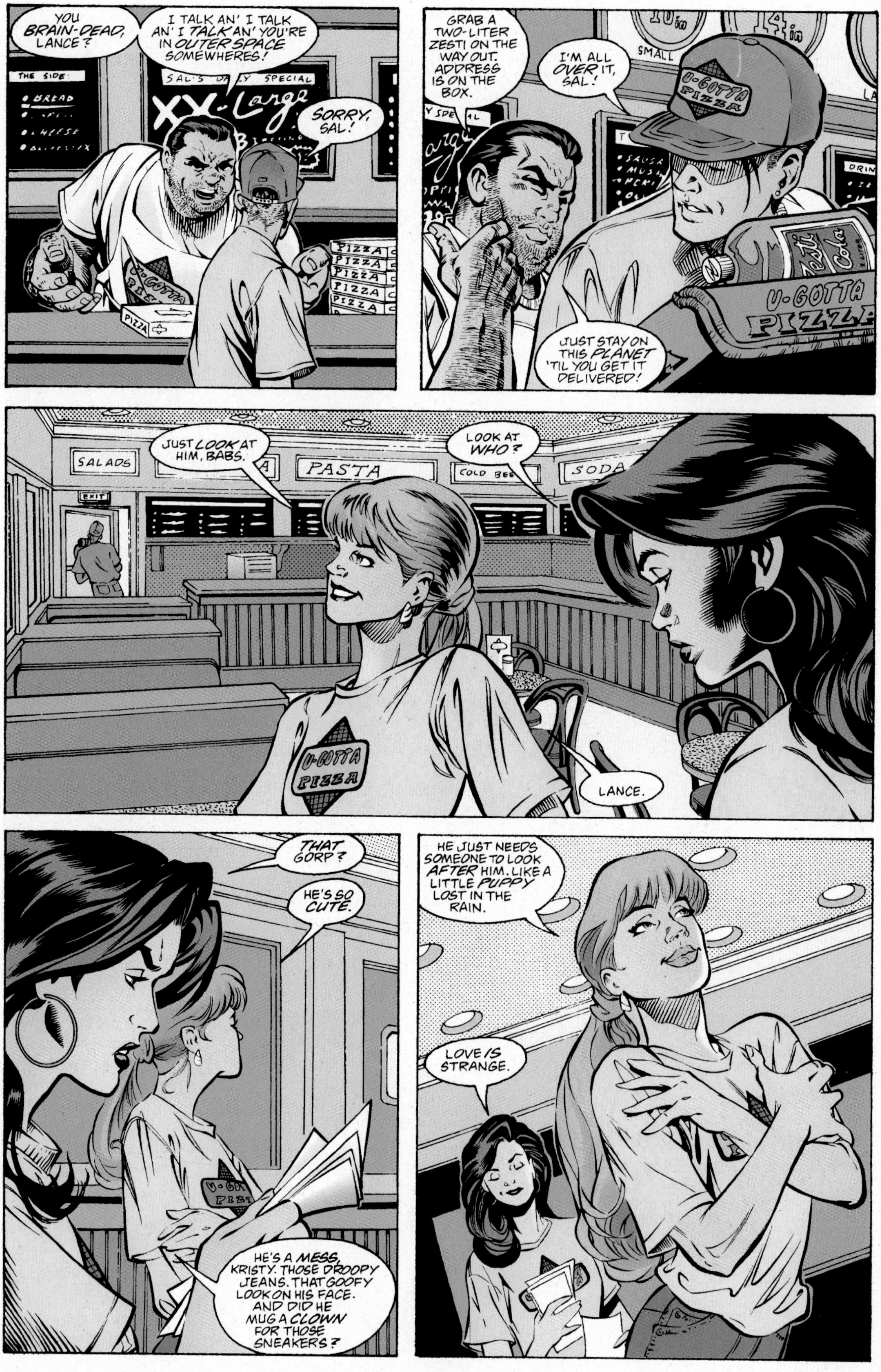
YOU BRAIN-DEAD, LANCE?
I TALK AN' I TALK AN' I TALK AN' YOU'RE IN OUTER SPACE SOMEWHERES!
SAL'S DAILY SPECIAL
XX-Large
SORRY, SAL!
PIZZA
GRAB A TWO-LITER ZESTI ON THE WAY OUT. ADDRESS IS ON THE BOX.
I'M ALL OVER IT, SAL!
SMALL
U-GOTTA PIZZA
Zesti Cola
JUST STAY ON THIS PLANET 'TIL YOU GET IT DELIVERED!
SALADS
PASTA
SODA
EXIT
JUST LOOK AT HIM, BABS.
LOOK AT WHO?
LANCE.
THAT GORP?
HE'S SO CUTE.
HE'S A MESS, KRISTY. THOSE DROOPY JEANS. THAT GOOFY LOOK ON HIS FACE. AND DID HE MUG A CLOWN FOR THOSE SNEAKERS?
HE JUST NEEDS SOMEONE TO LOOK AFTER HIM. LIKE A LITTLE PUPPY LOST IN THE RAIN.
LOVE IS STRANGE.

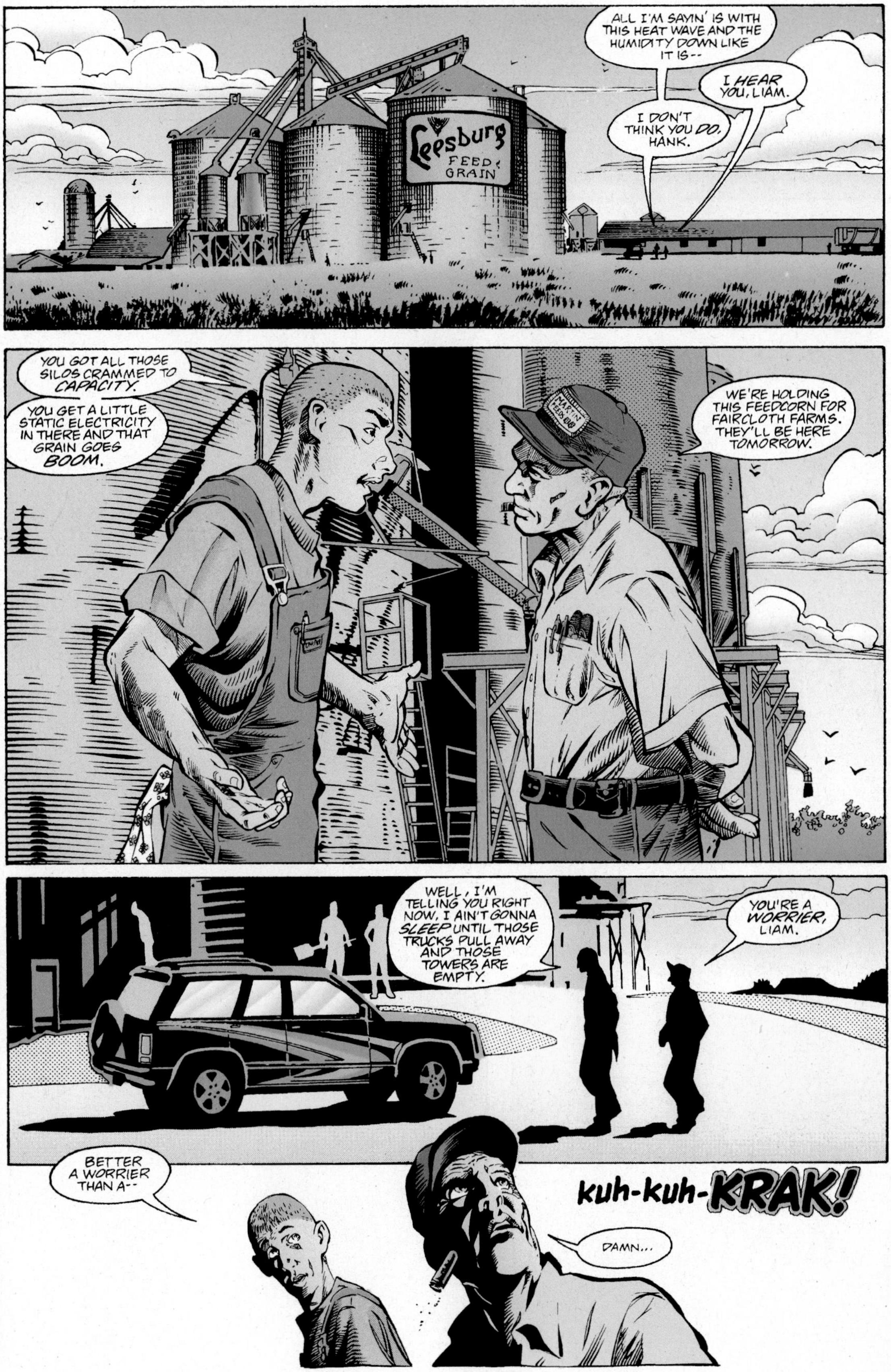
Leesburg FEED & GRAIN
ALL I'M SAYIN' IS WITH THIS HEAT WAVE AND THE HUMIDITY DOWN LIKE IT IS--
I HEAR YOU, LIAM.
I DON'T THINK YOU DO, HANK.
YOU GOT ALL THOSE SILOS CRAMMED TO CAPACITY.
YOU GET A LITTLE STATIC ELECTRICITY IN THERE AND THAT GRAIN GOES BOOM.
WE'RE HOLDING THIS FEEDCORN FOR FAIRCLOTH FARMS. THEY'LL BE HERE TOMORROW.
WELL, I'M TELLING YOU RIGHT NOW, I AIN'T GONNA SLEEP UNTIL THOSE TRUCKS PULL AWAY AND THOSE TOWERS ARE EMPTY.
YOU'RE A WORRIER, LIAM.
BETTER A WORRIER THAN A--
kuh-kuh-KRAK!
DAMN...

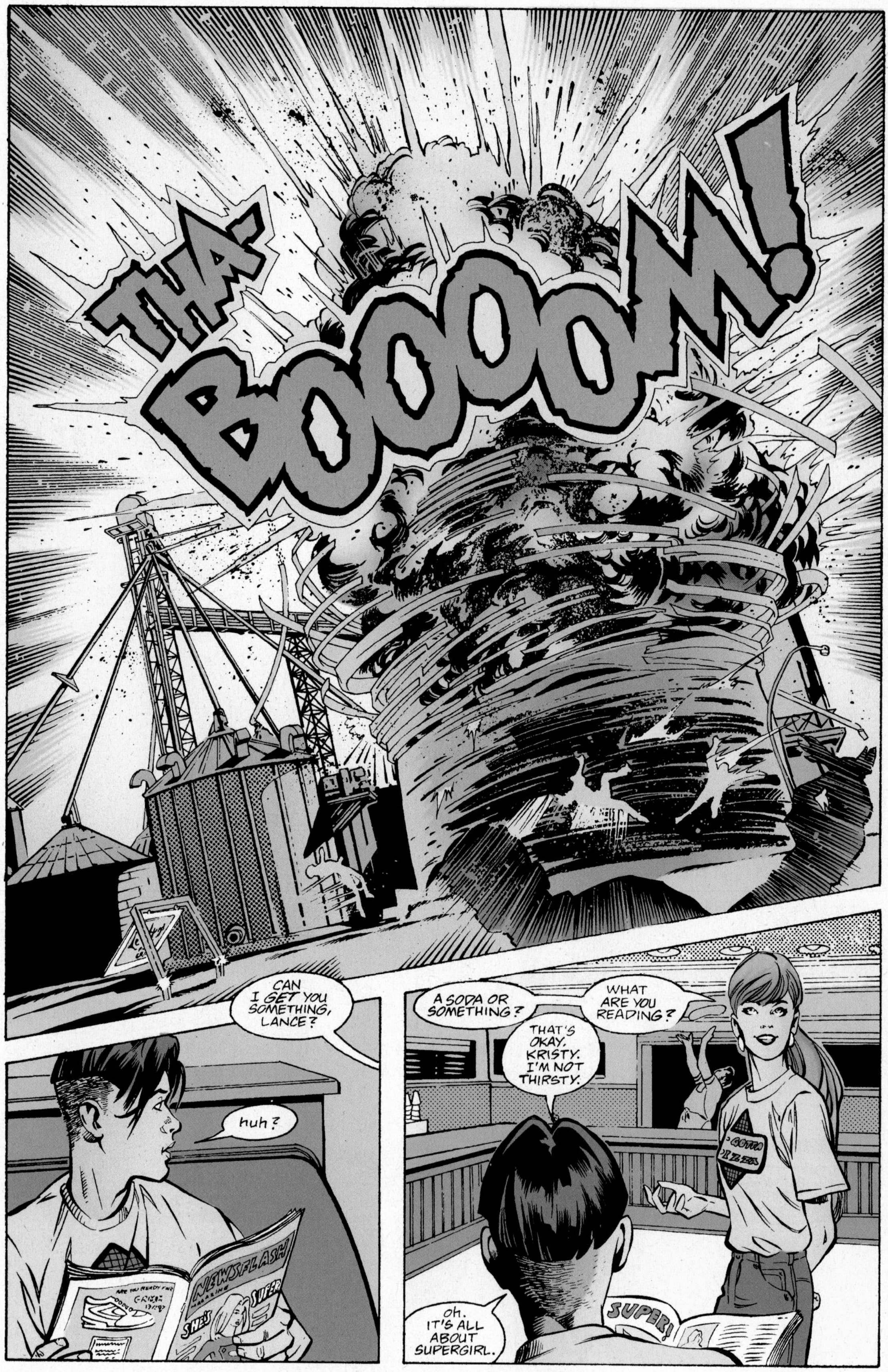
THA-BOOOOM!
CAN I GET YOU SOMETHING, LANCE?
huh?
A SODA OR SOMETHING?
WHAT ARE YOU READING?
THAT'S OKAY, KRISTY. I'M NOT THIRSTY.
oh. IT'S ALL ABOUT SUPERGIRL.
NEWSFLASH
SUPER!

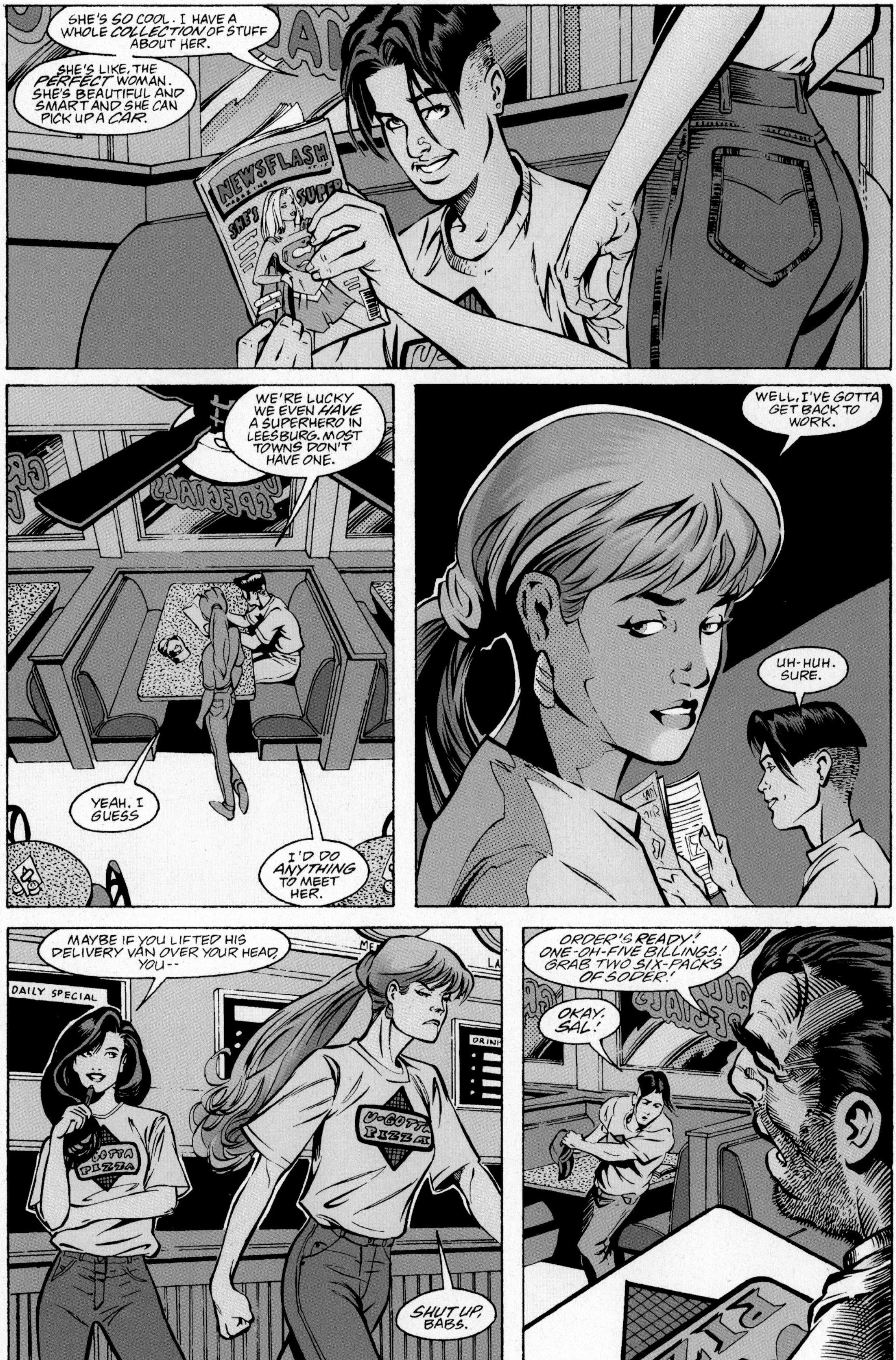

SHE'S SO COOL. I HAVE A WHOLE COLLECTION OF STUFF ABOUT HER.
SHE'S LIKE, THE PERFECT WOMAN. SHE'S BEAUTIFUL AND SMART AND SHE CAN PICK UP A CAR.
NEWSFLASH
SHE'S SUPER
WE'RE LUCKY WE EVEN HAVE A SUPERHERO IN LEESBURG. MOST TOWNS DON'T HAVE ONE.
SPECIALS
YEAH. I GUESS
I'D DO ANYTHING TO MEET HER.
WELL, I'VE GOTTA GET BACK TO WORK.
UH-HUH. SURE.
MAYBE IF YOU LIFTED HIS DELIVERY VAN OVER YOUR HEAD, YOU--
DAILY SPECIAL
U-GOTTA PIZZA
SHUT UP, BABS.
ORDER'S READY! ONE-OH-FIVE BILLINGS! GRAB TWO SIX-PACKS OF SODER!
OKAY, SAL!

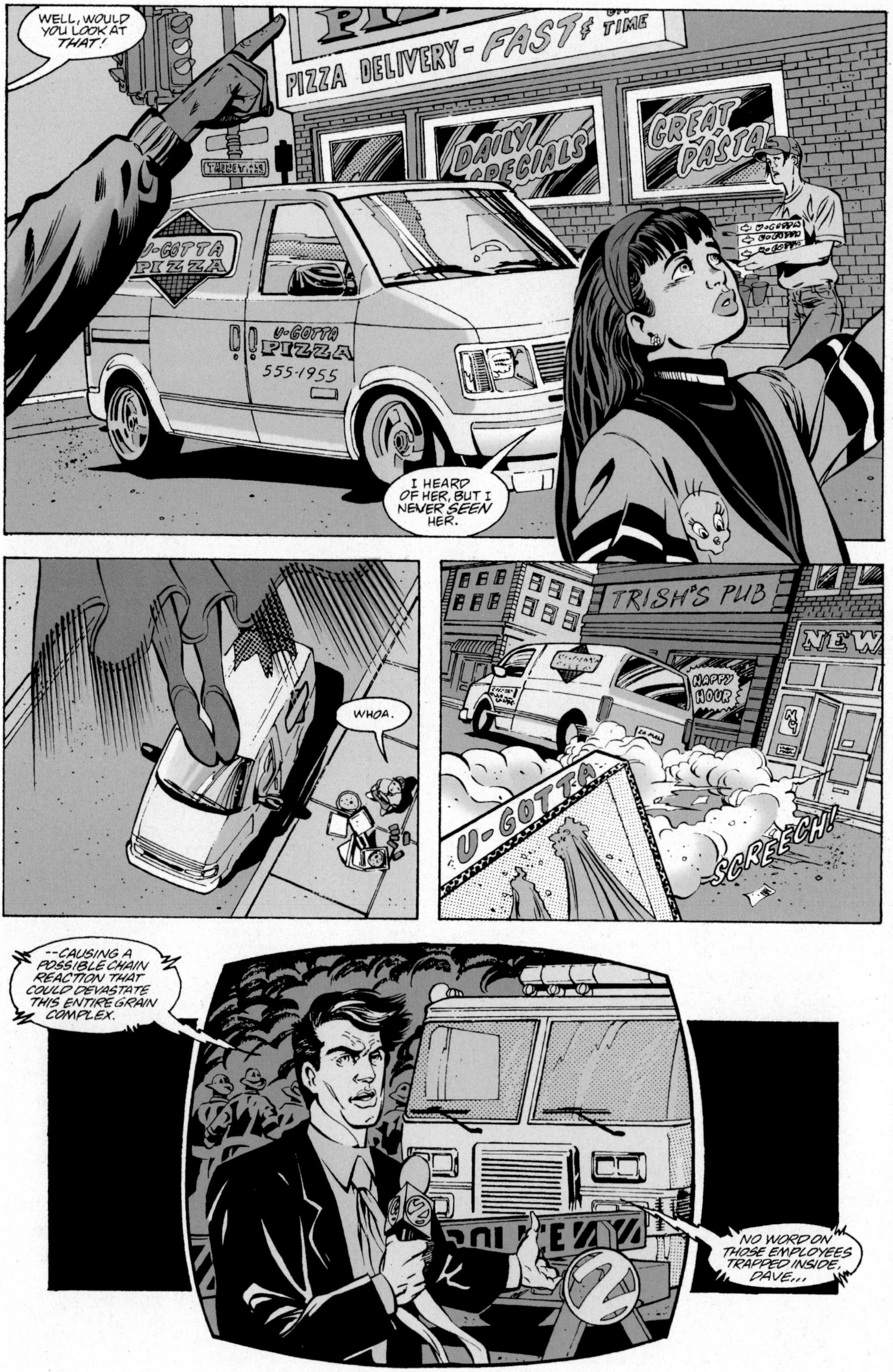

WELL, WOULD YOU LOOK AT *THAT!*
PIZZA DELIVERY- FAST & TIME
DAILY SPECIALS
GREAT PASTA
U-GOTTA PIZZA
U-GOTTA PIZZA 555-1955
I HEARD OF HER, BUT I NEVER *SEEN* HER.
WHOA.
TRISH'S PUB
HAPPY HOUR
U-GOTTA
SCREEECH!
--CAUSING A POSSIBLE CHAIN REACTION THAT COULD DEVASTATE THIS ENTIRE GRAIN COMPLEX.
NO WORD ON THOSE EMPLOYEES TRAPPED INSIDE, DAVE...

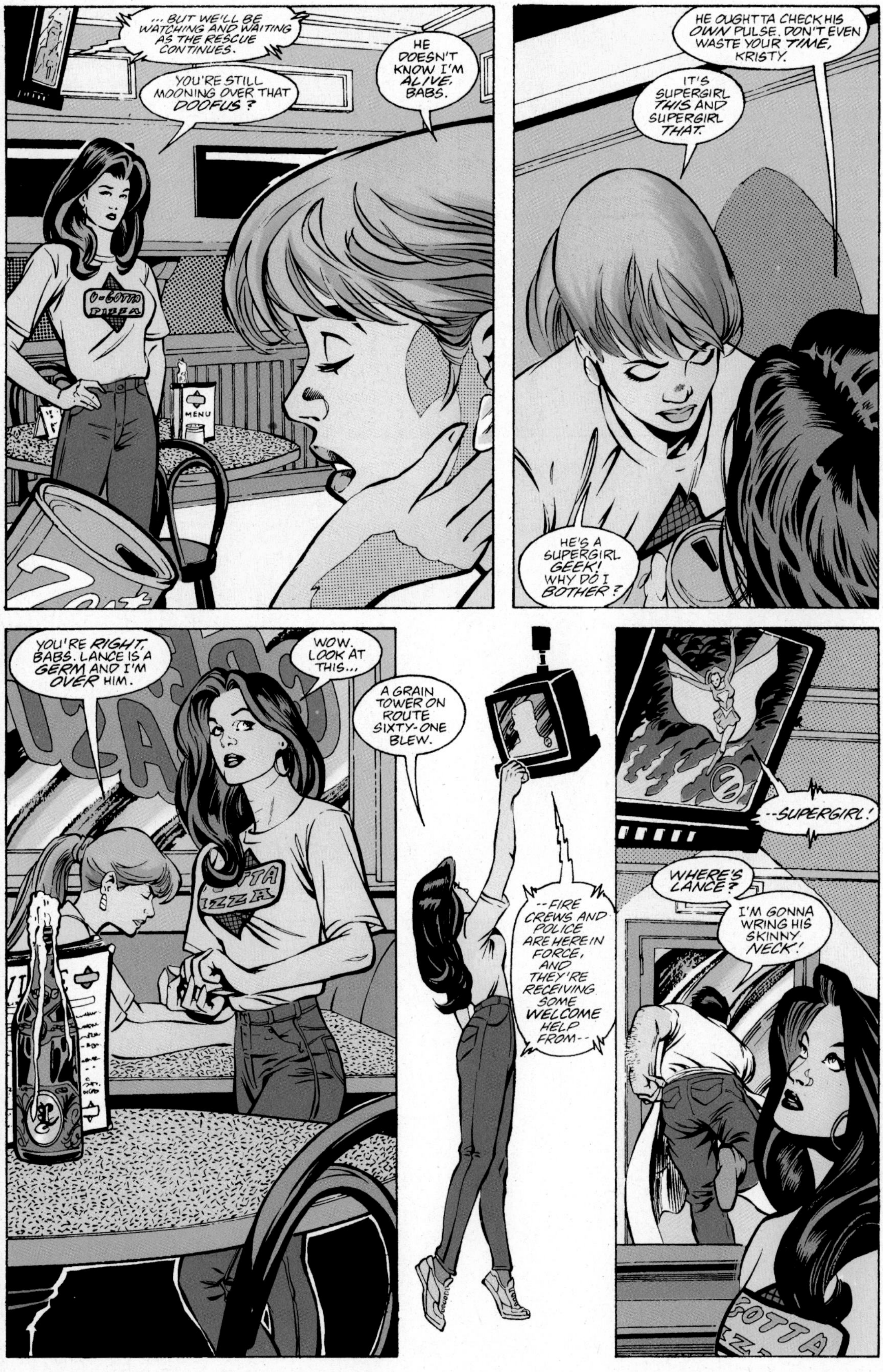
...BUT WE'LL BE WATCHING AND WAITING AS THE RESCUE CONTINUES.
YOU'RE STILL MOONING OVER THAT DOOFUS?
HE DOESN'T KNOW I'M ALIVE, BABS.
HE OUGHTTA CHECK HIS OWN PULSE. DON'T EVEN WASTE YOUR TIME, KRISTY.
IT'S SUPERGIRL THIS AND SUPERGIRL THAT.
HE'S A SUPERGIRL GEEK! WHY DO I BOTHER?
MENU
YOU'RE RIGHT, BABS. LANCE IS A GERM AND I'M OVER HIM.
WOW. LOOK AT THIS...
A GRAIN TOWER ON ROUTE SIXTY-ONE BLEW.
--FIRE CREWS AND POLICE ARE HERE IN FORCE, AND THEY'RE RECEIVING SOME WELCOME HELP FROM--
--SUPERGIRL!
WHERE'S LANCE?
I'M GONNA WRING HIS SKINNY NECK!

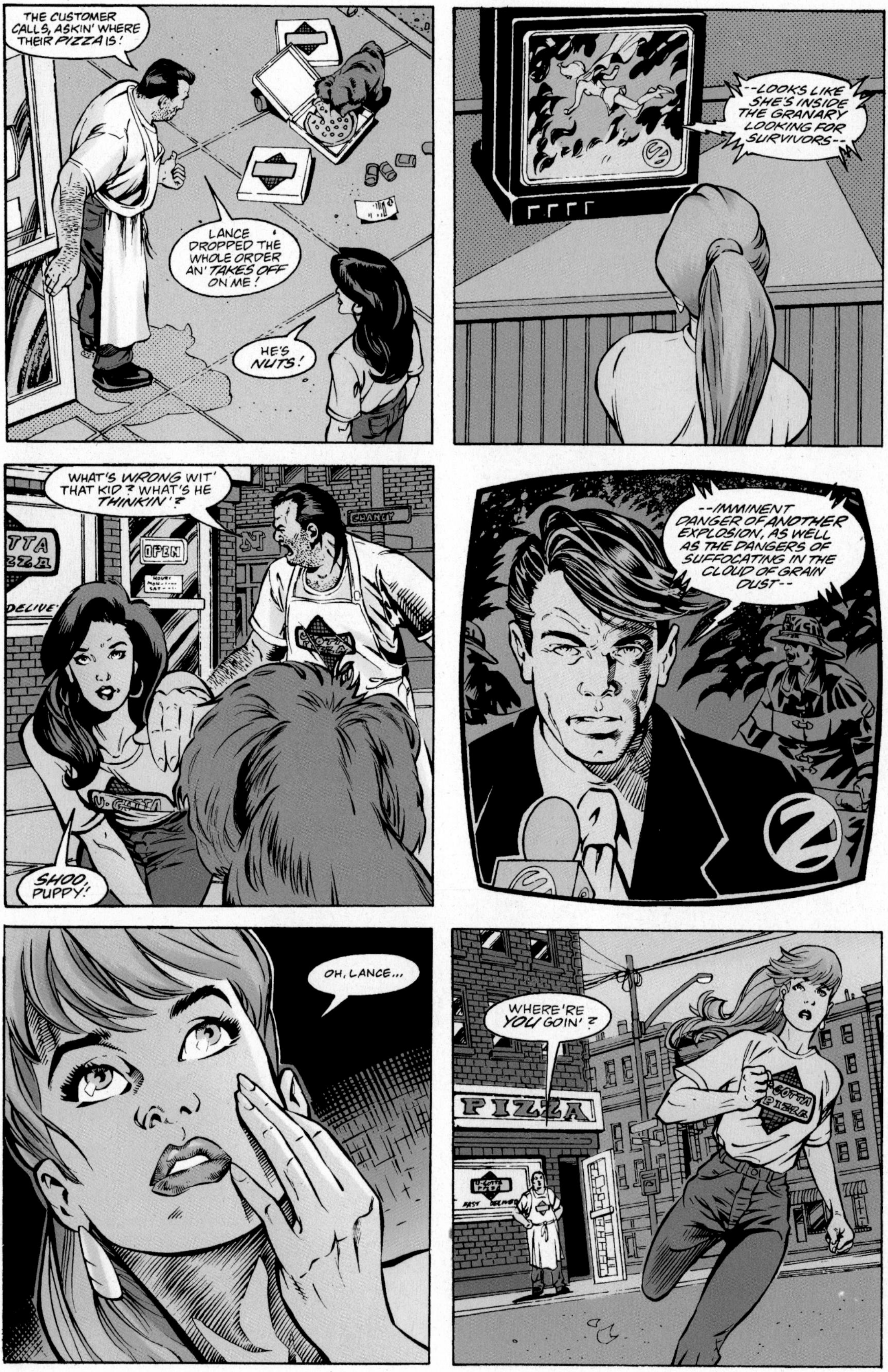
THE CUSTOMER CALLS, ASKIN' WHERE THEIR PIZZA IS!
LANCE DROPPED THE WHOLE ORDER AN' TAKES OFF ON ME!
HE'S NUTS!
--LOOKS LIKE SHE'S INSIDE THE GRANARY LOOKING FOR SURVIVORS--
WHAT'S WRONG WIT' THAT KID? WHAT'S HE THINKIN'?
SHOO, PUPPY!
--IMMINENT DANGER OF ANOTHER EXPLOSION, AS WELL AS THE DANGERS OF SUFFOCATING IN THE CLOUD OF GRAIN DUST--
OH, LANCE...
WHERE'RE YOU GOIN'?
PIZZA

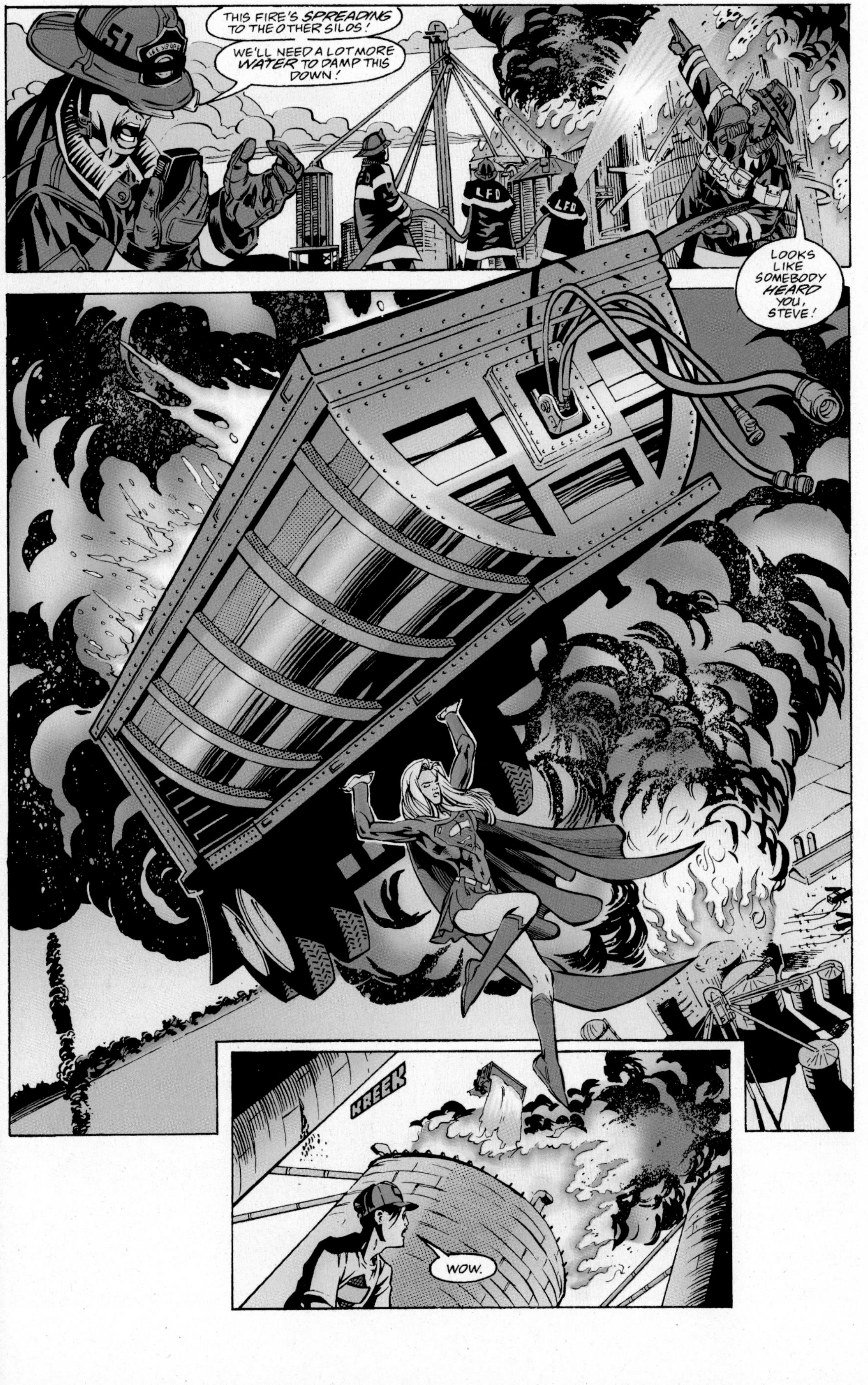
THIS FIRE'S SPREADING TO THE OTHER SILOS!
WE'LL NEED A LOT MORE WATER TO DAMP THIS DOWN!
LOOKS LIKE SOMEBODY HEARD YOU, STEVE!
KREEK
WOW.

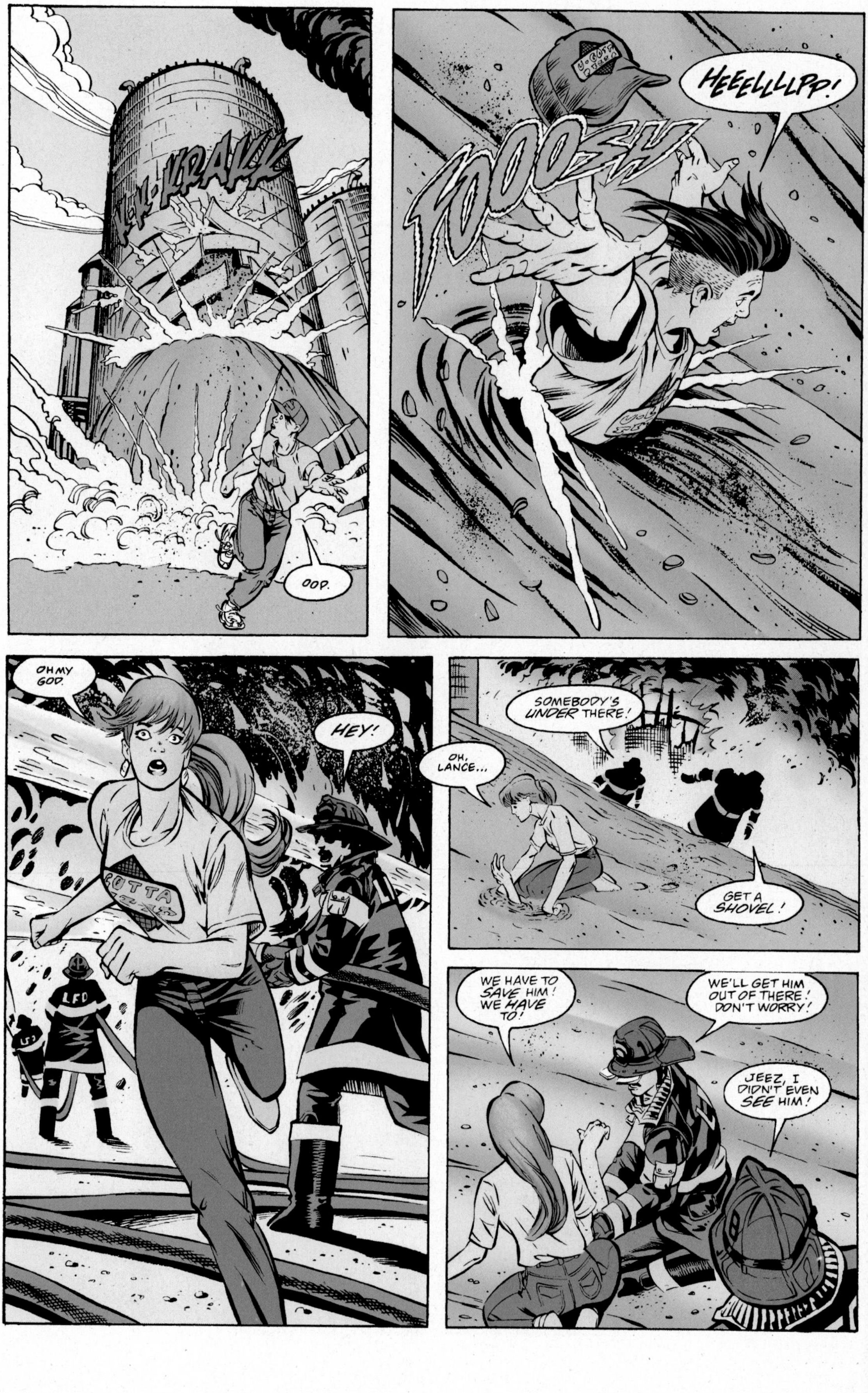
K-K-KRAKK
OOP.
FOOOSH
HEEELLLLPP!
OH MY GOD.
HEY!
OH, LANCE...
SOMEBODY'S UNDER THERE!
GET A SHOVEL!
WE HAVE TO SAVE HIM! WE HAVE TO!
WE'LL GET HIM OUT OF THERE! DON'T WORRY!
JEEZ, I DIDN'T EVEN SEE HIM!

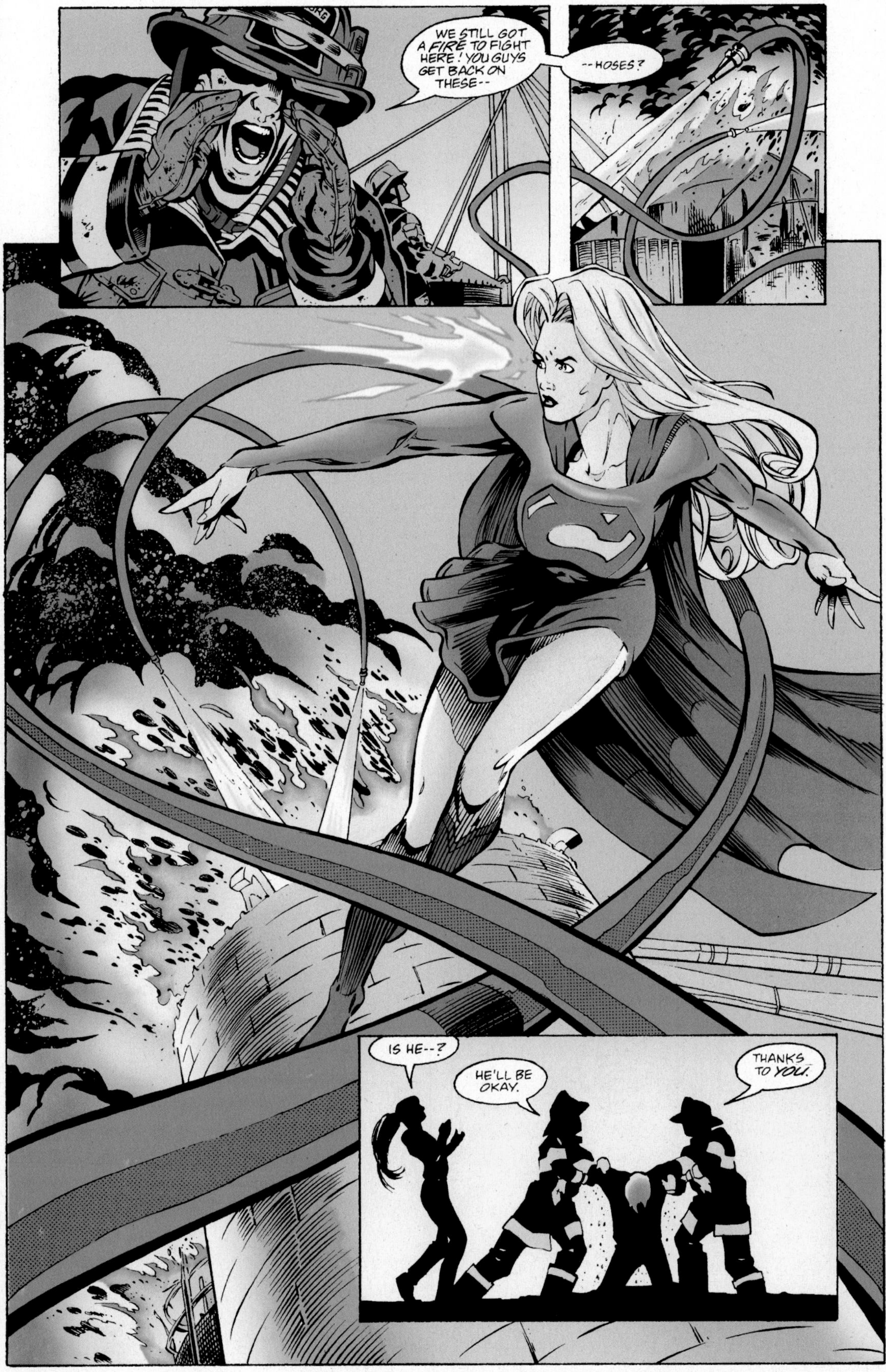

WE STILL GOT A FIRE TO FIGHT HERE! YOU GUYS GET BACK ON THESE--
--HOSES?
IS HE--?
HE'LL BE OKAY.
THANKS TO YOU.

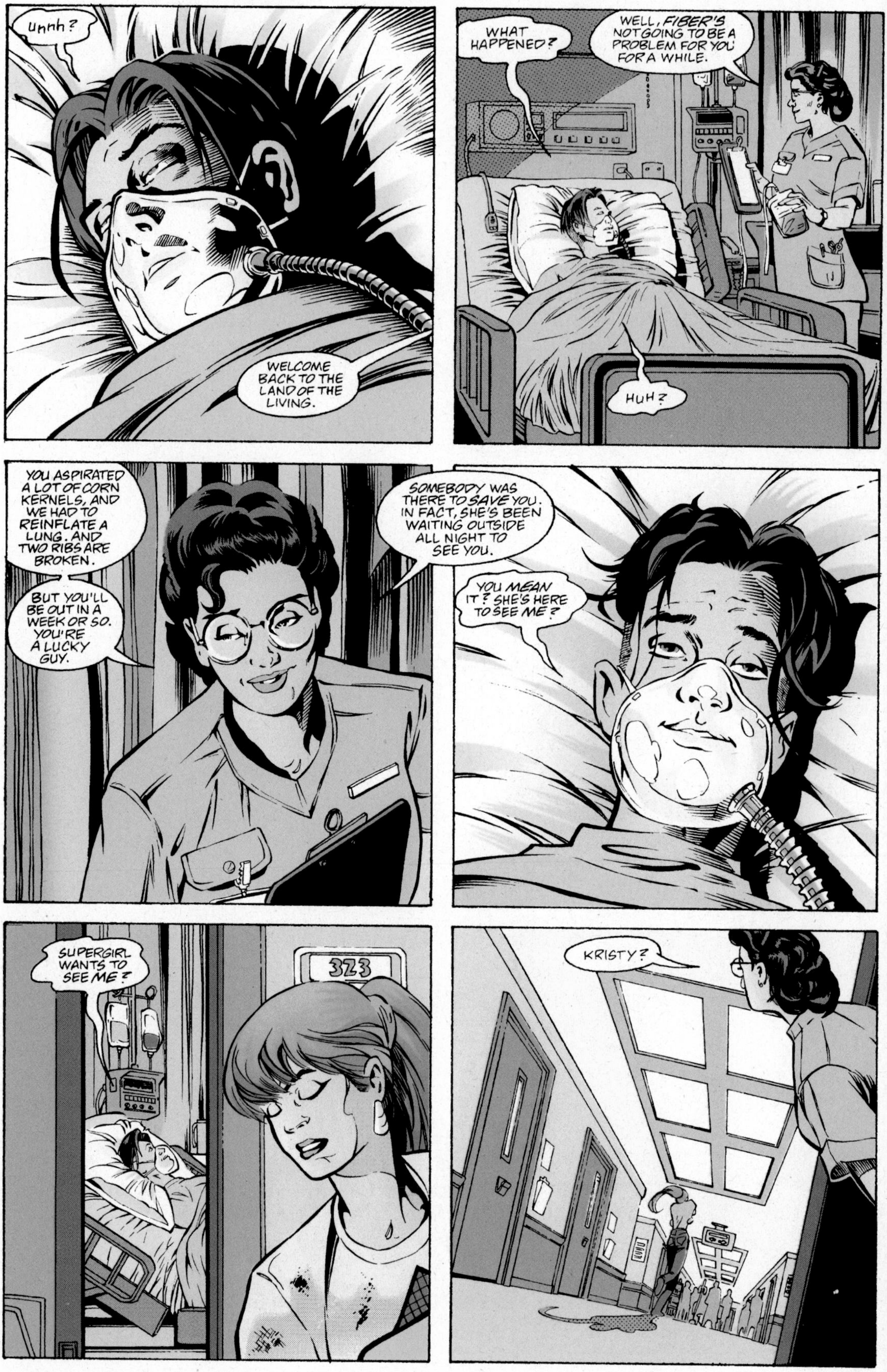
UNNH?
WELCOME BACK TO THE LAND OF THE LIVING.
WHAT HAPPENED?
WELL, FIBER'S NOT GOING TO BE A PROBLEM FOR YOU FOR A WHILE.
HUH?
YOU ASPIRATED A LOT OF CORN KERNELS, AND WE HAD TO REINFLATE A LUNG. AND TWO RIBS ARE BROKEN.
BUT YOU'LL BE OUT IN A WEEK OR SO. YOU'RE A LUCKY GUY.
SOMEBODY WAS THERE TO SAVE YOU. IN FACT, SHE'S BEEN WAITING OUTSIDE ALL NIGHT TO SEE YOU.
YOU MEAN IT? SHE'S HERE TO SEE ME?
SUPERGIRL WANTS TO SEE ME?
323
KRISTY?

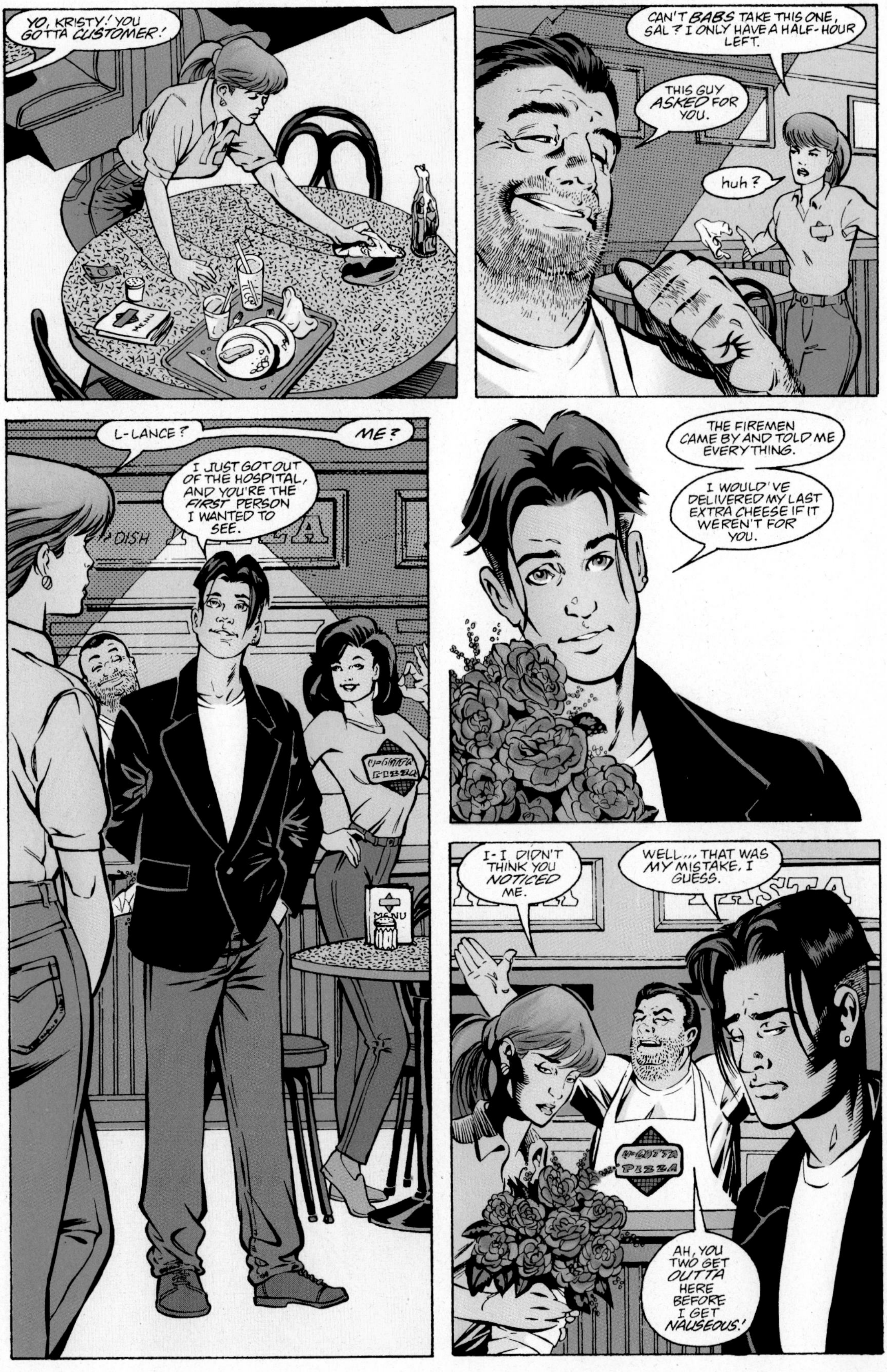
YO, KRISTY! YOU GOTTA CUSTOMER!
CAN'T BABS TAKE THIS ONE, SAL? I ONLY HAVE A HALF-HOUR LEFT.
THIS GUY ASKED FOR YOU.
huh?
L-LANCE?
ME?
I JUST GOT OUT OF THE HOSPITAL, AND YOU'RE THE FIRST PERSON I WANTED TO SEE.
MENU
THE FIREMEN CAME BY AND TOLD ME EVERYTHING.
I WOULD'VE DELIVERED MY LAST EXTRA CHEESE IF IT WEREN'T FOR YOU.
I-I DIDN'T THINK YOU NOTICED ME.
WELL... THAT WAS MY MISTAKE, I GUESS.
AH, YOU TWO GET OUTTA HERE BEFORE I GET NAUSEOUS!

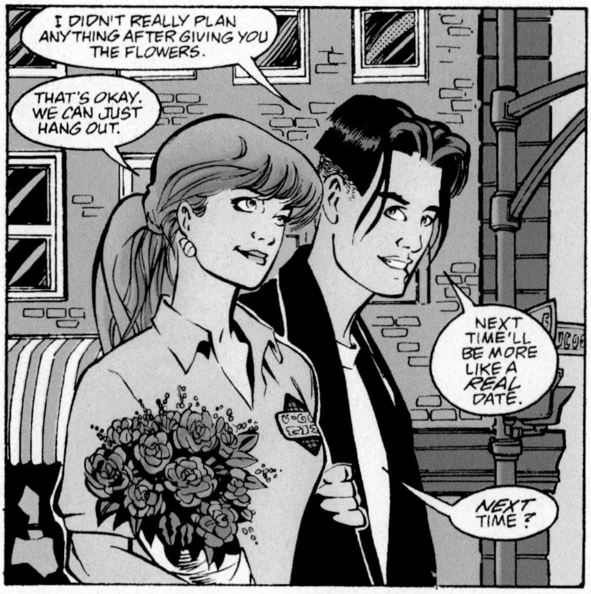
I DIDN'T REALLY PLAN ANYTHING AFTER GIVING YOU THE FLOWERS.
THAT'S OKAY. WE CAN JUST HANG OUT.
NEXT TIME'LL BE MORE LIKE A *REAL* DATE.
NEXT TIME?

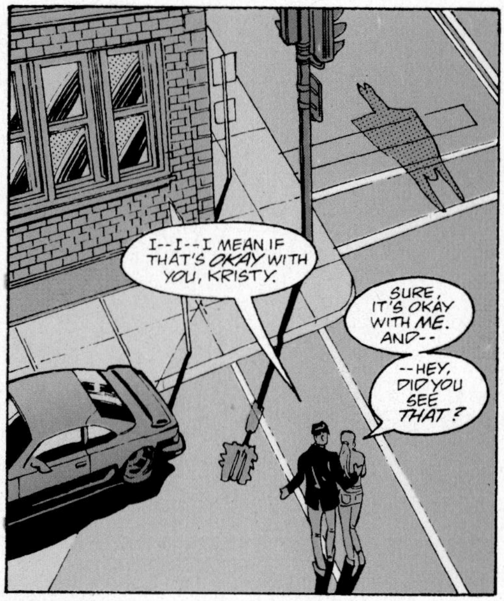
I--I--I MEAN IF THAT'S *OKAY* WITH YOU, KRISTY.
SURE, IT'S OKAY WITH *ME*. AND--
--HEY, DID YOU SEE *THAT*?

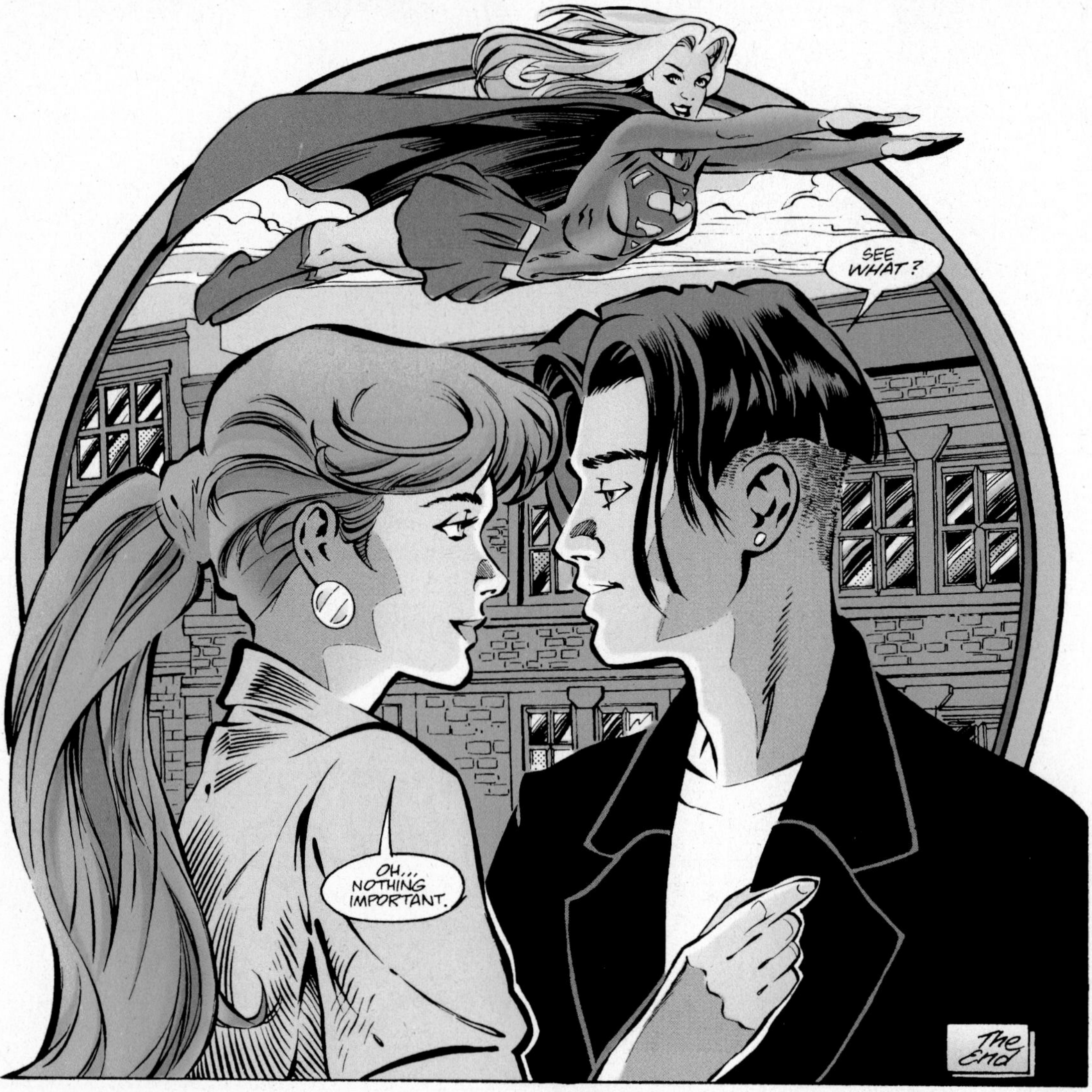
SEE *WHAT*?
OH... NOTHING IMPORTANT.
The End

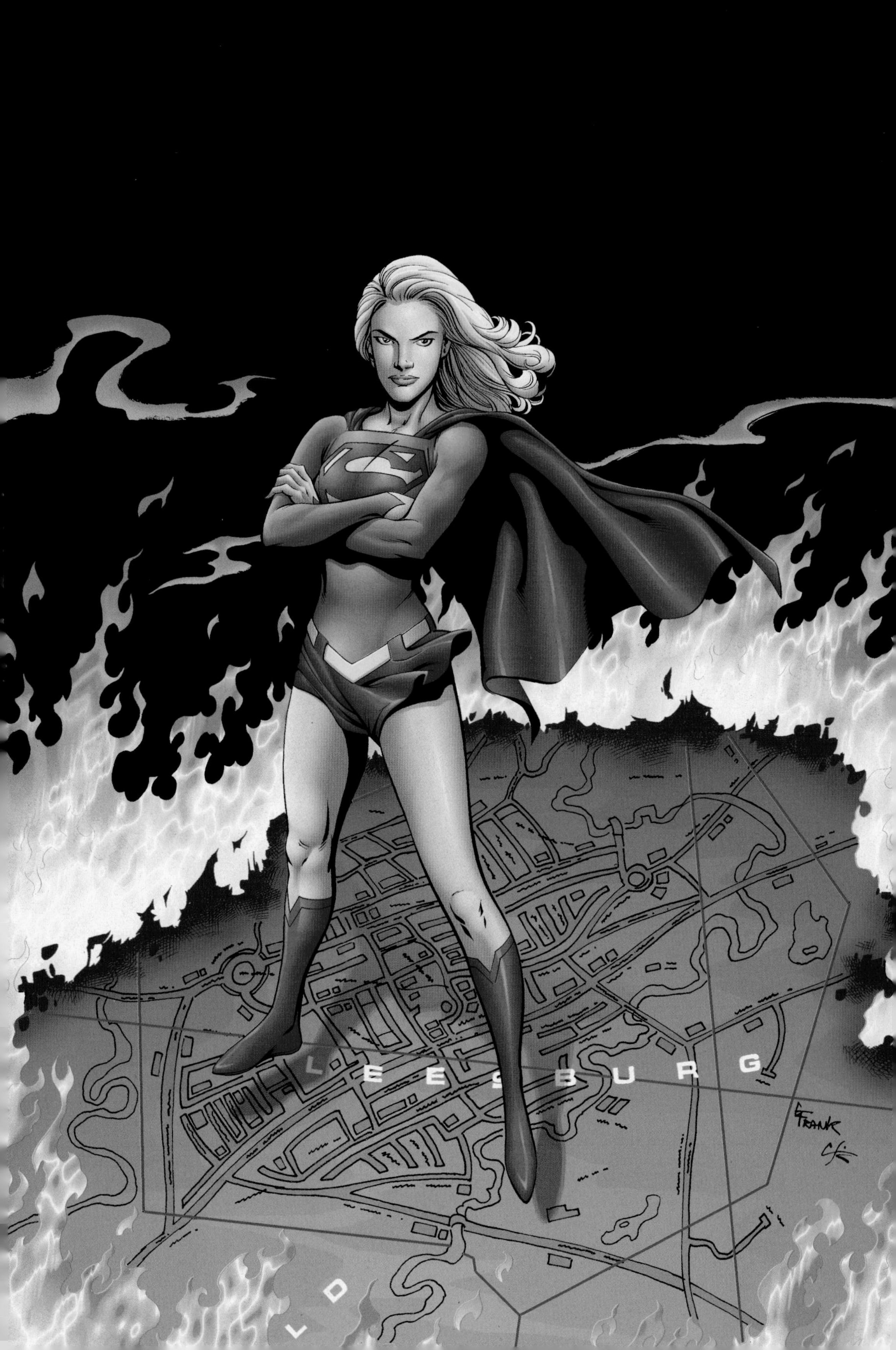
LEESBURG

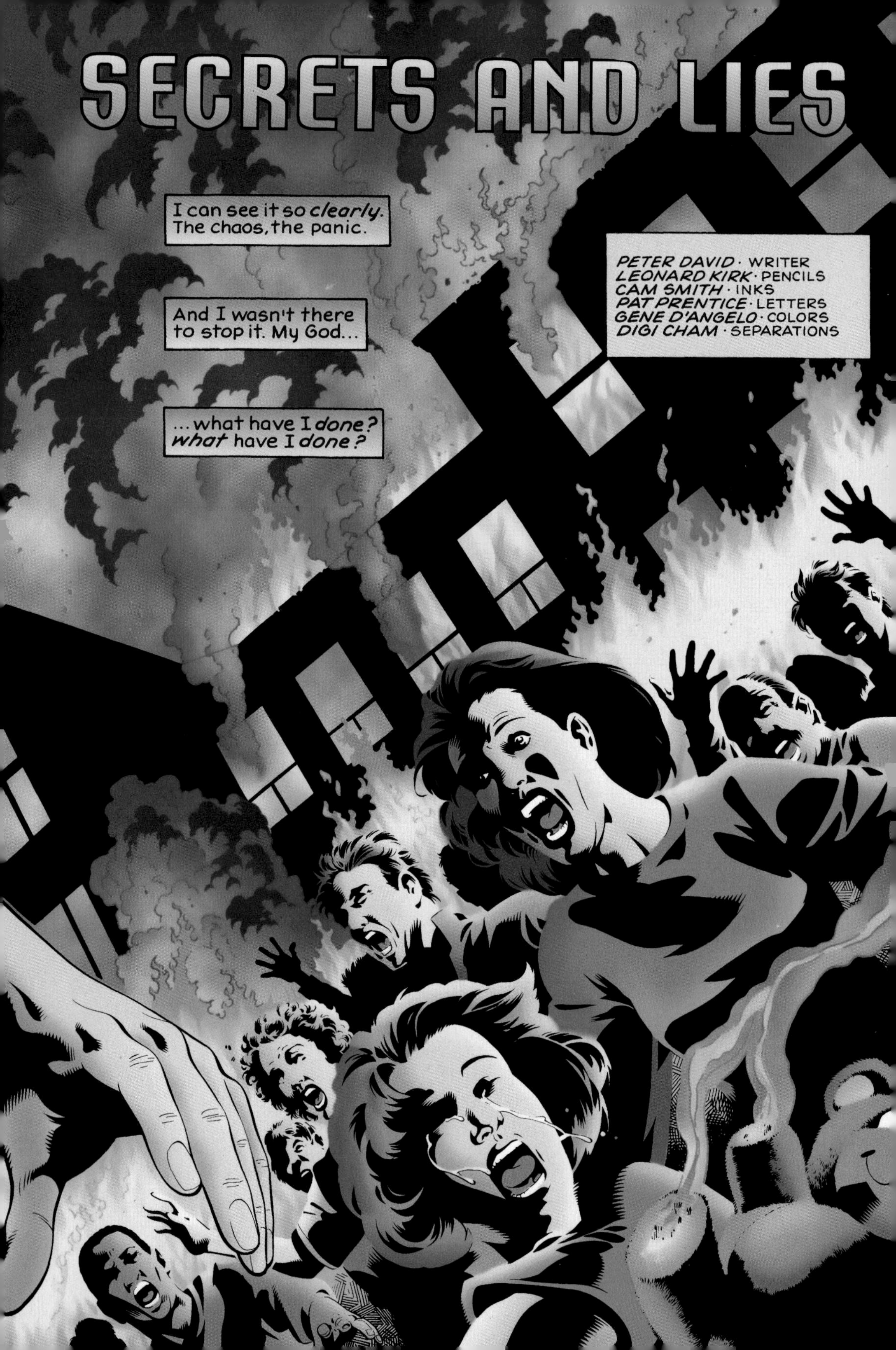
SECRETS AND LIES
I can see it so *clearly*. The chaos, the panic.
And I wasn't there to stop it. My God...
...what have I *done*? *what* have I *done*?
PETER DAVID · WRITER
LEONARD KIRK · PENCILS
CAM SMITH · INKS
PAT PRENTICE · LETTERS
GENE D'ANGELO · COLORS
DIGI CHAM · SEPARATIONS

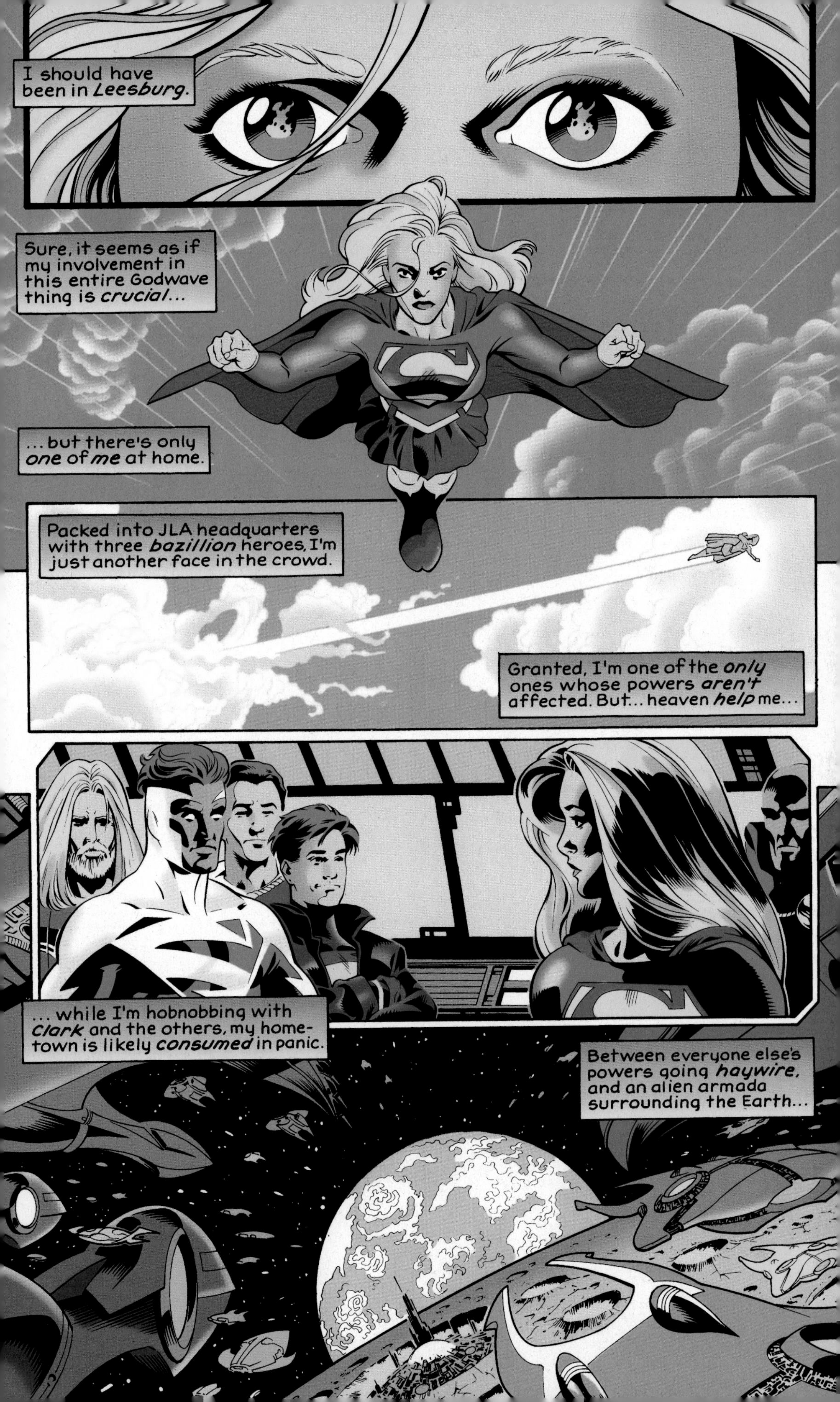
I should have been in *Leesburg*.
Sure, it seems as if my involvement in this entire Godwave thing is *crucial*...
...but there's only *one* of *me* at home.
Packed into JLA headquarters with three *bazillion* heroes, I'm just another face in the crowd.
Granted, I'm one of the *only* ones whose powers *aren't* affected. But... heaven *help* me...
... while I'm hobnobbing with *Clark* and the others, my hometown is likely *consumed* in panic.
Between everyone else's powers going *haywire*, and an alien armada surrounding the Earth...

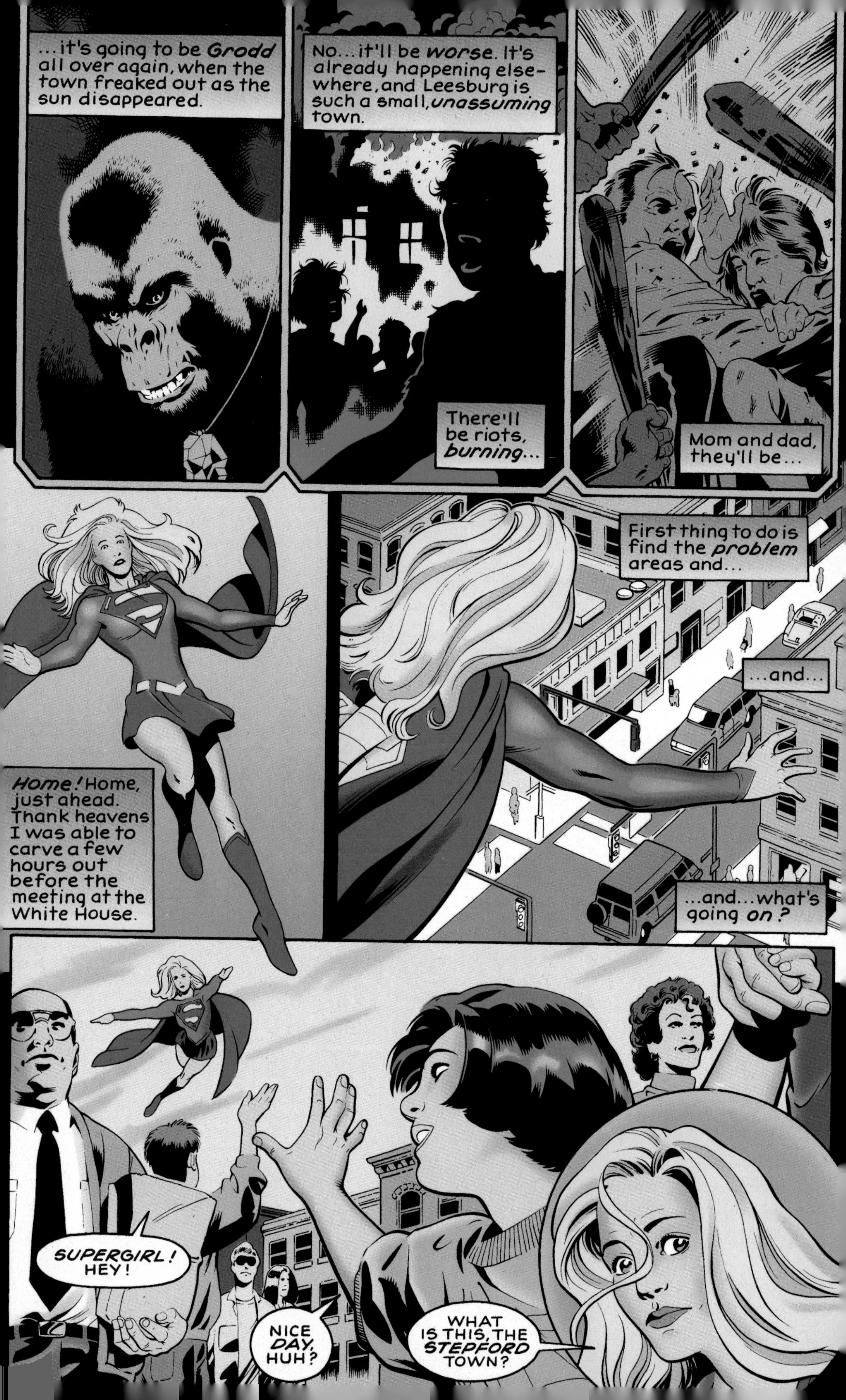
...it's going to be Grodd all over again, when the town freaked out as the sun disappeared.
No...it'll be worse. It's already happening elsewhere, and Leesburg is such a small, unassuming town.
There'll be riots, burning...
Mom and dad, they'll be...
Home! Home, just ahead. Thank heavens I was able to carve a few hours out before the meeting at the White House.
First thing to do is find the problem areas and...
...and...
...and...what's going on?
SUPERGIRL! HEY!
NICE DAY, HUH?
WHAT IS THIS, THE STEPFORD TOWN?

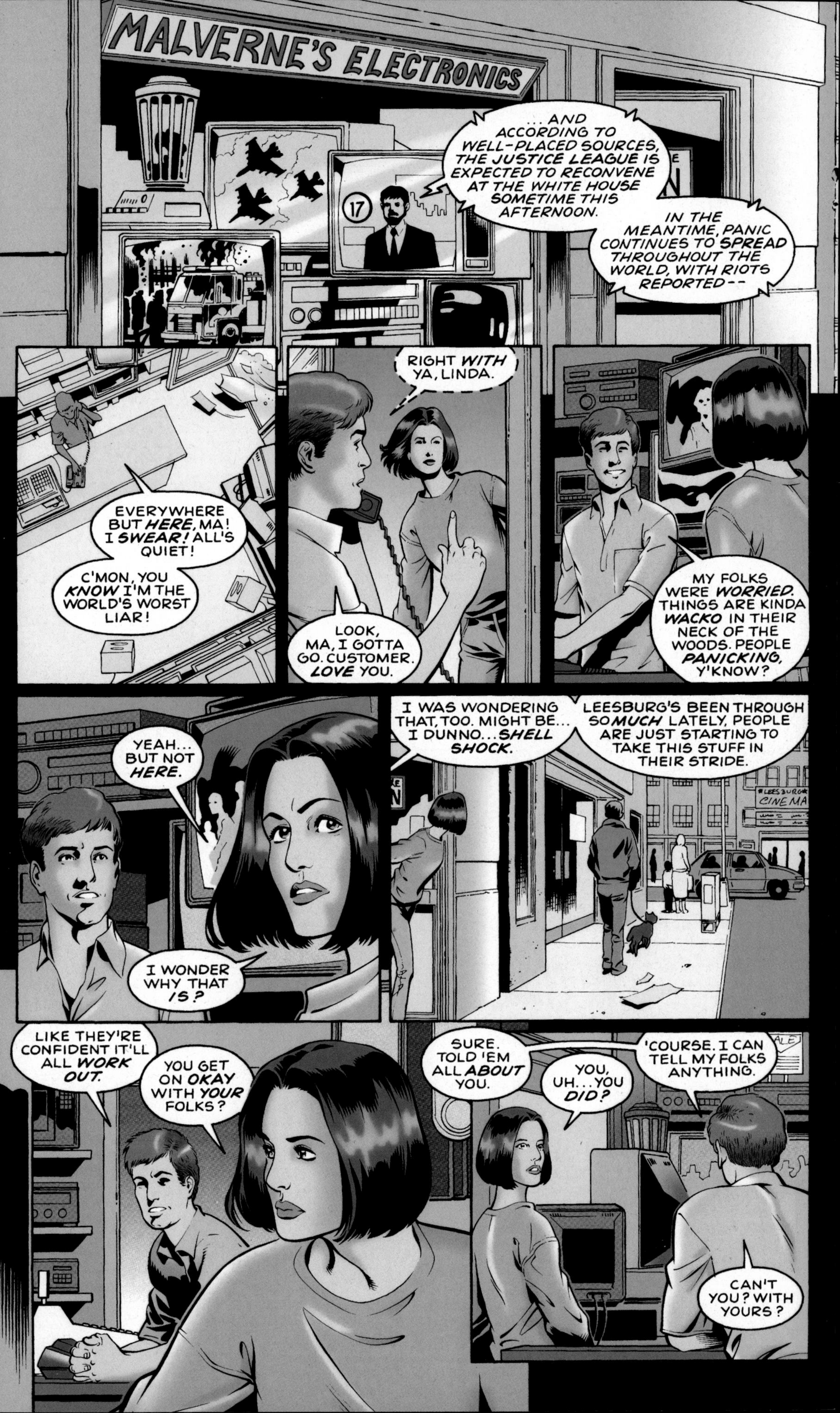
MALVERNE'S ELECTRONICS
17
...AND ACCORDING TO WELL-PLACED SOURCES, THE JUSTICE LEAGUE IS EXPECTED TO RECONVENE AT THE WHITE HOUSE SOMETIME THIS AFTERNOON.
IN THE MEANTIME, PANIC CONTINUES TO SPREAD THROUGHOUT THE WORLD, WITH RIOTS REPORTED--
EVERYWHERE BUT HERE, MA! I SWEAR! ALL'S QUIET!
C'MON, YOU KNOW I'M THE WORLD'S WORST LIAR!
RIGHT WITH YA, LINDA.
LOOK, MA, I GOTTA GO. CUSTOMER. LOVE YOU.
MY FOLKS WERE WORRIED. THINGS ARE KINDA WACKO IN THEIR NECK OF THE WOODS. PEOPLE PANICKING, Y'KNOW?
YEAH... BUT NOT HERE.
I WONDER WHY THAT IS?
I WAS WONDERING THAT, TOO. MIGHT BE... I DUNNO... SHELL SHOCK.
LEESBURG'S BEEN THROUGH SO MUCH LATELY, PEOPLE ARE JUST STARTING TO TAKE THIS STUFF IN THEIR STRIDE.
LEESBURG CINEMA
LIKE THEY'RE CONFIDENT IT'LL ALL WORK OUT.
YOU GET ON OKAY WITH YOUR FOLKS?
SURE. TOLD 'EM ALL ABOUT YOU.
YOU, UH...YOU DID?
'COURSE. I CAN TELL MY FOLKS ANYTHING.
CAN'T YOU? WITH YOURS?

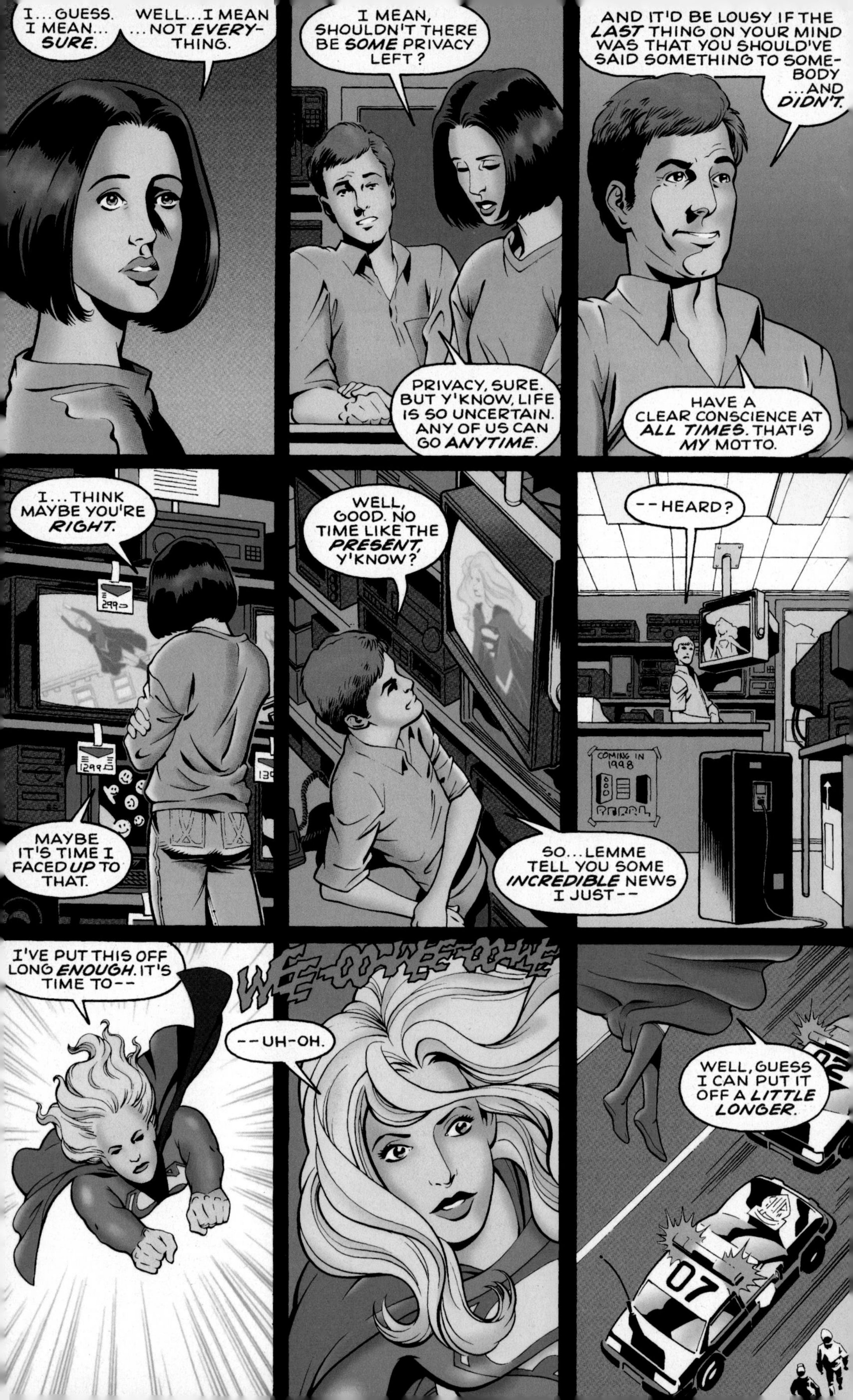
I... GUESS. I MEAN... SURE.
WELL... I MEAN ...NOT EVERY-THING.
I MEAN, SHOULDN'T THERE BE SOME PRIVACY LEFT?
PRIVACY, SURE. BUT Y'KNOW, LIFE IS SO UNCERTAIN. ANY OF US CAN GO ANYTIME.
AND IT'D BE LOUSY IF THE LAST THING ON YOUR MIND WAS THAT YOU SHOULD'VE SAID SOMETHING TO SOME-BODY ...AND DIDN'T.
HAVE A CLEAR CONSCIENCE AT ALL TIMES. THAT'S MY MOTTO.
I... THINK MAYBE YOU'RE RIGHT.
MAYBE IT'S TIME I FACED UP TO THAT.
WELL, GOOD. NO TIME LIKE THE PRESENT, Y'KNOW?
SO... LEMME TELL YOU SOME INCREDIBLE NEWS I JUST--
--HEARD?
COMING IN 1998
I'VE PUT THIS OFF LONG ENOUGH. IT'S TIME TO--
WEE-OO-WEE-OO-WEE
--UH-OH.
WELL, GUESS I CAN PUT IT OFF A LITTLE LONGER.
07

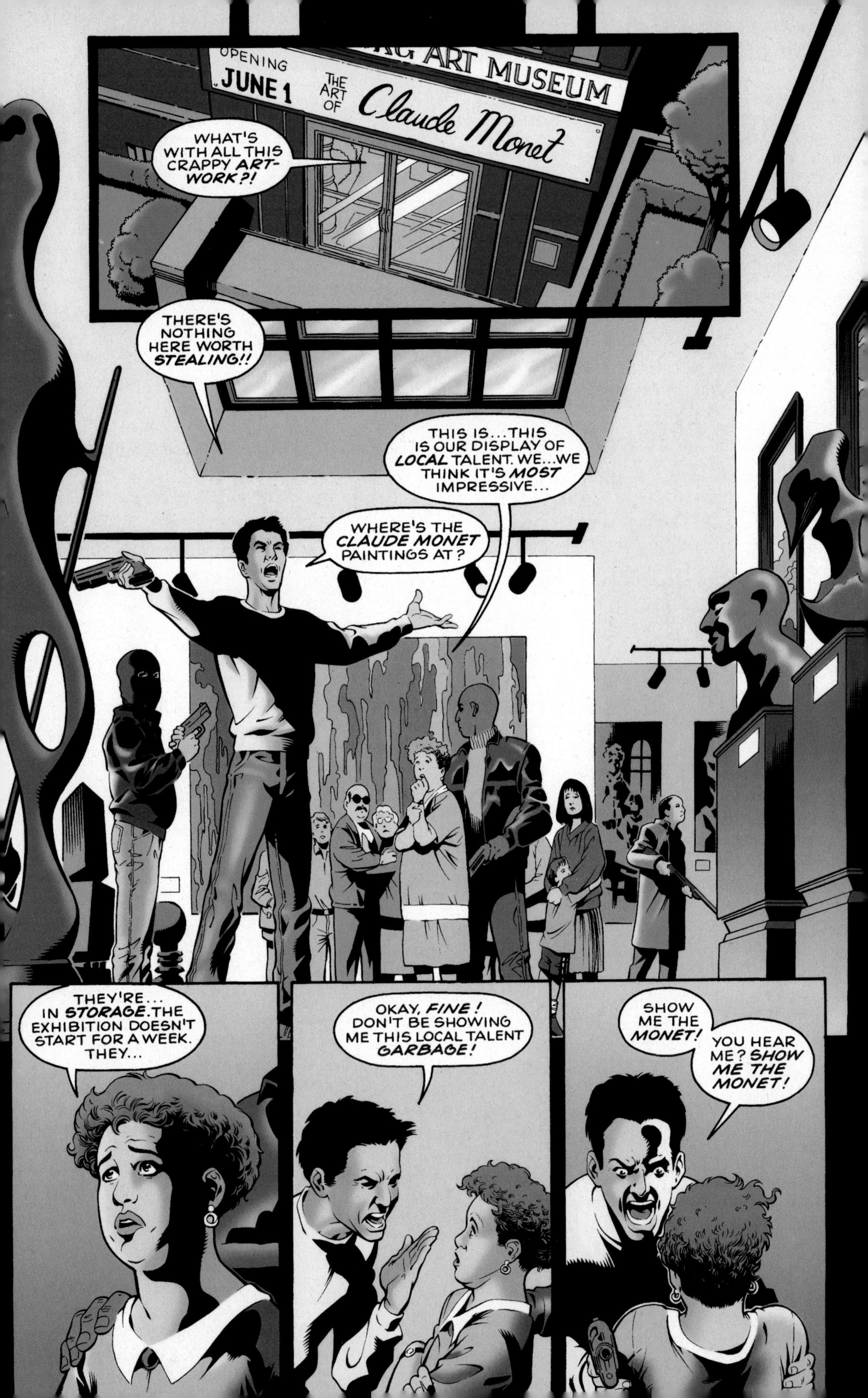
OPENING JUNE 1
ART MUSEUM
THE ART OF Claude Monet
WHAT'S WITH ALL THIS CRAPPY ART-WORK?!
THERE'S NOTHING HERE WORTH STEALING!!
THIS IS... THIS IS OUR DISPLAY OF LOCAL TALENT. WE... WE THINK IT'S MOST IMPRESSIVE...
WHERE'S THE CLAUDE MONET PAINTINGS AT?
THEY'RE... IN STORAGE. THE EXHIBITION DOESN'T START FOR A WEEK. THEY...
OKAY, FINE! DON'T BE SHOWING ME THIS LOCAL TALENT GARBAGE!
SHOW ME THE MONET!
YOU HEAR ME? SHOW ME THE MONET!

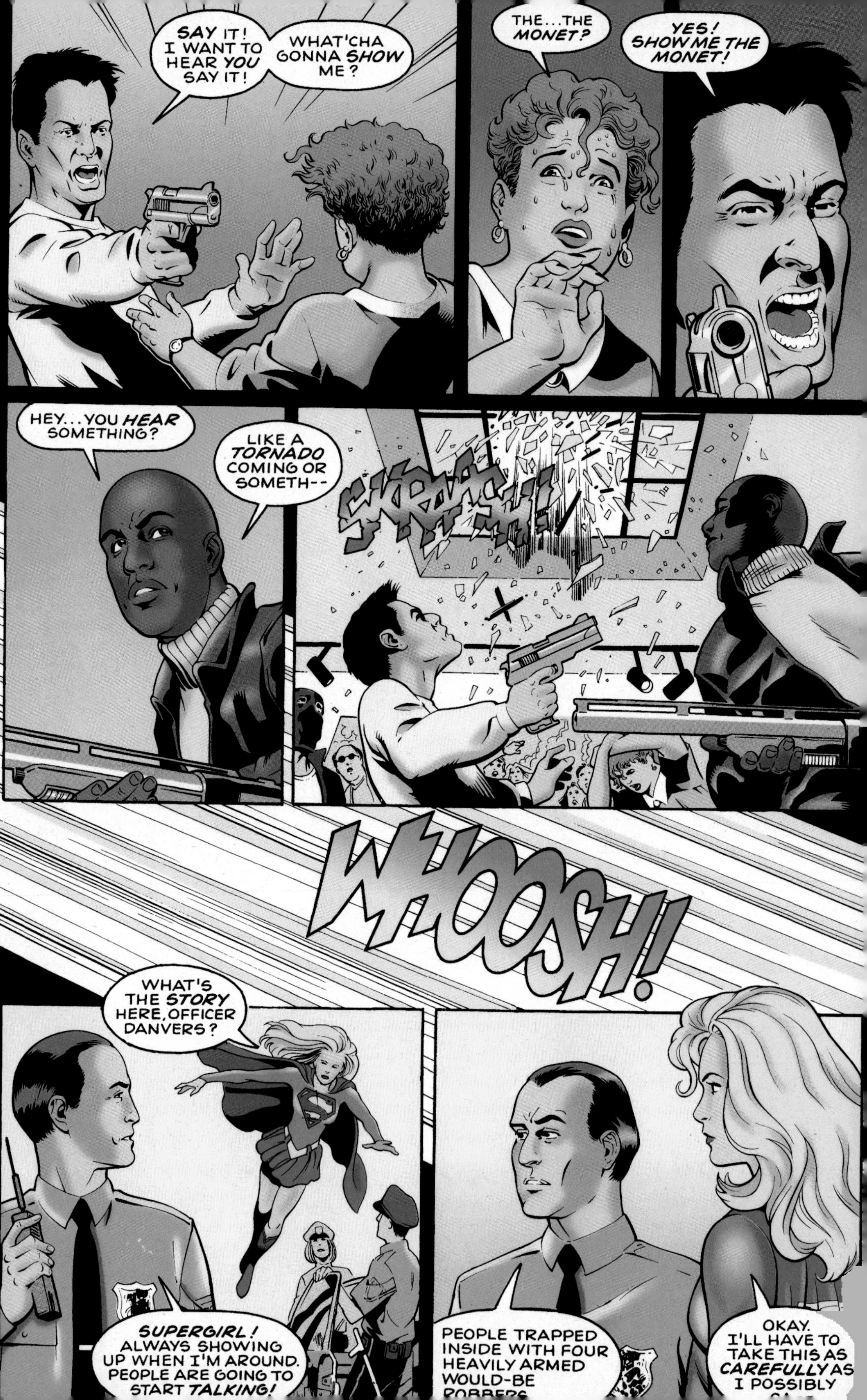
SAY IT! I WANT TO HEAR YOU SAY IT!
WHAT'CHA GONNA SHOW ME?
THE...THE MONET?
YES! SHOW ME THE MONET!
HEY...YOU HEAR SOMETHING?
LIKE A TORNADO COMING OR SOMETH--
WHOOSH!
WHAT'S THE STORY HERE, OFFICER DANVERS?
SUPERGIRL! ALWAYS SHOWING UP WHEN I'M AROUND. PEOPLE ARE GOING TO START TALKING!
PEOPLE TRAPPED INSIDE WITH FOUR HEAVILY ARMED WOULD-BE
OKAY. I'LL HAVE TO TAKE THIS AS CAREFULLY AS I POSSIBLY

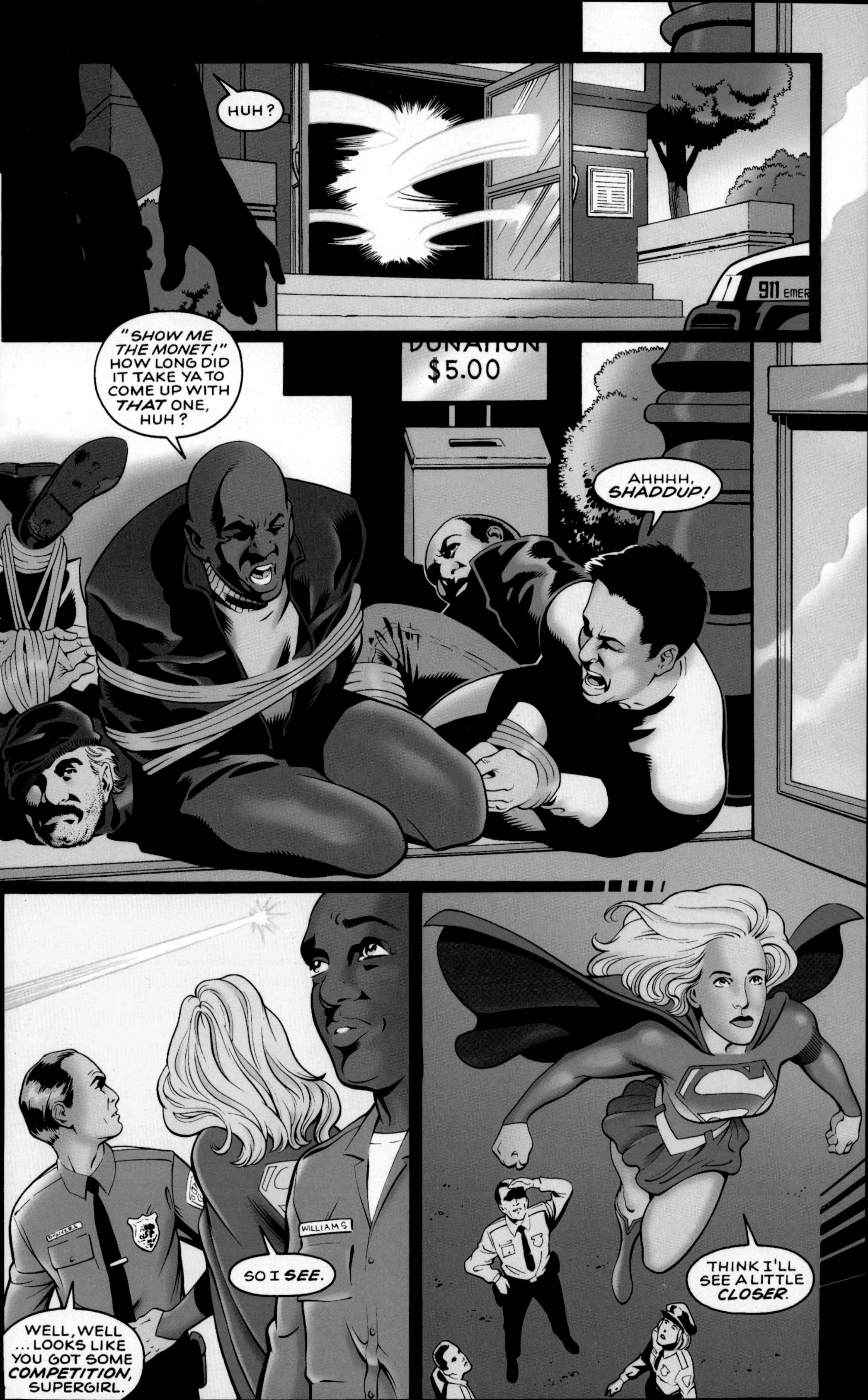
HUH?
911 EMER
$5.00
"SHOW ME THE MONET!" HOW LONG DID IT TAKE YA TO COME UP WITH *THAT* ONE, HUH?
AHHHH, *SHADDUP!*
WILLIAMS
WELL, WELL ...LOOKS LIKE YOU GOT SOME *COMPETITION*, SUPERGIRL.
SO I *SEE*.
THINK I'LL SEE A LITTLE *CLOSER*.

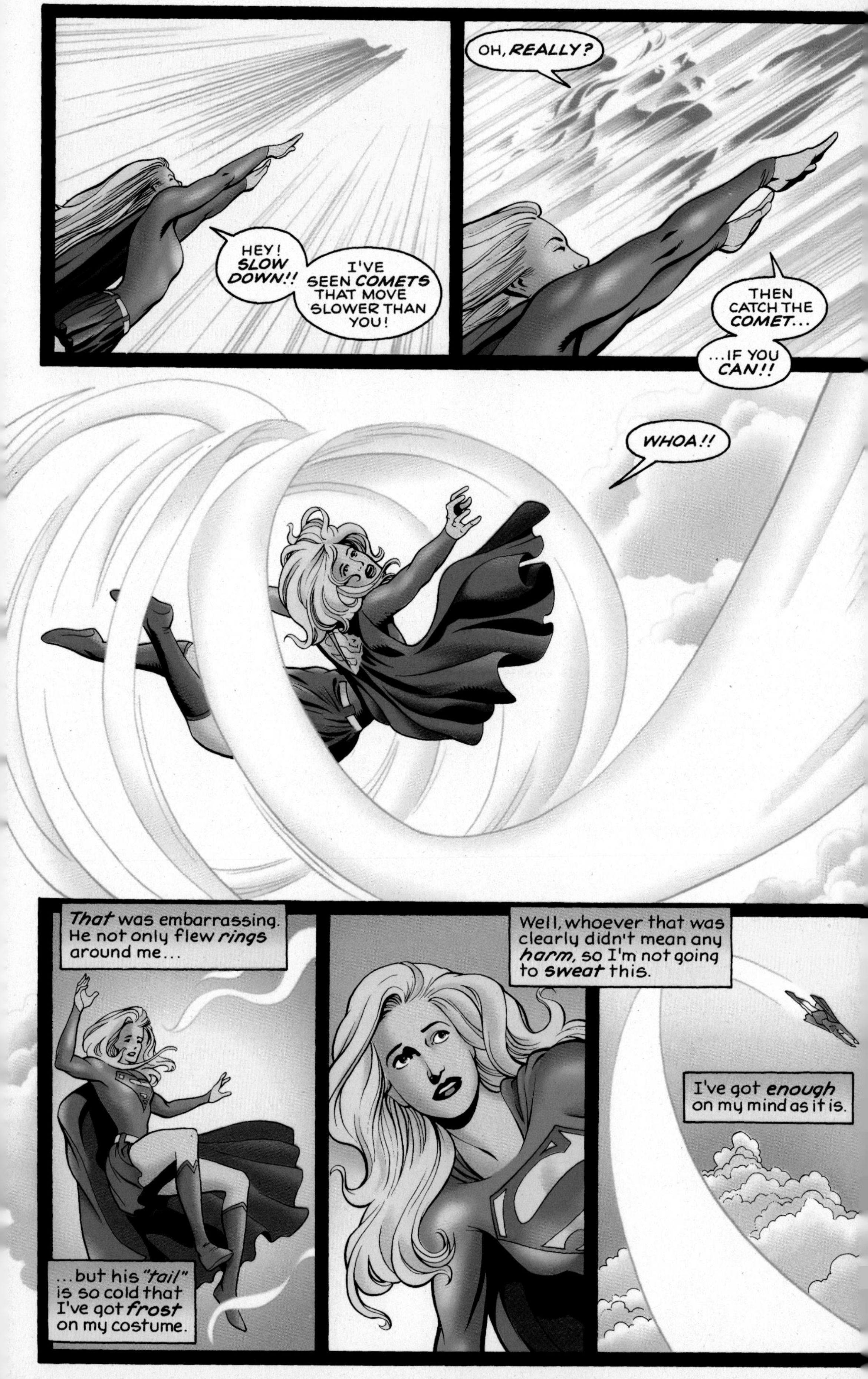
HEY! SLOW DOWN!!
I'VE SEEN COMETS THAT MOVE SLOWER THAN YOU!
OH, REALLY?
THEN CATCH THE COMET...
...IF YOU CAN!!
WHOA!!
That was embarrassing. He not only flew rings around me...
...but his "tail" is so cold that I've got frost on my costume.
Well, whoever that was clearly didn't mean any harm, so I'm not going to sweat this.
I've got enough on my mind as it is.

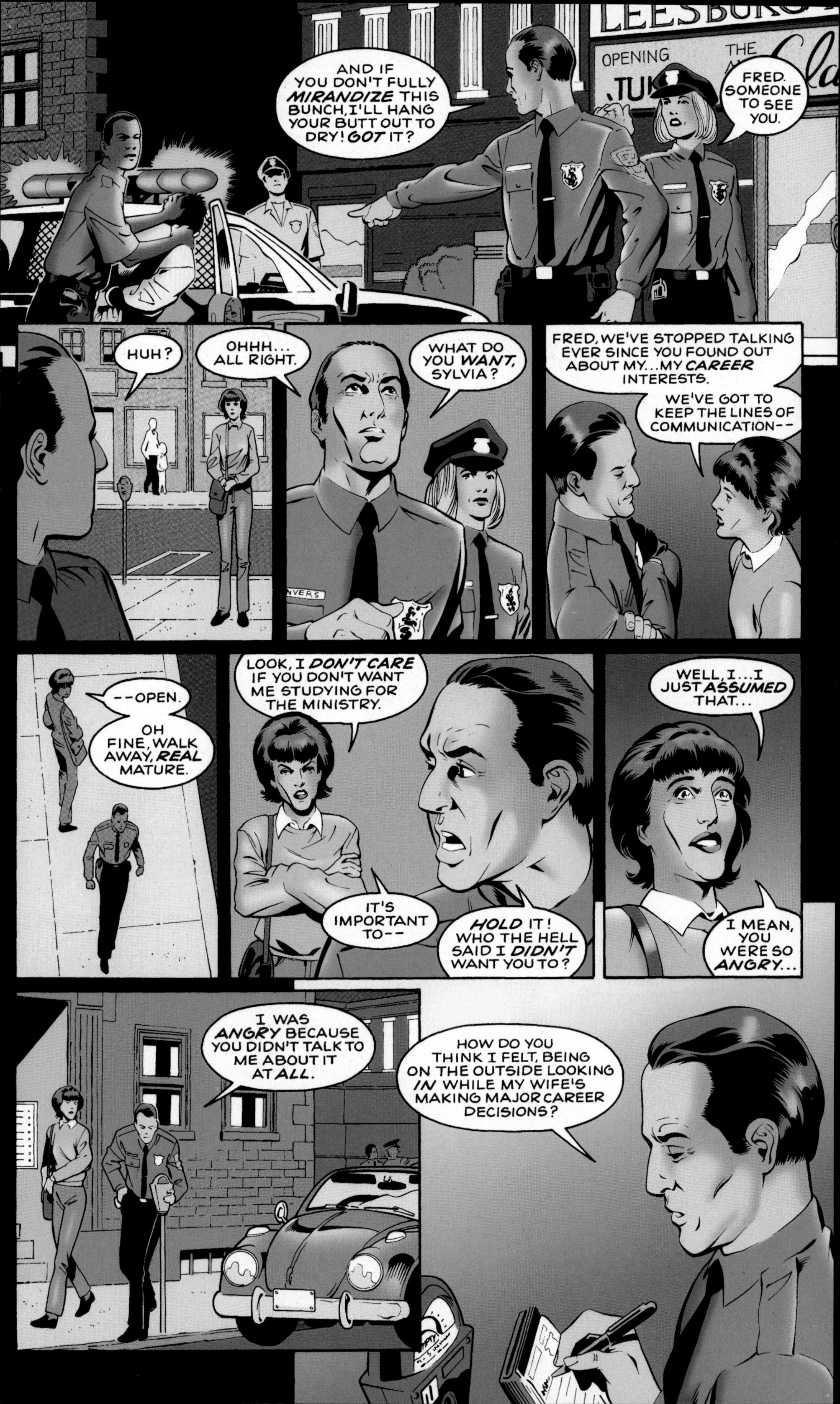

LEESBURG
OPENING
THE
AND IF YOU DON'T FULLY MIRANDIZE THIS BUNCH, I'LL HANG YOUR BUTT OUT TO DRY! GOT IT?
FRED. SOMEONE TO SEE YOU.
HUH?
OHHH... ALL RIGHT.
WHAT DO YOU WANT, SYLVIA?
FRED, WE'VE STOPPED TALKING EVER SINCE YOU FOUND OUT ABOUT MY...MY CAREER INTERESTS.
WE'VE GOT TO KEEP THE LINES OF COMMUNICATION--
--OPEN.
OH FINE, WALK AWAY, REAL MATURE.
LOOK, I DON'T CARE IF YOU DON'T WANT ME STUDYING FOR THE MINISTRY.
IT'S IMPORTANT TO--
HOLD IT! WHO THE HELL SAID I DIDN'T WANT YOU TO?
WELL, I...I JUST ASSUMED THAT...
I MEAN, YOU WERE SO ANGRY...
I WAS ANGRY BECAUSE YOU DIDN'T TALK TO ME ABOUT IT AT ALL.
HOW DO YOU THINK I FELT, BEING ON THE OUTSIDE LOOKING IN WHILE MY WIFE'S MAKING MAJOR CAREER DECISIONS?

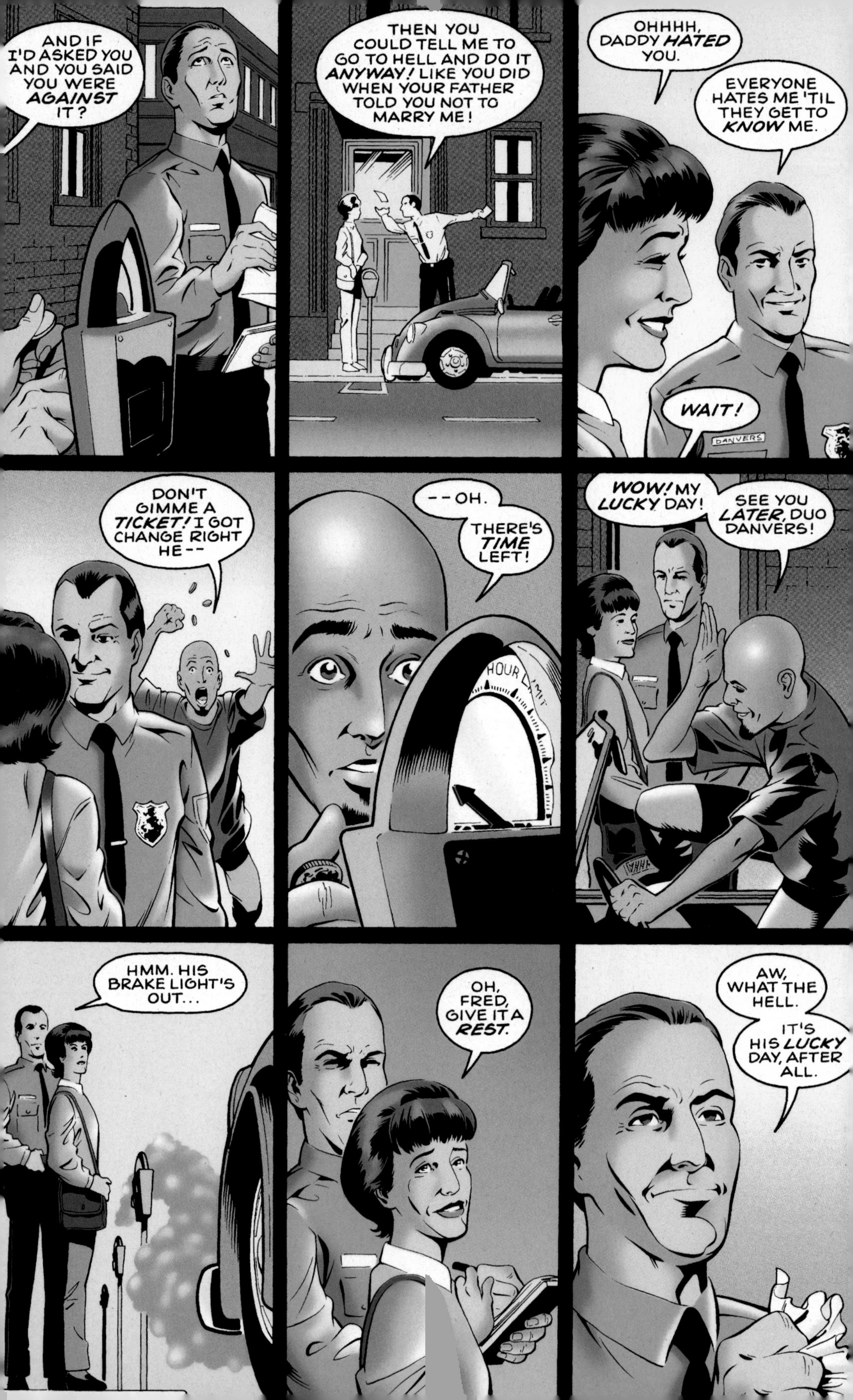
AND IF I'D ASKED YOU AND YOU SAID YOU WERE AGAINST IT?
THEN YOU COULD TELL ME TO GO TO HELL AND DO IT ANYWAY! LIKE YOU DID WHEN YOUR FATHER TOLD YOU NOT TO MARRY ME!
OHHHH, DADDY HATED YOU.
EVERYONE HATES ME 'TIL THEY GET TO KNOW ME.
WAIT!
DANVERS
DON'T GIMME A TICKET! I GOT CHANGE RIGHT HE--
--OH.
THERE'S TIME LEFT!
HOUR LIMIT
WOW! MY LUCKY DAY!
SEE YOU LATER, DUO DANVERS!
HMM. HIS BRAKE LIGHT'S OUT...
OH, FRED, GIVE IT A REST.
AW, WHAT THE HELL.
IT'S HIS LUCKY DAY, AFTER ALL.

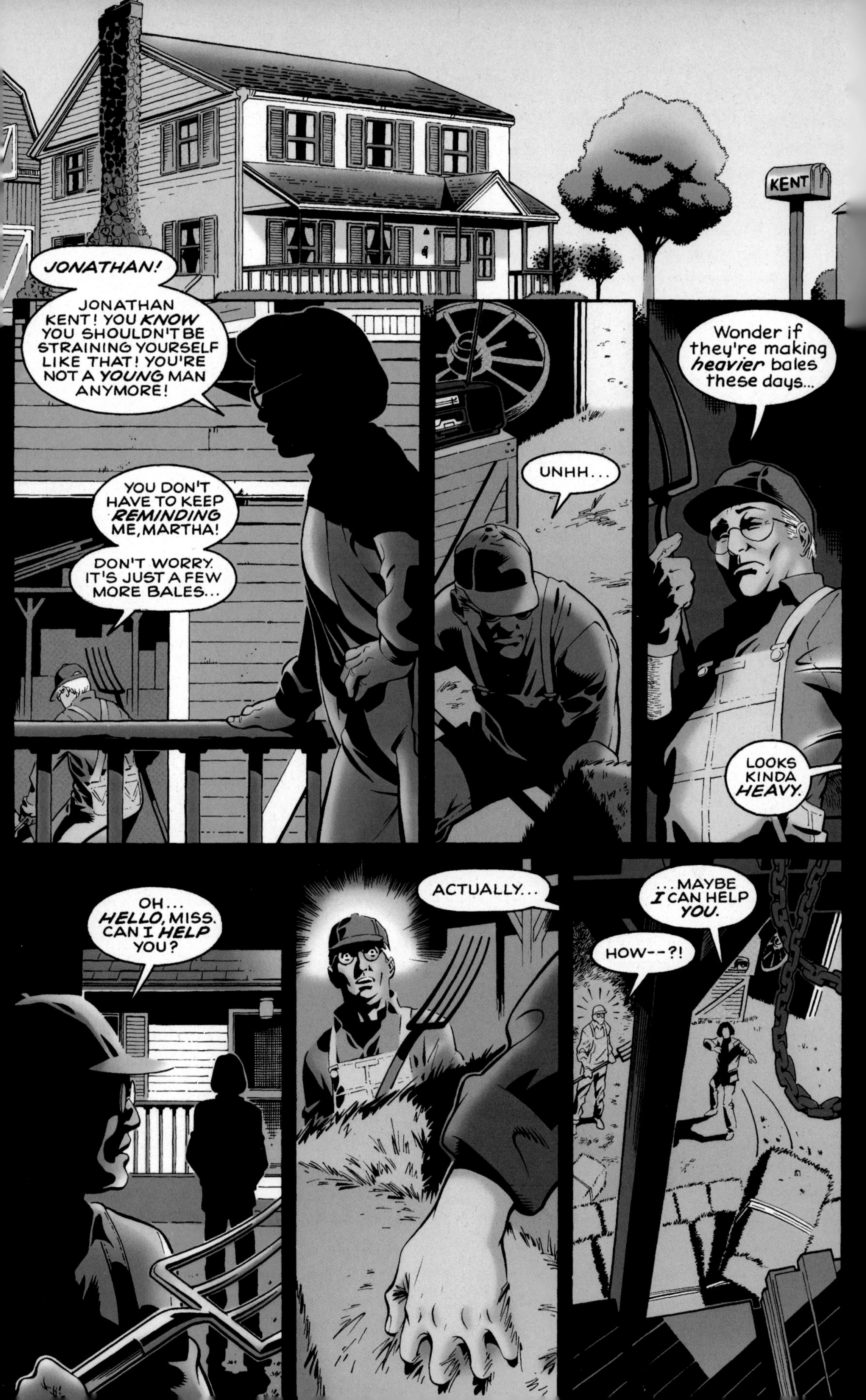
KENT
JONATHAN!
JONATHAN KENT! YOU KNOW YOU SHOULDN'T BE STRAINING YOURSELF LIKE THAT! YOU'RE NOT A YOUNG MAN ANYMORE!
YOU DON'T HAVE TO KEEP REMINDING ME, MARTHA!
DON'T WORRY. IT'S JUST A FEW MORE BALES...
UNHH...
Wonder if they're making heavier bales these days...
LOOKS KINDA HEAVY.
OH... HELLO, MISS. CAN I HELP YOU?
ACTUALLY...
...MAYBE I CAN HELP YOU.
HOW--?!

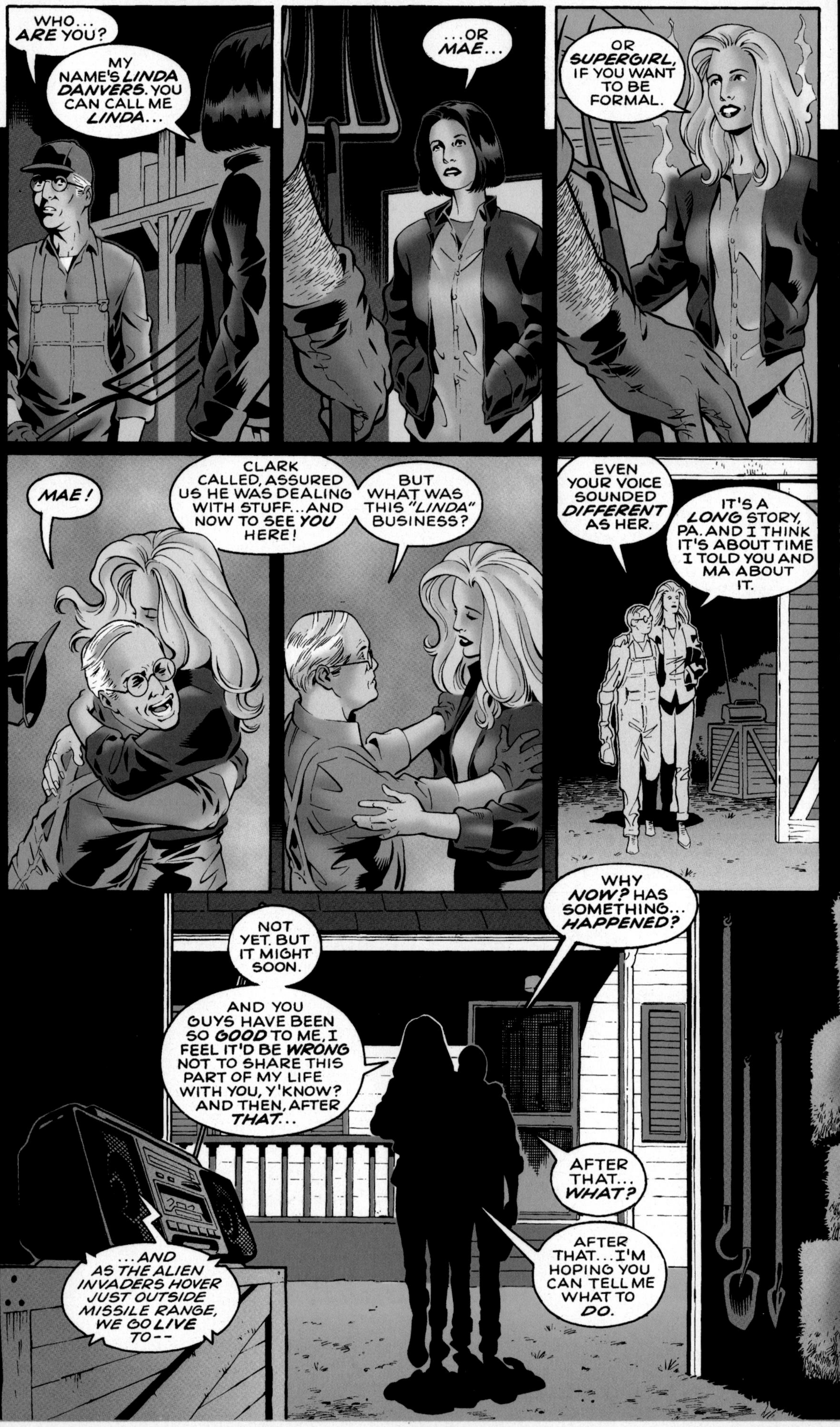
WHO... ARE YOU?
MY NAME'S LINDA DANVERS. YOU CAN CALL ME LINDA...
...OR MAE...
OR SUPERGIRL, IF YOU WANT TO BE FORMAL.
MAE!
CLARK CALLED, ASSURED US HE WAS DEALING WITH STUFF...AND NOW TO SEE YOU HERE!
BUT WHAT WAS THIS "LINDA" BUSINESS?
EVEN YOUR VOICE SOUNDED DIFFERENT AS HER.
IT'S A LONG STORY, PA. AND I THINK IT'S ABOUT TIME I TOLD YOU AND MA ABOUT IT.
WHY NOW? HAS SOMETHING... HAPPENED?
NOT YET. BUT IT MIGHT SOON.
AND YOU GUYS HAVE BEEN SO GOOD TO ME, I FEEL IT'D BE WRONG NOT TO SHARE THIS PART OF MY LIFE WITH YOU, Y'KNOW? AND THEN, AFTER THAT...
AFTER THAT... WHAT?
AFTER THAT...I'M HOPING YOU CAN TELL ME WHAT TO DO.
...AND AS THE ALIEN INVADERS HOVER JUST OUTSIDE MISSILE RANGE, WE GO LIVE TO--

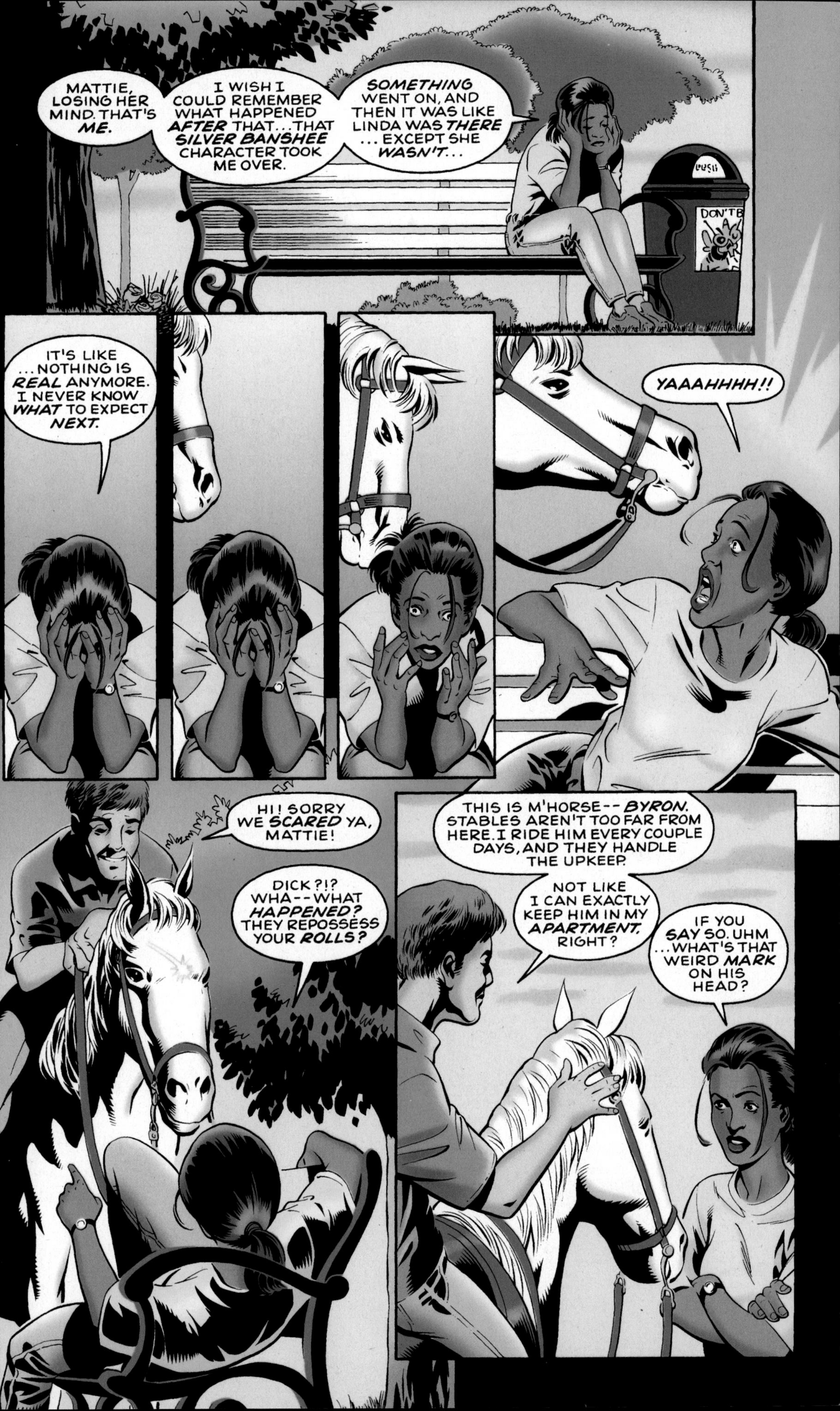
MATTIE, LOSING HER MIND. THAT'S ME.
I WISH I COULD REMEMBER WHAT HAPPENED AFTER THAT...THAT SILVER BANSHEE CHARACTER TOOK ME OVER.
SOMETHING WENT ON, AND THEN IT WAS LIKE LINDA WAS THERE ...EXCEPT SHE WASN'T...
PUSH
DON'T B
IT'S LIKE ...NOTHING IS REAL ANYMORE. I NEVER KNOW WHAT TO EXPECT NEXT.
YAAAHHHH!!
HI! SORRY WE SCARED YA, MATTIE!
DICK?!? WHA--WHAT HAPPENED? THEY REPOSSESS YOUR ROLLS?
THIS IS M'HORSE--BYRON. STABLES AREN'T TOO FAR FROM HERE. I RIDE HIM EVERY COUPLE DAYS, AND THEY HANDLE THE UPKEEP.
NOT LIKE I CAN EXACTLY KEEP HIM IN MY APARTMENT, RIGHT?
IF YOU SAY SO. UHM ...WHAT'S THAT WEIRD MARK ON HIS HEAD?

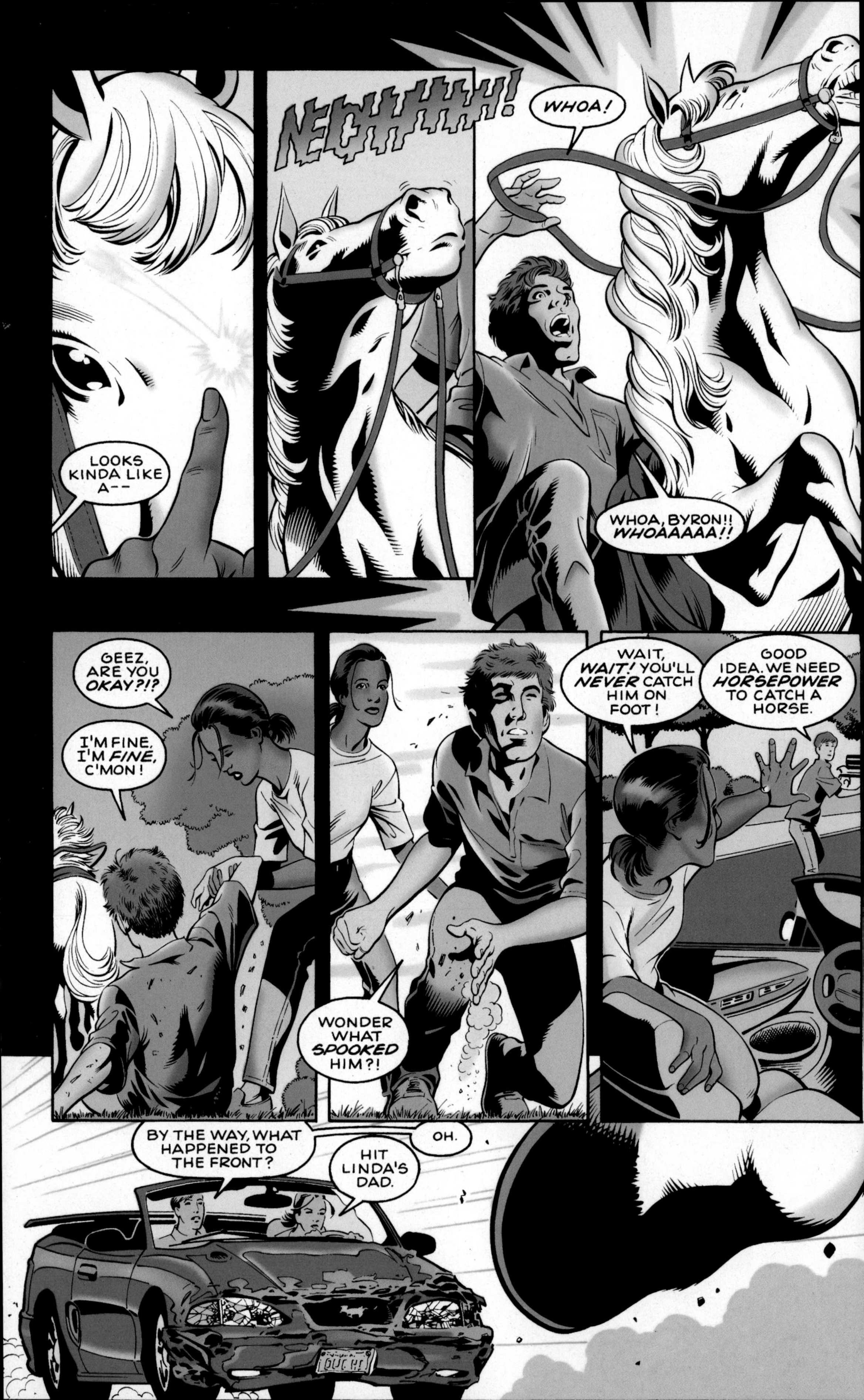
LOOKS KINDA LIKE A--
NEIGHHHH!
WHOA!
WHOA, BYRON!! WHOAAAAA!!
GEEZ, ARE YOU OKAY?!?
I'M FINE, I'M FINE, C'MON!
WONDER WHAT SPOOKED HIM?!
WAIT, WAIT! YOU'LL NEVER CATCH HIM ON FOOT!
GOOD IDEA. WE NEED HORSEPOWER TO CATCH A HORSE.
BY THE WAY, WHAT HAPPENED TO THE FRONT?
OH.
HIT LINDA'S DAD.
OUCH!

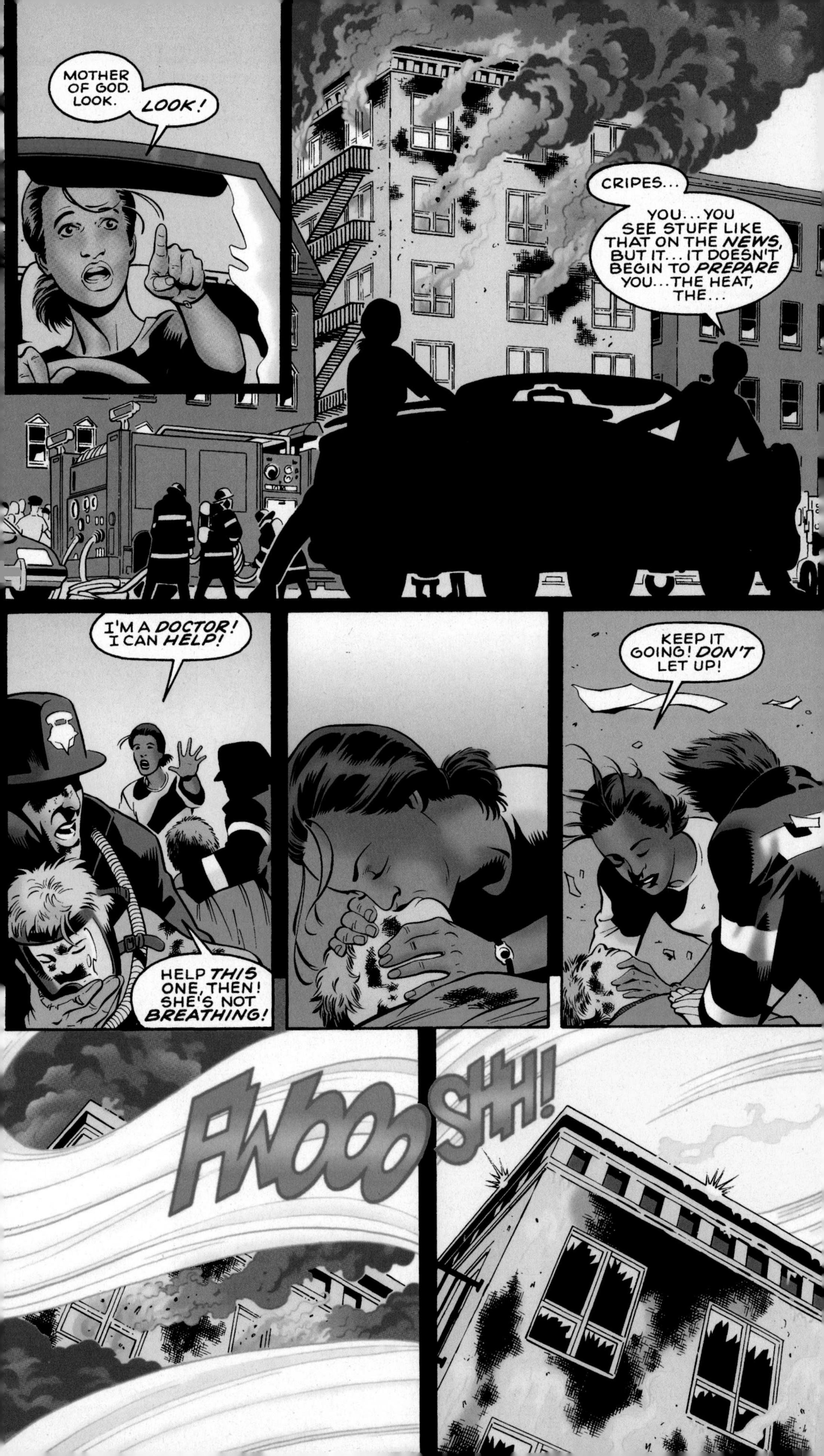

MOTHER OF GOD. LOOK. LOOK!
CRIPES...
YOU...YOU SEE STUFF LIKE THAT ON THE NEWS, BUT IT...IT DOESN'T BEGIN TO PREPARE YOU...THE HEAT, THE...
I'M A DOCTOR! I CAN HELP!
HELP THIS ONE, THEN! SHE'S NOT BREATHING!
KEEP IT GOING! DON'T LET UP!
FWOOOSHH!

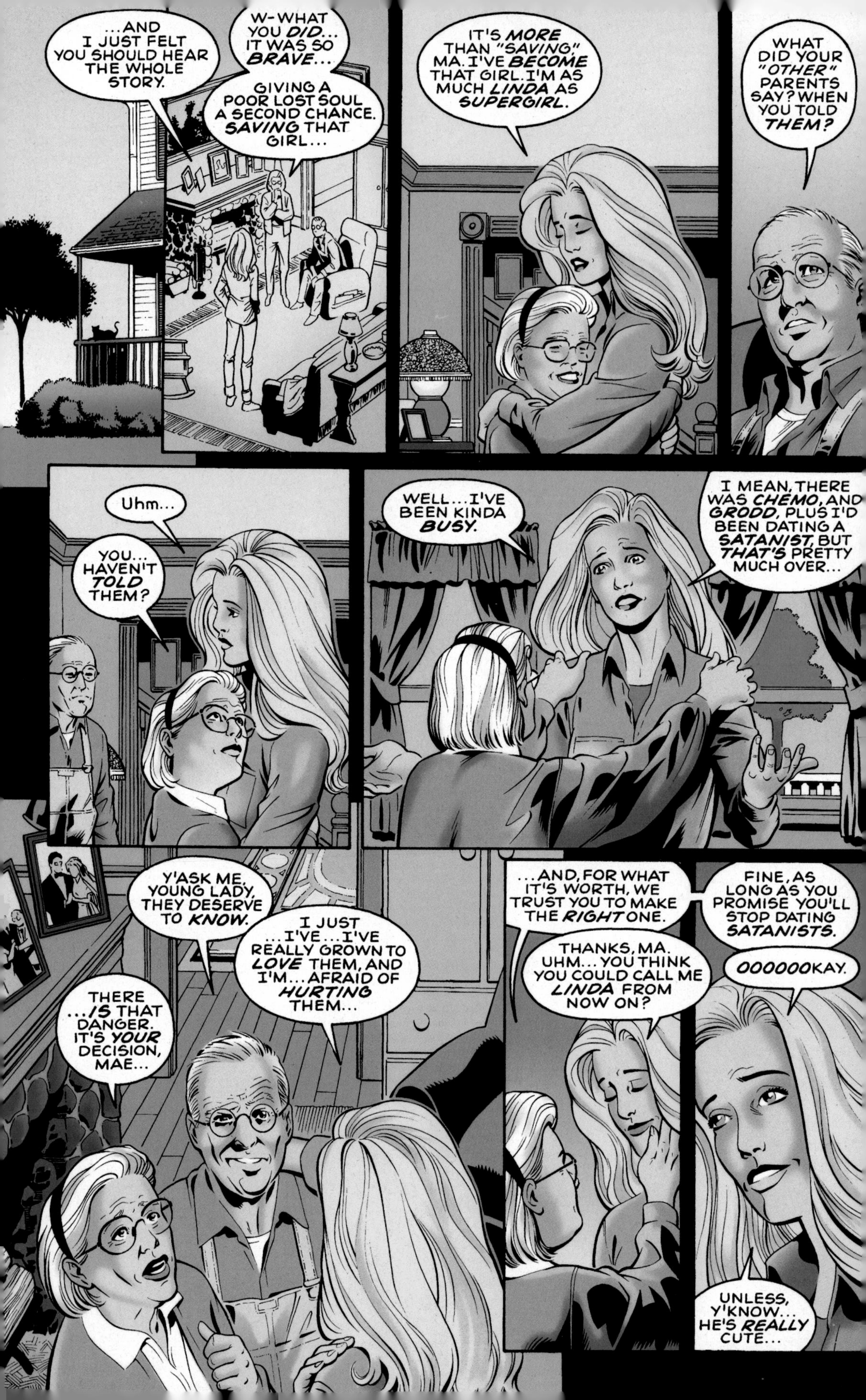
...AND I JUST FELT YOU SHOULD HEAR THE WHOLE STORY.
W-WHAT YOU DID... IT WAS SO BRAVE...
GIVING A POOR LOST SOUL A SECOND CHANCE. SAVING THAT GIRL...
IT'S MORE THAN "SAVING" MA. I'VE BECOME THAT GIRL. I'M AS MUCH LINDA AS SUPERGIRL.
WHAT DID YOUR "OTHER" PARENTS SAY? WHEN YOU TOLD THEM?
Uhm...
YOU... HAVEN'T TOLD THEM?
WELL... I'VE BEEN KINDA BUSY.
I MEAN, THERE WAS CHEMO, AND GRODD, PLUS I'D BEEN DATING A SATANIST, BUT THAT'S PRETTY MUCH OVER...
Y'ASK ME, YOUNG LADY, THEY DESERVE TO KNOW.
I JUST ...I'VE...I'VE REALLY GROWN TO LOVE THEM, AND I'M... AFRAID OF HURTING THEM...
THERE ...IS THAT DANGER. IT'S YOUR DECISION, MAE...
...AND, FOR WHAT IT'S WORTH, WE TRUST YOU TO MAKE THE RIGHT ONE.
THANKS, MA. UHM... YOU THINK YOU COULD CALL ME LINDA FROM NOW ON?
FINE, AS LONG AS YOU PROMISE YOU'LL STOP DATING SATANISTS.
OOOOOOKAY.
UNLESS, Y'KNOW... HE'S REALLY CUTE...

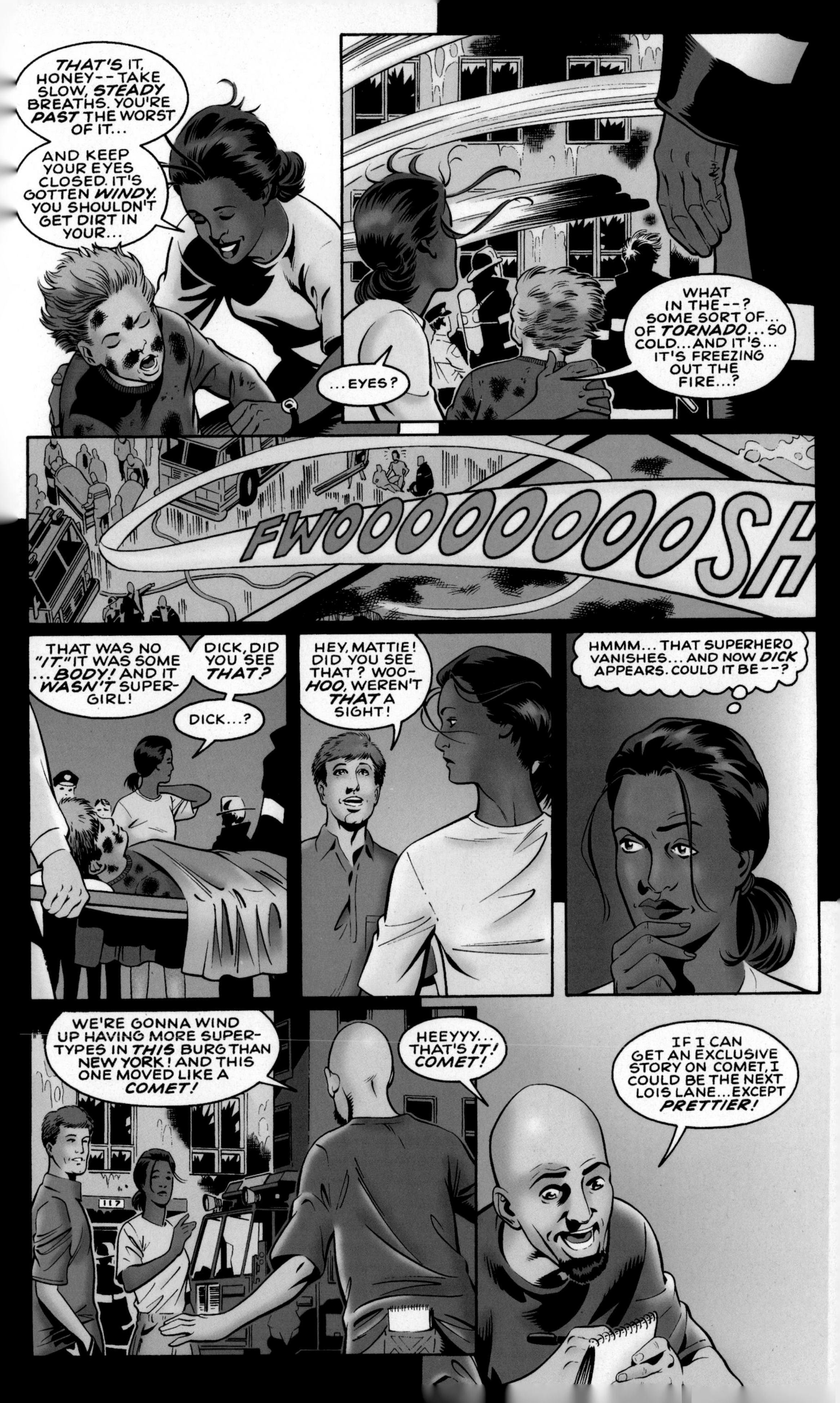

THAT'S IT, HONEY--TAKE SLOW, STEADY BREATHS. YOU'RE PAST THE WORST OF IT...
AND KEEP YOUR EYES CLOSED. IT'S GOTTEN WINDY. YOU SHOULDN'T GET DIRT IN YOUR...
...EYES?
WHAT IN THE--? SOME SORT OF... OF TORNADO...SO COLD...AND IT'S... IT'S FREEZING OUT THE FIRE...?
FWOOOOOOOOOSH
THAT WAS NO "IT." IT WAS SOME...BODY! AND IT WASN'T SUPER-GIRL!
DICK, DID YOU SEE THAT?
DICK...?
HEY, MATTIE! DID YOU SEE THAT? WOO-HOO, WEREN'T THAT A SIGHT!
HMMM... THAT SUPERHERO VANISHES... AND NOW DICK APPEARS. COULD IT BE--?
WE'RE GONNA WIND UP HAVING MORE SUPER-TYPES IN THIS BURG THAN NEW YORK! AND THIS ONE MOVED LIKE A COMET!
HEEYYY... THAT'S IT! COMET!
IF I CAN GET AN EXCLUSIVE STORY ON COMET, I COULD BE THE NEXT LOIS LANE...EXCEPT PRETTIER!

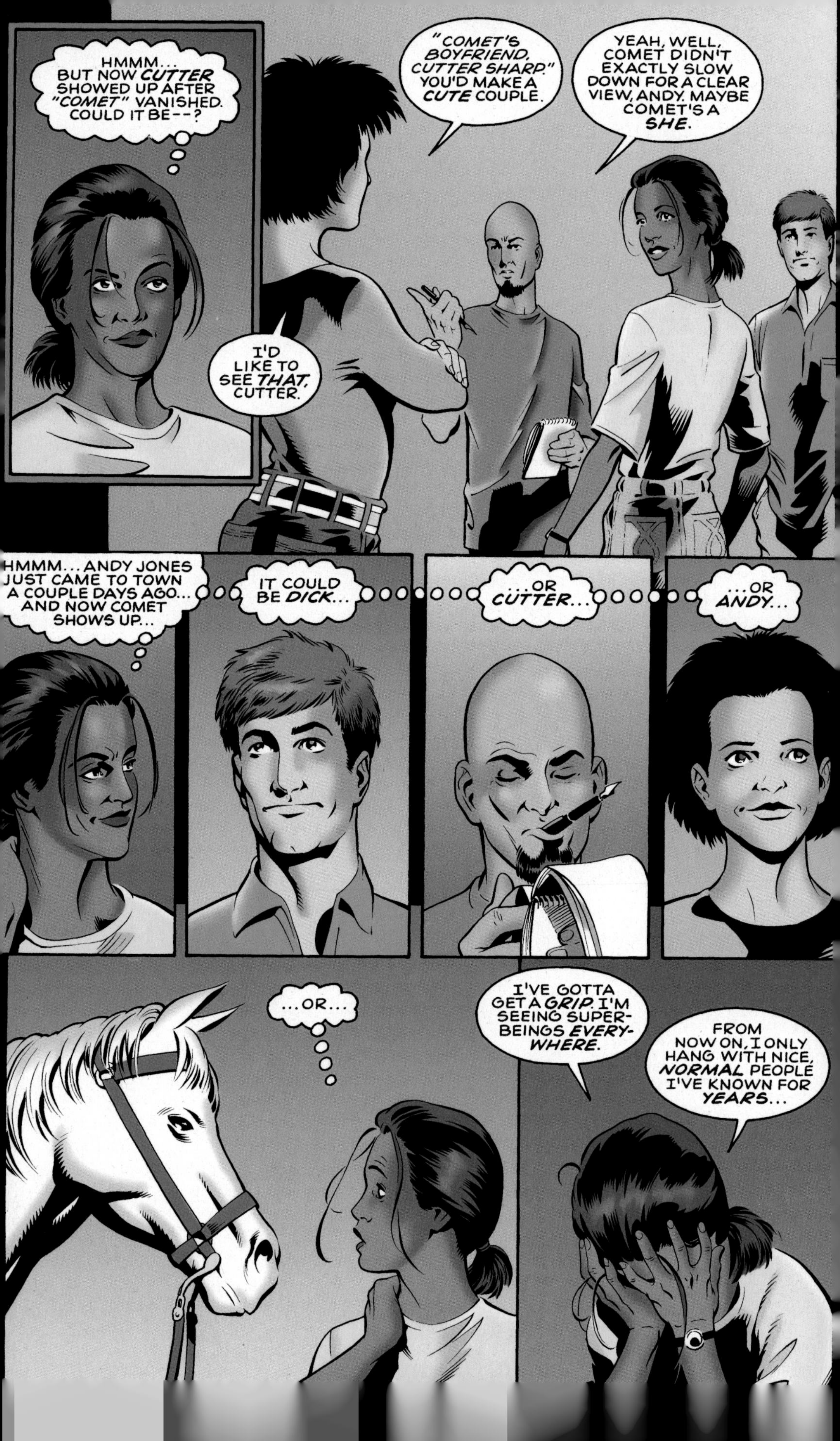
HMMM... BUT NOW CUTTER SHOWED UP AFTER "COMET" VANISHED. COULD IT BE--?
"COMET'S BOYFRIEND, CUTTER SHARP." YOU'D MAKE A CUTE COUPLE.
YEAH, WELL, COMET DIDN'T EXACTLY SLOW DOWN FOR A CLEAR VIEW, ANDY. MAYBE COMET'S A SHE.
I'D LIKE TO SEE THAT, CUTTER.
HMMM... ANDY JONES JUST CAME TO TOWN A COUPLE DAYS AGO... AND NOW COMET SHOWS UP...
IT COULD BE DICK...
...OR CUTTER...
...OR ANDY...
...OR...
I'VE GOTTA GET A GRIP. I'M SEEING SUPER-BEINGS EVERY-WHERE.
FROM NOW ON, I ONLY HANG WITH NICE, NORMAL PEOPLE I'VE KNOWN FOR YEARS...

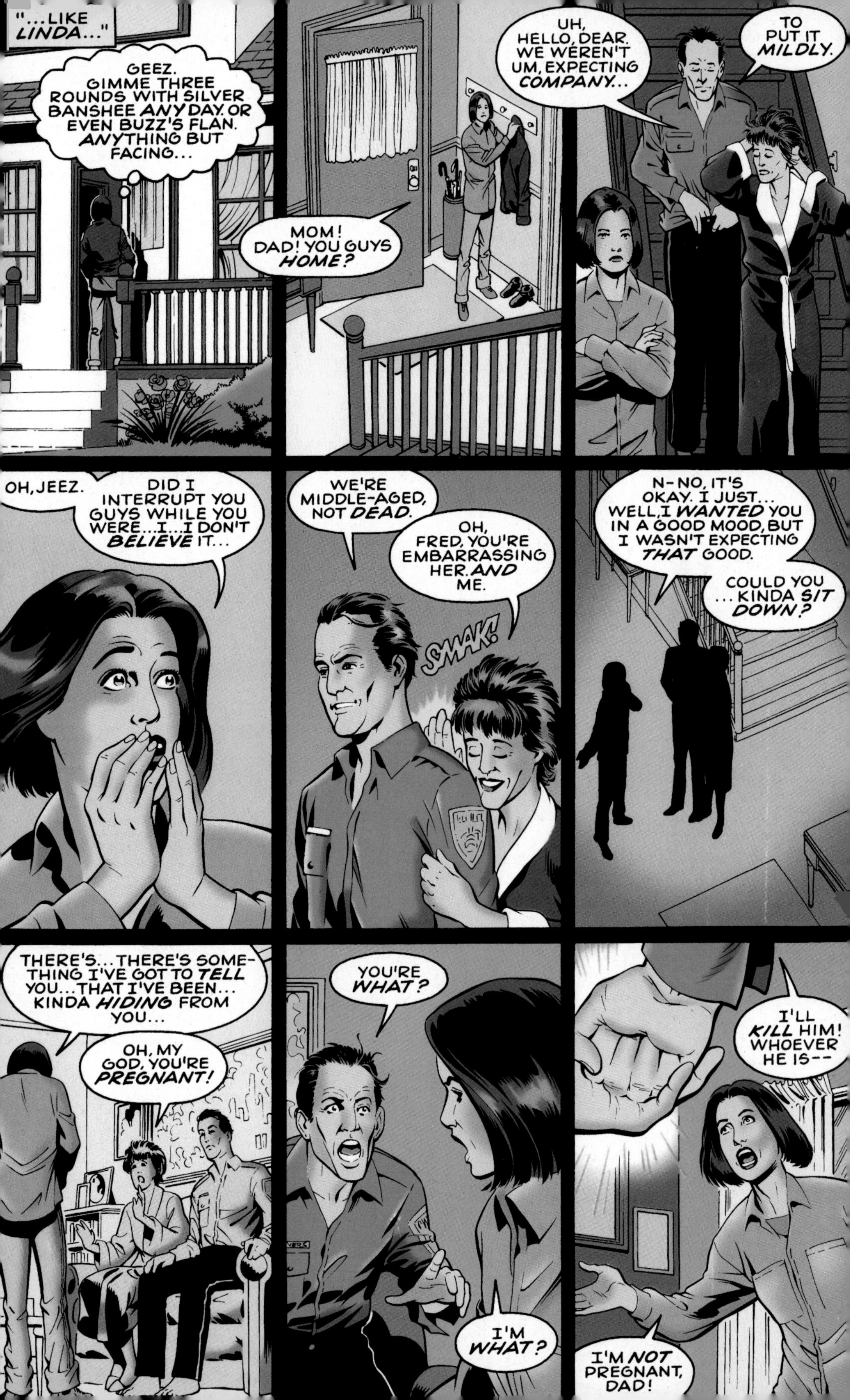
"...LIKE LINDA..."
GEEZ. GIMME THREE ROUNDS WITH SILVER BANSHEE ANY DAY. OR EVEN BUZZ'S FLAN. ANYTHING BUT FACING...
MOM! DAD! YOU GUYS HOME?
UH, HELLO, DEAR. WE WEREN'T UM, EXPECTING COMPANY...
TO PUT IT MILDLY.
OH, JEEZ.
DID I INTERRUPT YOU GUYS WHILE YOU WERE...I...I DON'T BELIEVE IT...
WE'RE MIDDLE-AGED, NOT DEAD.
OH, FRED, YOU'RE EMBARRASSING HER. AND ME.
SMAK!
N-NO, IT'S OKAY. I JUST... WELL, I WANTED YOU IN A GOOD MOOD, BUT I WASN'T EXPECTING THAT GOOD.
COULD YOU ...KINDA SIT DOWN?
THERE'S...THERE'S SOMETHING I'VE GOT TO TELL YOU...THAT I'VE BEEN... KINDA HIDING FROM YOU...
OH, MY GOD, YOU'RE PREGNANT!
YOU'RE WHAT?
I'M WHAT?
I'LL KILL HIM! WHOEVER HE IS--
I'M NOT PREGNANT, DAD!

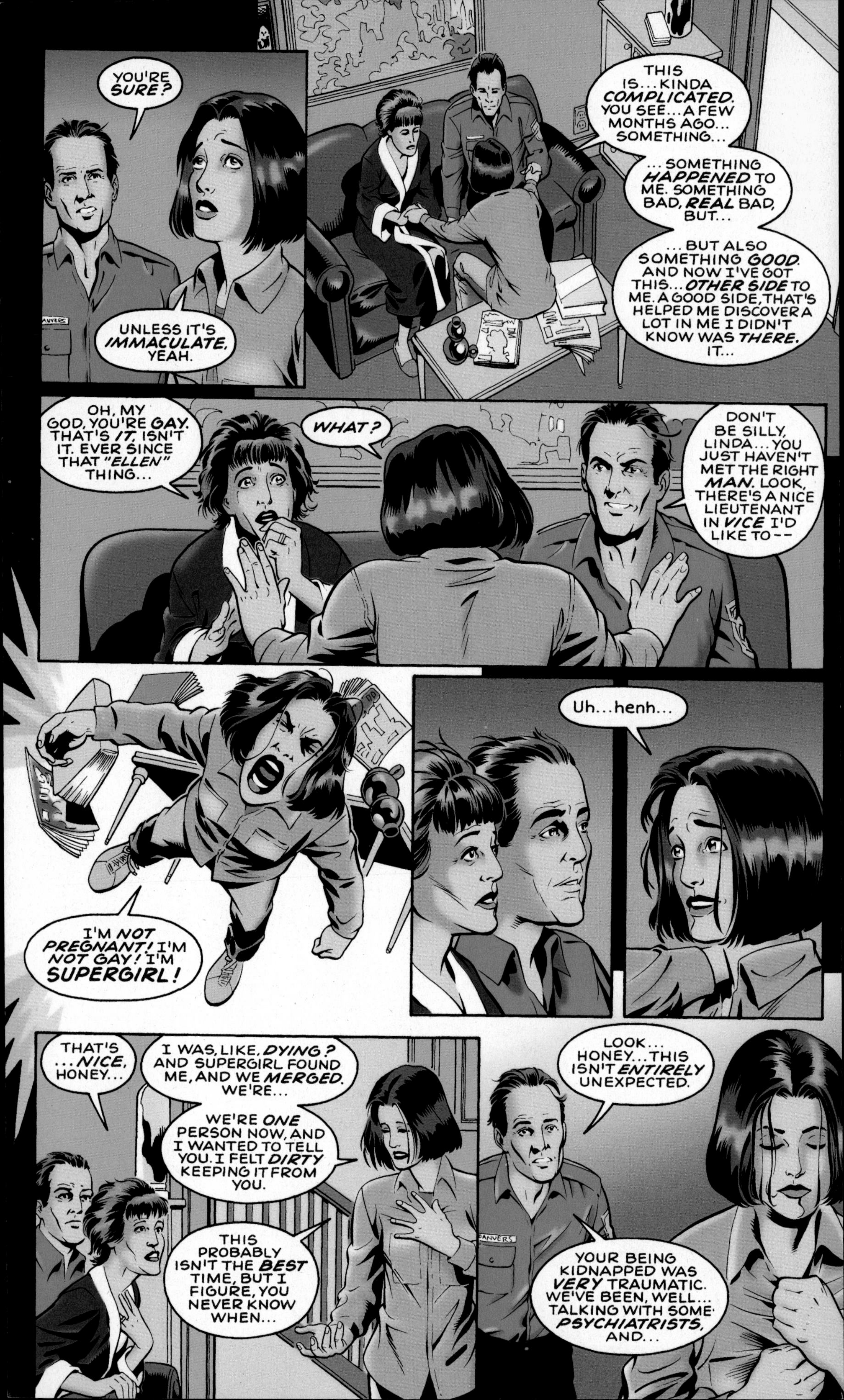
YOU'RE SURE?
UNLESS IT'S IMMACULATE, YEAH.
THIS IS... KINDA COMPLICATED. YOU SEE... A FEW MONTHS AGO... SOMETHING...
... SOMETHING HAPPENED TO ME. SOMETHING BAD, REAL BAD, BUT...
... BUT ALSO SOMETHING GOOD. AND NOW I'VE GOT THIS... OTHER SIDE TO ME. A GOOD SIDE, THAT'S HELPED ME DISCOVER A LOT IN ME I DIDN'T KNOW WAS THERE. IT...
OH, MY GOD, YOU'RE GAY. THAT'S IT, ISN'T IT. EVER SINCE THAT "ELLEN" THING...
WHAT?
DON'T BE SILLY, LINDA... YOU JUST HAVEN'T MET THE RIGHT MAN. LOOK, THERE'S A NICE LIEUTENANT IN VICE I'D LIKE TO--
I'M NOT PREGNANT! I'M NOT GAY! I'M SUPERGIRL!
Uh...henh...
THAT'S ...NICE, HONEY...
I WAS, LIKE, DYING? AND SUPERGIRL FOUND ME, AND WE MERGED. WE'RE...
WE'RE ONE PERSON NOW, AND I WANTED TO TELL YOU. I FELT DIRTY KEEPING IT FROM YOU.
THIS PROBABLY ISN'T THE BEST TIME, BUT I FIGURE, YOU NEVER KNOW WHEN...
LOOK... HONEY... THIS ISN'T ENTIRELY UNEXPECTED.
YOUR BEING KIDNAPPED WAS VERY TRAUMATIC. WE'VE BEEN, WELL... TALKING WITH SOME PSYCHIATRISTS, AND...

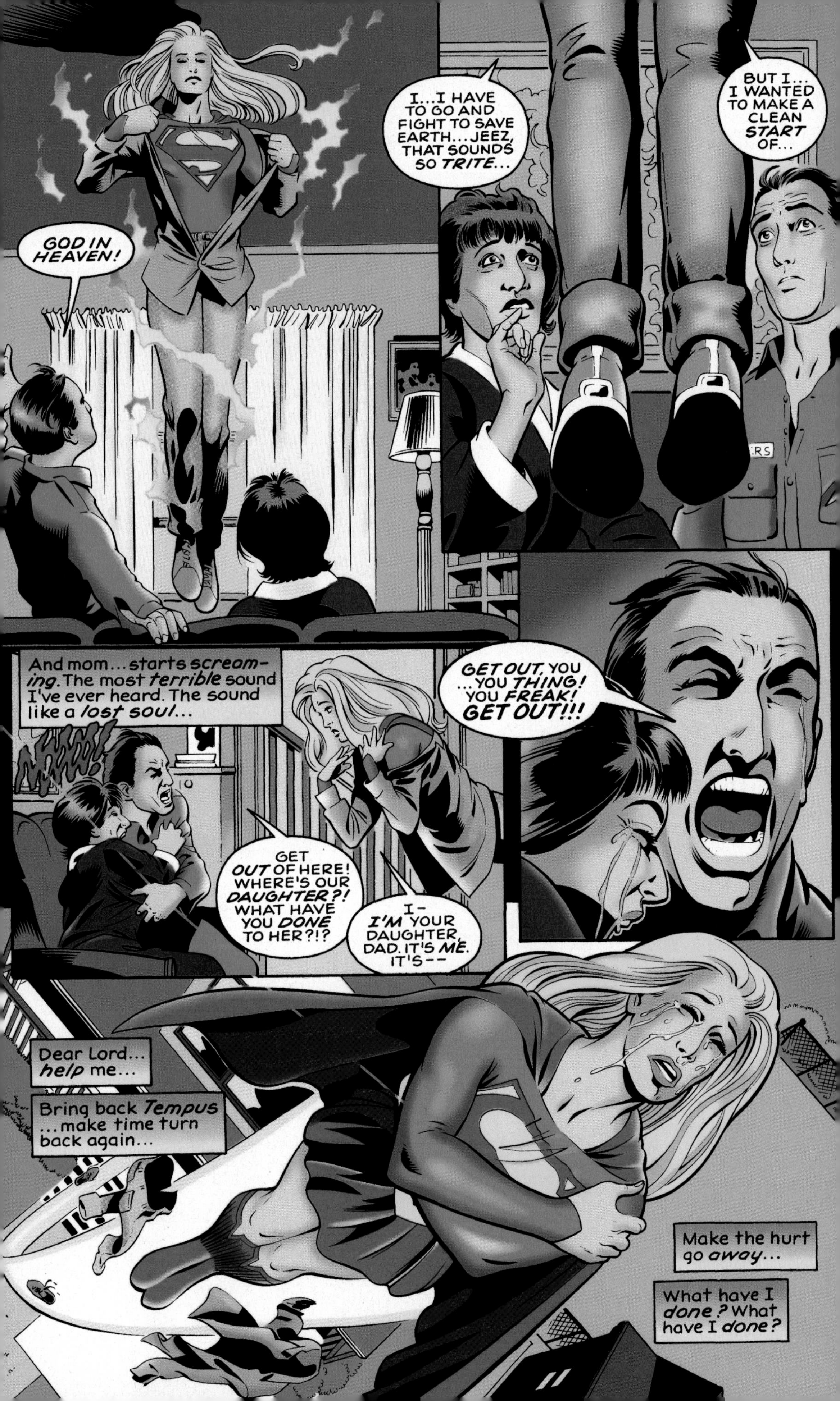
GOD IN HEAVEN!
I...I HAVE TO GO AND FIGHT TO SAVE EARTH...JEEZ, THAT SOUNDS SO TRITE...
BUT I... I WANTED TO MAKE A CLEAN START OF...
And mom...starts screaming. The most terrible sound I've ever heard. The sound like a lost soul...
GET OUT OF HERE! WHERE'S OUR DAUGHTER?! WHAT HAVE YOU DONE TO HER?!?
I- I'M YOUR DAUGHTER, DAD. IT'S ME. IT'S--
GET OUT, YOU ...YOU THING! YOU FREAK! GET OUT!!!
Dear Lord... help me...
Bring back Tempus ...make time turn back again...
Make the hurt go away...
What have I done? What have I done?

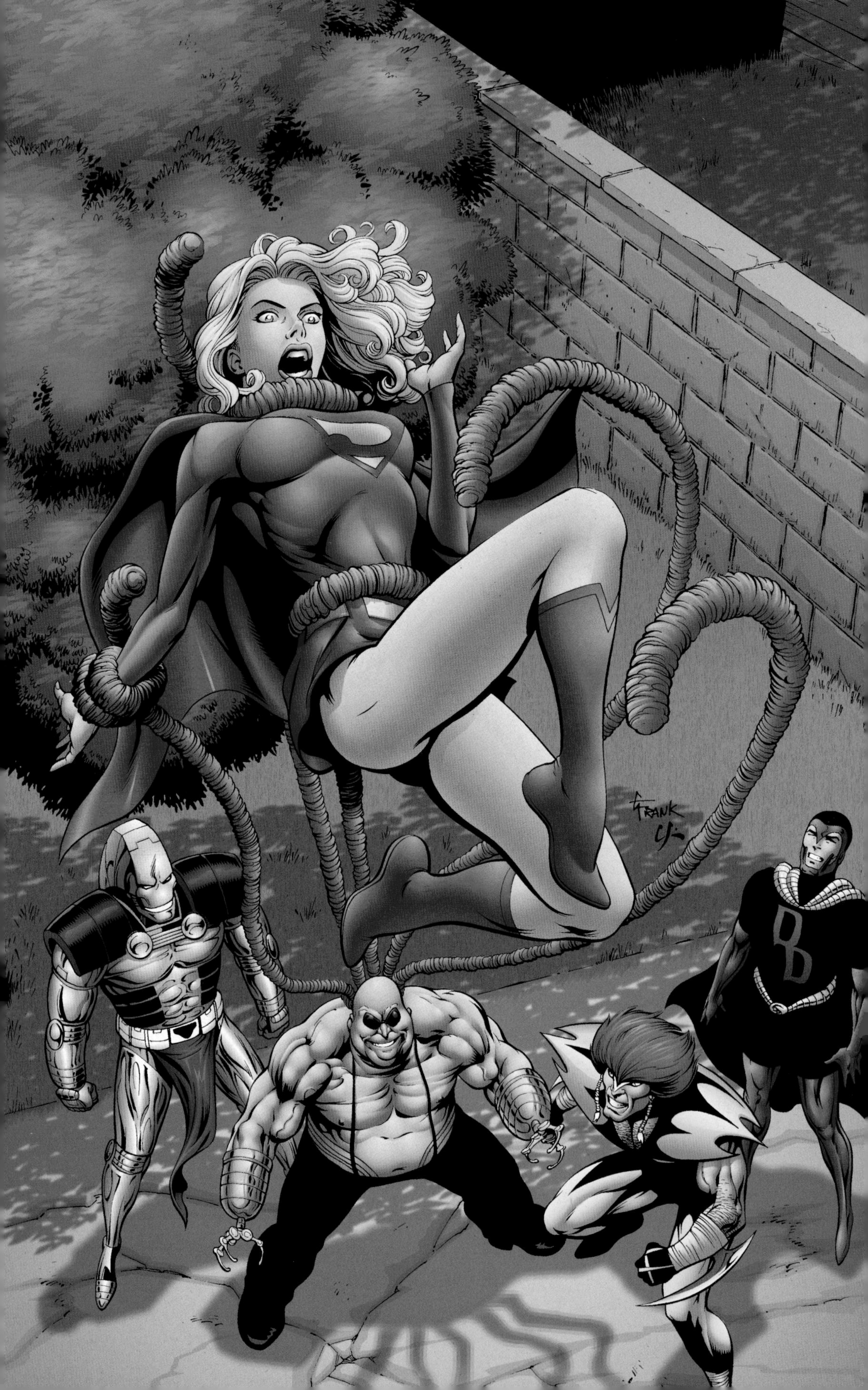

SUPERGIRL #15 cover by Gary Frank, Cam Smith and Patrick Martin

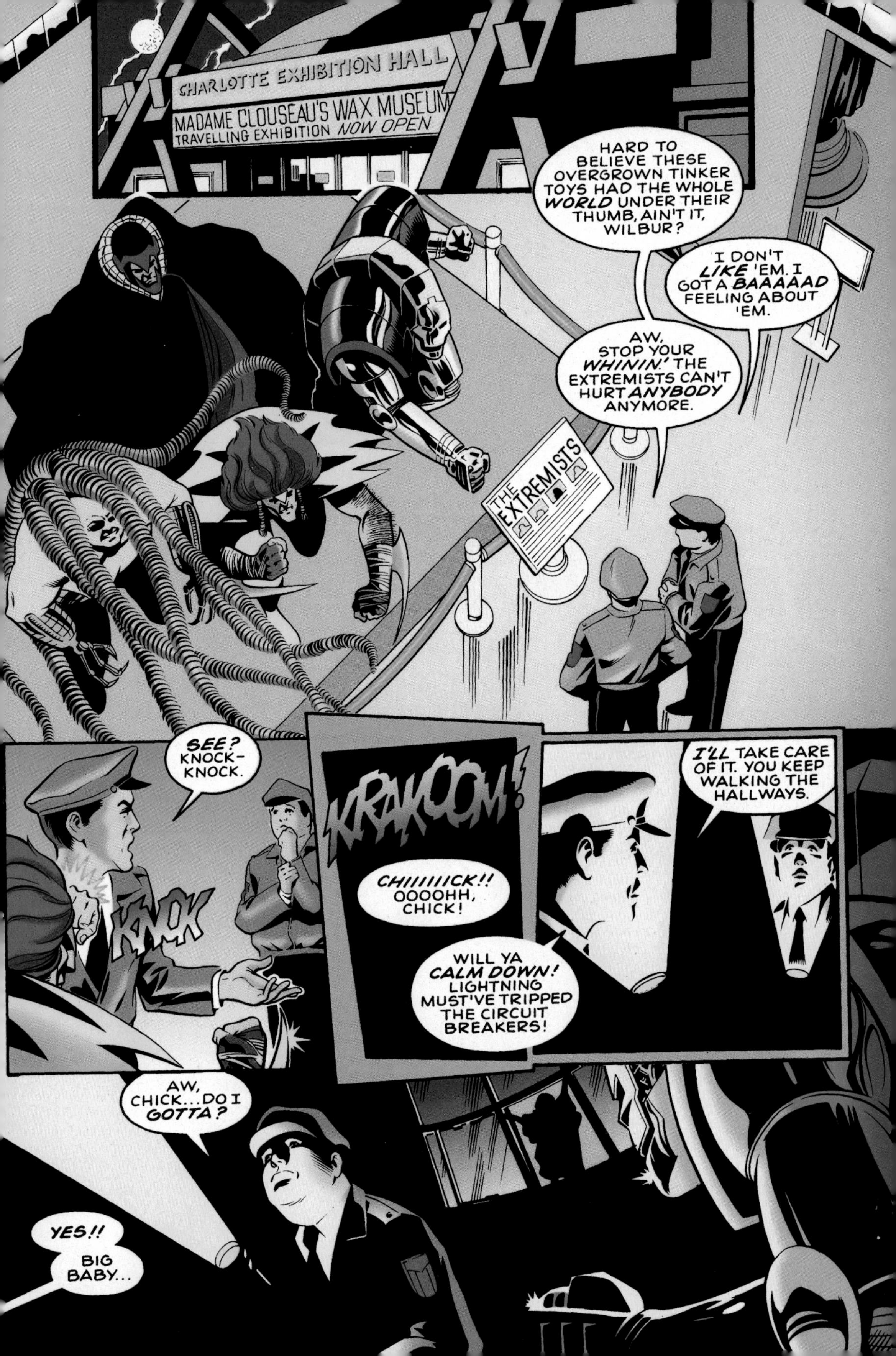
CHARLOTTE EXHIBITION HALL
MADAME CLOUSEAU'S WAX MUSEUM
TRAVELLING EXHIBITION NOW OPEN
HARD TO BELIEVE THESE OVERGROWN TINKER TOYS HAD THE WHOLE WORLD UNDER THEIR THUMB, AIN'T IT, WILBUR?
I DON'T LIKE 'EM. I GOT A BAAAAAD FEELING ABOUT 'EM.
AW, STOP YOUR WHININ.' THE EXTREMISTS CAN'T HURT ANYBODY ANYMORE.
THE EXTREMISTS
SEE? KNOCK-KNOCK.
KNOK
KRAKOOM!
CHIIIIIICK!! OOOOHH, CHICK!
WILL YA CALM DOWN! LIGHTNING MUST'VE TRIPPED THE CIRCUIT BREAKERS!
I'LL TAKE CARE OF IT. YOU KEEP WALKING THE HALLWAYS.
AW, CHICK...DO I GOTTA?
YES!!
BIG BABY...

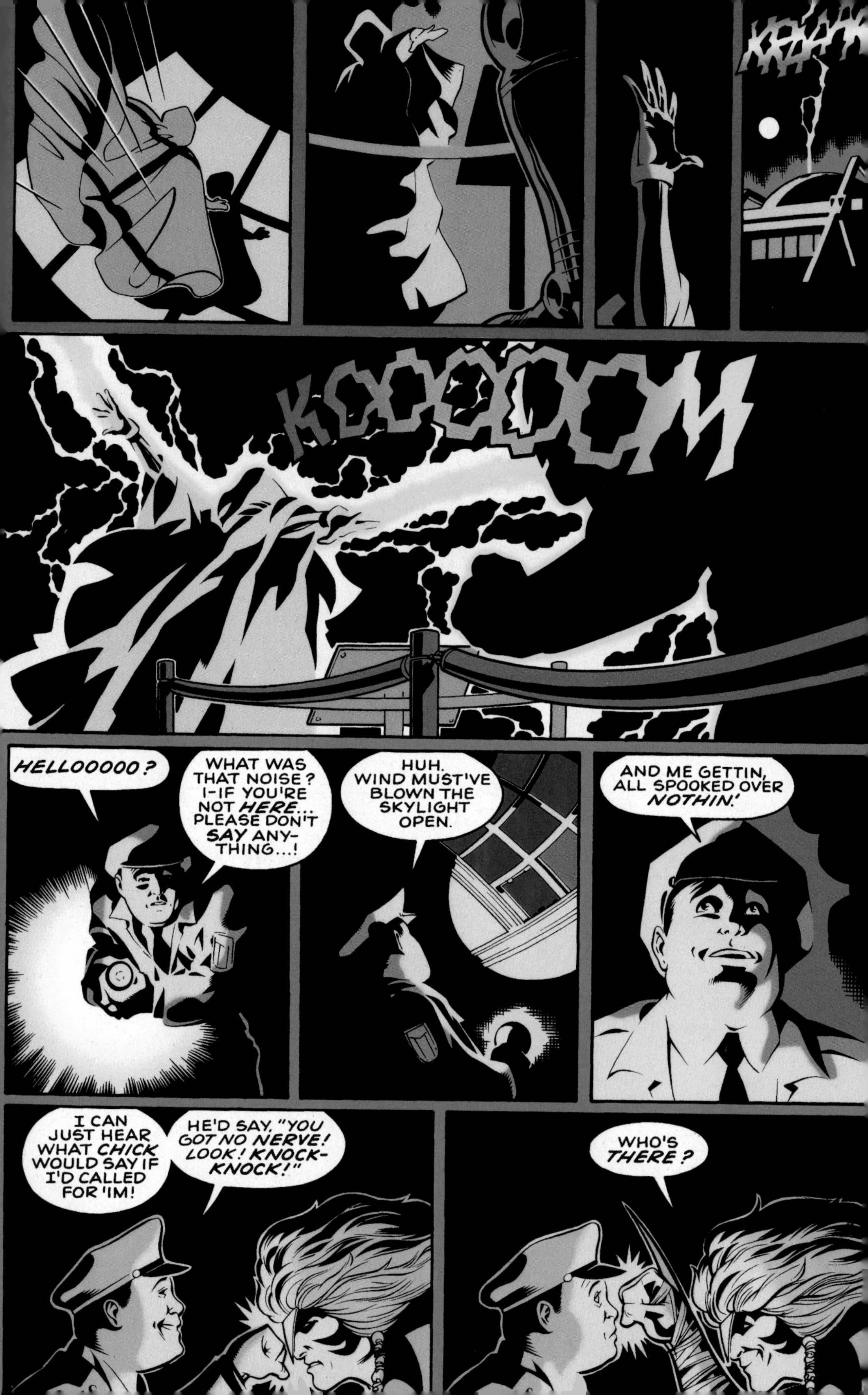
KRAAK
KOOOOOM
HELLOOOOO?
WHAT WAS THAT NOISE? I-IF YOU'RE NOT HERE... PLEASE DON'T SAY ANYTHING...!
HUH. WIND MUST'VE BLOWN THE SKYLIGHT OPEN.
AND ME GETTIN ALL SPOOKED OVER NOTHIN.'
I CAN JUST HEAR WHAT CHICK WOULD SAY IF I'D CALLED FOR 'IM!
HE'D SAY, "YOU GOT NO NERVE! LOOK! KNOCK-KNOCK!"
WHO'S THERE?

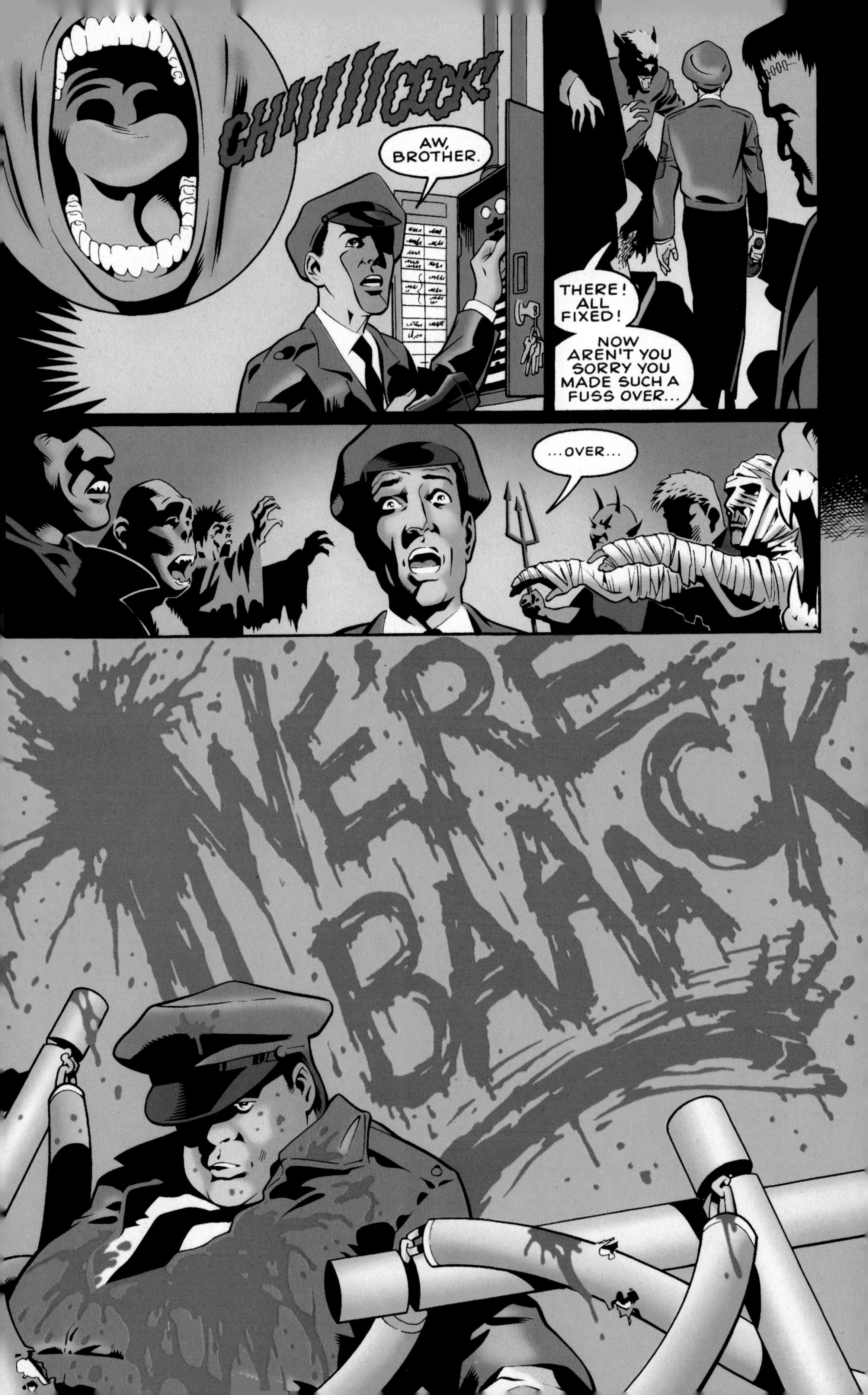
CHIIIIICCCK!
AW, BROTHER.
THERE! ALL FIXED!
NOW AREN'T YOU SORRY YOU MADE SUCH A FUSS OVER...
...OVER...
WE'RE BAAACK

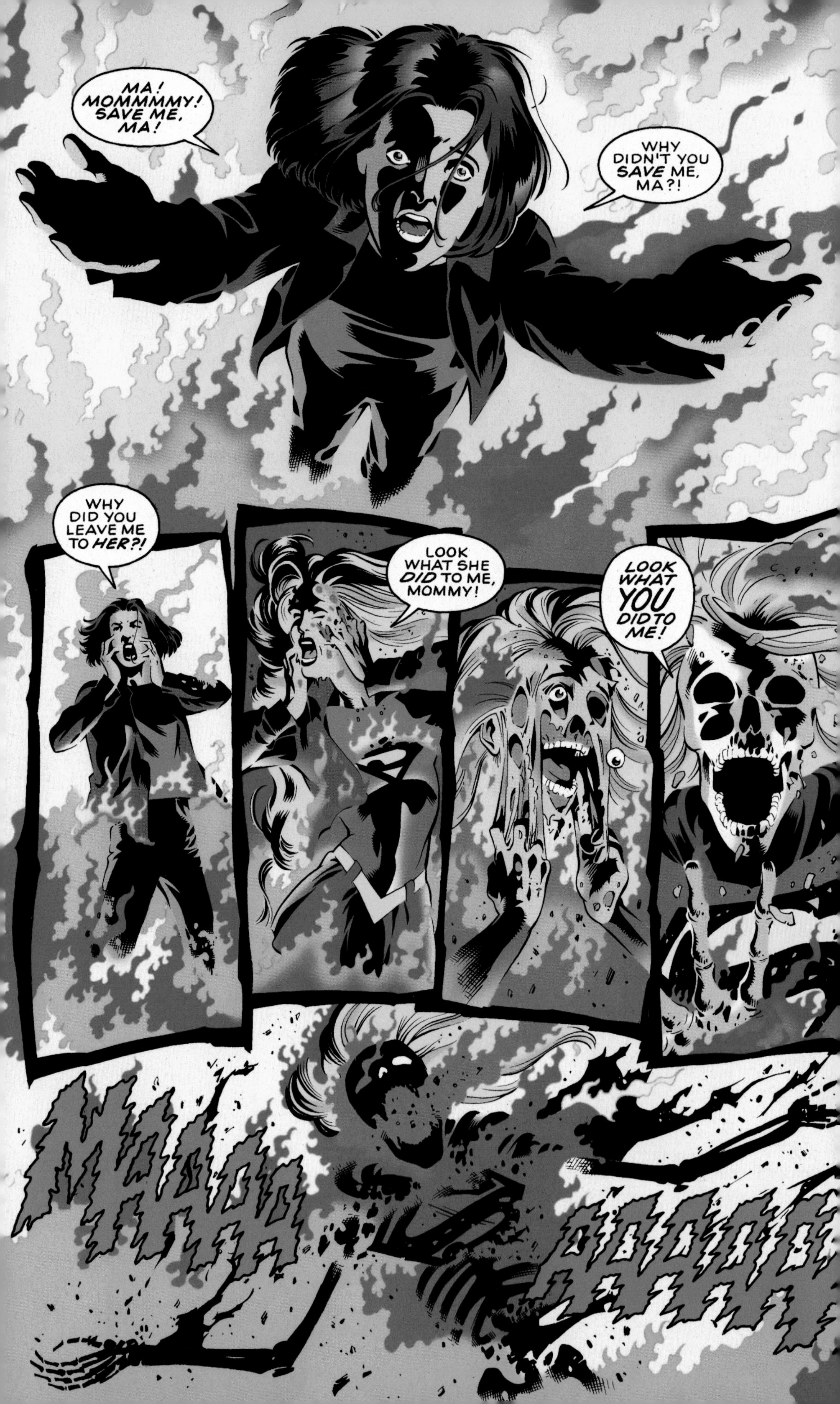

MA! MOMMMMY! SAVE ME, MA!
WHY DIDN'T YOU SAVE ME, MA?!
WHY DID YOU LEAVE ME TO HER?!
LOOK WHAT SHE DID TO ME, MOMMY!
LOOK WHAT YOU DID TO ME!

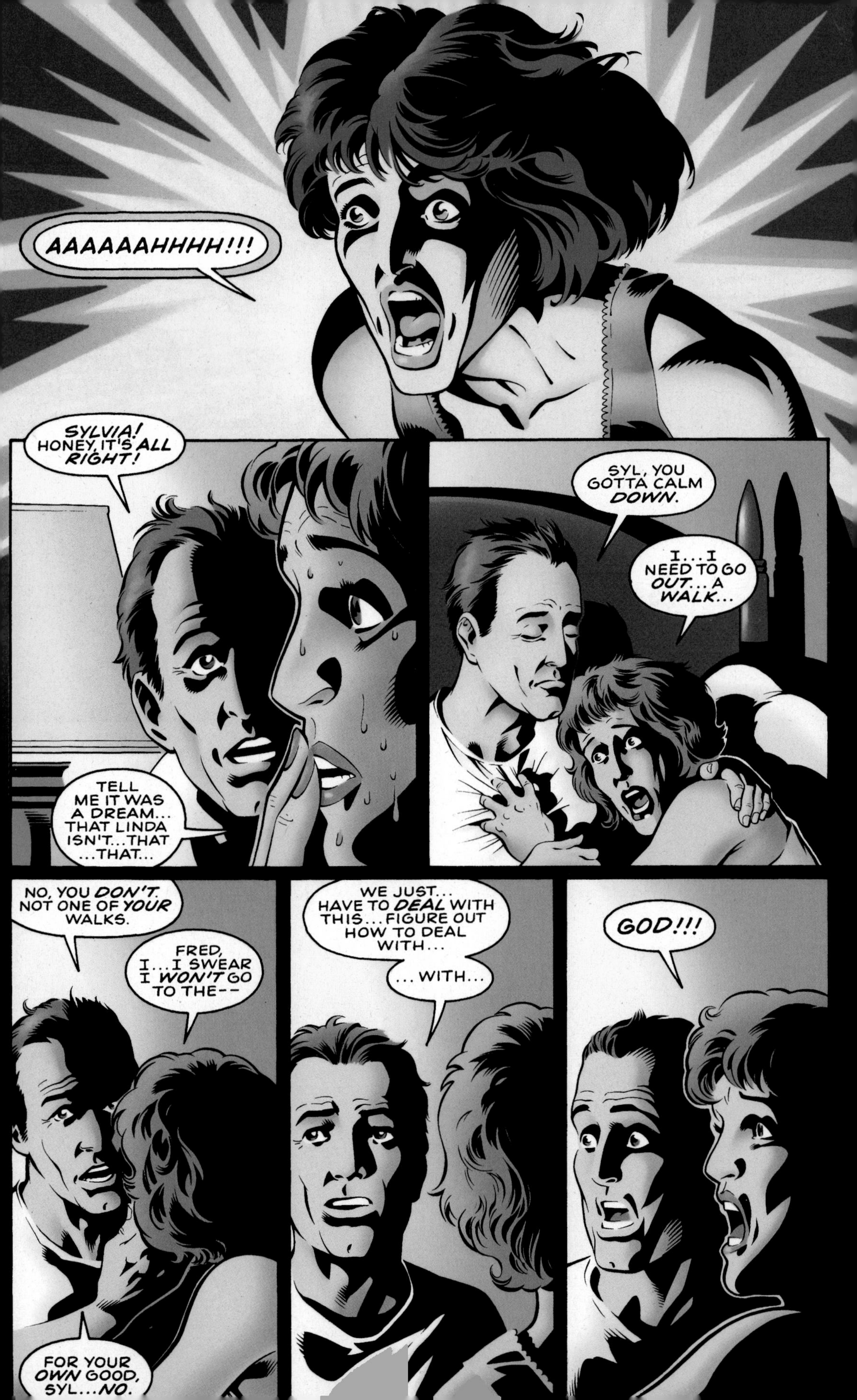
AAAAAAHHHH!!!
SYLVIA! HONEY, IT'S ALL RIGHT!
TELL ME IT WAS A DREAM... THAT LINDA ISN'T... THAT ...THAT...
SYL, YOU GOTTA CALM DOWN.
I...I NEED TO GO OUT... A WALK...
NO, YOU DON'T. NOT ONE OF YOUR WALKS.
FRED, I...I SWEAR I WON'T GO TO THE--
FOR YOUR OWN GOOD, SYL...NO.
WE JUST... HAVE TO DEAL WITH THIS... FIGURE OUT HOW TO DEAL WITH...
...WITH...
GOD!!!

GODS OF THE TWILIGHT

PETER DAVID, WRITER · LEONARD KIRK, PENCILLER

CAM SMITH, INKER · PAT PRENTICE, LETTERER

GENE D'ANGELO, COLORIST

DIGITAL CHAMELEON, SEPS

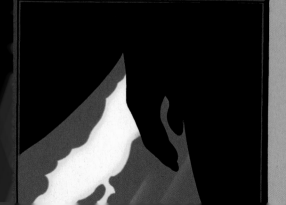

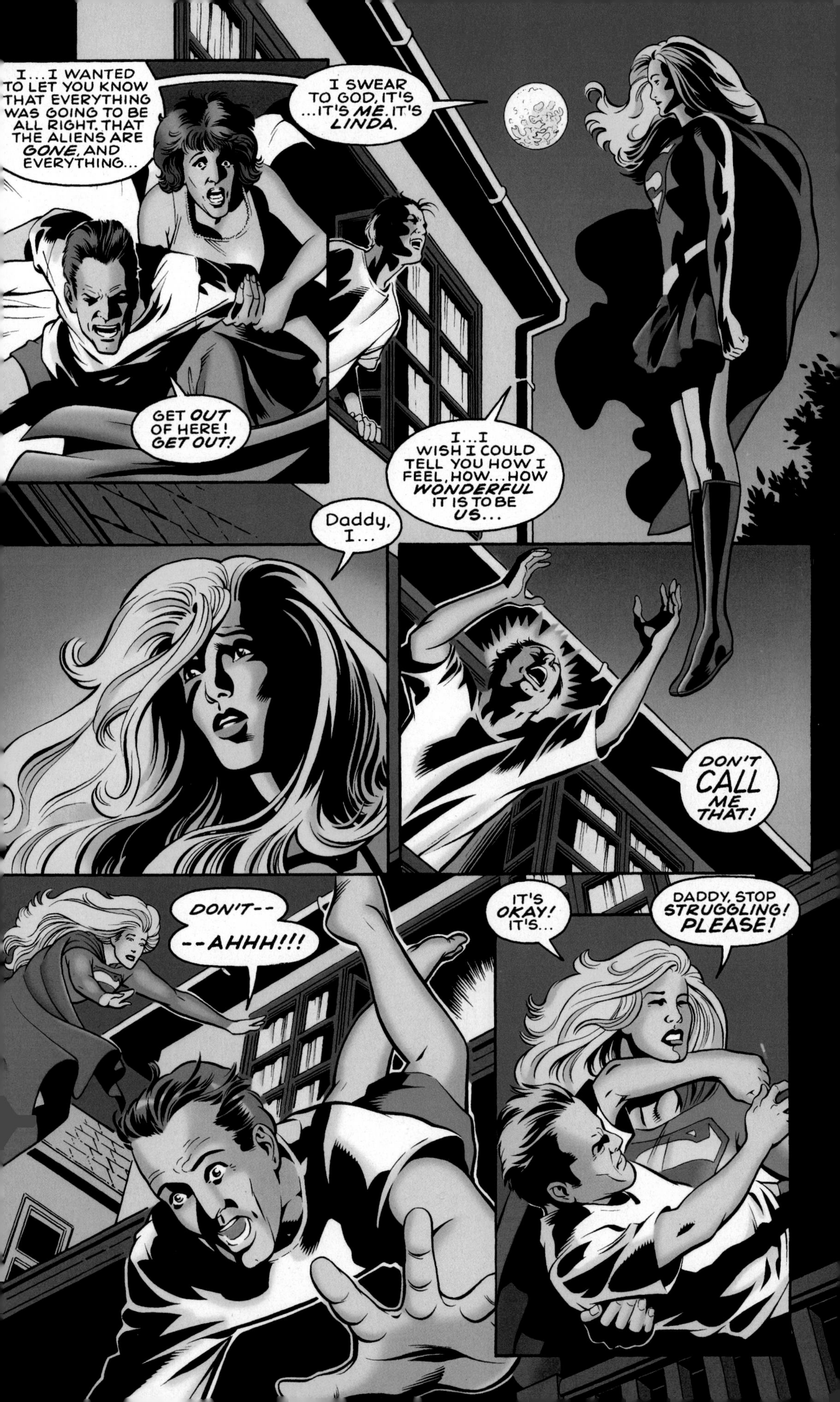
I... I WANTED TO LET YOU KNOW THAT EVERYTHING WAS GOING TO BE ALL RIGHT. THAT THE ALIENS ARE GONE, AND EVERYTHING...
I SWEAR TO GOD, IT'S ...IT'S ME. IT'S LINDA.
GET OUT OF HERE! GET OUT!
I...I WISH I COULD TELL YOU HOW I FEEL, HOW...HOW WONDERFUL IT IS TO BE US...
Daddy, I...
DON'T CALL ME THAT!
DON'T--
--AHHH!!!
IT'S OKAY! IT'S...
DADDY, STOP STRUGGLING! PLEASE!

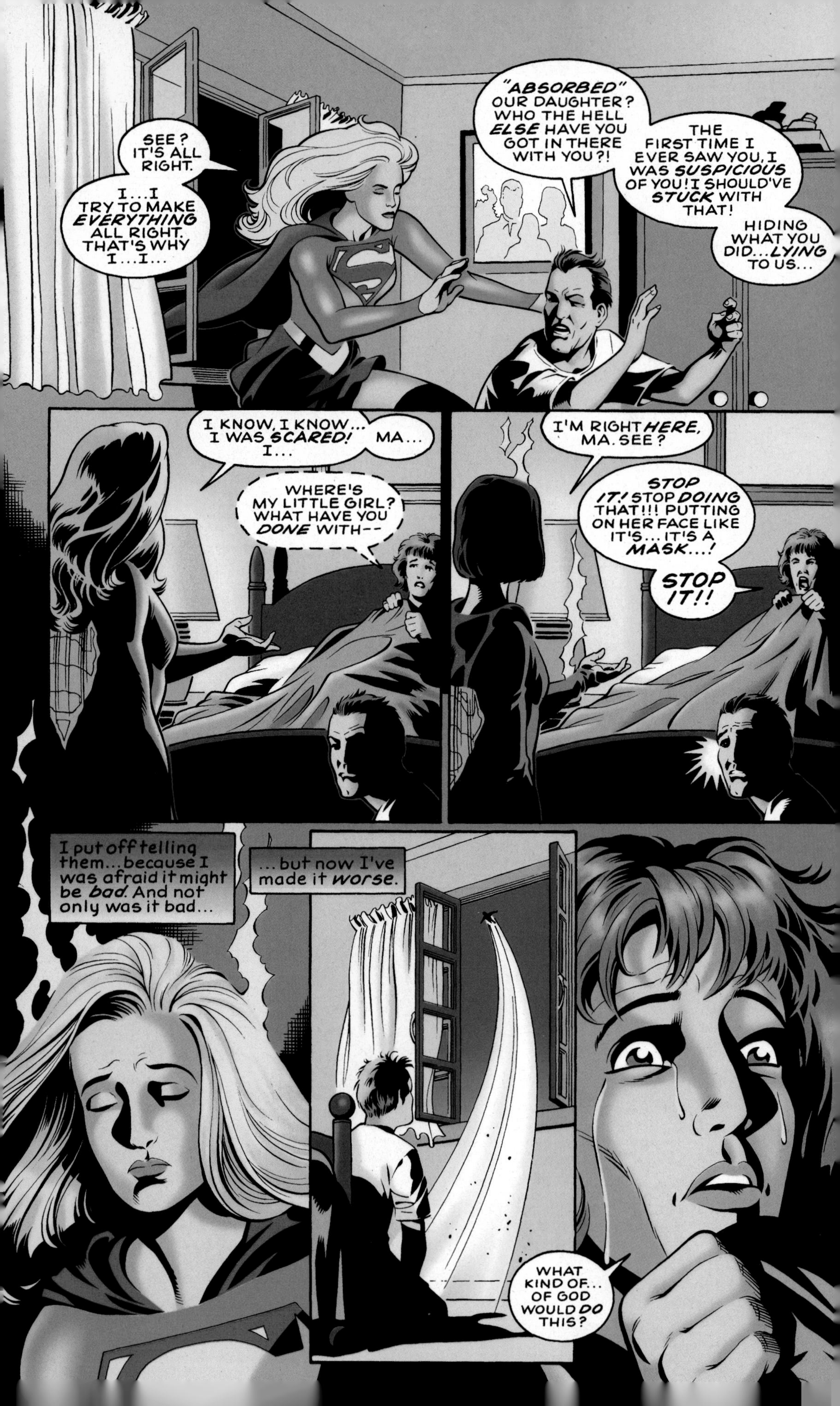

SEE? IT'S ALL RIGHT.
I...I TRY TO MAKE EVERYTHING ALL RIGHT. THAT'S WHY I...I...
"ABSORBED" OUR DAUGHTER? WHO THE HELL ELSE HAVE YOU GOT IN THERE WITH YOU?!
THE FIRST TIME I EVER SAW YOU, I WAS SUSPICIOUS OF YOU! I SHOULD'VE STUCK WITH THAT!
HIDING WHAT YOU DID...LYING TO US...
I KNOW, I KNOW... I WAS SCARED! I...
MA...
WHERE'S MY LITTLE GIRL? WHAT HAVE YOU DONE WITH--
I'M RIGHT HERE, MA. SEE?
STOP IT! STOP DOING THAT!!! PUTTING ON HER FACE LIKE IT'S... IT'S A MASK...!
STOP IT!!
I put off telling them...because I was afraid it might be bad. And not only was it bad...
...but now I've made it worse.
WHAT KIND OF... OF GOD WOULD DO THIS?

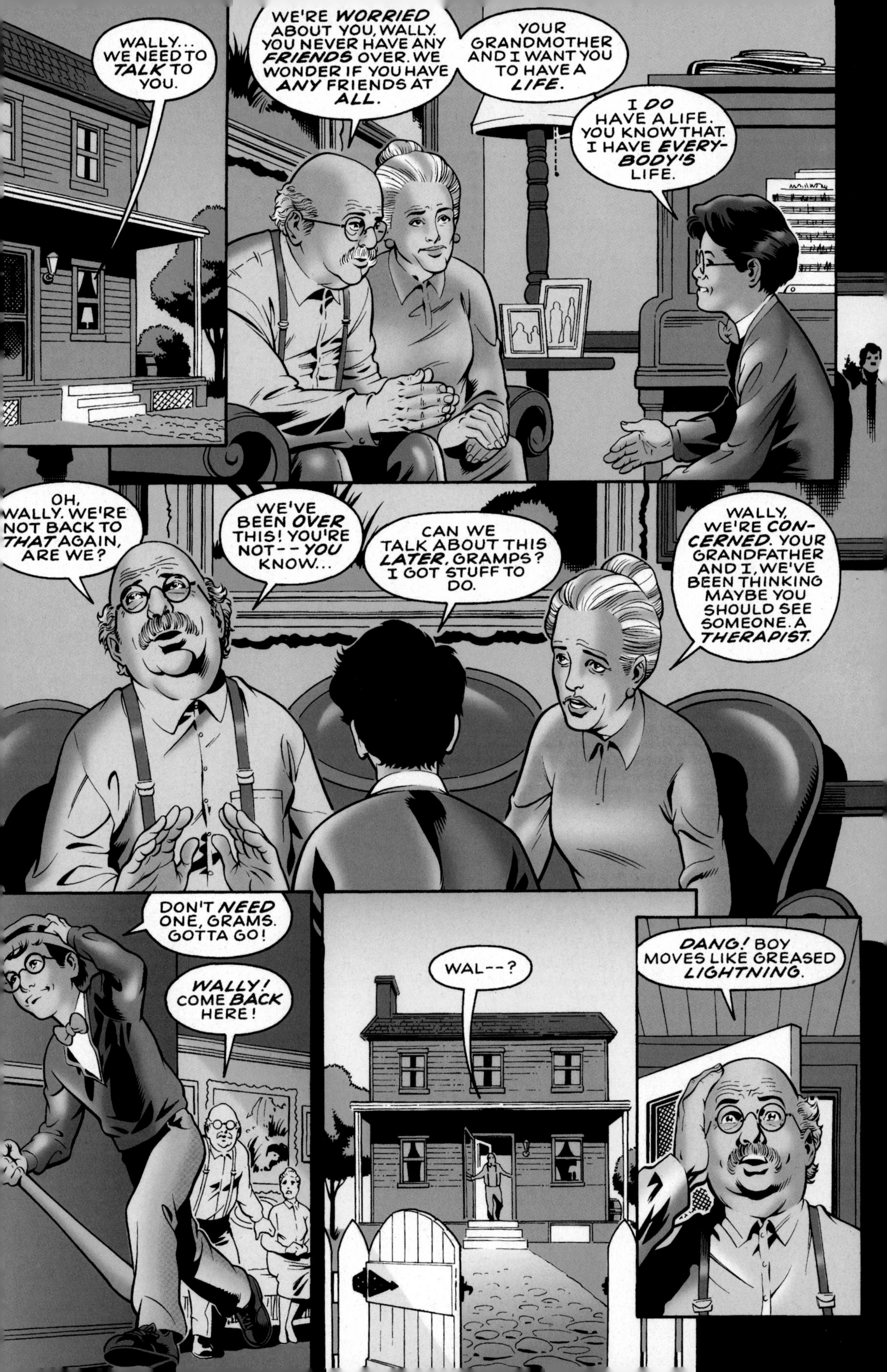
WALLY... WE NEED TO TALK TO YOU.
WE'RE WORRIED ABOUT YOU, WALLY. YOU NEVER HAVE ANY FRIENDS OVER. WE WONDER IF YOU HAVE ANY FRIENDS AT ALL.
YOUR GRANDMOTHER AND I WANT YOU TO HAVE A LIFE.
I DO HAVE A LIFE. YOU KNOW THAT. I HAVE EVERY-BODY'S LIFE.
OH, WALLY. WE'RE NOT BACK TO THAT AGAIN, ARE WE?
WE'VE BEEN OVER THIS! YOU'RE NOT-- YOU KNOW...
CAN WE TALK ABOUT THIS LATER, GRAMPS? I GOT STUFF TO DO.
WALLY, WE'RE CON-CERNED. YOUR GRANDFATHER AND I, WE'VE BEEN THINKING MAYBE YOU SHOULD SEE SOMEONE. A THERAPIST.
DON'T NEED ONE, GRAMS. GOTTA GO!
WALLY! COME BACK HERE!
WAL--?
DANG! BOY MOVES LIKE GREASED LIGHTNING.

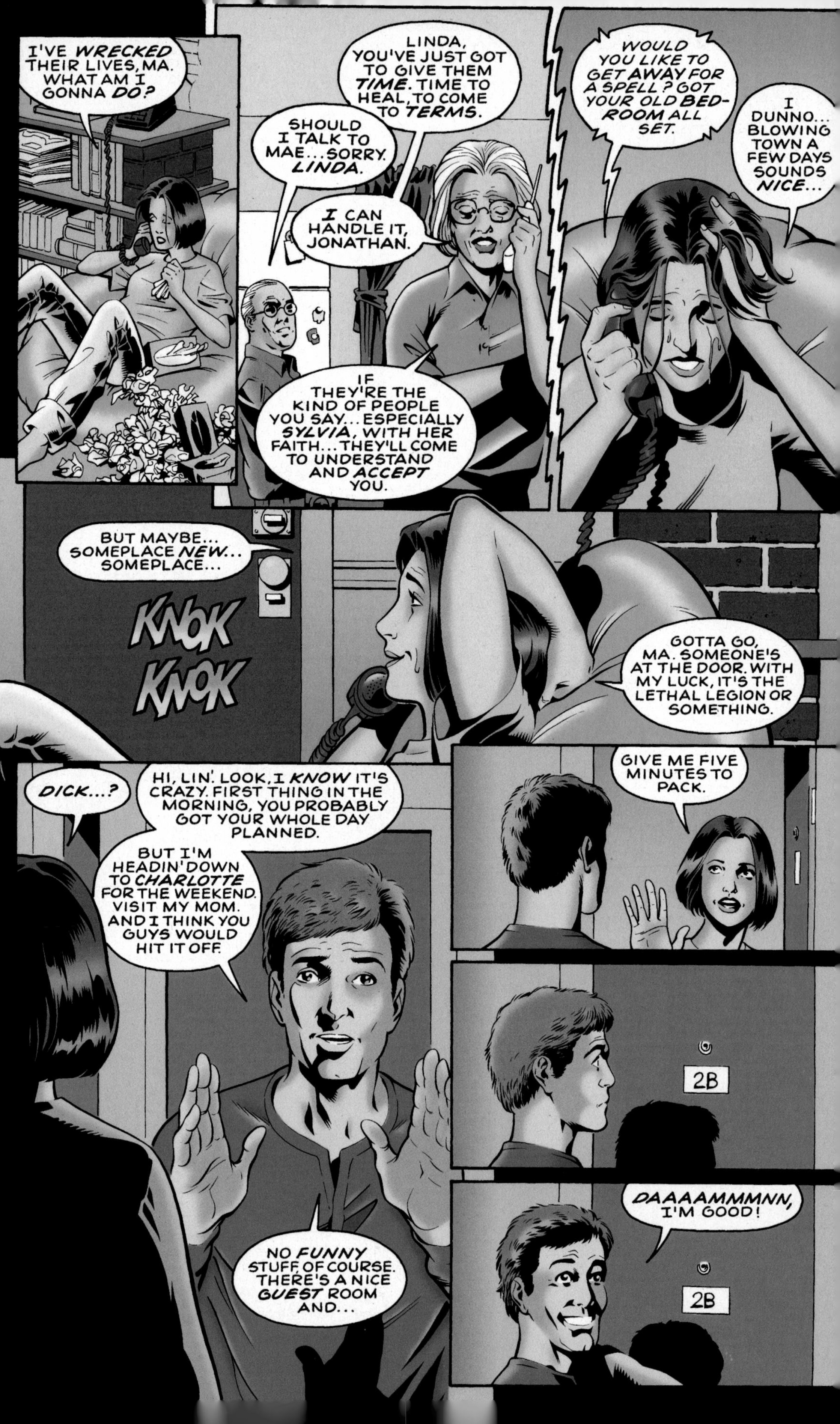
I'VE WRECKED THEIR LIVES, MA. WHAT AM I GONNA DO?
LINDA, YOU'VE JUST GOT TO GIVE THEM TIME. TIME TO HEAL, TO COME TO TERMS.
SHOULD I TALK TO MAE... SORRY. LINDA.
I CAN HANDLE IT, JONATHAN.
IF THEY'RE THE KIND OF PEOPLE YOU SAY... ESPECIALLY SYLVIA, WITH HER FAITH... THEY'LL COME TO UNDERSTAND AND ACCEPT YOU.
WOULD YOU LIKE TO GET AWAY FOR A SPELL? GOT YOUR OLD BED-ROOM ALL SET.
I DUNNO... BLOWING TOWN A FEW DAYS SOUNDS NICE...
BUT MAYBE... SOMEPLACE NEW... SOMEPLACE...
KNOK
KNOK
GOTTA GO, MA. SOMEONE'S AT THE DOOR. WITH MY LUCK, IT'S THE LETHAL LEGION OR SOMETHING.
DICK...?
HI, LIN'. LOOK, I KNOW IT'S CRAZY. FIRST THING IN THE MORNING, YOU PROBABLY GOT YOUR WHOLE DAY PLANNED.
BUT I'M HEADIN' DOWN TO CHARLOTTE FOR THE WEEKEND. VISIT MY MOM. AND I THINK YOU GUYS WOULD HIT IT OFF.
NO FUNNY STUFF, OF COURSE. THERE'S A NICE GUEST ROOM AND...
GIVE ME FIVE MINUTES TO PACK.
2B
DAAAAMMMNN, I'M GOOD!
2B

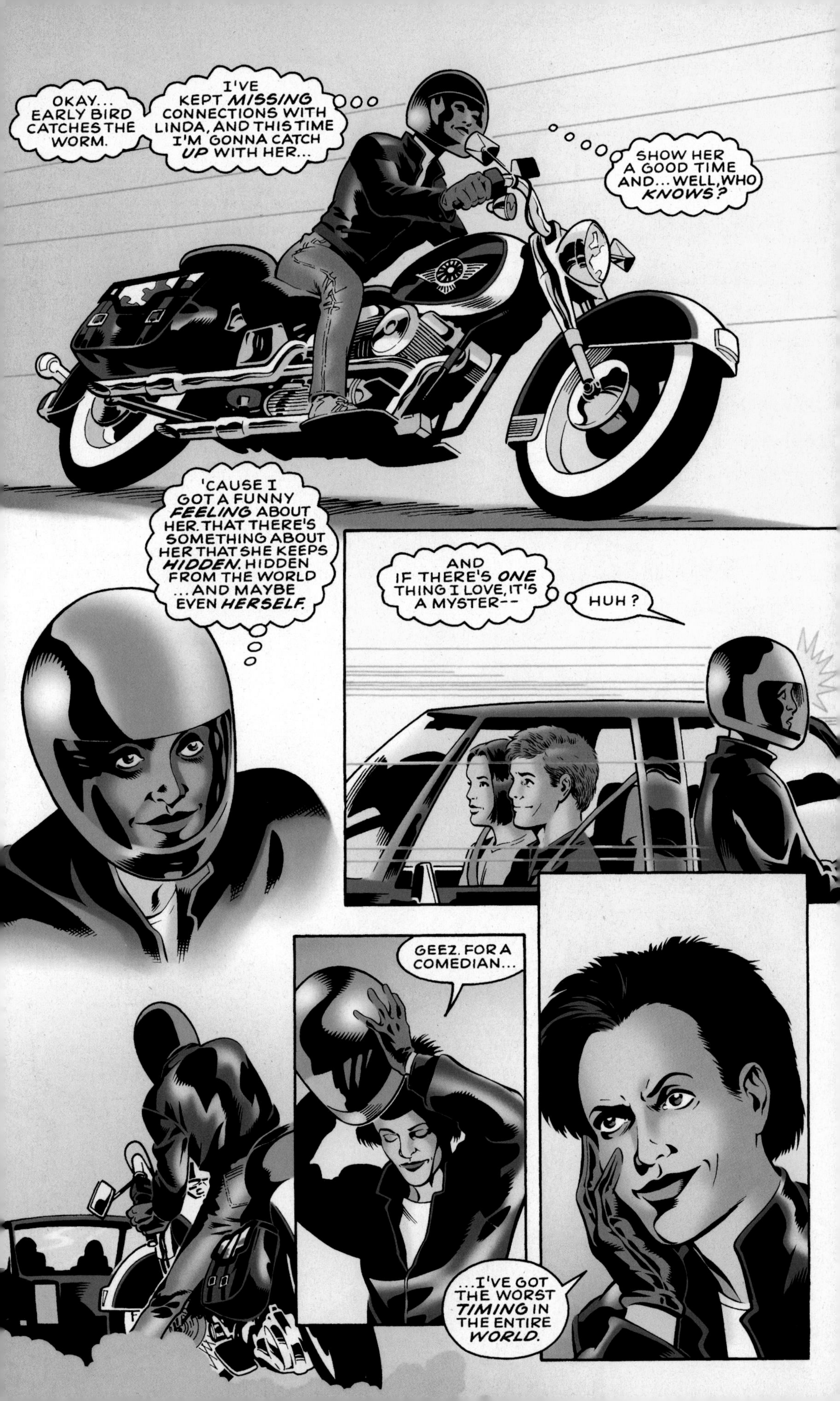

OKAY... EARLY BIRD CATCHES THE WORM.
I'VE KEPT MISSING CONNECTIONS WITH LINDA, AND THIS TIME I'M GONNA CATCH UP WITH HER...
SHOW HER A GOOD TIME AND... WELL, WHO KNOWS?
'CAUSE I GOT A FUNNY FEELING ABOUT HER. THAT THERE'S SOMETHING ABOUT HER THAT SHE KEEPS HIDDEN. HIDDEN FROM THE WORLD ...AND MAYBE EVEN HERSELF.
AND IF THERE'S ONE THING I LOVE, IT'S A MYSTER--
HUH?
GEEZ. FOR A COMEDIAN...
...I'VE GOT THE WORST TIMING IN THE ENTIRE WORLD.

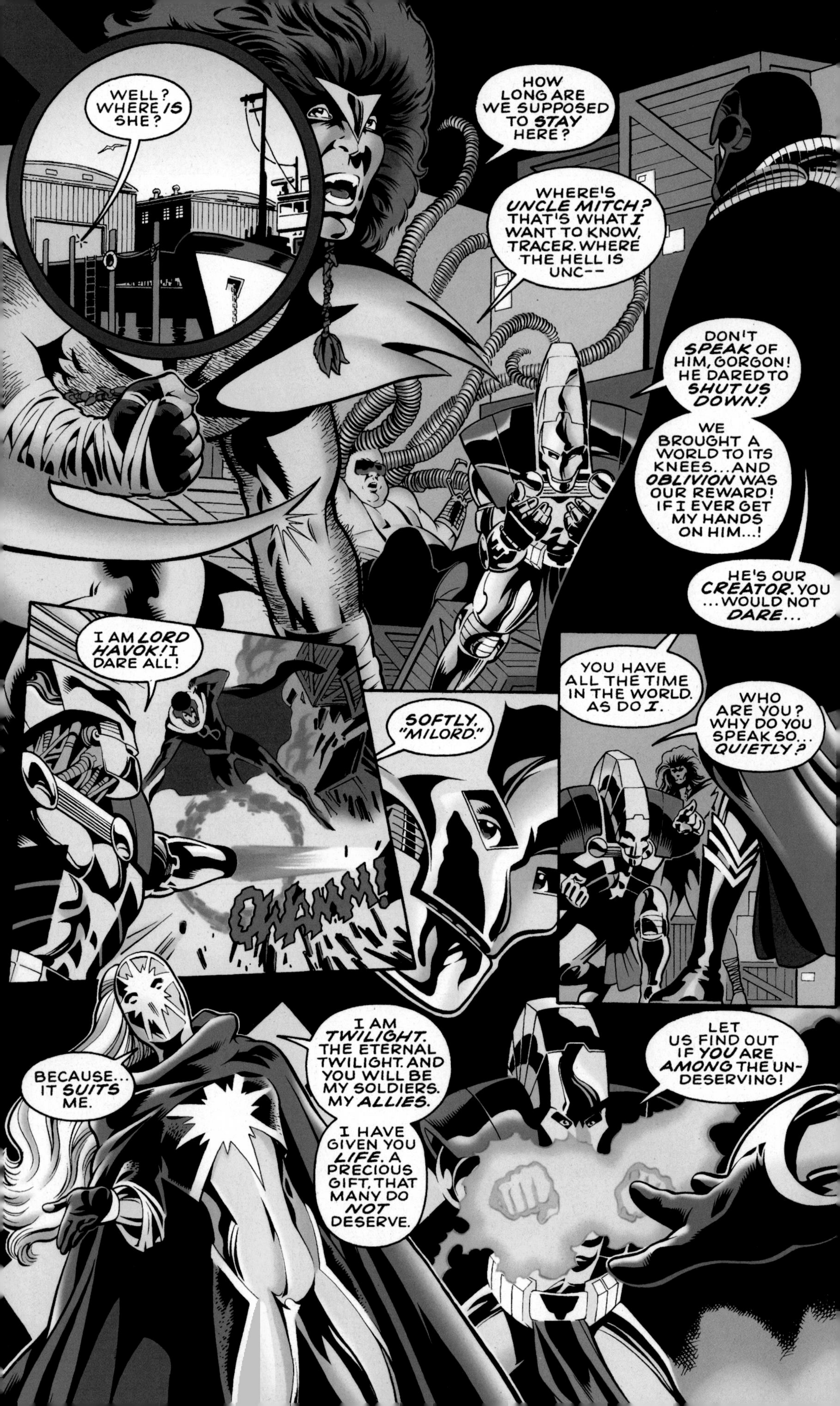
WELL? WHERE IS SHE?
HOW LONG ARE WE SUPPOSED TO STAY HERE?
WHERE'S UNCLE MITCH? THAT'S WHAT I WANT TO KNOW, TRACER. WHERE THE HELL IS UNC--
DON'T SPEAK OF HIM, GORGON! HE DARED TO SHUT US DOWN!
WE BROUGHT A WORLD TO ITS KNEES...AND OBLIVION WAS OUR REWARD! IF I EVER GET MY HANDS ON HIM...!
HE'S OUR CREATOR. YOU ...WOULD NOT DARE...
I AM LORD HAVOK! I DARE ALL!
QWAMM!
SOFTLY. "MILORD."
YOU HAVE ALL THE TIME IN THE WORLD. AS DO I.
WHO ARE YOU? WHY DO YOU SPEAK SO... QUIETLY?
BECAUSE... IT SUITS ME.
I AM TWILIGHT. THE ETERNAL TWILIGHT. AND YOU WILL BE MY SOLDIERS. MY ALLIES.
I HAVE GIVEN YOU LIFE. A PRECIOUS GIFT, THAT MANY DO NOT DESERVE.
LET US FIND OUT IF YOU ARE AMONG THE UN-DESERVING!

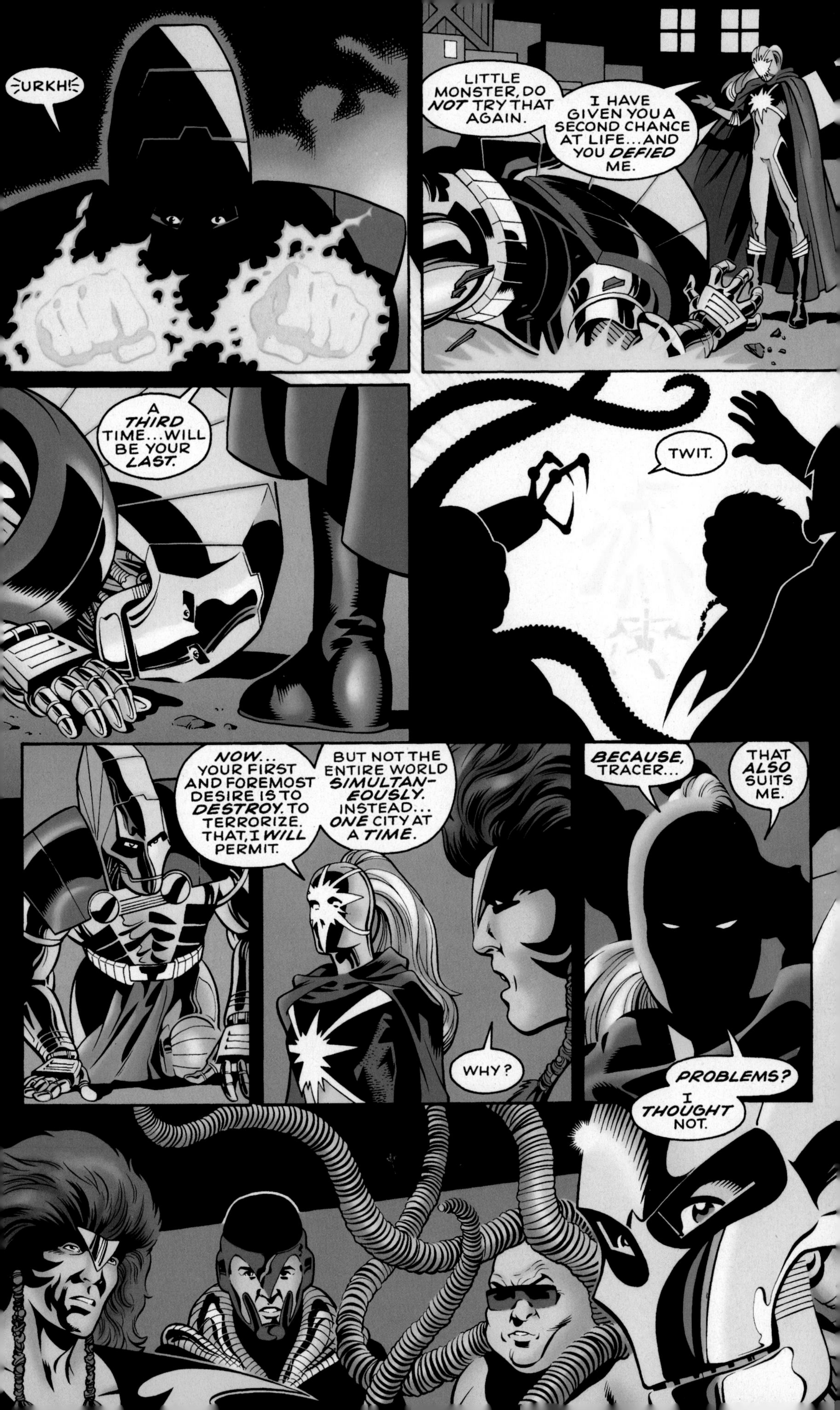
URKH!
LITTLE MONSTER, DO NOT TRY THAT AGAIN.
I HAVE GIVEN YOU A SECOND CHANCE AT LIFE...AND YOU DEFIED ME.
A THIRD TIME...WILL BE YOUR LAST.
TWIT.
NOW... YOUR FIRST AND FOREMOST DESIRE IS TO DESTROY. TO TERRORIZE. THAT, I WILL PERMIT.
BUT NOT THE ENTIRE WORLD SIMULTANEOUSLY. INSTEAD... ONE CITY AT A TIME.
WHY?
BECAUSE, TRACER...
THAT ALSO SUITS ME.
PROBLEMS? I THOUGHT NOT.

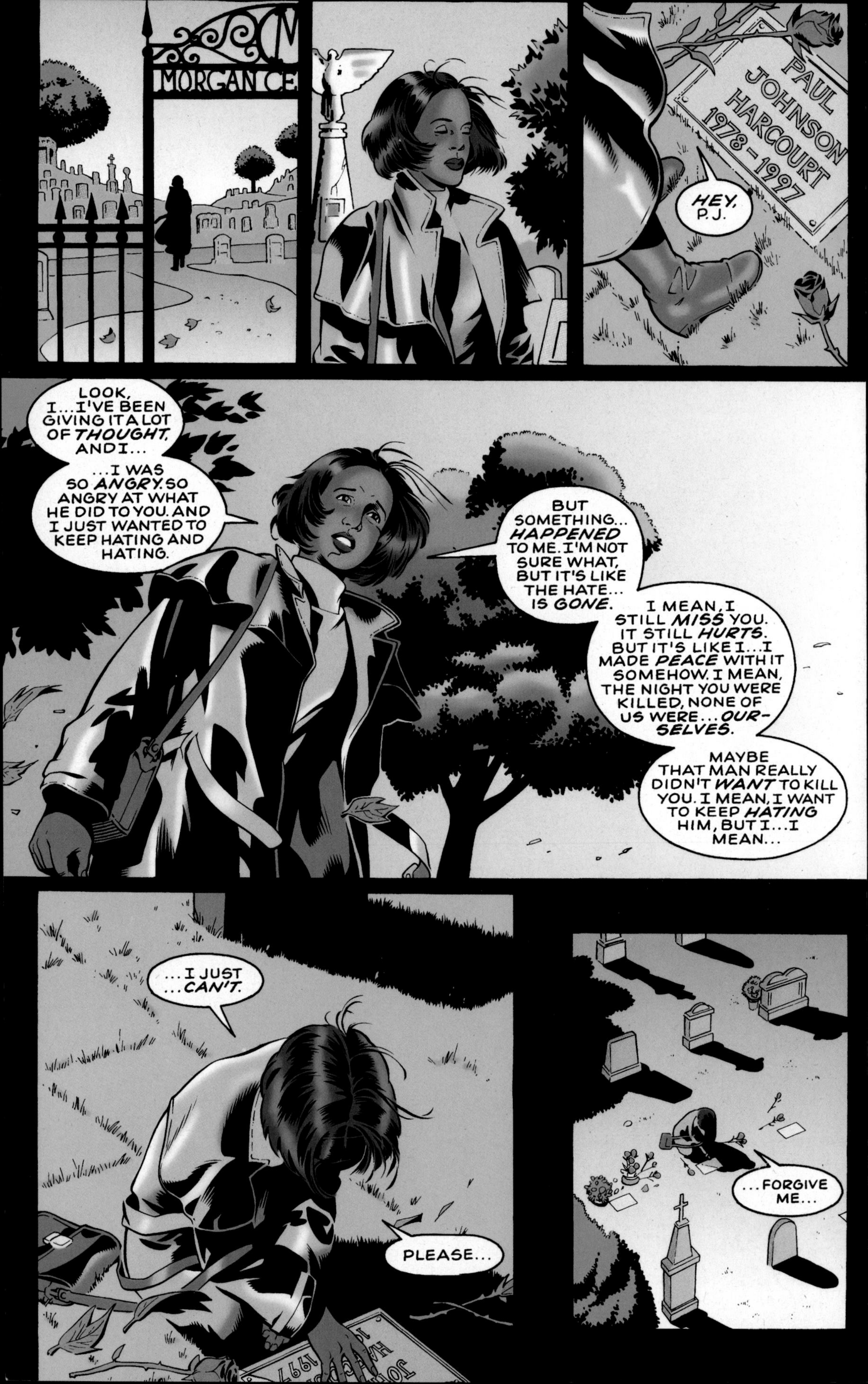
MORGAN CE
PAUL JOHNSON HARCOURT 1978-1997
HEY, P.J.
LOOK, I...I'VE BEEN GIVING IT A LOT OF THOUGHT, AND I...
...I WAS SO ANGRY. SO ANGRY AT WHAT HE DID TO YOU. AND I JUST WANTED TO KEEP HATING AND HATING.
BUT SOMETHING... HAPPENED TO ME. I'M NOT SURE WHAT, BUT IT'S LIKE THE HATE... IS GONE.
I MEAN, I STILL MISS YOU. IT STILL HURTS. BUT IT'S LIKE I...I MADE PEACE WITH IT SOMEHOW. I MEAN, THE NIGHT YOU WERE KILLED, NONE OF US WERE...OURSELVES.
MAYBE THAT MAN REALLY DIDN'T WANT TO KILL YOU. I MEAN, I WANT TO KEEP HATING HIM, BUT I...I MEAN...
...I JUST ...CAN'T.
PLEASE...
...FORGIVE ME...

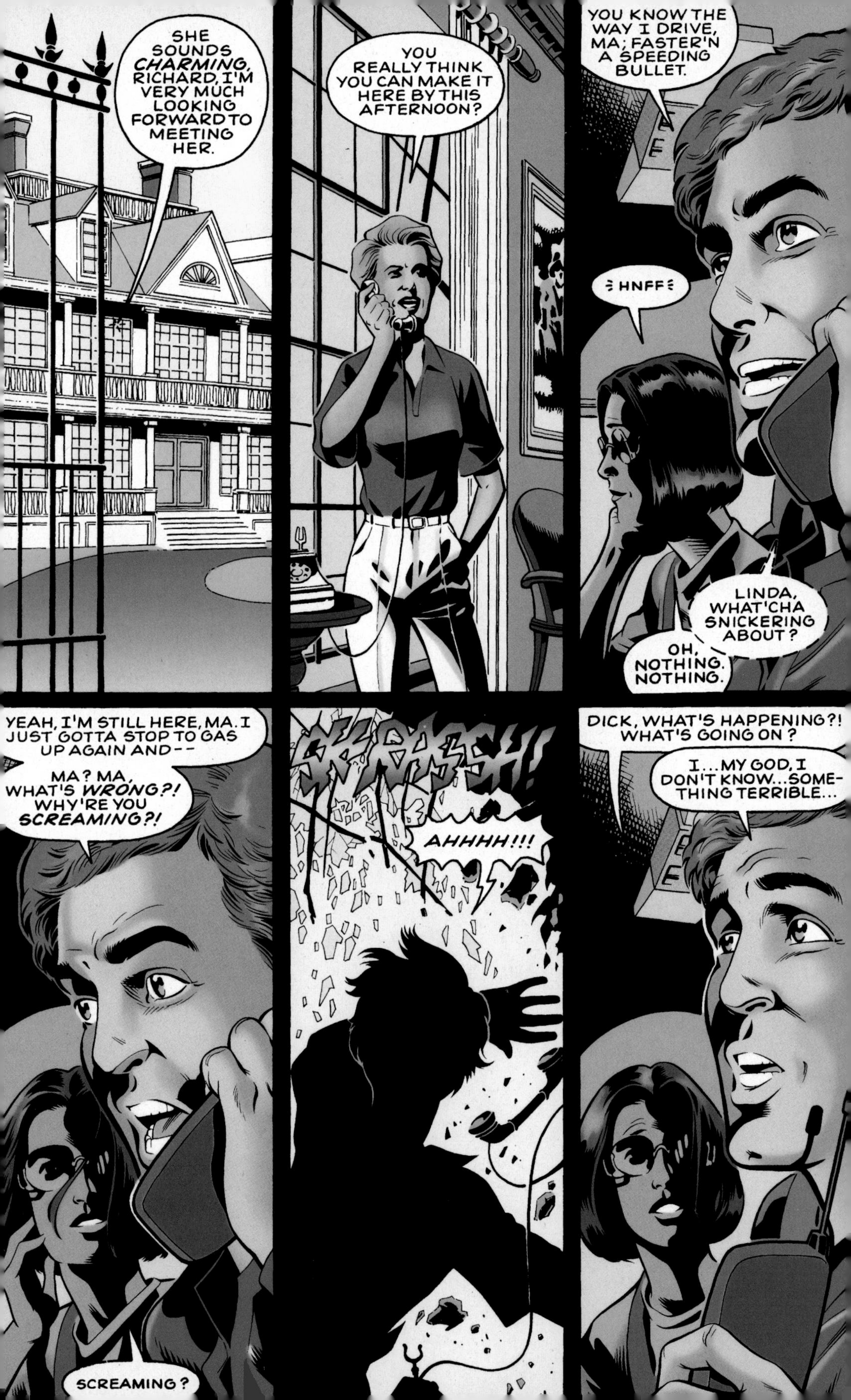
SHE SOUNDS *CHARMING*, RICHARD. I'M VERY MUCH LOOKING FORWARD TO MEETING HER.
YOU REALLY THINK YOU CAN MAKE IT HERE BY THIS AFTERNOON?
YOU KNOW THE WAY I DRIVE, MA; FASTER'N A SPEEDING BULLET.
HNFF
LINDA, WHAT'CHA SNICKERING ABOUT?
OH, NOTHING. NOTHING.
YEAH, I'M STILL HERE, MA. I JUST GOTTA STOP TO GAS UP AGAIN AND--
MA? MA, WHAT'S *WRONG?!* WHY'RE YOU *SCREAMING?!*
SCREAMING?
SKRASSH!
AHHHH!!!
DICK, WHAT'S HAPPENING?! WHAT'S GOING ON?
I...MY GOD, I DON'T KNOW...SOMETHING TERRIBLE...

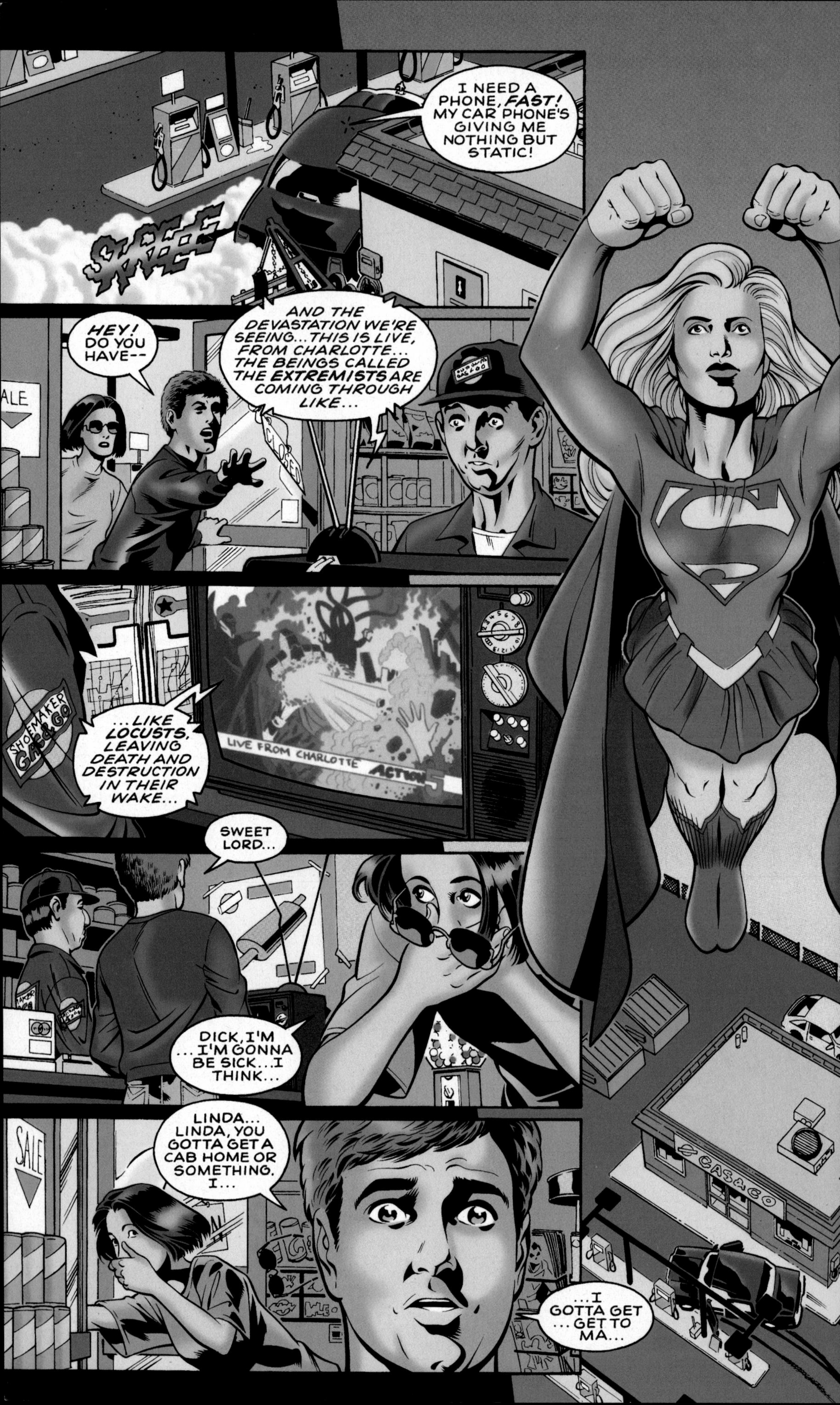
I NEED A PHONE, FAST! MY CAR PHONE'S GIVING ME NOTHING BUT STATIC!
SKREEE
HEY! DO YOU HAVE--
AND THE DEVASTATION WE'RE SEEING... THIS IS LIVE, FROM CHARLOTTE... THE BEINGS CALLED THE EXTREMISTS ARE COMING THROUGH LIKE...
CLOSED
...LIKE LOCUSTS, LEAVING DEATH AND DESTRUCTION IN THEIR WAKE...
SHOEMAKER GAS & GO
LIVE FROM CHARLOTTE
ACTION 5
SWEET LORD...
DICK, I'M ... I'M GONNA BE SICK... I THINK...
LINDA... LINDA, YOU GOTTA GET A CAB HOME OR SOMETHING. I...
SALE
...I GOTTA GET ... GET TO MA...
GASACO

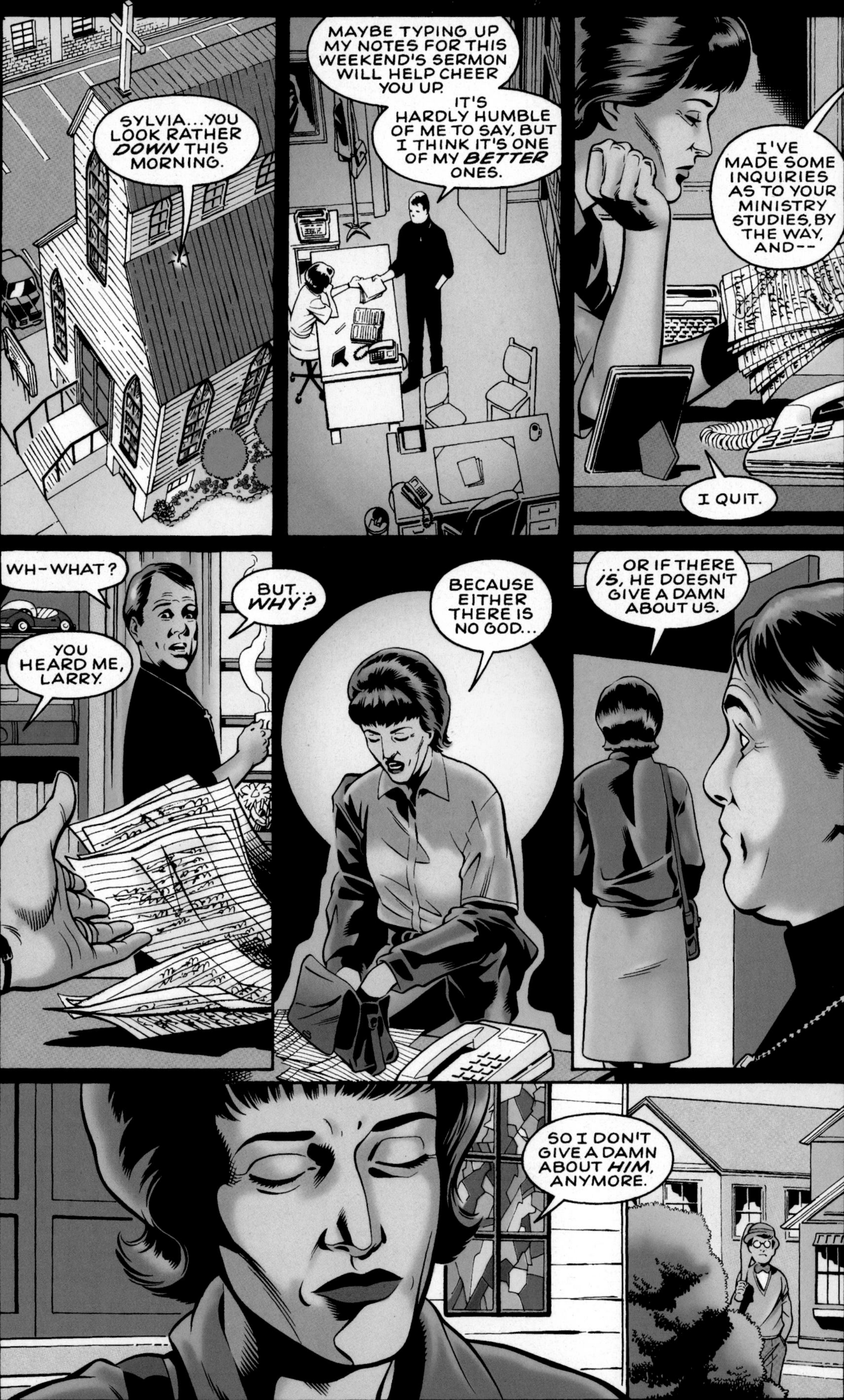
SYLVIA...YOU LOOK RATHER *DOWN* THIS MORNING.
MAYBE TYPING UP MY NOTES FOR THIS WEEKEND'S SERMON WILL HELP CHEER YOU UP.
IT'S HARDLY HUMBLE OF ME TO SAY, BUT I THINK IT'S ONE OF MY *BETTER* ONES.
I'VE MADE SOME INQUIRIES AS TO YOUR MINISTRY STUDIES, BY THE WAY, AND--
I QUIT.
WH-WHAT?
YOU HEARD ME, LARRY.
BUT... *WHY?*
BECAUSE EITHER THERE IS NO GOD...
...OR IF THERE *IS*, HE DOESN'T GIVE A DAMN ABOUT US.
SO I DON'T GIVE A DAMN ABOUT *HIM*, ANYMORE.

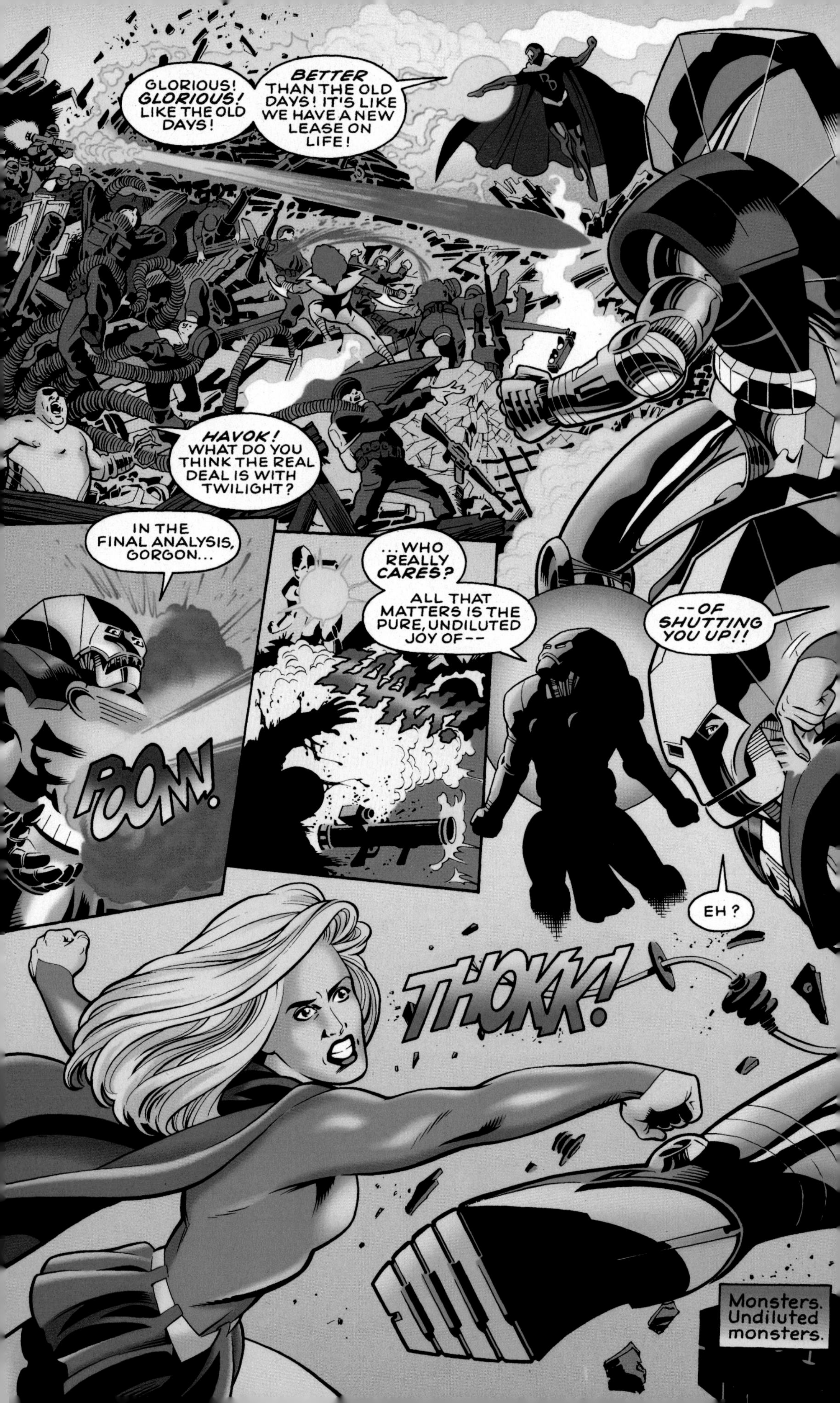
GLORIOUS! GLORIOUS! LIKE THE OLD DAYS!
BETTER THAN THE OLD DAYS! IT'S LIKE WE HAVE A NEW LEASE ON LIFE!
HAVOK! WHAT DO YOU THINK THE REAL DEAL IS WITH TWILIGHT?
IN THE FINAL ANALYSIS, GORGON...
POOM!
...WHO REALLY CARES?
ALL THAT MATTERS IS THE PURE, UNDILUTED JOY OF--
--OF SHUTTING YOU UP!!
EH?
THOKK!
Monsters. Undiluted monsters.

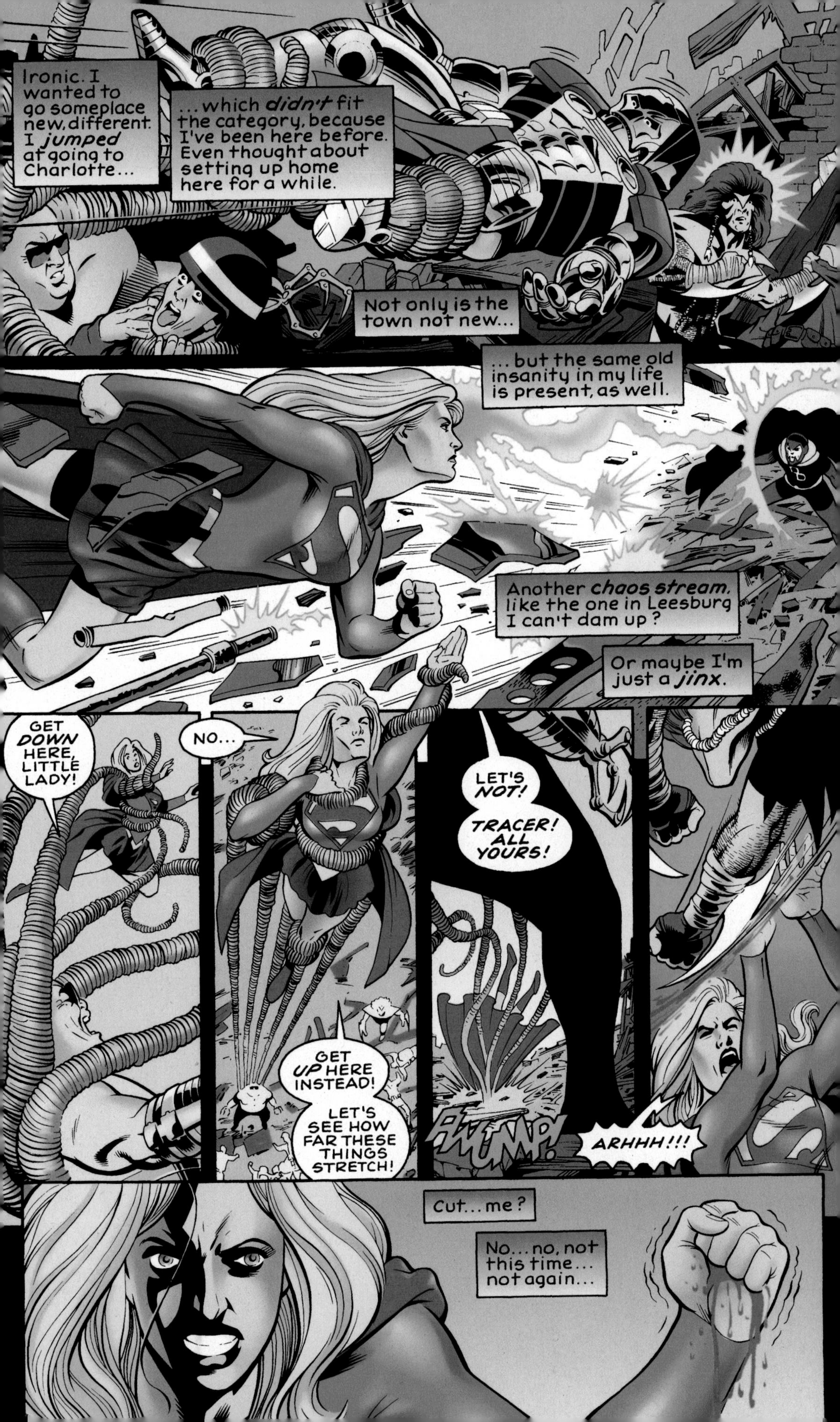

Ironic. I wanted to go someplace new, different. I jumped at going to Charlotte...
...which didn't fit the category, because I've been here before. Even thought about setting up home here for a while.
Not only is the town not new...
...but the same old insanity in my life is present, as well.
Another chaos stream, like the one in Leesburg I can't dam up?
Or maybe I'm just a jinx.
GET DOWN HERE, LITTLE LADY!
NO...
GET UP HERE INSTEAD!
LET'S SEE HOW FAR THESE THINGS STRETCH!
LET'S NOT!
TRACER! ALL YOURS!
FWUMP!
ARHHH!!!
Cut...me?
No...no, not this time... not again...

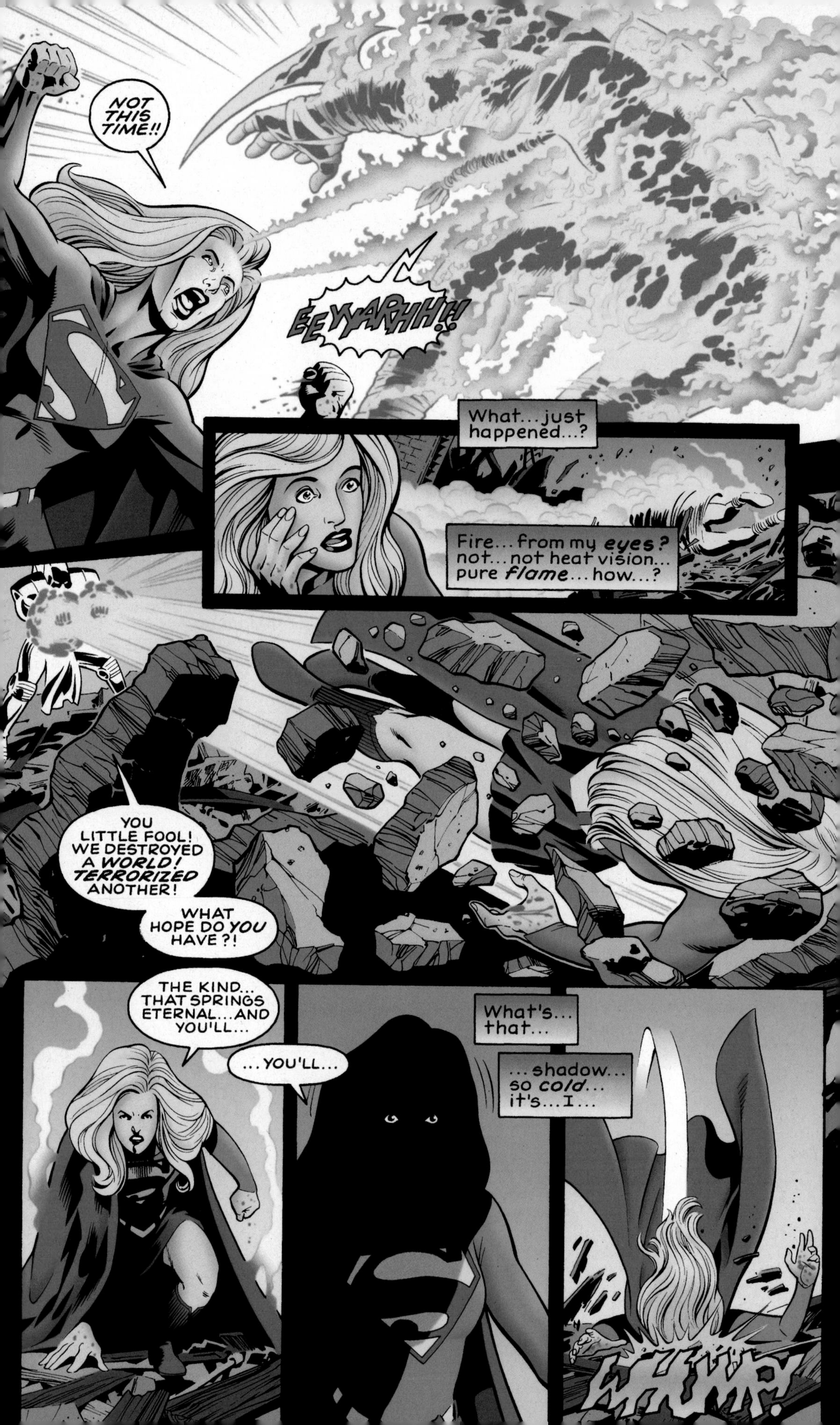
NOT THIS TIME!!
EEYYARHH!!
What... just happened...?
Fire... from my eyes? not... not heat vision... pure flame... how...?
YOU LITTLE FOOL! WE DESTROYED A WORLD! TERRORIZED ANOTHER!
WHAT HOPE DO YOU HAVE?!
THE KIND... THAT SPRINGS ETERNAL... AND YOU'LL...
...YOU'LL...
What's... that...
...shadow... so cold... it's... I...

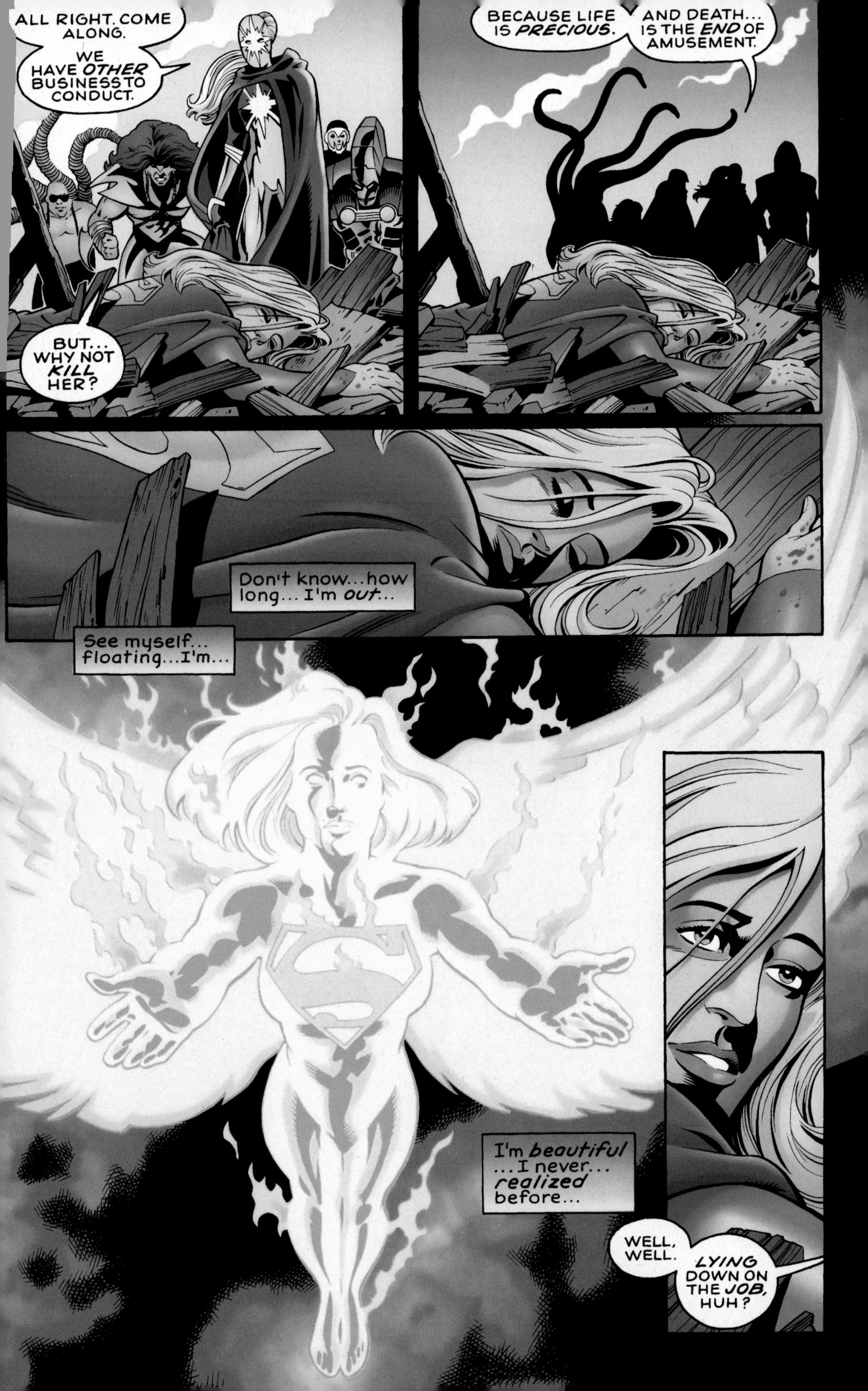
ALL RIGHT. COME ALONG.
WE HAVE OTHER BUSINESS TO CONDUCT.
BUT... WHY NOT KILL HER?
BECAUSE LIFE IS PRECIOUS.
AND DEATH... IS THE END OF AMUSEMENT.
Don't know...how long... I'm out...
See myself... floating...I'm...
I'm beautiful ...I never... realized before...
WELL, WELL.
LYING DOWN ON THE JOB, HUH?

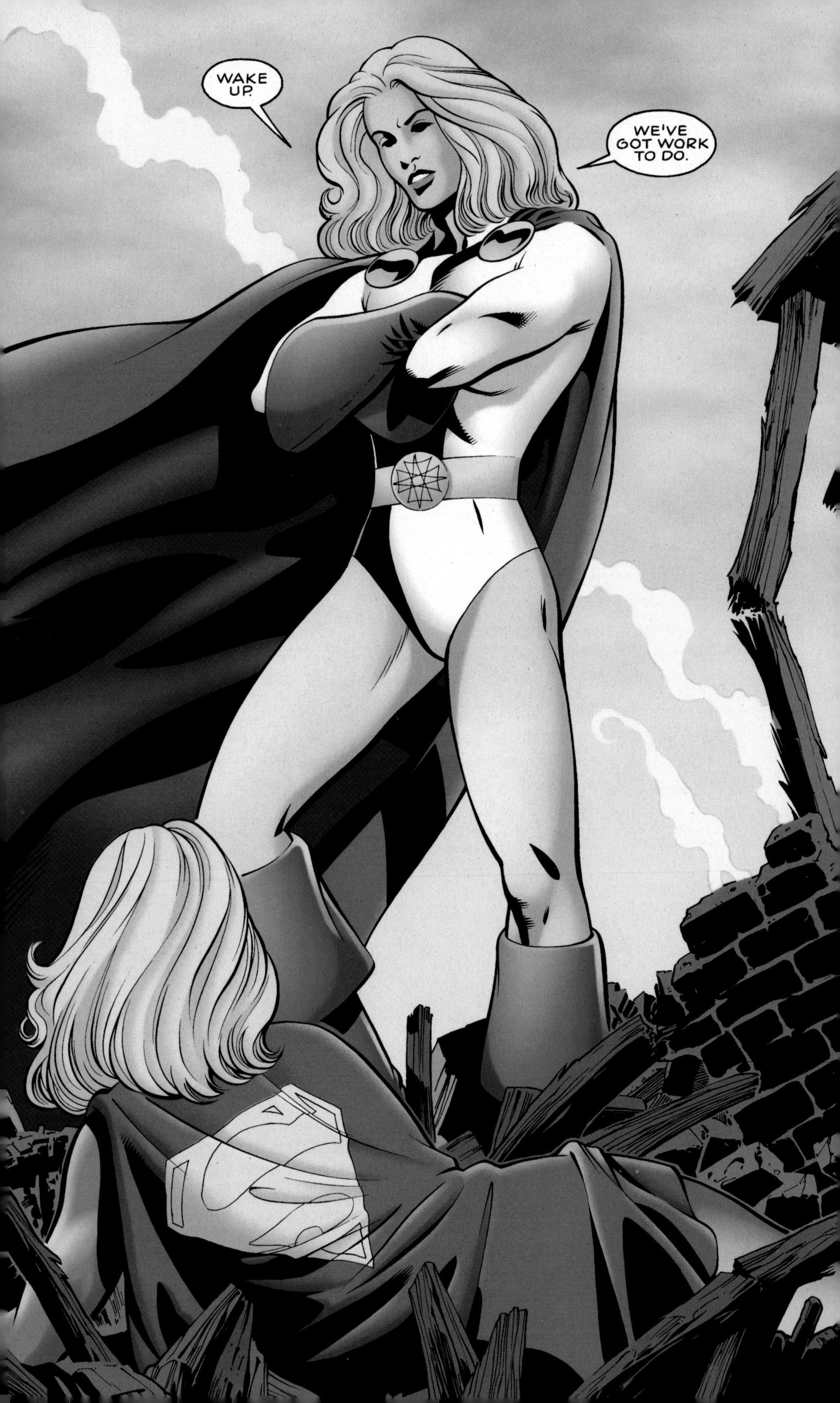
WAKE UP.
WE'VE GOT WORK TO DO.

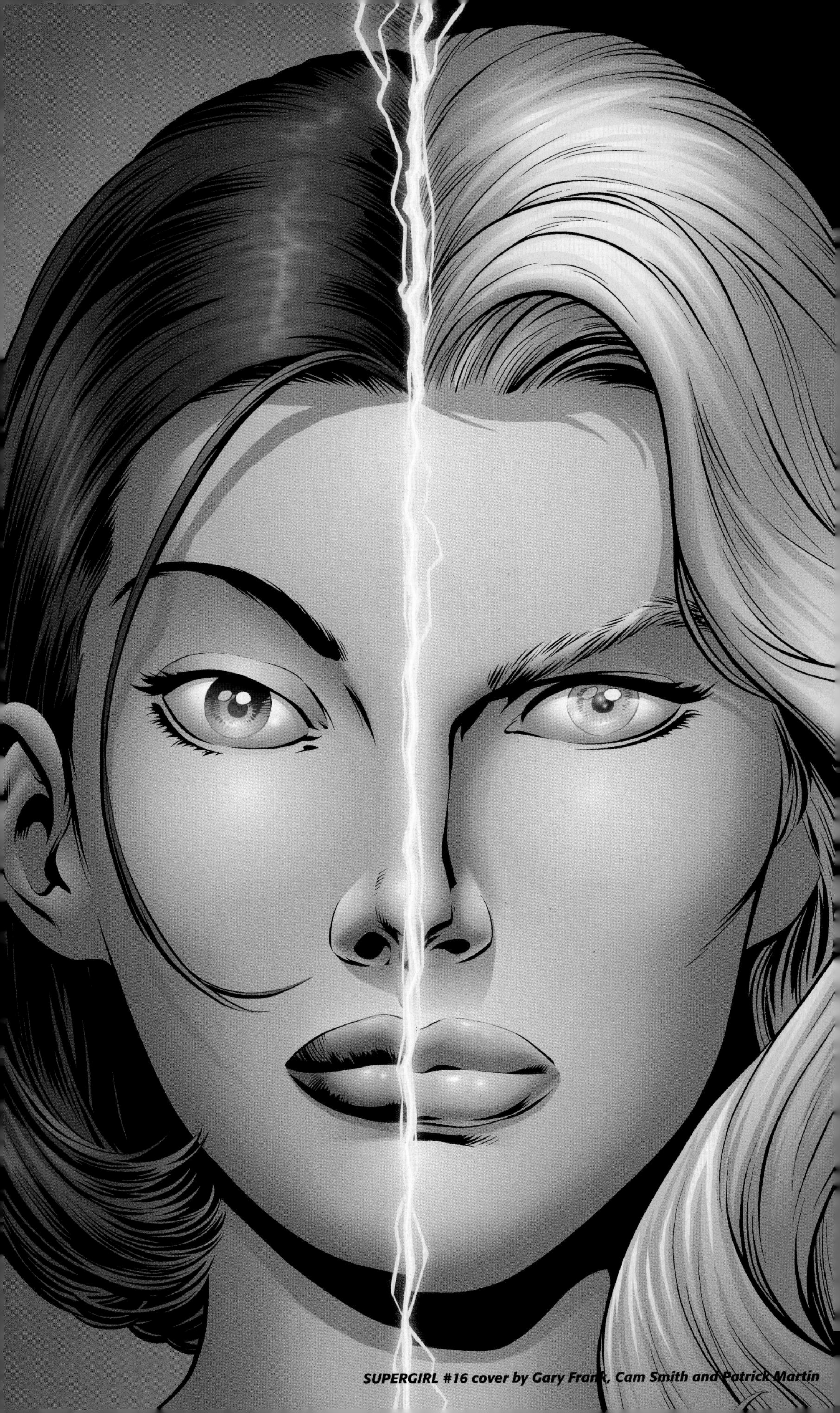

SUPERGIRL #16 cover by Gary Frank, Cam Smith and Patrick Martin

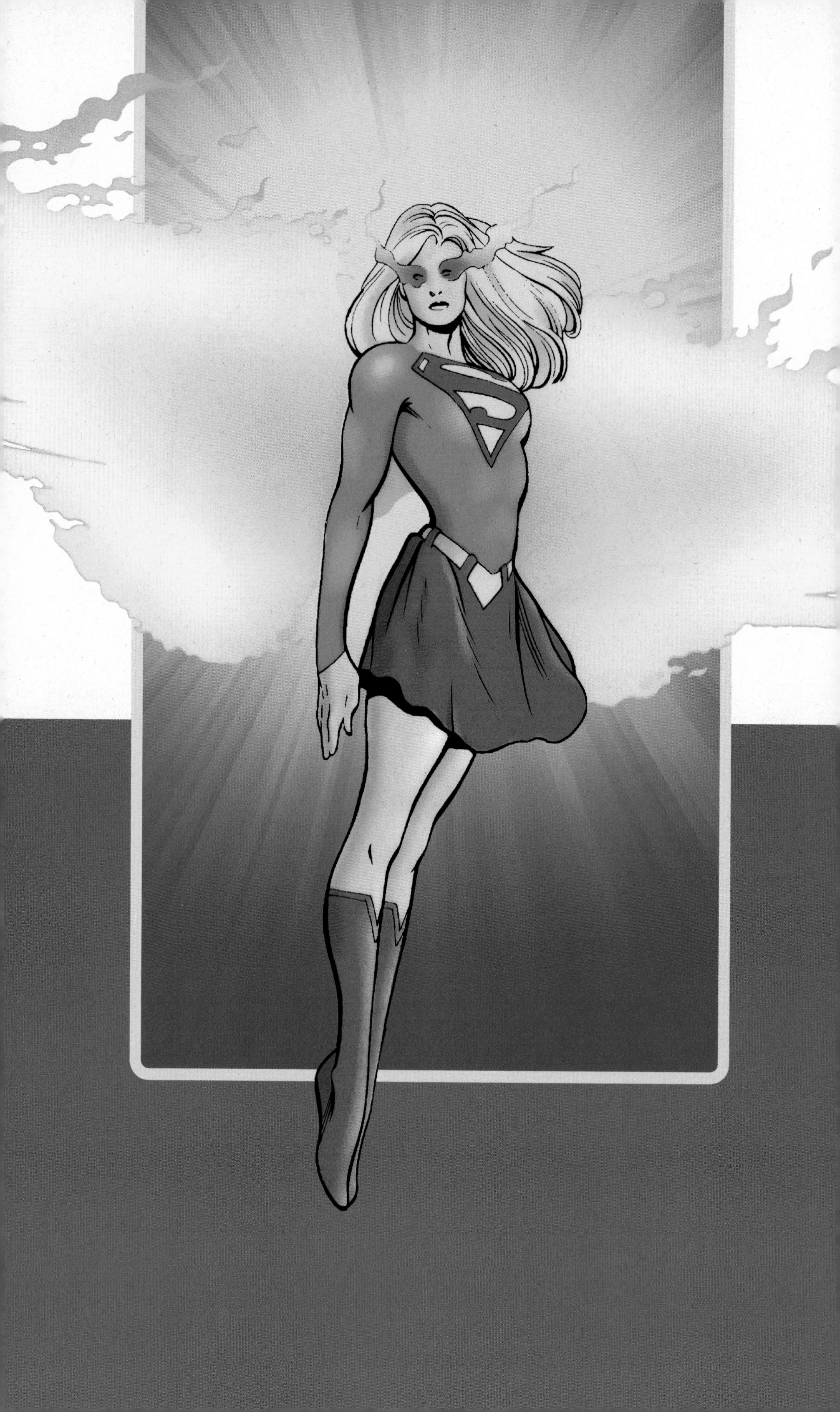

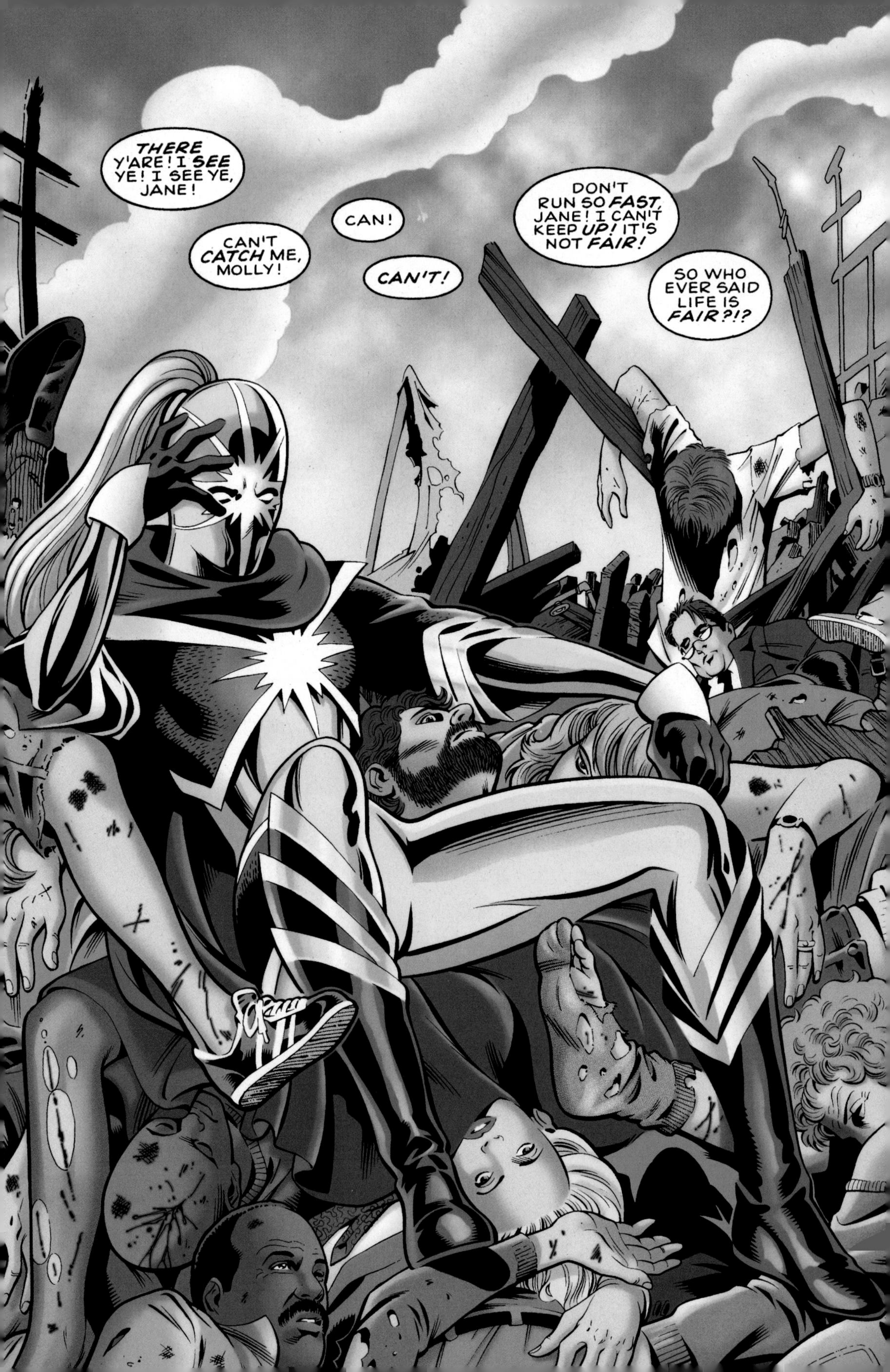
THERE Y'ARE! I SEE YE! I SEE YE, JANE!
CAN'T CATCH ME, MOLLY!
CAN!
CAN'T!
DON'T RUN SO FAST, JANE! I CAN'T KEEP UP! IT'S NOT FAIR!
SO WHO EVER SAID LIFE IS FAIR?!?

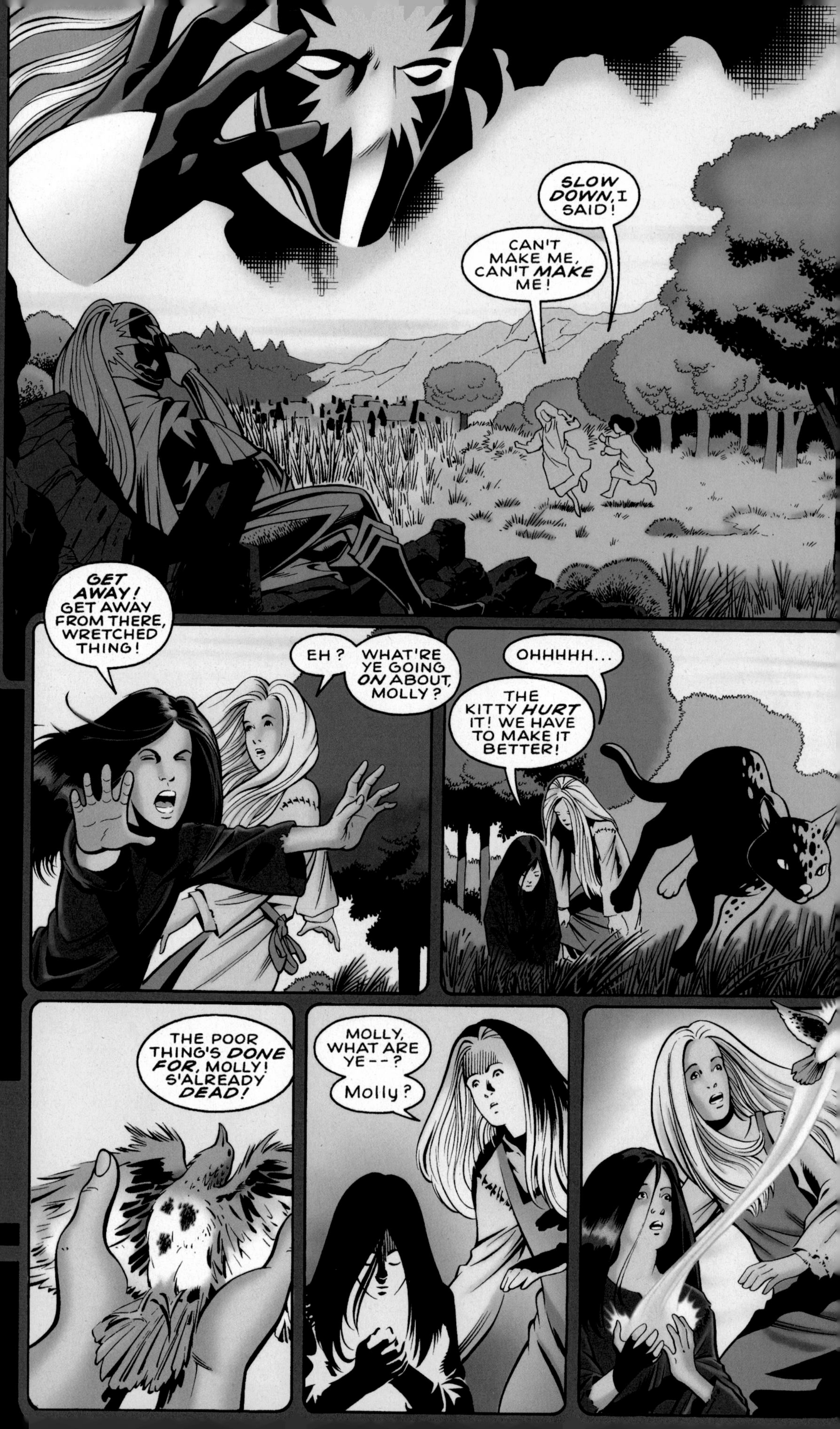
SLOW DOWN, I SAID!
CAN'T MAKE ME, CAN'T MAKE ME!
GET AWAY! GET AWAY FROM THERE, WRETCHED THING!
EH?
WHAT'RE YE GOING ON ABOUT, MOLLY?
OHHHHH...
THE KITTY HURT IT! WE HAVE TO MAKE IT BETTER!
THE POOR THING'S DONE FOR, MOLLY! S'ALREADY DEAD!
MOLLY, WHAT ARE YE--?
Molly?

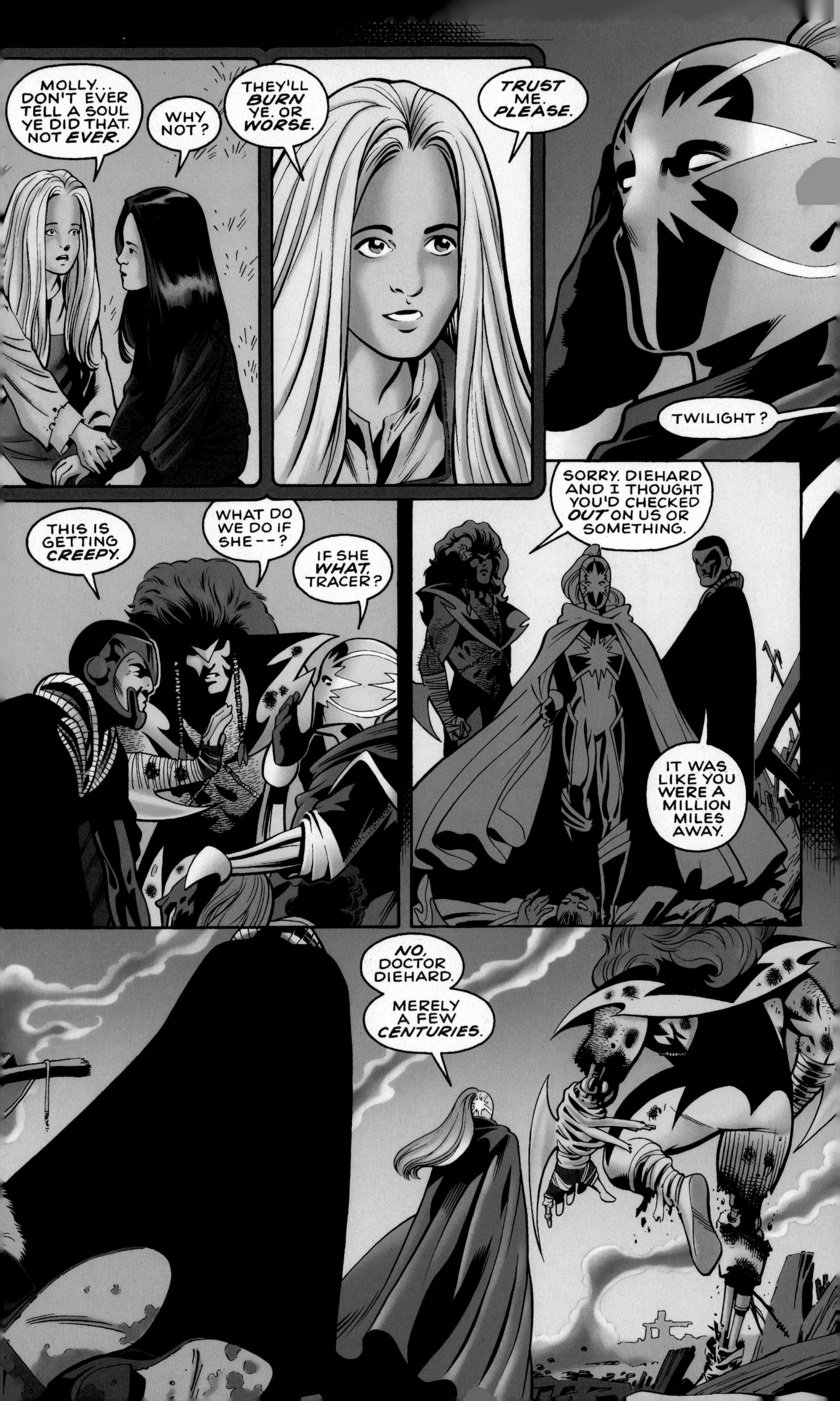

MOLLY... DON'T EVER TELL A SOUL YE DID THAT. NOT EVER.
WHY NOT?
THEY'LL BURN YE. OR WORSE.
TRUST ME. PLEASE.
TWILIGHT?
THIS IS GETTING CREEPY.
WHAT DO WE DO IF SHE--?
IF SHE WHAT, TRACER?
SORRY. DIEHARD AND I THOUGHT YOU'D CHECKED OUT ON US OR SOMETHING.
IT WAS LIKE YOU WERE A MILLION MILES AWAY.
NO, DOCTOR DIEHARD.
MERELY A FEW CENTURIES.

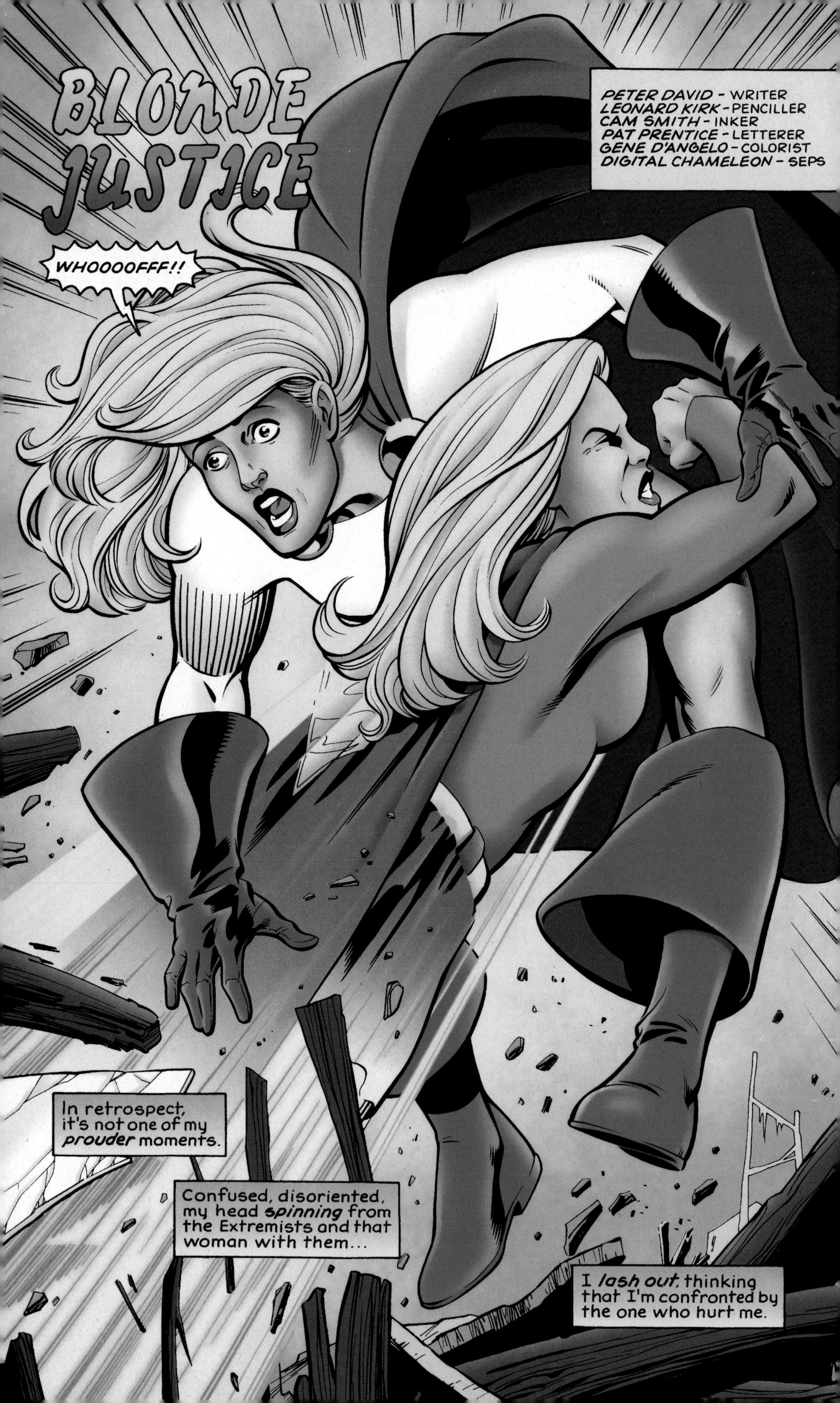
BLONDE JUSTICE
PETER DAVID - WRITER
LEONARD KIRK - PENCILLER
CAM SMITH - INKER
PAT PRENTICE - LETTERER
GENE D'ANGELO - COLORIST
DIGITAL CHAMELEON - SEPS
WHOOOOFFF!!
In retrospect, it's not one of my *prouder* moments.
Confused, disoriented, my head *spinning* from the Extremists and that woman with them...
I *lash out*, thinking that I'm confronted by the one who hurt me.

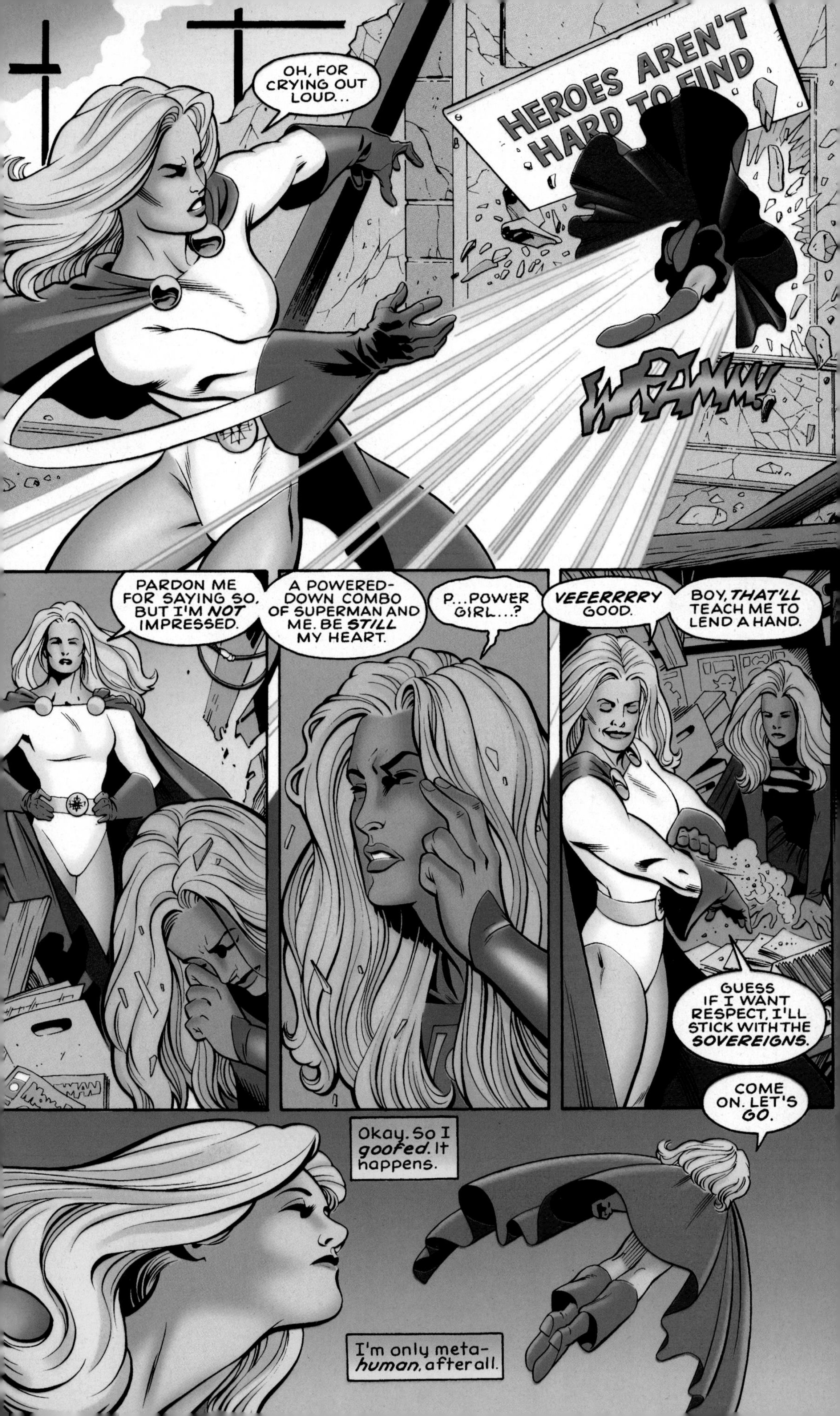
OH, FOR CRYING OUT LOUD...
HEROES AREN'T HARD TO FIND
WHAMM!
PARDON ME FOR SAYING SO, BUT I'M NOT IMPRESSED.
A POWERED-DOWN COMBO OF SUPERMAN AND ME. BE STILL MY HEART.
P...POWER GIRL...?
VEEERRRRY GOOD.
BOY, THAT'LL TEACH ME TO LEND A HAND.
GUESS IF I WANT RESPECT, I'LL STICK WITH THE SOVEREIGNS.
COME ON. LET'S GO.
Okay. So I goofed. It happens.
I'm only meta-human, after all.

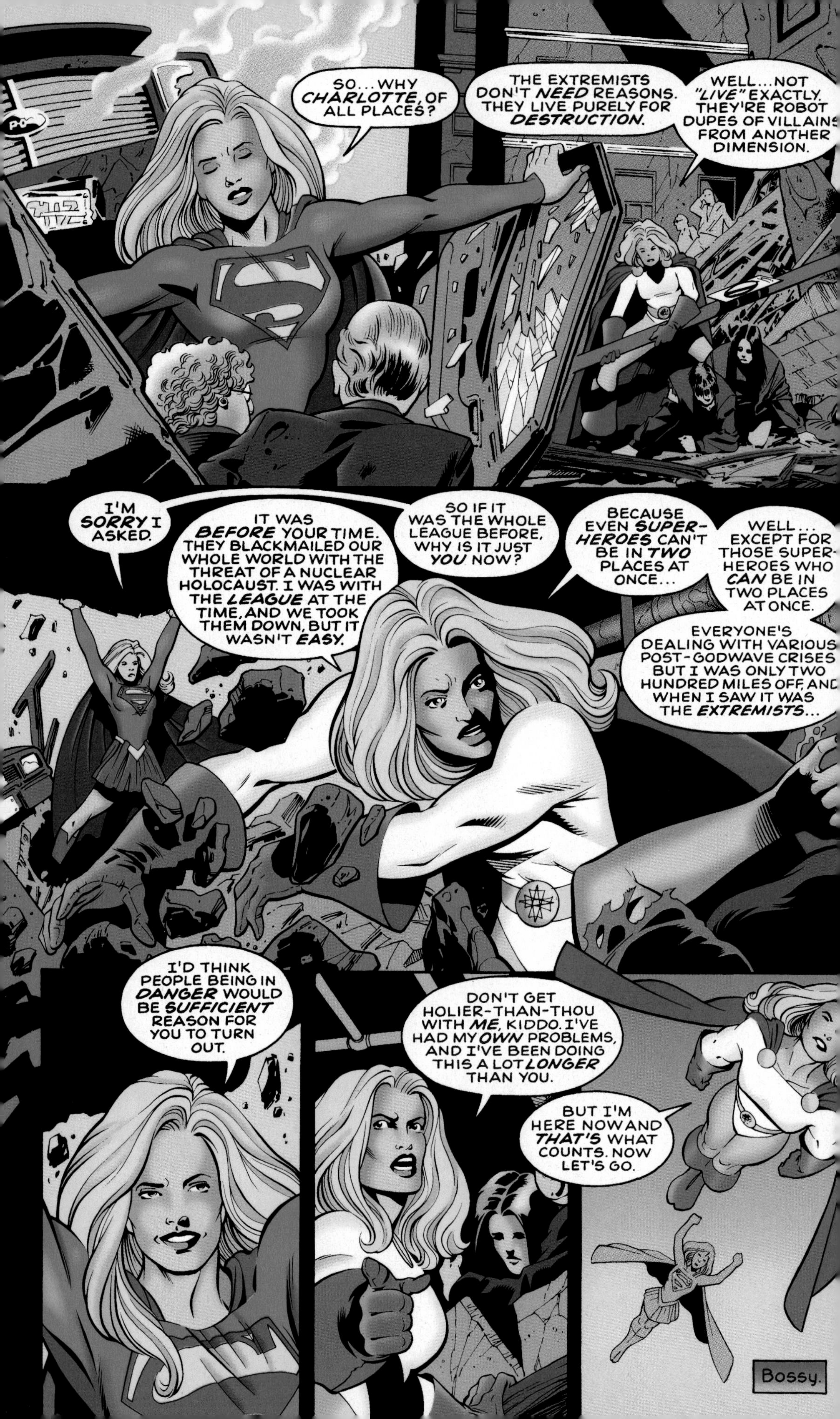
SO... WHY CHARLOTTE, OF ALL PLACES?
THE EXTREMISTS DON'T NEED REASONS. THEY LIVE PURELY FOR DESTRUCTION.
WELL... NOT "LIVE" EXACTLY. THEY'RE ROBOT DUPES OF VILLAINS FROM ANOTHER DIMENSION.
I'M SORRY I ASKED.
IT WAS BEFORE YOUR TIME. THEY BLACKMAILED OUR WHOLE WORLD WITH THE THREAT OF A NUCLEAR HOLOCAUST. I WAS WITH THE LEAGUE AT THE TIME, AND WE TOOK THEM DOWN, BUT IT WASN'T EASY.
SO IF IT WAS THE WHOLE LEAGUE BEFORE, WHY IS IT JUST YOU NOW?
BECAUSE EVEN SUPER-HEROES CAN'T BE IN TWO PLACES AT ONCE...
WELL... EXCEPT FOR THOSE SUPER-HEROES WHO CAN BE IN TWO PLACES AT ONCE.
EVERYONE'S DEALING WITH VARIOUS POST-GODWAVE CRISES BUT I WAS ONLY TWO HUNDRED MILES OFF, AND WHEN I SAW IT WAS THE EXTREMISTS...
I'D THINK PEOPLE BEING IN DANGER WOULD BE SUFFICIENT REASON FOR YOU TO TURN OUT.
DON'T GET HOLIER-THAN-THOU WITH ME, KIDDO. I'VE HAD MY OWN PROBLEMS, AND I'VE BEEN DOING THIS A LOT LONGER THAN YOU.
BUT I'M HERE NOW AND THAT'S WHAT COUNTS. NOW LET'S GO.
Bossy.

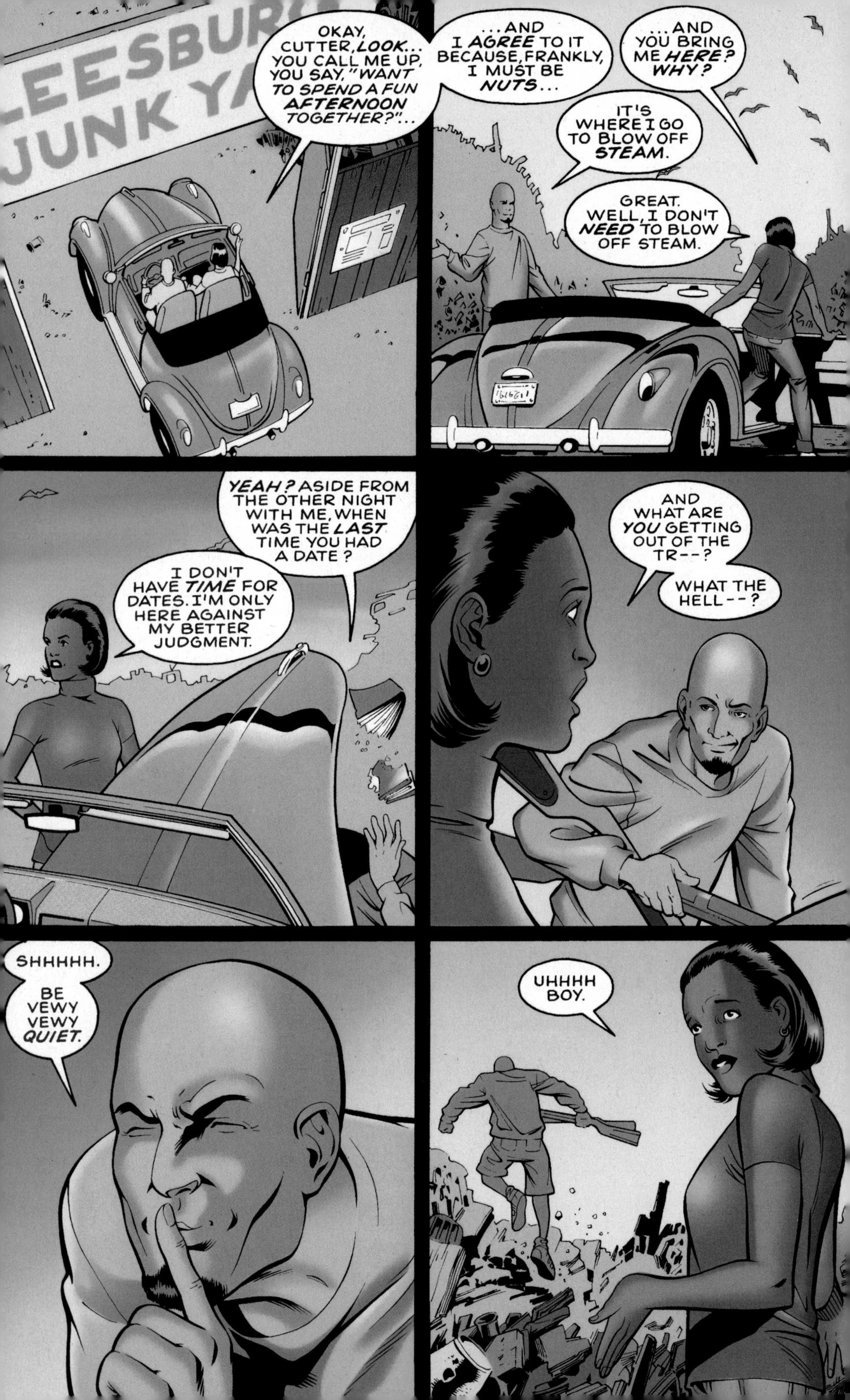
LEESBURG
JUNK YA
OKAY, CUTTER, LOOK... YOU CALL ME UP, YOU SAY, "WANT TO SPEND A FUN AFTERNOON TOGETHER?"...
...AND I AGREE TO IT BECAUSE, FRANKLY, I MUST BE NUTS...
...AND YOU BRING ME HERE? WHY?
IT'S WHERE I GO TO BLOW OFF STEAM.
GREAT. WELL, I DON'T NEED TO BLOW OFF STEAM.
YEAH? ASIDE FROM THE OTHER NIGHT WITH ME, WHEN WAS THE LAST TIME YOU HAD A DATE?
I DON'T HAVE TIME FOR DATES. I'M ONLY HERE AGAINST MY BETTER JUDGMENT.
AND WHAT ARE YOU GETTING OUT OF THE TR--?
WHAT THE HELL--?
SHHHHH.
BE VEWY VEWY QUIET.
UHHHH BOY.

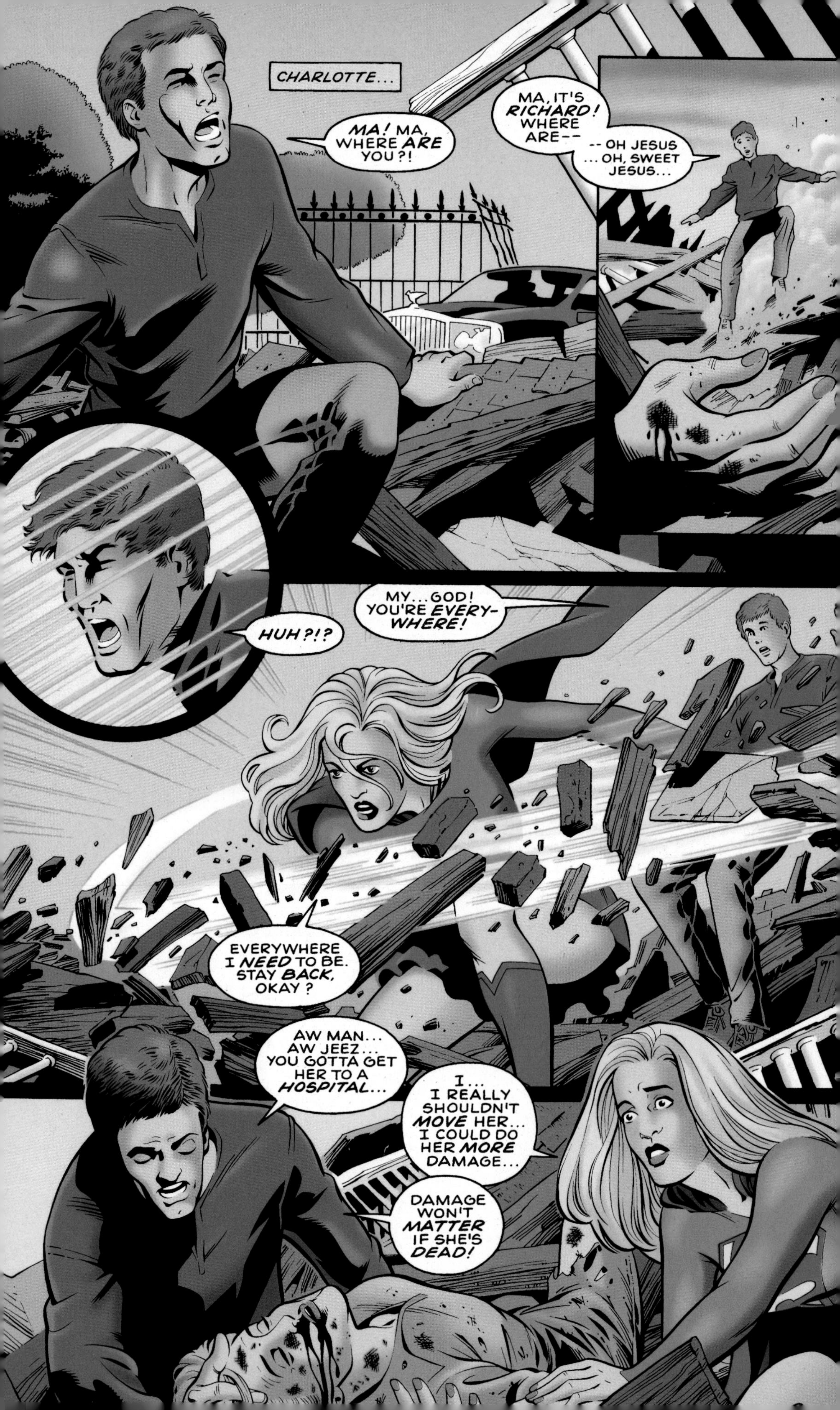
CHARLOTTE...
MA! MA, WHERE ARE YOU?!
MA, IT'S RICHARD! WHERE ARE--
-- OH JESUS ... OH, SWEET JESUS...
HUH?!?
MY... GOD! YOU'RE EVERY-WHERE!
EVERYWHERE I NEED TO BE. STAY BACK, OKAY?
AW MAN... AW JEEZ... YOU GOTTA GET HER TO A HOSPITAL...
I... I REALLY SHOULDN'T MOVE HER... I COULD DO HER MORE DAMAGE...
DAMAGE WON'T MATTER IF SHE'S DEAD!

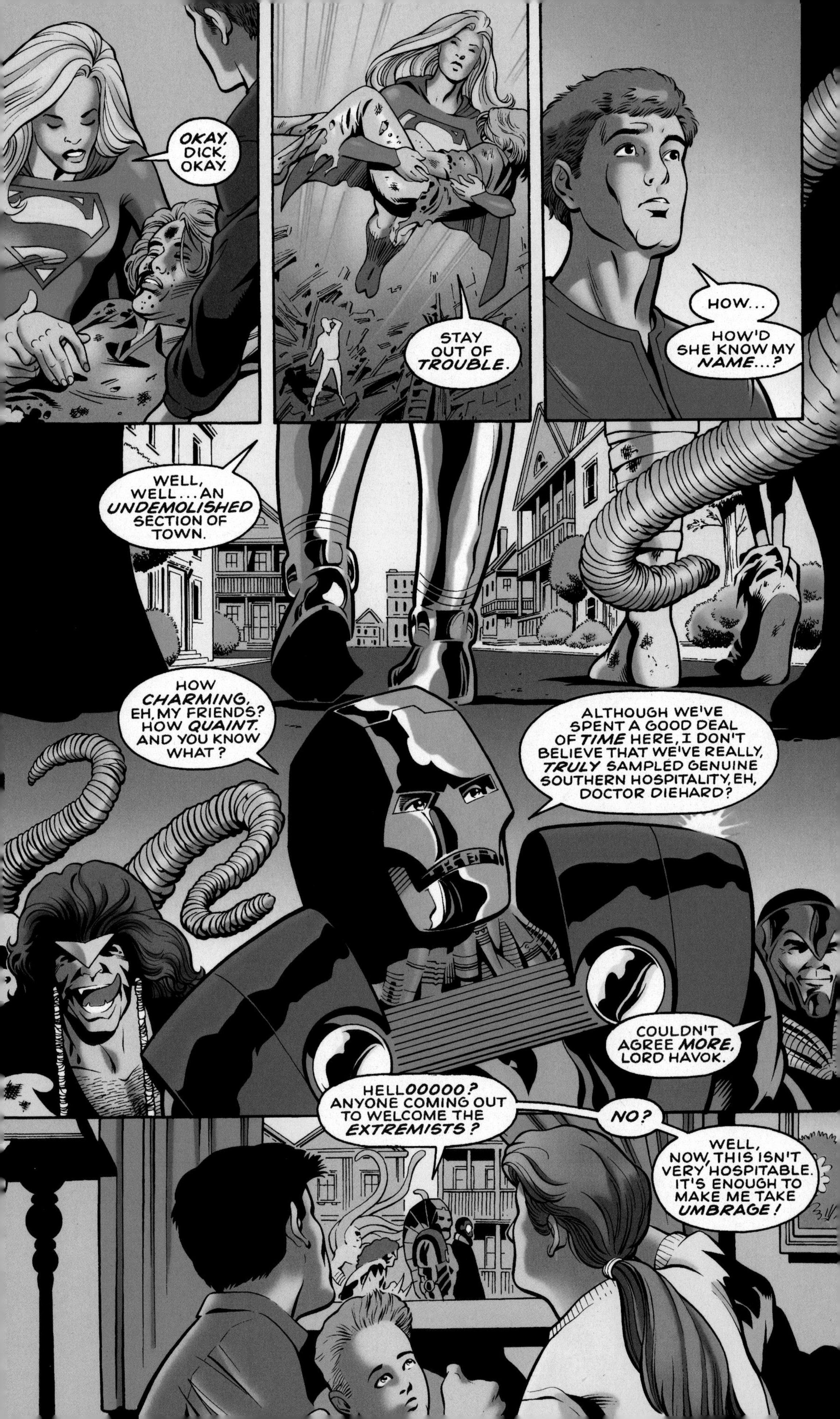
OKAY, DICK, OKAY.
STAY OUT OF TROUBLE.
HOW...
HOW'D SHE KNOW MY NAME...?
WELL, WELL... AN UNDEMOLISHED SECTION OF TOWN.
HOW CHARMING, EH, MY FRIENDS? HOW QUAINT. AND YOU KNOW WHAT?
ALTHOUGH WE'VE SPENT A GOOD DEAL OF TIME HERE, I DON'T BELIEVE THAT WE'VE REALLY, TRULY SAMPLED GENUINE SOUTHERN HOSPITALITY, EH, DOCTOR DIEHARD?
COULDN'T AGREE MORE, LORD HAVOK.
HELLOOOOO? ANYONE COMING OUT TO WELCOME THE EXTREMISTS?
NO?
WELL, NOW, THIS ISN'T VERY HOSPITABLE. IT'S ENOUGH TO MAKE ME TAKE UMBRAGE!

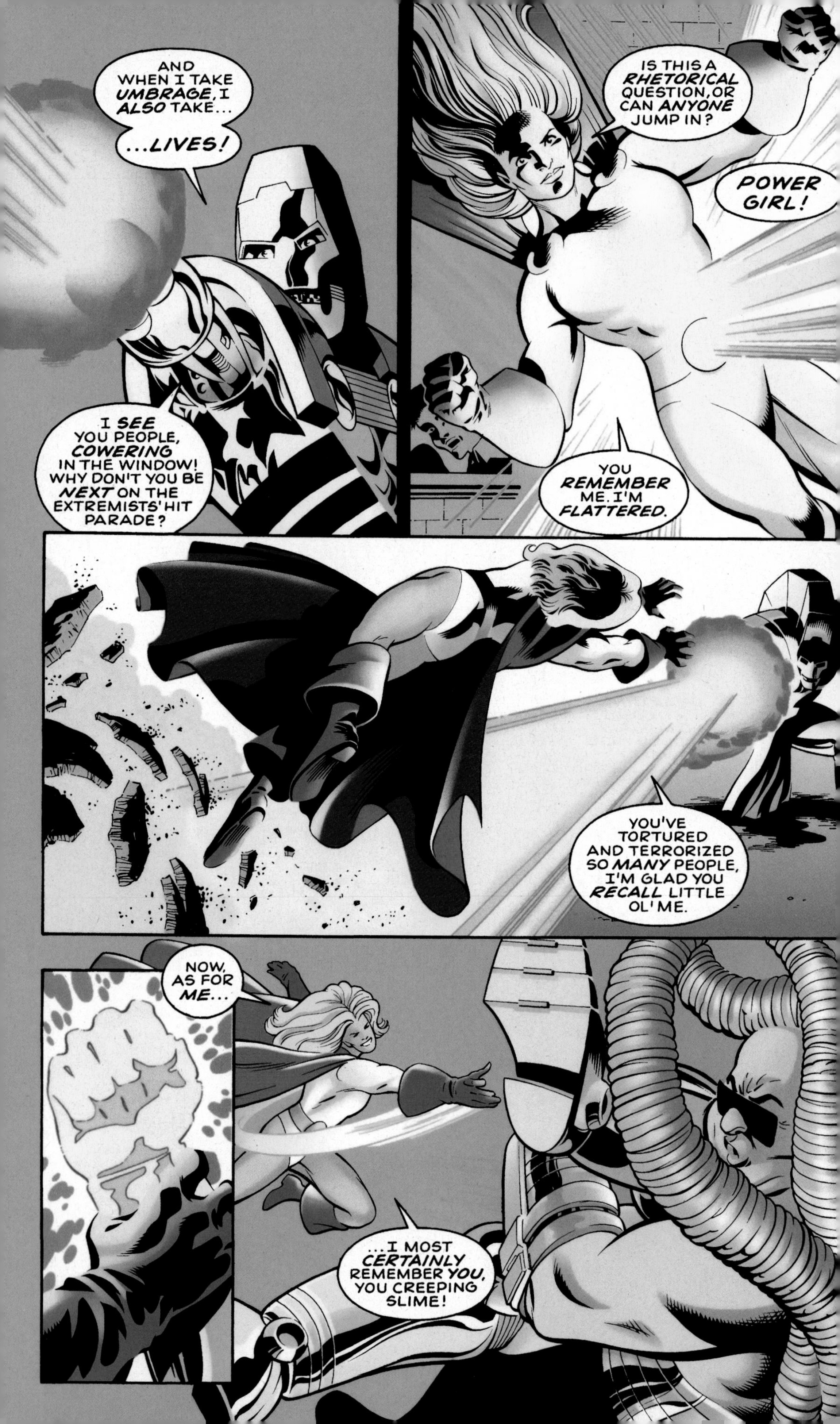
AND WHEN I TAKE UMBRAGE, I ALSO TAKE...
...LIVES!
I SEE YOU PEOPLE, COWERING IN THE WINDOW! WHY DON'T YOU BE NEXT ON THE EXTREMISTS' HIT PARADE?
IS THIS A RHETORICAL QUESTION, OR CAN ANYONE JUMP IN?
POWER GIRL!
YOU REMEMBER ME. I'M FLATTERED.
YOU'VE TORTURED AND TERRORIZED SO MANY PEOPLE, I'M GLAD YOU RECALL LITTLE OL' ME.
NOW, AS FOR ME...
...I MOST CERTAINLY REMEMBER YOU, YOU CREEPING SLIME!

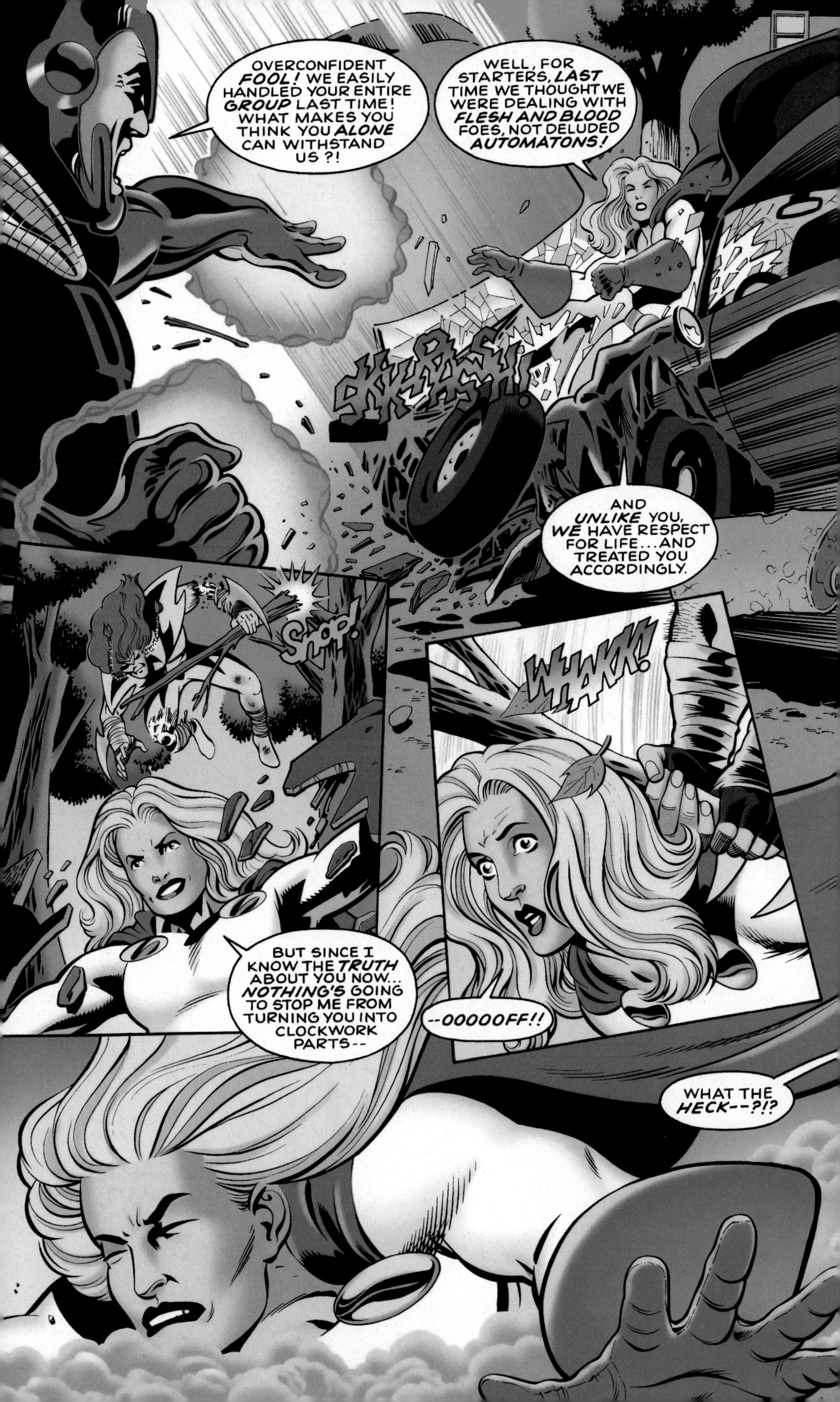
OVERCONFIDENT FOOL! WE EASILY HANDLED YOUR ENTIRE GROUP LAST TIME! WHAT MAKES YOU THINK YOU ALONE CAN WITHSTAND US?!
WELL, FOR STARTERS, LAST TIME WE THOUGHT WE WERE DEALING WITH FLESH AND BLOOD FOES, NOT DELUDED AUTOMATONS!
SKRASSH!
AND UNLIKE YOU, WE HAVE RESPECT FOR LIFE...AND TREATED YOU ACCORDINGLY.
SNAP!
BUT SINCE I KNOW THE TRUTH ABOUT YOU NOW... NOTHING'S GOING TO STOP ME FROM TURNING YOU INTO CLOCKWORK PARTS--
WHAKK!
--OOOOOFF!!
WHAT THE HECK--?!?

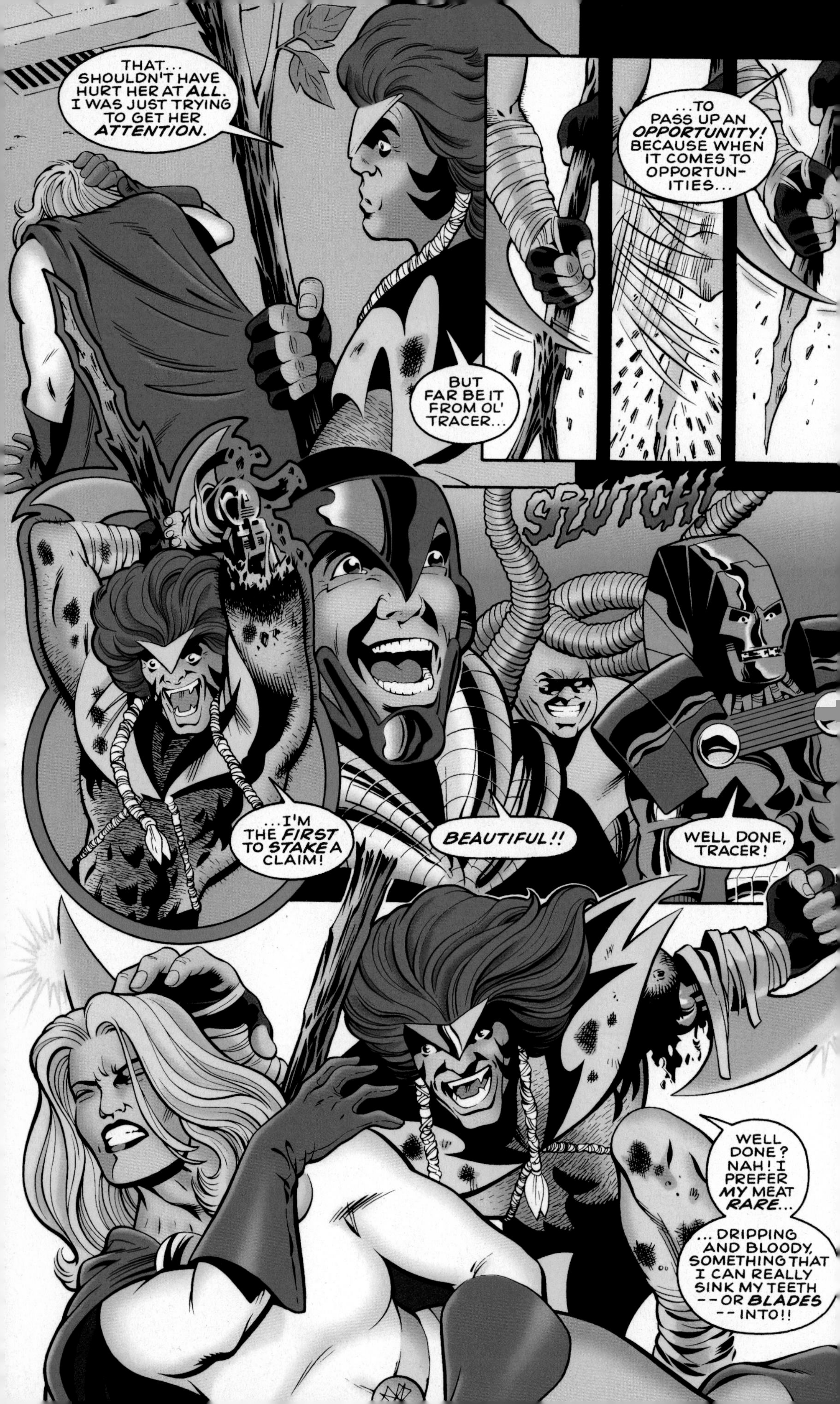

THAT... SHOULDN'T HAVE HURT HER AT ALL. I WAS JUST TRYING TO GET HER ATTENTION.
BUT FAR BE IT FROM OL' TRACER...
...TO PASS UP AN OPPORTUNITY! BECAUSE WHEN IT COMES TO OPPORTUN-ITIES...
SPLUTCH!
...I'M THE FIRST TO STAKE A CLAIM!
BEAUTIFUL!!
WELL DONE, TRACER!
WELL DONE? NAH! I PREFER MY MEAT RARE...
...DRIPPING AND BLOODY, SOMETHING THAT I CAN REALLY SINK MY TEETH --OR BLADES-- INTO!!

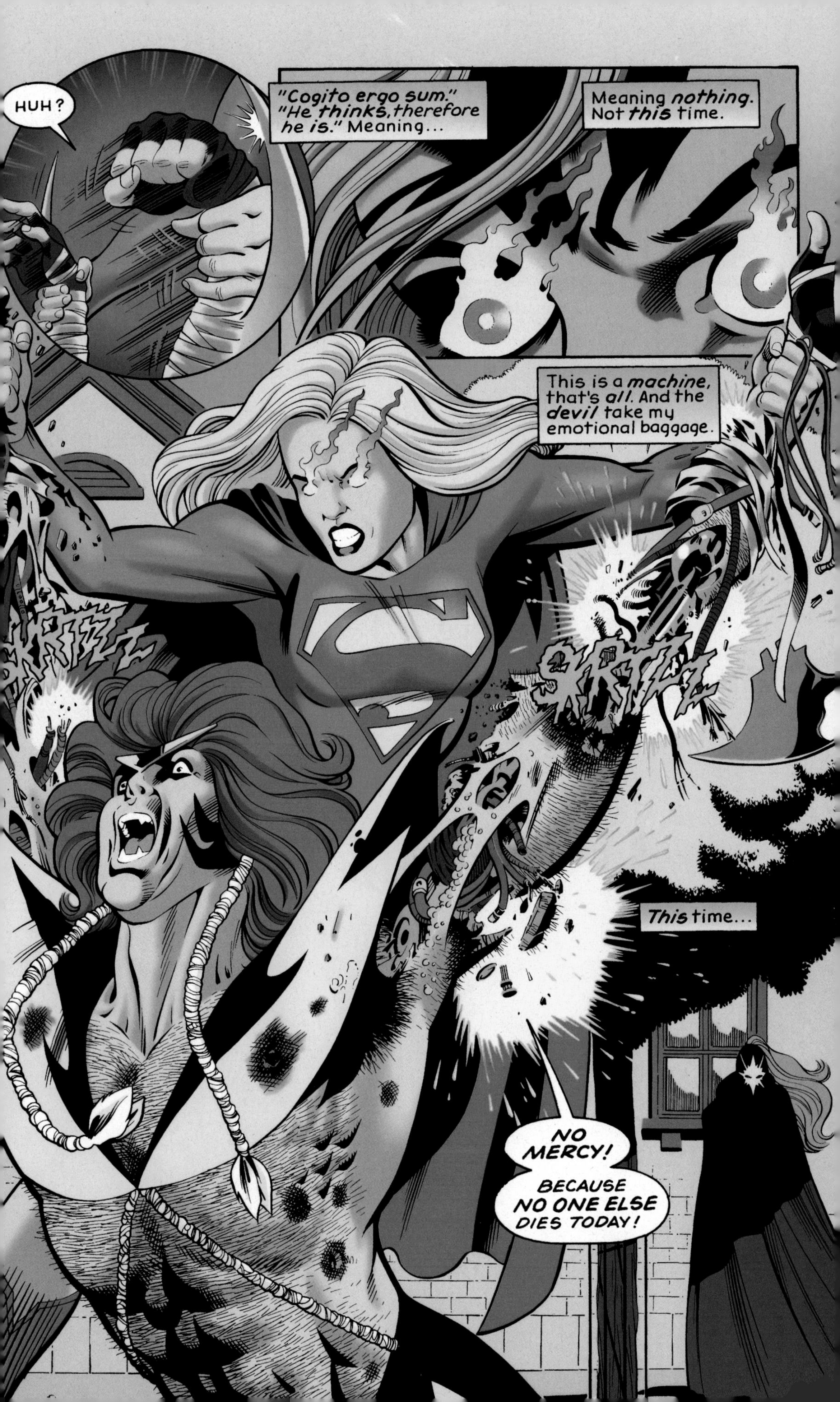
HUH?
"Cogito ergo sum." "He thinks, therefore he is." Meaning...
Meaning nothing. Not this time.
This is a machine, that's all. And the devil take my emotional baggage.
SKRITZ
SKRITZ
This time...
NO MERCY!
BECAUSE NO ONE ELSE DIES TODAY!

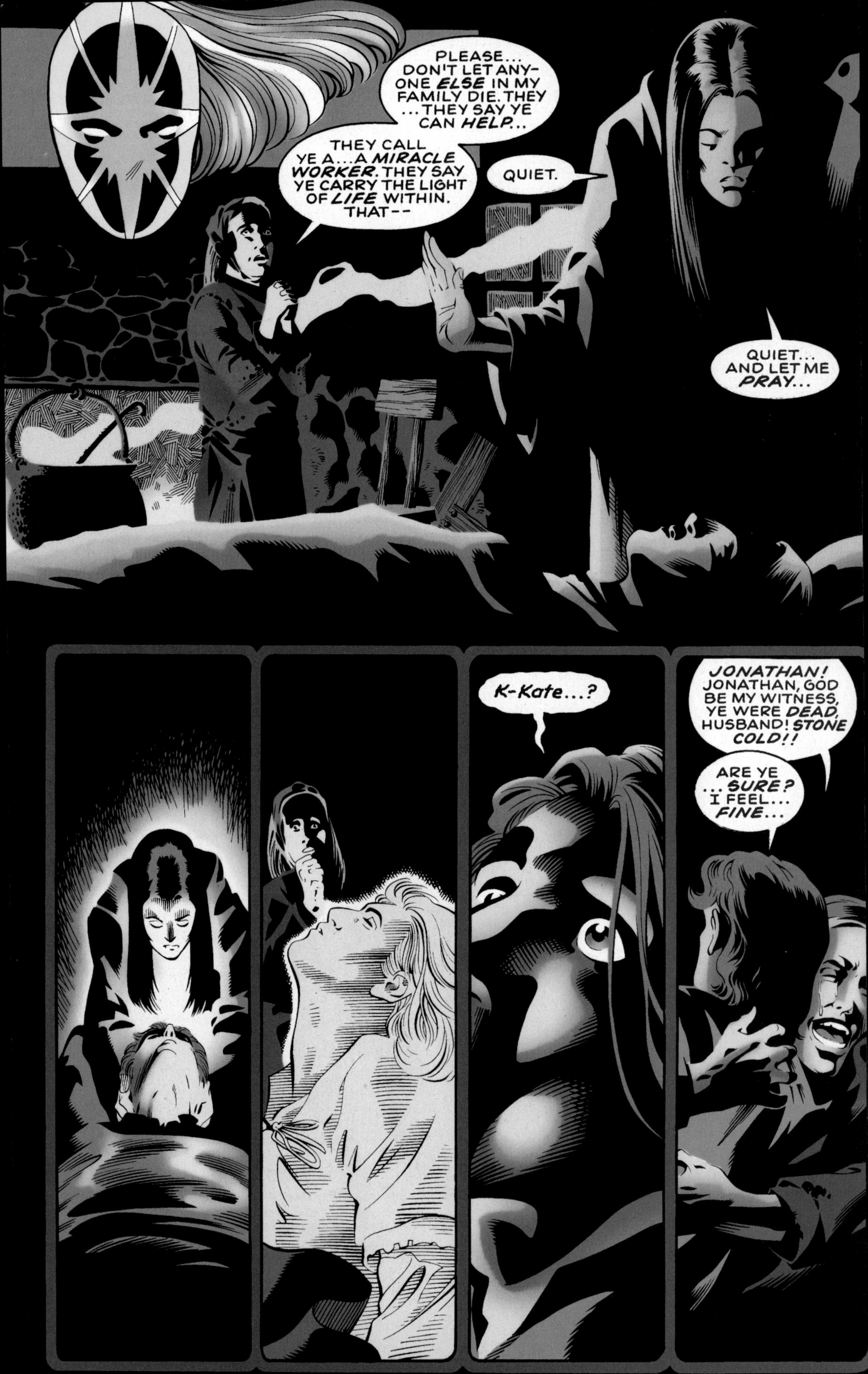
PLEASE... DON'T LET ANY-ONE ELSE IN MY FAMILY DIE. THEY ...THEY SAY YE CAN HELP...
THEY CALL YE A...A MIRACLE WORKER. THEY SAY YE CARRY THE LIGHT OF LIFE WITHIN. THAT--
QUIET.
QUIET... AND LET ME PRAY...
K-Kate...?
JONATHAN! JONATHAN, GOD BE MY WITNESS, YE WERE DEAD, HUSBAND! STONE COLD!!
ARE YE ...SURE? I FEEL... FINE...

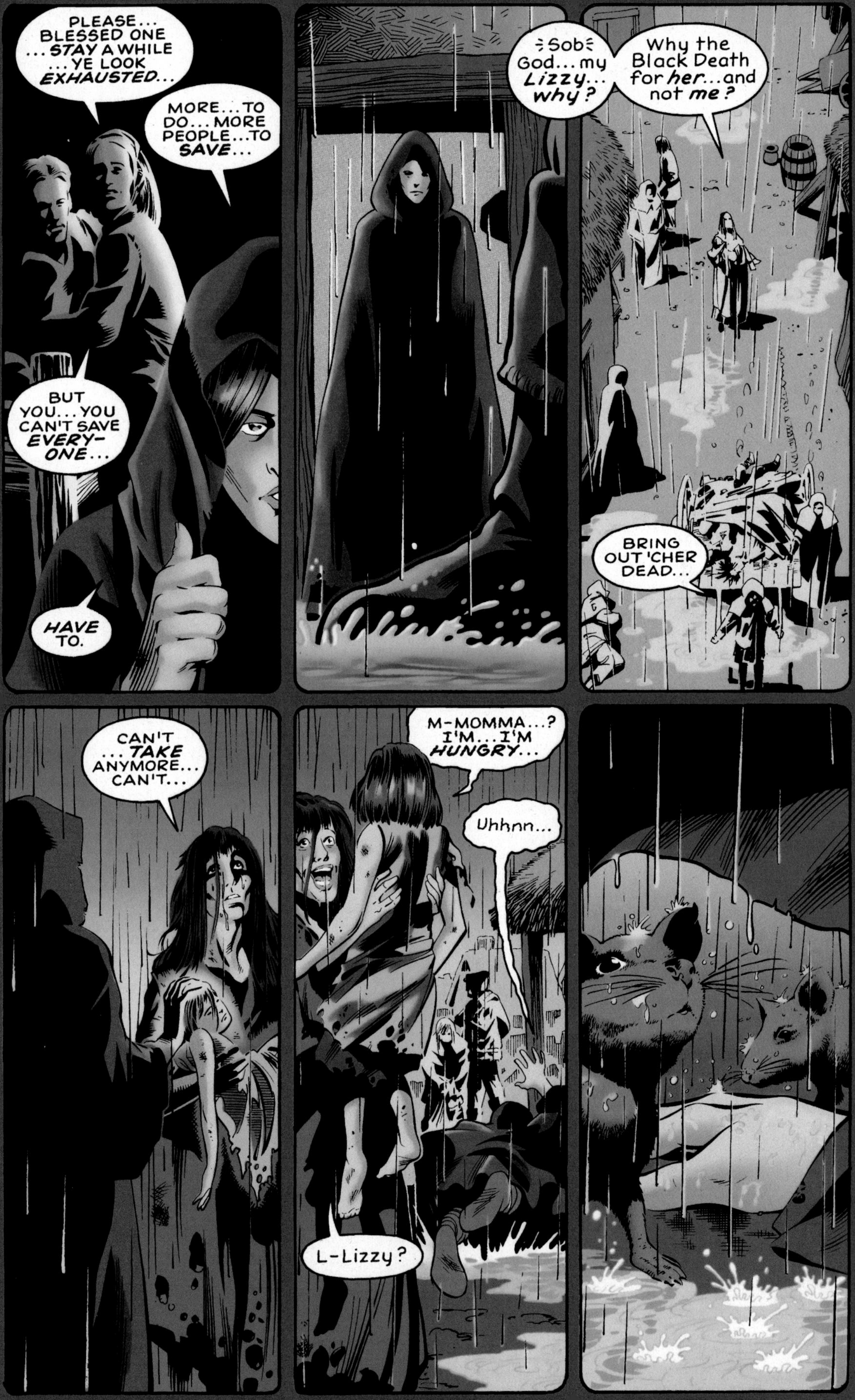
PLEASE... BLESSED ONE ...STAY A WHILE ...YE LOOK EXHAUSTED...
MORE...TO DO...MORE PEOPLE...TO SAVE...
BUT YOU...YOU CAN'T SAVE EVERY-ONE...
HAVE TO.
Sob God...my Lizzy... why?
Why the Black Death for her...and not me?
BRING OUT 'CHER DEAD...
CAN'T ...TAKE ANYMORE... CAN'T...
M-MOMMA...? I'M...I'M HUNGRY...
Uhhnn...
L-Lizzy?

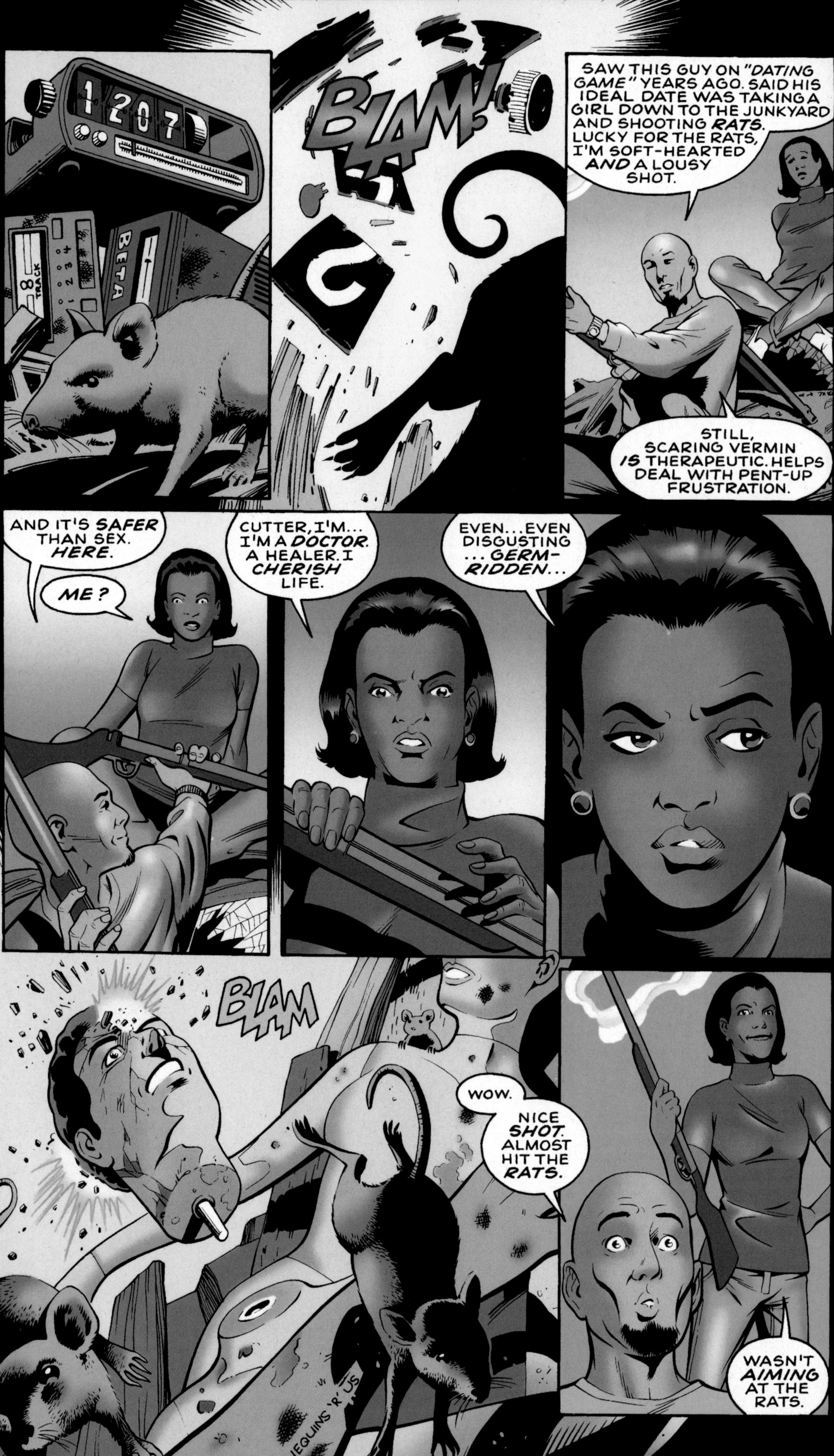
1207
8 TRACK
BETA
BLAM!
SAW THIS GUY ON "DATING GAME" YEARS AGO. SAID HIS IDEAL DATE WAS TAKING A GIRL DOWN TO THE JUNKYARD AND SHOOTING RATS. LUCKY FOR THE RATS, I'M SOFT-HEARTED AND A LOUSY SHOT.
STILL, SCARING VERMIN IS THERAPEUTIC. HELPS DEAL WITH PENT-UP FRUSTRATION.
AND IT'S SAFER THAN SEX. HERE.
ME?
CUTTER, I'M... I'M A DOCTOR. A HEALER. I CHERISH LIFE.
EVEN... EVEN DISGUSTING ...GERM-RIDDEN...
BLAM
WOW.
NICE SHOT. ALMOST HIT THE RATS.
WASN'T AIMING AT THE RATS.
NEQUINS 'R' US

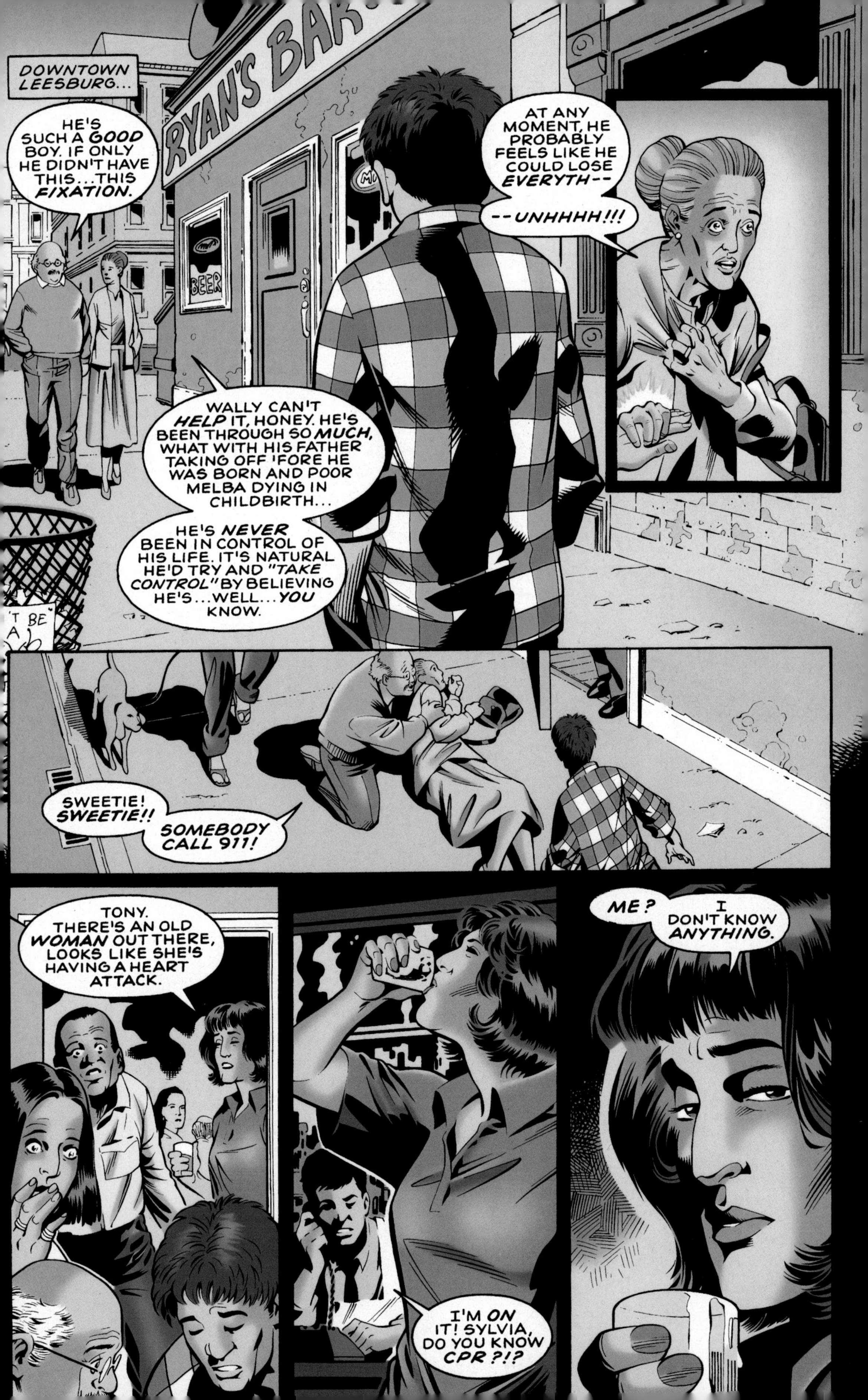

DOWNTOWN LEESBURG...
RYAN'S BAR
HE'S SUCH A GOOD BOY. IF ONLY HE DIDN'T HAVE THIS...THIS FIXATION.
WALLY CAN'T HELP IT, HONEY. HE'S BEEN THROUGH SO MUCH, WHAT WITH HIS FATHER TAKING OFF 'FORE HE WAS BORN AND POOR MELBA DYING IN CHILDBIRTH...
HE'S NEVER BEEN IN CONTROL OF HIS LIFE. IT'S NATURAL HE'D TRY AND "TAKE CONTROL" BY BELIEVING HE'S...WELL...YOU KNOW.
BEER
AT ANY MOMENT, HE PROBABLY FEELS LIKE HE COULD LOSE EVERYTH--
--UNHHHH!!!
SWEETIE! SWEETIE!!
SOMEBODY CALL 911!
TONY. THERE'S AN OLD WOMAN OUT THERE, LOOKS LIKE SHE'S HAVING A HEART ATTACK.
I'M ON IT! SYLVIA, DO YOU KNOW CPR?!?
ME?
I DON'T KNOW ANYTHING.

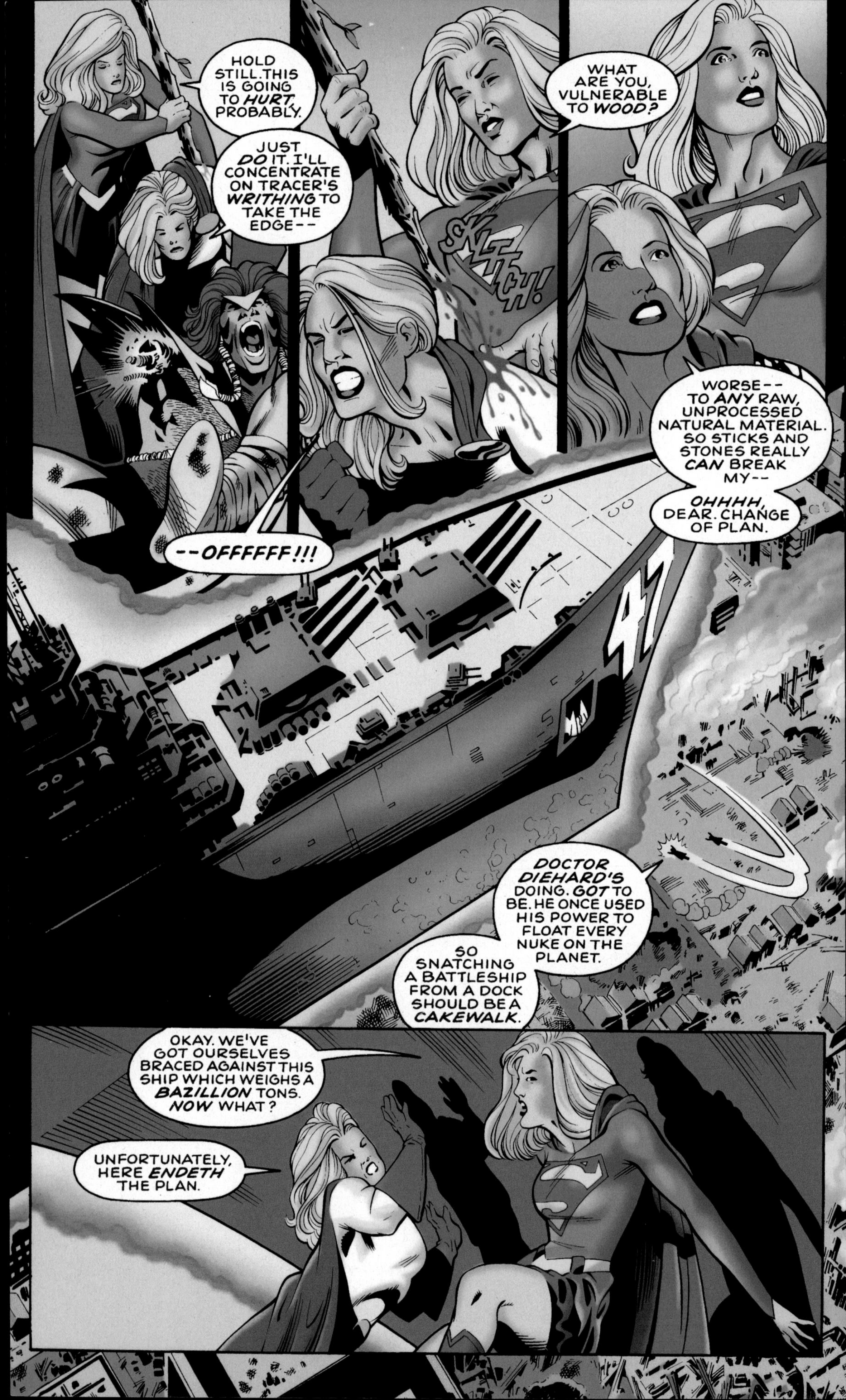
HOLD STILL. THIS IS GOING TO HURT, PROBABLY.
JUST DO IT. I'LL CONCENTRATE ON TRACER'S WRITHING TO TAKE THE EDGE--
--OFFFFFF!!!
SKLTCH!
WHAT ARE YOU, VULNERABLE TO WOOD?
WORSE-- TO ANY RAW, UNPROCESSED NATURAL MATERIAL. SO STICKS AND STONES REALLY CAN BREAK MY--
OHHHH, DEAR. CHANGE OF PLAN.
47
DOCTOR DIEHARD'S DOING. GOT TO BE. HE ONCE USED HIS POWER TO FLOAT EVERY NUKE ON THE PLANET.
SO SNATCHING A BATTLESHIP FROM A DOCK SHOULD BE A CAKEWALK.
OKAY. WE'VE GOT OURSELVES BRACED AGAINST THIS SHIP WHICH WEIGHS A BAZILLION TONS. NOW WHAT?
UNFORTUNATELY, HERE ENDETH THE PLAN.

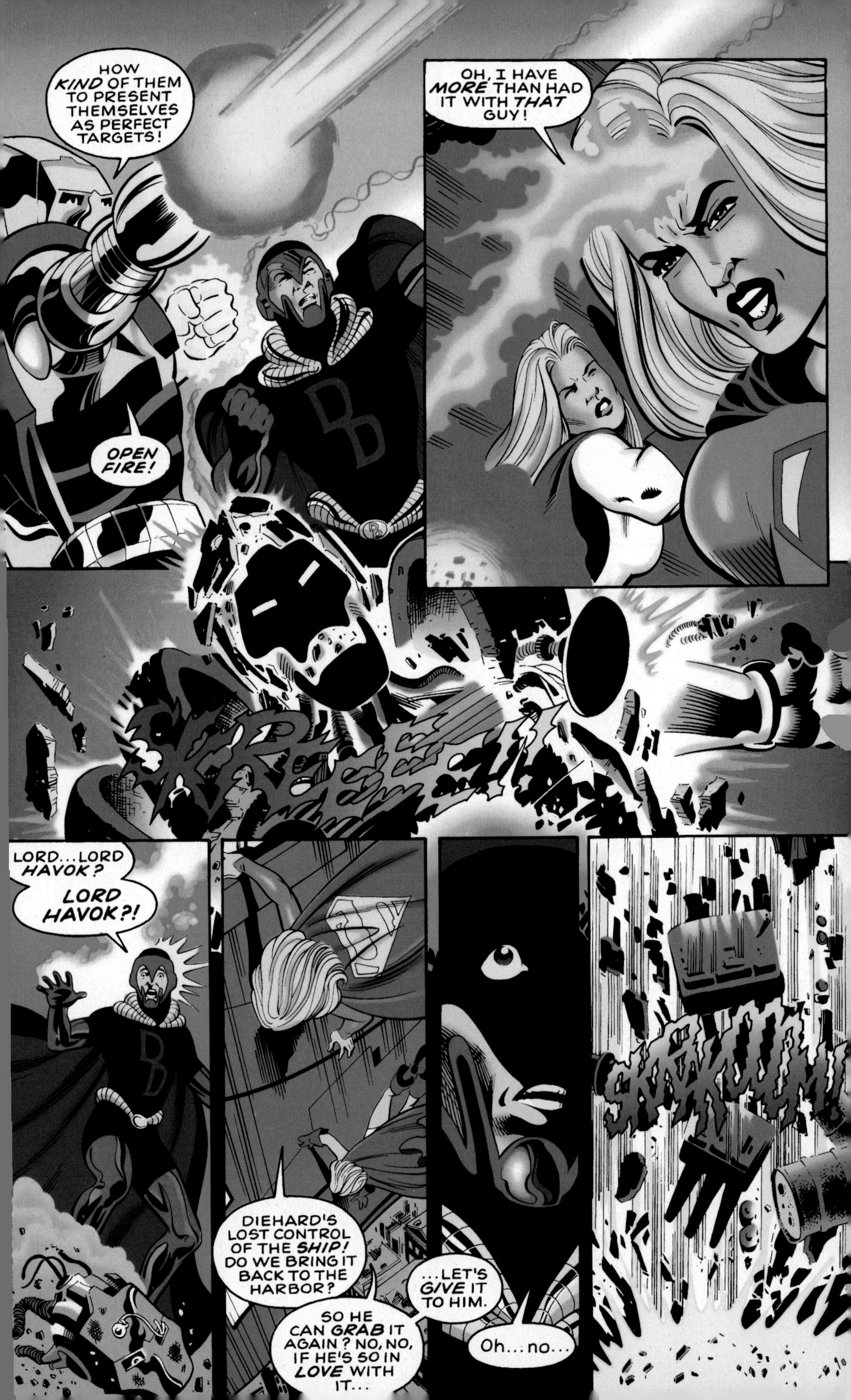
HOW KIND OF THEM TO PRESENT THEMSELVES AS PERFECT TARGETS!
OPEN FIRE!
OH, I HAVE MORE THAN HAD IT WITH THAT GUY!
LORD... LORD HAVOK?
LORD HAVOK?!
DIEHARD'S LOST CONTROL OF THE SHIP! DO WE BRING IT BACK TO THE HARBOR?
SO HE CAN GRAB IT AGAIN? NO, NO, IF HE'S SO IN LOVE WITH IT...
...LET'S GIVE IT TO HIM.
Oh... no...
SKKKUMM!

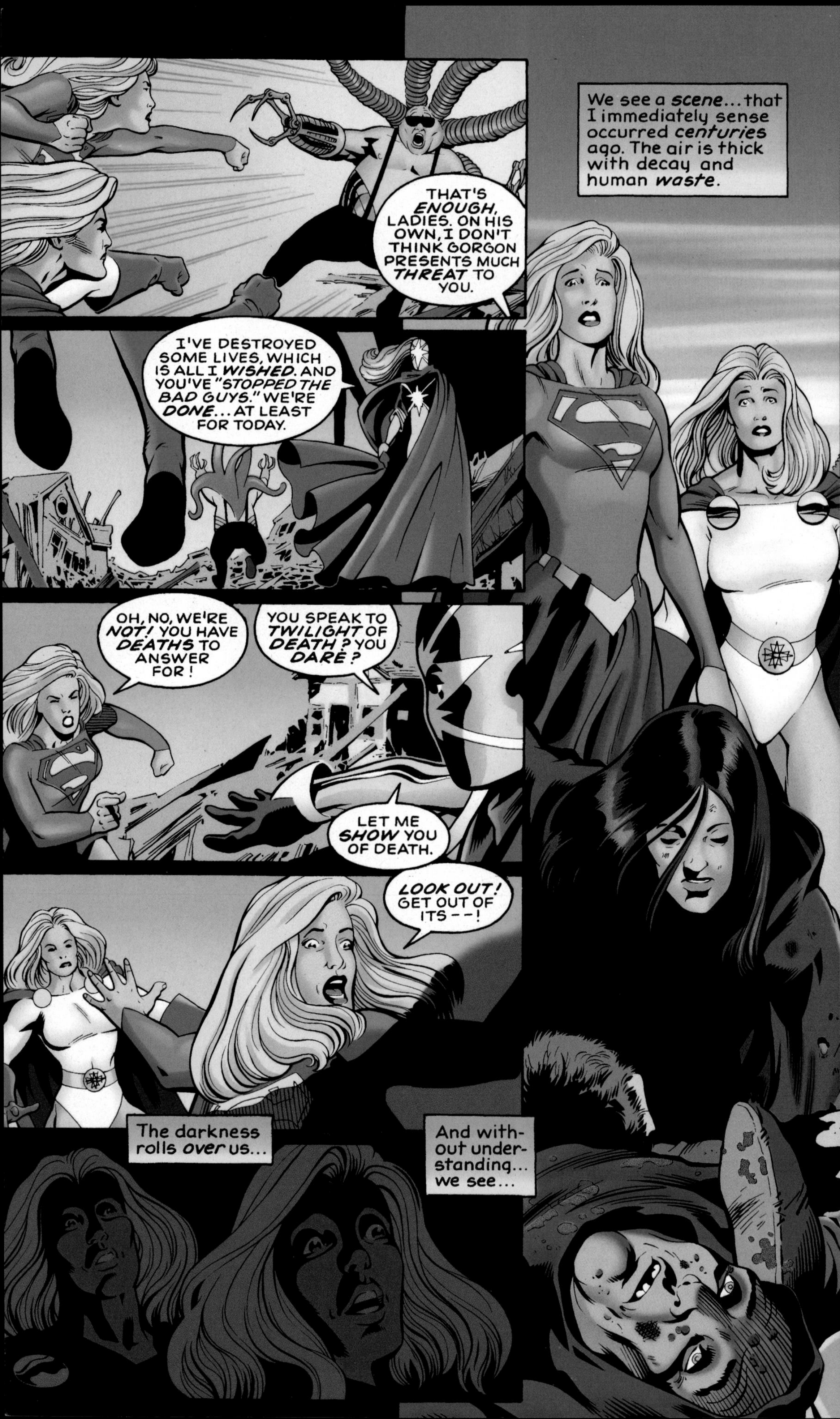

THAT'S ENOUGH, LADIES. ON HIS OWN, I DON'T THINK GORGON PRESENTS MUCH THREAT TO YOU.
I'VE DESTROYED SOME LIVES, WHICH IS ALL I WISHED. AND YOU'VE "STOPPED THE BAD GUYS." WE'RE DONE... AT LEAST FOR TODAY.
OH, NO, WE'RE NOT! YOU HAVE DEATHS TO ANSWER FOR!
YOU SPEAK TO TWILIGHT OF DEATH? YOU DARE?
LET ME SHOW YOU OF DEATH.
LOOK OUT! GET OUT OF ITS --!
The darkness rolls over us...
And without understanding... we see...
We see a scene... that I immediately sense occurred centuries ago. The air is thick with decay and human waste.

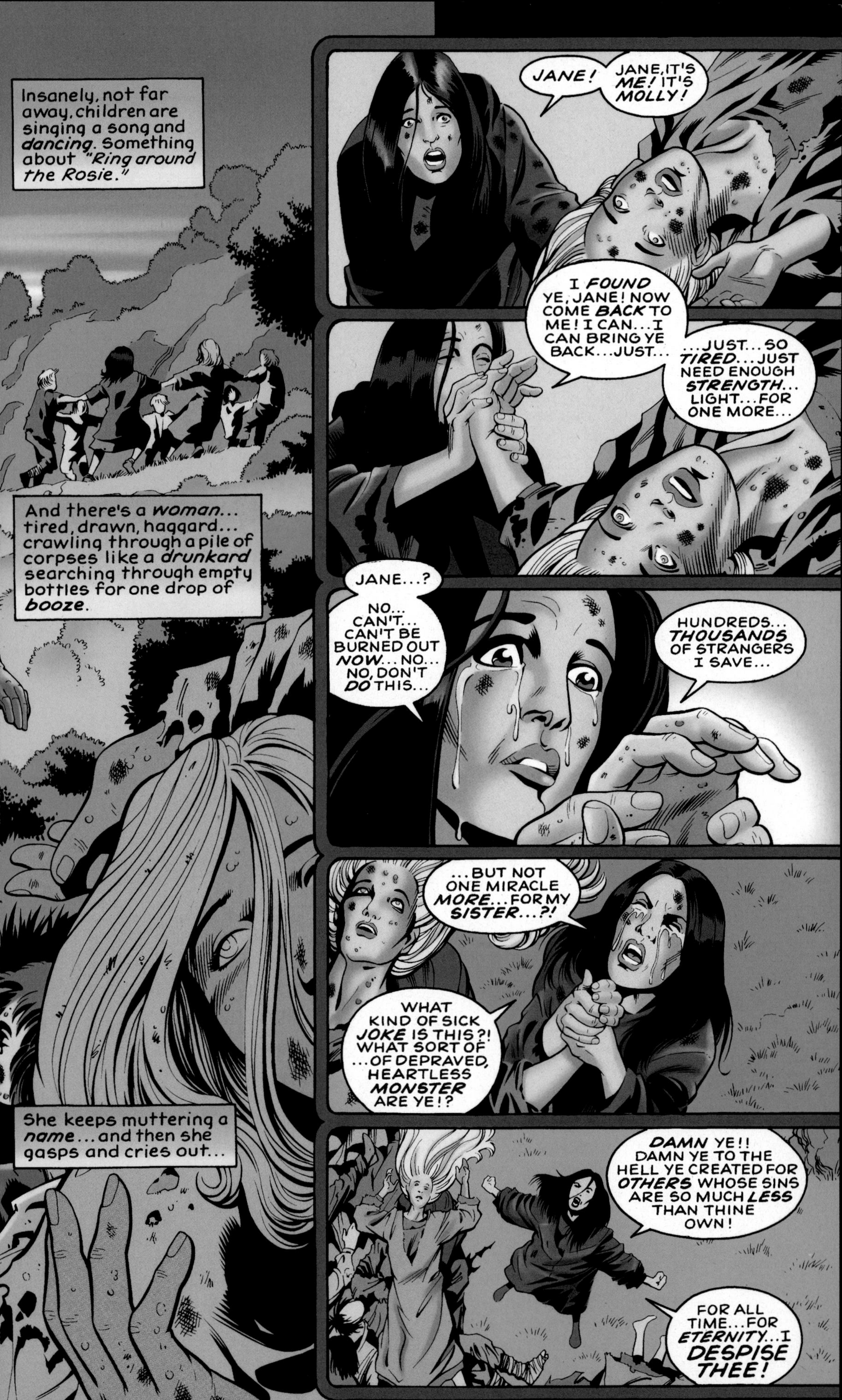

Insanely, not far away, children are singing a song and dancing. Something about "Ring around the Rosie."
JANE!
JANE, IT'S ME! IT'S MOLLY!
I FOUND YE, JANE! NOW COME BACK TO ME! I CAN... I CAN BRING YE BACK... JUST...
...JUST... SO TIRED... JUST NEED ENOUGH STRENGTH... LIGHT... FOR ONE MORE...
And there's a woman... tired, drawn, haggard... crawling through a pile of corpses like a drunkard searching through empty bottles for one drop of booze.
JANE...?
NO... CAN'T... CAN'T BE BURNED OUT NOW... NO... NO, DON'T DO THIS...
HUNDREDS... THOUSANDS OF STRANGERS I SAVE...
...BUT NOT ONE MIRACLE MORE... FOR MY SISTER...?!
WHAT KIND OF SICK JOKE IS THIS?! WHAT SORT OF ...OF DEPRAVED, HEARTLESS MONSTER ARE YE!?
She keeps muttering a name... and then she gasps and cries out...
DAMN YE!! DAMN YE TO THE HELL YE CREATED FOR OTHERS WHOSE SINS ARE SO MUCH LESS THAN THINE OWN!
FOR ALL TIME... FOR ETERNITY... I DESPISE THEE!

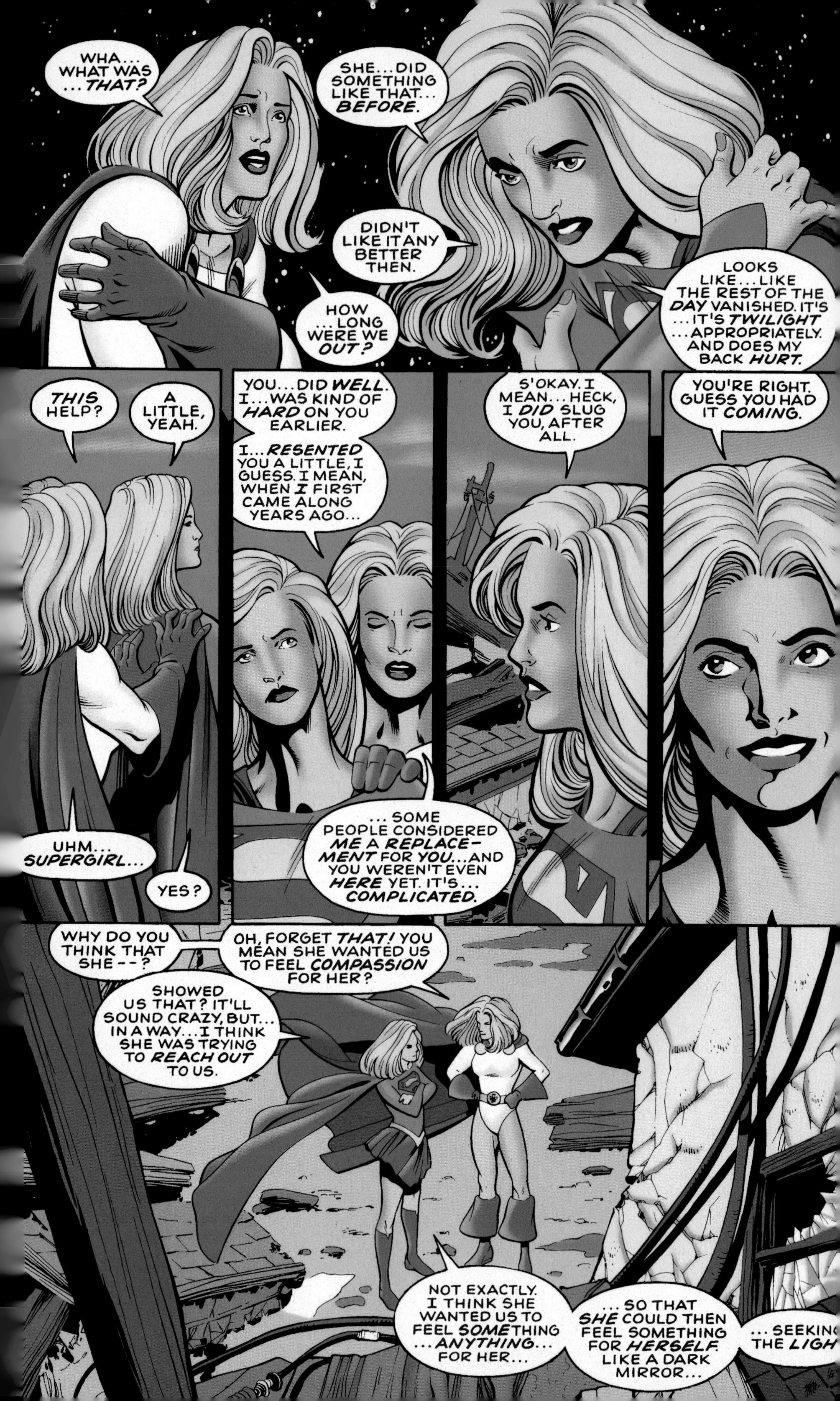

WHA... WHAT WAS ...THAT?
SHE...DID SOMETHING LIKE THAT... BEFORE.
DIDN'T LIKE IT ANY BETTER THEN.
HOW ...LONG WERE WE OUT?
LOOKS LIKE...LIKE THE REST OF THE DAY VANISHED. IT'S ...IT'S TWILIGHT ...APPROPRIATELY. AND DOES MY BACK HURT.
THIS HELP?
A LITTLE, YEAH.
UHM... SUPERGIRL...
YES?
YOU...DID WELL. I...WAS KIND OF HARD ON YOU EARLIER.
I...RESENTED YOU A LITTLE, I GUESS. I MEAN, WHEN I FIRST CAME ALONG YEARS AGO...
...SOME PEOPLE CONSIDERED ME A REPLACE-MENT FOR YOU...AND YOU WEREN'T EVEN HERE YET. IT'S... COMPLICATED.
S'OKAY. I MEAN... HECK, I DID SLUG YOU, AFTER ALL.
YOU'RE RIGHT. GUESS YOU HAD IT COMING.
WHY DO YOU THINK THAT SHE--?
OH, FORGET THAT! YOU MEAN SHE WANTED US TO FEEL COMPASSION FOR HER?
SHOWED US THAT? IT'LL SOUND CRAZY, BUT... IN A WAY...I THINK SHE WAS TRYING TO REACH OUT TO US.
NOT EXACTLY. I THINK SHE WANTED US TO FEEL SOMETHING ...ANYTHING... FOR HER...
...SO THAT SHE COULD THEN FEEL SOMETHING FOR HERSELF. LIKE A DARK MIRROR...
...SEEKIN THE LIGH

SUPERGIRL #17 cover by Gary Frank, Cam Smith and Patrick Martin

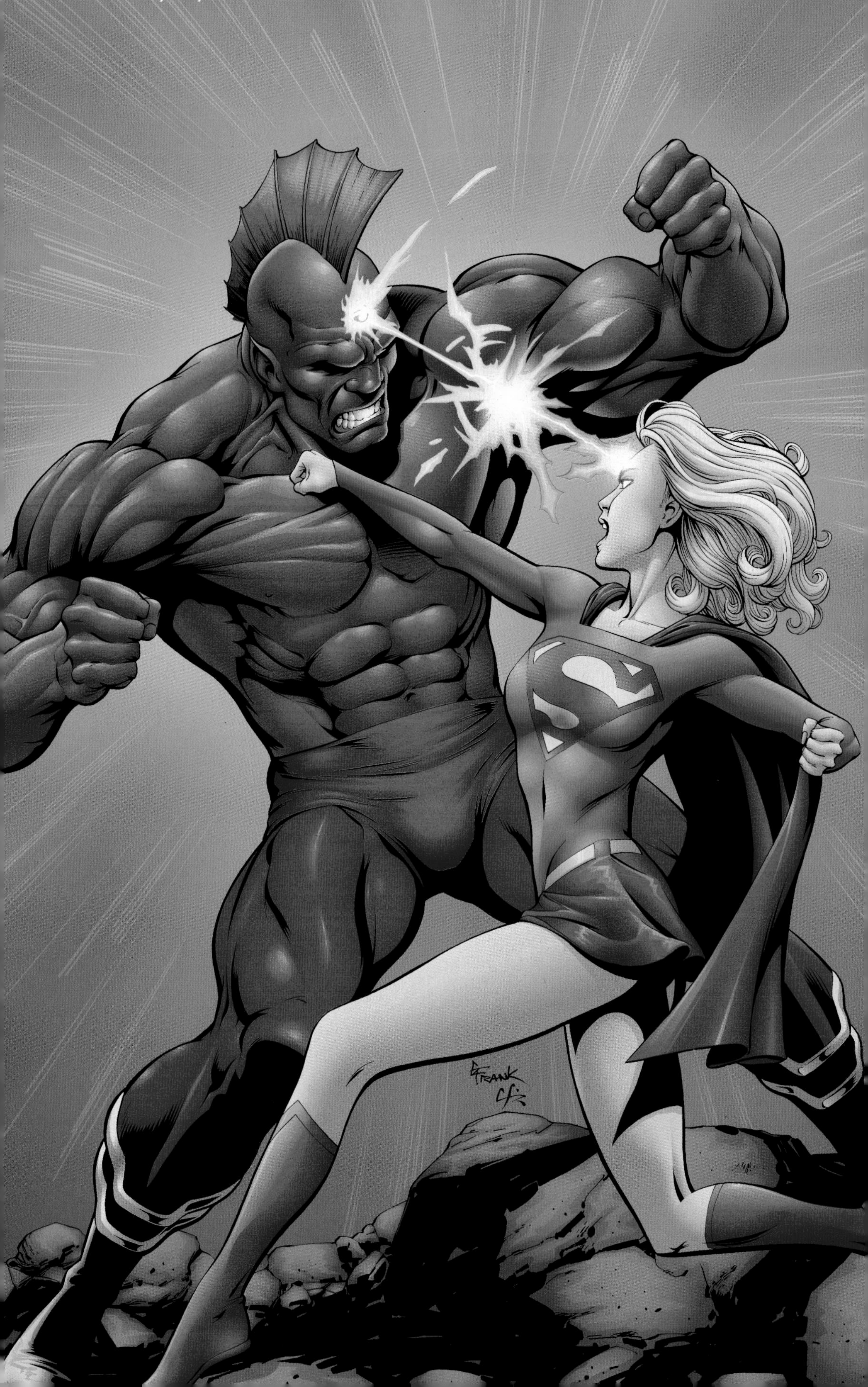

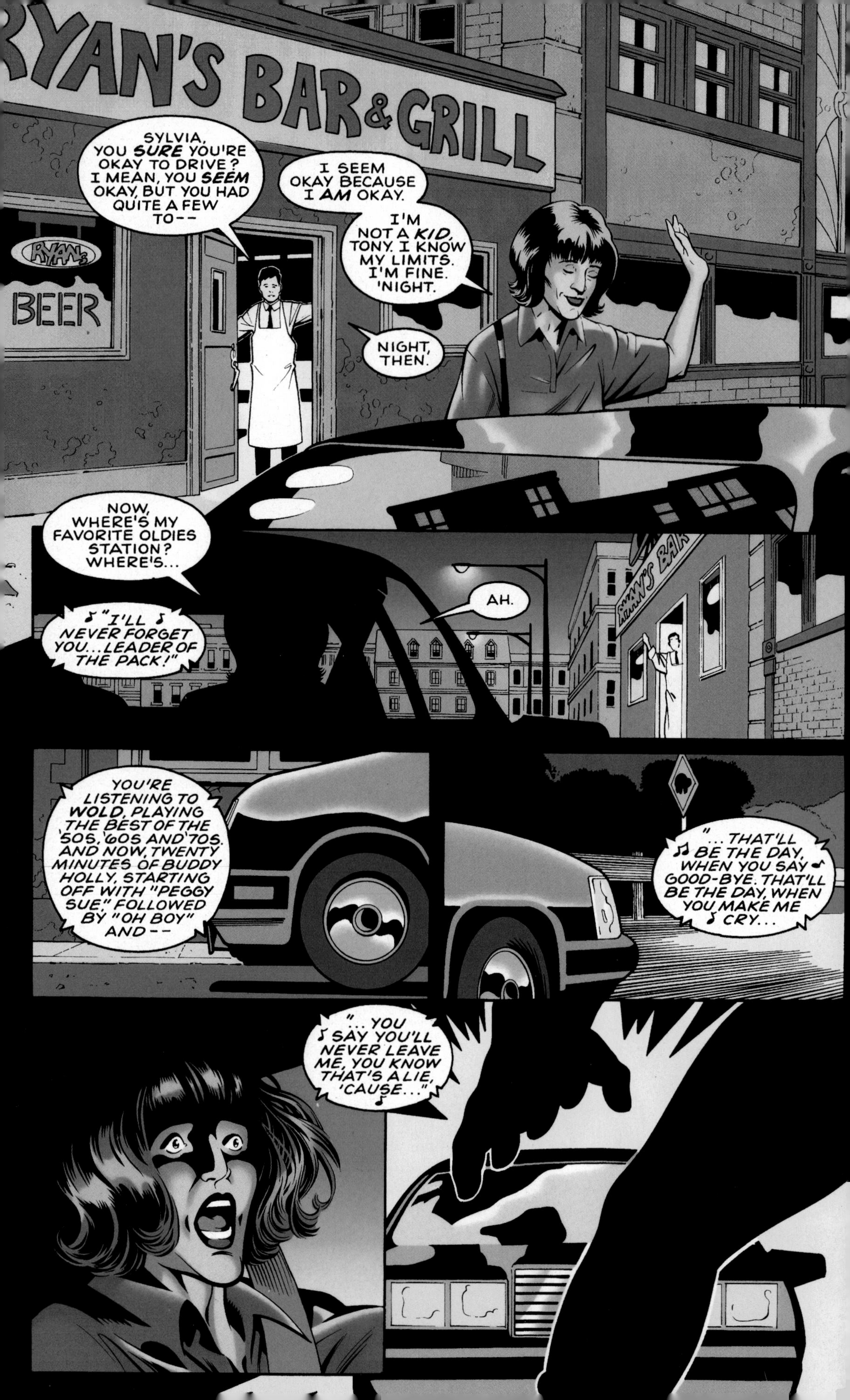
RYAN'S BAR & GRILL
RYAN'S
BEER
SYLVIA, YOU *SURE* YOU'RE OKAY TO DRIVE? I MEAN, YOU *SEEM* OKAY, BUT YOU HAD QUITE A FEW TO--
I SEEM OKAY BECAUSE I *AM* OKAY.
I'M NOT A *KID*, TONY. I KNOW MY LIMITS. I'M FINE. 'NIGHT.
NIGHT, THEN.
NOW, WHERE'S MY FAVORITE OLDIES STATION? WHERE'S...
AH.
"I'LL NEVER FORGET YOU...LEADER OF THE PACK!"
YOU'RE LISTENING TO WOLD, PLAYING THE BEST OF THE '50S, '60S AND '70S. AND NOW, TWENTY MINUTES OF BUDDY HOLLY, STARTING OFF WITH "PEGGY SUE," FOLLOWED BY "OH BOY" AND--
"...THAT'LL BE THE DAY, WHEN YOU SAY GOOD-BYE. THAT'LL BE THE DAY, WHEN YOU MAKE ME CRY...
"...YOU SAY YOU'LL NEVER LEAVE ME, YOU KNOW THAT'S A LIE, 'CAUSE..."

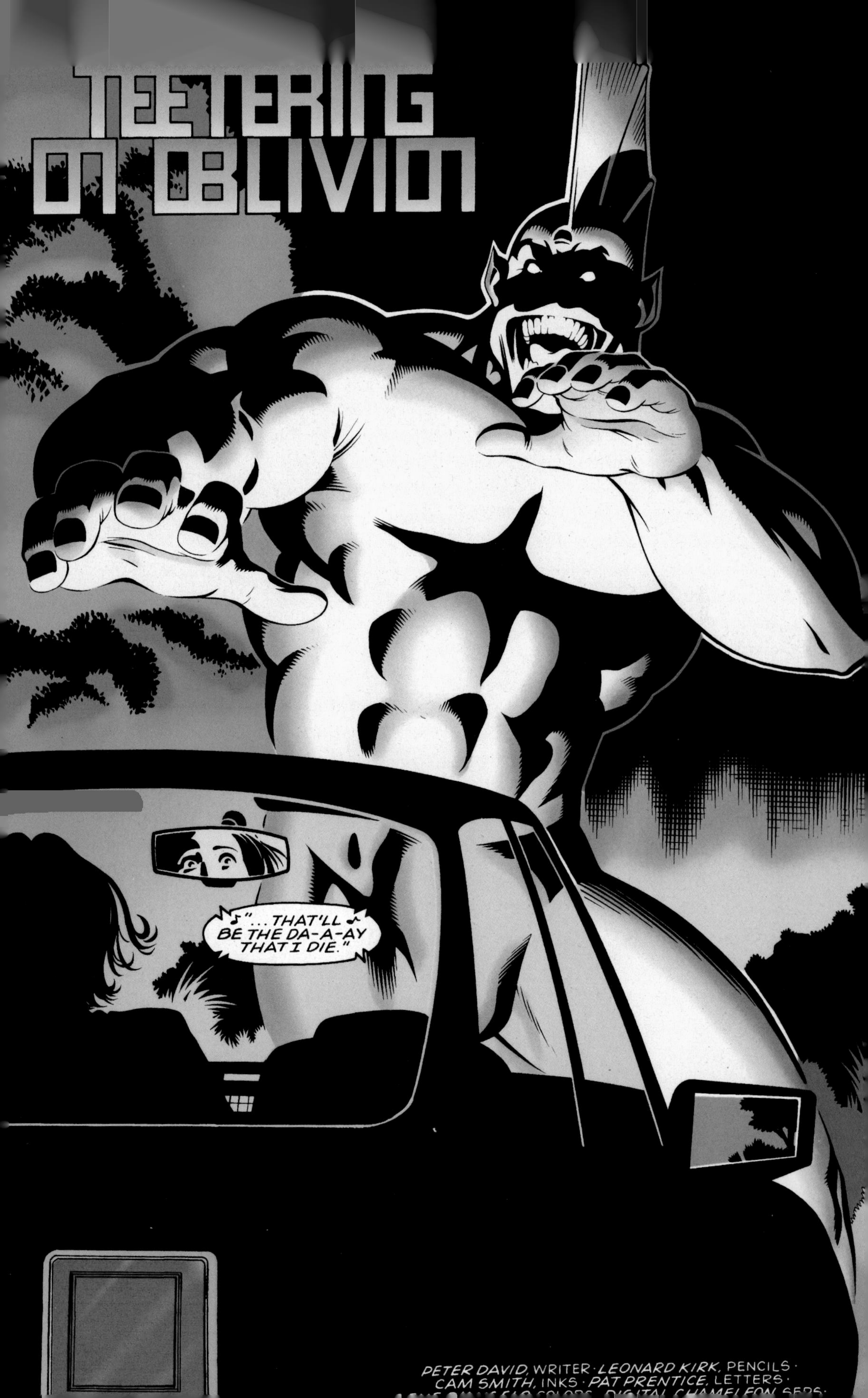
TEETERING ON OBLIVION
"...THAT'LL BE THE DA-A-AY THAT I DIE."
PETER DAVID, WRITER · LEONARD KIRK, PENCILS ·
CAM SMITH, INKS · PAT PRENTICE, LETTERS ·

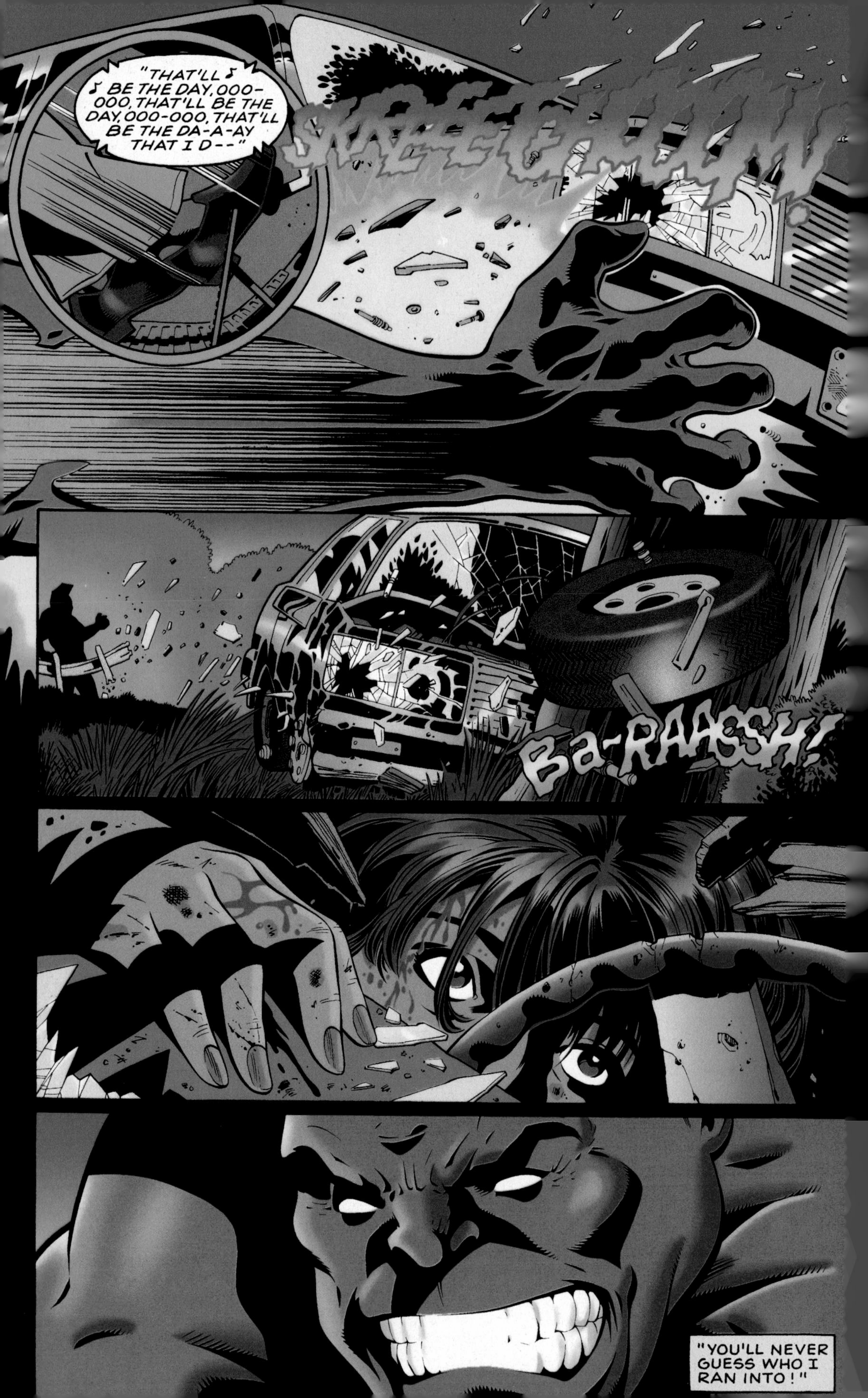
"THAT'LL ♪ ♪ BE THE DAY, OOO-OOO, THAT'LL BE THE DAY, OOO-OOO, THAT'LL BE THE DA-A-AY THAT I D--"
SKRREEEEEEEEEEEEEEEEEEEEEEEEEEEEEEEEEEEEEEEEEEEEEEEEEEEEEEEEEEEEEEEEEEEEEEEEEEEEEE
Ba-RAAASSH!
"YOU'LL NEVER GUESS WHO I RAN INTO!"

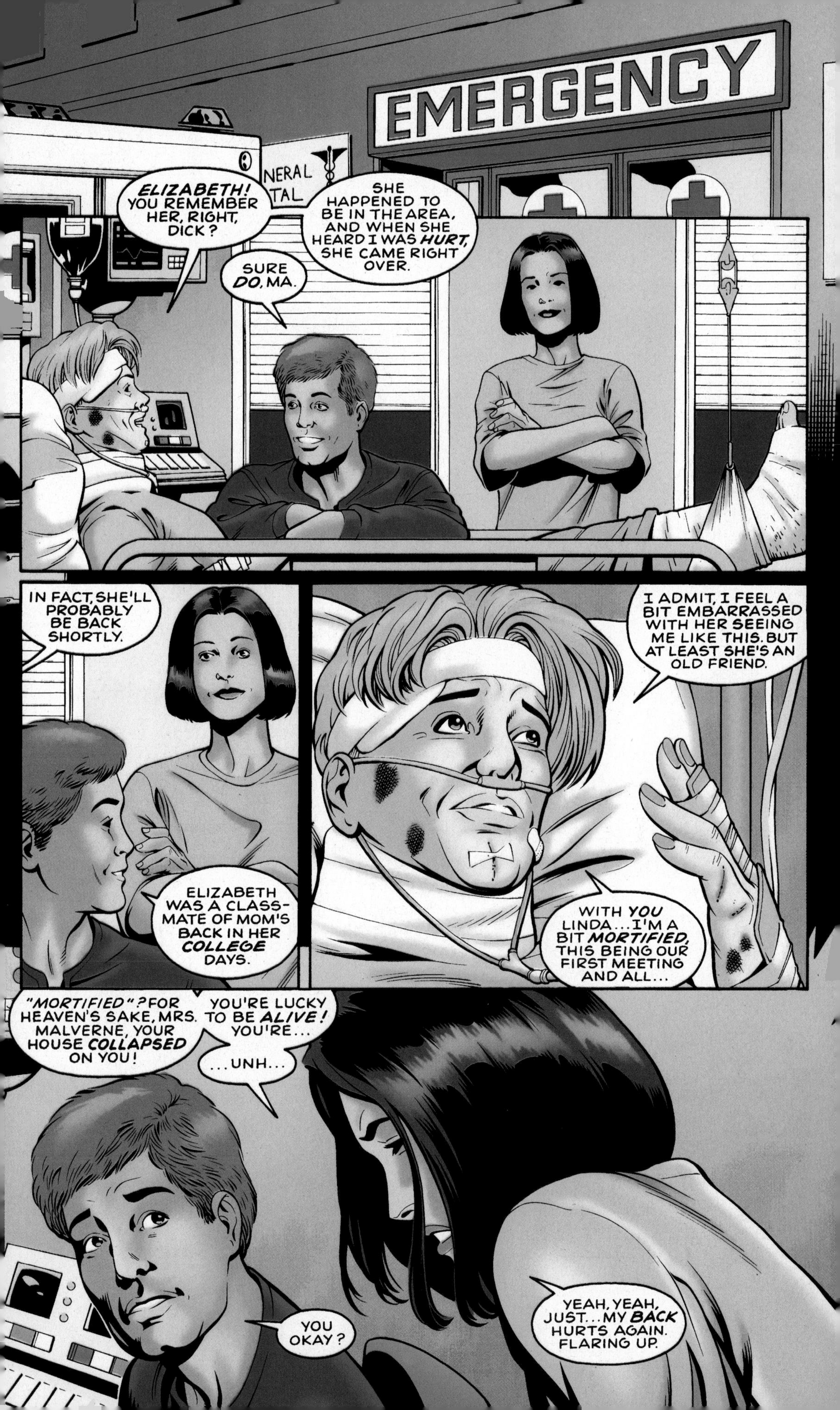
EMERGENCY
NERAL
TAL
ELIZABETH! YOU REMEMBER HER, RIGHT, DICK?
SHE HAPPENED TO BE IN THE AREA, AND WHEN SHE HEARD I WAS HURT, SHE CAME RIGHT OVER.
SURE DO, MA.
IN FACT, SHE'LL PROBABLY BE BACK SHORTLY.
ELIZABETH WAS A CLASSMATE OF MOM'S BACK IN HER COLLEGE DAYS.
I ADMIT, I FEEL A BIT EMBARRASSED WITH HER SEEING ME LIKE THIS. BUT AT LEAST SHE'S AN OLD FRIEND.
WITH YOU LINDA...I'M A BIT MORTIFIED, THIS BEING OUR FIRST MEETING AND ALL...
"MORTIFIED"? FOR HEAVEN'S SAKE, MRS. MALVERNE, YOUR HOUSE COLLAPSED ON YOU!
YOU'RE LUCKY TO BE ALIVE! YOU'RE...
...UNH...
YOU OKAY?
YEAH, YEAH, JUST...MY BACK HURTS AGAIN. FLARING UP.

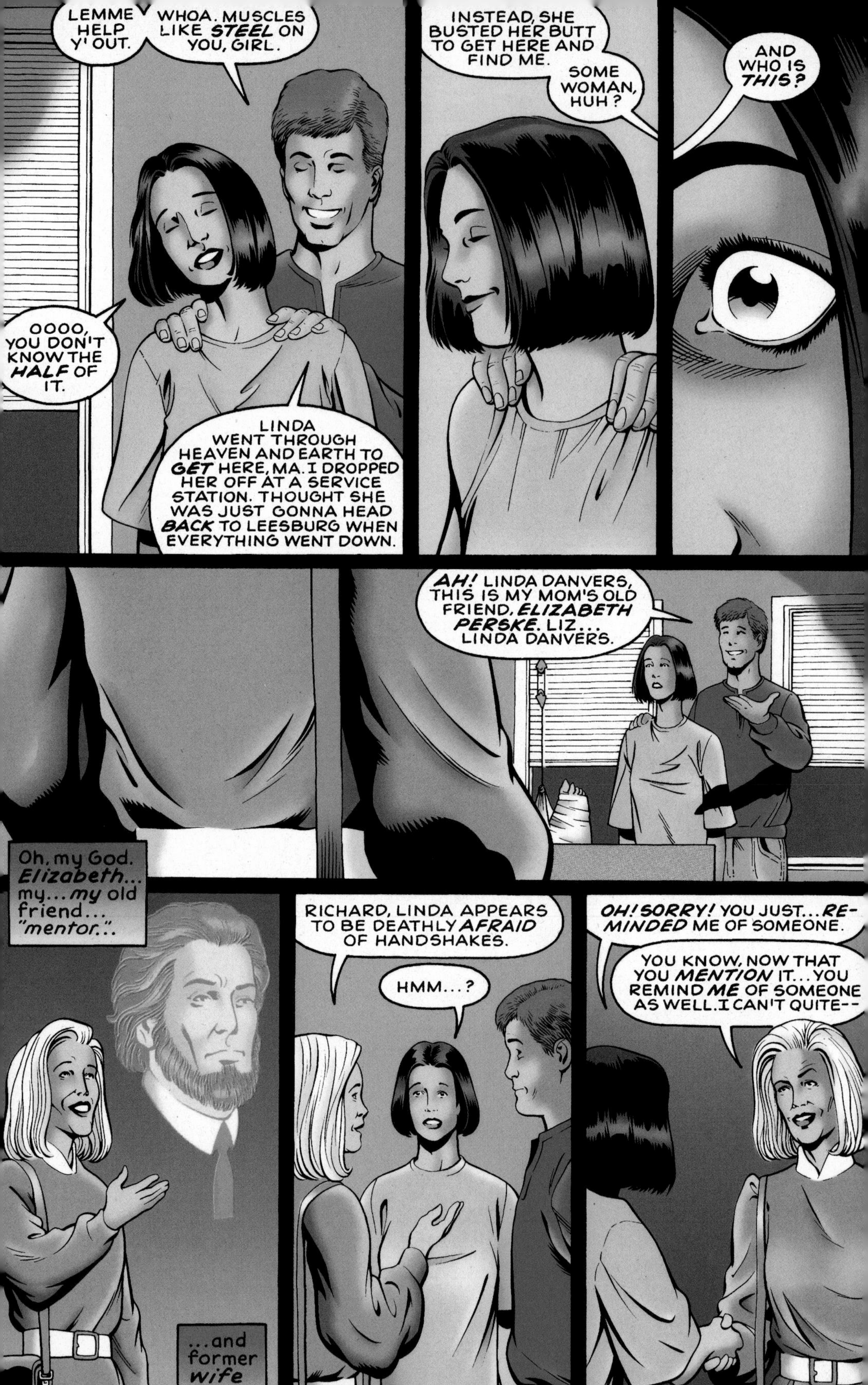
LEMME HELP Y' OUT.
WHOA. MUSCLES LIKE STEEL ON YOU, GIRL.
OOOO, YOU DON'T KNOW THE HALF OF IT.
LINDA WENT THROUGH HEAVEN AND EARTH TO GET HERE, MA. I DROPPED HER OFF AT A SERVICE STATION. THOUGHT SHE WAS JUST GONNA HEAD BACK TO LEESBURG WHEN EVERYTHING WENT DOWN.
INSTEAD, SHE BUSTED HER BUTT TO GET HERE AND FIND ME.
SOME WOMAN, HUH?
AND WHO IS THIS?
AH! LINDA DANVERS, THIS IS MY MOM'S OLD FRIEND, ELIZABETH PERSKE. LIZ... LINDA DANVERS.
Oh, my God. Elizabeth... my... my old friend... "mentor."...
...and former wife of Lex Luthor.
RICHARD, LINDA APPEARS TO BE DEATHLY AFRAID OF HANDSHAKES.
HMM...?
OH! SORRY! YOU JUST... REMINDED ME OF SOMEONE.
YOU KNOW, NOW THAT YOU MENTION IT... YOU REMIND ME OF SOMEONE AS WELL. I CAN'T QUITE--

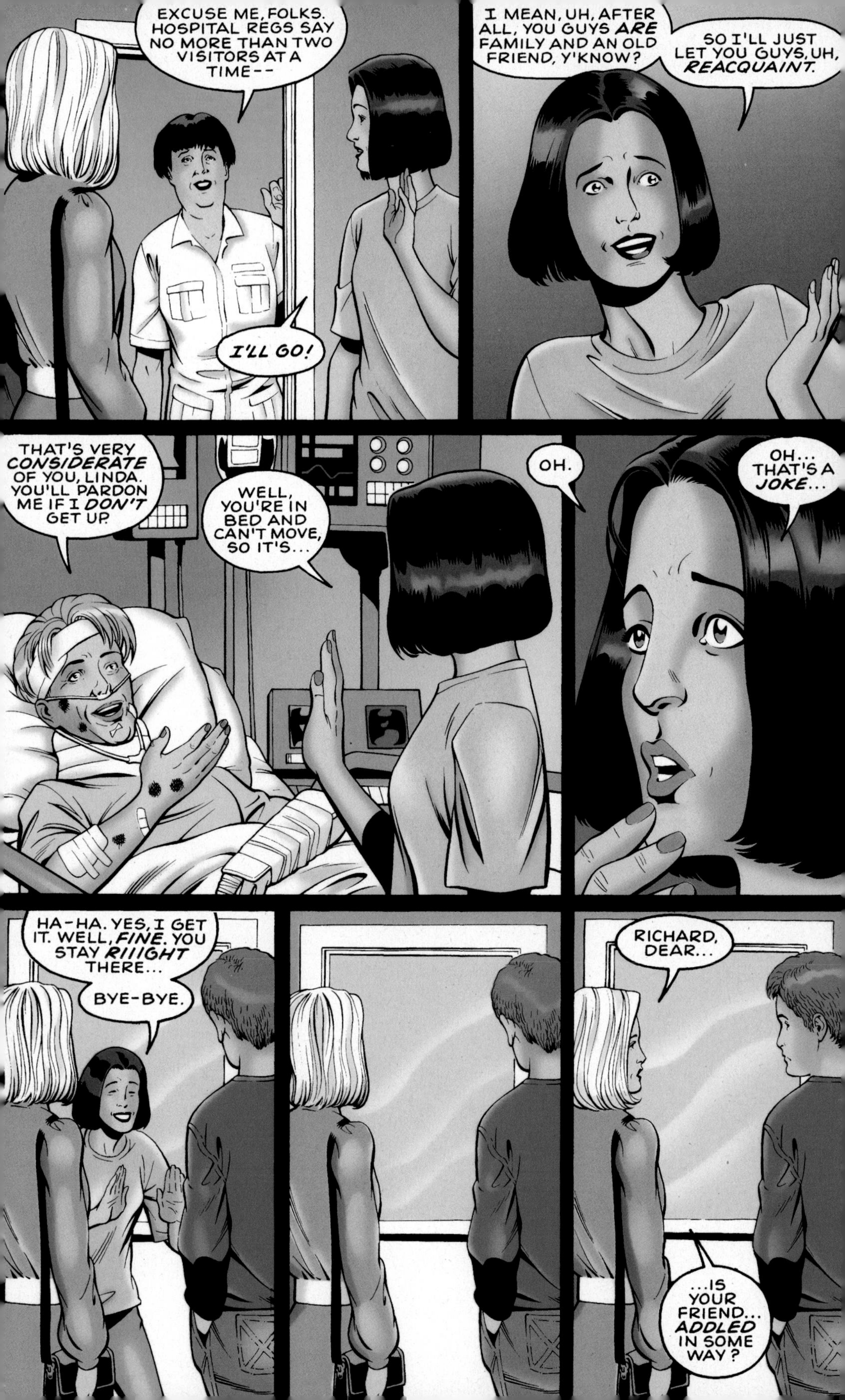
EXCUSE ME, FOLKS. HOSPITAL REGS SAY NO MORE THAN TWO VISITORS AT A TIME--
I'LL GO!
I MEAN, UH, AFTER ALL, YOU GUYS ARE FAMILY AND AN OLD FRIEND, Y'KNOW?
SO I'LL JUST LET YOU GUYS, UH, REACQUAINT.
THAT'S VERY CONSIDERATE OF YOU, LINDA. YOU'LL PARDON ME IF I DON'T GET UP.
WELL, YOU'RE IN BED AND CAN'T MOVE, SO IT'S...
OH.
OH... THAT'S A JOKE...
HA-HA. YES, I GET IT. WELL, FINE. YOU STAY RIIIGHT THERE...
BYE-BYE.
RICHARD, DEAR...
...IS YOUR FRIEND... ADDLED IN SOME WAY?

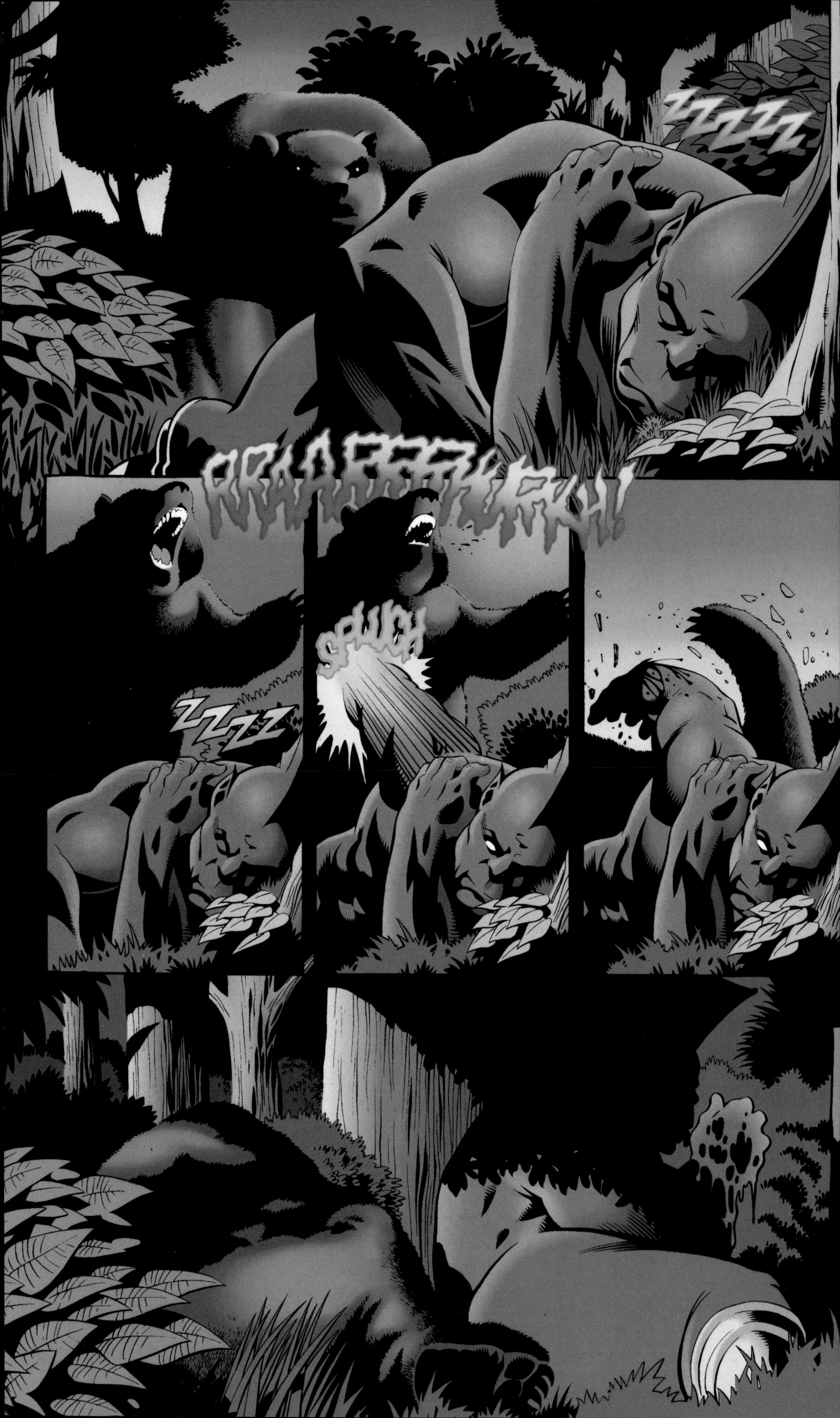
ZZZZZ
RRAARRRUKKH!
ZZZZZ
SPLUCH

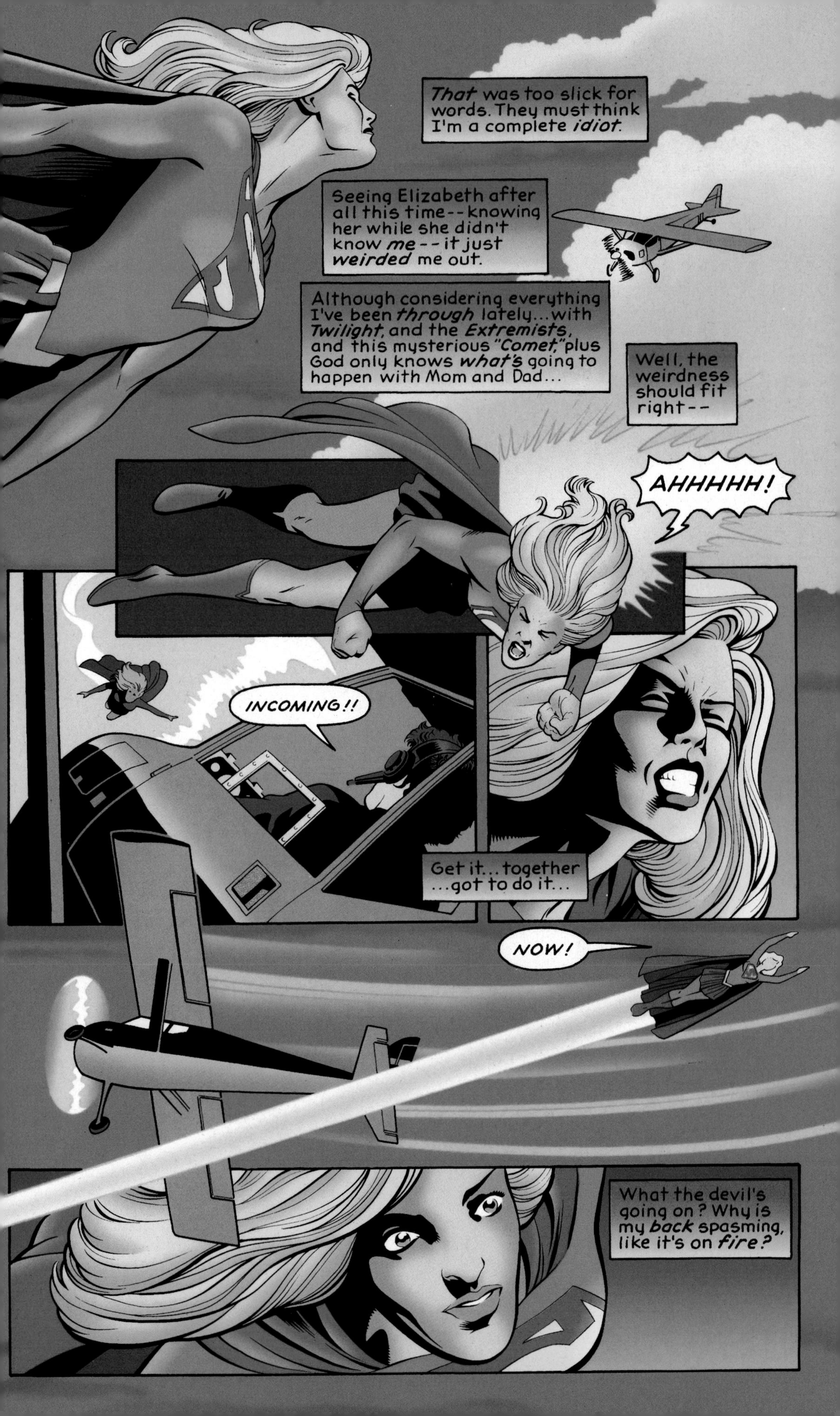
That was too slick for words. They must think I'm a complete idiot.
Seeing Elizabeth after all this time--knowing her while she didn't know me--it just weirded me out.
Although considering everything I've been through lately...with Twilight, and the Extremists, and this mysterious "Comet," plus God only knows what's going to happen with Mom and Dad...
Well, the weirdness should fit right--
AHHHHH!
INCOMING!!
Get it...together ...got to do it...
NOW!
What the devil's going on? Why is my back spasming, like it's on fire?

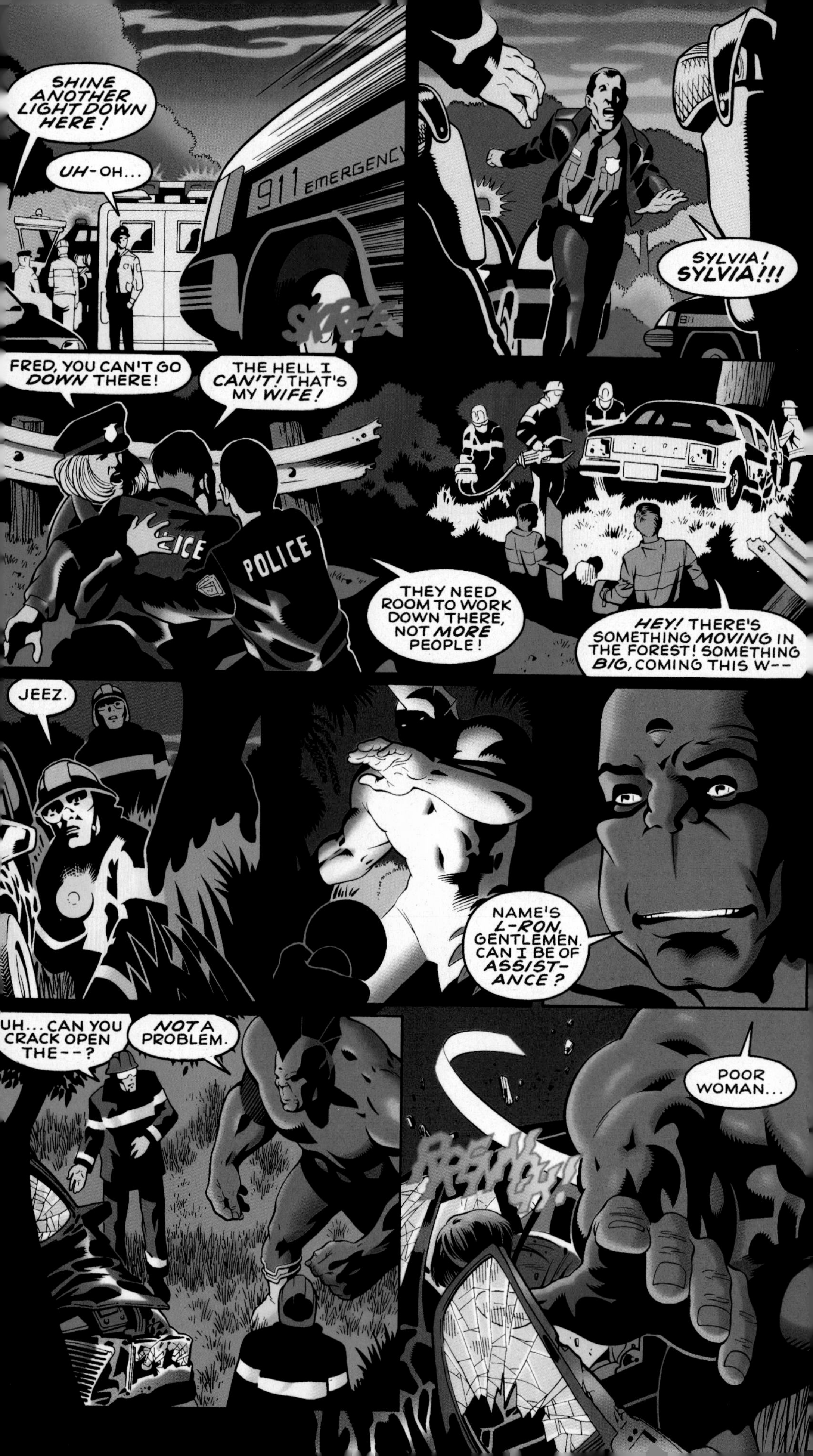
SHINE ANOTHER LIGHT DOWN HERE!
UH-OH...
911 EMERGENCY
SKREE
SYLVIA! SYLVIA!!!
FRED, YOU CAN'T GO DOWN THERE!
THE HELL I CAN'T! THAT'S MY WIFE!
POLICE
THEY NEED ROOM TO WORK DOWN THERE, NOT MORE PEOPLE!
HEY! THERE'S SOMETHING MOVING IN THE FOREST! SOMETHING BIG, COMING THIS W--
JEEZ.
NAME'S L-RON, GENTLEMEN. CAN I BE OF ASSIST-ANCE?
UH... CAN YOU CRACK OPEN THE--?
NOT A PROBLEM.
POOR WOMAN...

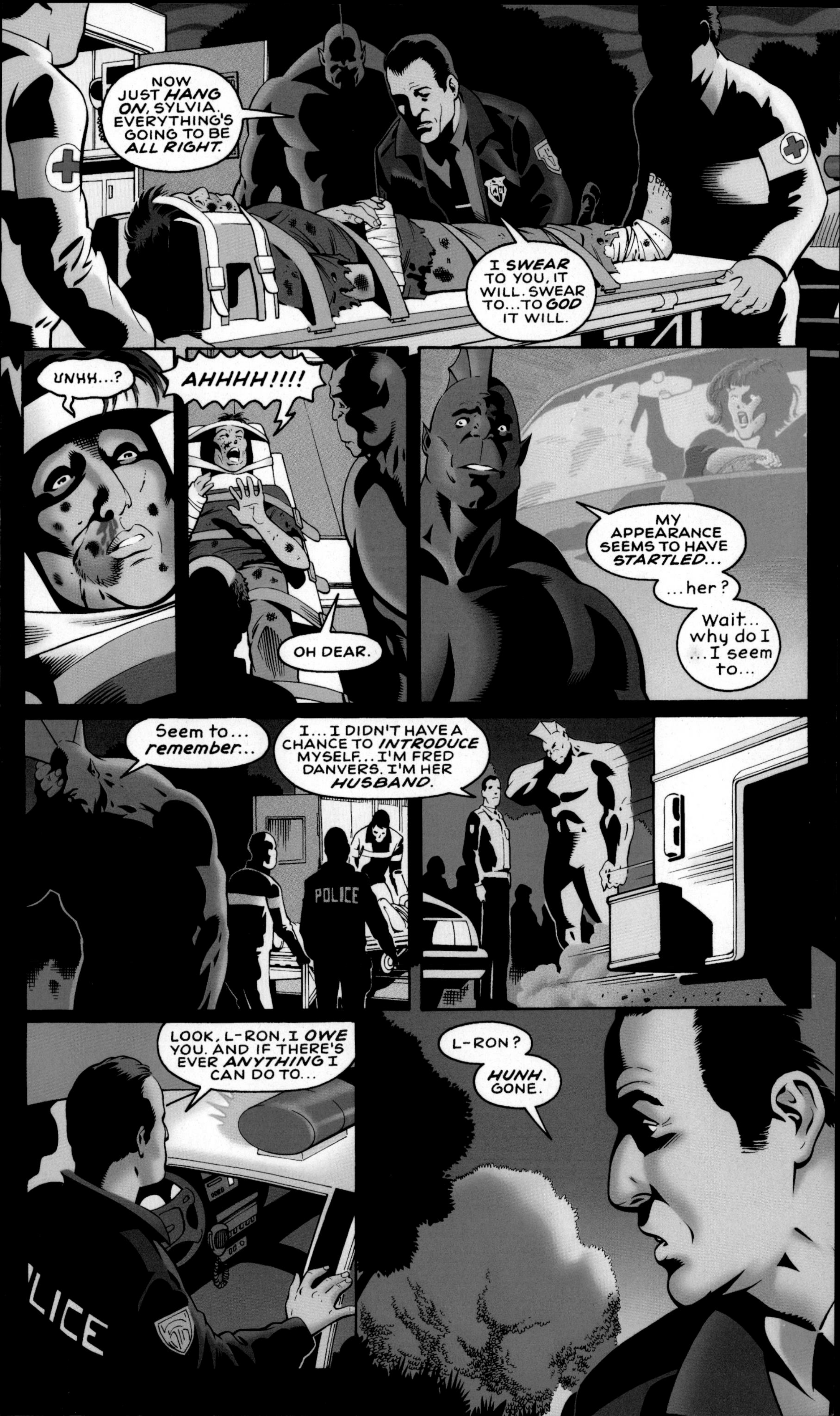
NOW JUST HANG ON, SYLVIA. EVERYTHING'S GOING TO BE ALL RIGHT.
I SWEAR TO YOU, IT WILL. SWEAR TO... TO GOD IT WILL.
UNHH...?
AHHHH!!!!
OH DEAR.
MY APPEARANCE SEEMS TO HAVE STARTLED...
...her?
Wait... why do I ...I seem to...
Seem to... remember...
I... I DIDN'T HAVE A CHANCE TO INTRODUCE MYSELF... I'M FRED DANVERS. I'M HER HUSBAND.
POLICE
LOOK, L-RON, I OWE YOU. AND IF THERE'S EVER ANYTHING I CAN DO TO...
L-RON?
HUNH. GONE.
LICE

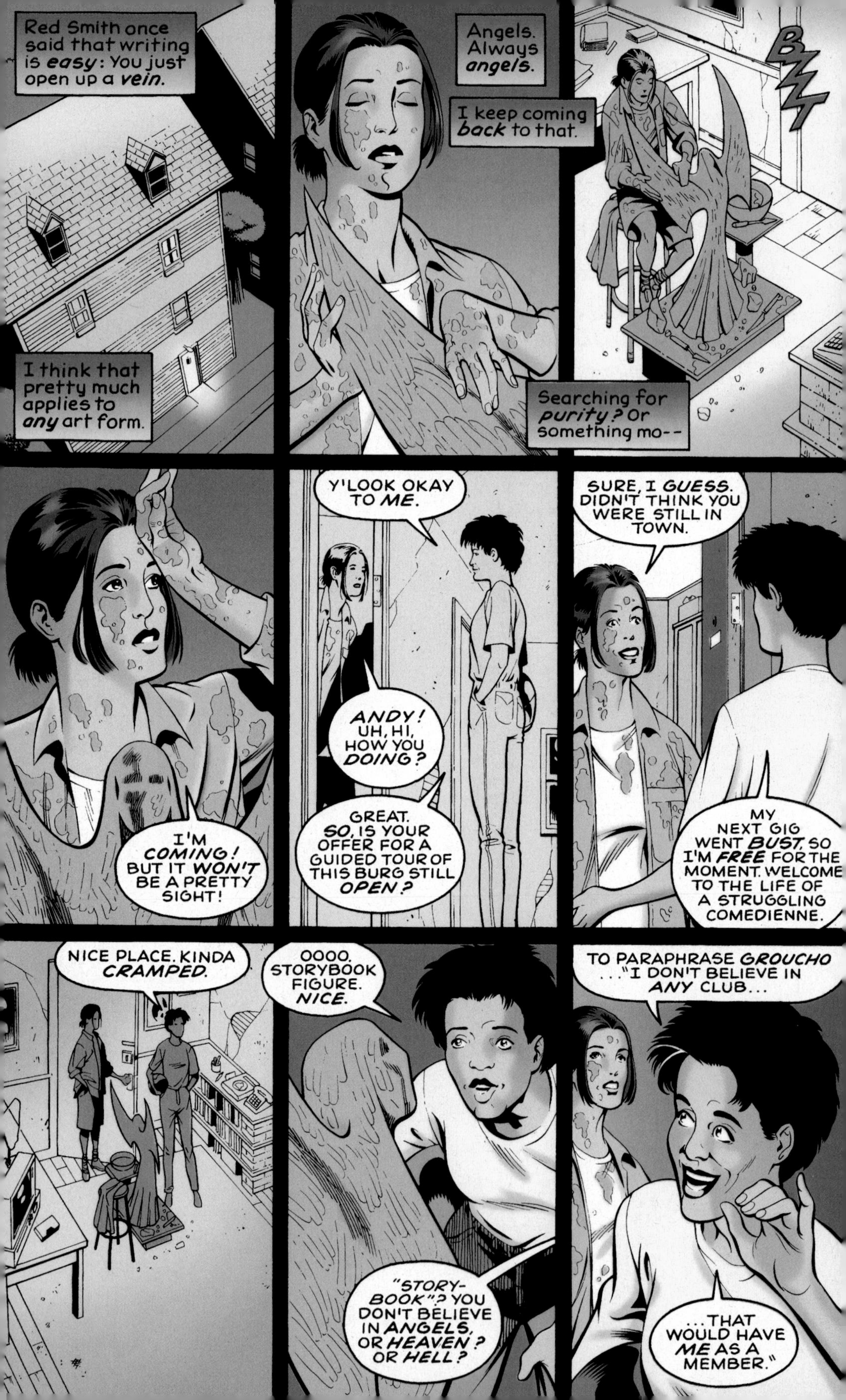
Red Smith once said that writing is *easy*: You just open up a *vein*.
I think that pretty much applies to *any* art form.
Angels. Always *angels*.
I keep coming *back* to that.
BZZT
Searching for *purity*? Or something mo--
I'M *COMING*! BUT IT *WON'T* BE A PRETTY SIGHT!
Y'LOOK OKAY TO *ME*.
ANDY! UH, HI, HOW YOU *DOING*?
GREAT. *SO*, IS YOUR OFFER FOR A GUIDED TOUR OF THIS BURG STILL *OPEN*?
SURE, I *GUESS*. DIDN'T THINK YOU WERE STILL IN TOWN.
MY NEXT GIG WENT *BUST*, SO I'M *FREE* FOR THE MOMENT. WELCOME TO THE LIFE OF A STRUGGLING COMEDIENNE.
NICE PLACE. KINDA *CRAMPED*.
OOOO. STORYBOOK FIGURE. *NICE*.
"STORY-BOOK"? YOU DON'T BELIEVE IN *ANGELS*, OR *HEAVEN*? OR *HELL*?
TO PARAPHRASE *GROUCHO* . . . "I DON'T BELIEVE IN *ANY* CLUB . . .
. . . THAT WOULD HAVE *ME* AS A MEMBER."

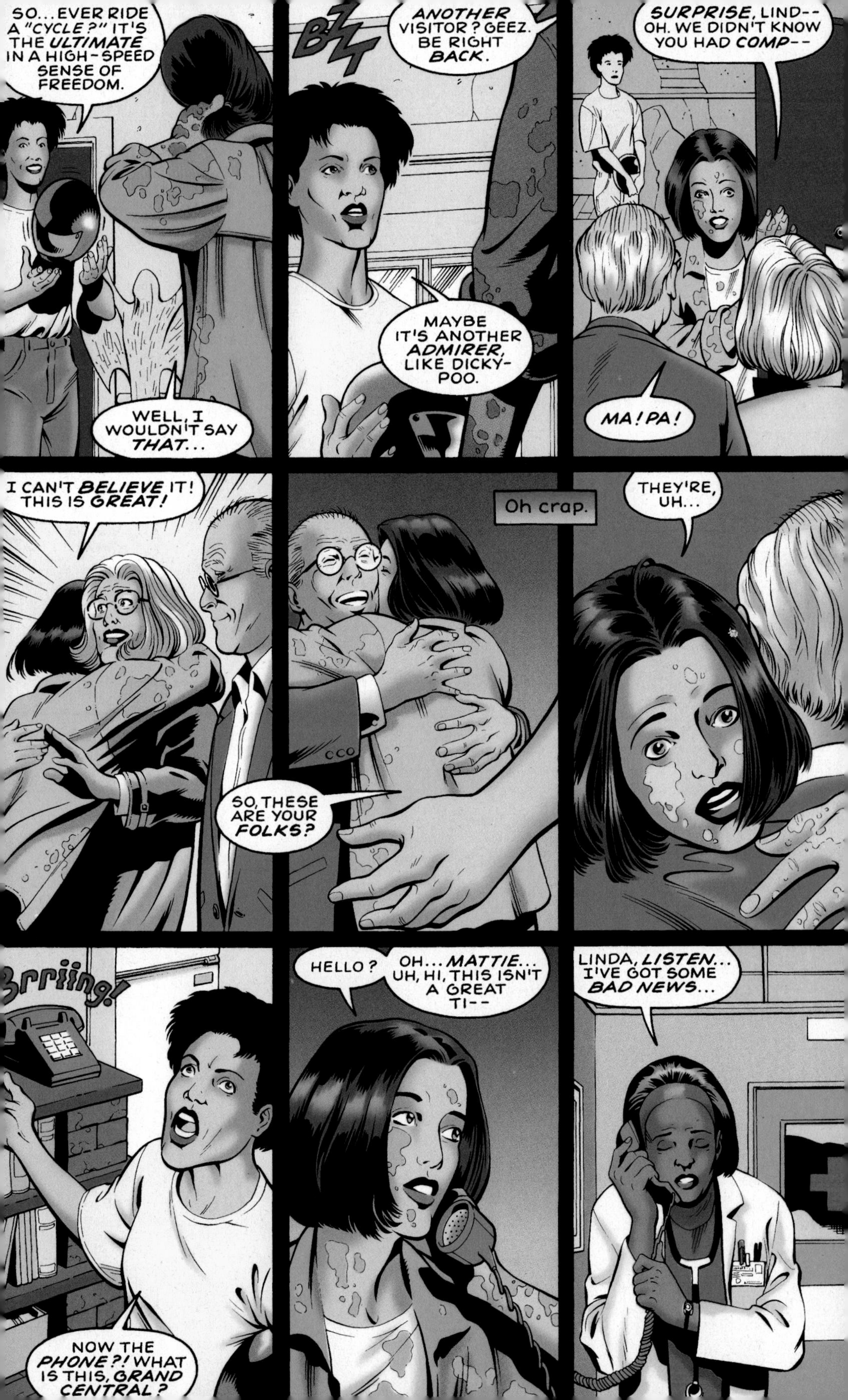
SO... EVER RIDE A "CYCLE?" IT'S THE ULTIMATE IN A HIGH-SPEED SENSE OF FREEDOM.
WELL, I WOULDN'T SAY THAT...
BZZT
ANOTHER VISITOR? GEEZ. BE RIGHT BACK.
MAYBE IT'S ANOTHER ADMIRER, LIKE DICKY-POO.
SURPRISE, LIND-- OH. WE DIDN'T KNOW YOU HAD COMP--
MA! PA!
I CAN'T BELIEVE IT! THIS IS GREAT!
Oh crap.
SO, THESE ARE YOUR FOLKS?
THEY'RE, UH...
Brriing!
NOW THE PHONE?! WHAT IS THIS, GRAND CENTRAL?
HELLO?
OH... MATTIE... UH, HI, THIS ISN'T A GREAT TI--
LINDA, LISTEN... I'VE GOT SOME BAD NEWS...

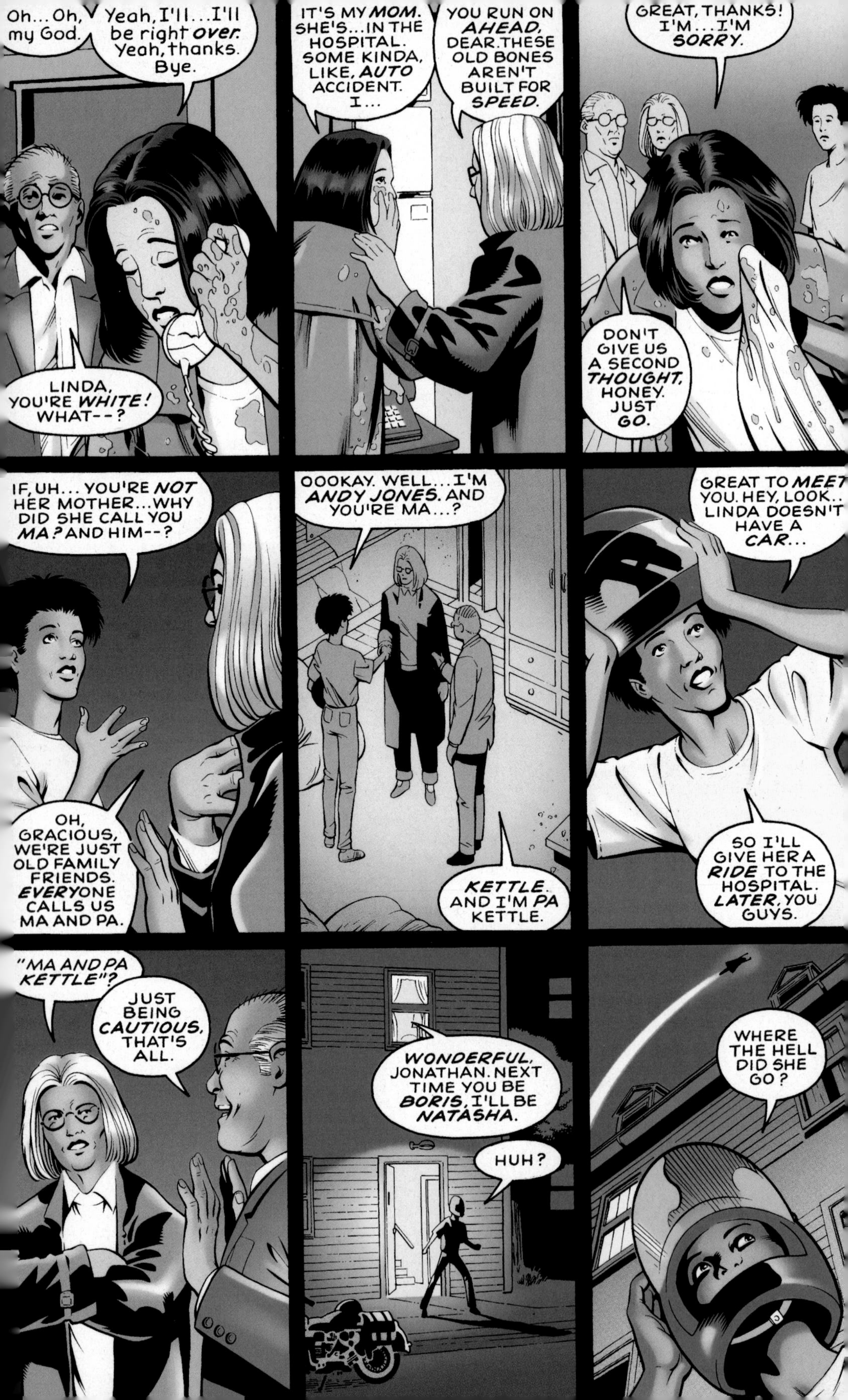

Oh... Oh, my God.
Yeah, I'll... I'll be right over. Yeah, thanks. Bye.
LINDA, YOU'RE WHITE! WHAT--?
IT'S MY MOM. SHE'S... IN THE HOSPITAL. SOME KINDA, LIKE, AUTO ACCIDENT. I...
YOU RUN ON AHEAD, DEAR. THESE OLD BONES AREN'T BUILT FOR SPEED.
GREAT, THANKS! I'M... I'M SORRY.
DON'T GIVE US A SECOND THOUGHT, HONEY. JUST GO.
IF, UH... YOU'RE NOT HER MOTHER... WHY DID SHE CALL YOU MA? AND HIM--?
OH, GRACIOUS, WE'RE JUST OLD FAMILY FRIENDS. EVERYONE CALLS US MA AND PA.
OOOKAY. WELL... I'M ANDY JONES. AND YOU'RE MA...?
KETTLE. AND I'M PA KETTLE.
GREAT TO MEET YOU. HEY, LOOK.. LINDA DOESN'T HAVE A CAR...
SO I'LL GIVE HER A RIDE TO THE HOSPITAL. LATER, YOU GUYS.
"MA AND PA KETTLE"?
JUST BEING CAUTIOUS, THAT'S ALL.
WONDERFUL, JONATHAN. NEXT TIME YOU BE BORIS, I'LL BE NATASHA.
HUH?
WHERE THE HELL DID SHE GO?

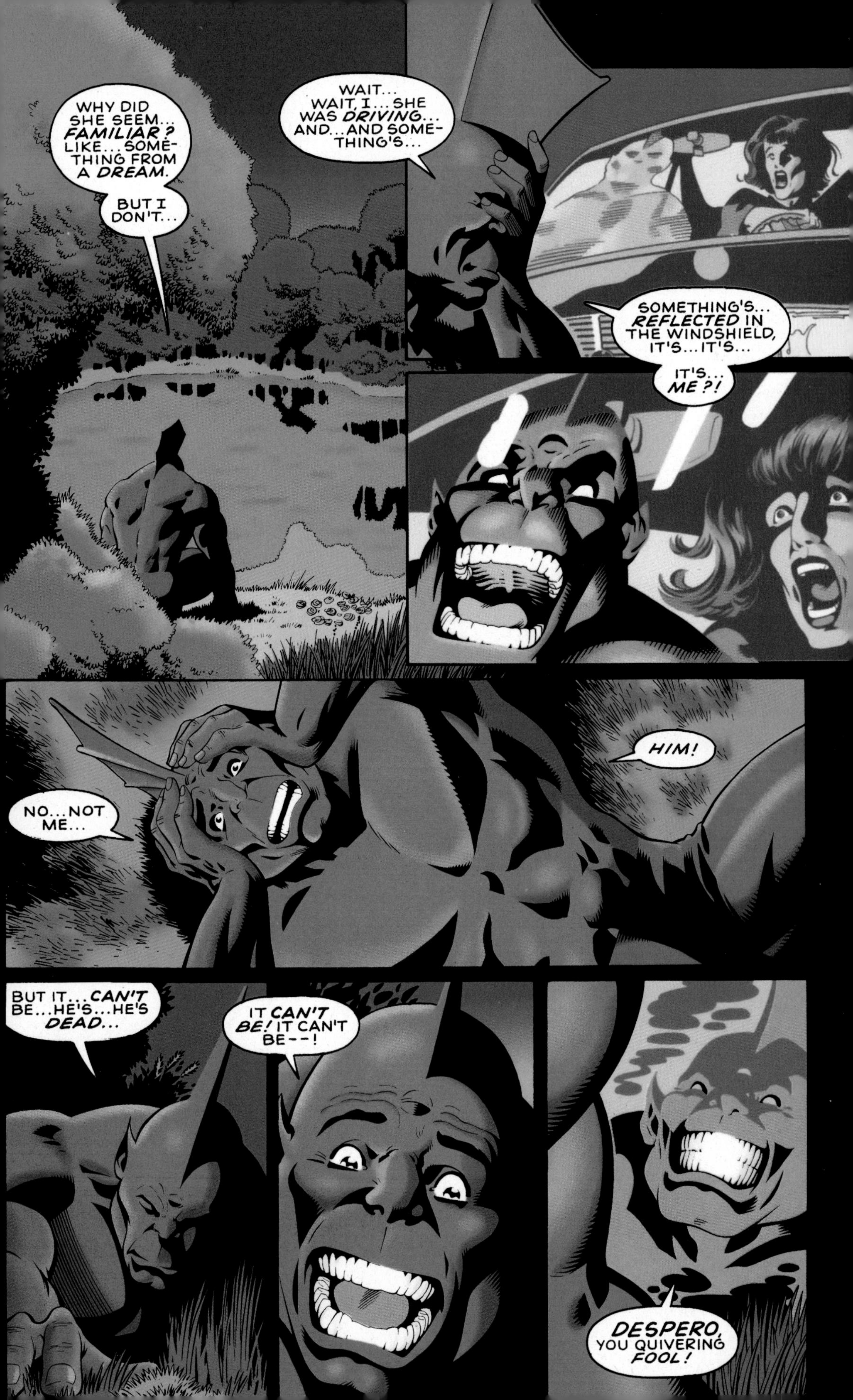

WHY DID SHE SEEM... FAMILIAR? LIKE... SOME-THING FROM A DREAM.
BUT I DON'T...
WAIT... WAIT, I... SHE WAS DRIVING... AND... AND SOME-THING'S...
SOMETHING'S... REFLECTED IN THE WINDSHIELD, IT'S... IT'S...
IT'S... ME?!
HIM!
NO... NOT ME...
BUT IT... CAN'T BE... HE'S... HE'S DEAD...
IT CAN'T BE! IT CAN'T BE--!
DESPERO, YOU QUIVERING FOOL!

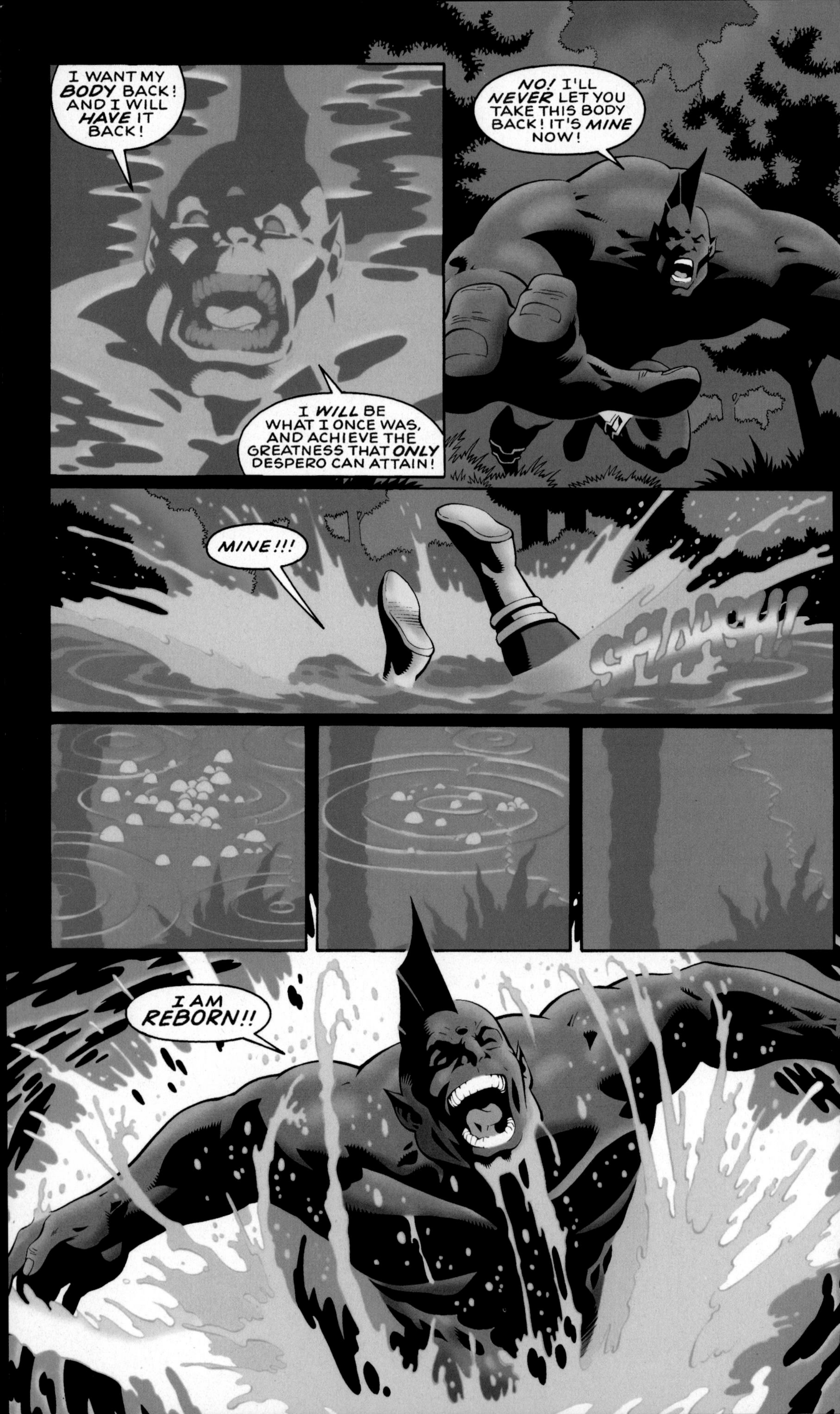
I WANT MY BODY BACK! AND I WILL HAVE IT BACK!
I WILL BE WHAT I ONCE WAS, AND ACHIEVE THE GREATNESS THAT ONLY DESPERO CAN ATTAIN!
NO! I'LL NEVER LET YOU TAKE THIS BODY BACK! IT'S MINE NOW!
MINE!!!
SPLASH!!
I AM REBORN!!

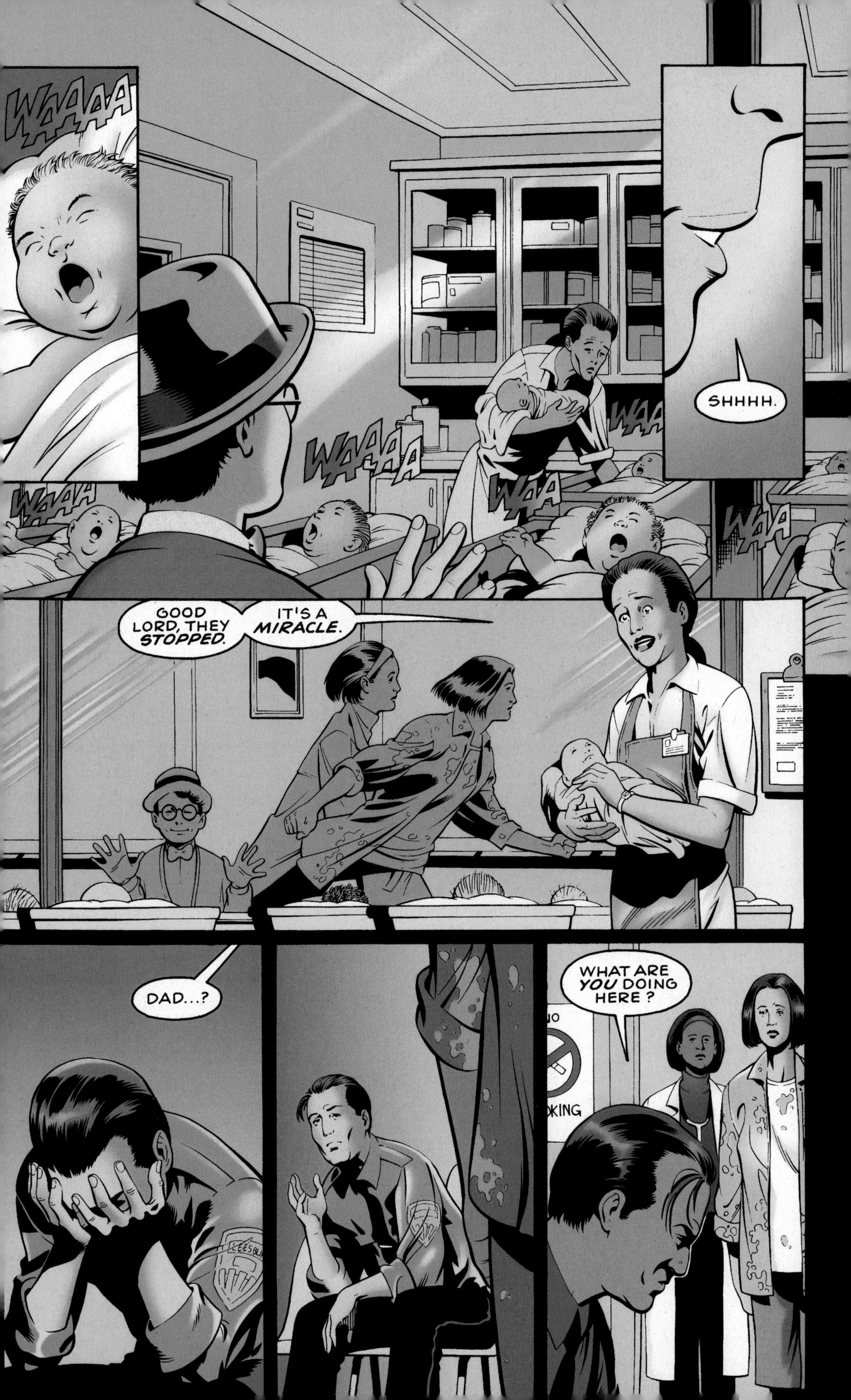
WAAAA
SHHHH.
WAAAA
WAA
WAA
WAAA
WAA
GOOD LORD, THEY STOPPED.
IT'S A MIRACLE.
DAD...?
WHAT ARE YOU DOING HERE ?

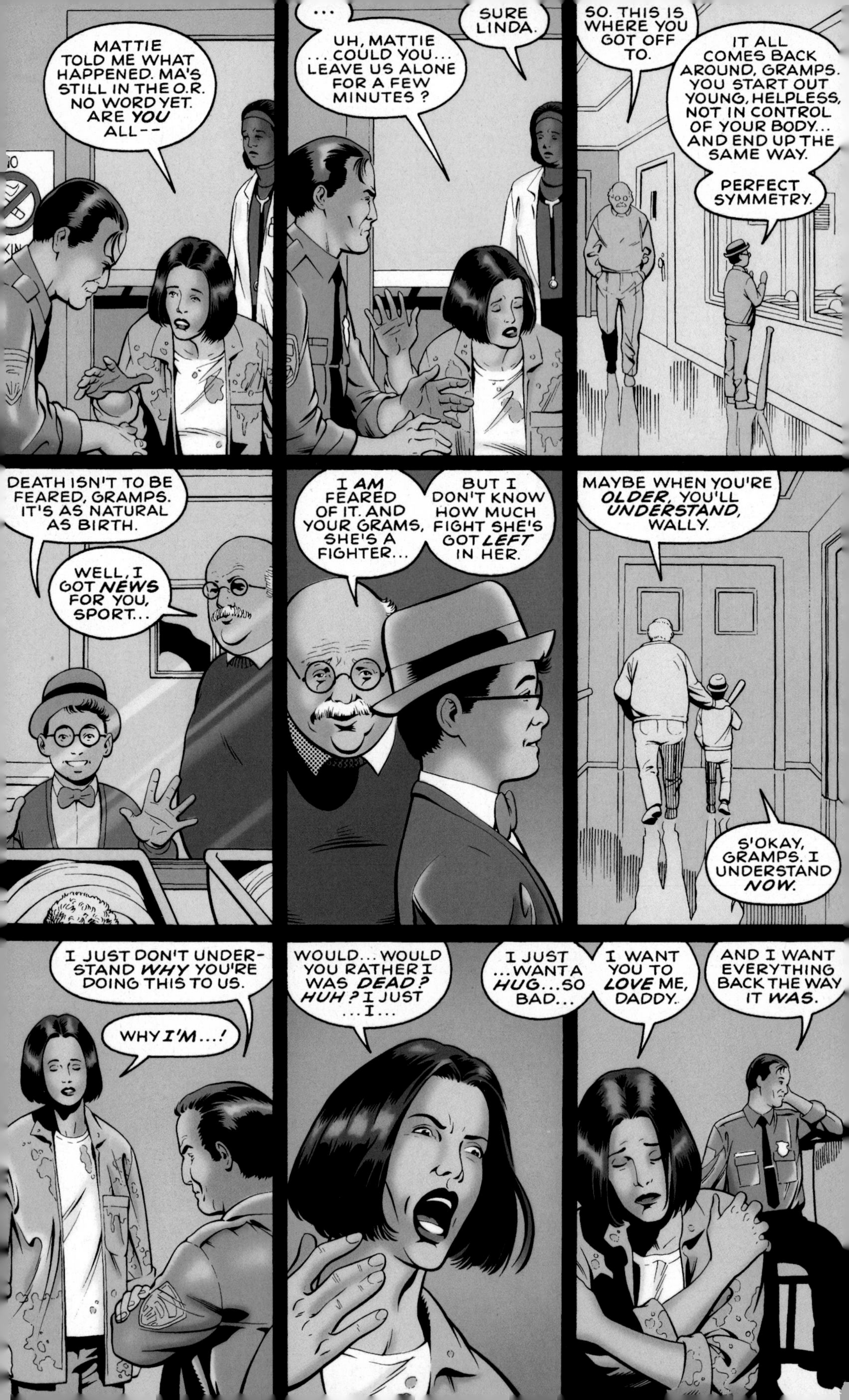
MATTIE TOLD ME WHAT HAPPENED. MA'S STILL IN THE O.R. NO WORD YET. ARE YOU ALL--
...
UH, MATTIE ...COULD YOU... LEAVE US ALONE FOR A FEW MINUTES?
SURE LINDA.
SO. THIS IS WHERE YOU GOT OFF TO.
IT ALL COMES BACK AROUND, GRAMPS. YOU START OUT YOUNG, HELPLESS, NOT IN CONTROL OF YOUR BODY... AND END UP THE SAME WAY.
PERFECT SYMMETRY.
DEATH ISN'T TO BE FEARED, GRAMPS. IT'S AS NATURAL AS BIRTH.
WELL, I GOT NEWS FOR YOU, SPORT...
I AM FEARED OF IT. AND YOUR GRAMS, SHE'S A FIGHTER...
BUT I DON'T KNOW HOW MUCH FIGHT SHE'S GOT LEFT IN HER.
MAYBE WHEN YOU'RE OLDER, YOU'LL UNDERSTAND, WALLY.
S'OKAY, GRAMPS. I UNDERSTAND NOW.
I JUST DON'T UNDERSTAND WHY YOU'RE DOING THIS TO US.
WHY I'M...!
WOULD... WOULD YOU RATHER I WAS DEAD? HUH? I JUST ...I...
I JUST ...WANT A HUG...SO BAD...
I WANT YOU TO LOVE ME, DADDY.
AND I WANT EVERYTHING BACK THE WAY IT WAS.

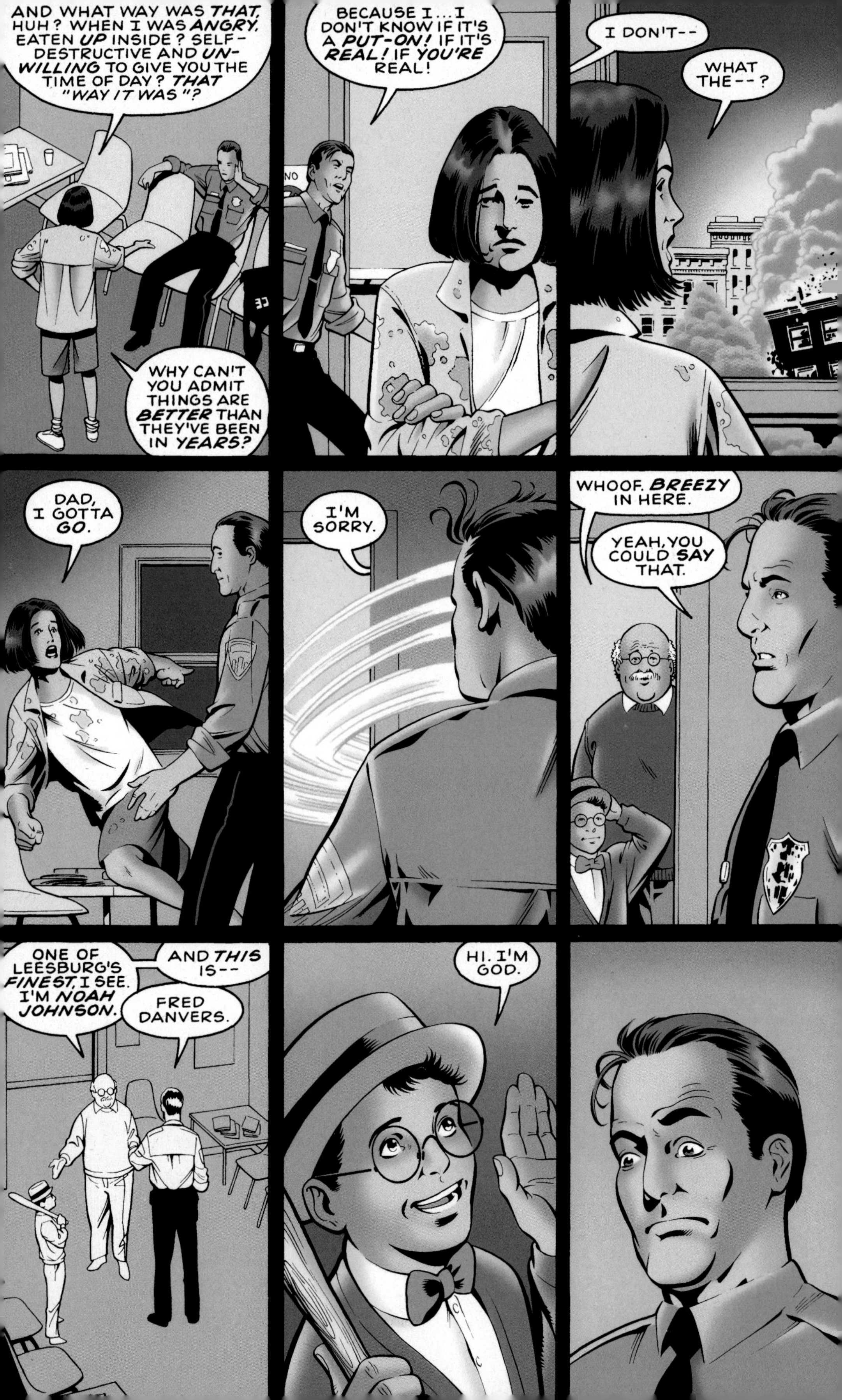
AND WHAT WAY WAS THAT, HUH? WHEN I WAS ANGRY, EATEN UP INSIDE? SELF-DESTRUCTIVE AND UNWILLING TO GIVE YOU THE TIME OF DAY? THAT "WAY IT WAS"?
WHY CAN'T YOU ADMIT THINGS ARE BETTER THAN THEY'VE BEEN IN YEARS?
BECAUSE I...I DON'T KNOW IF IT'S A PUT-ON! IF IT'S REAL! IF YOU'RE REAL!
I DON'T--
WHAT THE--?
DAD, I GOTTA GO.
I'M SORRY.
WHOOF. BREEZY IN HERE.
YEAH, YOU COULD SAY THAT.
ONE OF LEESBURG'S FINEST, I SEE. I'M NOAH JOHNSON.
AND THIS IS--
FRED DANVERS.
HI. I'M GOD.

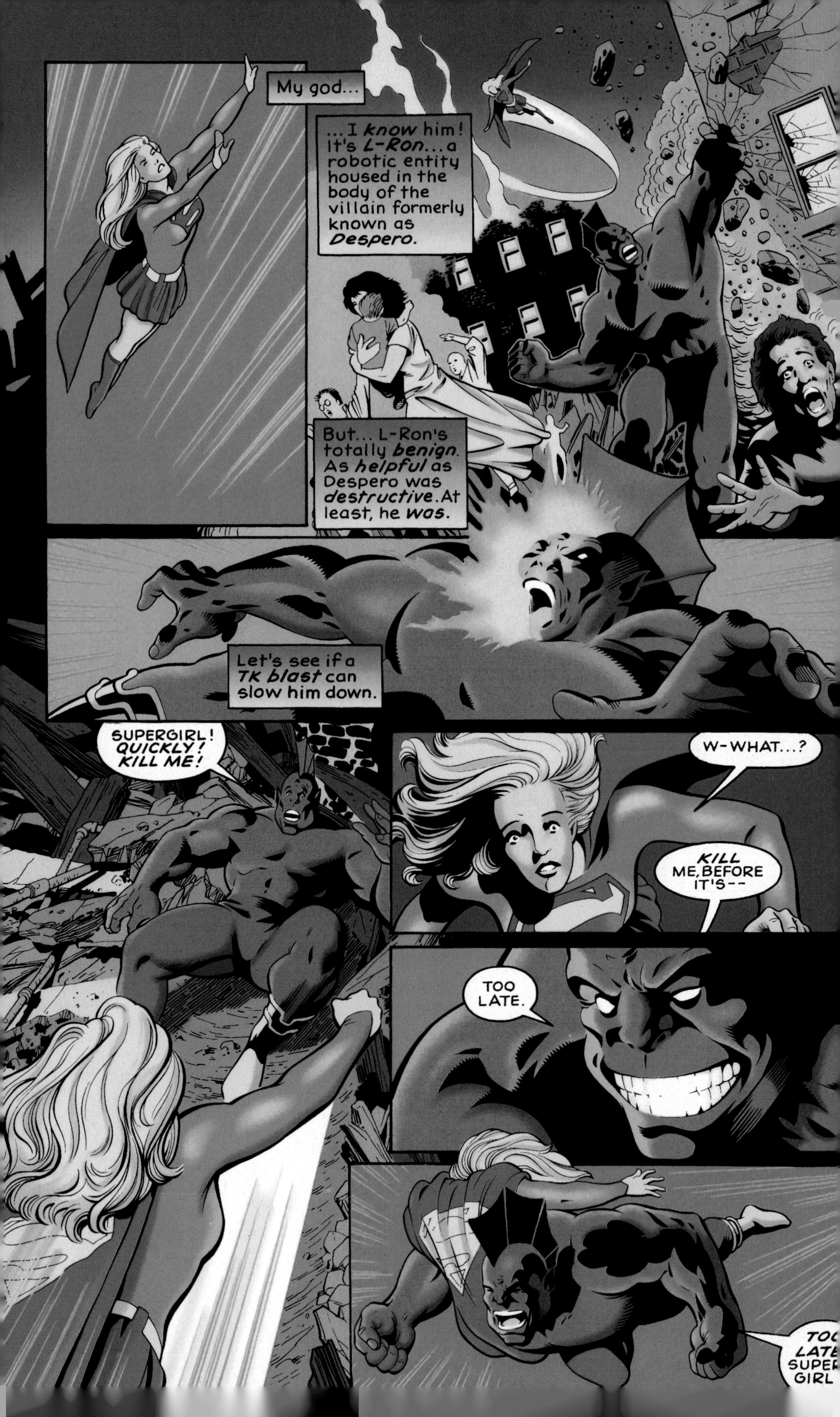
My god...
...I know him! It's L-Ron...a robotic entity housed in the body of the villain formerly known as Despero.
But... L-Ron's totally benign. As helpful as Despero was destructive. At least, he was.
Let's see if a TK blast can slow him down.
SUPERGIRL! QUICKLY! KILL ME!
W-WHAT...?
KILL ME, BEFORE IT'S--
TOO LATE.

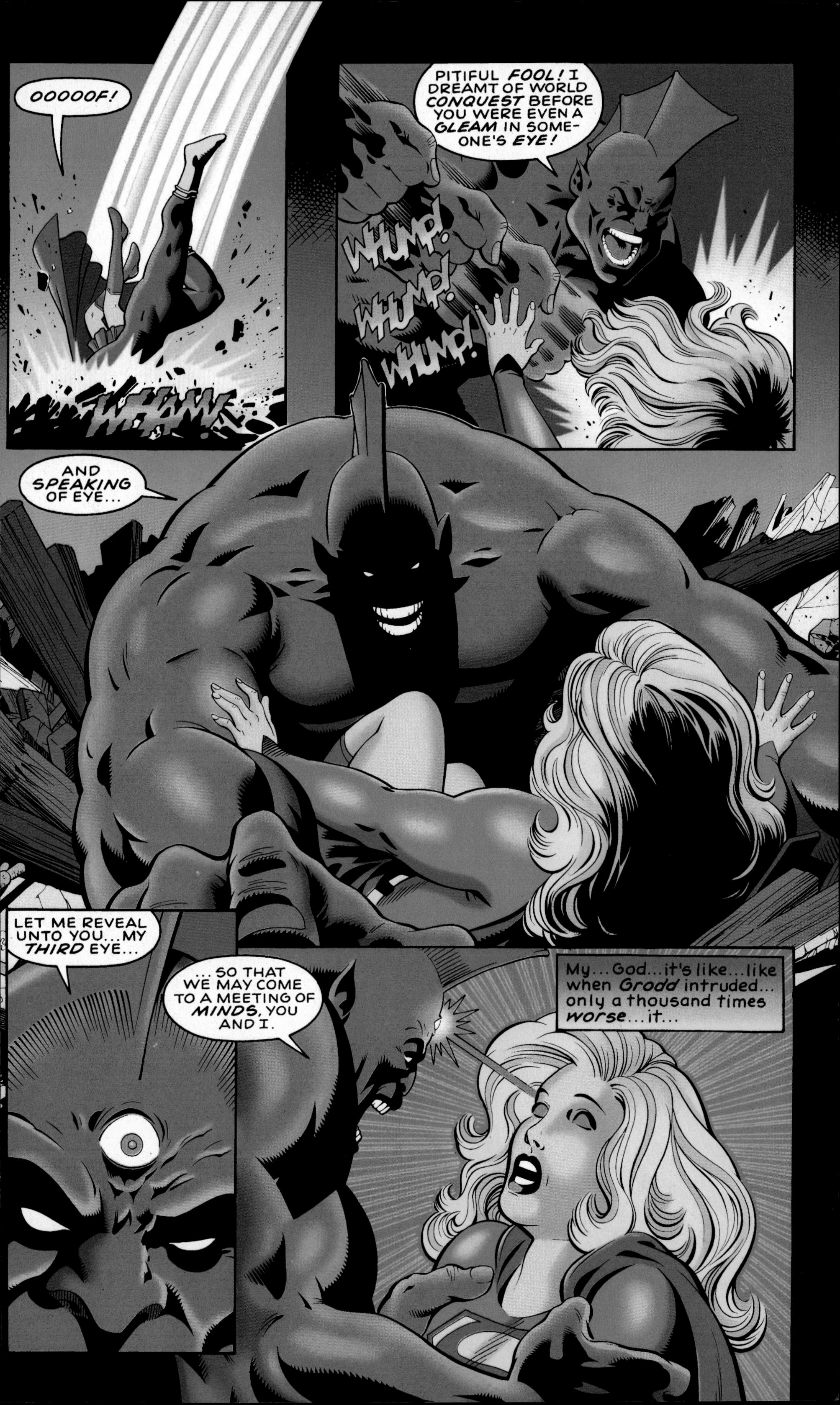
OOOOOF!
WHAM!
PITIFUL FOOL! I DREAMT OF WORLD CONQUEST BEFORE YOU WERE EVEN A GLEAM IN SOME-ONE'S EYE!
WHUMP! WHUMP! WHUMP!
AND SPEAKING OF EYE...
LET ME REVEAL UNTO YOU...MY THIRD EYE...
...SO THAT WE MAY COME TO A MEETING OF MINDS, YOU AND I.
My...God...it's like...like when Grodd intruded...only a thousand times worse...it...

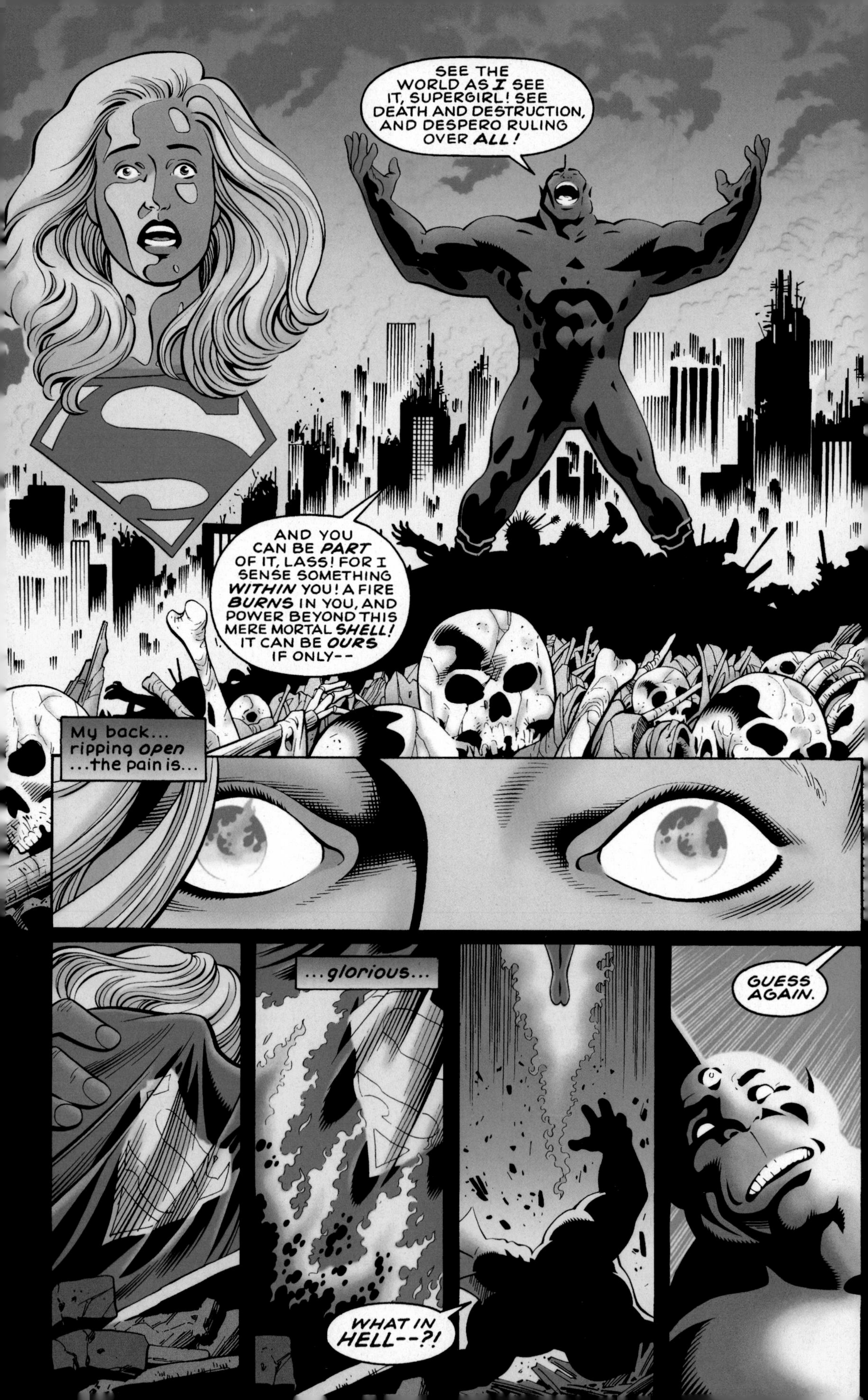
SEE THE WORLD AS I SEE IT, SUPERGIRL! SEE DEATH AND DESTRUCTION, AND DESPERO RULING OVER ALL!
AND YOU CAN BE PART OF IT, LASS! FOR I SENSE SOMETHING WITHIN YOU! A FIRE BURNS IN YOU, AND POWER BEYOND THIS MERE MORTAL SHELL! IT CAN BE OURS IF ONLY--
My back... ripping open ...the pain is...
...glorious...
WHAT IN HELL--?!
GUESS AGAIN.

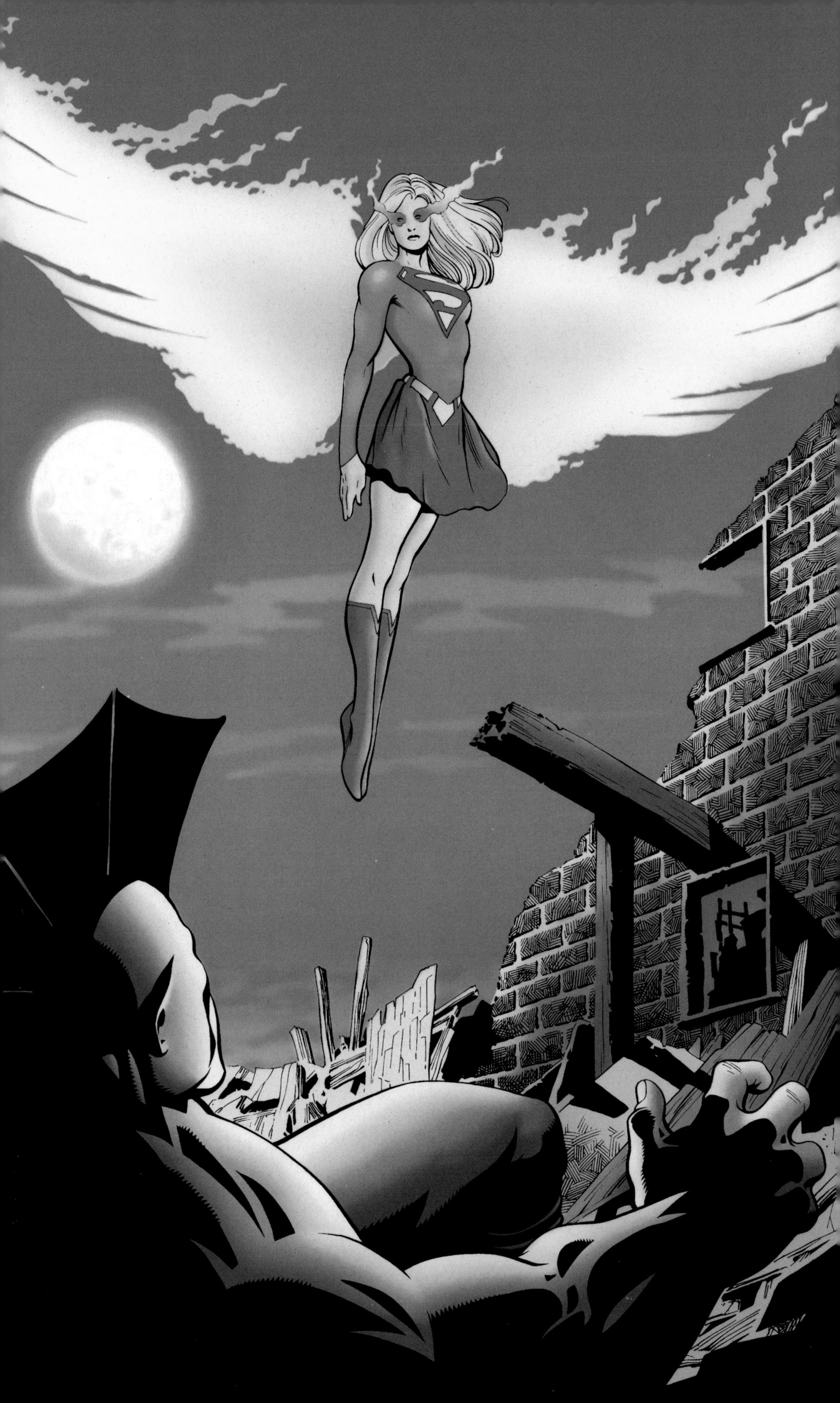

SUPERGIRL #18 cover by Gary Frank, Cam Smith and Patrick Marti

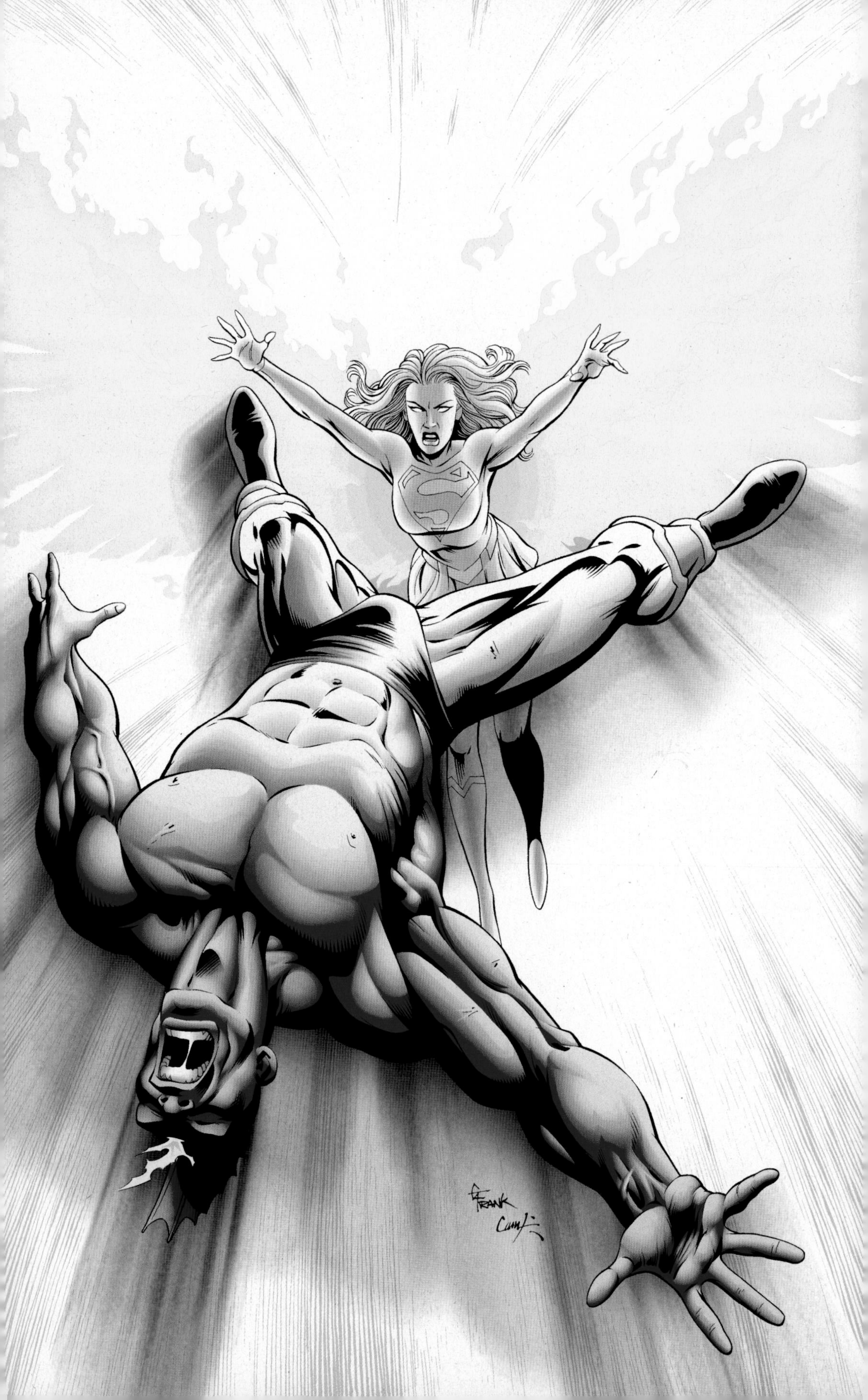

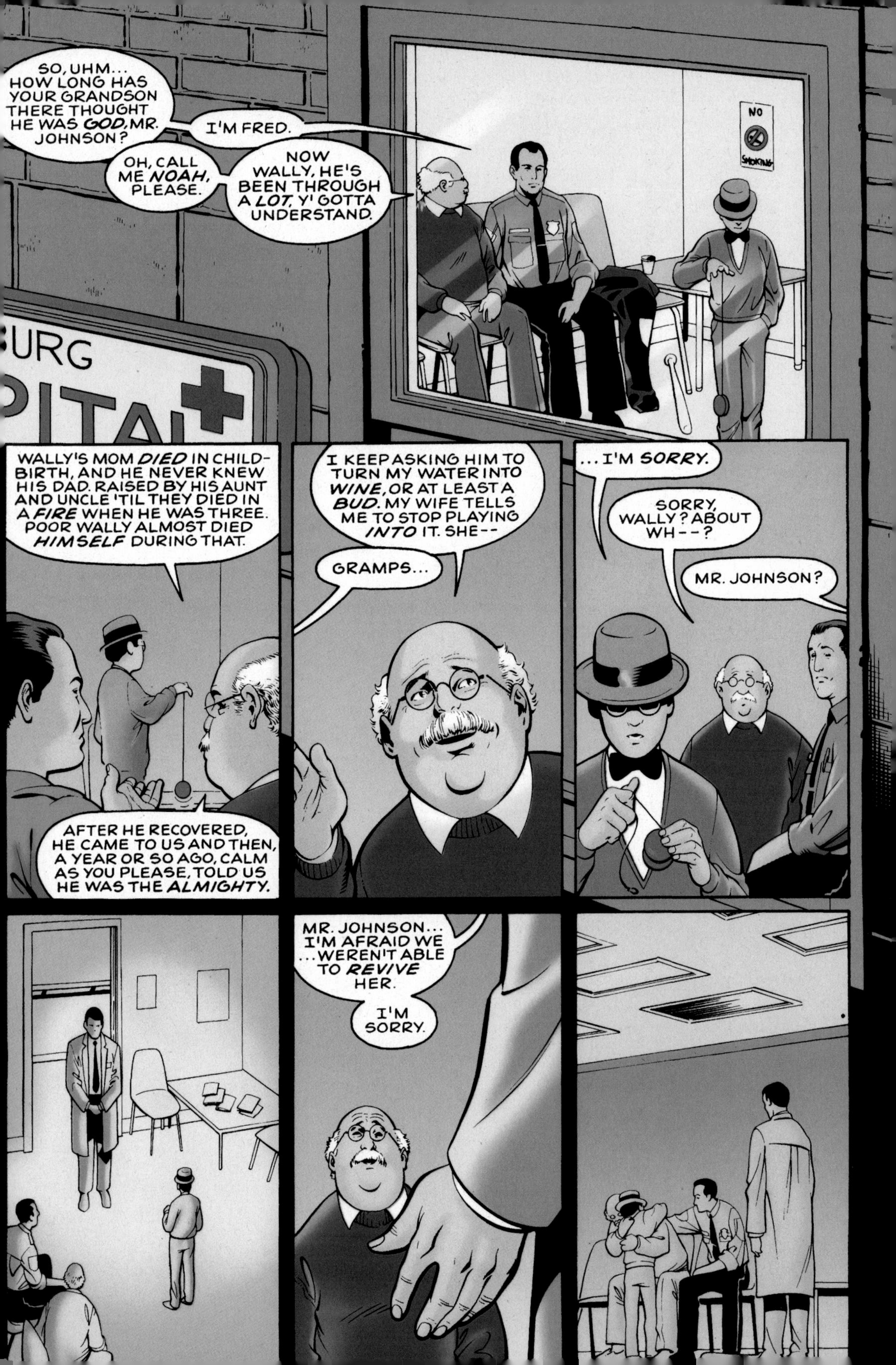

SO, UHM... HOW LONG HAS YOUR GRANDSON THERE THOUGHT HE WAS GOD, MR. JOHNSON?
I'M FRED.
OH, CALL ME NOAH, PLEASE.
NOW WALLY, HE'S BEEN THROUGH A LOT, Y' GOTTA UNDERSTAND.
NO SMOKING
URG
PITAL
WALLY'S MOM DIED IN CHILD-BIRTH, AND HE NEVER KNEW HIS DAD. RAISED BY HIS AUNT AND UNCLE 'TIL THEY DIED IN A FIRE WHEN HE WAS THREE. POOR WALLY ALMOST DIED HIMSELF DURING THAT.
AFTER HE RECOVERED, HE CAME TO US AND THEN, A YEAR OR SO AGO, CALM AS YOU PLEASE, TOLD US HE WAS THE ALMIGHTY.
I KEEP ASKING HIM TO TURN MY WATER INTO WINE, OR AT LEAST A BUD. MY WIFE TELLS ME TO STOP PLAYING INTO IT. SHE--
GRAMPS...
...I'M SORRY.
SORRY, WALLY? ABOUT WH--?
MR. JOHNSON?
MR. JOHNSON... I'M AFRAID WE ...WEREN'T ABLE TO REVIVE HER.
I'M SORRY.

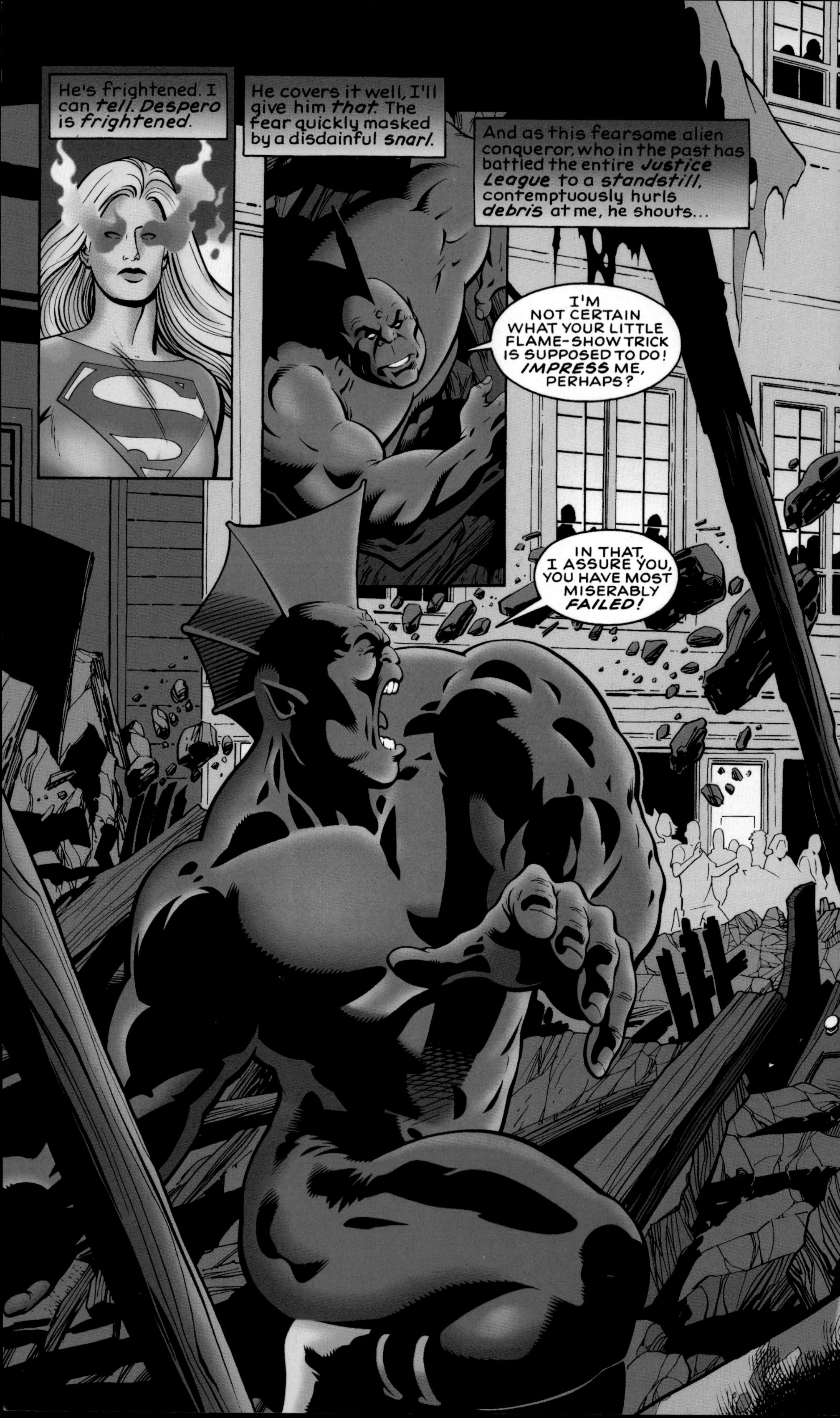
He's frightened. I can tell. Despero is frightened.
He covers it well, I'll give him that. The fear quickly masked by a disdainful snarl.
And as this fearsome alien conqueror, who in the past has battled the entire Justice League to a standstill, contemptuously hurls debris at me, he shouts...
I'M NOT CERTAIN WHAT YOUR LITTLE FLAME-SHOW TRICK IS SUPPOSED TO DO! IMPRESS ME, PERHAPS?
IN THAT, I ASSURE YOU, YOU HAVE MOST MISERABLY FAILED!

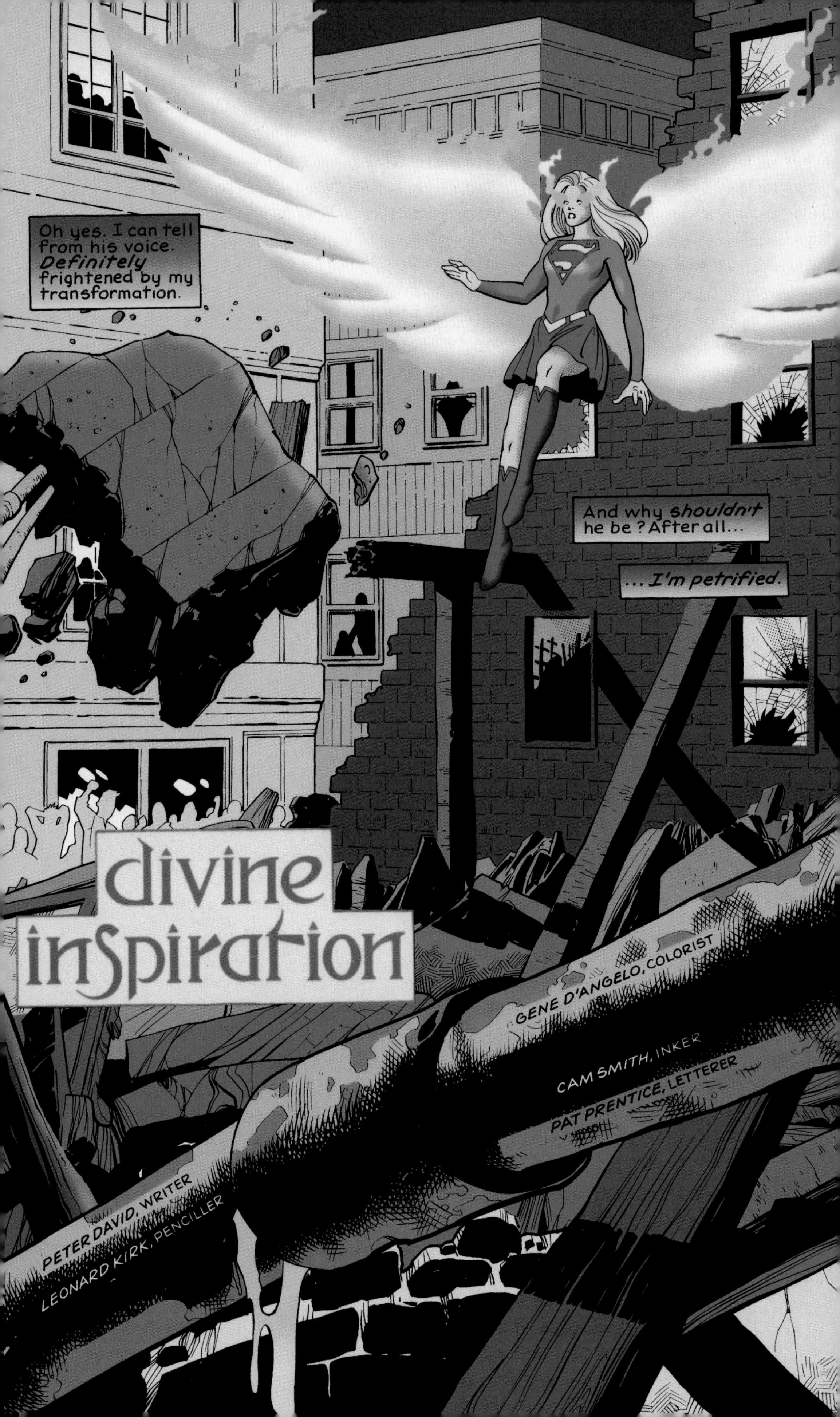

Oh yes. I can tell from his voice. *Definitely* frightened by my transformation.
And why *shouldn't* he be? After all...
...*I'm petrified.*
divine inspiration
GENE D'ANGELO, COLORIST
CAM SMITH, INKER
PAT PRENTICE, LETTERER
PETER DAVID, WRITER
LEONARD KIRK, PENCILLER

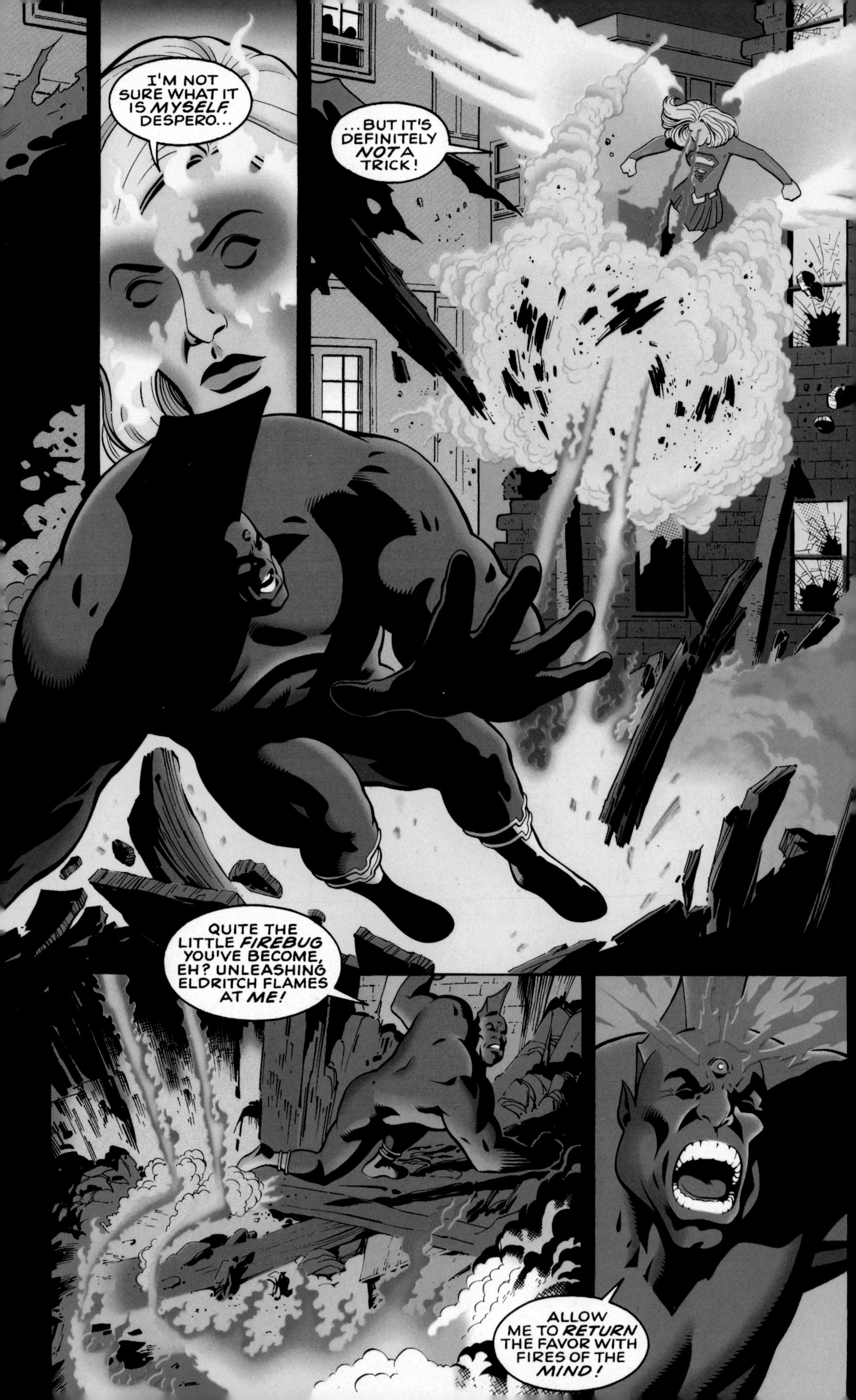
I'M NOT SURE WHAT IT IS MYSELF, DESPERO...
...BUT IT'S DEFINITELY NOT A TRICK!
QUITE THE LITTLE FIREBUG YOU'VE BECOME, EH? UNLEASHING ELDRITCH FLAMES AT ME!
ALLOW ME TO RETURN THE FAVOR WITH FIRES OF THE MIND!

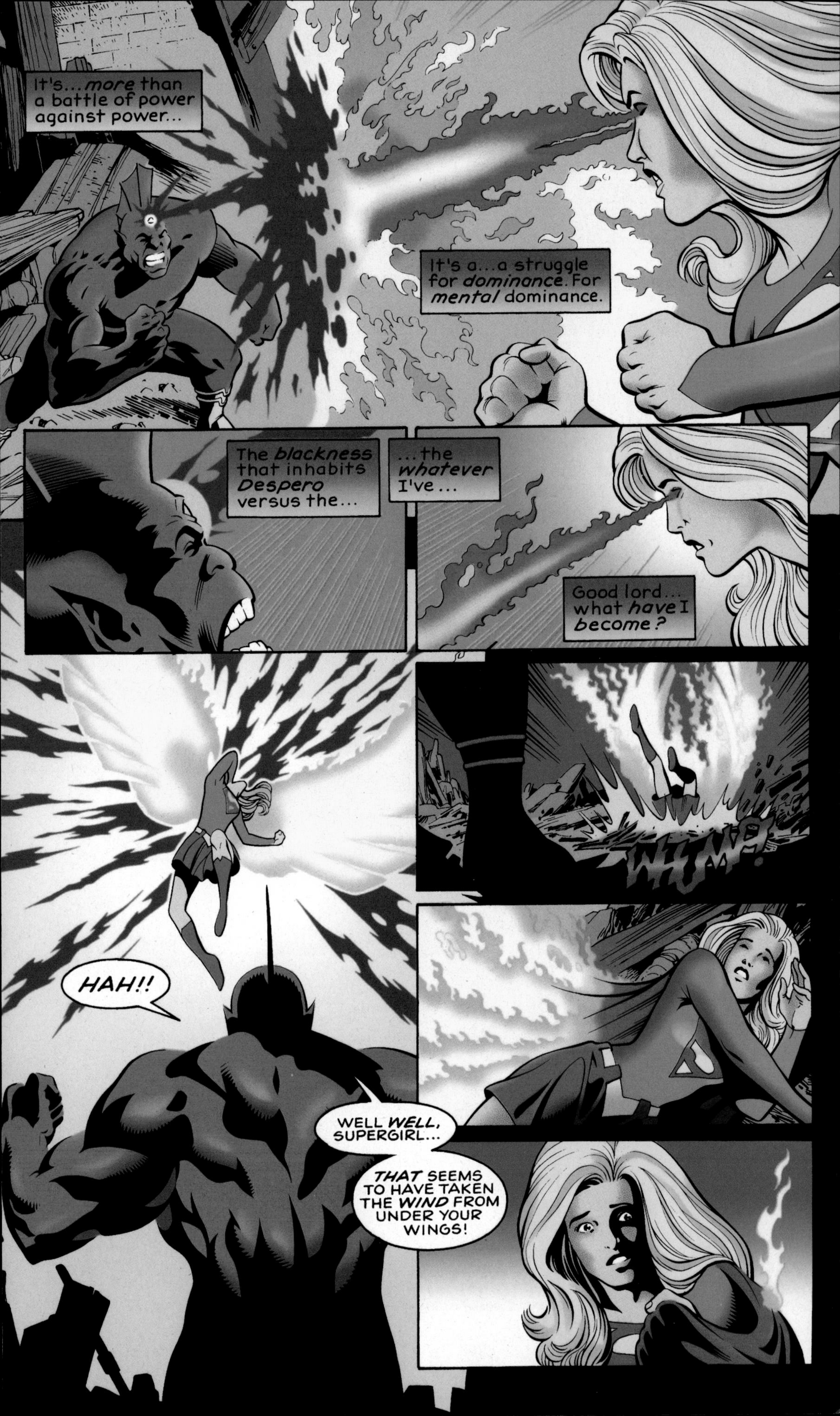
It's... *more* than a battle of power against power...
It's a... a struggle for *dominance*. For *mental* dominance.
The *blackness* that inhabits *Despero* versus the...
...the *whatever* I've...
Good lord... what *have* I *become*?
WHUMP!
HAH!!
WELL *WELL*, SUPERGIRL...
THAT SEEMS TO HAVE TAKEN THE *WIND* FROM UNDER YOUR WINGS!

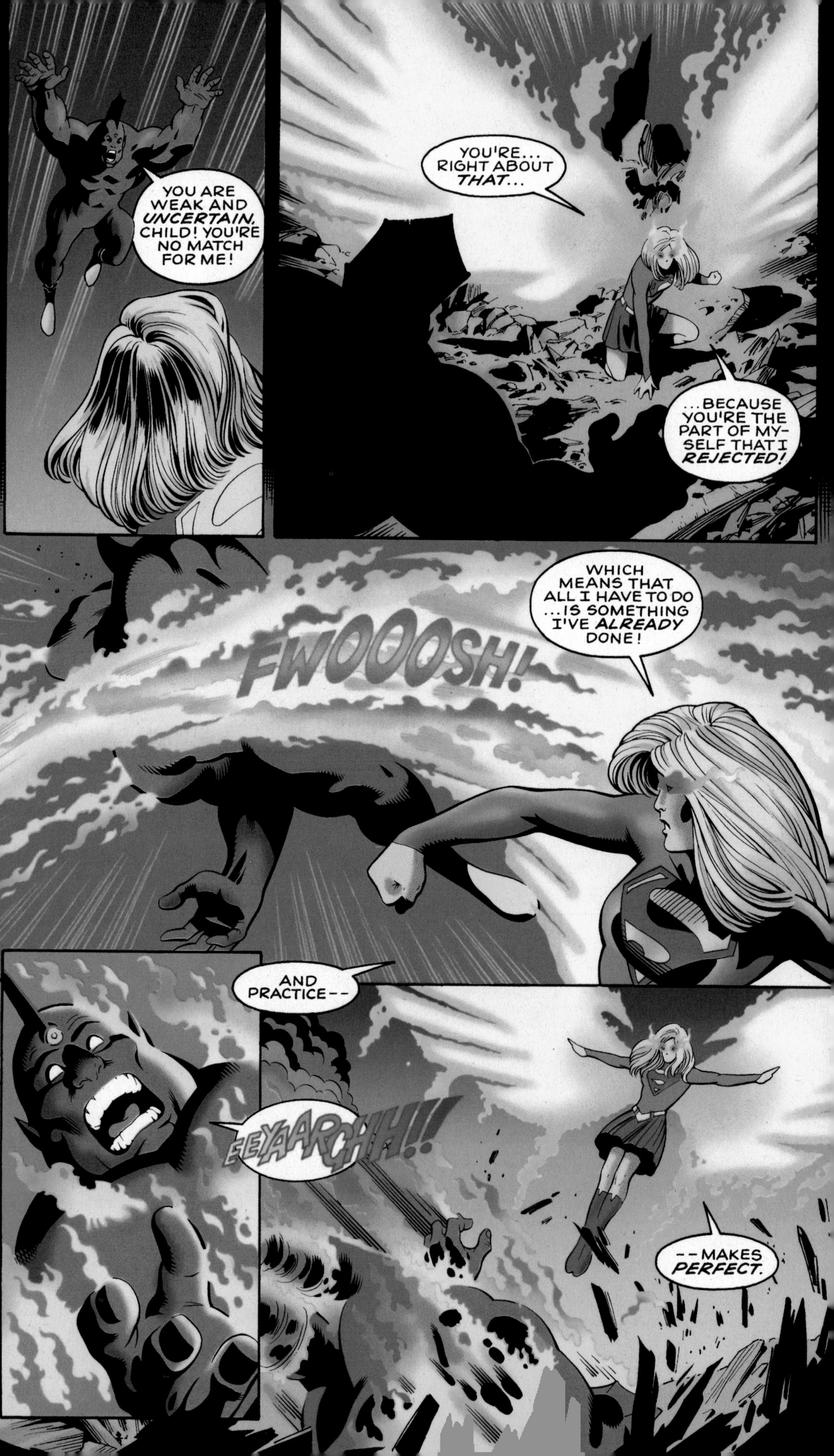
YOU ARE WEAK AND UNCERTAIN, CHILD! YOU'RE NO MATCH FOR ME!
YOU'RE... RIGHT ABOUT THAT...
...BECAUSE YOU'RE THE PART OF MY-SELF THAT I REJECTED!
WHICH MEANS THAT ALL I HAVE TO DO ...IS SOMETHING I'VE ALREADY DONE!
FWOOOSH!
AND PRACTICE--
EEYAARGHH!!
--MAKES PERFECT.

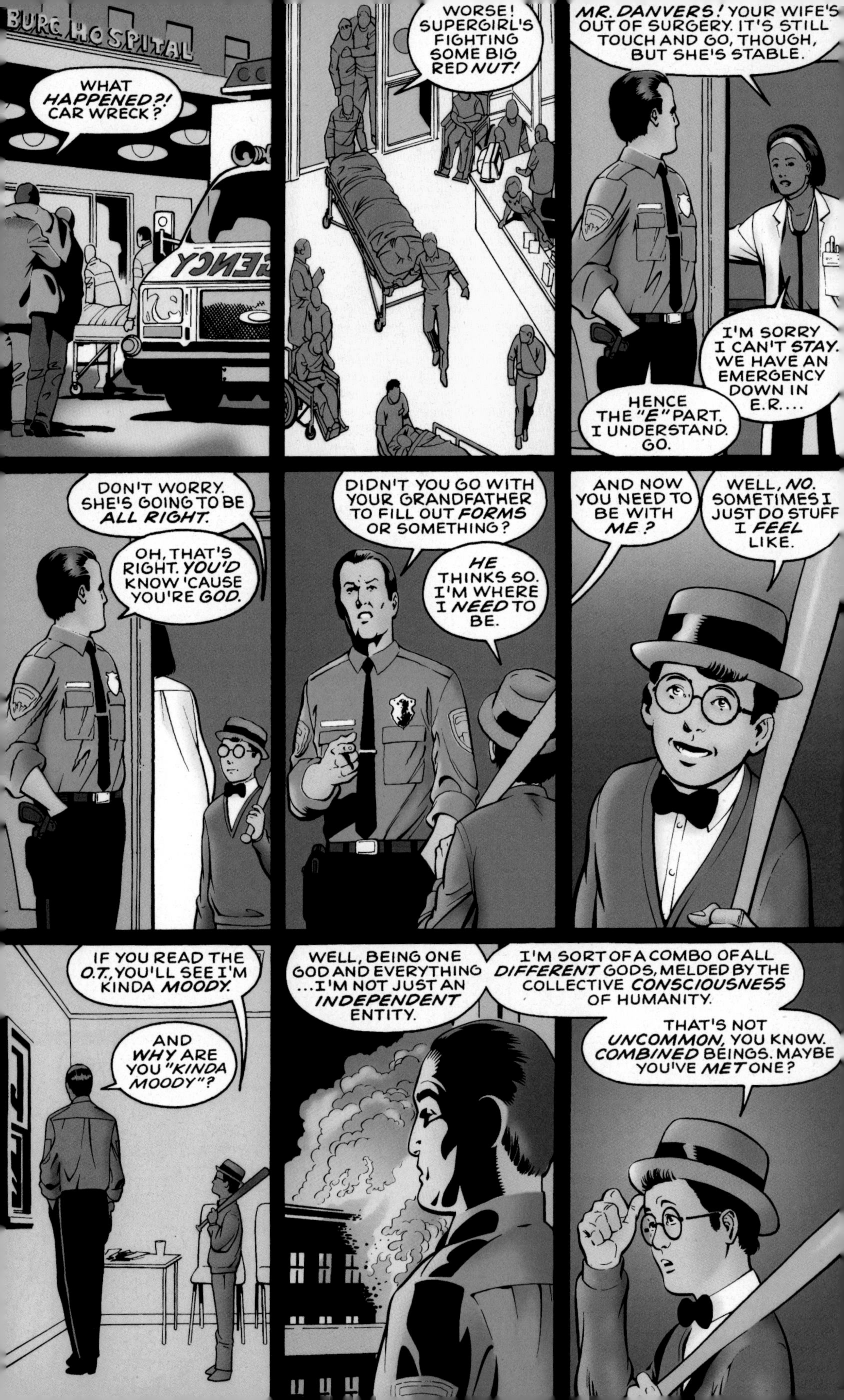
BURG HOSPITAL
WHAT HAPPENED?! CAR WRECK?
ENCY
WORSE! SUPERGIRL'S FIGHTING SOME BIG RED NUT!
MR. DANVERS! YOUR WIFE'S OUT OF SURGERY. IT'S STILL TOUCH AND GO, THOUGH, BUT SHE'S STABLE.
I'M SORRY I CAN'T STAY. WE HAVE AN EMERGENCY DOWN IN E.R....
HENCE THE "E" PART. I UNDERSTAND. GO.
DON'T WORRY. SHE'S GOING TO BE ALL RIGHT.
OH, THAT'S RIGHT. YOU'D KNOW 'CAUSE YOU'RE GOD.
DIDN'T YOU GO WITH YOUR GRANDFATHER TO FILL OUT FORMS OR SOMETHING?
HE THINKS SO. I'M WHERE I NEED TO BE.
AND NOW YOU NEED TO BE WITH ME?
WELL, NO. SOMETIMES I JUST DO STUFF I FEEL LIKE.
IF YOU READ THE O.T., YOU'LL SEE I'M KINDA MOODY.
AND WHY ARE YOU "KINDA MOODY"?
WELL, BEING ONE GOD AND EVERYTHING ...I'M NOT JUST AN INDEPENDENT ENTITY.
I'M SORT OF A COMBO OF ALL DIFFERENT GODS, MELDED BY THE COLLECTIVE CONSCIOUSNESS OF HUMANITY.
THAT'S NOT UNCOMMON, YOU KNOW. COMBINED BEINGS. MAYBE YOU'VE MET ONE?

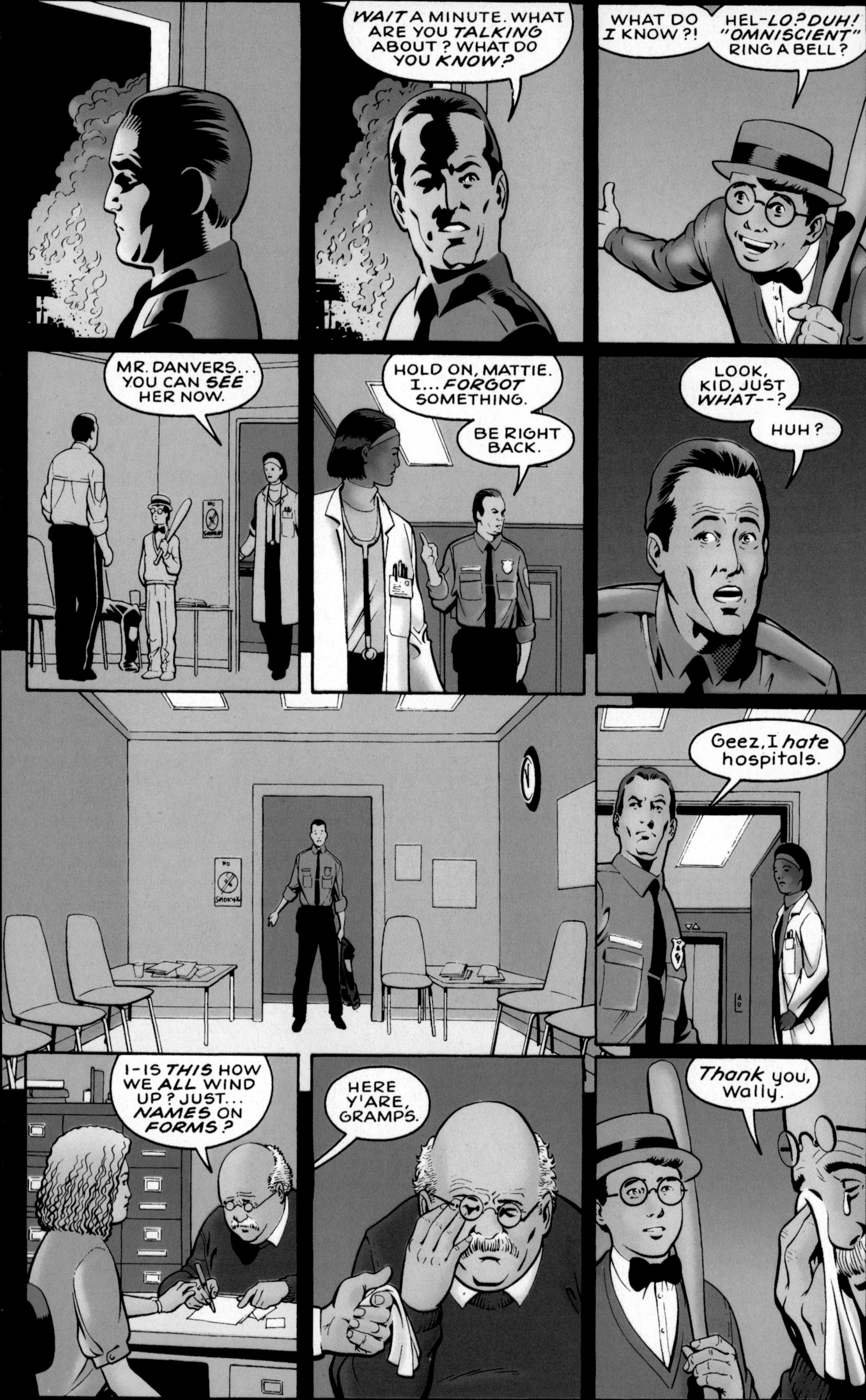
WAIT A MINUTE. WHAT ARE YOU TALKING ABOUT? WHAT DO YOU KNOW?
WHAT DO I KNOW?!
HEL-LO? DUH! "OMNISCIENT" RING A BELL?
MR. DANVERS... YOU CAN SEE HER NOW.
HOLD ON, MATTIE. I... FORGOT SOMETHING.
BE RIGHT BACK.
LOOK, KID, JUST WHAT--?
HUH?
Geez, I hate hospitals.
I-IS THIS HOW WE ALL WIND UP? JUST... NAMES ON FORMS?
HERE Y'ARE, GRAMPS.
Thank you, Wally.

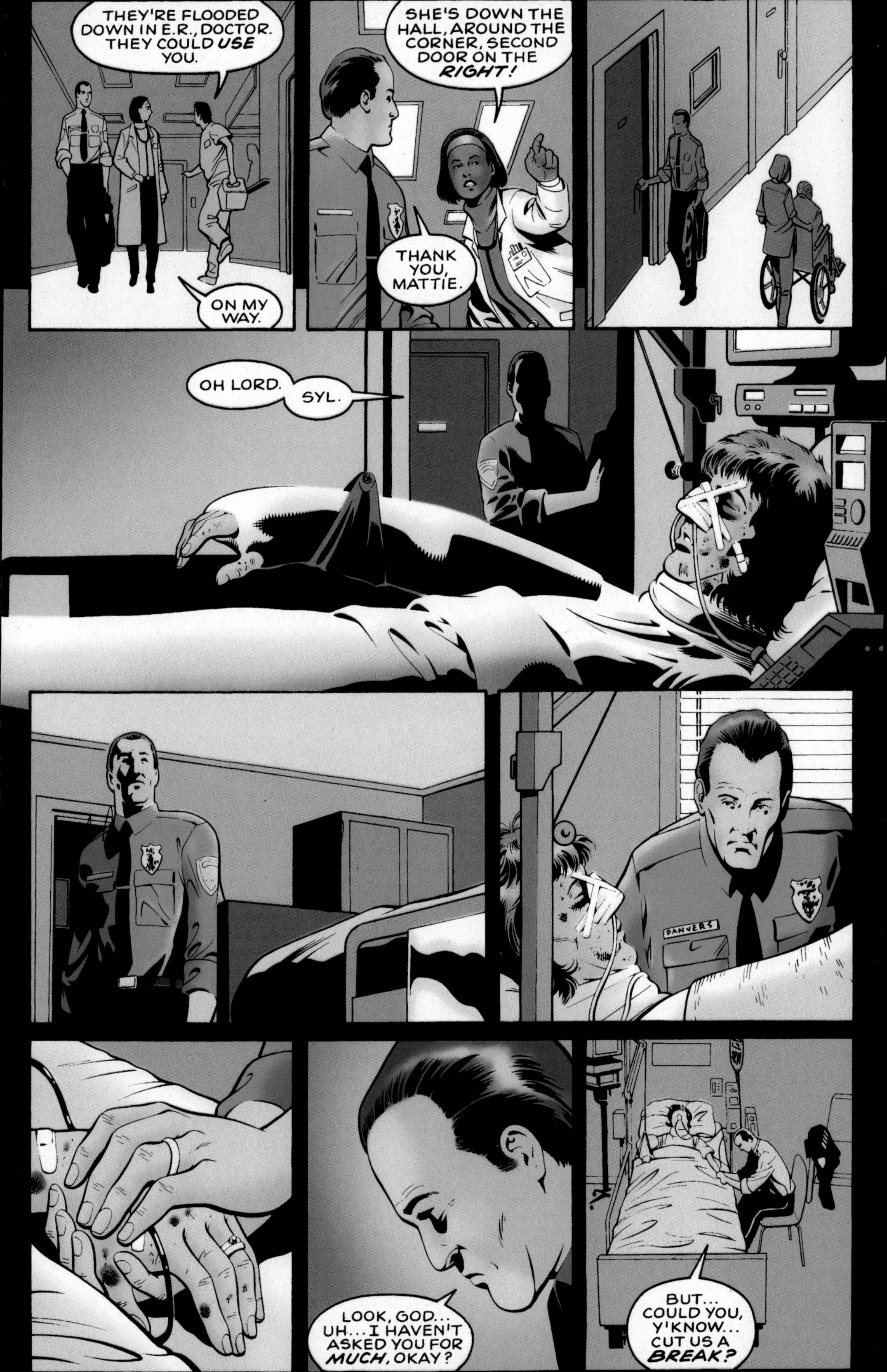
THEY'RE FLOODED DOWN IN E.R., DOCTOR. THEY COULD USE YOU.
ON MY WAY.
SHE'S DOWN THE HALL, AROUND THE CORNER, SECOND DOOR ON THE RIGHT!
THANK YOU, MATTIE.
OH LORD.
SYL.
DANVERS
LOOK, GOD... UH... I HAVEN'T ASKED YOU FOR MUCH, OKAY?
BUT... COULD YOU, Y'KNOW... CUT US A BREAK?

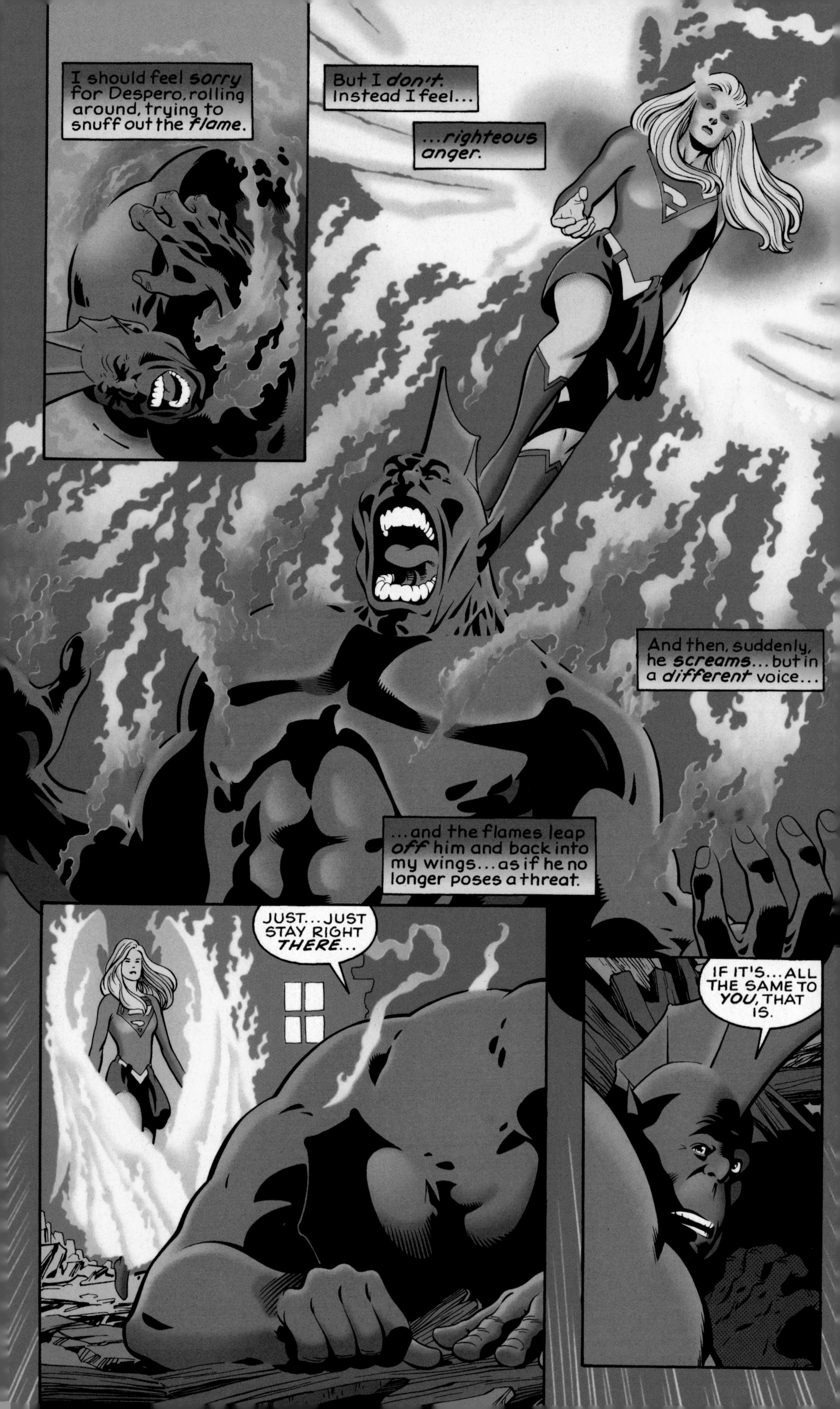
I should feel *sorry* for Despero, rolling around, trying to snuff out the *flame*.
But I *don't*. Instead I feel...
...*righteous anger*.
And then, suddenly, he *screams*... but in a *different* voice...
...and the flames leap *off* him and back into my wings... as if he no longer poses a threat.
JUST... JUST STAY RIGHT *THERE*...
IF IT'S... ALL THE SAME TO *YOU*, THAT IS.

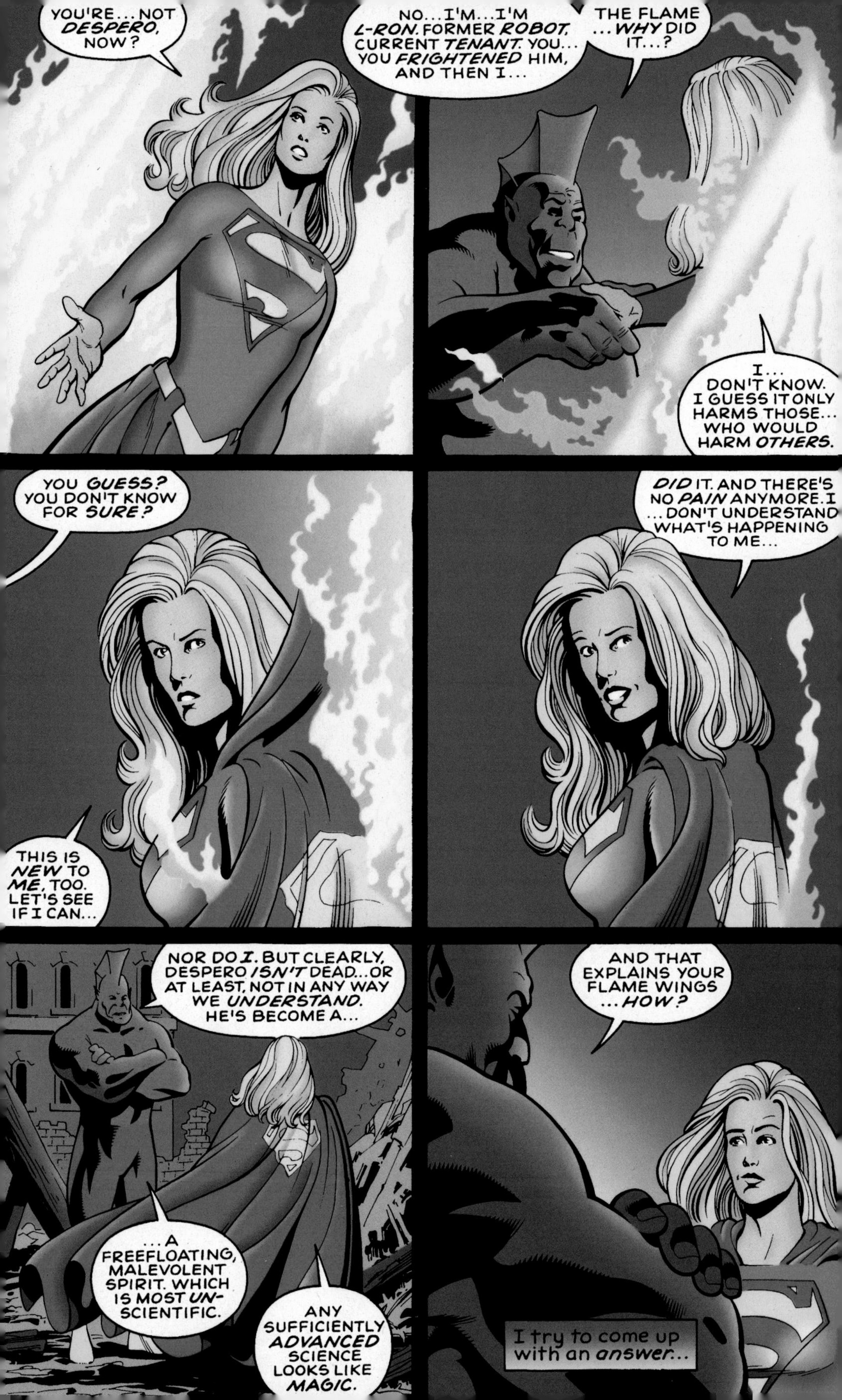
YOU'RE... NOT DESPERO, NOW?
NO... I'M... I'M L-RON. FORMER ROBOT, CURRENT TENANT. YOU... YOU FRIGHTENED HIM, AND THEN I...
THE FLAME ...WHY DID IT...?
I... DON'T KNOW. I GUESS IT ONLY HARMS THOSE... WHO WOULD HARM OTHERS.
YOU GUESS? YOU DON'T KNOW FOR SURE?
THIS IS NEW TO ME, TOO. LET'S SEE IF I CAN...
DID IT. AND THERE'S NO PAIN ANYMORE. I ...DON'T UNDERSTAND WHAT'S HAPPENING TO ME...
NOR DO I. BUT CLEARLY, DESPERO ISN'T DEAD...OR AT LEAST, NOT IN ANY WAY WE UNDERSTAND. HE'S BECOME A...
...A FREEFLOATING, MALEVOLENT SPIRIT. WHICH IS MOST UN-SCIENTIFIC.
ANY SUFFICIENTLY ADVANCED SCIENCE LOOKS LIKE MAGIC.
AND THAT EXPLAINS YOUR FLAME WINGS ...HOW?
I try to come up with an answer...

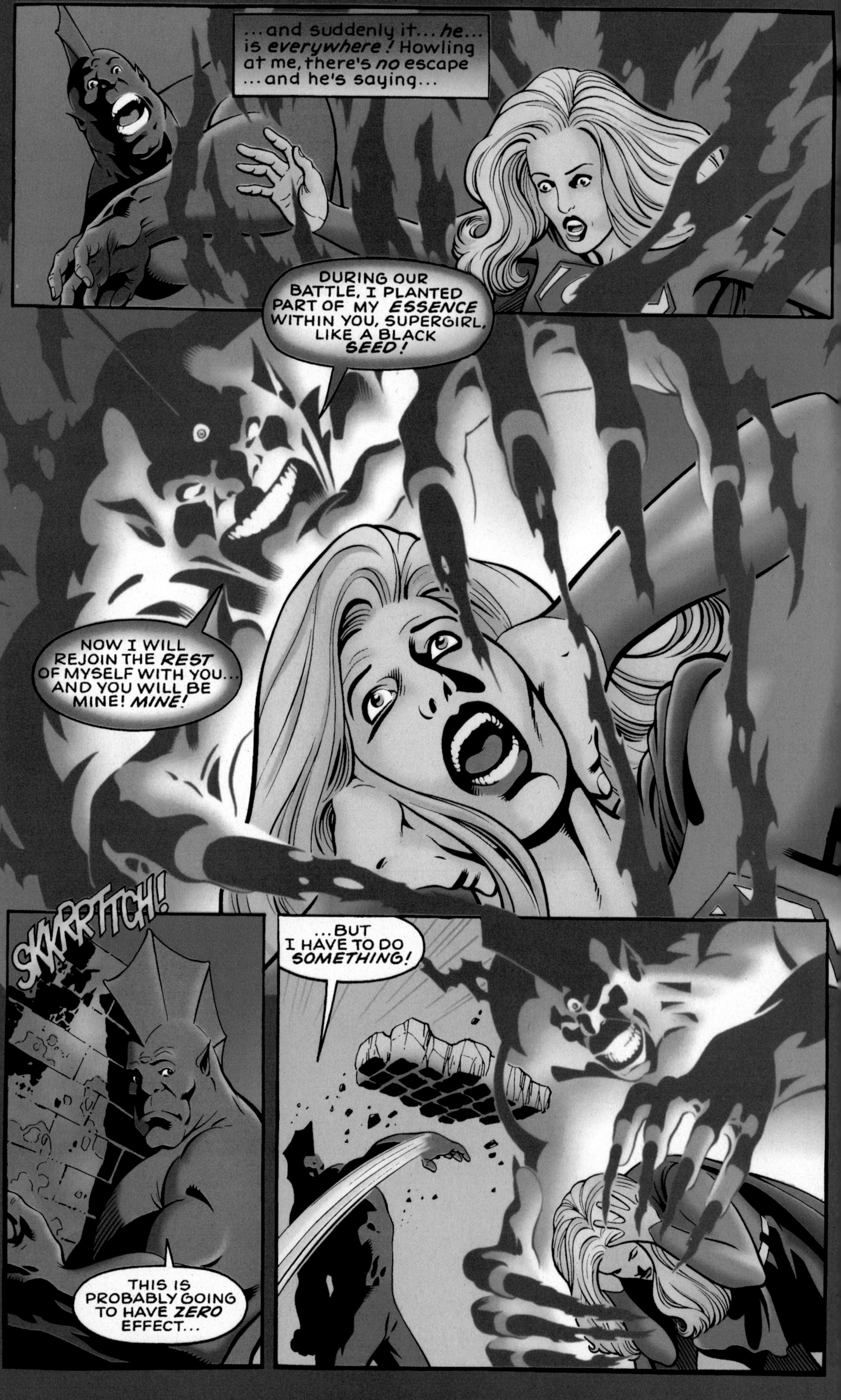
...and suddenly it... he... is everywhere! Howling at me, there's no escape ...and he's saying...
DURING OUR BATTLE, I PLANTED PART OF MY ESSENCE WITHIN YOU, SUPERGIRL, LIKE A BLACK SEED!
NOW I WILL REJOIN THE REST OF MYSELF WITH YOU... AND YOU WILL BE MINE! MINE!
SKKRRTTCH!
THIS IS PROBABLY GOING TO HAVE ZERO EFFECT...
...BUT I HAVE TO DO SOMETHING!

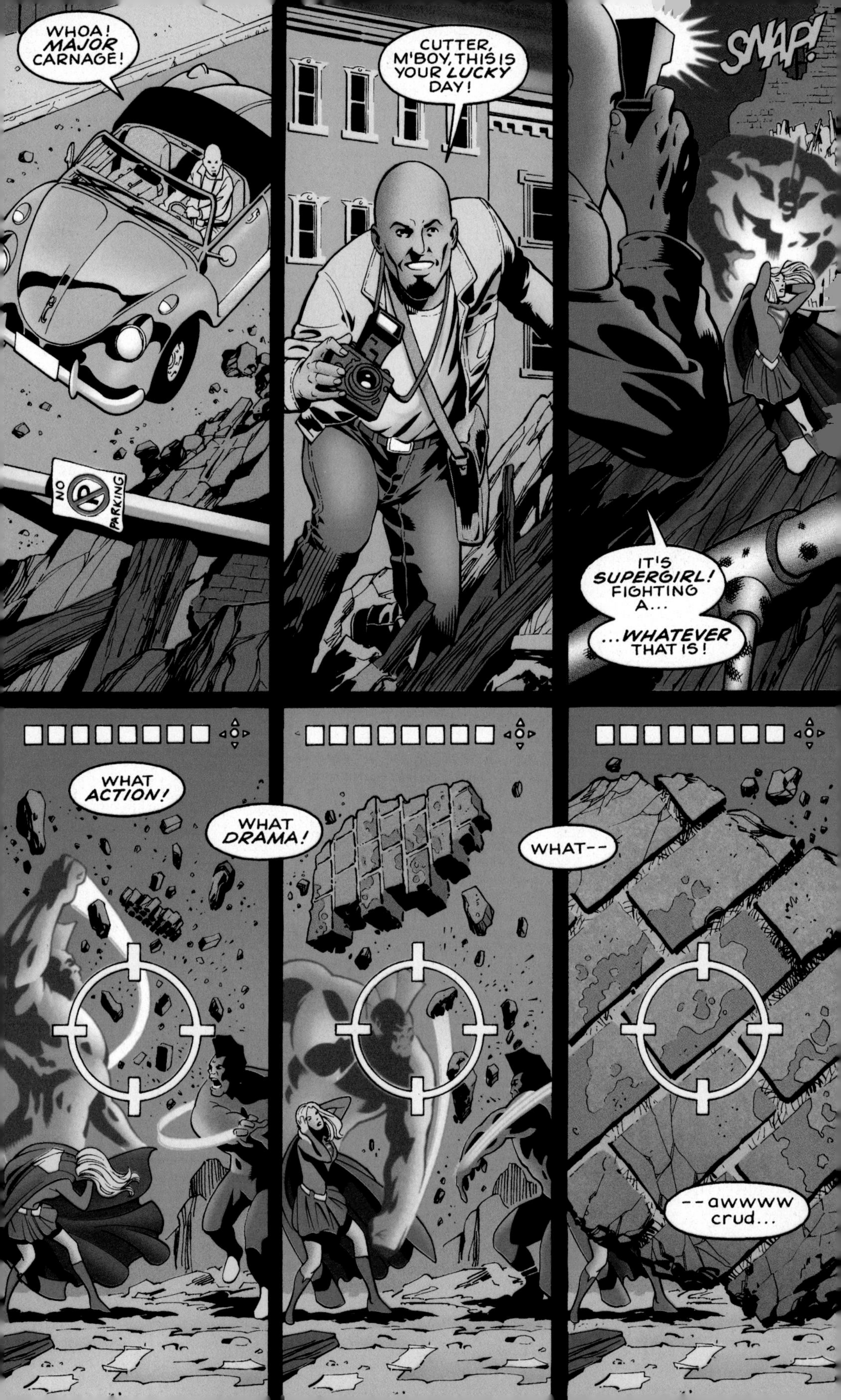
WHOA! MAJOR CARNAGE!
NO PARKING
CUTTER, M'BOY, THIS IS YOUR LUCKY DAY!
SNAP!
IT'S SUPERGIRL! FIGHTING A...
...WHATEVER THAT IS!
WHAT ACTION!
WHAT DRAMA!
WHAT--
--awwww crud...

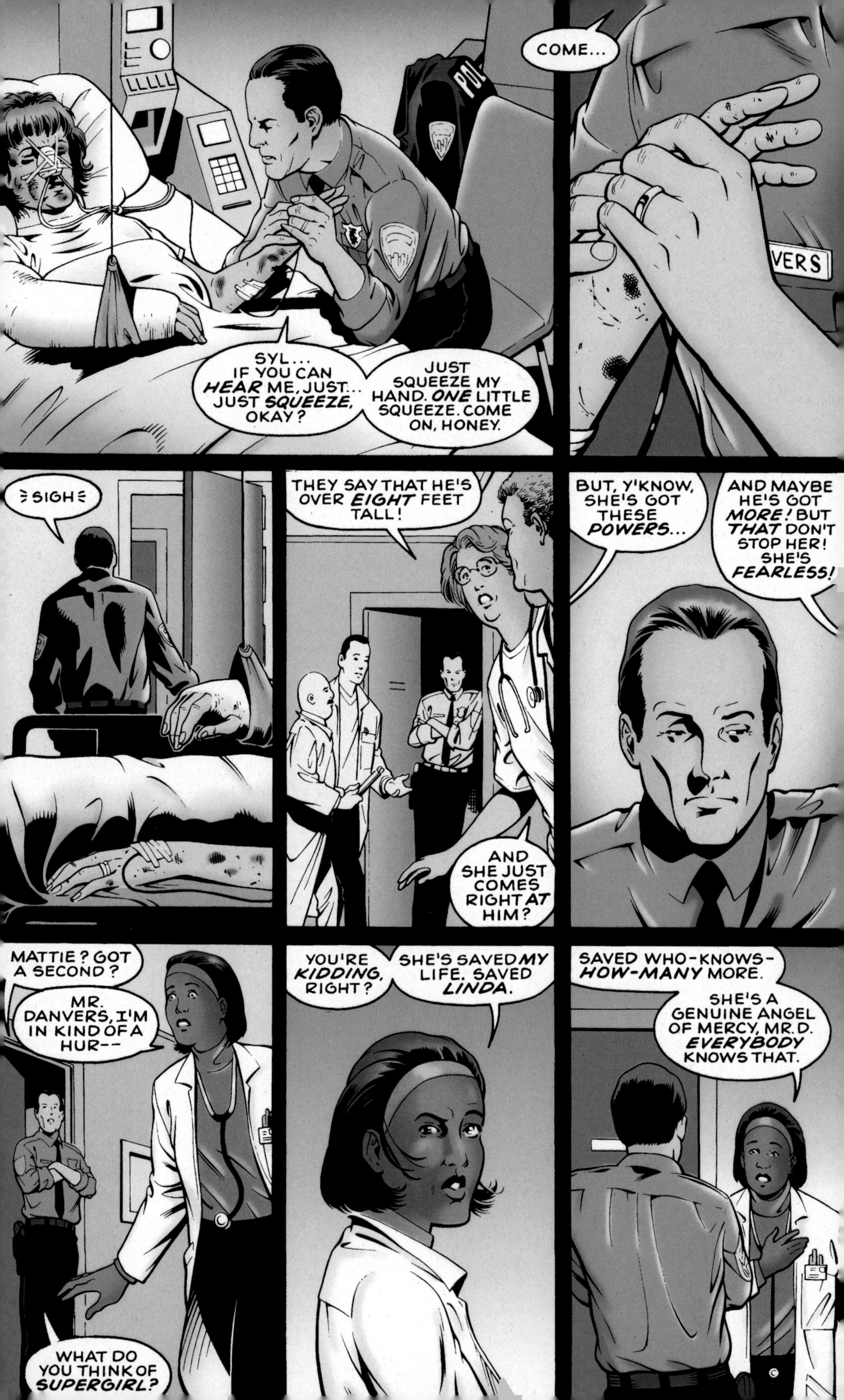
SYL... IF YOU CAN HEAR ME, JUST... JUST SQUEEZE, OKAY?
JUST SQUEEZE MY HAND. ONE LITTLE SQUEEZE. COME ON, HONEY.
COME...
VERS
SIGH
THEY SAY THAT HE'S OVER EIGHT FEET TALL!
AND SHE JUST COMES RIGHT AT HIM?
BUT, Y'KNOW, SHE'S GOT THESE POWERS...
AND MAYBE HE'S GOT MORE! BUT THAT DON'T STOP HER! SHE'S FEARLESS!
MATTIE? GOT A SECOND?
MR. DANVERS, I'M IN KIND OF A HUR--
WHAT DO YOU THINK OF SUPERGIRL?
YOU'RE KIDDING, RIGHT?
SHE'S SAVED MY LIFE. SAVED LINDA.
SAVED WHO-KNOWS-HOW-MANY MORE.
SHE'S A GENUINE ANGEL OF MERCY, MR. D. EVERYBODY KNOWS THAT.

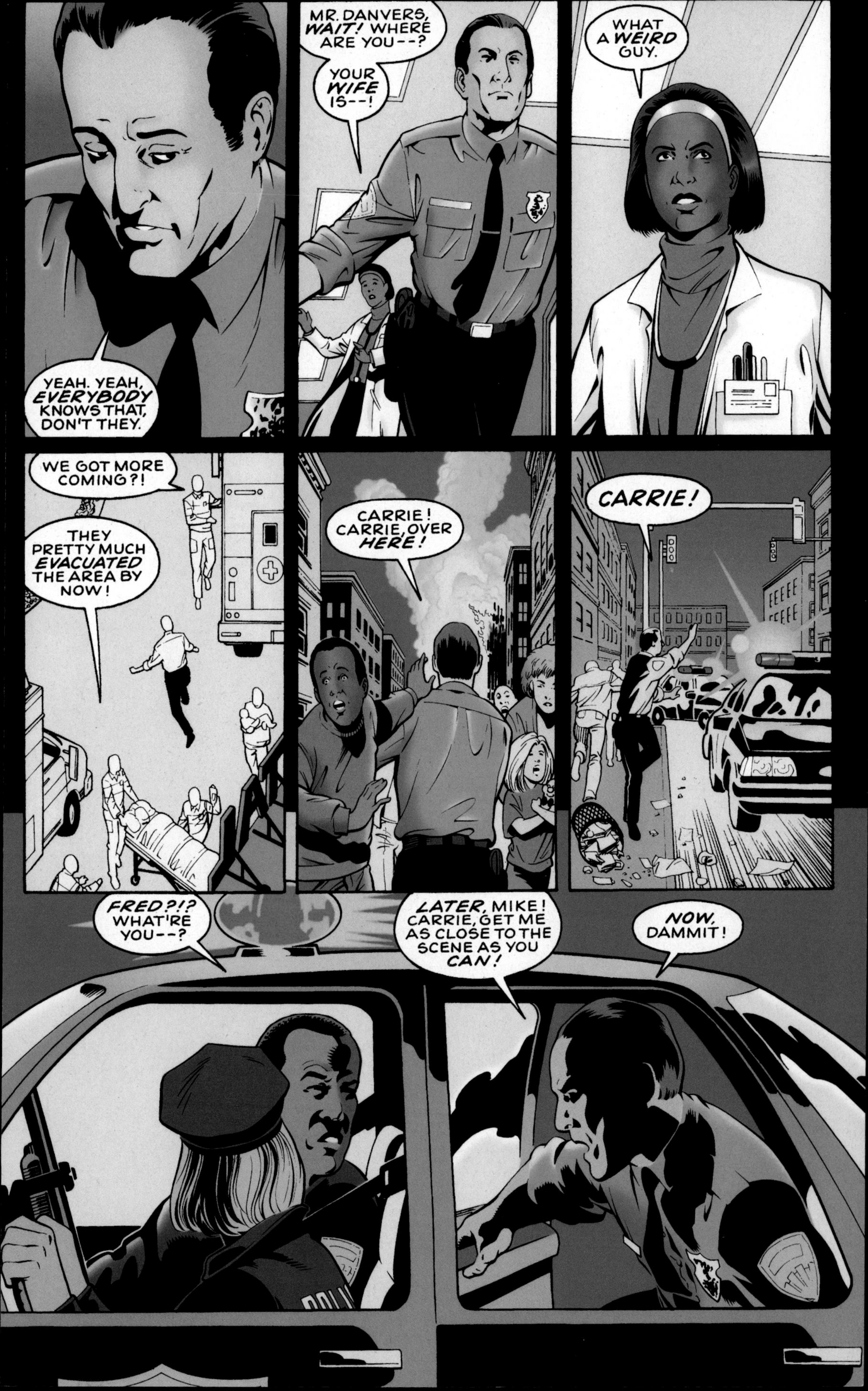
YEAH. YEAH, EVERYBODY KNOWS THAT, DON'T THEY.
MR. DANVERS, WAIT! WHERE ARE YOU--?
YOUR WIFE IS--!
WHAT A WEIRD GUY.
WE GOT MORE COMING?!
THEY PRETTY MUCH EVACUATED THE AREA BY NOW!
CARRIE! CARRIE, OVER HERE!
CARRIE!
FRED?!? WHAT'RE YOU--?
LATER, MIKE! CARRIE, GET ME AS CLOSE TO THE SCENE AS YOU CAN!
NOW, DAMMIT!

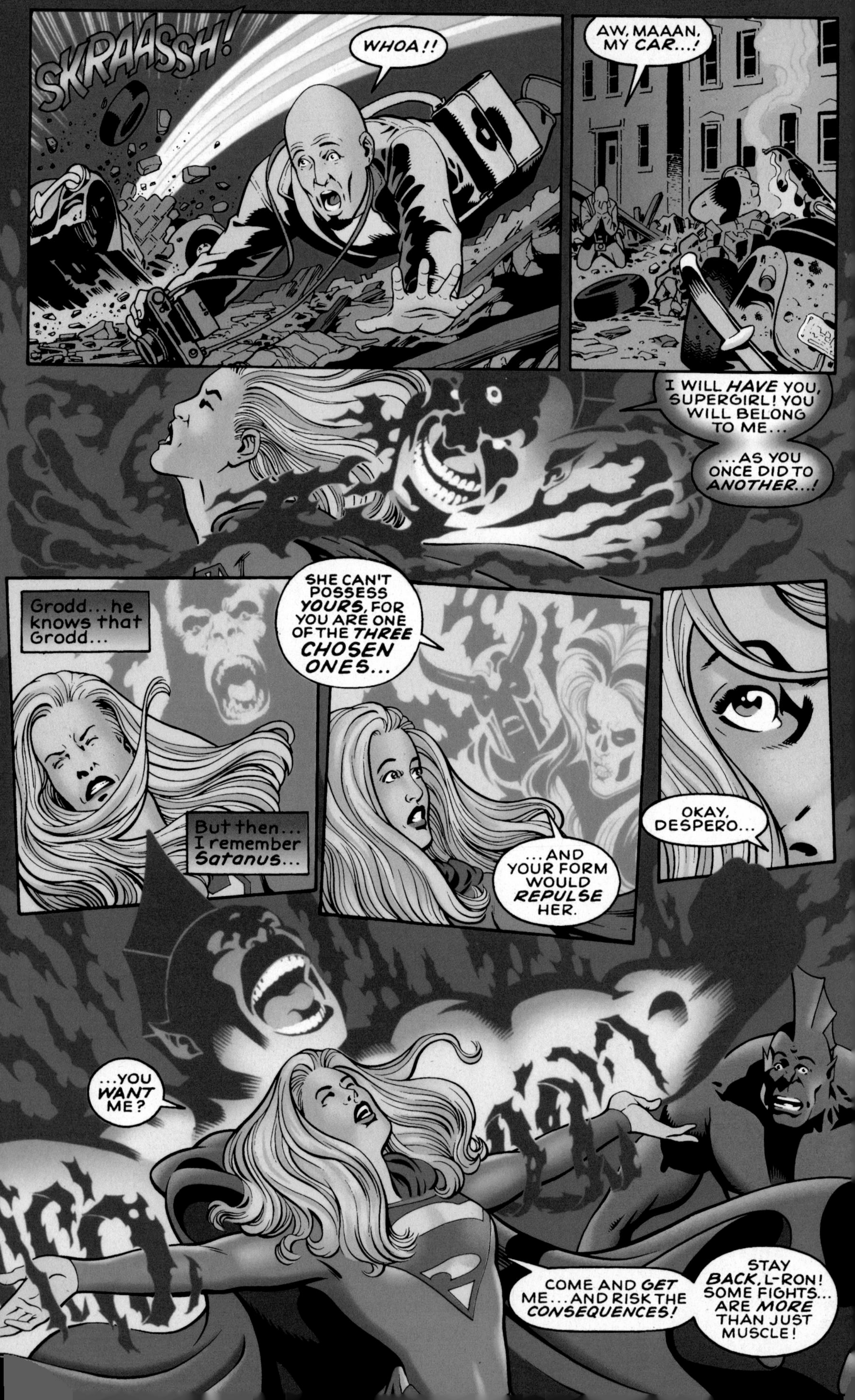
SKRAASSH!
WHOA!!
AW, MAAAN, MY CAR...!
I WILL HAVE YOU, SUPERGIRL! YOU WILL BELONG TO ME...
...AS YOU ONCE DID TO ANOTHER...!
Grodd... he knows that Grodd...
But then... I remember Satanus...
SHE CAN'T POSSESS YOURS, FOR YOU ARE ONE OF THE THREE CHOSEN ONES...
...AND YOUR FORM WOULD REPULSE HER.
OKAY, DESPERO...
...YOU WANT ME?
COME AND GET ME... AND RISK THE CONSEQUENCES!
STAY BACK, L-RON! SOME FIGHTS... ARE MORE THAN JUST MUSCLE!

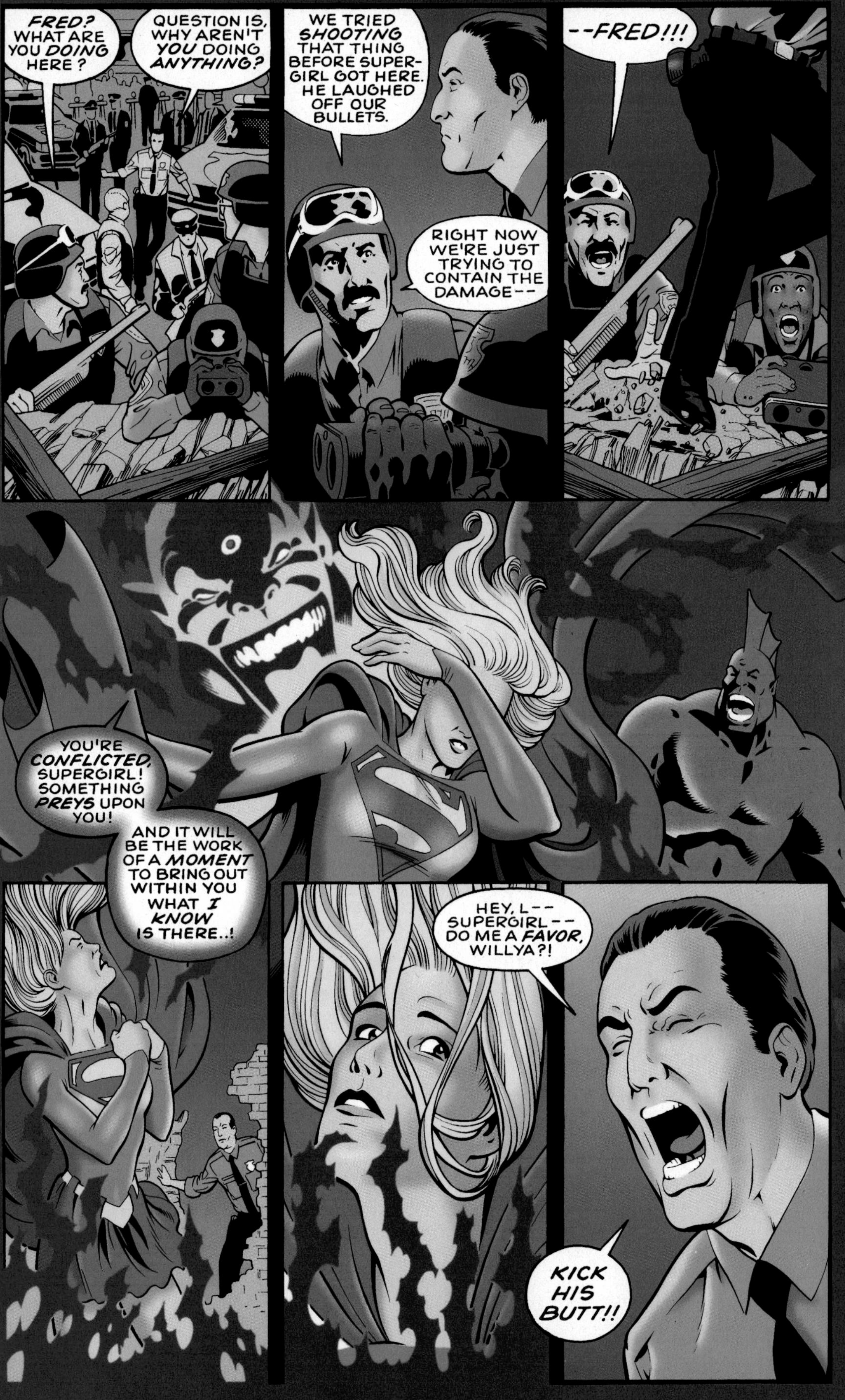
FRED? WHAT ARE YOU DOING HERE?
QUESTION IS, WHY AREN'T YOU DOING ANYTHING?
WE TRIED SHOOTING THAT THING BEFORE SUPER-GIRL GOT HERE. HE LAUGHED OFF OUR BULLETS.
RIGHT NOW WE'RE JUST TRYING TO CONTAIN THE DAMAGE--
--FRED!!!
YOU'RE CONFLICTED, SUPERGIRL! SOMETHING PREYS UPON YOU!
AND IT WILL BE THE WORK OF A MOMENT TO BRING OUT WITHIN YOU WHAT I KNOW IS THERE..!
HEY, L-- SUPERGIRL-- DO ME A FAVOR, WILLYA?!
KICK HIS BUTT!!

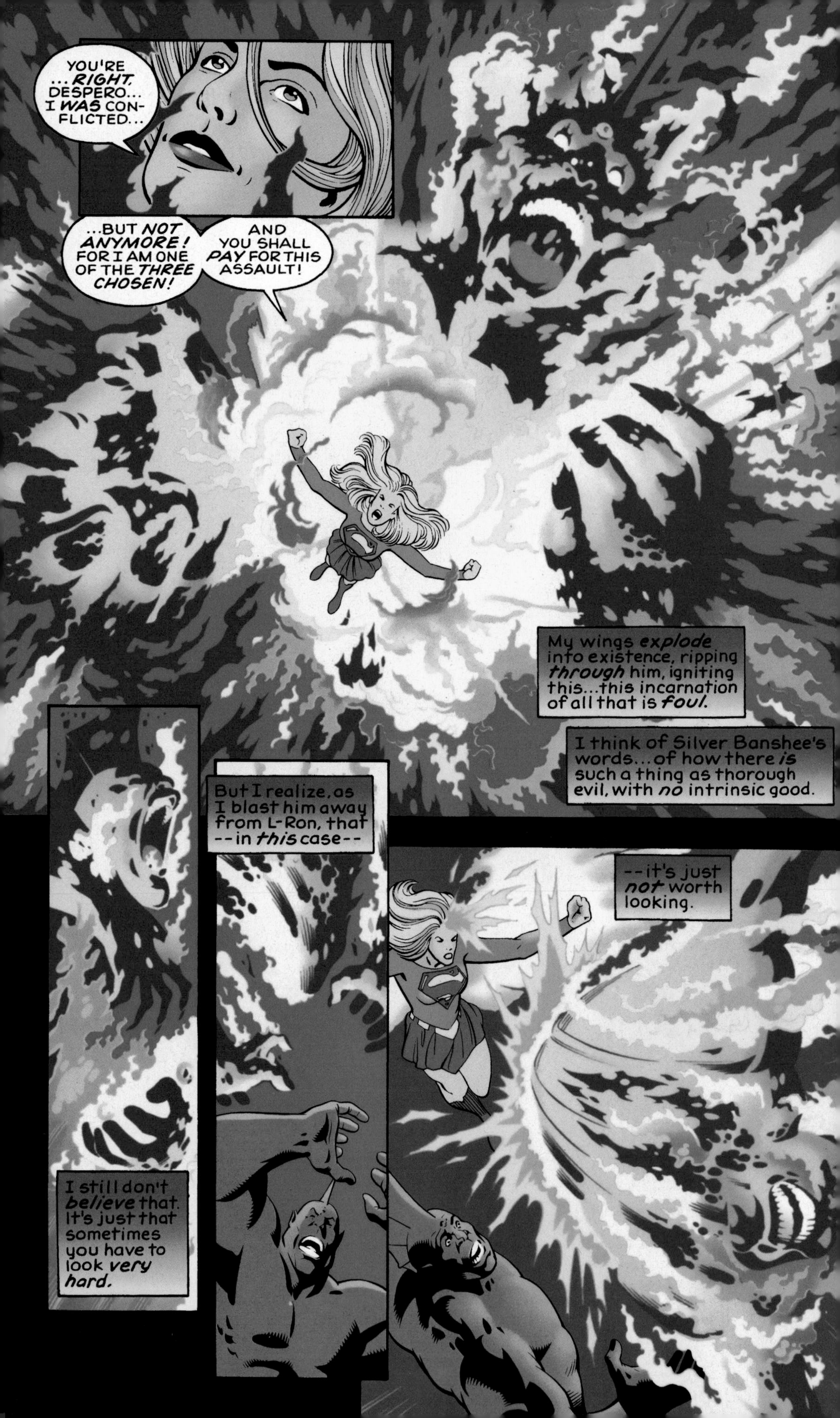
YOU'RE ...RIGHT, DESPERO... I WAS CONFLICTED...
...BUT NOT ANYMORE! FOR I AM ONE OF THE THREE CHOSEN!
AND YOU SHALL PAY FOR THIS ASSAULT!
My wings explode into existence, ripping through him, igniting this...this incarnation of all that is foul.
I think of Silver Banshee's words...of how there is such a thing as thorough evil, with no intrinsic good.
I still don't believe that. It's just that sometimes you have to look very hard.
But I realize, as I blast him away from L-Ron, that --in this case--
--it's just not worth looking.

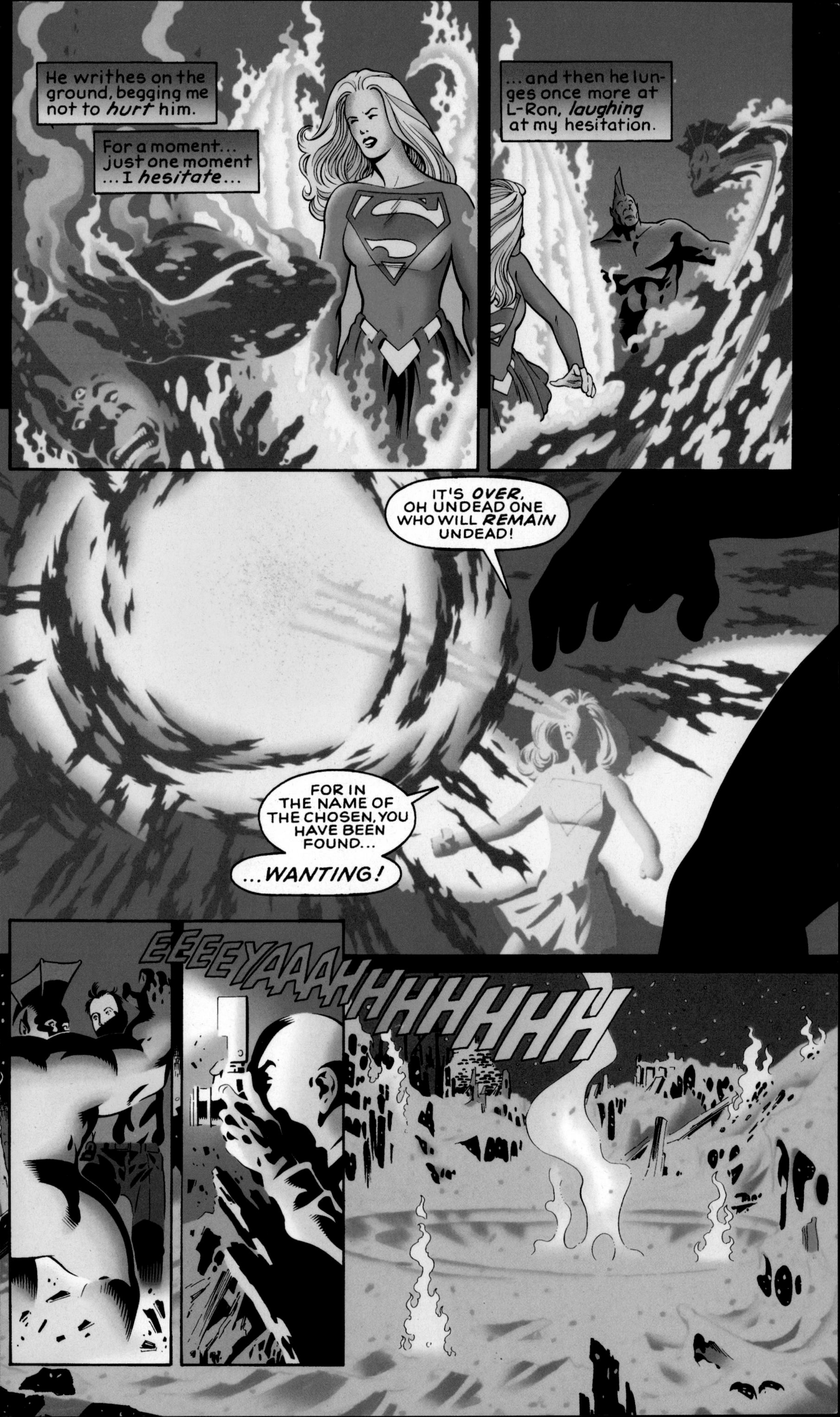
He writhes on the ground, begging me not to *hurt* him.
For a moment... just one moment ...I *hesitate*...
...and then he lunges once more at L-Ron, *laughing* at my hesitation.
IT'S *OVER*, OH UNDEAD ONE WHO WILL *REMAIN* UNDEAD!
FOR IN THE NAME OF THE CHOSEN, YOU HAVE BEEN FOUND...
...*WANTING!*
EEEEYAAAHHHHHHHH

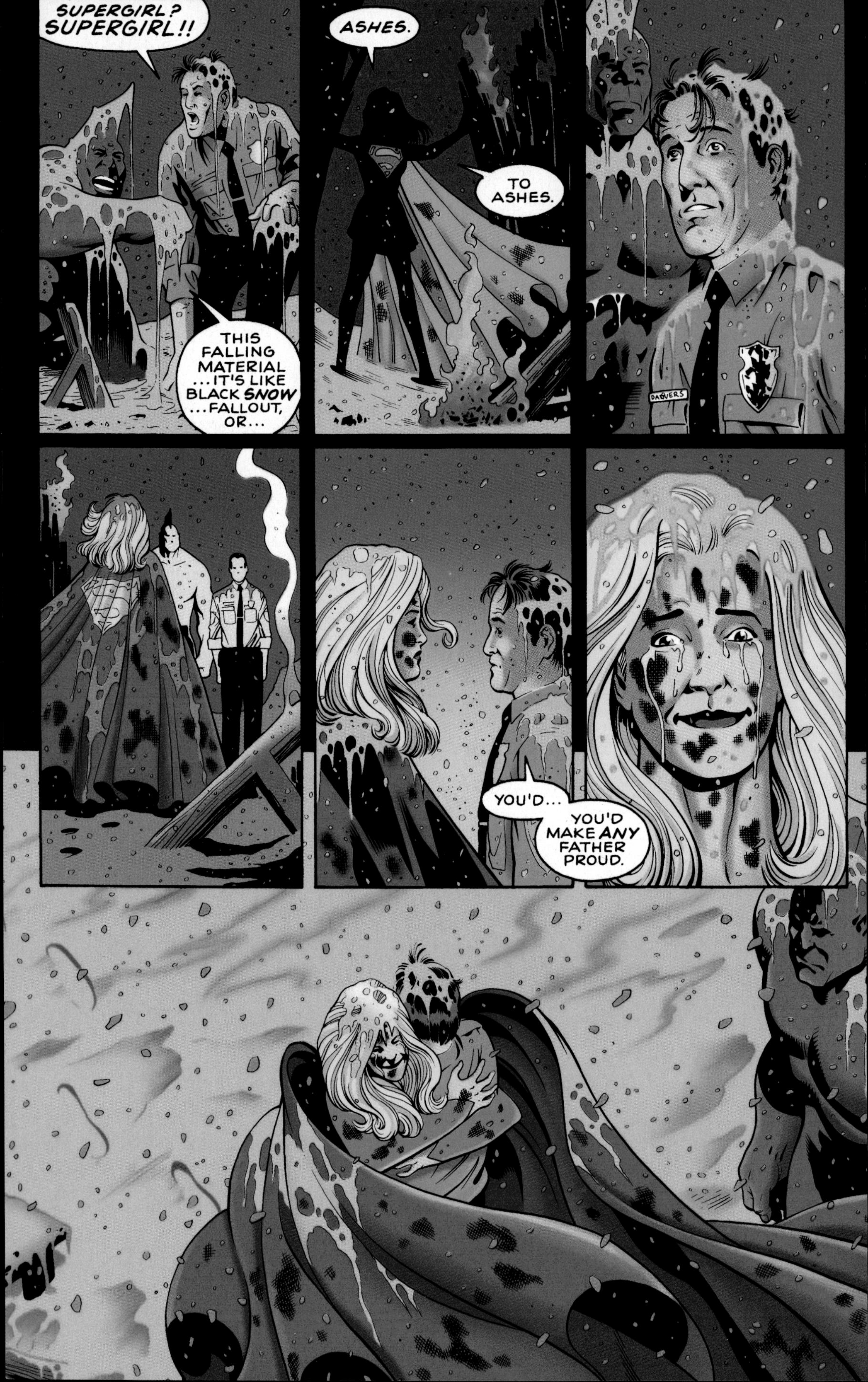
SUPERGIRL? SUPERGIRL!!
THIS FALLING MATERIAL ...IT'S LIKE BLACK SNOW ...FALLOUT, OR...
ASHES.
TO ASHES.
DABVERS
YOU'D...
YOU'D MAKE ANY FATHER PROUD.

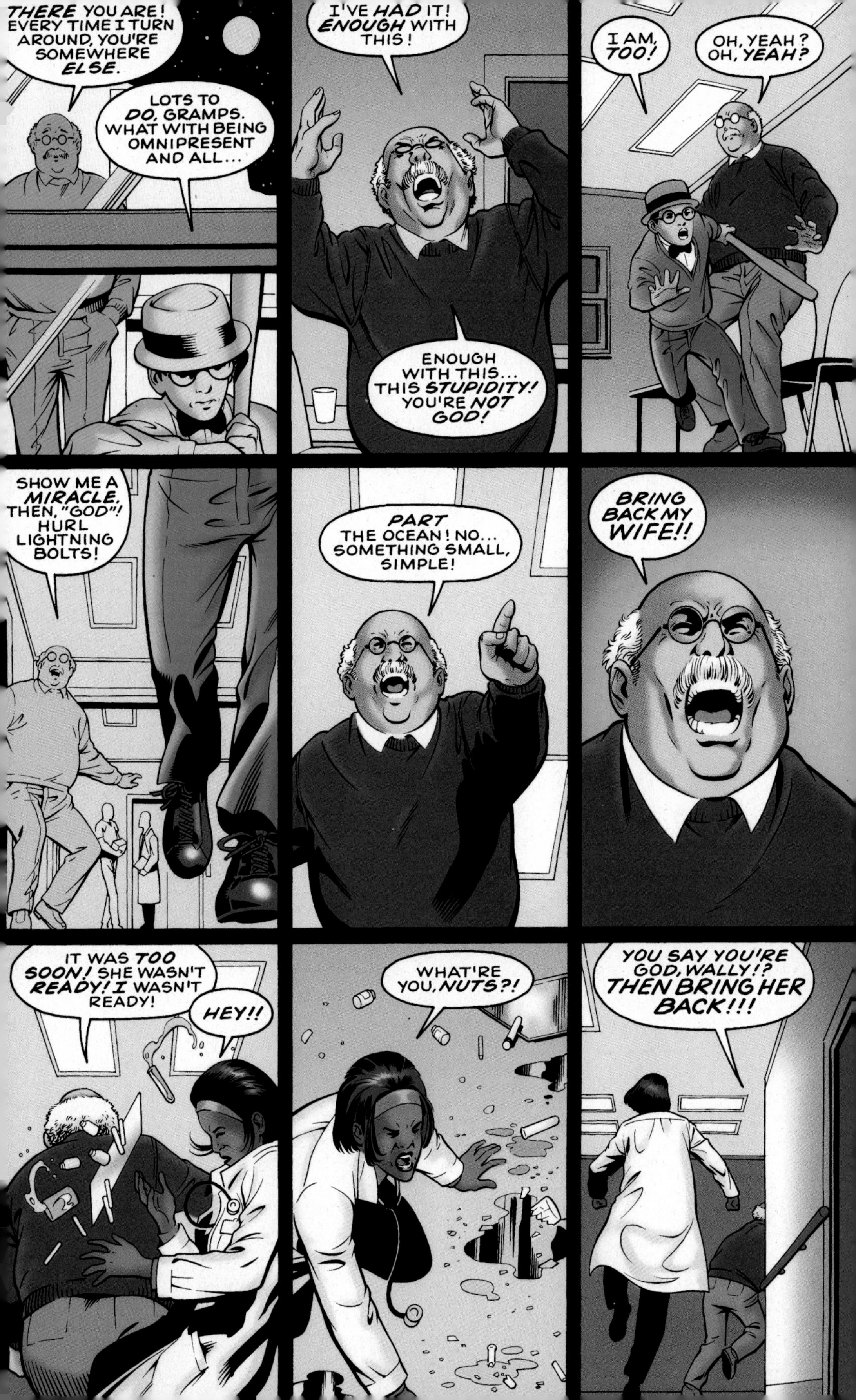
THERE YOU ARE! EVERY TIME I TURN AROUND, YOU'RE SOMEWHERE ELSE.
LOTS TO DO, GRAMPS. WHAT WITH BEING OMNIPRESENT AND ALL...
I'VE HAD IT! ENOUGH WITH THIS!
ENOUGH WITH THIS... THIS STUPIDITY! YOU'RE NOT GOD!
I AM, TOO!
OH, YEAH? OH, YEAH?
SHOW ME A MIRACLE, THEN, "GOD"! HURL LIGHTNING BOLTS!
PART THE OCEAN! NO... SOMETHING SMALL, SIMPLE!
BRING BACK MY WIFE!!
IT WAS TOO SOON! SHE WASN'T READY! I WASN'T READY!
HEY!!
WHAT'RE YOU, NUTS?!
YOU SAY YOU'RE GOD, WALLY!? THEN BRING HER BACK!!!

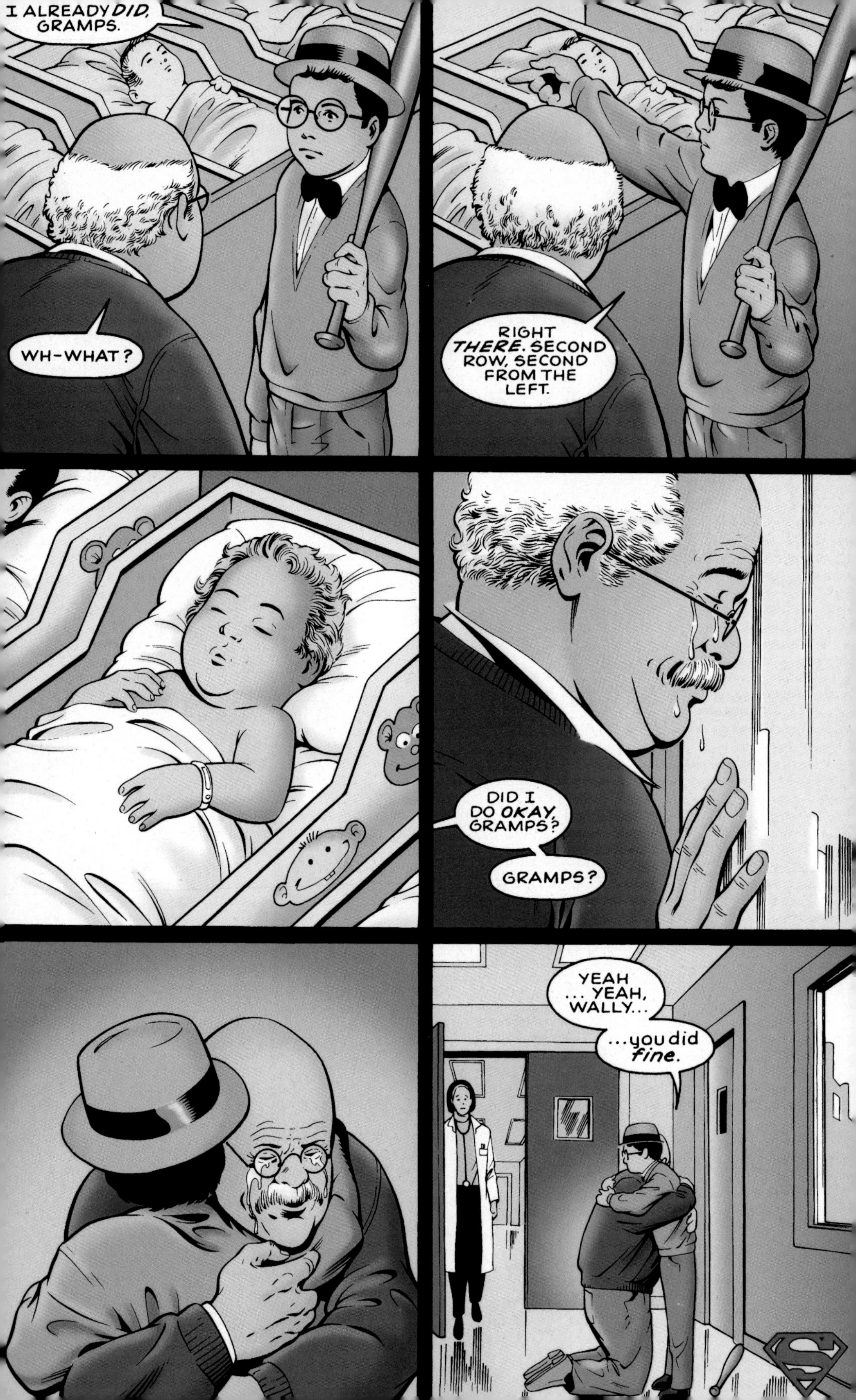
I ALREADY DID, GRAMPS.
WH-WHAT?
RIGHT THERE. SECOND ROW, SECOND FROM THE LEFT.
DID I DO OKAY, GRAMPS?
GRAMPS?
YEAH ...YEAH, WALLY...
...you did fine.

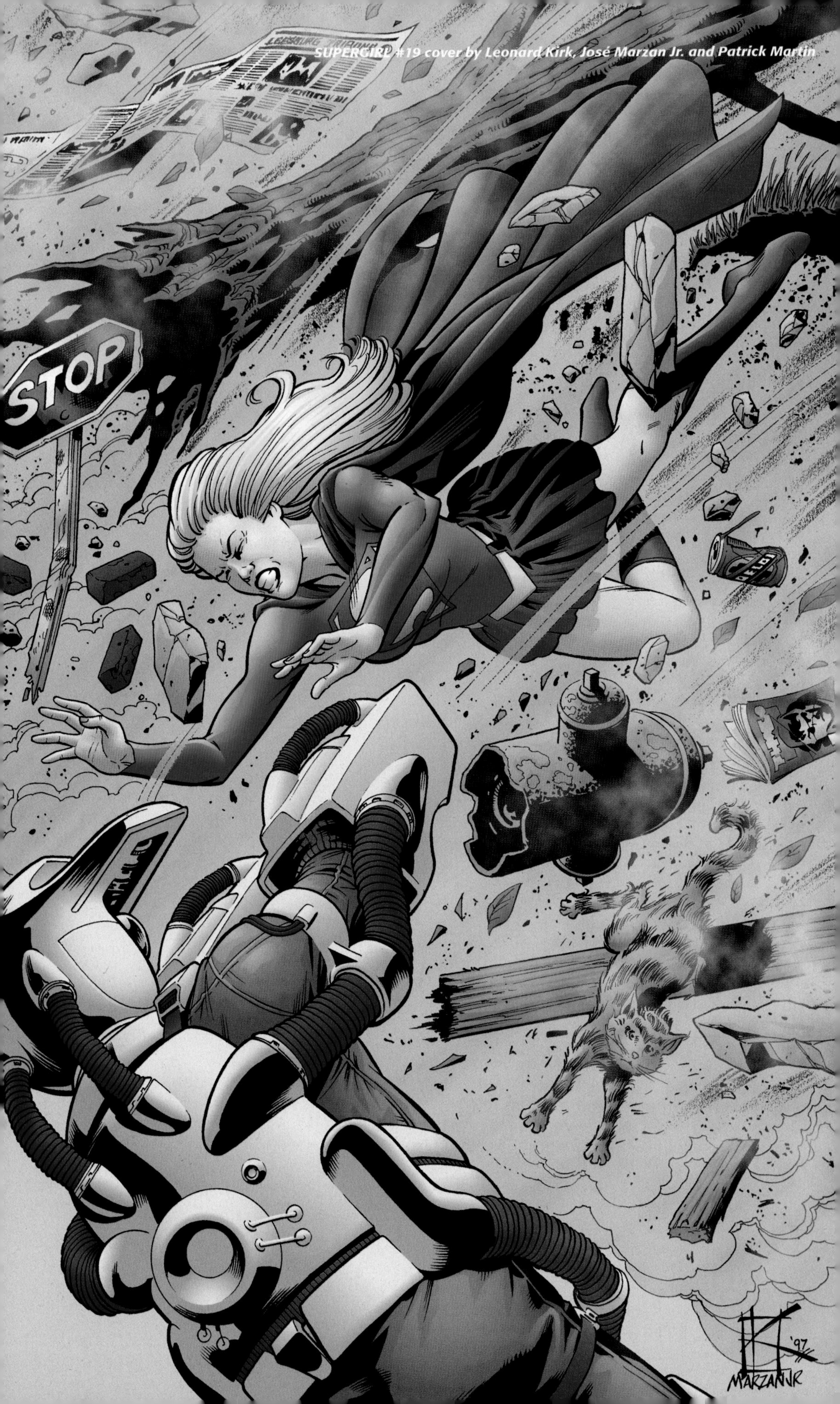
STOP
'97
MARZANJR

SUPERGIRL #19 cover by Leonard Kirk, José Marzan Jr. and Patrick Martin

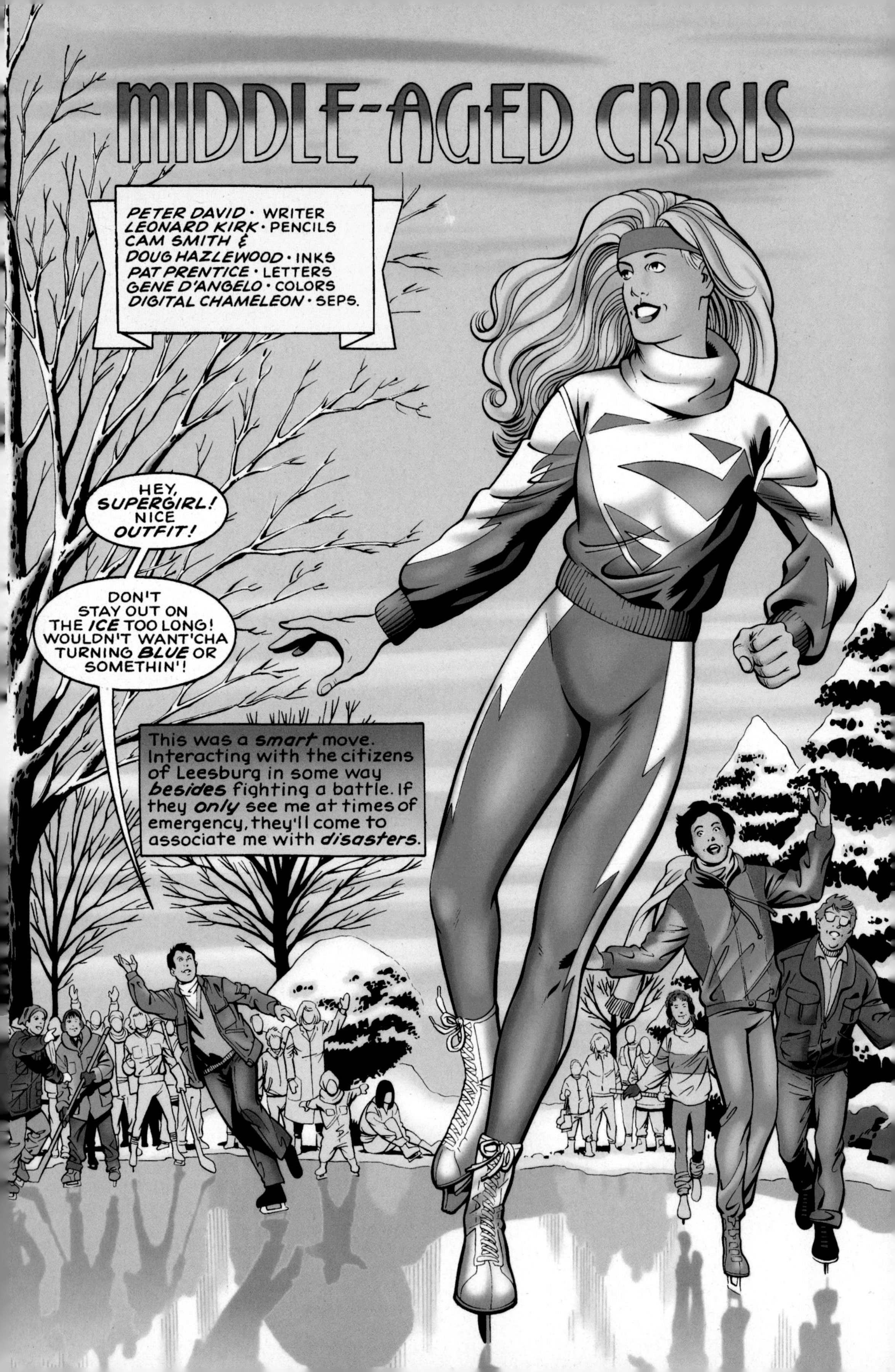
MIDDLE-AGED CRISIS
PETER DAVID • WRITER
LEONARD KIRK • PENCILS
CAM SMITH &
DOUG HAZLEWOOD • INKS
PAT PRENTICE • LETTERS
GENE D'ANGELO • COLORS
DIGITAL CHAMELEON • SEPS.
HEY, SUPERGIRL! NICE OUTFIT!
DON'T STAY OUT ON THE ICE TOO LONG! WOULDN'T WANT'CHA TURNING BLUE OR SOMETHIN'!
This was a smart move. Interacting with the citizens of Leesburg in some way besides fighting a battle. If they only see me at times of emergency, they'll come to associate me with disasters.

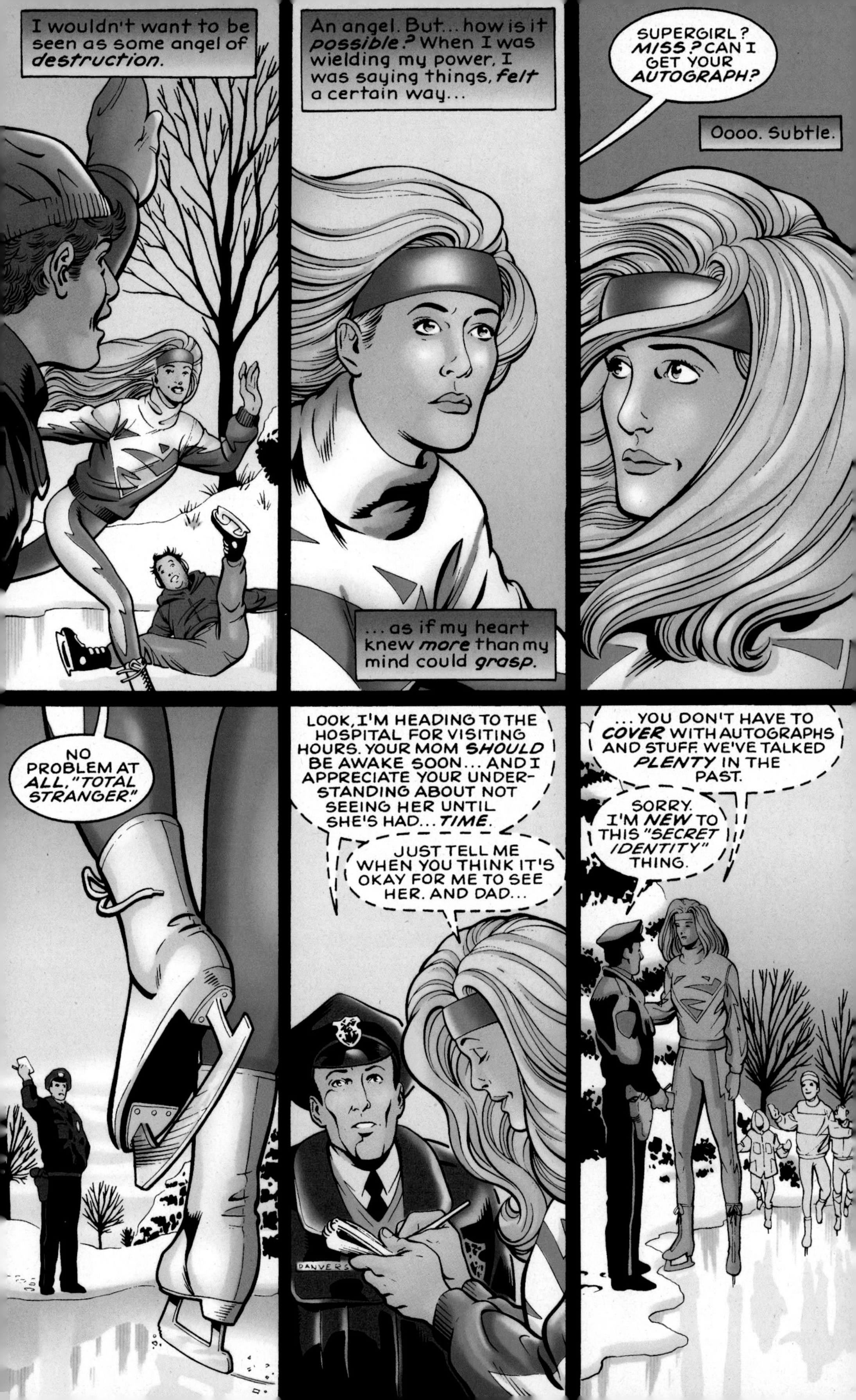

I wouldn't want to be seen as some angel of *destruction*.
An angel. But... how is it *possible?* When I was wielding my power, I was saying things, *felt* a certain way...
...as if my heart knew *more* than my mind could *grasp*.
SUPERGIRL? *MISS?* CAN I GET YOUR *AUTOGRAPH?*
Oooo. Subtle.
NO PROBLEM AT *ALL*, "*TOTAL STRANGER*."
LOOK, I'M HEADING TO THE HOSPITAL FOR VISITING HOURS. YOUR MOM *SHOULD* BE AWAKE SOON... AND I APPRECIATE YOUR UNDER-STANDING ABOUT NOT SEEING HER UNTIL SHE'S HAD... *TIME*.
JUST TELL ME WHEN YOU THINK IT'S OKAY FOR ME TO SEE HER. AND DAD...
DANVERS
...YOU DON'T HAVE TO *COVER* WITH AUTOGRAPHS AND STUFF. WE'VE TALKED *PLENTY* IN THE PAST.
SORRY. I'M *NEW* TO THIS "*SECRET IDENTITY*" THING.

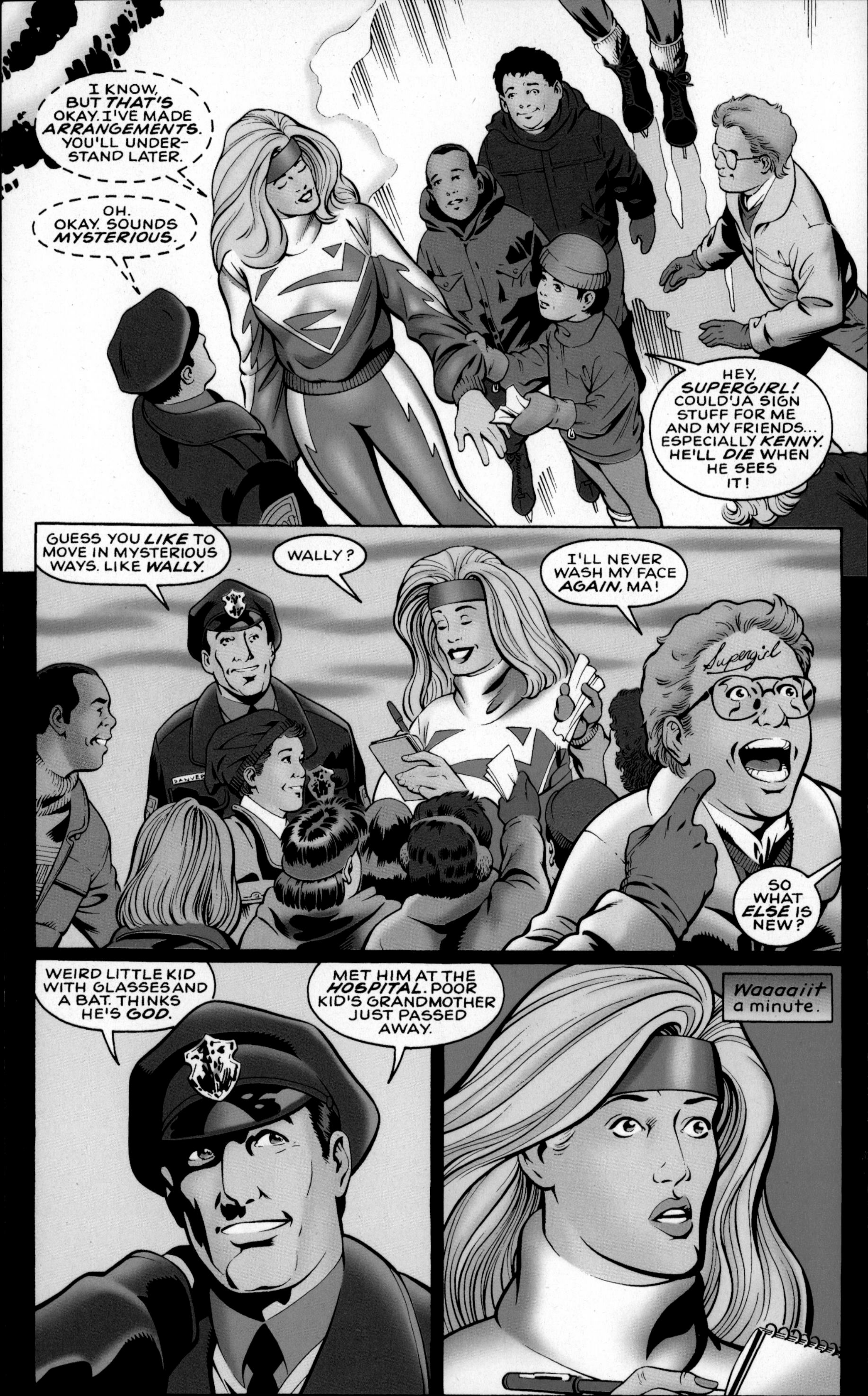
I KNOW, BUT THAT'S OKAY. I'VE MADE ARRANGEMENTS. YOU'LL UNDERSTAND LATER.
OH. OKAY. SOUNDS MYSTERIOUS.
HEY, SUPERGIRL! COULD'JA SIGN STUFF FOR ME AND MY FRIENDS... ESPECIALLY KENNY. HE'LL DIE WHEN HE SEES IT!
GUESS YOU LIKE TO MOVE IN MYSTERIOUS WAYS. LIKE WALLY.
WALLY?
I'LL NEVER WASH MY FACE AGAIN, MA!
Supergirl
SO WHAT ELSE IS NEW?
WEIRD LITTLE KID WITH GLASSES AND A BAT. THINKS HE'S GOD.
MET HIM AT THE HOSPITAL. POOR KID'S GRANDMOTHER JUST PASSED AWAY.
Waaaaiit a minute.

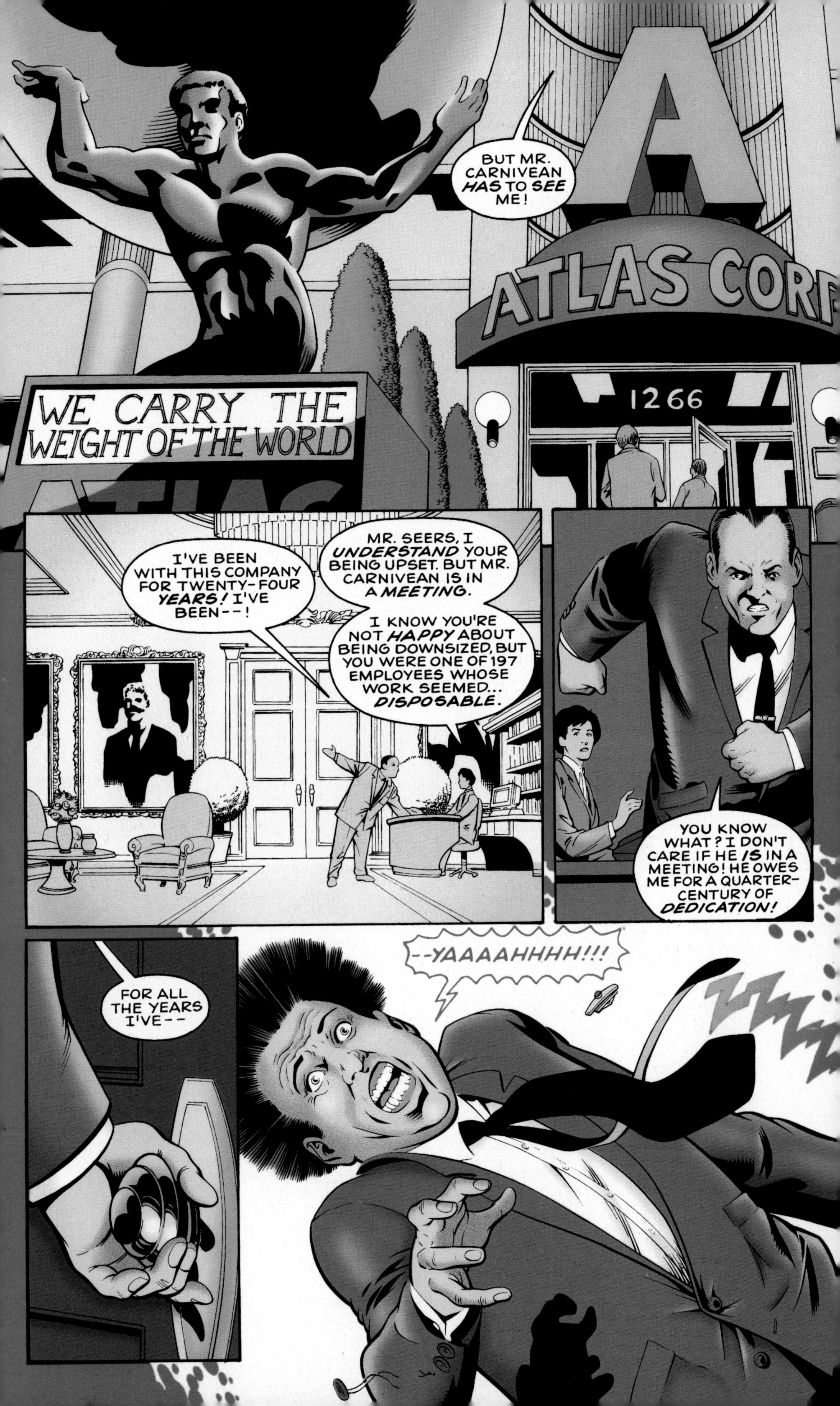

BUT MR. CARNIVEAN HAS TO SEE ME!
ATLAS CORP
WE CARRY THE WEIGHT OF THE WORLD
1266
I'VE BEEN WITH THIS COMPANY FOR TWENTY-FOUR YEARS! I'VE BEEN--!
MR. SEERS, I UNDERSTAND YOUR BEING UPSET. BUT MR. CARNIVEAN IS IN A MEETING.
I KNOW YOU'RE NOT HAPPY ABOUT BEING DOWNSIZED, BUT YOU WERE ONE OF 197 EMPLOYEES WHOSE WORK SEEMED... DISPOSABLE.
YOU KNOW WHAT? I DON'T CARE IF HE IS IN A MEETING! HE OWES ME FOR A QUARTER-CENTURY OF DEDICATION!
FOR ALL THE YEARS I'VE--
--YAAAAHHHH!!!

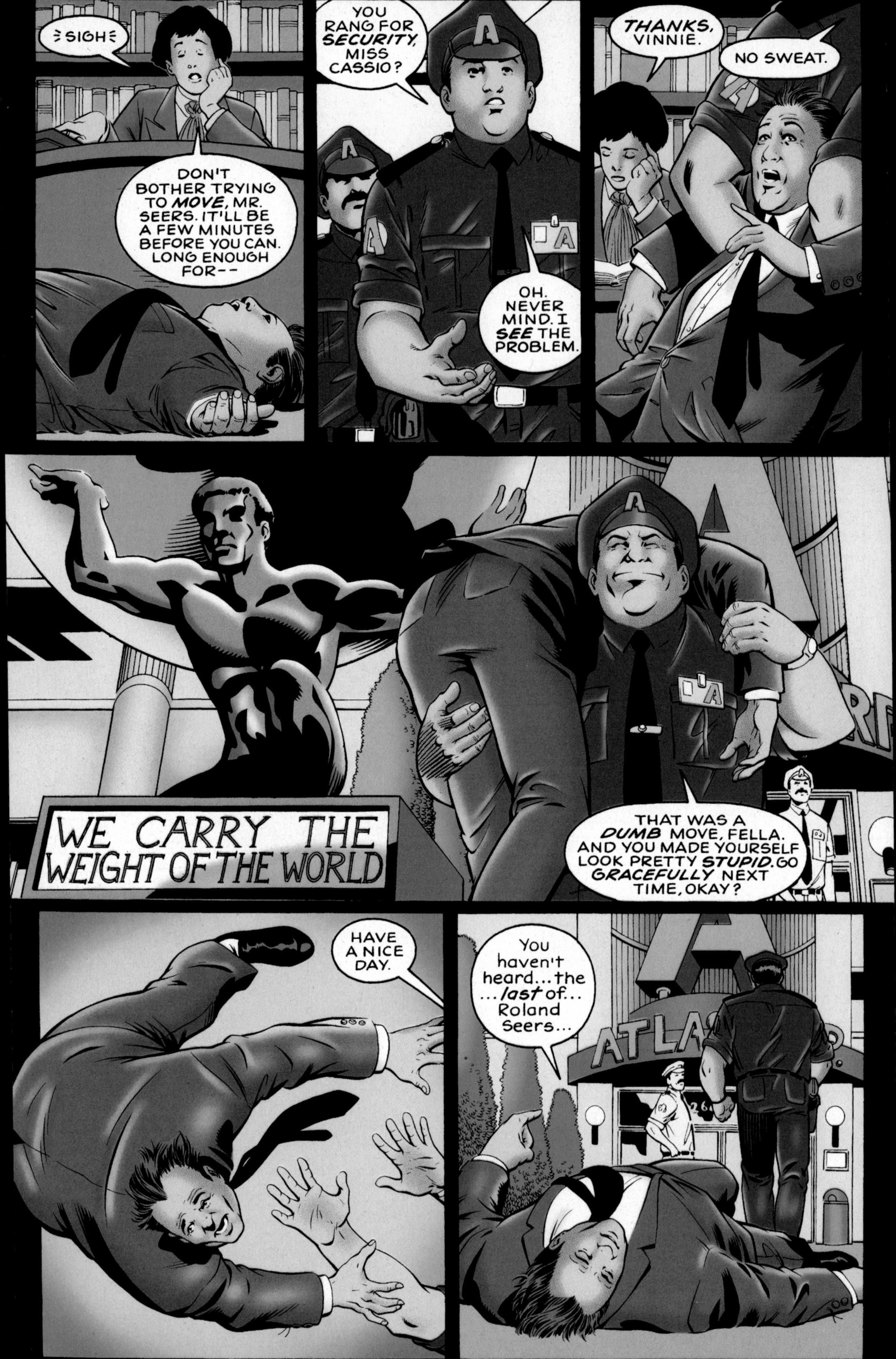

SIGH
DON'T BOTHER TRYING TO MOVE, MR. SEERS. IT'LL BE A FEW MINUTES BEFORE YOU CAN. LONG ENOUGH FOR--
YOU RANG FOR SECURITY, MISS CASSIO?
OH. NEVER MIND. I SEE THE PROBLEM.
THANKS, VINNIE.
NO SWEAT.
WE CARRY THE WEIGHT OF THE WORLD
THAT WAS A DUMB MOVE, FELLA. AND YOU MADE YOURSELF LOOK PRETTY STUPID. GO GRACEFULLY NEXT TIME, OKAY?
HAVE A NICE DAY.
You haven't heard... the ...last of... Roland Seers...

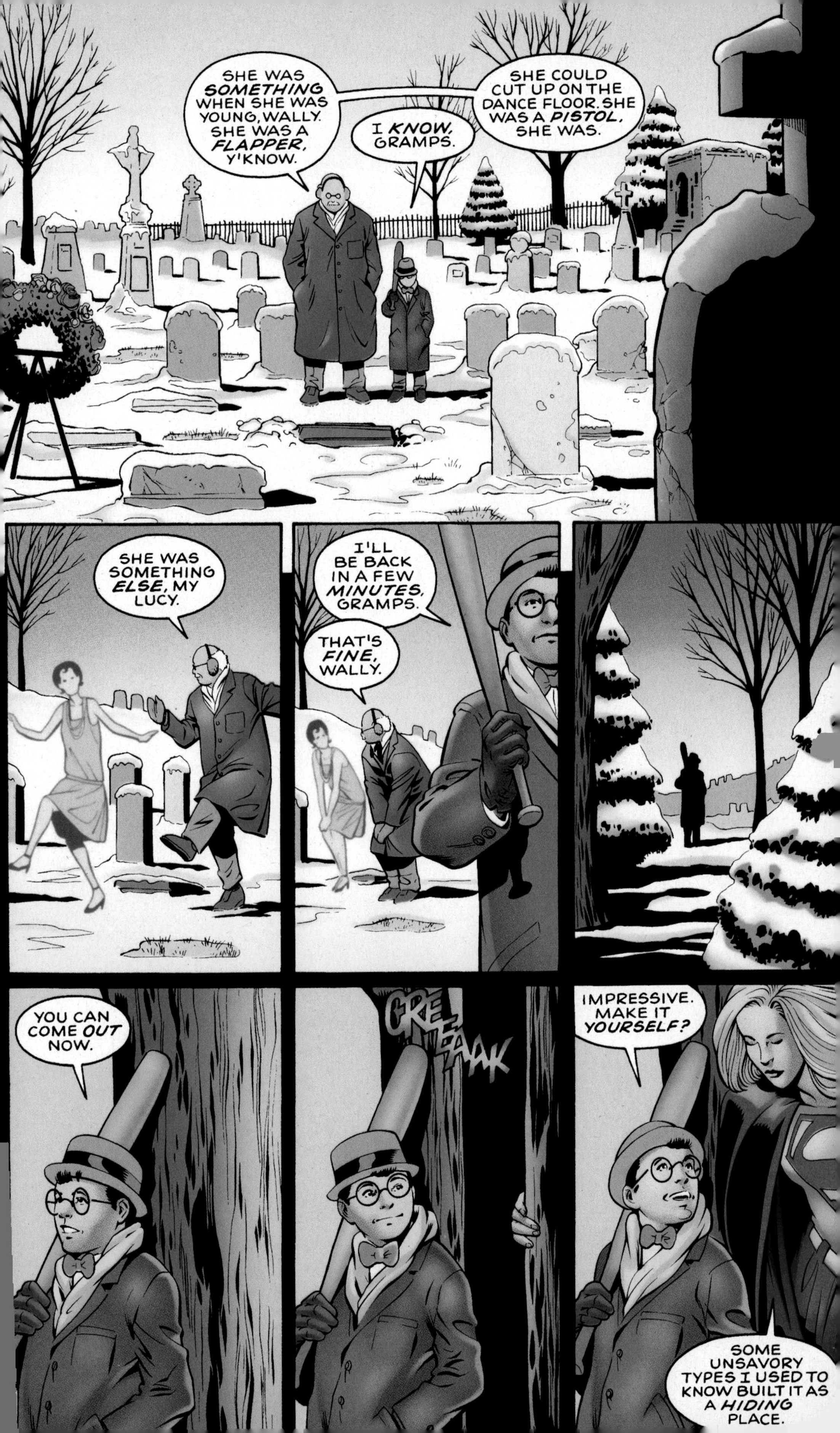
SHE WAS SOMETHING WHEN SHE WAS YOUNG, WALLY. SHE WAS A FLAPPER, Y'KNOW.
SHE COULD CUT UP ON THE DANCE FLOOR. SHE WAS A PISTOL, SHE WAS.
I KNOW, GRAMPS.
SHE WAS SOMETHING ELSE, MY LUCY.
I'LL BE BACK IN A FEW MINUTES, GRAMPS.
THAT'S FINE, WALLY.
YOU CAN COME OUT NOW.
CREEEAAAK
IMPRESSIVE. MAKE IT YOURSELF?
SOME UNSAVORY TYPES I USED TO KNOW BUILT IT AS A HIDING PLACE.

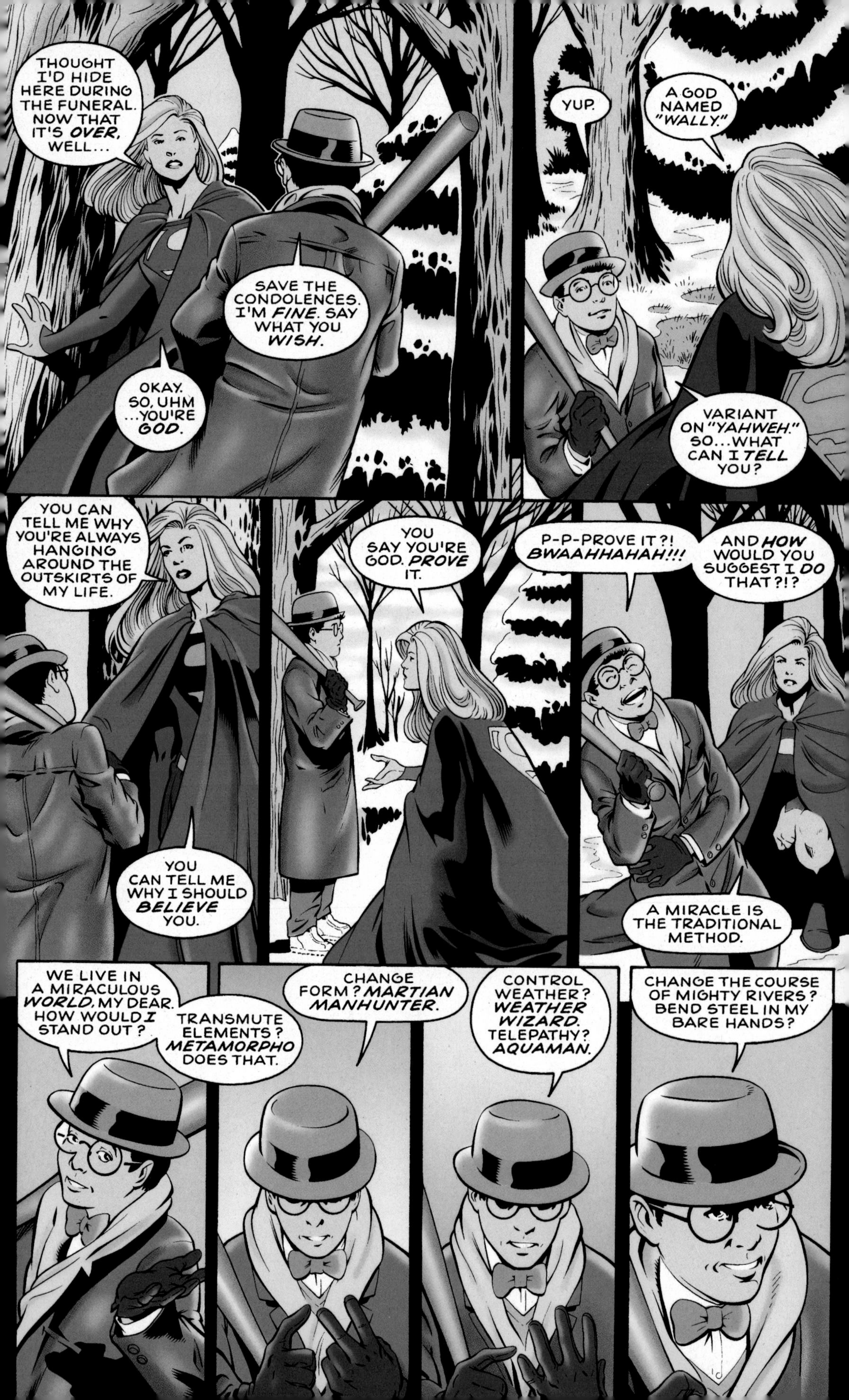
THOUGHT I'D HIDE HERE DURING THE FUNERAL. NOW THAT IT'S *OVER*, WELL...
SAVE THE CONDOLENCES. I'M *FINE*. SAY WHAT YOU *WISH*.
OKAY. SO, UHM ...YOU'RE *GOD*.
YUP.
A GOD NAMED *"WALLY."*
VARIANT ON "*YAHWEH*." SO...WHAT CAN I *TELL* YOU?
YOU CAN TELL ME WHY YOU'RE ALWAYS HANGING AROUND THE OUTSKIRTS OF MY LIFE.
YOU CAN TELL ME WHY I SHOULD *BELIEVE* YOU.
YOU SAY YOU'RE GOD. *PROVE* IT.
P-P-PROVE IT?! *BWAAHHAHAH!!!*
AND *HOW* WOULD YOU SUGGEST I *DO* THAT?!?
A MIRACLE IS THE TRADITIONAL METHOD.
WE LIVE IN A MIRACULOUS *WORLD*, MY DEAR. HOW WOULD *I* STAND OUT?
TRANSMUTE ELEMENTS? *METAMORPHO* DOES THAT.
CHANGE FORM? *MARTIAN MANHUNTER*.
CONTROL WEATHER? *WEATHER WIZARD*. TELEPATHY? *AQUAMAN*.
CHANGE THE COURSE OF MIGHTY RIVERS? BEND STEEL IN MY BARE HANDS?

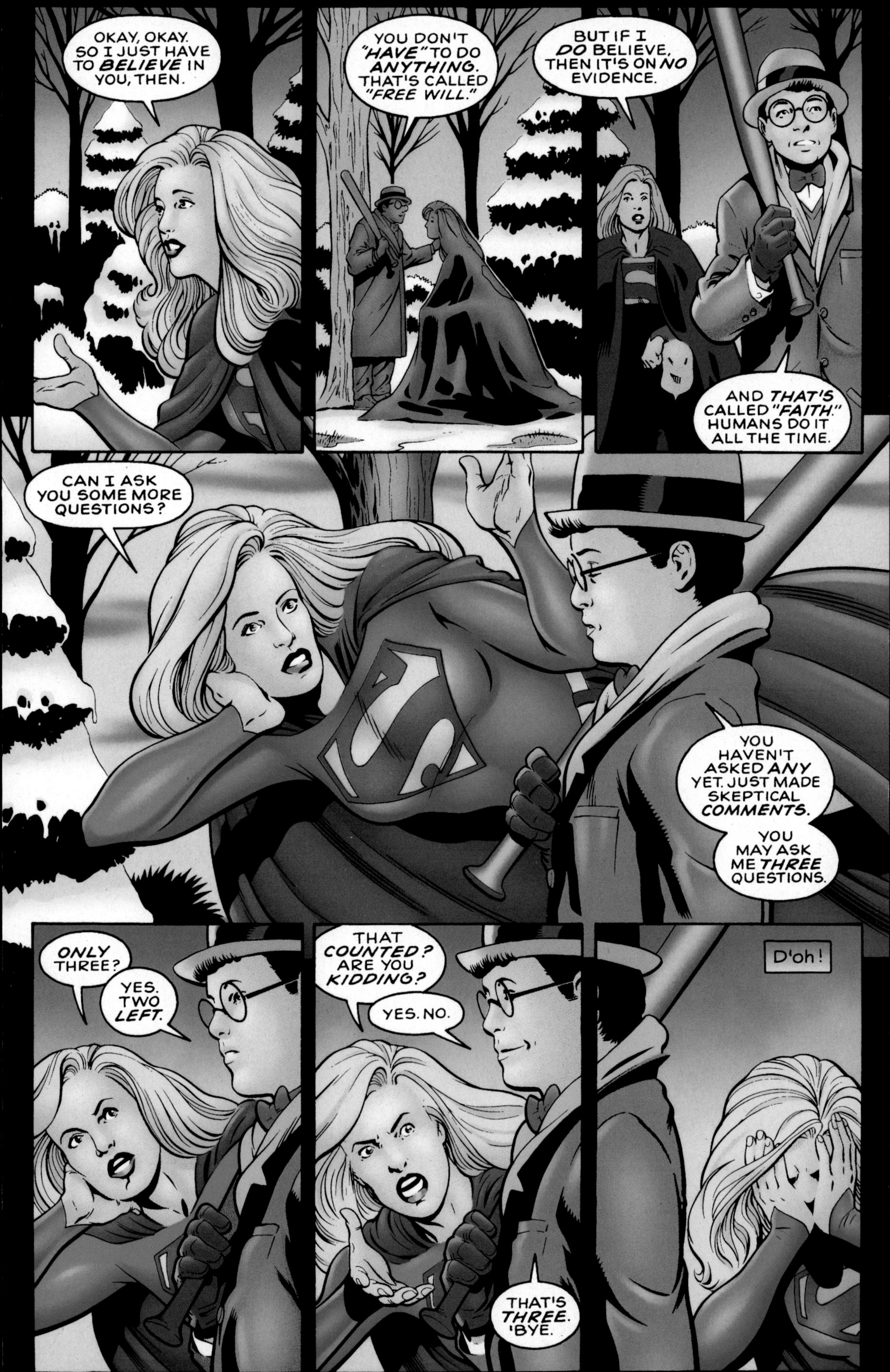
OKAY, OKAY. SO I JUST HAVE TO *BELIEVE* IN YOU, THEN.
YOU DON'T *"HAVE"* TO DO *ANYTHING*. THAT'S CALLED *"FREE WILL."*
BUT IF I *DO* BELIEVE, THEN IT'S ON *NO* EVIDENCE.
AND *THAT'S* CALLED *"FAITH."* HUMANS DO IT ALL THE TIME.
CAN I ASK YOU SOME MORE QUESTIONS?
YOU HAVEN'T ASKED *ANY* YET. JUST MADE SKEPTICAL *COMMENTS*.
YOU MAY ASK ME *THREE* QUESTIONS.
ONLY THREE?
YES. TWO *LEFT*.
THAT *COUNTED?* ARE YOU *KIDDING?*
YES. NO.
THAT'S *THREE*. 'BYE.
D'oh!

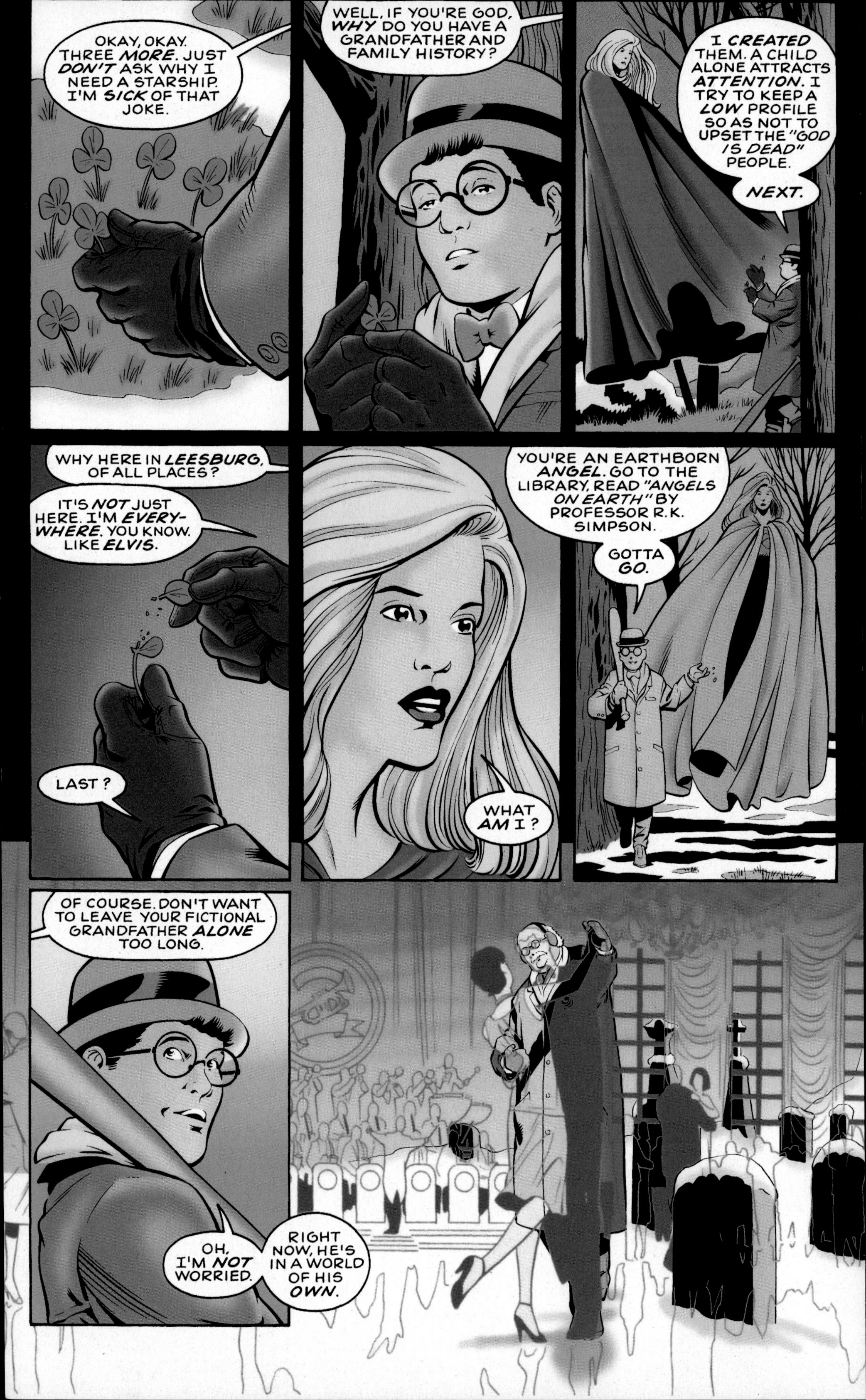
OKAY, OKAY. THREE MORE. JUST DON'T ASK WHY I NEED A STARSHIP. I'M SICK OF THAT JOKE.
WELL, IF YOU'RE GOD, WHY DO YOU HAVE A GRANDFATHER AND FAMILY HISTORY?
I CREATED THEM. A CHILD ALONE ATTRACTS ATTENTION. I TRY TO KEEP A LOW PROFILE SO AS NOT TO UPSET THE "GOD IS DEAD" PEOPLE.
NEXT.
WHY HERE IN LEESBURG, OF ALL PLACES?
IT'S NOT JUST HERE. I'M EVERY-WHERE. YOU KNOW. LIKE ELVIS.
LAST?
WHAT AM I?
YOU'RE AN EARTHBORN ANGEL. GO TO THE LIBRARY, READ "ANGELS ON EARTH" BY PROFESSOR R.K. SIMPSON.
GOTTA GO.
OF COURSE. DON'T WANT TO LEAVE YOUR FICTIONAL GRANDFATHER ALONE TOO LONG.
OH, I'M NOT WORRIED.
RIGHT NOW, HE'S IN A WORLD OF HIS OWN.

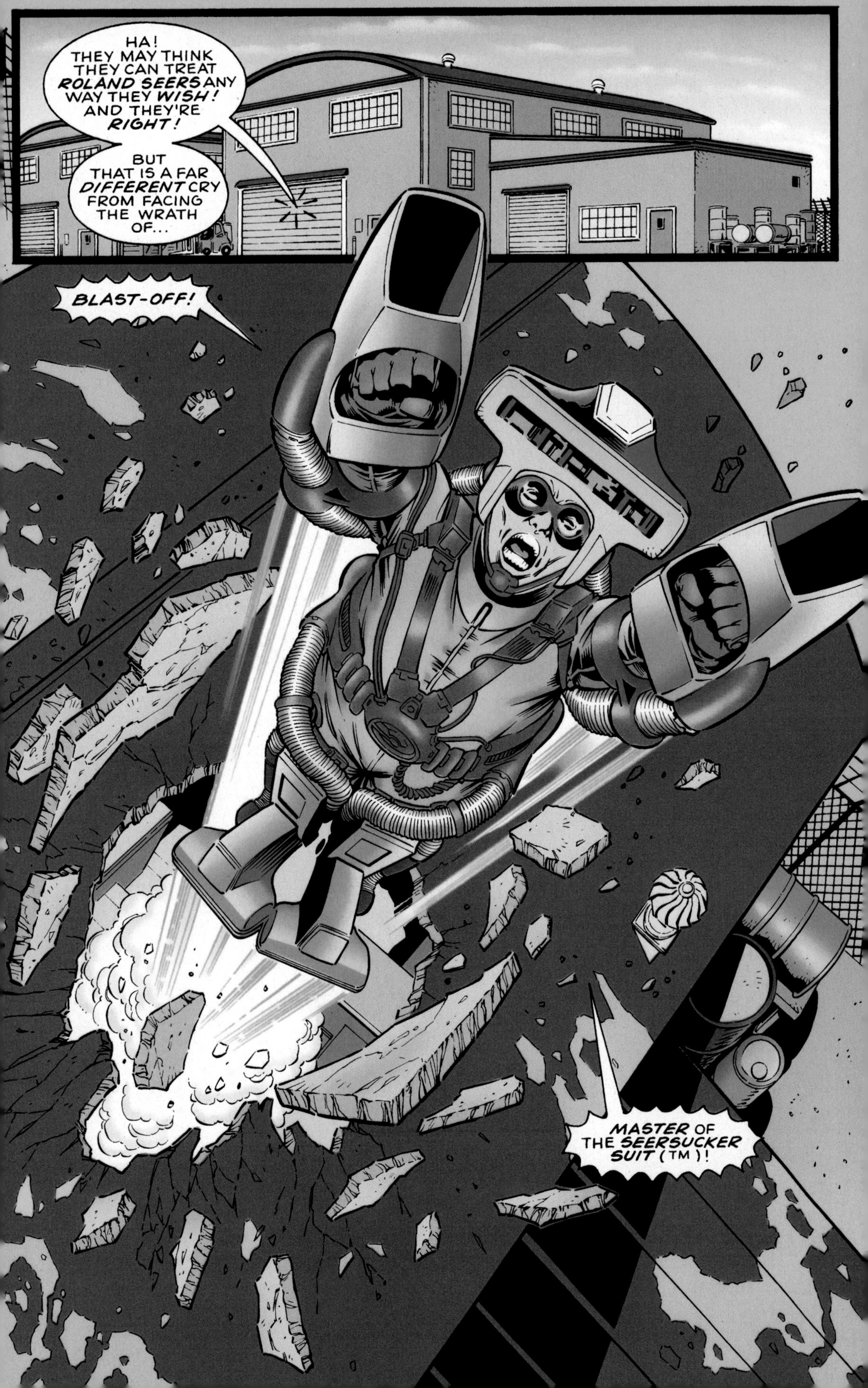
HA! THEY MAY THINK THEY CAN TREAT ROLAND SEERS ANY WAY THEY WISH! AND THEY'RE RIGHT!
BUT THAT IS A FAR DIFFERENT CRY FROM FACING THE WRATH OF...
BLAST-OFF!
MASTER OF THE SEERSUCKER SUIT (TM)!

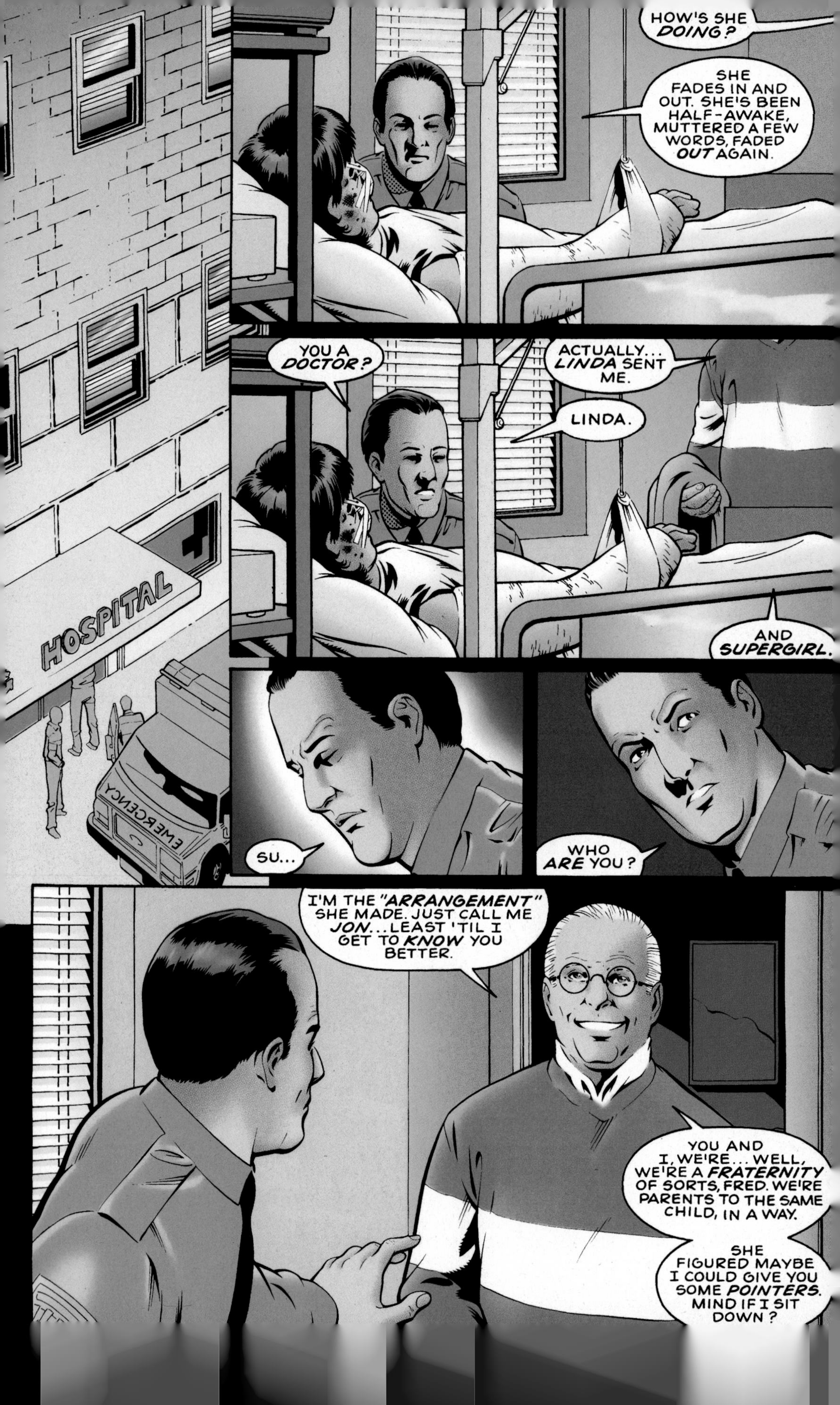
HOW'S SHE DOING?
SHE FADES IN AND OUT. SHE'S BEEN HALF-AWAKE, MUTTERED A FEW WORDS, FADED OUT AGAIN.
HOSPITAL
EMERGENCY
YOU A DOCTOR?
ACTUALLY... LINDA SENT ME.
LINDA.
AND SUPERGIRL.
SU...
WHO ARE YOU?
I'M THE "ARRANGEMENT" SHE MADE. JUST CALL ME JON... LEAST 'TIL I GET TO KNOW YOU BETTER.
YOU AND I, WE'RE... WELL, WE'RE A FRATERNITY OF SORTS, FRED. WE'RE PARENTS TO THE SAME CHILD, IN A WAY.
SHE FIGURED MAYBE I COULD GIVE YOU SOME POINTERS. MIND IF I SIT DOWN?

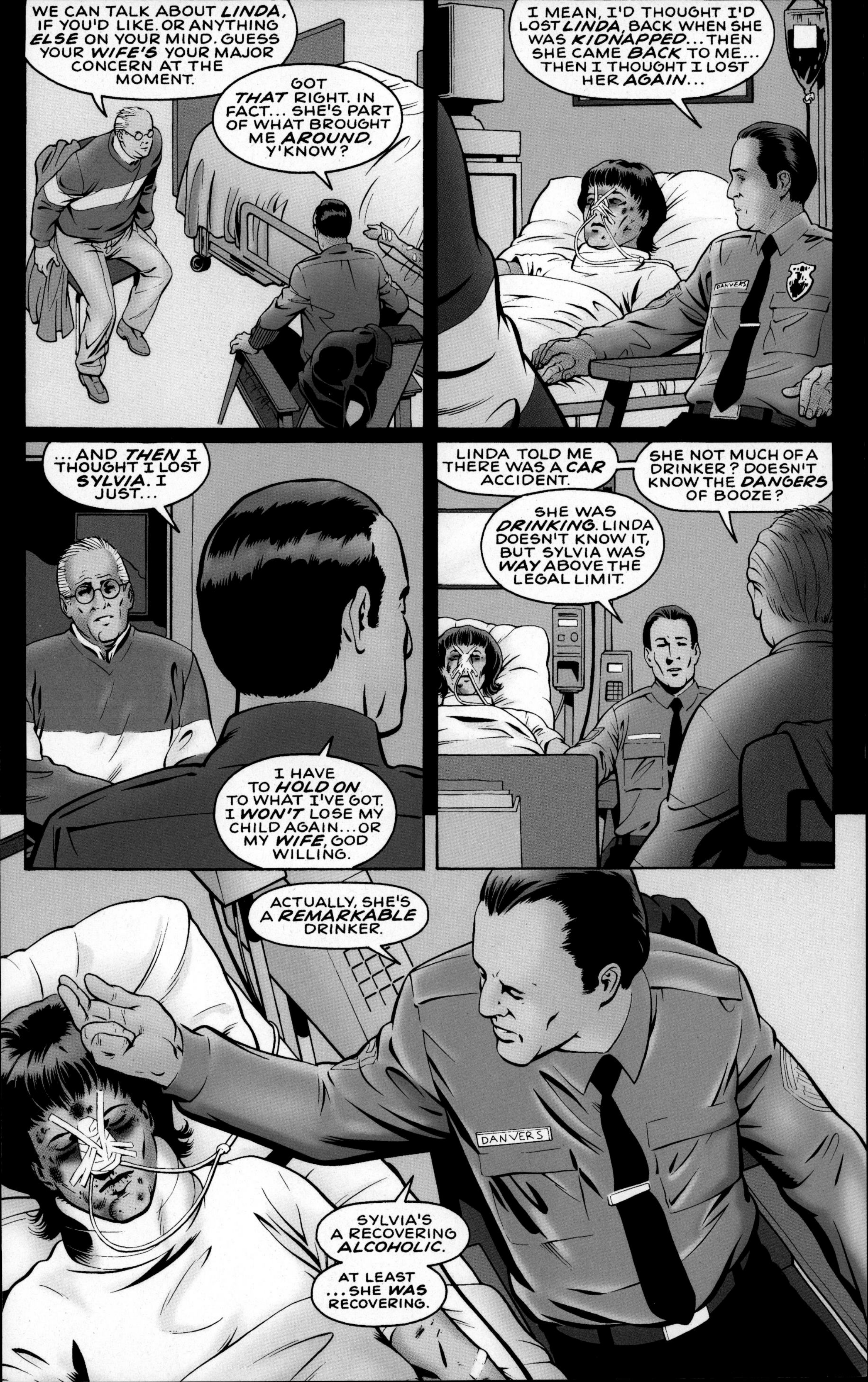
WE CAN TALK ABOUT LINDA, IF YOU'D LIKE. OR ANYTHING ELSE ON YOUR MIND. GUESS YOUR WIFE'S YOUR MAJOR CONCERN AT THE MOMENT.
GOT THAT RIGHT. IN FACT... SHE'S PART OF WHAT BROUGHT ME AROUND, Y'KNOW?
I MEAN, I'D THOUGHT I'D LOST LINDA, BACK WHEN SHE WAS KIDNAPPED... THEN SHE CAME BACK TO ME... THEN I THOUGHT I LOST HER AGAIN...
DANVERS
...AND THEN I THOUGHT I LOST SYLVIA. I JUST...
I HAVE TO HOLD ON TO WHAT I'VE GOT. I WON'T LOSE MY CHILD AGAIN...OR MY WIFE, GOD WILLING.
LINDA TOLD ME THERE WAS A CAR ACCIDENT.
SHE NOT MUCH OF A DRINKER? DOESN'T KNOW THE DANGERS OF BOOZE?
SHE WAS DRINKING. LINDA DOESN'T KNOW IT, BUT SYLVIA WAS WAY ABOVE THE LEGAL LIMIT.
ACTUALLY, SHE'S A REMARKABLE DRINKER.
DANVERS
SYLVIA'S A RECOVERING ALCOHOLIC.
AT LEAST ...SHE WAS RECOVERING.

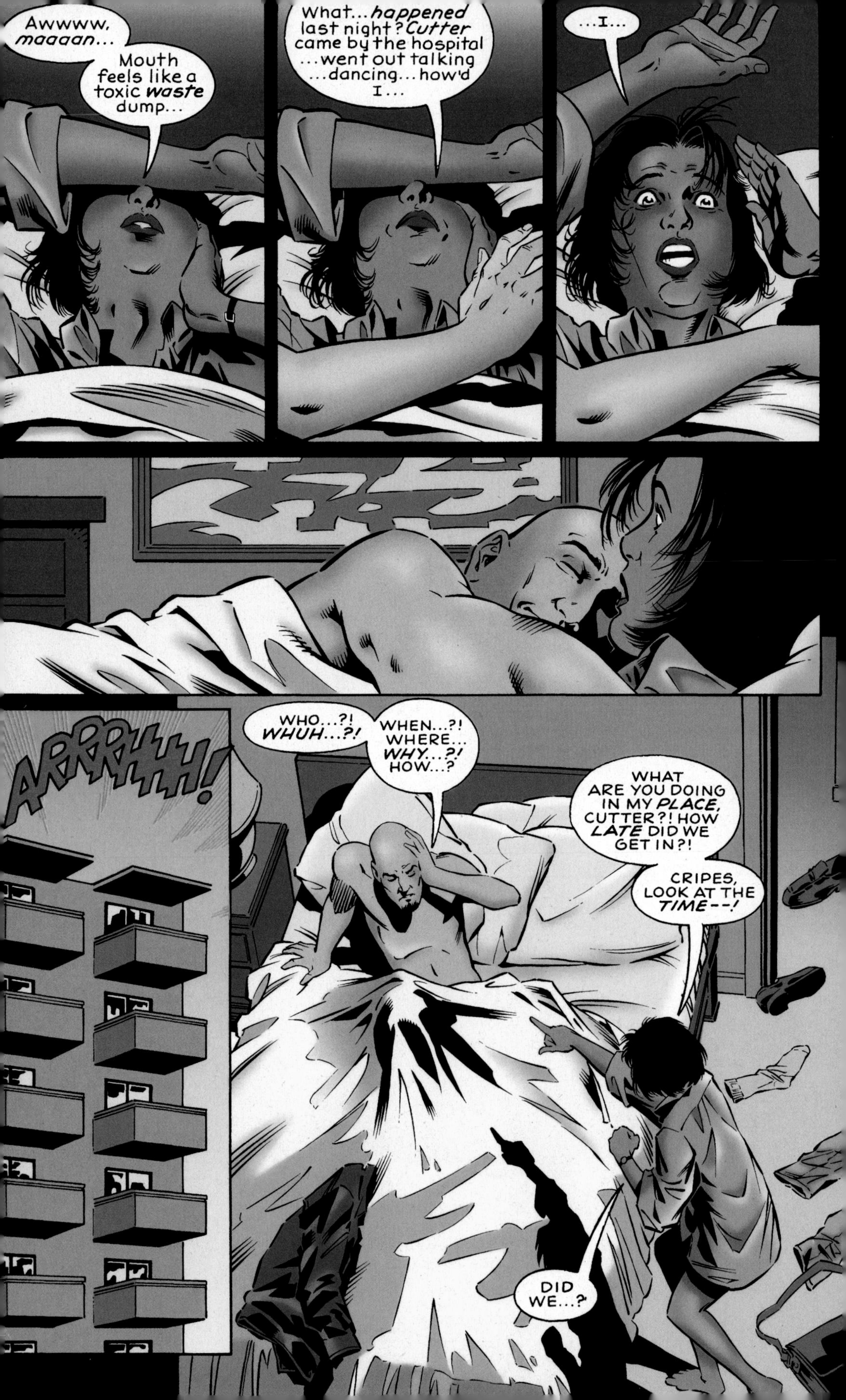
Awwww, maaaan... Mouth feels like a toxic waste dump...
What... happened last night? Cutter came by the hospital ...went out talking ...dancing... how'd I...
...I...
ARRRHHH!
WHO...?! WHUH...?!
WHEN...?! WHERE... WHY...?! HOW...?
WHAT ARE YOU DOING IN MY PLACE, CUTTER?! HOW LATE DID WE GET IN?!
CRIPES, LOOK AT THE TIME--!
DID WE...?

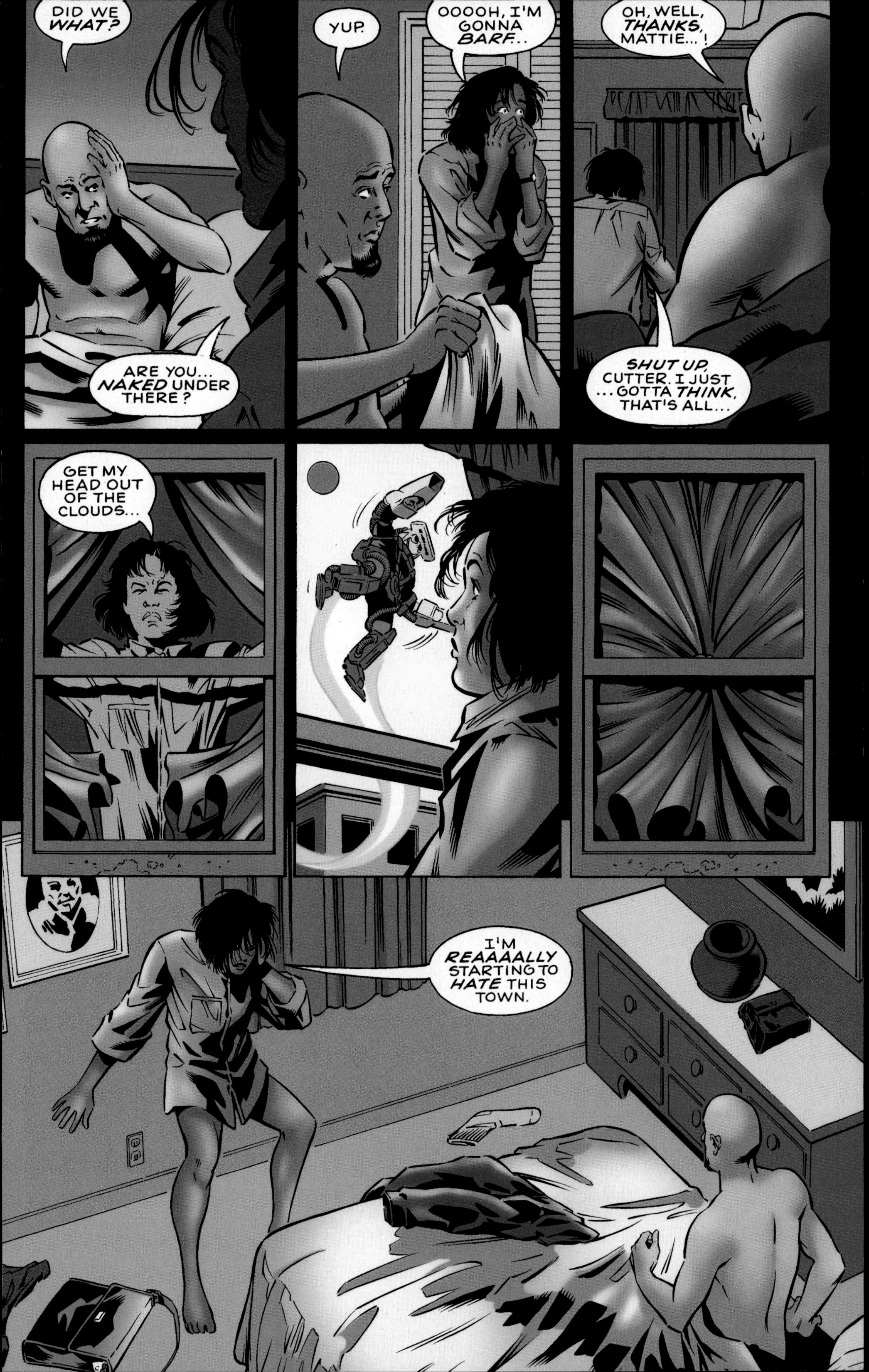
DID WE *WHAT?*
ARE YOU... *NAKED* UNDER THERE?
YUP.
OOOOH, I'M GONNA *BARF*...
OH, WELL, *THANKS,* MATTIE...!
SHUT UP, CUTTER. I JUST ...GOTTA *THINK,* THAT'S ALL...
GET MY HEAD OUT OF THE CLOUDS...
I'M *REAAAALLY* STARTING TO *HATE* THIS TOWN.

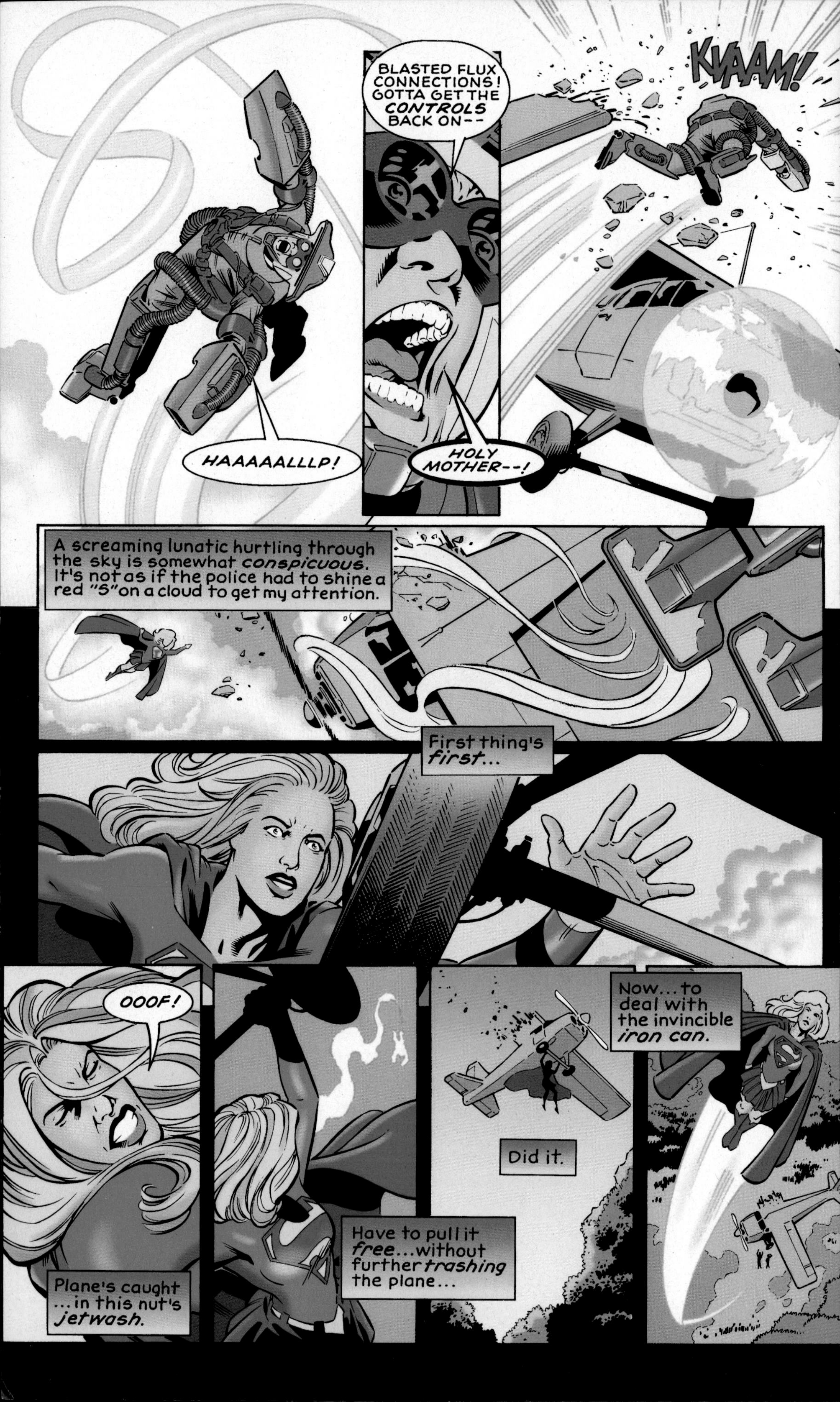
HAAAAALLLP!
BLASTED FLUX CONNECTIONS! GOTTA GET THE CONTROLS BACK ON--
HOLY MOTHER--!
KVAAM!
A screaming lunatic hurtling through the sky is somewhat conspicuous. It's not as if the police had to shine a red "S" on a cloud to get my attention.
First thing's first...
OOOF!
Plane's caught ...in this nut's jetwash.
Have to pull it free...without further trashing the plane...
Did it.
Now...to deal with the invincible iron can.

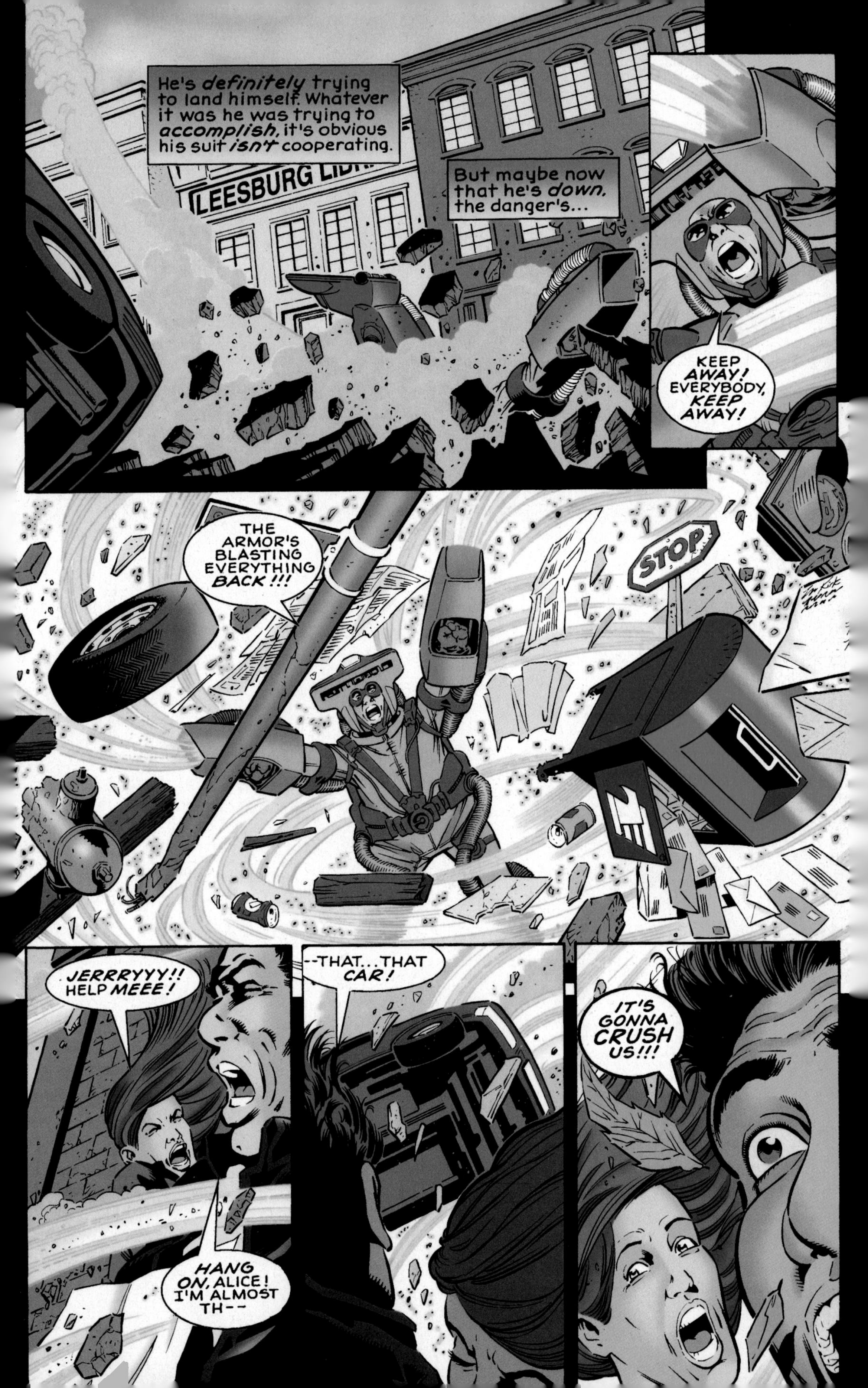
He's definitely trying to land himself. Whatever it was he was trying to accomplish, it's obvious his suit isn't cooperating.
LEESBURG LIBR
But maybe now that he's down, the danger's...
KEEP AWAY! EVERYBODY, KEEP AWAY!
THE ARMOR'S BLASTING EVERYTHING BACK!!!
STOP
JERRRYYY!! HELP MEEE!
HANG ON, ALICE! I'M ALMOST TH--
--THAT...THAT CAR!
IT'S GONNA CRUSH US!!!

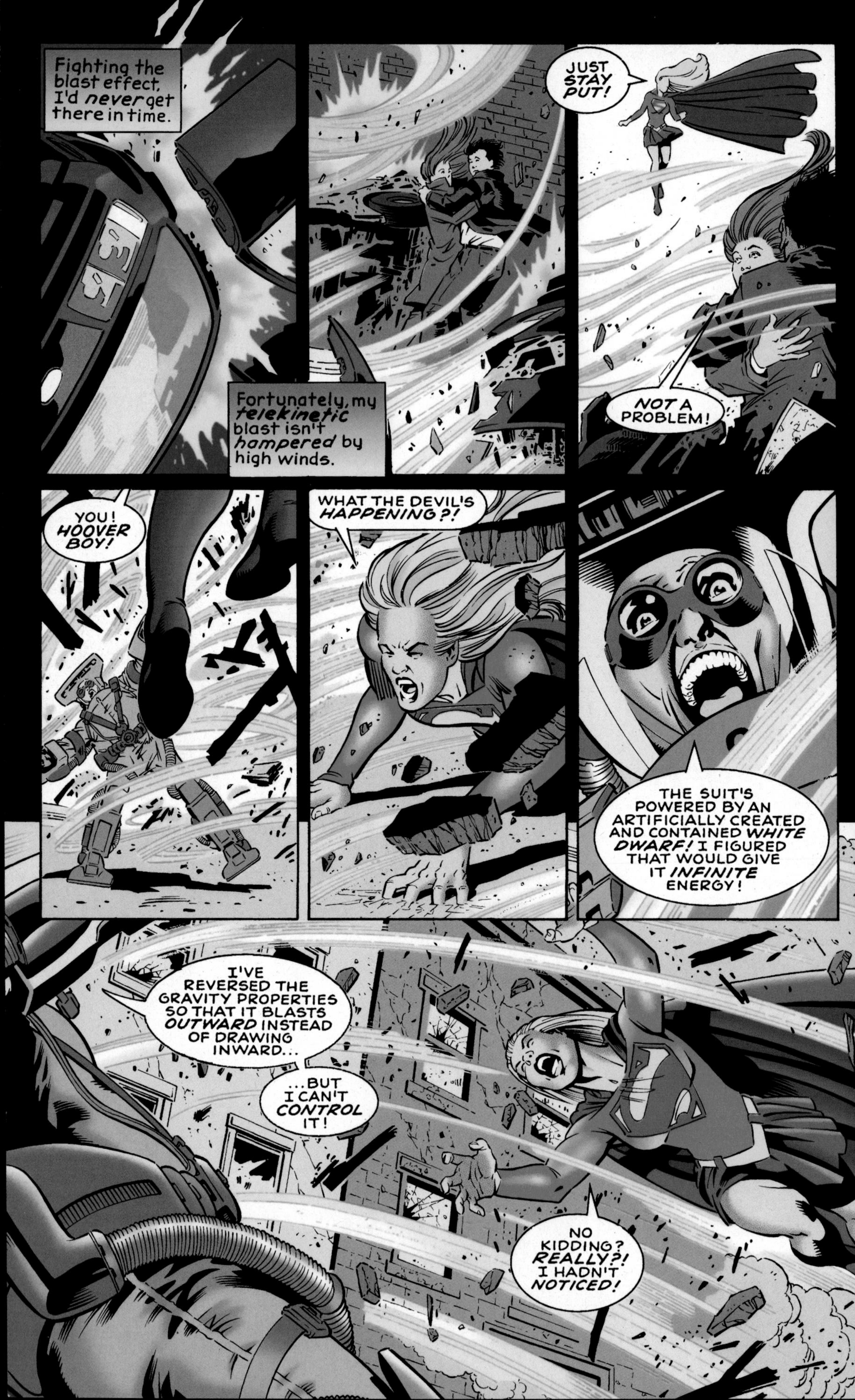
Fighting the blast effect, I'd *never* get there in time.
Fortunately, my *telekinetic* blast isn't *hampered* by high winds.
JUST *STAY PUT!*
NOT A PROBLEM!
YOU! *HOOVER BOY!*
WHAT THE DEVIL'S *HAPPENING?!*
THE SUIT'S POWERED BY AN ARTIFICIALLY CREATED AND CONTAINED *WHITE DWARF!* I FIGURED THAT WOULD GIVE IT *INFINITE* ENERGY!
I'VE REVERSED THE GRAVITY PROPERTIES SO THAT IT BLASTS *OUTWARD* INSTEAD OF DRAWING INWARD...
...BUT I CAN'T *CONTROL* IT!
NO KIDDING? *REALLY?!* I HADN'T *NOTICED!*

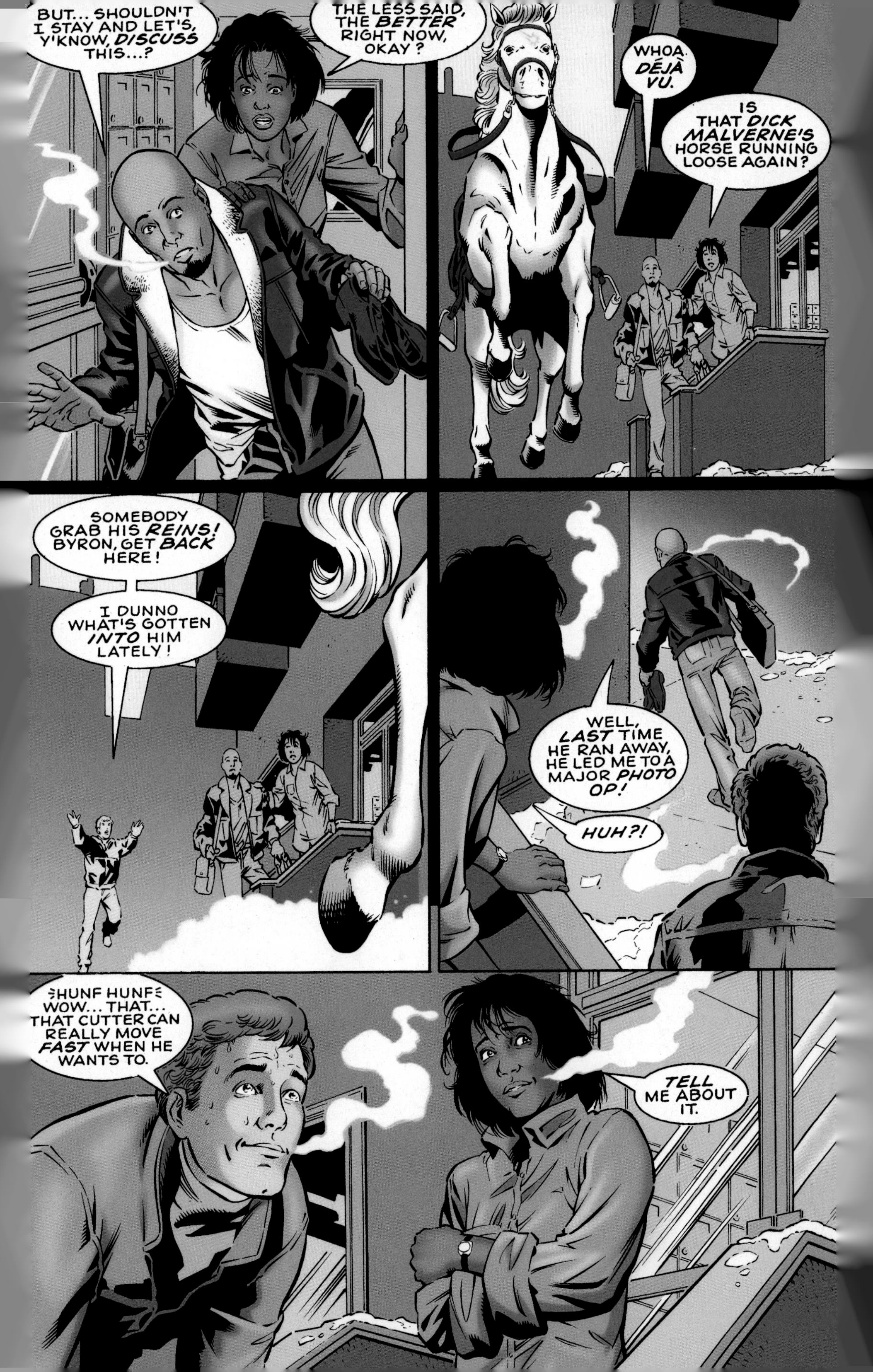
BUT... SHOULDN'T I STAY AND LET'S, Y'KNOW, DISCUSS THIS...?
THE LESS SAID, THE BETTER RIGHT NOW, OKAY?
WHOA. DÉJÀ VU.
IS THAT DICK MALVERNE'S HORSE RUNNING LOOSE AGAIN?
SOMEBODY GRAB HIS REINS! BYRON, GET BACK HERE!
I DUNNO WHAT'S GOTTEN INTO HIM LATELY!
WELL, LAST TIME HE RAN AWAY, HE LED ME TO A MAJOR PHOTO OP!
HUH?!
HUNF HUNF WOW... THAT... THAT CUTTER CAN REALLY MOVE FAST WHEN HE WANTS TO.
TELL ME ABOUT IT.

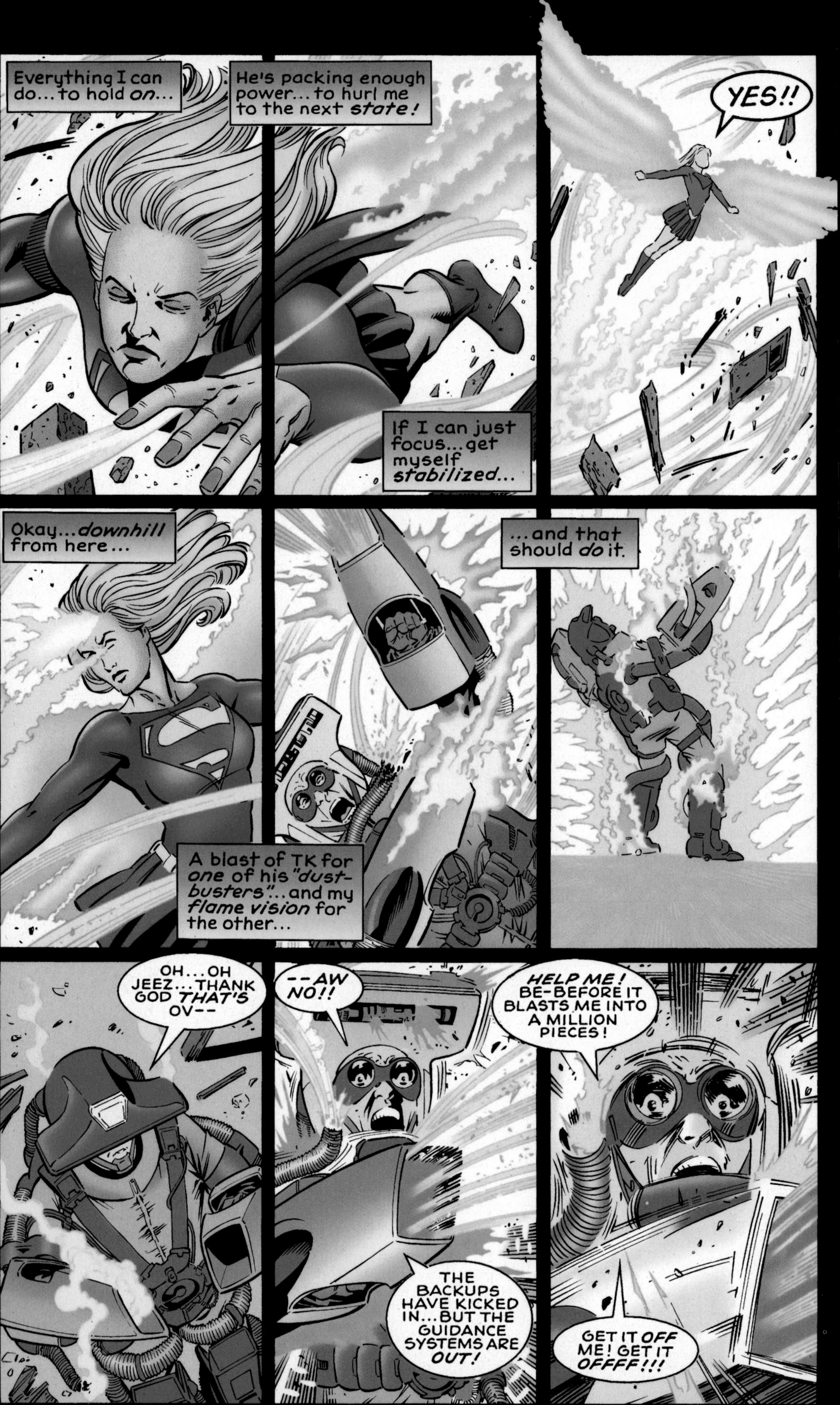

Everything I can do... to hold on...
He's packing enough power... to hurl me to the next state!
If I can just focus... get myself stabilized...
YES!!
Okay... downhill from here...
A blast of TK for one of his "dust-busters"... and my flame vision for the other...
...and that should do it.
OH... OH JEEZ... THANK GOD THAT'S OV--
--AW NO!!
THE BACKUPS HAVE KICKED IN... BUT THE GUIDANCE SYSTEMS ARE OUT!
HELP ME! BE-BEFORE IT BLASTS ME INTO A MILLION PIECES!
GET IT OFF ME! GET IT OFFFF!!!

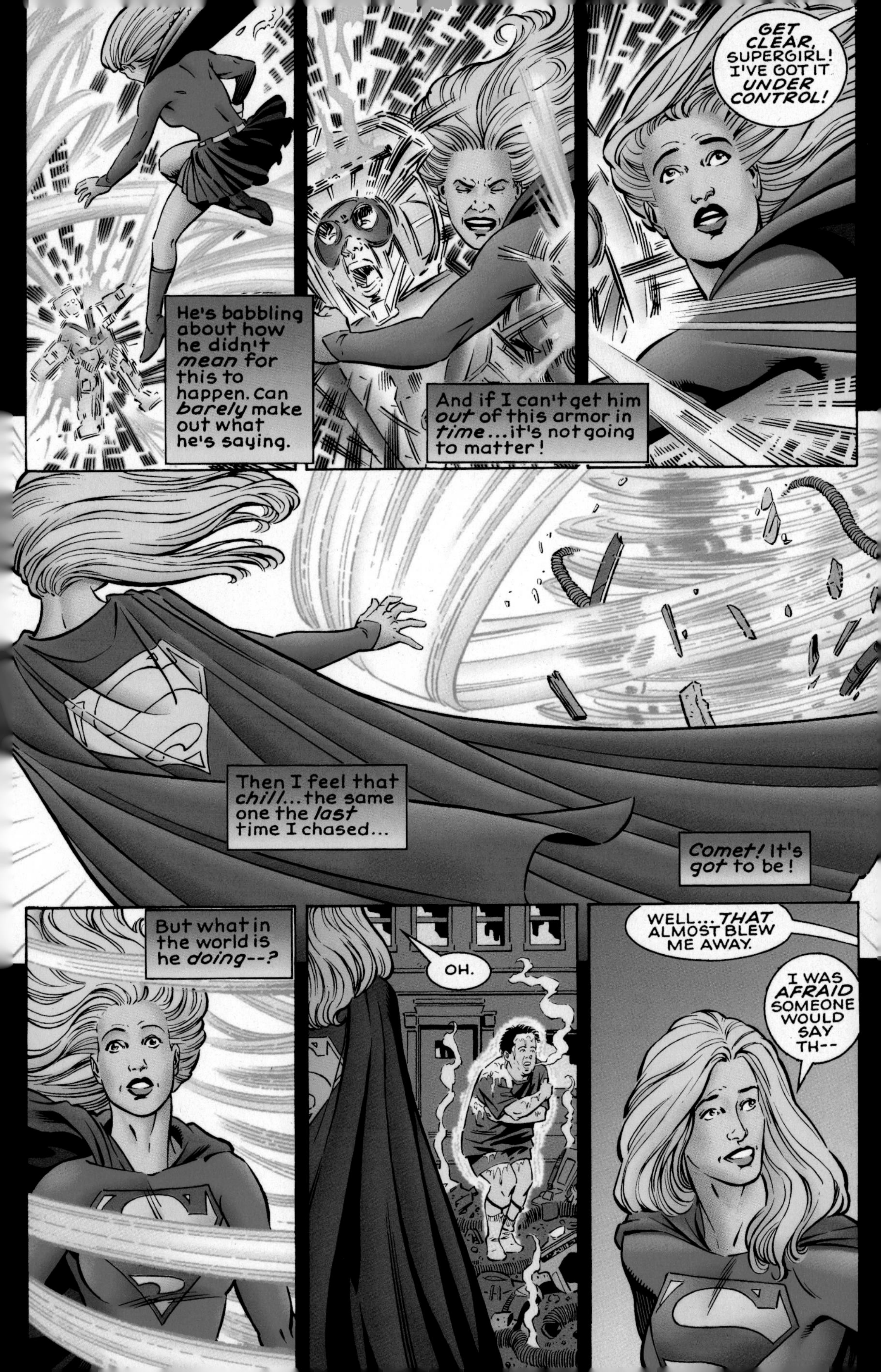
GET CLEAR, SUPERGIRL! I'VE GOT IT UNDER CONTROL!
He's babbling about how he didn't mean for this to happen. Can barely make out what he's saying.
And if I can't get him out of this armor in time... it's not going to matter!
Then I feel that chill... the same one the last time I chased...
Comet! It's got to be!
But what in the world is he doing--?
OH.
WELL... THAT ALMOST BLEW ME AWAY.
I WAS AFRAID SOMEONE WOULD SAY TH--

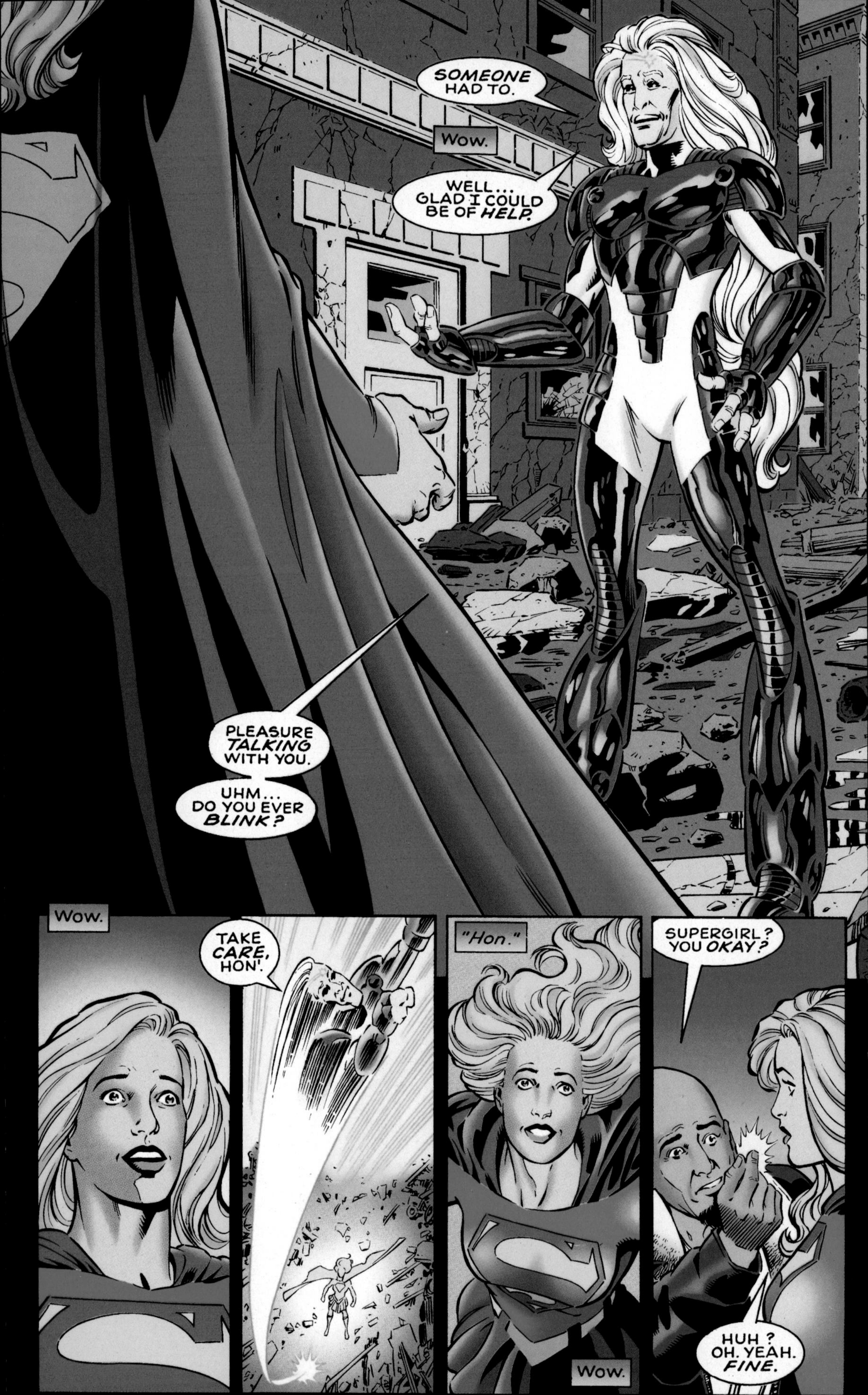
SOMEONE HAD TO.
Wow.
WELL... GLAD I COULD BE OF HELP.
PLEASURE TALKING WITH YOU.
UHM... DO YOU EVER BLINK?
Wow.
TAKE CARE, HON'.
"Hon."
Wow.
SUPERGIRL? YOU OKAY?
HUH? OH. YEAH. FINE.

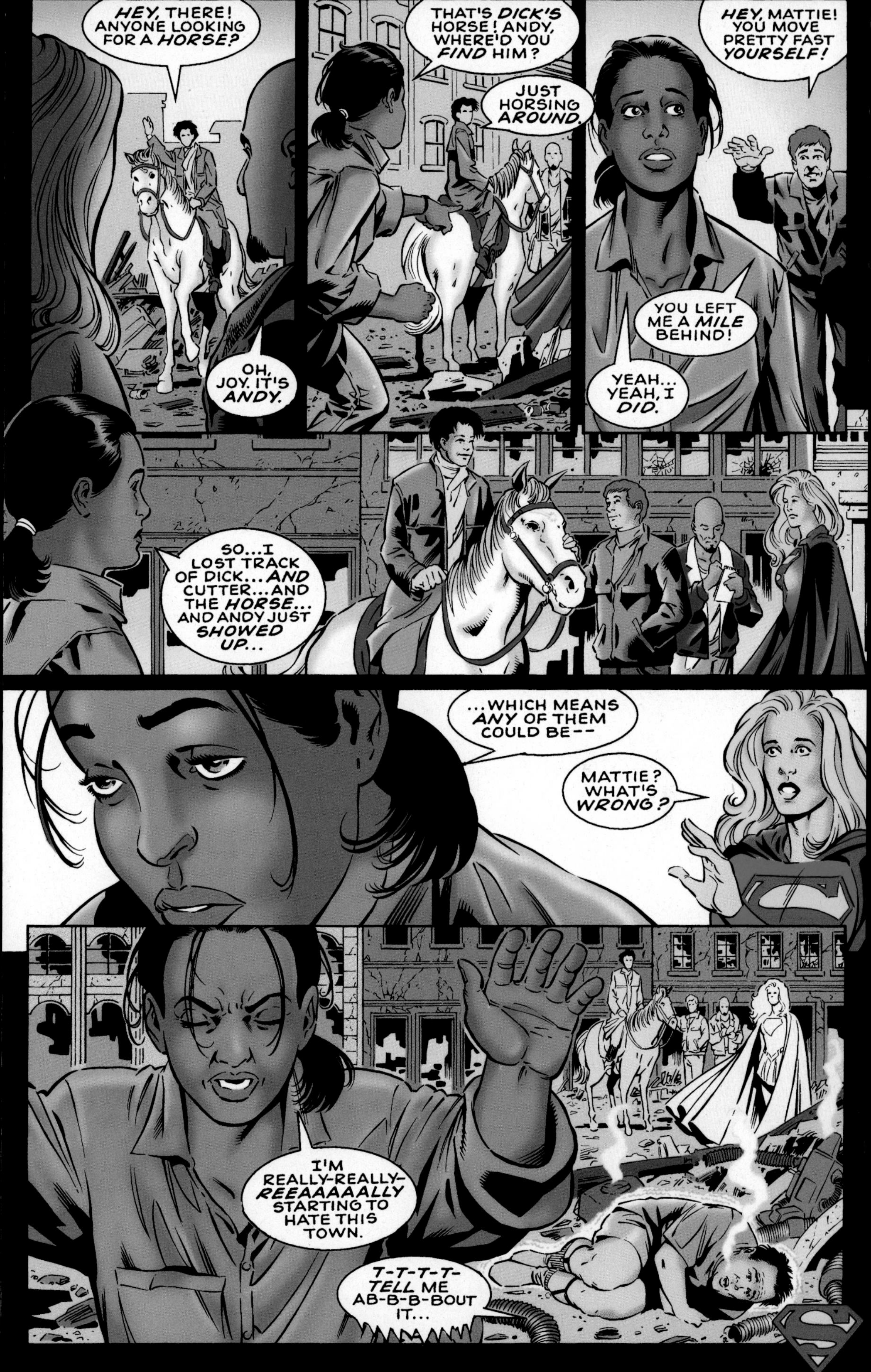
HEY, THERE! ANYONE LOOKING FOR A HORSE?
OH, JOY. IT'S ANDY.
THAT'S DICK'S HORSE! ANDY, WHERE'D YOU FIND HIM?
JUST HORSING AROUND.
HEY, MATTIE! YOU MOVE PRETTY FAST YOURSELF!
YOU LEFT ME A MILE BEHIND!
YEAH... YEAH, I DID.
SO...I LOST TRACK OF DICK...AND CUTTER...AND THE HORSE... AND ANDY JUST SHOWED UP...
...WHICH MEANS ANY OF THEM COULD BE--
MATTIE? WHAT'S WRONG?
I'M REALLY-REALLY-REEAAAAALLY STARTING TO HATE THIS TOWN.
T-T-T-T-TELL ME AB-B-B-BOUT IT...

SUPERGIRL #20 cover by Ron Frenz, Leonard Kirk, José Marzan Jr. and Patrick Martin

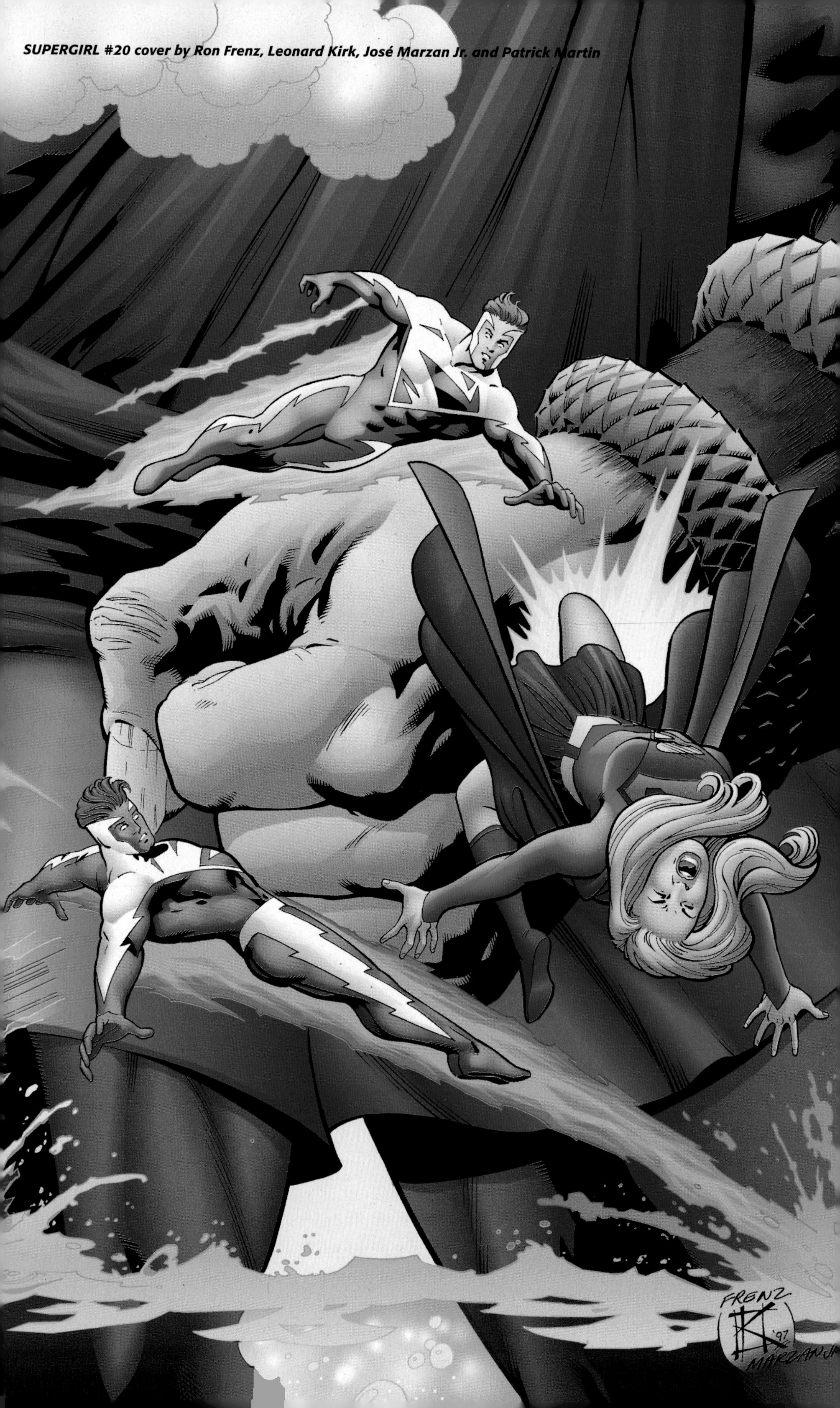
FRENZ
'97
MARZAN

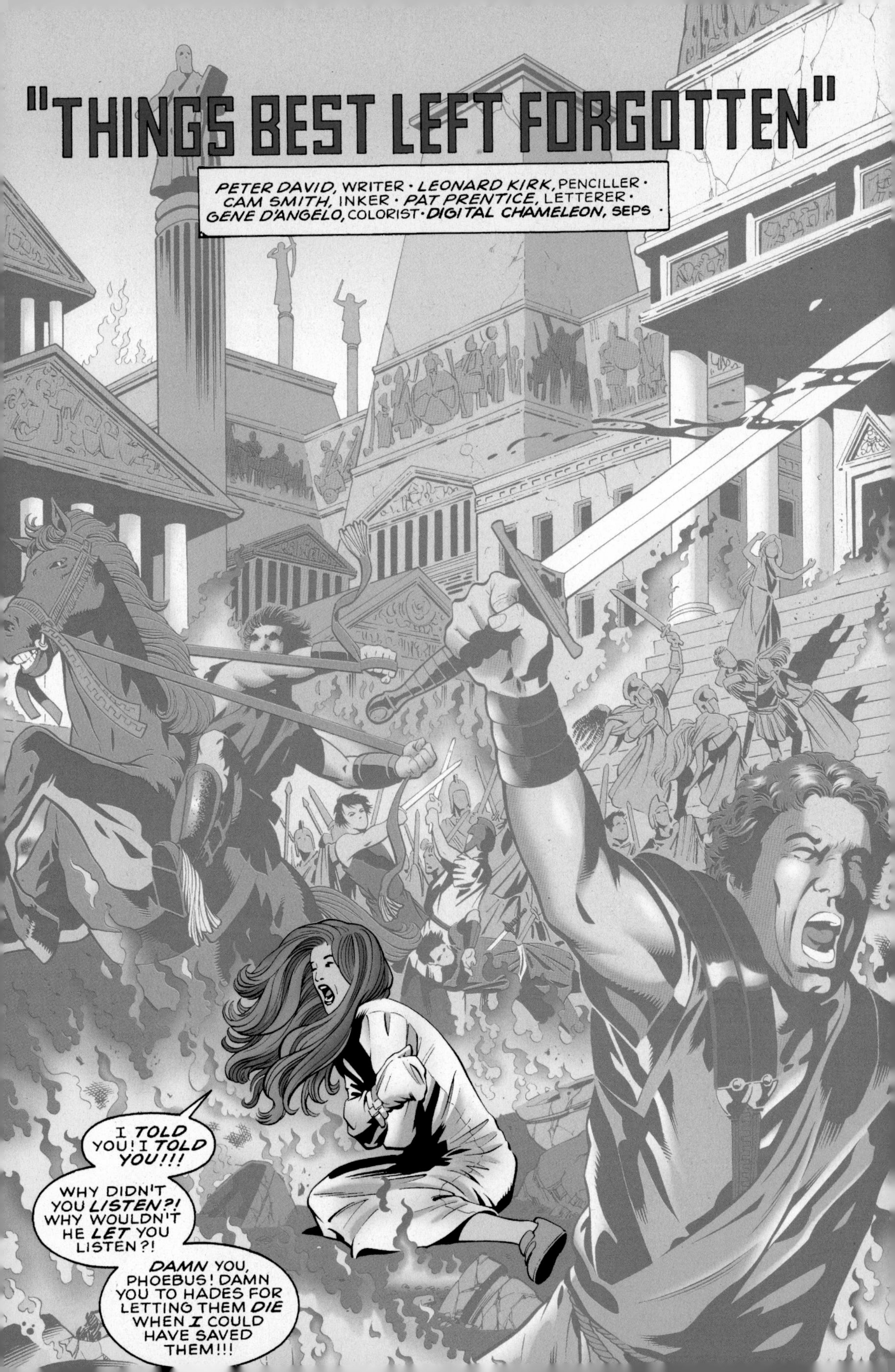
"THINGS BEST LEFT FORGOTTEN"
PETER DAVID, WRITER · LEONARD KIRK, PENCILLER · CAM SMITH, INKER · PAT PRENTICE, LETTERER · GENE D'ANGELO, COLORIST · DIGITAL CHAMELEON, SEPS ·
I TOLD YOU! I TOLD YOU!!!
WHY DIDN'T YOU LISTEN?! WHY WOULDN'T HE LET YOU LISTEN?!
DAMN YOU, PHOEBUS! DAMN YOU TO HADES FOR LETTING THEM DIE WHEN I COULD HAVE SAVED THEM!!!

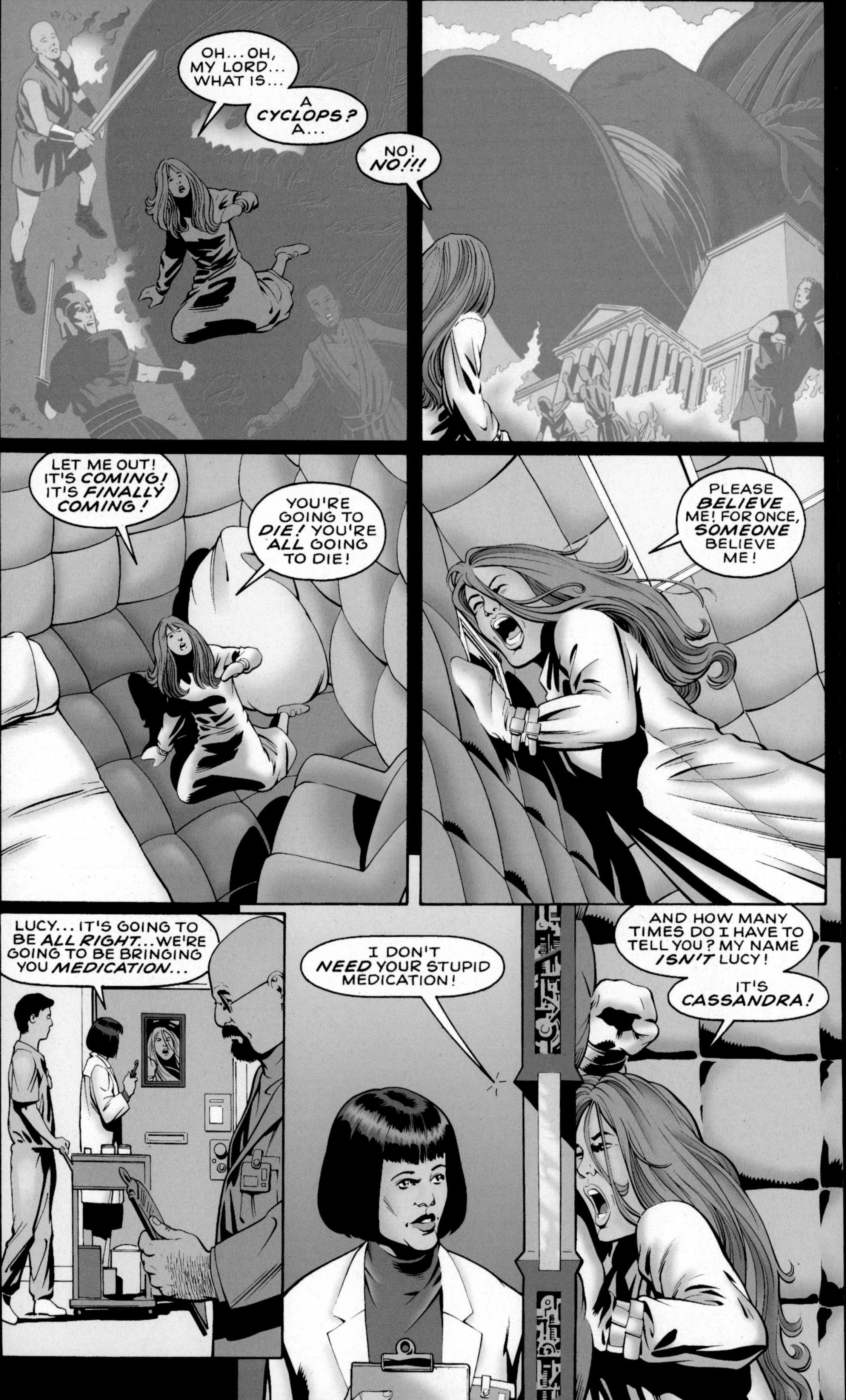
OH... OH, MY LORD... WHAT IS... A CYCLOPS? A...
NO! NO!!!
LET ME OUT! IT'S COMING! IT'S FINALLY COMING!
YOU'RE GOING TO DIE! YOU'RE ALL GOING TO DIE!
PLEASE BELIEVE ME! FOR ONCE, SOMEONE BELIEVE ME!
LUCY... IT'S GOING TO BE ALL RIGHT... WE'RE GOING TO BE BRINGING YOU MEDICATION...
I DON'T NEED YOUR STUPID MEDICATION!
AND HOW MANY TIMES DO I HAVE TO TELL YOU? MY NAME ISN'T LUCY!
IT'S CASSANDRA!

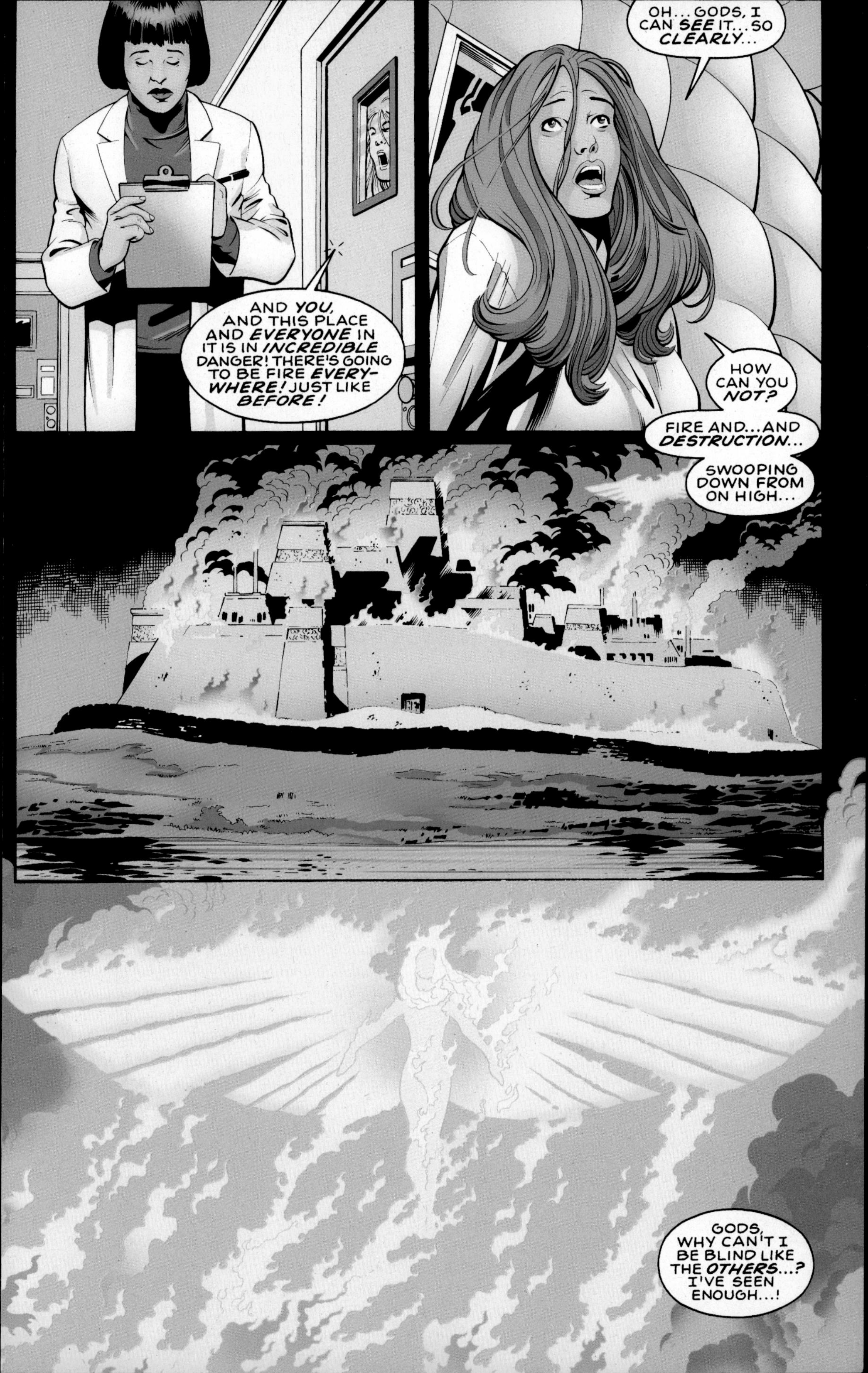
AND YOU, AND THIS PLACE AND EVERYONE IN IT IS IN INCREDIBLE DANGER! THERE'S GOING TO BE FIRE EVERY-WHERE! JUST LIKE BEFORE!
OH...GODS, I CAN SEE IT...SO CLEARLY...
HOW CAN YOU NOT?
FIRE AND...AND DESTRUCTION...
SWOOPING DOWN FROM ON HIGH...
GODS, WHY CAN'T I BE BLIND LIKE THE OTHERS...? I'VE SEEN ENOUGH...!

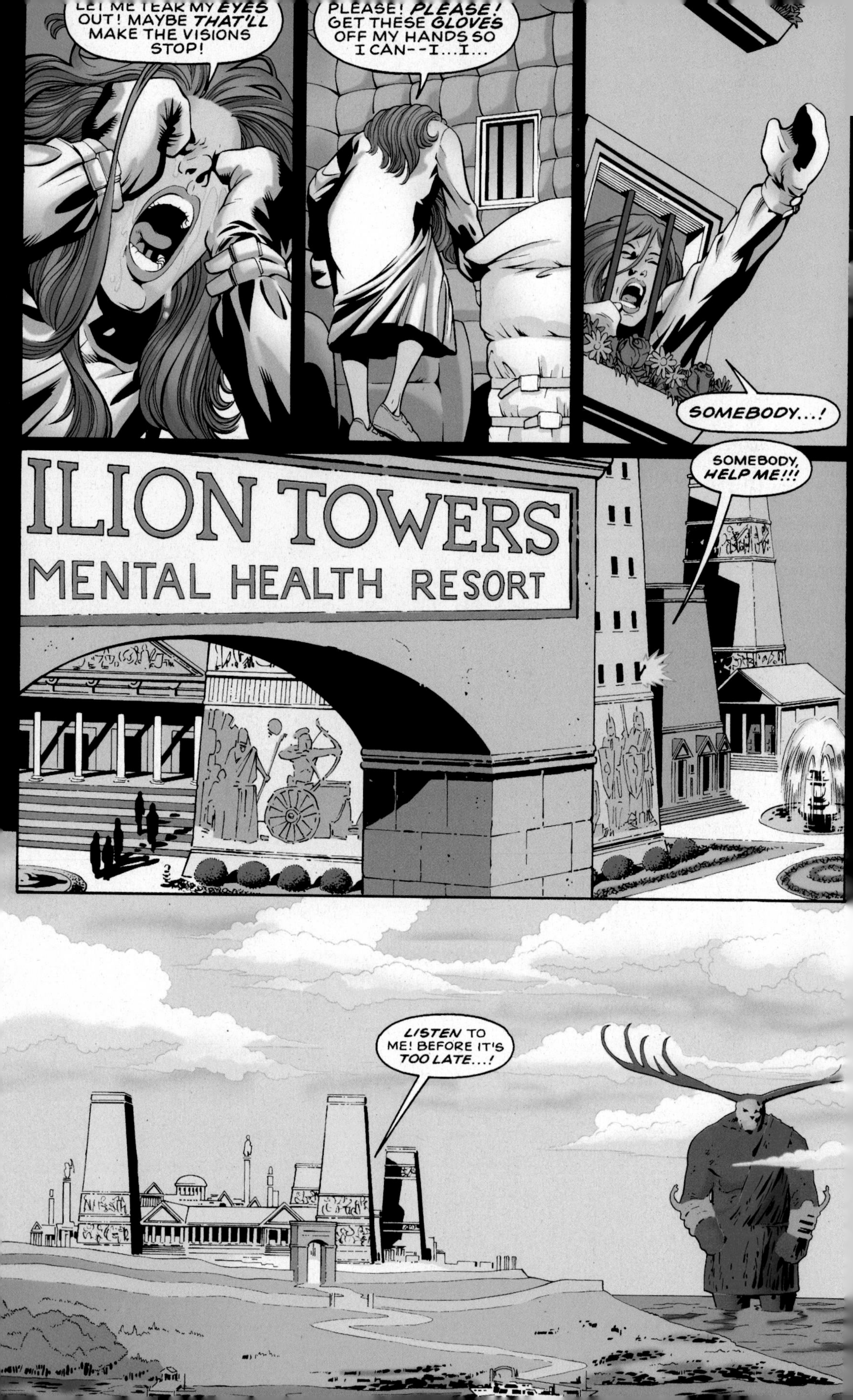

LET ME TEAR MY EYES OUT! MAYBE THAT'LL MAKE THE VISIONS STOP!
PLEASE! PLEASE! GET THESE GLOVES OFF MY HANDS SO I CAN--I...I...
SOMEBODY...!
ILION TOWERS
MENTAL HEALTH RESORT
SOMEBODY, HELP ME!!!
LISTEN TO ME! BEFORE IT'S TOO LATE...!

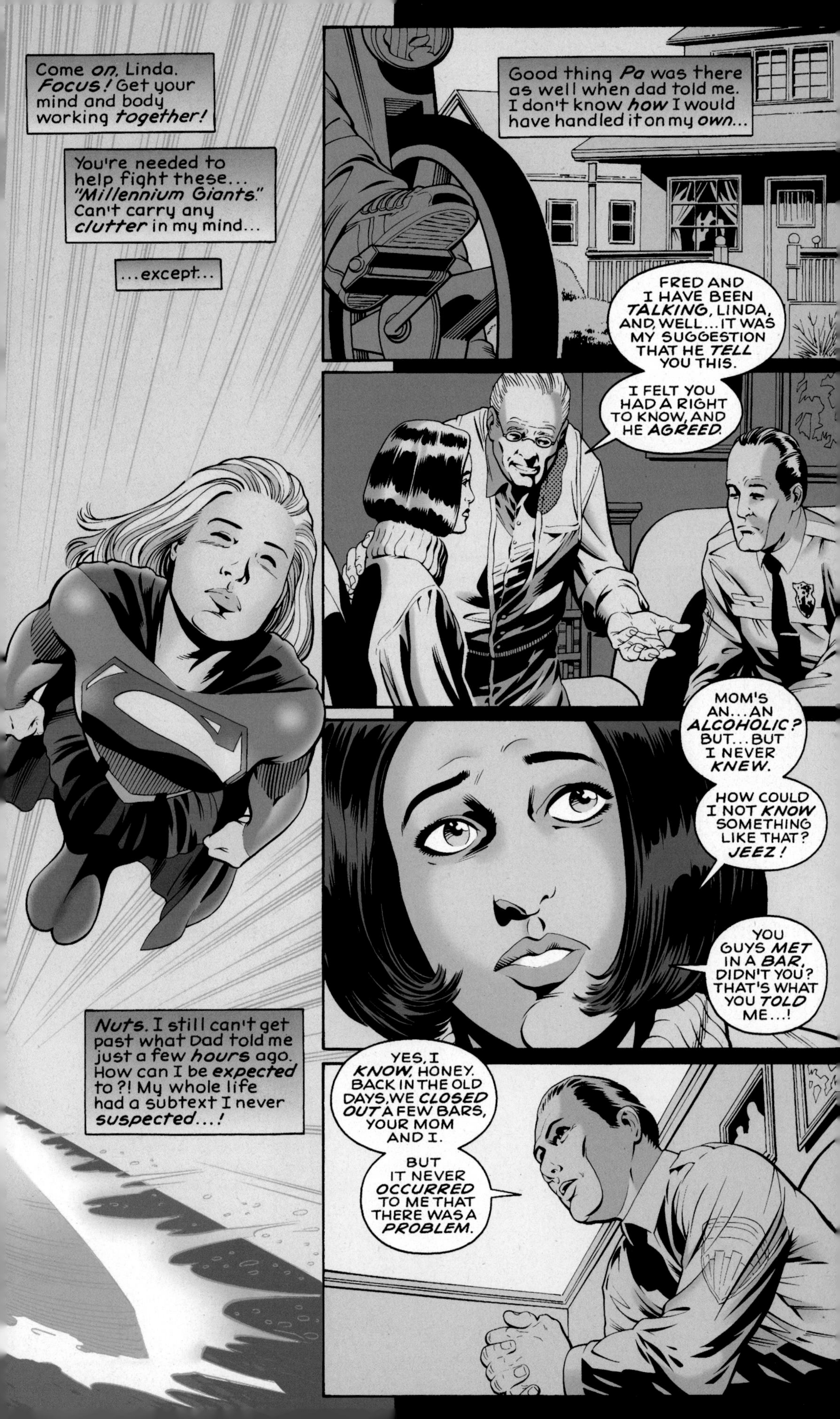
Come on, Linda. Focus! Get your mind and body working together!
You're needed to help fight these... "Millennium Giants." Can't carry any clutter in my mind...
...except...
Good thing Pa was there as well when dad told me. I don't know how I would have handled it on my own...
FRED AND I HAVE BEEN TALKING, LINDA, AND, WELL... IT WAS MY SUGGESTION THAT HE TELL YOU THIS.
I FELT YOU HAD A RIGHT TO KNOW, AND HE AGREED.
MOM'S AN... AN ALCOHOLIC? BUT... BUT I NEVER KNEW.
HOW COULD I NOT KNOW SOMETHING LIKE THAT? JEEZ!
YOU GUYS MET IN A BAR, DIDN'T YOU? THAT'S WHAT YOU TOLD ME...!
Nuts. I still can't get past what Dad told me just a few hours ago. How can I be expected to?! My whole life had a subtext I never suspected...!
YES, I KNOW, HONEY. BACK IN THE OLD DAYS, WE CLOSED OUT A FEW BARS, YOUR MOM AND I.
BUT IT NEVER OCCURRED TO ME THAT THERE WAS A PROBLEM.

Panel 1: "WE LOVED GOING OUT, DOING THE TOWN. I'D FINALLY FOUND A GIRL I COULD *PARTY* WITH."

Panel 2: "I THINK HER *OLD MAN* BOOZED IT, TOO. WHACKED HER AROUND. MAYBE PART OF THE REASON SHE MARRIED ME WAS TO GET *AWAY* FROM HIM."

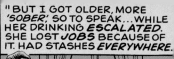

Panel 3: "BUT I GOT OLDER, MORE *'SOBER,'* SO TO SPEAK...WHILE HER DRINKING *ESCALATED.* SHE LOST *JOBS* BECAUSE OF IT. HAD STASHES *EVERYWHERE.*"

Panel 4: "I REALIZED SHE NEEDED *HELP* BUT SHE WOULDN'T *DO* ANYTHING ABOUT IT."

EXIT

"FINALLY, I WALKED *OUT.* I'D HAD *ENOUGH.* WE WERE PRETTY MUCH *THROUGH.*"

Panel 5: AND... AND WHAT *HAPPENED?*

YOU DID. YOUR MOTHER DISCOVERED SHE WAS PREGNANT A COUPLE WEEKS AFTER I'D *LEFT* HER. SHE WOULDN'T HAVE AN ABORTION, DIDN'T *BELIEVE* IN IT.

Panel 6: BUT SHE KNEW ALCOHOL WOULD HURT YOU. SHE TOOK IT AS, WELL ...A *SIGN.* A SIGN IT WAS TIME TO DO THE RIGHT THING.

Panel 7: "ONE OF THE AA STEPS IS AFFIRMING YOUR BELIEF IN *GOD* AND PUTTING YOURSELF INTO HIS HANDS. ME, I WAS NEVER MUCH FOR THAT, BUT I FIGURED, ANYTHING THAT DID THE JOB, *GREAT.*"

Panel 8: "YOUR MOTHER EMBRACED IT *COMPLETELY.* BECAME THE SINGLE MOST DEVOUT WOMAN I'VE EVER *KNOWN.*"

Panel 9: "WASN'T *EASY* AT FIRST. SHE WANTED THE BOOZE SO BAD IT JUST ATE HER *UP.* BUT SHE *NEVER* LOST SIGHT OF THE GOAL."

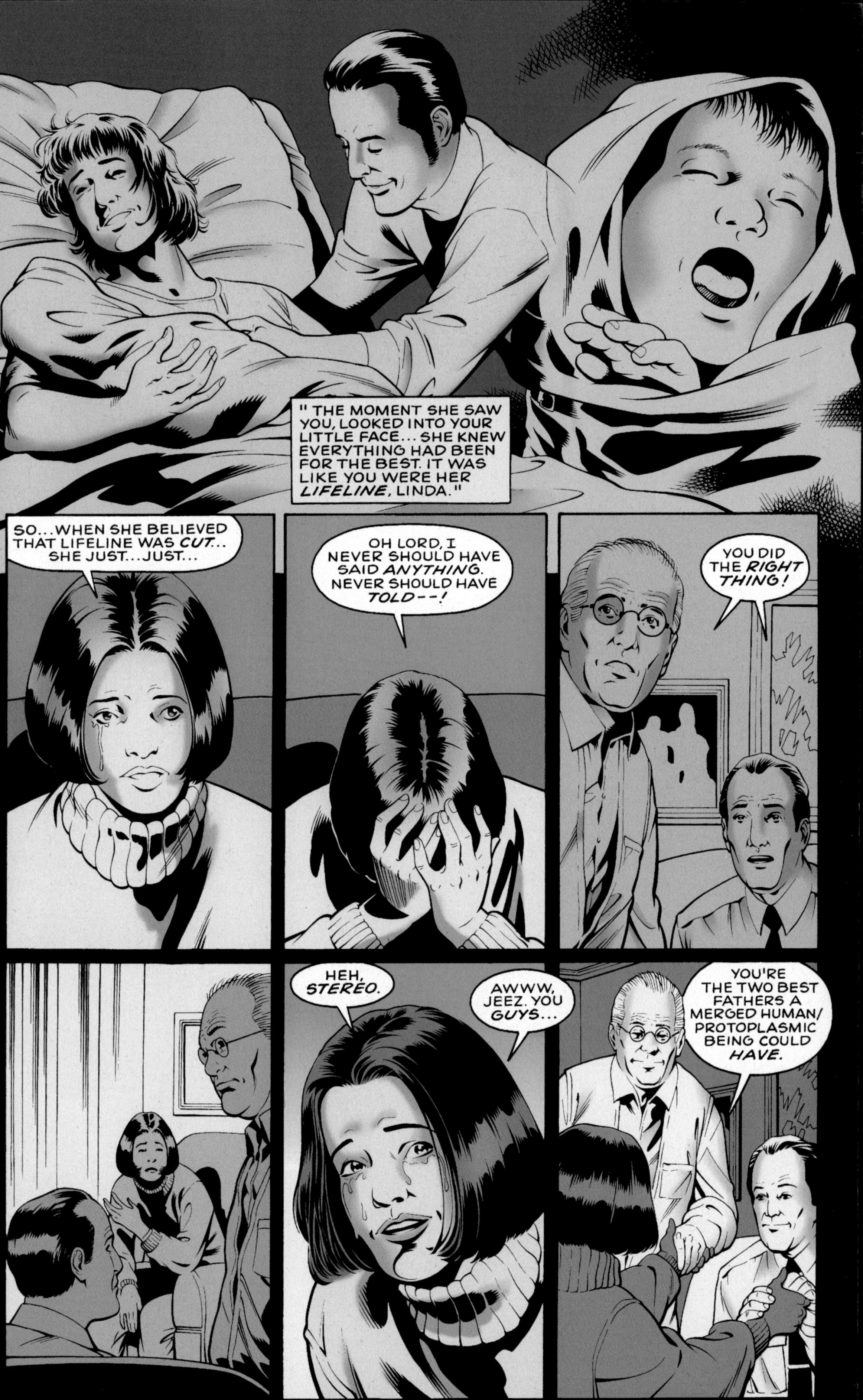
"THE MOMENT SHE SAW YOU, LOOKED INTO YOUR LITTLE FACE... SHE KNEW EVERYTHING HAD BEEN FOR THE BEST. IT WAS LIKE YOU WERE HER *LIFELINE*, LINDA."
SO...WHEN SHE BELIEVED THAT LIFELINE WAS *CUT*... SHE JUST...JUST...
OH LORD, I NEVER SHOULD HAVE SAID *ANYTHING*. NEVER SHOULD HAVE *TOLD--!*
YOU DID THE *RIGHT THING!*
HEH, *STEREO.*
AWWW, JEEZ. YOU *GUYS*...
YOU'RE THE TWO BEST FATHERS A MERGED HUMAN/ PROTOPLASMIC BEING COULD *HAVE.*

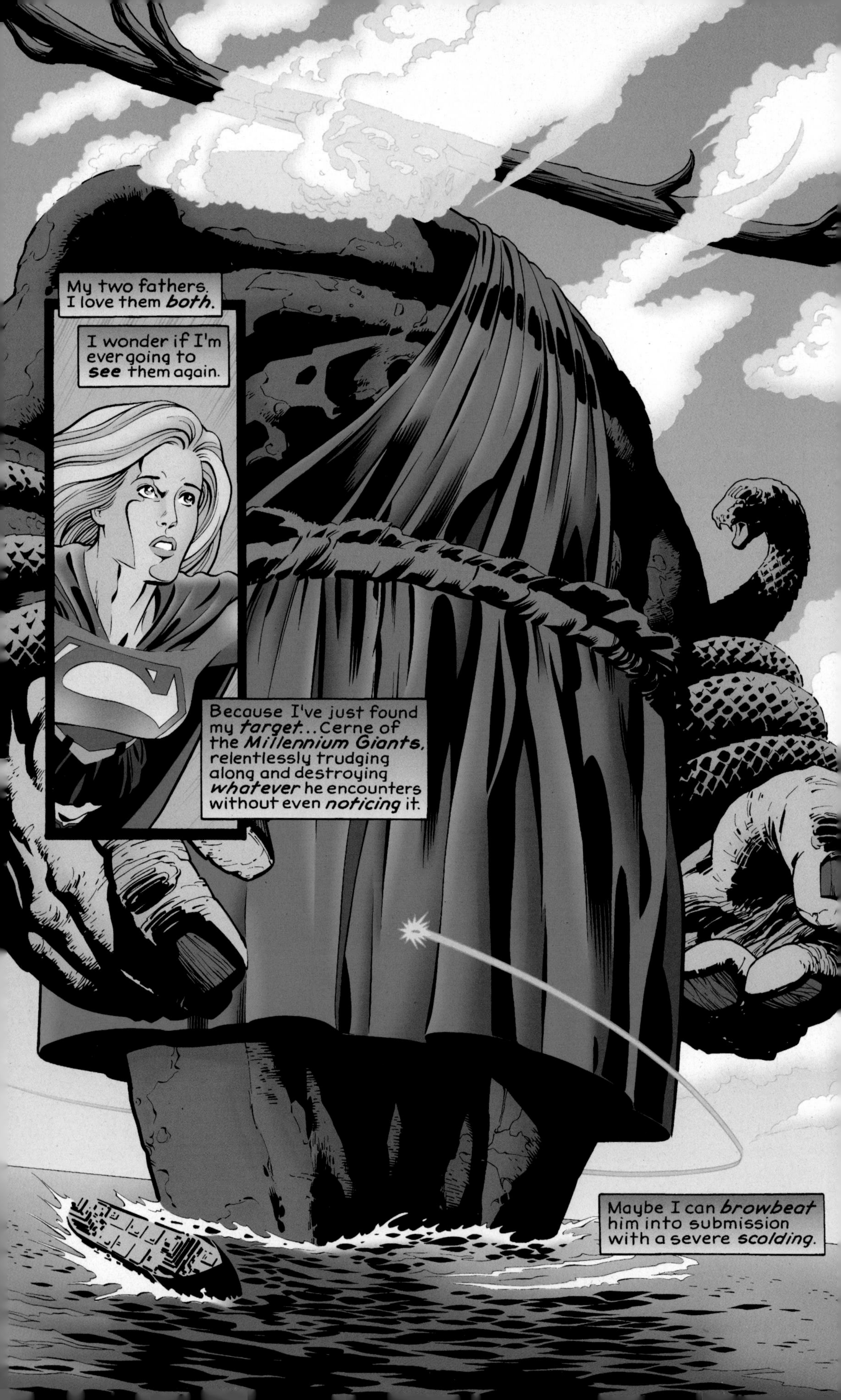
My two fathers. I love them *both*.
I wonder if I'm ever going to **see** them again.
Because I've just found my *target*...Cerne of the *Millennium Giants*, relentlessly trudging along and destroying ***whatever*** he encounters without even *noticing* it.
Maybe I can *browbeat* him into submission with a severe *scolding*.

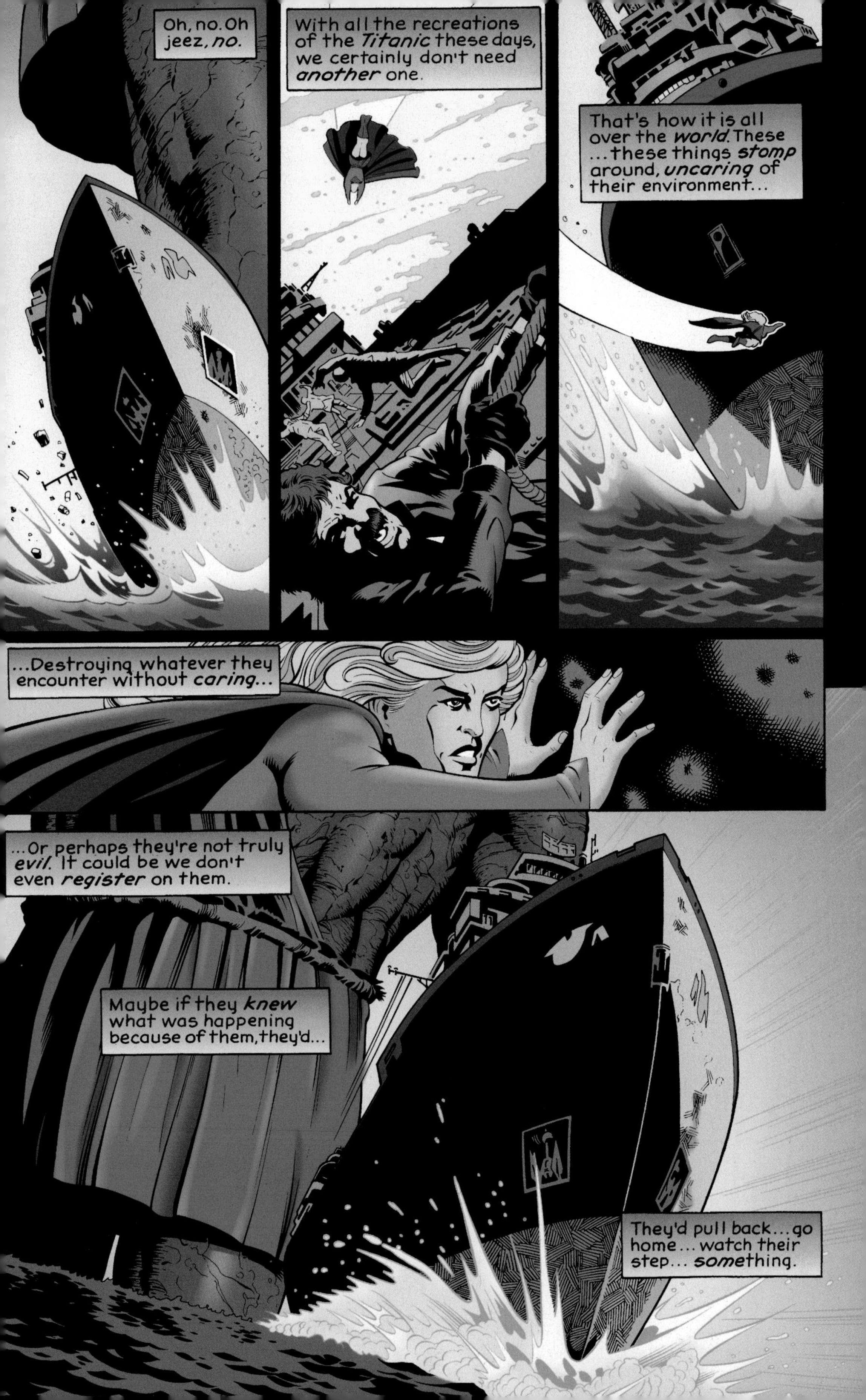
Oh, no. Oh jeez, *no.*
With all the recreations of the *Titanic* these days, we certainly don't need *another* one.
That's how it is all over the *world.* These ...these things *stomp* around, *uncaring* of their environment...
...Destroying whatever they encounter without *caring*...
...Or perhaps they're not truly *evil.* It could be we don't even *register* on them.
Maybe if they *knew* what was happening because of them, they'd...
They'd pull back...go home... watch their step... *some*thing.

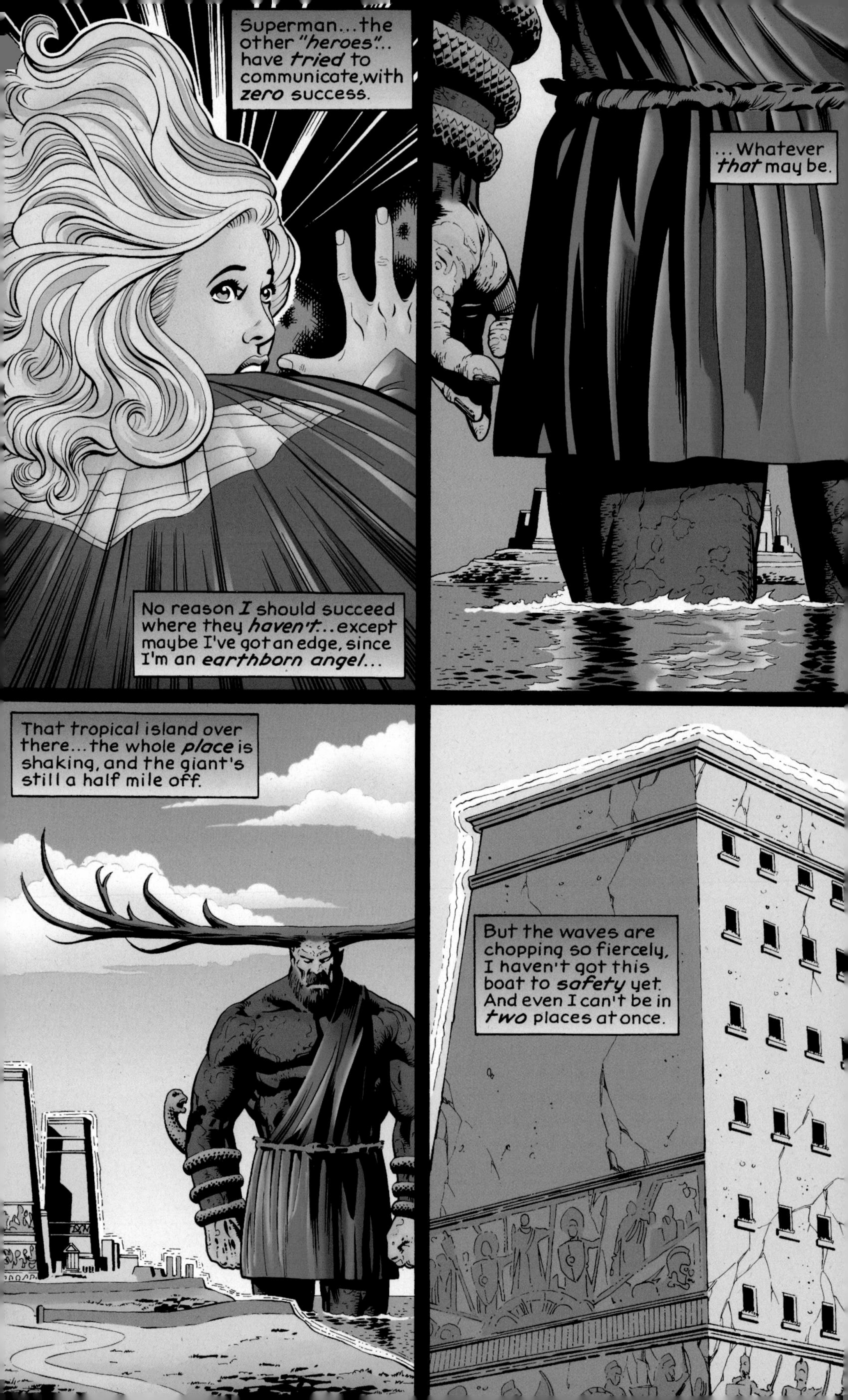
Superman... the other "heroes"... have tried to communicate, with zero success.
No reason I should succeed where they haven't... except maybe I've got an edge, since I'm an earthborn angel...
...Whatever that may be.
That tropical island over there... the whole place is shaking, and the giant's still a half mile off.
But the waves are chopping so fiercely, I haven't got this boat to safety yet. And even I can't be in two places at once.

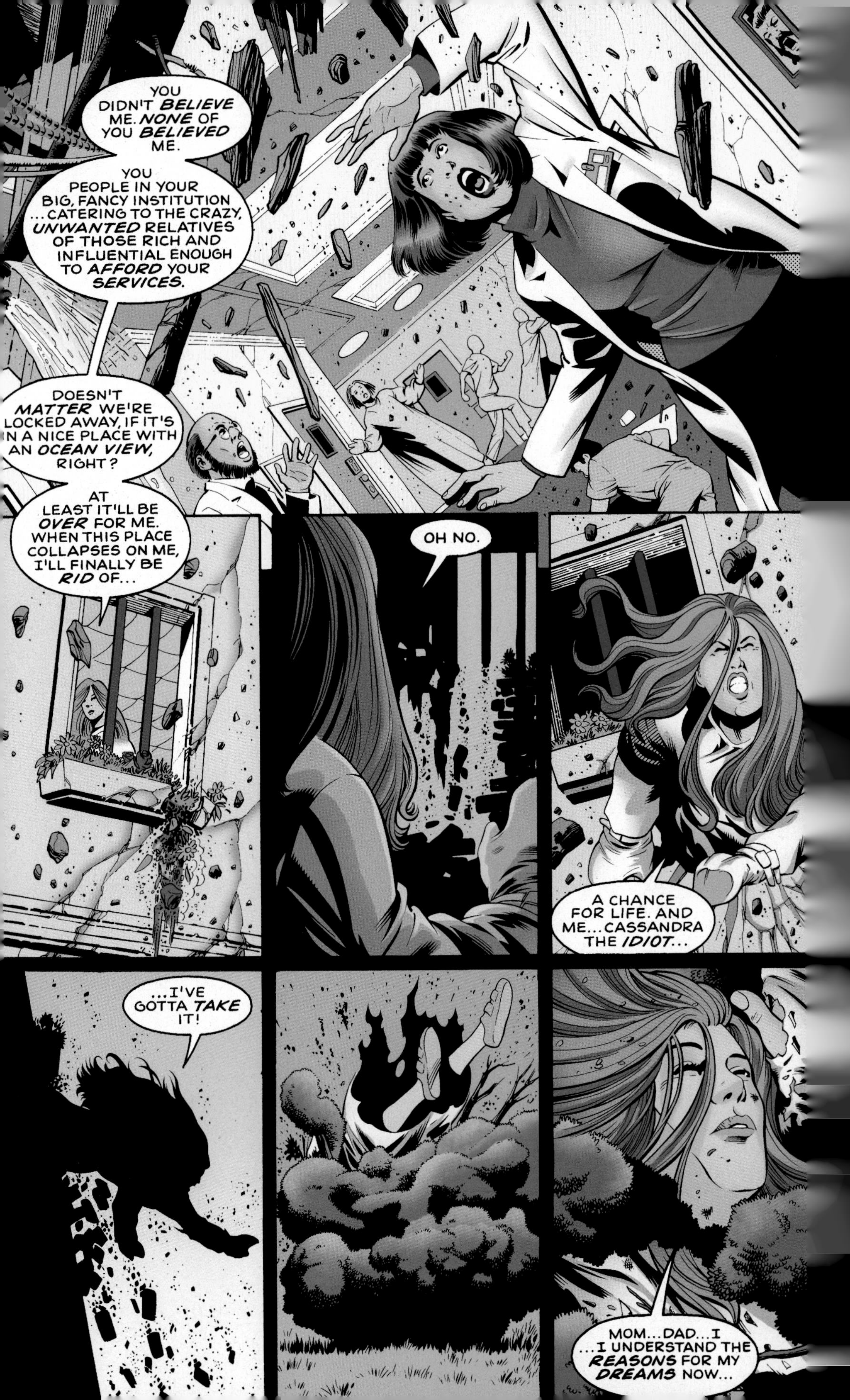
YOU DIDN'T BELIEVE ME. NONE OF YOU BELIEVED ME.
YOU PEOPLE IN YOUR BIG, FANCY INSTITUTION ...CATERING TO THE CRAZY, UNWANTED RELATIVES OF THOSE RICH AND INFLUENTIAL ENOUGH TO AFFORD YOUR SERVICES.
DOESN'T MATTER WE'RE LOCKED AWAY, IF IT'S IN A NICE PLACE WITH AN OCEAN VIEW, RIGHT?
AT LEAST IT'LL BE OVER FOR ME. WHEN THIS PLACE COLLAPSES ON ME, I'LL FINALLY BE RID OF...
OH NO.
A CHANCE FOR LIFE. AND ME...CASSANDRA THE IDIOT...
...I'VE GOTTA TAKE IT!
MOM...DAD...I ...I UNDERSTAND THE REASONS FOR MY DREAMS NOW...

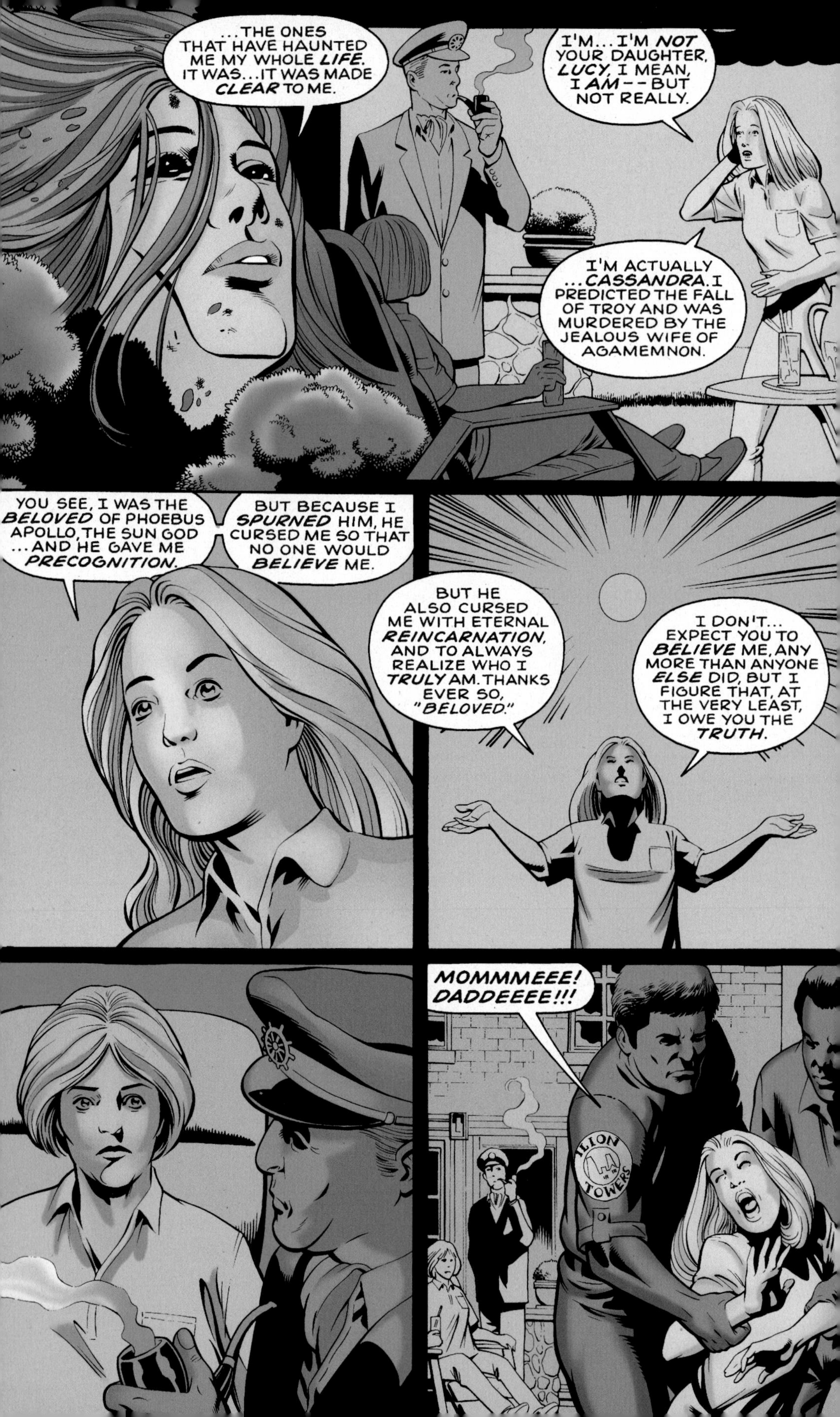
...THE ONES THAT HAVE HAUNTED ME MY WHOLE LIFE. IT WAS...IT WAS MADE CLEAR TO ME.
I'M...I'M NOT YOUR DAUGHTER, LUCY, I MEAN, I AM--BUT NOT REALLY.
I'M ACTUALLY ...CASSANDRA. I PREDICTED THE FALL OF TROY AND WAS MURDERED BY THE JEALOUS WIFE OF AGAMEMNON.
YOU SEE, I WAS THE BELOVED OF PHOEBUS APOLLO, THE SUN GOD ...AND HE GAVE ME PRECOGNITION.
BUT BECAUSE I SPURNED HIM, HE CURSED ME SO THAT NO ONE WOULD BELIEVE ME.
BUT HE ALSO CURSED ME WITH ETERNAL REINCARNATION, AND TO ALWAYS REALIZE WHO I TRULY AM. THANKS EVER SO, "BELOVED."
I DON'T... EXPECT YOU TO BELIEVE ME, ANY MORE THAN ANYONE ELSE DID, BUT I FIGURE THAT, AT THE VERY LEAST, I OWE YOU THE TRUTH.
MOMMMEEE! DADDEEEE!!!
ILION TOWERS

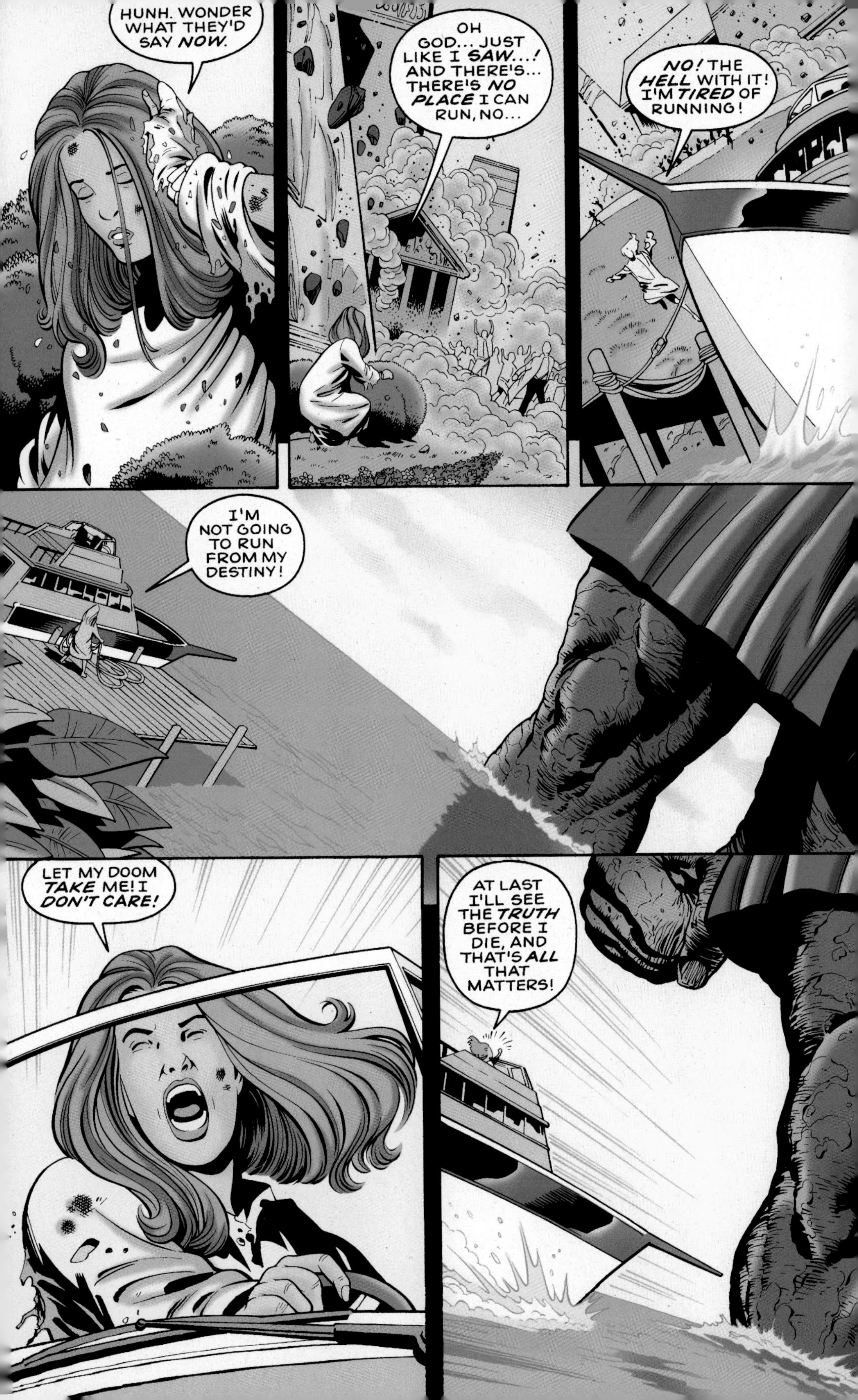
HUNH. WONDER WHAT THEY'D SAY NOW.
OH GOD... JUST LIKE I SAW...! AND THERE'S... THERE'S NO PLACE I CAN RUN, NO...
NO! THE HELL WITH IT! I'M TIRED OF RUNNING!
I'M NOT GOING TO RUN FROM MY DESTINY!
LET MY DOOM TAKE ME! I DON'T CARE!
AT LAST I'LL SEE THE TRUTH BEFORE I DIE, AND THAT'S ALL THAT MATTERS!

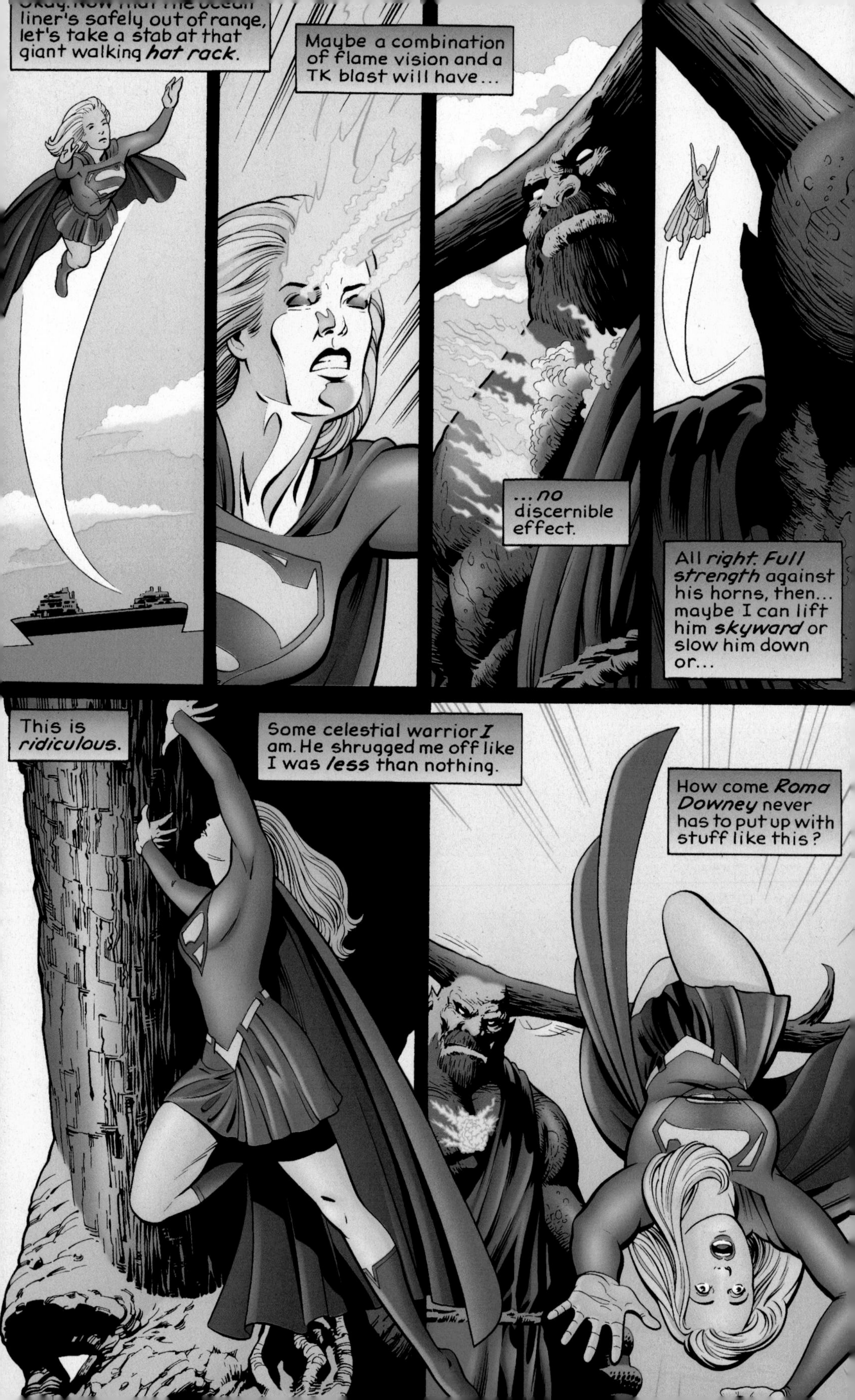
liner's safely out of range, let's take a stab at that giant walking *hat rack*.
Maybe a combination of flame vision and a TK blast will have...
...*no* discernible effect.
All *right. Full strength* against his horns, then... maybe I can lift him *skyward* or slow him down or...
This is *ridiculous*.
Some celestial warrior *I* am. He shrugged me off like I was *less* than nothing.
How come *Roma Downey* never has to put up with stuff like this?

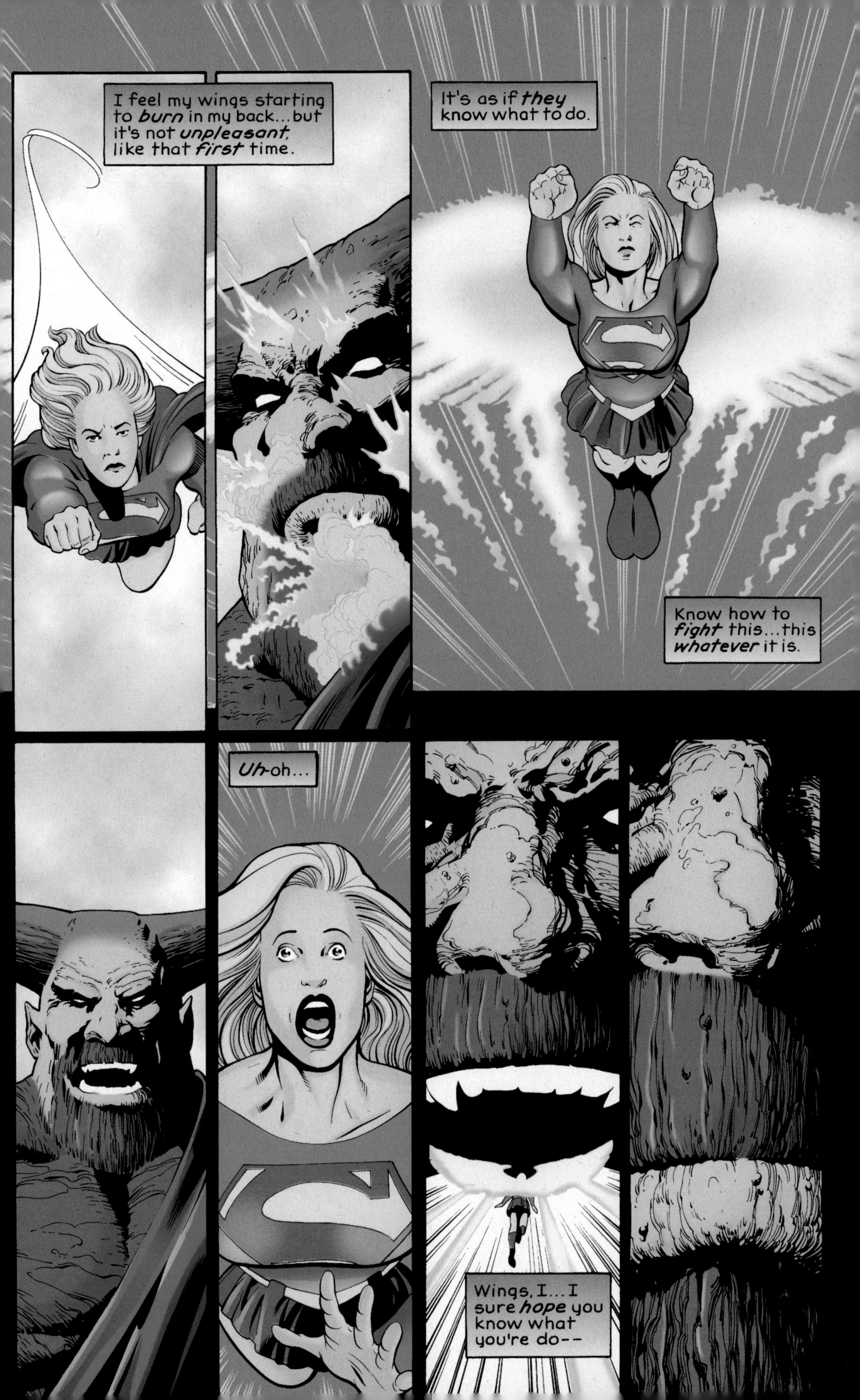
I feel my wings starting to burn in my back...but it's not unpleasant, like that first time.
It's as if they know what to do.
Know how to fight this...this whatever it is.
Uh-oh...
Wings, I...I sure hope you know what you're do--

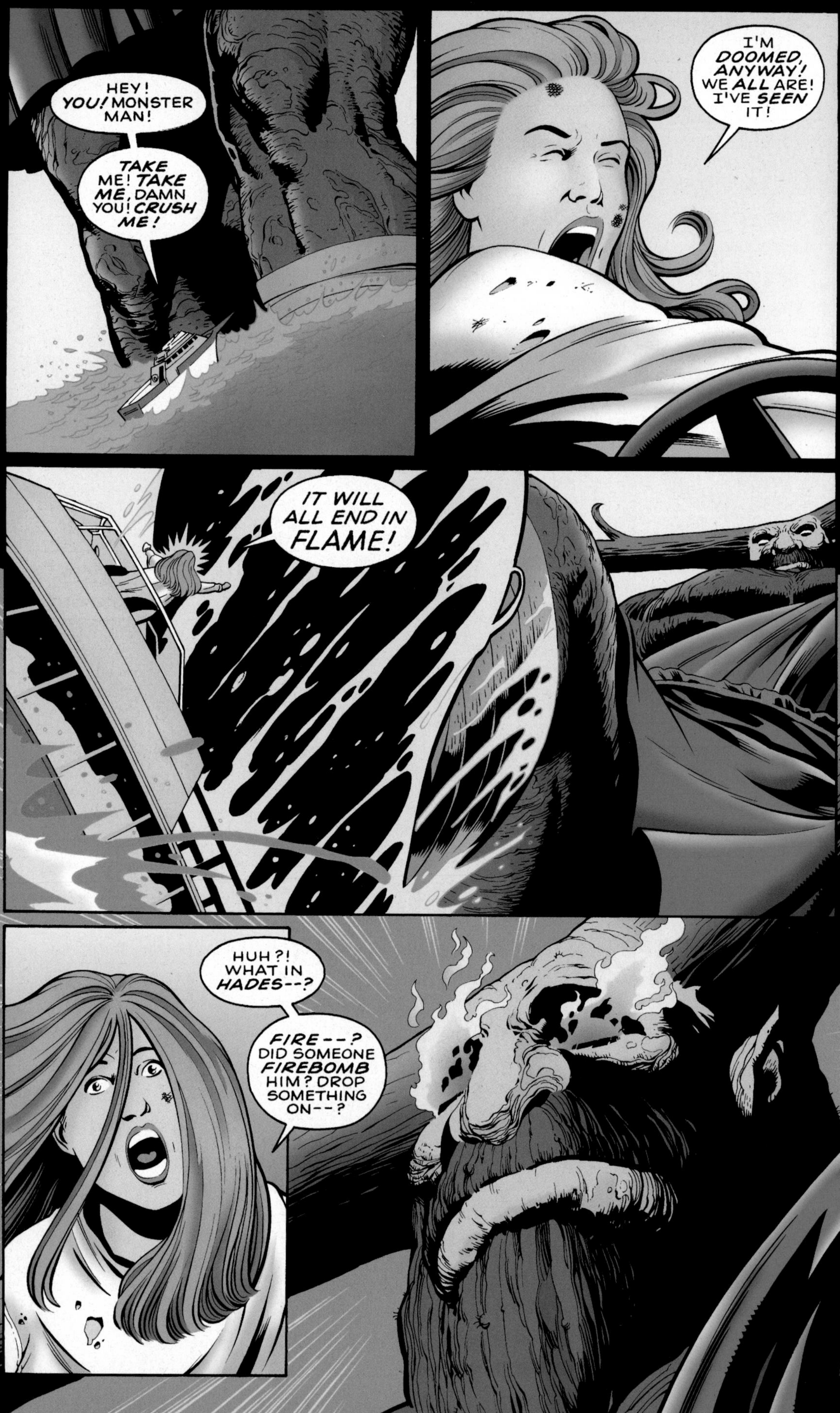

HEY! YOU! MONSTER MAN!
TAKE ME! TAKE ME, DAMN YOU! CRUSH ME!
I'M DOOMED, ANYWAY! WE ALL ARE! I'VE SEEN IT!
IT WILL ALL END IN FLAME!
HUH?! WHAT IN HADES--?
FIRE--? DID SOMEONE FIREBOMB HIM? DROP SOMETHING ON--?

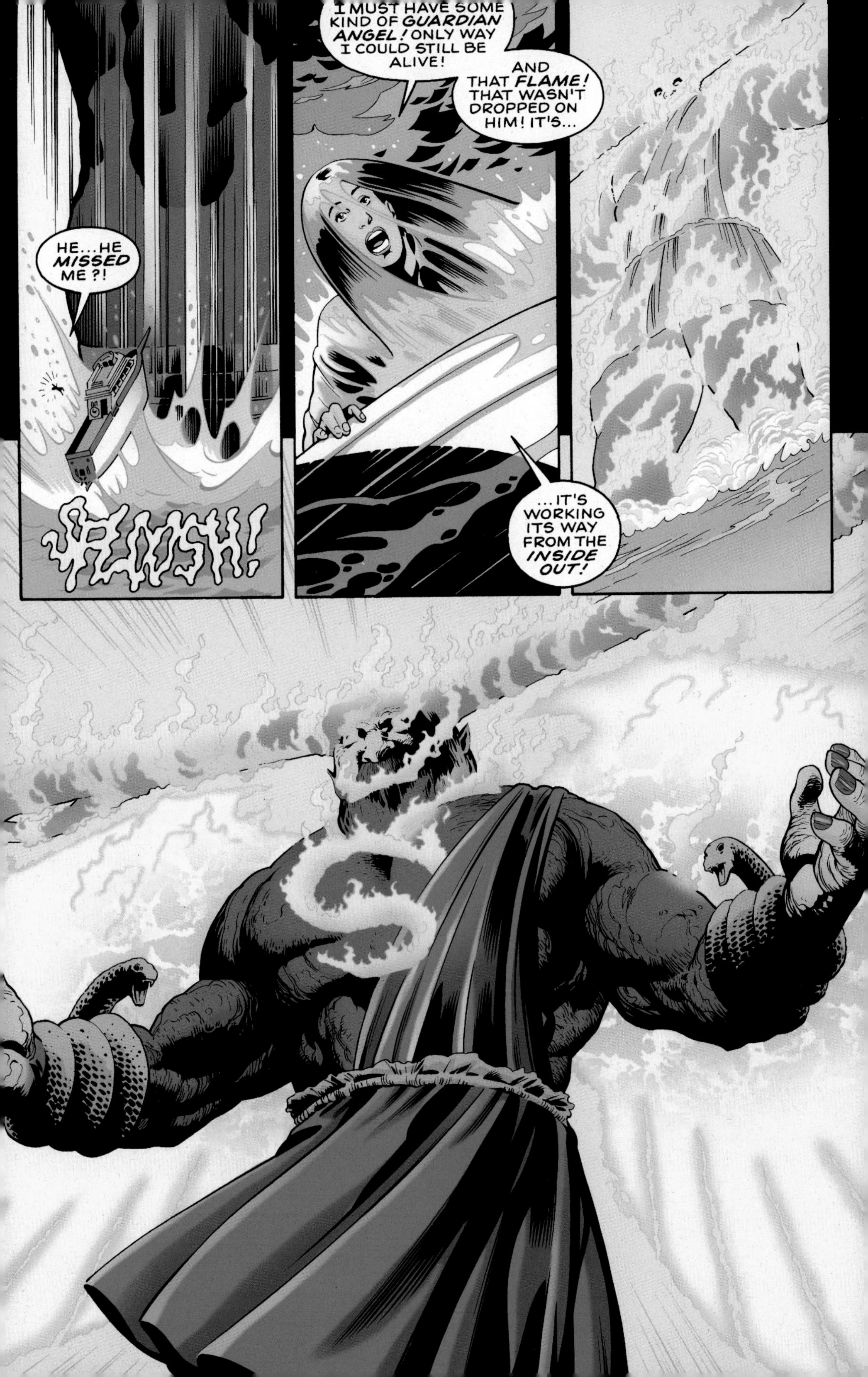
HE...HE MISSED ME?!
SPLOOSH!
I MUST HAVE SOME KIND OF GUARDIAN ANGEL! ONLY WAY I COULD STILL BE ALIVE!
AND THAT FLAME! THAT WASN'T DROPPED ON HIM! IT'S...
...IT'S WORKING ITS WAY FROM THE INSIDE OUT!

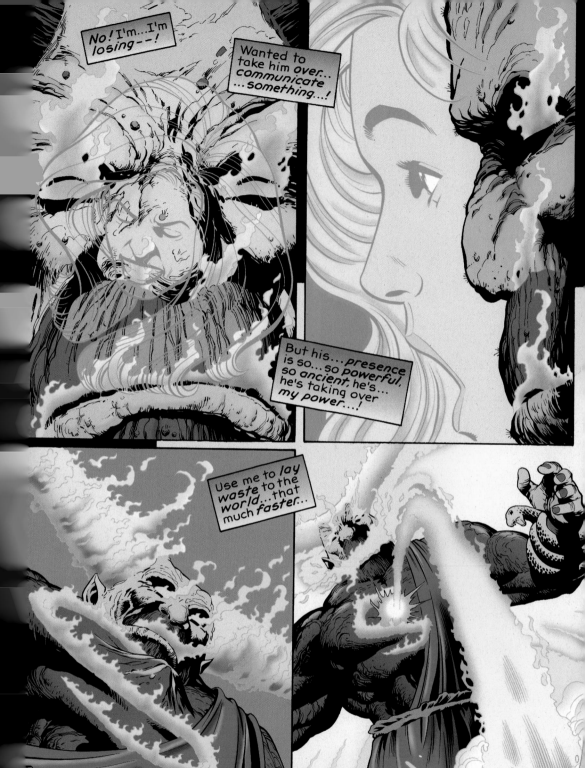

No! I'm...I'm losing--!

Wanted to take him over... communicate ...something...!

But his...presence is so...so powerful, so ancient, he's taking over my power...!

Use me to lay waste to the world...that much faster...

Got to get out ...before it's...

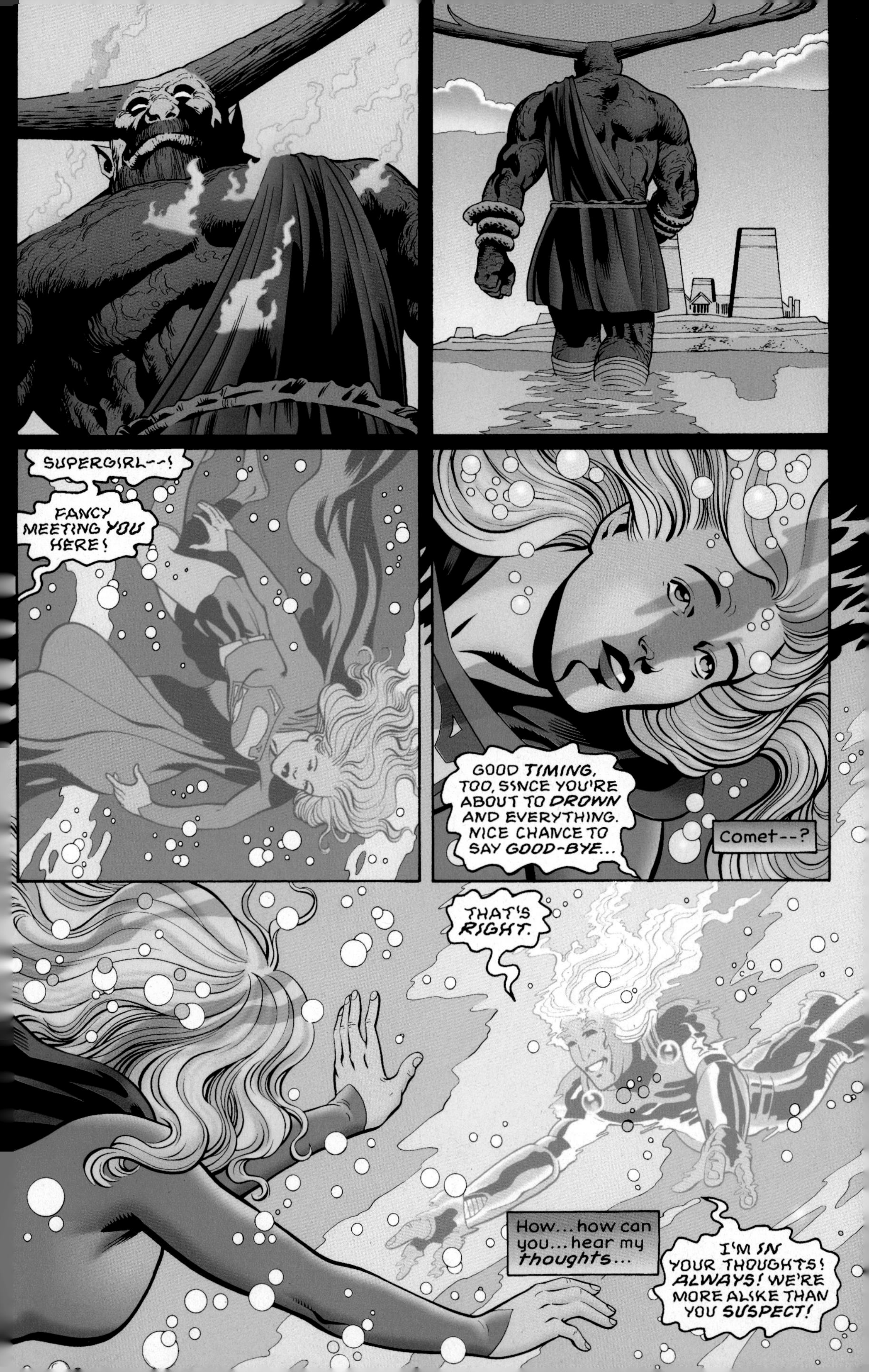
SUPERGIRL--!
FANCY MEETING YOU HERE!
GOOD TIMING, TOO, SINCE YOU'RE ABOUT TO DROWN AND EVERYTHING. NICE CHANCE TO SAY GOOD-BYE...
Comet--?
THAT'S RIGHT.
How... how can you... hear my thoughts...
I'M IN YOUR THOUGHTS! ALWAYS! WE'RE MORE ALIKE THAN YOU SUSPECT!

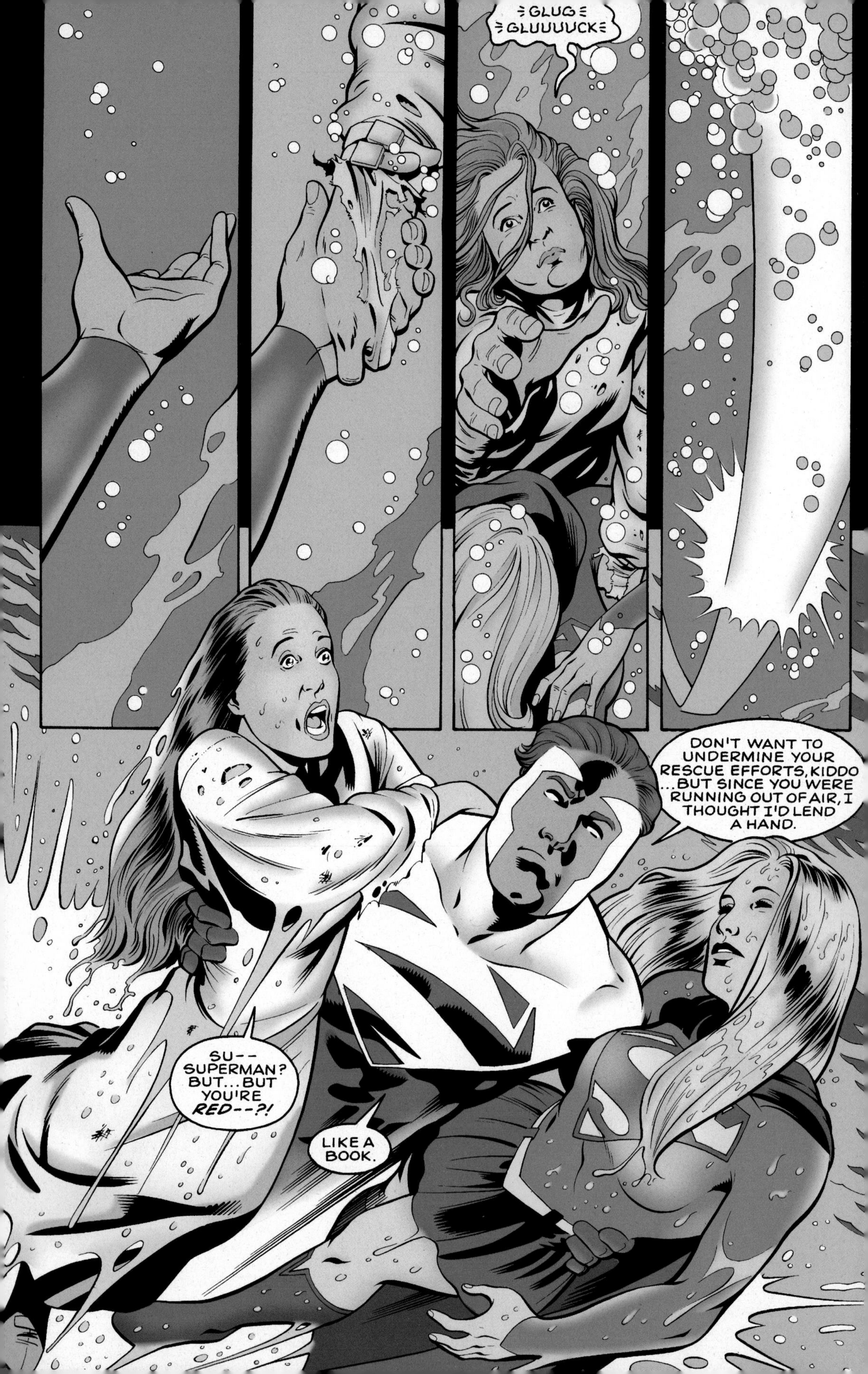
GLUG GLUUUUCK
DON'T WANT TO UNDERMINE YOUR RESCUE EFFORTS, KIDDO ...BUT SINCE YOU WERE RUNNING OUT OF AIR, I THOUGHT I'D LEND A HAND.
SU-- SUPERMAN? BUT...BUT YOU'RE *RED*--?!
LIKE A BOOK.

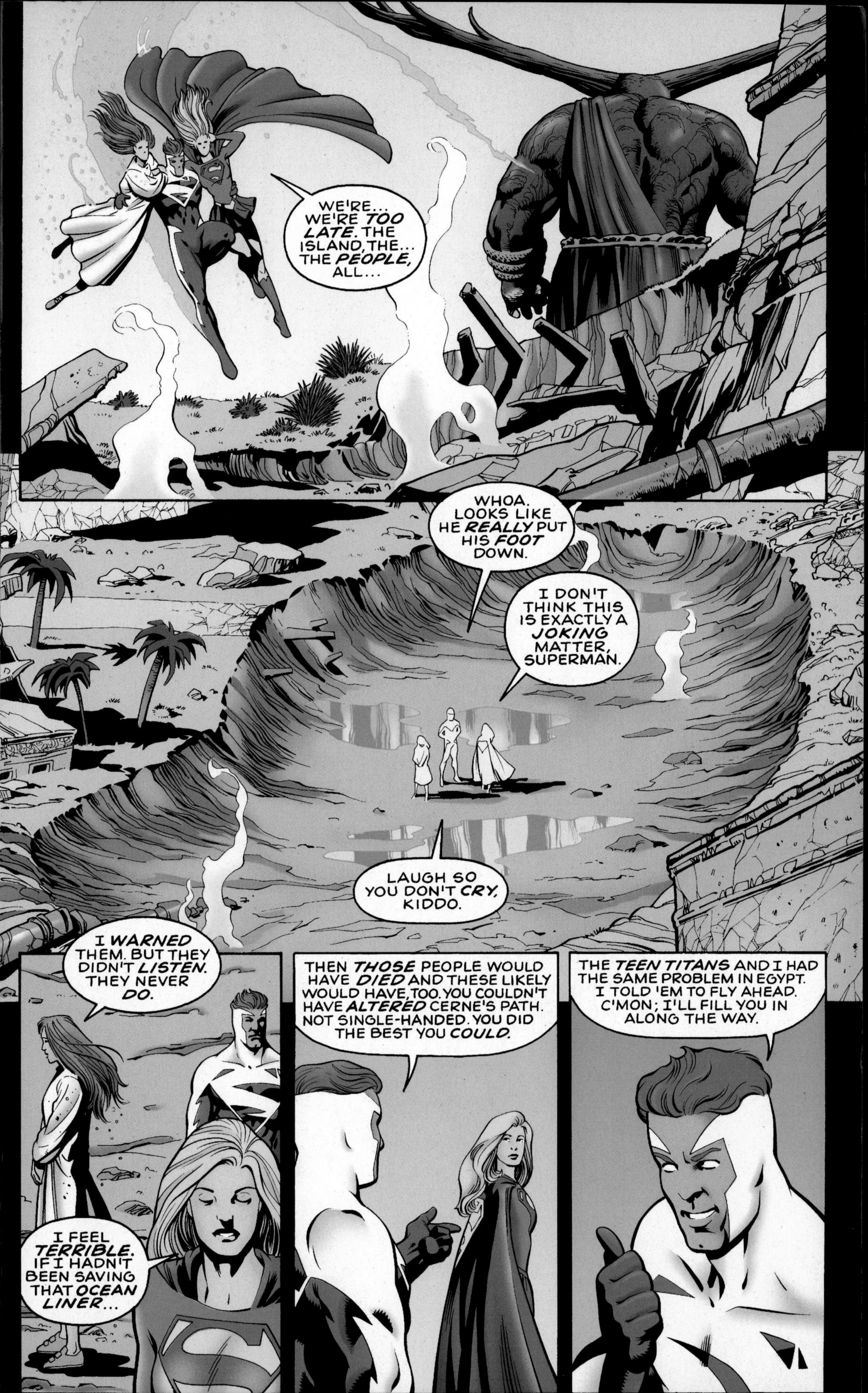
WE'RE... WE'RE TOO LATE. THE ISLAND, THE... THE PEOPLE, ALL...
WHOA. LOOKS LIKE HE REALLY PUT HIS FOOT DOWN.
I DON'T THINK THIS IS EXACTLY A JOKING MATTER, SUPERMAN.
LAUGH SO YOU DON'T CRY, KIDDO.
I WARNED THEM. BUT THEY DIDN'T LISTEN. THEY NEVER DO.
I FEEL TERRIBLE. IF I HADN'T BEEN SAVING THAT OCEAN LINER...
THEN THOSE PEOPLE WOULD HAVE DIED AND THESE LIKELY WOULD HAVE, TOO. YOU COULDN'T HAVE ALTERED CERNE'S PATH. NOT SINGLE-HANDED. YOU DID THE BEST YOU COULD.
THE TEEN TITANS AND I HAD THE SAME PROBLEM IN EGYPT. I TOLD 'EM TO FLY AHEAD. C'MON; I'LL FILL YOU IN ALONG THE WAY.

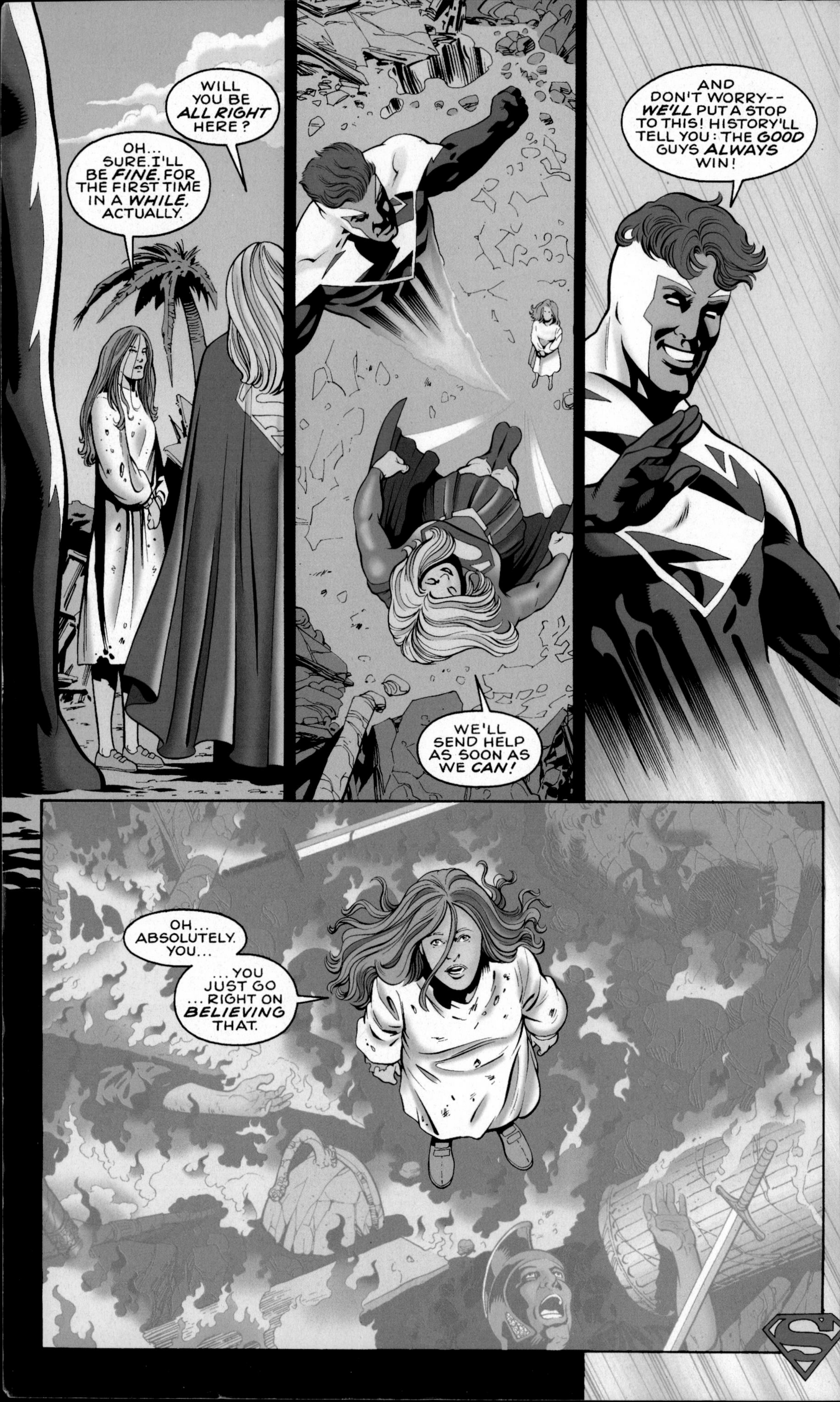
WILL YOU BE ALL RIGHT HERE?
OH... SURE. I'LL BE FINE. FOR THE FIRST TIME IN A WHILE, ACTUALLY.
WE'LL SEND HELP AS SOON AS WE CAN!
AND DON'T WORRY-- WE'LL PUT A STOP TO THIS! HISTORY'LL TELL YOU: THE GOOD GUYS ALWAYS WIN!
OH... ABSOLUTELY. YOU...
...YOU JUST GO ...RIGHT ON BELIEVING THAT.

"Greg Rucka and company have created a compelling narrative for fans of the Amazing Amazon."– **NERDIST**

"(A) heartfelt and genuine take on Diana's origin."– **NEWSARAMA**

DC UNIVERSE REBIRTH

WONDER WOMAN

VOL. 1: THE LIES
GREG RUCKA
with LIAM SHARP

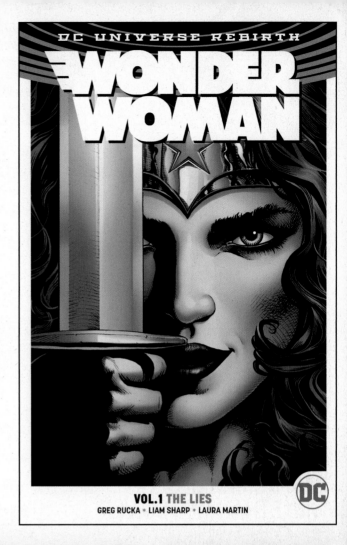

**JUSTICE LEAGUE VOL. 1:
THE EXTINCTION MACHINES**

**SUPERGIRL VOL. 1:
REIGN OF THE SUPERMEN**

**BATGIRL VOL. 1:
BEYOND BURNSIDE**

Get more DC graphic novels wherever comics and books are sold!

DC UNIVERSE REBIRTH

GREEN LANTERNS

VOL. 1: RAGE PLANET

SAM HUMPHRIES
with ETHAN VAN SCIVER

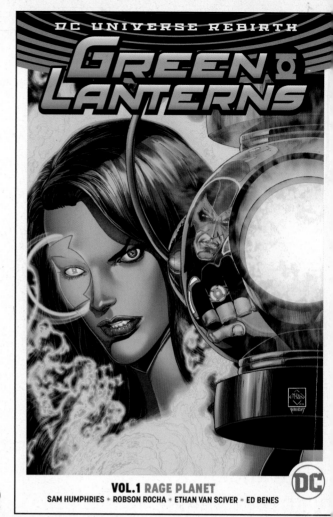

DC UNIVERSE REBIRTH

GREEN LANTERNS

VOL. 1 RAGE PLANET

SAM HUMPHRIES * ROBSON ROCHA * ETHAN VAN SCIVER * ED BENES

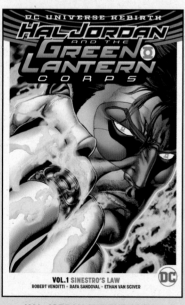

VOL. 1 SINESTRO'S LAW
ROBERT VENDITTI * RAFA SANDOVAL * ETHAN VAN SCIVER

HAL JORDAN AND THE GREEN LANTERN CORPS VOL. 1: SINESTRO'S LAW

VOL. 1 THE DEATH & LIFE OF OLIVER QUEEN
BENJAMIN PERCY * OTTO SCHMIDT * JUAN FERREYRA

GREEN ARROW VOL. 1: THE DEATH & LIFE OF OLIVER QUEEN

VOL. 1 WHO IS ORACLE?
JULIE BENSON * SHAWNA BENSON * CLAIRE ROE

BATGIRL AND THE BIRDS OF PREY VOL. 1: WHO IS ORACLE?

Get more DC graphic novels wherever comics and books are sold!